Advances in Computer Vision and Pattern Recognition

More information about this series at http://www.springer.com/series/4205

Paul L. Rosin · Yu-Kun Lai ·
Ling Shao · Yonghuai Liu
Editors

RGB-D Image Analysis and Processing

 Springer

Editors
Paul L. Rosin
School of Computer Science
and Informatics
Cardiff University
Cardiff, UK

Yu-Kun Lai
School of Computer Science
and Informatics
Cardiff University
Cardiff, UK

Ling Shao
IEEE
University of East Anglia
Norwich, UK

Yonghuai Liu
Department of Computer Science
Edge Hill University
Ormskirk, UK

ISSN 2191-6586   ISSN 2191-6594   (electronic)
Advances in Computer Vision and Pattern Recognition
ISBN 978-3-030-28605-7   ISBN 978-3-030-28603-3   (eBook)
https://doi.org/10.1007/978-3-030-28603-3

This Springer imprint is published by the registered company Springer Nature Switzerland AG
The registered company address is: Gewerbestrasse 11, 6330 Cham, Switzerland

Preface

Colours become weaker in proportion to their distance from the person who is looking at them.
Leonardo da Vinci, *Treatise on Painting*, 1651.

Leonardo da Vinci used *aerial perspective*, as defined above, to good effect. Nevertheless, for thousands of years, artists have had to struggle to capture depth in their images. It was only with the introduction of RGB-D sensors in recent years that capturing depth along with colour has become possible. Moreover, Microsoft's release of the immensely successful Kinect for the mass consumer market in 2010 was literally a game changer, making real-time RGB-D cameras more affordable, accessible, widespread, mainstream and more fun! While the Kinect was designed for home game controller applications, researchers and practitioners quickly realised that its ability as a natural user interface could be deployed in many other scenarios. And so today, RGB-D cameras are ubiquitous, ranging from expensive industrial scanners to webcams and smartphones.

Recent years have continued to see technical developments on RGB-D sensors, both in terms of hardware and software. Data capture is now relatively mature, but understanding and analysing the data remains challenging. Not surprisingly, giving its overwhelming success in many areas, deep learning has also been applied to RGB-D; not only is it effective at processing RGB-D images, but is increasingly used for the challenging task of monocular depth estimation, i.e. creating the -D directly from a single standard (i.e. passive) RGB image. However, despite all these advances, there remain many challenges, ensuring the continuation of active research and development in RGB-D. At the data acquisition stages (depending on which sensing technology is used), examples are coping with general scenes and unconstrained conditions, reflections, transparent surfaces and background light. Subsequent processing typically needs to be performed to remove noise, replace missing depth values and merge sequential RGB-D scans or multiple RGB-D camera outputs to reconstruct objects and scenes. Mid-level processing then consists of tasks such as segmentation and object detection, which remain active research topics both within the RGB-D community as well as the general computer vision community.

This book is structured to reflect such a breakdown into RGB-D data acquisition and processing followed by RGB-D data analysis, which then sets the scene for the final section on RGB-D applications. A set of chapters has been assembled to provide a thorough introduction to the area, with sufficient technical detail to prepare the reader for research and development with RGB-D imagery.

The future will continue to see increasing takeup of RGB-D. The wide availability of RGB-D sensors means that more data is becoming available, consequently facilitating improvements to be made via machine learning. In addition, further improvements in both the hardware and software will help extend the range of possible applications. As RGB-D sensors become smaller and reduce their power consumption, then emerging uses, that would have been impractical just a few years ago, are becoming more widespread and mainstream. Some examples are wearable RGB-D systems (e.g. providing navigation for the visually impaired), face recognition on mobile phones (biometrics), online shopping (e.g. virtual try-on for clothing), 3D mapping using drones and many more applications in health care, gaming, industry, etc. The improved capability to capture 3D environment and shapes also facilitates downstream applications, such as Augmented Reality and 3D printing.

In the future, RGB-D sensing can continue to draw from developments in the core technologies of image processing and computer vision. And just as Leonardo da Vinci's inventive mind was forever seeking out new ways of interpreting the world, we believe researchers will continue to be pushing RGB-D sensing forward to new approaches and applications in the future.

July 2019   Paul L. Rosin
Cardiff University, Cardiff, UK

Yu-Kun Lai
Cardiff University, Cardiff, UK

Ling Shao
Inception Institute of Artificial Intelligence, Abu Dhabi
United Arab Emirates

Yonghuai Liu
Edge Hill University, Ormskirk, UK

Contents

Contributors

Alireza Asvadi Laboratory of Medical Information Processing (LaTIM), University of Western Brittany, Brest, France

Amir Atapour-Abarghouei Department of Computer Science, Durham University, Durham, UK

Ines Ayed Departament de Ciències Matemàtiques i Informàtica, GresCom Lab, Ecole Supèrieure des Communications de Tunis, Universitè de Carthage, tunis, Tunisia

Sven Behnke Autonomous Intelligent Systems, Computer Science Institute VI University of Bonn, Bonn, Germany

Mohammed Bennamoun University of Western Australia, Crawley, WA, Australia

Toby P. Breckon Departments of Engineering & Computer Science, Durham University, Durham, UK

Hao Chen Department of Mechanical Engineering, City University of Hong Kong, Hong Kong SAR, China

Javier Civera I3A, Universidad de Zaragoza, Zaragoza, Spain

Runmin Cong Beijing Key Laboratory of Advanced Information Science and Network Technology, Institute of Information Science, Beijing Jiaotong University, Beijing, China

Emanuele Frontoni Department of Information Engineering, Università Politecnica delle Marche, Ancona, Italy

Huazhu Fu Inception Institute of Artificial Intelligence, Abu Dhabi, United Arab Emirates

Guillermo Garcia-Hernando Department of Electrical-Electronic Engineering, Imperial Computer Vision and Learning Lab (ICVL), Imperial College, London, UK

Liuhao Ge Institute for Media Innovation, Nanyang Technological University Singapore, Singapore, Singapore

Gabriele Guidi Department of Mechanical Engineering, Politecnico di Milano, Milan, Italy

Jean-Yves Guillemaut Centre for Vision, Speech and Signal Processing & University of Surrey, Guildford, UK

Adrian Hilton Centre for Vision, Speech and Signal Processing & University of Surrey, Guildford, UK

Antoni Jaume-i-Capó Departament de Ciències Matemàtiques i Informàtica, Universitat de les Illes Balears, Palma (Illes Balears), Spain

Zhongyu Jiang Tianjin University, Tianjin, China

Tae-Kyun Kim Department of Electrical-Electronic Engineering, Imperial Computer Vision and Learning Lab (ICVL), Imperial College, London, UK

Hamid Laga Murdoch University, Perth, WA, Australia;
The Phenomics and Bioinformatics Research Centre, University of South Australia, Adelaide, SA, Australia

Yu-Kun Lai School of Computer Science and Informatics, Cardiff University, Cardiff, UK

Seong Hun Lee I3A, Universidad de Zaragoza, Zaragoza, Spain

Kun Li Tianjin University, Tianjin, China

Nadia Magnenat Thalmann Institute for Media Innovation, Nanyang Technological University Singapore, Singapore, Singapore

Charles Malleson Centre for Vision, Speech and Signal Processing & University of Surrey, Guildford, UK

Gledson Melotti Department of Electrical and Computer Engineering (DEEC), University of Coimbra, Coimbra, Portugal

Oscar Meruvia-Pastor Department of Computer Science, Memorial University of Newfoundland, St. John's, NL, Canada

Gabriel Moyà-Alcover Departament de Ciències Matemàtiques i Informàtica, Universitat de les Illes Balears, Palma (Illes Balears), Spain

Marina Paolanti Department of Information Engineering, Universitá Politecnica delle Marche, Ancona, Italy

Rocco Pietrini Department of Information Engineering, Universitá Politecnica delle Marche, Ancona, Italy

Cristiano Premebida Department of Aeronautical and Automotive Engineering (AAE), Loughborough University, Loughborough, UK

Tongwei Ren Software Institute, Nanjing University, Nanjing, China

Pablo Rodríguez-Gonzálvez Department of Mining Technology, Topography and Structures, Universidad de León, Ponferrada, Spain

Caner Sahin Department of Electrical-Electronic Engineering, Imperial Computer Vision and Learning Lab (ICVL), Imperial College, London, UK

Max Schwarz Autonomous Intelligent Systems, Computer Science Institute VI University of Bonn, Bonn, Germany

Juil Sock Department of Electrical-Electronic Engineering, Imperial Computer Vision and Learning Lab (ICVL), Imperial College, London, UK

Susanna Spinsante Dipartimento di Ingegneria dell'Informazione, Università Politecnica delle Marche, Ancona, Italy

Javier Varona Departament de Ciències Matemàtiques i Informàtica, Universitat de les Illes Balears, Palma (Illes Balears), Spain

Isaac Ronald Ward University of Western Australia, Crawley, WA, Australia

Jingyu Yang Tianjin University, Tianjin, China

Xinchen Ye Dalian University of Technology, Dalian, China

Junsong Yuan Department of Computer Science and Engineering, State University of New York at Buffalo, Buffalo, NY, USA

Ao Zhang Software Institute, Nanjing University, Nanjing, China

Song-Hai Zhang Department of Computer Science and Technology, Tsinghua University, Beijing, China

Hongyuan Zhu Institute for Infocomm Research, Agency for Science, Technology and Research, Singapore, Singapore

Michael Zollhöfer Stanford University, Stanford, CA, USA

Part I
RGB-D Data Acquisition and Processing

Part I of this book focuses on RGB-D data acquisition and processing. The two main approaches for capturing RGB-D images are passive and active sensing. In addition, with the rise of deep learning, monocular depth estimation has become possible, and is becoming increasingly popular. For the first two approaches, the images often have missing values (i.e. holes) which need to be filled, or low-resolution depth maps which need to be upsampled. RGB-D video enables active depth capture in which the sensor moves within a static scene, with the individual captures fused to produce a 3D reconstruction of the scene. Multiple RGB-D cameras can also be deployed, which facilitates reconstruction of dynamic scenes. Since low-cost RGB-D sensors will not have top quality data, it is important to consider a metrological analysis of their performance.

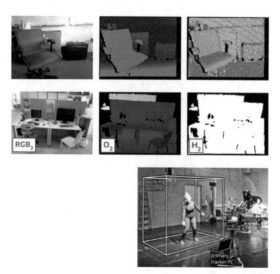

An RGB-D camera jointly captures colour and depth images, the latter describing the 3D geometry of the scene. The RGB-D acquisition process is described in Chap. 1. Along with the RGB-D image, the second row of images shows the hole mask indicating missing depth values, as described in Chap. 2. The third row shows a multiple camera setup using Kinects to capture a performer's motion (Chap. 7).

Chapter 1
Commodity RGB-D Sensors: Data Acquisition

Michael Zollhöfer

Abstract Over the past 10 years, we have seen a democratization of range sensing technology. While previously range sensors have been highly expensive and only accessible to a few domain experts, such sensors are nowadays ubiquitous and can even be found in the latest generation of mobile devices, e.g., current smartphones. This democratization of range sensing technology was started with the release of the Microsoft Kinect, and since then many different commodity range sensors followed its lead, such as the Primesense Carmine, Asus Xtion Pro, and the Structure Sensor from Occipital. The availability of cheap range sensing technology led to a big leap in research, especially in the context of more powerful static and dynamic reconstruction techniques, starting from 3D scanning applications, such as KinectFusion, to highly accurate face and body tracking approaches. In this chapter, we have a detailed look into the different types of existing range sensors. We discuss the two fundamental types of commodity range sensing techniques in detail, namely passive and active sensing, and we explore the principles these technologies are based on. Our focus is on modern active commodity range sensors based on time of flight and structured light. We conclude by discussing the noise characteristics, working ranges, and types of errors made by the different sensing modalities.

1.1 Introduction

Modern conventional color cameras are ubiquitous in our society and enable us to capture precious memories in a persistent and digital manner. These recordings are represented as millions of three channel pixels that encode the amount of red, green, and blue light that reached the sensor at a corresponding sensor location and time. Unfortunately, color images are an inherently flat 2D representation, since most of the 3D scene informations is lost during the process of image formation.

M. Zollhöfer (✉)
Stanford University, 353 Serra Mall, Stanford, CA 94305, USA
e-mail: zollhoefer@cs.stanford.edu

© Springer Nature Switzerland AG 2019
P. L. Rosin et al. (eds.), *RGB-D Image Analysis and Processing*,
Advances in Computer Vision and Pattern Recognition,
https://doi.org/10.1007/978-3-030-28603-3_1

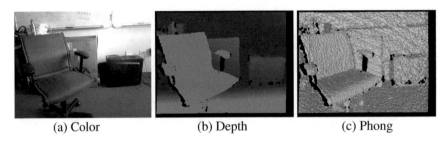

| (a) Color | (b) Depth | (c) Phong |

Fig. 1.1 An RGB-D camera jointly captures color (a) and depth (b) images. The depth image encodes the distance to the scene on a per-pixel basis. Green color means that this part of the scene is close to the camera and red means that it is far away. The Phong shaded image (c) is an alternative visualization of the 3D geometry

Over the past 10 years, we have seen a democratization of a new class of cameras that enables the dense measurement of the 3D geometry of the observed scene, thus overcoming the mentioned limitation of conventional color cameras. These so-called *range* or *depth sensors* perform a dense per-pixel measurement of scene depth, i.e., the distance to the observed points in the scene. These measured depth values are normally exposed to the user in the form of a *depth image*, which is a 2.5-dimensional representation of the visible parts of the scene. An *RGB-D sensor* is the combination of a conventional color camera (RGB) with such a depth sensor (D). It enables the joint capture of scene appearance and scene geometry at real-time frame rates based on a stream of color $\mathscr{C}$ and depth images $\mathscr{D}$. Figure 1.1 shows an example of such a color (a) and depth image pair (b). The phong-shaded image (c) is an alternative visualization of the captured 3D geometry that better illustrates the accuracy of the obtained depth measurements. Current RGB-D sensors provide a live stream of color and depth at over 30 Hz.

Starting with the *Microsoft Kinect*, over the past 10 years a large number of commodity RGB-D sensors have been developed, such as the *Primesense Carmine*, *Asus Xtion Pro*, *Creative Senz3D*, *Microsoft Kinect One*, *Intel Realsense*, and the *Structure Sensor*. While previous range sensors [8, 9, 19] were highly expensive and only accessible to a few domain experts, range sensors are nowadays ubiquitous and can even be found in the latest generation of mobile devices. Current sensors have a small form factor, are affordable, and accessible for everyday use to a broad audience. The availability of cheap range sensing technology led to a big leap in research [10], especially in the context of more powerful static and dynamic reconstruction techniques, starting from 3D scanning applications, such as KinectFusion, to highly accurate face and body tracking approaches. One very recent example is the current Apple iPhone X that employs the range data captured by an off-the-shelf depth sensor as part of its face identification system.

In the following, we review the technical foundations of such camera systems. We will start by reviewing the *Pinhole Camera* model and perspective projections. Afterward, we will introduce the ideas behind both *passive* as well as *active* depth sensing approaches and explain their fundamental working principles. More specifically, we will discuss how commodity RGB-D sensors based on *Stereo Vision* (SV), *Structured Light* (SL), and *Time of Flight* (ToF) technology work. We conclude by comparing the different depth sensing modalities and discussing their advantages and disadvantages.

1.2 Projective Camera Geometry

We start by reviewing the *Pinhole Camera* model, which is a simplified version of the projective geometry of real-world cameras, since it is a basic building block for many types of depth sensors. An illustration of the perspective projection defined by the *Pinhole Camera* model can be found in Fig. 1.2. A 3D point $\mathbf{v} = (\mathbf{v}_x, \mathbf{v}_y, \mathbf{v}_z)^T \in \mathbb{R}^3$ in camera space is mapped to the sensor plane (green) based on a perspective projection [6]. The resulting point $\mathbf{p} = (\mathbf{p}_x, \mathbf{p}_y)^T \in \mathbb{R}^2$ on the sensor depends on the intrinsic properties of the camera, i.e., its focal length f and the principal point $\mathbf{c} = (\mathbf{c}_x, \mathbf{c}_y)^T$. Let us first assume that the principal point is at the center of the sensor plane, i.e., $\mathbf{c} = (0, 0)^T$. In the following, we show how to compute the 2D position $\mathbf{p}$ on the image plane given a 3D point $\mathbf{x}$ and the intrinsic camera parameters. By applying the geometric rule of equal triangles, the following relation can be obtained, see also Fig. 1.2 for an illustration:

$$\frac{\mathbf{p}_x}{f} = \frac{\mathbf{v}_x}{\mathbf{v}_z} \, . \tag{1.1}$$

With the same reasoning, a similar relation also holds for the y-component. Reordering and solving for $\mathbf{p}$ leads to the fundamental equations of perspective projection that describe how a 3D point $\mathbf{v}$ is projected to the sensor plane:

$$\mathbf{p}_x = \frac{f \cdot \mathbf{v}_x}{\mathbf{v}_z} \, , \tag{1.2}$$

$$\mathbf{p}_y = \frac{f \cdot \mathbf{v}_y}{\mathbf{v}_z} \, . \tag{1.3}$$

The same mapping can be more concisely represented in matrix-vector notation by using homogeneous coordinates. Let $\mathbf{K}$ be the intrinsic camera matrix:

$$\mathbf{K} = \begin{bmatrix} f & s & \mathbf{c}_x \\ 0 & f & \mathbf{c}_y \\ 0 & 0 & 1 \end{bmatrix} \, . \tag{1.4}$$

Here, s is an additional skew parameter [7] and $\mathbf{c}$ specifies the principal point, which we assumed to be zero so far. Given the definition of $\mathbf{K}$, the perspective projection can be represented as $\hat{\mathbf{p}} = \mathbf{K}\mathbf{v}$, where $\hat{\mathbf{p}} \in \mathbb{R}^3$ are the homogeneous coordinates of the 2D point $\mathbf{p}$. The intrinsic camera parameters can be obtained based on camera

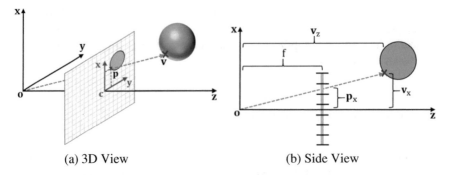

(a) 3D View   (b) Side View

Fig. 1.2 Perspective camera geometry. The image sensor is shown in green. The *Pinhole Camera* model describes how a point $v \in \mathbb{R}^3$ is mapped to a location $p \in \mathbb{R}^2$ on the sensor. The z-axis is the cameras viewing direction and the x-axis is the up-vector. The perspective projection is defined by the camera's focal length f and the principal point c. The focal length f is the distance between the sensor plane and the origin o of the camera coordinate system

calibration routines [3, 18]. The *Pinhole Camera* model is one of the basic building blocks of range sensing approaches. It makes a few simplifying assumptions, such as that the lens is perfect, i.e., that there are no lens distortions. Lens distortion [16] can be tackled in a preprocessing step by calibrating the camera.

1.3 Passive Range Sensing

Similar to human 3D vision, passive range sensing is implemented based on the input of two or multiple [15] conventional monochrome or color cameras. Here, the term "passive" refers to the fact that passive sensors do not modify the scene to obtain the scene depth. The special case of obtaining depth measurements based on only two cameras [17] is known as *stereo* or *binocular reconstruction*. These systems are quite cheap and have a low-power consumption, since they are based on two normal color cameras. The basic setup of such a stereo camera system is illustrated in Fig. 1.3.

Scene depth can be estimated based on a computational process called *triangulation*. The first step in the estimation of scene depth is finding correspondences between the two camera views, i.e., pixels in the two images that observe the same 3D position in the scene. From these two corresponding points, the 3D position of the point that gave rise to these two observations can be computed via triangulation, i.e., by intersecting two rays cast through the detected point correspondences. Finding corresponding points between two different camera views is, in general, a highly challenging problem. Normally, the search is based on local color descriptor matching or on solving an optimization problem. One way to simplify this search is by exploiting the epipolar geometry between the two camera views. This reduces the 2D search problem to a 1D search along a line. Still, solving the correspondence problem requires sufficient local intensity and color variation in the recorded images,

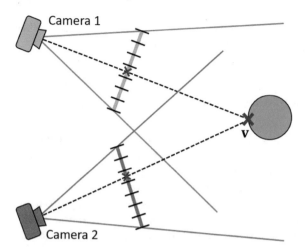

Fig. 1.3 Stereo reconstruction. Similar to human vision, stereo approaches employ two cameras to obtain observations of the scene from two slightly different viewpoints. In the first step of stereo reconstruction, the corresponding points in both images are computed, i.e., pixels of the images that observe the same 3D point in the scene. Based on these matches, the 3D position can be found via triangulation, i.e., by intersecting two rays cast through the detected point correspondences

i.e., enough features. Therefore, passive stereo reconstruction techniques work well in highly textured regions of the scene, but the search for correspondences might fail in featureless regions, which can result in missing depth information. Active depth sensing approaches aim at alleviating this problem.

1.4 Active Range Sensing

Besides passive range sensing approaches, such as the stereo cameras discussed in the last section, there are also active techniques for range sensing. Here, the term "active" refers to the fact that these sensors actively modify the scene to simplify the reconstruction problem. There are two classes of active approaches [13], which are based on different working principles, the so-called *Time of Flight* (ToF) and *Structured Light* (SL) cameras. Structured Light cameras project a unique pattern into the scene to add additional features for matching and thus simplify feature matching and depth computation. Therefore, they address the challenges passive reconstruction approaches face with featureless regions in the scene. On the other hand, Time of Flight cameras emit a (potentially modulated) light pulse and measure its round trip time or phase shift. Since Time-of-Flight cameras do not rely on color or texture to measure distance, they also do not struggle with texture-less scenes. In both of the cases, modern commodity sensors normally work in the *infrared* (IR) domain to not interfere with human vision and enable the simultaneous capture of scene appearance. In the following, we discuss both of these technologies in more detail and highlight their advantages and disadvantages.

1.4.1 Time-of-Flight Sensors

Besides passive binocular vision, many animals have implemented active range sensing approaches, e.g., the sonar used by whales is based on measuring the round trip time of a sound wave. As the name already suggests, the basic working principle of a Time-of-Flight camera is based on measuring the time of flight of an emitted light pulse [5]. More specifically, a light pulse is sent out from an emitter, it then traverses the scene until it hits an object and is reflected back to the Time-of-Flight camera, where a sensor records its arrival. In general, there are two different types of Time-of-Flight cameras.

The first class, *Pulsed Time-of-Flight cameras*, measures the round trip time of a light pulse based on rapid shutters and a clock. For Pulsed Time-of-Flight cameras, due to the constant known speed of light, the round trip distance can be computed by measuring the delay between sending and receiving the light pulse. The scene depth can then be computed as half of the measured round trip distance:

$$\text{Depth} = \frac{\text{Speed of Light} \times \text{Round Trip Time}}{2} . \tag{1.5}$$

There are two types of pulsed Time-of-Flight cameras. Point-wise Time-of-Flight sensors use a pan-tilt mechanism to obtain a time sequence of point measurements. This technique is also known as *Light Detection And Ranging* (LiDAR). Matrix-based Time-of-Flight cameras estimate a complete depth image for every time step based on a CMOS or CCD image sensor. They employ light pulses generated by a laser that are a few nanoseconds apart. Current commodity sensors belong to the second category, while Light Detection And Ranging is more employed for long-range outdoor sensing, e.g., in the context of self-driving cars. Due to the immensely high speed of light of approximately 300,000 km per second, the used clock for measuring the travel time has to be highly accurate, otherwise the depth measurements are imprecise.

The second type of Time-of-Flight camera uses a time-modulated light pulse and measures the phase shift between the emitted and returning pulse. For *Modulated Time-of-Flight* cameras, the light pulse is normally modulated by a continuous wave. A phase detector is used to estimate the phase of the returning light pulse. Afterward, the scene depth is obtained by the correlation between phase shift and scene depth. Multi-frequency techniques can be employed to further improve the accuracy of the obtained depth measurements and the effective sensing range of the cameras. Examples of current commodity Time-of-Flight cameras that are based on modulated time of flight include the Microsoft Kinect One and the Creative Senz3D.

1.4.2 Structured Light Sensors

Structured light sensing, similar to stereo reconstruction, is based on triangulation. The key idea is to replace one of the two cameras in a stereo system by a projector. The projector can be interpreted as an inverse camera. By projecting a known unique structured pattern [14] into the scene, additional artificial features are introduced into the scene. This drastically simplifies correspondence matching, thus the quality of the reconstruction does not depend on the amount of natural color features in the scene. Some sensors, such as the Microsoft Kinect, project a unique dot pattern [4], others project a temporal sequence of black and white stripes. Structured Light cameras are widespread and often used in research. The commodity sensors of this category normally work in the infrared domain to not interfere with human vision and enable the simultaneous capture of an additional color image. Examples of commodity sensors based on this technology are the Microsoft Kinect, Primesense Carmine, Asus Xtion Pro, and Intel Realsense. Actually, the Intel Realsense is a hybrid of a passive and active sensing approach. One problem of structured light cameras is that the sun's infrared radiation can saturate the sensor, making the pattern indiscernible. This results in missing depth information. The Intel Realsense alleviates this problem by combining active and passive vision. To this end, it combines two infrared cameras with one infrared projector that is used to add additional features to the scene. If the projector is overpowered by the ambient scene illumination the Intel Realsense defaults to standard stereo matching between two captured infrared images. Normal working ranges for such commodity sensors are between 0.5 and 12 m. Similar to stereo systems, the accuracy of such sensors directly depends on the distance to the scene, i.e., the accuracy degrades with increasing distance. The captured depth and color images of RGB-D sensors are not aligned, since the infrared and the color sensor are at different spatial locations, but the depth map can be mapped to the color image if the position and orientation of the two sensors is known.

1.5 Comparison of the Sensing Technologies

So far, we have discussed the most prevalent technologies for obtaining depth measurements. More specifically, we had a look at passive stereo reconstruction and active structured light as well as time-of-flight sensing. These three types of approaches are based on different physical and computational principles and thus have different advantages and disadvantages. For example, they have differing working ranges and noise characteristics. It is important to understand the advantages and disadvantages of the different technologies to be able to pick the right sensor for the application one wants to build. In the following, we compare the discussed three technologies in detail.

1.5.1   Passive Stereo Sensing

Stereo reconstruction is based on finding correspondences between points observed in both camera views and triangulation to obtain the depth measurements. Thus, the quality and density of the depth map directly depends on the amount of color and texture features in the scene. More specifically, the quality and density of the depth measurements degrades with a decreasing amount of available features. One extreme case, that is often found in indoor scenes, are walls of uniform color, which can not be reconstructed, since no reliable matches between the left and right camera can be found. Similar to uniformly colored objects, also low light, e.g., scanning in a dark room, can heavily impact the ability to compute reliable matches. Repeated structures and symmetries in the scene can lead to wrong feature associations. In this case, multiple equally good matches exist and sophisticated pruning strategies and local smoothness assumptions are required to select the correct match. Passive stereo is a triangulation-based technique. Therefore, it requires a baseline between the two cameras, which leads to a larger form factor of the device. Similar to all approaches based on triangulation, the quality of the depth measurements degrades with increasing distance to the scene and improves for larger baselines. The noise characteristics of stereo vision systems have been extensively studied [2]. One significant advantage of passive stereo systems is that multiple devices do not interfere with each other. This is in contrast to most active sensing technologies. In addition, stereo sensing can have a large working range if a sufficiently large baseline between the two cameras is used. Since stereo systems are built from off-the-shelf monochrome or color cameras, they are cheap to build and are quite energy efficient. One great use case for passive stereo sensing is outdoor 3D scene reconstruction.

1.5.2   Structured Light Sensing

Active range sensing techniques, such as structured light sensing, remove one of the fundamental problems of passive approaches, i.e., the assumption that the scene naturally contains a large amount of color or texture features. This is made possible, since the projected pattern introduces additional features into the scene which can be used for feature matching. For example, this allows to reconstruct even completely uniformly colored objects, but comes at the price of a higher energy consumption of the sensor, since the scene has to be actively illuminated. In addition, structured light sensors do not work under strong sunlight, since the sensor will be oversaturated by the sun's strong IR radiation and thus the projected pattern is not visible. Due to the projection of a structured pattern, a few problems might occur: If the projected pattern is partially occluded from the sensor's viewpoint, which is especially a problem at depth discontinuities in the scene, the depth cannot be reliably computed. Normally, this leads to missing depth estimates around the object silhouette, which leads to a slightly "shrunken" reconstruction. This also complicates the reconstruction of thin objects. The projected pattern might also be absorbed by dark objects, reflected by specular objects, or refracted by transparent objects, all of these situations might lead to wrong or missing depth estimates. Active structured light depth sensing technology has a limited working range, normally up to 15 m, since otherwise too much energy would be required to consistently illuminate the scene. The noise characteristics of structured light sensors have been extensively studied [11, 12]. Using multiple sensors at the same time might result in a loss of depth accuracy due to interference of multiple overlapping patterns, since the correspondences can not be reliably computed. Geometric structures that are smaller than the distance between the projected points are lost. One great use case for structured light sensing is the face identification system of the current Apple iPhone X.

1.5.3   Time-of-Flight Sensing

In contrast to stereo vision and structured light, Time-of-Flight cameras are based on a different physical measurement principle, i.e., measuring time of flight/phase shift of a light pulse instead of triangulation. This leads to a different set of failure modes and drastically different noise characteristics. One of the biggest artifacts in time-of-flight depth images are the so-called "flying pixels" at depth discontinuities. Flying pixels have depth values between the fore- and background values that exist in reality. They appear if the light pulse is reflected back by multiple parts of the scene and then measured at the same sensor location. This is related to the much wider class of multi-path interference effects ToF cameras suffer from, i.e, multiple indirect light paths being captured by the sensor. Examples of this are multi-path effects caused by materials that exhibit reflections or refractions, e.g., mirrors or glass. Even in relatively diffuse scenes, indirect bounces of the light pulse might influence the reconstruction quality. Dark materials do not reflect light. Therefore, no returning light pulse can be measured which leads to holes in the depth map. Similar to other active sensing modalities, Time of Flight suffers from interference between multiple sensors if they use the same phase shift. This can be alleviated by using different modulation frequencies for each sensor. Similar to active Structured Light, Time-of-Flight depth sensing struggles under strong sunlight. Since Time-of-Flight cameras require a certain integration time to obtain a good signal-to-noise ratio, fast motions lead to motion-blurred depth estimates. The noise characteristics of Time-of-Flight cameras have been extensively studied [1]. One great use case for time-of-flight sensors is body tracking in the living room to enable immersive gaming experiences.

1.6 Conclusion and Outlook

We had a detailed look into the different types of existing range sensors. All depth sensing techniques have their own advantages and disadvantages and it is important to pick the right sensor for the application one wants to build. In the future, higher resolution sensors and projectors will further help to increase the achievable quality of depth measurements. On the software side, deep learning techniques have the potential to further improve the captured depth data by learning depth denoising, upsampling, and super-resolution. This will lead to an even wider democratization of range sensing technology and many more compelling new use cases.

References

1. Belhedi A, Bartoli A, Bourgeois S, Gay-Bellile V, Hamrouni K, Sayd P (2015) Noise modelling in time-of-flight sensors with application to depth noise removal and uncertainty estimation in three-dimensional measurement. IET Comput Vis 9(6):967–977
2. Bier A, Luchowski L (2009) Error analysis of stereo calibration and reconstruction. In: Gagalowicz A, Philips W (eds) Computer vision/computer graphics collaboration techniques. Springer, Berlin, pp 230–241
3. Bradski G, Kaehler A (2013) Learning OpenCV: computer vision in C++ with the OpenCV Library, 2nd edn. O'Reilly Media, Inc, Sebastopol (2013)
4. Cruz L, Lucio D, Velho L (2012) Kinect and RGBD images: challenges and applications. In: Proceedings of the 2012 25th SIBGRAPI conference on graphics, patterns and images tutorials, SIBGRAPI-T '12, pp. 36–49. IEEE Computer Society, Washington, DC (2012). https://doi.org/10.1109/SIBGRAPI-T.2012.13
5. Foix S, Alenya G, Torras C (2011) Lock-in time-of-flight (ToF) cameras: a survey. IEEE Sens J 11(9):1917–1926. https://doi.org/10.1109/JSEN.2010.2101060
6. Forsyth DA, Ponce J (2002) Computer vision: a modern approach. Prentice Hall Professional Technical Reference (2002)
7. Hartley R, Zisserman A (2000) Multiple view geometry in computer vision. Cambridge University Press, New York
8. Huhle B, Jenke P, Straßer W (2008) On-the-fly scene acquisition with a handy multi-sensor system. IJISTA 5(3/4):255–263
9. Lindner M, Kolb A, Hartmann K (2007) Data-fusion of PMD-based distance-information and high-resolution RGB-images. In: International symposium on signals, circuits and systems, vol 1, pp 1–4. https://doi.org/10.1109/ISSCS.2007.4292666
10. Magnor M, Grau O, Sorkine-Hornung O, Theobalt C (eds.) (2015) Digital representations of the real world: how to capture, model, and render visual reality. A K Peters/CRC Press, Massachusetts
11. Mallick T, Das PP, Majumdar AK (2014) Characterizations of noise in kinect depth images: a review. IEEE Sens J 14(6):1731–1740. https://doi.org/10.1109/JSEN.2014.2309987
12. Nguyen CV, Izadi S, Lovell D (2012) Modeling kinect sensor noise for improved 3D reconstruction and tracking. In: Proceedings of the 2012 second international conference on 3D imaging, modeling, processing, visualization and transmission, 3DIMPVT '12, pp. 524–530. IEEE Computer Society, Washington, DC (2012). https://doi.org/10.1109/3DIMPVT.2012.84
13. Sarbolandi H, Lefloch D, Kolb A (2015) Kinect range sensing: structured-light versus time-of-flight kinect. Comput Vis Image Underst 139:1–20. https://doi.org/10.1016/j.cviu.2015.05.006

14. Saty TP, Gupta RK (2007) Model and algorithms for point cloud construction using digital projection patterns
15. Seitz SM, Curless B, Diebel J, Scharstein D, Szeliski R (2006) A comparison and evaluation of multi-view stereo reconstruction algorithms. In: Proceedings of the 2006 IEEE computer society conference on computer vision and pattern recognition, CVPR '06, vol 1, pp 519–528. IEEE Computer Society, Washington, DC (2006). https://doi.org/10.1109/CVPR.2006.19
16. Sturm P, Ramalingam S, Tardif JP, Gasparini S, Barreto JA (2011) Camera models and fundamental concepts used in geometric computer vision. Found Trends Comput Graph Vis 6(1-2), 1–183. https://doi.org/10.1561/0600000023
17. Tippetts B, Lee DJ, Lillywhite K, Archibald J (2016) Review of stereo vision algorithms and their suitability for resource-limited systems. J Real-Time Image Process 11(1):5–25. https://doi.org/10.1007/s11554-012-0313-2
18. Zhang Z (2000) A flexible new technique for camera calibration. IEEE Trans Pattern Anal Mach Intell 22(11):1330–1334. https://doi.org/10.1109/34.888718
19. Zollhöfer M, Nießner M, Izadi S, Rehmann C, Zach C, Fisher M, Wu C, Fitzgibbon A, Loop C, Theobalt C, Stamminger M (2014) Real-time non-rigid reconstruction using an RGB-D camera. ACM Trans Graph 33(4), 156:1–156:12. https://doi.org/10.1145/2601097.2601165

Chapter 2
Dealing with Missing Depth: Recent Advances in Depth Image Completion and Estimation

Amir Atapour-Abarghouei and Toby P. Breckon

Abstract Even though obtaining 3D information has received significant attention in scene capture systems in recent years, there are currently numerous challenges within scene depth estimation which is one of the fundamental parts of any 3D vision system focusing on RGB-D images. This has lead to the creation of an area of research where the goal is to complete the missing 3D information post capture. In many downstream applications, incomplete scene depth is of limited value, and thus, techniques are required to *fill the holes* that exist in terms of both missing depth and colour scene information. An analogous problem exists within the scope of scene filling post object removal in the same context. Although considerable research has resulted in notable progress in the synthetic expansion or reconstruction of missing colour scene information in both statistical and structural forms, work on the plausible completion of missing scene depth is contrastingly limited. Furthermore, recent advances in machine learning using deep neural networks have enabled complete depth estimation in a monocular or stereo framework circumnavigating the need for any completion post-processing, hence increasing both efficiency and functionality. In this chapter, a brief overview of the advances in the state-of-the-art approaches within RGB-D completion is presented while noting related solutions in the space of traditional texture synthesis and colour image completion for hole filling. Recent advances in employing learning-based techniques for this and related depth estimation tasks are also explored and presented.

A. Atapour-Abarghouei (✉)
Department of Computer Science, Durham University, Durham, UK
e-mail: amir.atapour-abarghouei@durham.ac.uk

T. P. Breckon
Departments of Engineering & Computer Science, Durham University, Durham, UK
e-mail: toby.breckon@durham.ac.uk

© Springer Nature Switzerland AG 2019
P. L. Rosin et al. (eds.), *RGB-D Image Analysis and Processing*,
Advances in Computer Vision and Pattern Recognition,
https://doi.org/10.1007/978-3-030-28603-3_2

15

2.1 Introduction

Three-dimensional scene understanding has received increasing attention within the research community in recent years due to its ever-growing applicability and widespread use in real-world scenarios such as security systems, manufacturing and future vehicle autonomy. As mentioned in Chap. 1, a number of limitations pertaining to environmental conditions, inter-object occlusion and sensor capabilities still remain despite the extensive recent work and many promising accomplishments of 3D sensing technologies [33, 134, 149, 158]. It is due to these challenges that a novel area of research has emerged mostly focusing on refining and completing missing scene depth to increase the quality of the depth information for better downstream applicability.

Although traditional RGB image inpainting and texture synthesis approaches have been previously utilized to address scene depth completion [7, 39, 64], challenges regarding efficiency, depth continuity, surface relief and local feature preservation have hindered flawless operation against high expectations of plausibility and accuracy in 3D images [4]. In this vein, this chapter provides a brief overview of the recent advances in scene depth completion, covering commonly used approaches designed to refine depth images acquired through imperfect means.

Moreover, recent progress in the area of monocular depth estimation [6, 44, 55, 152] has lead to a cheap and innovative alternative to completely replace other more expensive and performance-limited depth-sensing approaches such as stereo correspondence [129], structure from motion [27, 41] and depth from shading and light diffusion [1, 132] among others. Apart from computationally intensive demands and careful calibration requirements, these conventional depth-sensing techniques suffer from a variety of quality issues including depth inhomogeneity, missing or invalid values and alike, which is why the need for depth completion and refinement in post-processing arises in the first place.

As a result, generating complete scene depth from a single image using a learning-based approach can be of significant value. Consequently, a small portion of this chapter is dedicated to covering the state-of-the-art monocular depth estimation techniques capable of producing complete depth which would eliminate any need for depth completion or refinement.

2.2 Missing Depth

As explained in the previous chapter, different depth-sensing approaches can lead to various issues within the acquired scene depth, which in turn make depth completion and refinement an important post-processing step.

Passive scene-sensing approaches such as stereo correspondence [129] have long been established as a reliable method of dense depth acquisition. Although stereo imaging is well equipped to estimate depth where highly granular texture is present, even the smallest of issues in calibration and synchronization can lead to noisy, invalid

Fig. 2.1 Examples of depth acquired via stereo correspondence (top), structured light device (bottom left) and time-of-flight camera (bottom right). **RGB:** colour image; **D:** depth image; **H:** hole mask indication missing depth values

or missing depth values. Additionally, missing values are prevalent in sections of the scene that contain occluded regions (i.e. groups of pixels that are seen in one image but not the other), featureless surfaces, sparse information for a scene object such as shrubbery, unclear object boundaries, very distant objects and alike. Such issues can be seen in Fig. 2.1 (top), wherein the binary mask marks where the missing depth values are in a disparity image calculated via a stereo correspondence algorithm [65].

On the other hand, consumer devices such as structured light and time-of-flight cameras are active range sensors that are more widely utilized for a variety of purposes due to their low cost and wide availability in the commercial market with factory calibration settings [14, 23, 46].

However, due to a number of shortcomings such as external illumination interference [23], ambient light saturation [46], inaccurate light pattern detection in the presence of motion [125] and active light path error caused by reflective surfaces or occlusion [126], consumer structured light devices can result in missing depth or noisy values that are best handled by removal and subsequent filling. An example of such a depth image and its missing values can be seen in Fig. 2.1 (bottom left). Time-of-flight cameras can also suffer from complications detrimental to output deployment due to issues such as external illumination interference [123], light scattering caused by semi-transparent surfaces [59, 72] and depth offset for non-reflective objects [96]. Such issues are exemplified in Fig. 2.1 (bottom right).

Completing depth images, captured through these active or passive depth-sensing technologies, can lead to significant performance boost in any 3D vision application even though many current systems simply cope with challenges created by noisy and incomplete depth images without any post-processing. In the next section, we will focus on various approaches to the problem of image completion in the context of RGB-D imagery.

2.3 RGB-D Completion

While object removal, inpainting and surface completion [2, 15, 17–20, 36, 43, 133] has been a long-standing problem addressed within the literature in the past few decades, depth completion is a relatively new area of research with its own challenges and limitations. However, scene depth is still represented and processed in the form of images, and some researchers still directly apply classical RGB image inpainting methods to depth images or use depth completion approaches heavily inspired by RGB completion techniques. Consequently, an overview of image inpainting within the context of scene colour image (RGB) can be beneficial for a better understanding of the multi-facet subject of depth filling. In the following section, relevant image inpainting methods are briefly discussed before moving on to a more detailed description of the depth completion literature.

2.3.1 RGB Image Inpainting

Inpainting deals with the issue of a plausibly completing a target region within the image often created as a result of removing a certain portion of the scene. Early image inpainting approaches attempted to smoothly propagate the isophotes (lines within the image with similar intensity values) into this target area. However, most of these approaches [15, 133] tend to ignore an important aspect significant to an observer's sense of plausibility, which is the high-frequency spatial component of the image or texture. Consequently, later inpainting techniques began to incorporate ideas from the field of texture synthesis (in which the objective is to generate a large texture region given a smaller sample of texture without visible artefacts of repetition within the larger region [42, 43, 118]) into the inpainting process to compensate for the lack of texture commonly found in the target region post completion [2, 36, 79] (exemplar-based inpainting).

In one of the most seminal works on image inpainting [15], the problem is addressed using higher order partial differential equations and anisotropic diffusion to propagate pixel values along isophote directions (Fig. 2.2). The approach demonstrated remarkable progress in the area at the time but more importantly, it contained a set of guidelines for image inpainting created after extensive consultations with scene composition experts, which have now standardized the functionalities of an inpainting algorithm. These remain highly relevant even in depth completion:

- **1:** Upon completion of the inpainting process, the target region must be consistent with the known region of the image to preserve global continuity.
- **2:** The structures present within the known region must be propagated and linked into the target region.

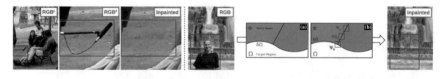

Fig. 2.2 Left: results of [15]. The foreground microphone has been removed and inpainted, but the texture is not accurate, leading to a perception of blurring. **Right:** an example of the results and process of exemplar-based inpainting [36]

- **3:** The structures formed within the target region must be filled with colours consistent with the known region.
- **4:** Texture must be added into the target region after or during the inpainting process.

Improved inpainting approaches were subsequently proposed employing a variety of solutions including the fast marching method [133], total variational (TV) models [28, 121], and exemplar-based techniques [16, 36]. In one such approach, the authors of [36] follow traditional exemplar-based texture synthesis methods [43] by prioritizing the order of filling based on the strength of the gradient along the target region boundary. Although the authors of [36] are not the first to carry out inpainting via exemplar-based synthesis [16], previous approaches are all lacking in either structure propagation or defining a suitable filling order that could prevent the introduction of blurring or distortion in shapes and structures. This exemplar-based method [36] is not only capable of handling two-dimensional texture but can plausibly propagate linear structures within the image. An example of the results of this method can be seen in Fig. 2.2 (right), in which water texture has been plausibly synthesized after the person is removed from the image. However, this approach cannot cope with curved structures and is heavily dependent on the existence of similar pixel neighbourhoods in the known region for plausible completion. Even though the approach relies on fine reflectance texture within the image to prioritize patches and can fail when dealing with large objects in more smooth depth images (Fig. 2.3—left), it has been a great step towards focusing on granular texture within the image completion literature.

Other image completion techniques have also been proposed that would address different challenges in the inpainting process. For instance, certain methods use schemes such as reformulating the problem as metric labelling [85], energy minimization [12, 140], Markov random field models with labels assigned to patches [83], models represented as an optimal graph labelling problem, where the shift-map (the relative shift of every pixel in the output from its source in the input) represents the selected label and is solved by graph cuts [119], and the use of *Laplacian pyramids* [91] instead of the gradient operator in a patch correspondence search framework due to the advantageous qualities of Laplacian pyramids, such as isotropy, rotation invariance and lighter computation. There have also been attempts to complete images in an exemplar-based framework using external databases of semantically similar images [60, 141] (Fig. 2.3—right).

Deep neural networks have recently revolutionized the state of the art in many computer vision tasks such as image stylization [52, 54, 76, 80], super-resolution [111, 138] and colourization [156]. Image completion has also seen its fair share of progress using such techniques. In [113], an approach is proposed that is capable of predicting missing regions in an RGB image via adversarial training of a generative model [56]. In a related work, the authors of [150] utilize an analogous framework with similar loss functions to map the input image with missing or corrupted regions to a latent vector, which in turn is passed through their generator network that recovers the target content. The approach in [146] proposes a joint optimization framework

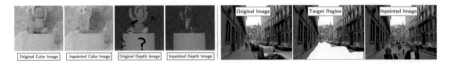

Fig. 2.3 **Left:** results of exemplar-based inpainting [36] applied to RGB and depth images. Note that the objective is to remove the object (baby) from both the RGB and depth images and to fill the already existing holes (pre-removal) in the depth image. The approach is significantly more effective when applied to colour images. **Right:** result of exemplar-based inpainting using an external database [60]

composed of two separate networks, a content encoder, based on [113], which is tasked to preserve contextual structures within the image, and a texture network, which enforces similarity of the fine texture within and without the target region using neural patches [95]. The model is capable of completing higher resolution images than [113, 150] but at the cost of greater inference time since the final output is not achievable via a single forward pass through the network.

More recently, significantly better results have been achieved using [73], which improves on the model in [113] by introducing global and local discriminators as adversarial loss components. The global discriminator assesses whether the completed image is coherent as a whole, while the local discriminator concentrates on small areas within the target region to enforce local consistency. Similarly, the authors of [151] train a fully convolutional neural network capable of not only synthesizing geometric image structures but also explicitly using image features surrounding the target region as reference during training to make better predictions.

While these learning approaches are highly capable of generating perceptually plausible outputs despite the significant corruption applied to the input, when it comes to depth, they are incapable of producing high-quality outputs due in part to the significantly higher number of target regions (holes) both large and small over the smoother surfaces in depth images. Examples of these novel approaches applied to depth images can be seen in Fig. 2.4, which indicates how ineffective learning-based RGB image inpainting approaches can be within the depth modality [4].

While RGB completion techniques in various forms have previously been used with or without modifications [100, 144, 154] to complete depth images, significant differences between RGB and depth images prevent a successful deployment of RGB inpainting techniques to perform depth completion. For instance, the lack of

Fig. 2.4 Results of global and local completion (GLC) [73] compared to inpainting with contextual attention (ICA) ([151]) applied to depth images

reflectance colour texture in depth images, large featureless regions within the depth, overly smooth or blurred depth which can obscure object geometry, holes overlapping with object boundaries and unclear stopping points that mark the termination of structure continuation all contribute to the fact that specifically designed approaches are required to handle the completion of depth images, leading to the importance of the existing literature on depth completion.

Consequently, RGB inpainting is not the focus of this chapter and is only covered here to give context to the relevant literature on depth completion. As such, the reader is invited to refer to the wide-expanding surveys that already exist on the issues of texture synthesis and inpainting within the context of RGB images [58, 78, 131, 139].

2.3.2 Depth Filling

One of the most important steps in addressing any problem, such as that of depth completion, is to focus on how the problem can be formulated. Numerous research works have attempted to solve the depth filling problem by concentrating on different challenges within the domain. In this section, a general overview of the most common formulations of the depth completion problem is presented before moving on to discussing a brief taxonomy of the depth filling literature.

2.3.2.1 Problem Formulation

Reformulating any ill-posed problem such as depth completion can lead to solutions suitable for particular requirements pertaining to certain situations, including time, computation, accuracy and alike. In this section, some of the most common ways in which depth filling has been posed and solved as a problem, and the effects each reformulation can have on the results are discussed.

Formulating the image completion and de-noising problem as **anisotropic diffusion** [115] has proven very successful in the context of RGB images [10, 15, 22]. Such solutions have therefore also made their way into the domain of depth image completion, since the smoothing and edge-preserving qualities of the diffusion-based solutions are highly desirable when dealing with depth information. This is primarily because image gradients are stronger where depth discontinuities are most likely and scene depth is often locally smooth within a single object.

Anisotropic diffusion is a nonlinear partial differential equation scheme [115] which can be described as a space-variant transformation of an input image. It can therefore generate a family of smoothed parametrized images, each of which corresponds with a filter that depends on the local statistics of the input image.

More formally, if $I(\cdot, t)$ is a family of parametrized images, then the anisotropic diffusion is

$$I_t = div(c(x, y, t)\nabla I) = c(x, y, t)\Delta I = \nabla c \cdot \nabla I, \qquad (2.1)$$

where div is the divergence operator, ∇ and Δ denote the gradient and Laplacian operators, respectively, and $c(x, y, t)$ is the diffusion coefficient, which can be a constant or a function of the image gradient.

In [136], Eq. 2.1 is discretized via a 4-neighbourhood scheme, and the corresponding RGB image is used to guide the depth diffusion in an iterative process. The depth image is completed at a lower spatial resolution, and the iterative colour-guided anisotropic diffusion subsequently corrects the depth image as it is upsampled step by step.

The work of [107] demonstrates another example of the use of diffusion in depth completion. The process begins by extracting edges from the corresponding RGB image captured via a structured light device, and then the smooth and edge regions undergo different diffusion algorithms. The separation of these regions before the diffusion process is performed based on the observation that surfaces which need to be smooth in the depth may be textured in the RGB image, and object boundaries within the depth image can be missed during the RGB edge extraction process due to the potentially low contrast in the RGB view of the scene.

While smooth surfaces and strong object boundaries can be very desirable traits in a depth image, the implementation of an anisotropic diffusion method requires discretization, which can lead to numerical stability issues and is computationally intensive. The longer runtime of diffusion-based methods makes them intractable within real-time applications.

Energy minimization is another formulation of the completion problem which has seen significant success in the domain of RGB image inpainting [12, 140] and has consequently been used in depth filling as well.

Energy minimization relies on certain assumptions made about the image, using which an energy function is designed. Essentially, prior knowledge about images and sensing devices is modelled via regularization terms that form the energy function. This function is subsequently optimized, which leads to the completion and enhancement of the image based on the criteria set by the different terms within the function. The approaches addressing the depth completion problem in this manner often produce accurate and plausible results but more importantly, the capability of these approaches to focus on specific features within the image based on the terms added to the energy function is highly advantageous.

For example, the energy function in [31] models the common features of a depth image captured using a structured light device. The noise model of the device and the structure information of the depth image are taken into account using terms added to the energy function, performing regularization during the minimization process. Similarly, the authors of [103] assume a linear correlation between depth and RGB values within small local neighbourhoods. An additional regularization term based on [11] enforces sparsity in vertical and horizontal gradients of the depth image, resulting in sharper object boundaries with less noise. The energy function in [63] includes a data term that favours pixels surrounding hole boundaries and a smoothing term that encourages locally smoother surfaces within the depth image. While this leads to better geometric and structural coherency within the scene, surface relief and texture are lost in the resulting depth image.

The lack of accurate surface relief and texture is in fact a very common challenge with many depth completion techniques. This issue can be addressed by solving depth completion as an **exemplar-based inpainting** problem, which has seen enormous success in RGB images [36]. Most exemplar-based inpainting techniques operate on the assumption that the information needed to complete the target region (with respect to both texture and structural continuity) is contained within the known regions of the image. As a result, plausible image completion can be achieved, at least in part, by copying and pasting patches, sometimes in a very specific order [36], from the known regions of the image into the target region.

However, there can be major pitfalls with using an exemplar-based technique to complete missing values in a depth image. For instance, the lack of reflectance colour texture on a smooth surface which leads to unified depth can confuse an exemplar-based approach to a great degree. As can be seen in Fig. 2.3 (left), the notable exemplar-based inpainting method of [36] is capable of filling the target region post object removal from the RGB image in a plausible way due to existence of visible colour texture in the background but for a depth image, where no colour texture is present and the background only consists of a flat plane, the results are not nearly as impressive (Fig. 2.3—left). Please note that the goal is to remove an object (the baby) from both the RGB and depth images and plausibly complete the remaining holes post removal and at the same time fill the existing holes in the depth image (represented by black markings on the depth image).

Nevertheless, just as various depth completion techniques take advantage of other inpainting approaches such as [133], with or without modifications [100, 144, 154], exemplar-based image inpainting has also left its mark on depth completion.

For instance, in [7], object removal and depth completion of RGB-D images is carried out by decomposing the image into separate high and low spatial frequency components by means of Butterworth filtering in Fourier space. After the disentanglement of high and low frequency images, the high-frequency information (object boundaries and texture relief) is filled using a classic texture synthesis method [43] reformulated as a pixel-by-pixel exemplar-based inpainting approach and enhanced by means of query expansion within the search space, and the low frequency component (underlying shape geometry) is completed via [2]. The results are then recombined in the frequency domain to generate the final output. As can be seen in Fig. 2.5, the produced images are sharp and with no additional artefacts.

Fig. 2.5 Example of the results of [7]. An object has been removed from the RGB-D image and the missing values in the depth image have been completed

Fig. 2.6 Example of the results of exemplar-based RGB-D completion [5] as opposed to exemplar-based RGB completion applied to depth images from the Middlebury dataset [66]. The artefacts are marked with red boxes

Exemplar-based completion also makes an appearance in [9], which performs object removal in multi-view images with an extracted depth image, and uses both structure propagation and structure-guided filling to complete the images. The target region is completed in one of a set of multi-view photographs casually taken in a scene. The obtained images are first used to estimate depth via structure from motion. Structure propagation and structure-guided completion are employed to create the final results after an initial RGB-D completion step. The individual steps of this algorithm use the inpainting method in [140], and the patch-based exemplar-based completion approach of [38] to generate the results.

The work in [5] extends on the seminal RGB inpainting technique of [36] to create an exemplar-based approach explicitly designed to complete depth images. This is achieved by adding specific terms focusing on the characteristics of depth images into the priority function, which determines which patches take precedence in the filling order. By introducing texture and boundary terms, the authors of [5] ensure that surface relief and texture are well preserved in the depth image after completion, leading to more plausible results with fewer artefacts. As can be seen in Fig. 2.6, the RGB completion technique [36] applied to depth images produces many undesirable artefacts while [5] generates sharper depth outputs.

Even though solving the depth filling problem using an exemplar-based framework has the potential to produce outputs in which structural continuity within the scene is preserved and granular relief texture is accurately and consistently replicated in the missing depth regions, there are still many challenges the completion process must contend with. For instance, if the scene depth is not of a fronto-parallel view, there is no guarantee that correct depth values can be predicted for the missing regions via patch sampling even if the patches undergo different transformations such as rotation, scale, shear, aspect ratio, keystone corrections, gain and bias colour adjustments, and other photometric transformations in the search space when trying to find similar patches to sample from [4].

To combat some of these issues, **matrix completion** has recently emerged as an interesting formulation of the image completion problem, especially since it has been observed [104] that similar patches in an RGB-D image lie in a low-dimensional subspace and can be approximated by a matrix with a low rank. The approach in [104] presents a linear algebraic method for low-rank matrix completion-based depth image enhancement to simultaneously remove noise and complete depth images using the corresponding RGB images, even if they contain heavily visible noise. In order to accomplish simultaneous de-noising and completion, the low-rank subspace constraint is enforced on a matrix with RGB-D patches via incomplete factorization,

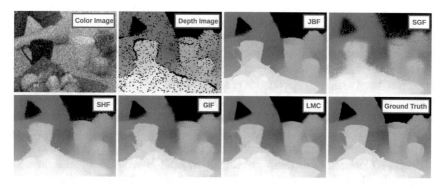

Fig. 2.7 Demonstrating the results of the matrix completion technique of [104] using low-rank operations (denoted by LMC) compared to joint bilateral filtering (JBF) [122], structure-guided fusion (SGF) [120], spatio-temporal hole filling (SHF) [25] and guided inpainting and filtering (GIF) [100]

which results in capturing the potentially scene-dependent image structures both in the depth and colour space.

The rank differs from patch to patch depending on the image structures, so a method is proposed to automatically estimate a rank number based on the data. Figure 2.7 demonstrates the performance capabilities of this approach compared to other depth completion methods, such as joint bilateral filtering (JBF) [122], structure-guided fusion (SGF) [120], spatio-temporal hole filling (SHF) [25] and guided inpainting and filtering (GIF) [100]. This approach [104] generates particularly impressive results in that the input RGB image is very noisy (Fig. 2.7—Colour Image). Before the comparisons, a de-noising method [37] is applied to the noisy RGB image used as an input for the comparators.

The work in [145] points out, however, that the low-rank assumption does not fully take advantage of the characteristics of depth images. Sparse gradient regularization can naively penalize non-zero gradients within the image but based on statistical observations, it is demonstrated that despite most pixels having zero gradients, there is still a relatively significant number of pixels with gradients of 1. Therefore, a low-gradient regularization scheme is proposed in which the penalty for gradient 1 is reduced while non-zero gradients are penalized to allow for gradual changes within the depth image. This regularization approach is subsequently integrated with the low-rank regularization for depth completion.

More recently, with the advent of deep neural network, many image generation problems such as RGB inpainting [73, 113, 146, 150, 151] are essentially formulated as an **image-to-image translation** problem using a mapping function approximated by a deep network directly supervised on ground truth samples. However, as can be seen in Fig. 2.4, networks designed to complete RGB images might not work well when it comes to depth. A significant obstacle to creating a neural network trained to complete scene depth is the lack of hole-free ground truth depth images available.

To overcome this problem, the authors of [157] create a dataset of RGB-D images based on available surface meshes reconstructed from multi-view RGB-D scans of large environments [29]. Reconstructed meshes from different camera poses are rendered, which produces a supply of complete RGB-D images. This data is subsequently utilized to train a network that produces dense surface normals and occlusion boundaries. The outputs are then combined with raw depth data provided by a consumer RGB-D sensor to predict all depth pixels including those missing (holes).

While the formulation of a problem plays a significant role in the quality of the solution, the desired outcome of depth completion is highly dependent on a variety of factors, including the availability of the input data, the information domain, computational requirements and alike. In the following section, a brief discussion of the most successful depth completion techniques in the literature is provided.

2.3.2.2   A Taxonomy of Depth Completion

Within the literature, different depth completion techniques are often designed around the information domain available as the input or required as the output. Some techniques only utilize the spatial information locally contained within the image, while some take advantage of the temporal information extracted from a video sequence used to complete or homogenize the scene depth, and there are some that are based on a combination of both (Fig. 2.8 and Table 2.1).

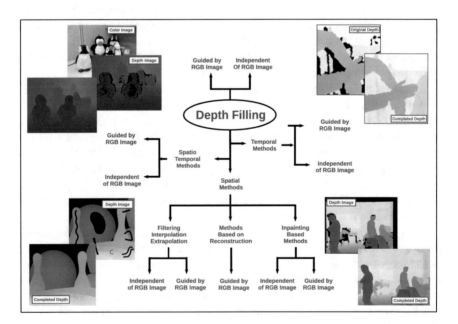

Fig. 2.8 A diagrammatic taxonomy of depth filling based on inputs and the information domain used during the completion process

Table 2.1 A taxonomy of depth filling completion based on the information domain used during the filling process

Categories	Subcategories	Examples
Spatial-based methods	Filtering, interpolation, extrapolation	[3, 89, 92, 108, 117, 148]
	Inpainting-based	[39, 64, 100, 120, 136]
	Reconstruction-based	[30, 31, 103, 147]
Temporal-based methods		[13, 48, 75, 106, 130]
Spatio-temporal-based methods		[24, 25, 122, 137]

Spatial-based depth completion approaches use the neighbouring pixel values and other information available in a single RGB-D image to complete any missing or invalid data in the depth image. Even though there are clear limitations to using this type of approach, such as a possible lack of specific information that can be construed as useful to a particular target region (hole) in the scene depth, there are many important advantages. For instance, when temporal and motion information is taken into consideration for depth completion, filling one frame in a video requires processing multiple consecutive frames around it and so either the processing has to be done offline or if real-time results are needed, the results of each frame will appear with a delay. However, if there is no dependence on other frames, with an efficient spatial-based method, real-time results can be generated without any delay.

One of the simplest, yet not always the best, approaches to using the spatial information within a single RGB-D frame is to employ a *filtering* mechanism to scene depth. Some common filters of choice would be the median filter [88] or the Gaussian filter [155] but with their use comes significant blurring effects and loss of texture and sharp object boundaries. However, there are image filtering techniques with edge-preserving qualities, such as the bilateral filter [135] and non-local filter [21]. On the other hand, these filters will not only preserve edges at object boundaries but the undesirable depth discontinuities caused by depth-sensing issues as well.

There have been attempts to use the visual information present in the colour component of the RGB-D image to improve the accuracy of the depth completion results within or near object boundaries. This notion has also been utilized to reduce the noise in depth images generated by upsampling procedures [49, 82], where the goal is to increase the sharpness, accuracy and the resolution of the depth image. Moreover, it can also be used to assist filtering approaches, as can be seen in methods such as joint bilateral filtering [116], joint trilateral filtering [102] and alike.

A fast and non-approximate linear-time guided filtering method is proposed in [61]. The output is generated based on the contents of a guidance image. It can transfer the structures of the guidance image into the output and has edge-preserving qualities like the bilateral filter but can perform even better near object boundaries and edges by avoiding reversal artefacts. Due to its efficiency and performance, it has been used as the basis for several depth completion methods [100, 147].

Fig. 2.9 Left: example of the result of neighbouring pixel distribution (NPD) approach [148] compared to temporal-based completion (TBC) of [106]; **right:** example of depth completion using cross-bilateral filtering [112]

The approach in [148] completes depth images based on the depth distribution of pixels adjacent to the holes after labelling each hole and dilating each labelled hole to get the value of the surrounding pixels. Cross-bilateral filtering is subsequently used to refine the results. In Fig. 2.9 (left), the results are compared with the temporal-based method in [106], which will be discussed subsequently.

Similarly, in [92], object boundaries are first extracted, and then a discontinuity-adaptive smoothing filter is applied based on the distance of the object boundary and the quantity of depth discontinuities. The approach in [112] proposes a propagation method, inspired by [110], that makes use of a cross-bilateral filter to fill the holes in the image (as can be seen in Fig. 2.9—right).

In [108], an approach based on weighted mode filtering and a joint histogram of the RGB and depth image is used. A weight value is calculated based on the colour similarity between the target and neighbouring pixels on the RGB image and used for counting each bin on the joint histogram of the depth image. The authors of [109], on the other hand, use adaptive cross-trilateral median filtering to reduce the noise and inaccuracies commonly found in scene depth obtained via stereo correspondence. Parameters of the filter are adapted to the local structures, and a confidence kernel is employed in selecting the filter weights to reduce the number of mismatches.

In an attempt to handle the false contours and noisy artefacts in depth estimated via stereo correspondence, the authors of [89] employ a joint multilateral filter that consists of kernels measuring proximity of depth samples, similarity between the sample values and similarity between the corresponding colour values. The shape of the filter is adaptive to brightness variations.

Various *interpolation* and *extrapolation* methods using the spatial information within RGB-D images have also appeared in the depth completion literature. For instance, an object-aware non-parametric interpolation method is proposed in [3], which utilizes a segmentation step [8] and redefines and identifies holes within a set of 12 completion cases with each hole existing in a single row of a single object. The depth pattern is then propagated into hole regions accordingly. Figure 2.10 demonstrates the efficacy of the approach [3] compared to [2, 7, 63, 100, 133]. Additionally, the approach [3] functions in a manner of milliseconds, making it highly effective in real-time application, as can be seen in Table 2.2.

There are other interpolation techniques that complete depth images horizontally or vertically within target boundaries by calculating a normalized distance between opposite points of the border (horizontally or vertically) and interpolating the pixels

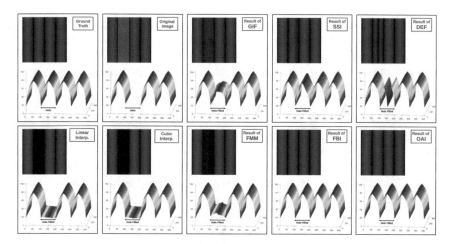

Fig. 2.10 Comparing the results of guided inpainting and filtering (GIF) [100], second-order smoothing inpainting (SSI) [63], fast marching-based inpainting (FMM) [133], Fourier-based inpainting (FBI) [7], diffusion-based exemplar filling (DEF) [2], object-aware interpolation (OAI) [3] and linear and cubic interpolation using a synthetic test image with available ground truth depth

Table 2.2 Average RMSE, PBMP and runtime (test images from Middlebury [66])

Method	Error (lower, better)		Runtime (ms)	Method	Error (lower, better)		Runtime (ms)
	RMSE	PBMP			RMSE	PBMP	
Linear Inter.	1.3082	0.0246	25.12	Cubic Inter.	1.3501	0.0236	27.85
GIF [100]	0.7797	0.0383	3.521e3	SSI [63]	3.7382	0.0245	51.56e3
FMM [133]	1.0117	0.0365	4.31e3	DEF [2]	0.6188	0.0030	8.25e5
FBI [7]	0.6944	0.0058	3.84e6	OAI [3]	0.4869	0.0016	99.09

accordingly [117]. These approaches can face performance challenges when the target region (hole) covers parts of certain structures that are neither horizontal nor vertical. To prevent this potential issue, the authors of [117] propose a multi-directional extrapolation technique that uses the neighbouring texture features to estimate the direction in which extrapolation is to take place, rather than using the classic horizontal or vertical directions that create obvious deficiencies in the completed image.

Similarly, the authors of [51] present a segmentation-based interpolation technique to upsample, refine and enhance depth images. The strategy uses segmentation methods that combine depth and RGB information [35, 105] in the presence of texture. Alternatively, when the image is not highly textured, segmentation techniques based on graph cuts [47] can be used to identify the surfaces and objects in the RGB image, which are assumed to align with those in the depth image. The low-resolution depth image is later projected on the segmented RGB image and interpolation is subsequently performed on the output.

While spatial-based depth completion strategies using filtering, interpolation and extrapolation techniques are among the most used and most efficient methods, traditional *inpainting-based* techniques (normally used for RGB images, Sect. 2.3.1) can yield more promising results in terms of accuracy and plausibility despite being computationally expensive.

The approach in [120] attempts to recover the missing depth information using a fusion-based method integrated with a non-local filtering strategy. Object boundaries and other stopping points that mark the termination of structure continuation process are not easy to locate in depth images which generally have little or no texture, or the boundaries or stopping points might be in the target region within the depth image. The RGB image is thus used to assist with spotting the boundaries, and their corresponding positions in the depth image are estimated according to calibration parameters. The inpainting framework follows the work of [22] that takes advantage of a scheme similar to the non-local means scheme to make more accurate predictions for pixel values based on image textures. To solve the issue of structure propagation termination, a weight function is proposed in the inpainting framework that takes the geometric distance, depth similarity and structure information within the RGB image into account.

The fast marching method-based inpainting of [133] has achieved promising success in RGB inpainting (Sect. 2.3.1). The work of [100] improves upon this approach for depth completion by using the RGB image to guide the depth inpainting process. By assuming that the adjacent pixels that have similar colour values have a higher probability of having similar depth values as well, an additional *colour term* is introduced into the weighting function to increase the contribution of the pixels with the same colour. The order of filling is also changed so that the pixels near edges and object boundaries are filled later, in order to produce sharper edges. However, even with all the improvements, this guided depth inpainting method is still not immune to noise and added artefacts around object boundaries (as can be seen in Figs. 2.11—bottom, 2.7 and Fig. 2.12); therefore, the guided filter [61] is used in the post-processing stage to refine the depth image.

The work in [144] introduces an exemplar-based inpainting method to prevent the common blurring effects produced while completing the scene depth in novel views synthesized through depth image-based rendering. In the two separate stages of warped depth image hole filling and warped RGB image completion, the focus is mainly on depth-assisted colour completion with texture. The depth image is assumed to be only a greyscale image with no texture and is therefore filled using any available background information (i.e. depth pixels are filled by being assigned the minimum of the neighbouring values). The assumptions that depth images have no texture, that texture and relief are not of any significant importance in depth images, and depth holes can be plausibly filled using neighbouring background values are obviously not true and lead to ignoring the utter importance of accurate 3D information in the state of the art. As a result, although the inpainting method proposed in [144] to complete newly synthesized views based on depth is reasonable, the depth filling itself is lacking.

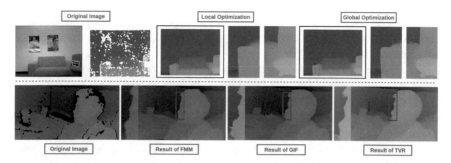

Fig. 2.11 **Top:** local and global framework of [31]. The energy function is made up of a fidelity term (generated depth data characteristics) and a regularization term (joint bilateral and joint trilateral kernels). Local filtering can be used instead of global filtering to make parallelization possible. **Bottom:** example of the results of depth completion using energy minimization with TV regularization (TVR) [103] compared to fast marching method-based inpainting (FMM) [133] and guided inpainting and filtering (GIF) [100]. The energy function assumes that in small local neighbourhoods, depth and colour values are linearly correlated

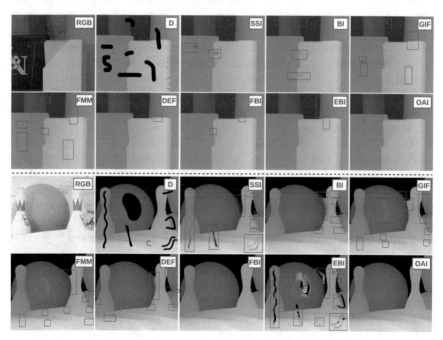

Fig. 2.12 Comparing the results of guided inpainting and filtering (GIF) [100], second-order smoothing inpainting (SSI) [63], fast marching-based inpainting (FMM) [133], Fourier-based inpainting (FBI) [7], diffusion-based exemplar filling (DEF) [2], object-aware interpolation (OAI) [3] and bilinear interpolation (BI) using examples from the Middlebury dataset [66]

An anisotropic diffusion-based method is proposed in [136] that can have real-time capabilities by means of a GPU. The RGB image is used to guide the diffusion in the depth image, which saves computation in the multi-scale pyramid scheme since the RGB image does not change. In order to guarantee the alignment of the object boundaries in the RGB and the depth image, anisotropic diffusion is also applied to object boundaries.

Although inpainting-based depth filling techniques can produce reasonable and efficient results, there is a possibility of blurring, ringing, and added artefacts especially around object boundaries, sharp discontinuities and highly textured regions. In *reconstruction-based* methods, however, missing depth values are predicted using common synthesis approaches. Since a closed-loop strategy is mostly used to resolve the reconstruction coefficients in terms of the minimization of residuals, higher levels of accuracy can be accomplished in depth completion. There are numerous different models found in the literature that are used to represent the depth completion problem as such.

For instance, in [30, 31], energy minimization is used to solve the depth completion problem, specifically depth generated by consumer depth sensors. The energy function consists of a fidelity term that considers the characteristics of consumer device generated depth data and a regularization term that incorporates the joint bilateral kernel and the joint trilateral kernel. The joint bilateral filter is tuned to incorporate the structure information and the joint trilateral kernel is adapted to the noise model of consumer device generated depth data. Since the approach is relatively computationally expensive, local filtering is used to approximate the global optimization framework in order to make parallelization possible, which brings forth the long-pondered question of accuracy versus efficiency. A comparison between examples of the results generated through both local and global frameworks can be seen in Fig. 2.11 (top).

The work of [93] in image matting inspired [103] to design an energy function based on the assumption that in small local neighbourhoods, there is a linear correlation between depth and RGB values. To remove noise and create sharper object boundaries and edges, a regularization term originally proposed in [11] is added to the energy function, which makes the gradient of the depth image both horizontally and vertically sparse, resulting in less noise and sharper edges. A comparison between the results of this method and inpainting methods in [100, 133] is shown in Fig. 2.11 (bottom).

Figure 2.12 contains a qualitative comparison of some of the spatial-based depth filling methods [3, 3, 63, 100], RGB completion techniques [2, 36, 133], and bilinear interpolation over examples from the Middlebury dataset [66]. Table 2.2 presents the numerical evaluation of the same approaches by comparing their root mean square error (RMSE), percentage of bad matching pixels (PBMP), and their runtime. As you can see, even though spatial-based methods are certainly capable of achieving real-time results (unlike temporal-based methods), the current literature epitomizes the long-standing trade-off between accuracy and efficiency. Many of these methods are capable of filling only small holes [3] and others are extremely inefficient [7]. Any future work will need to work towards achieving higher standards of accuracy and plausibility in shorter periods of time.

Certain depth completion techniques in the literature take advantage of the motion and temporal information contained within a video sequence to complete and refine depth images [13, 106]. One of these **temporal-based** approaches, commonly used as a comparator in the literature, is the method proposed in [106] which utilizes motion information and the difference between the depth values in the current image and those in the consecutive frames to fill holes by giving the pixels the weighted average values of the corresponding pixels in other frames. Although the results are mostly plausible, one drawback is that the value of the edges of objects cannot be accurately estimated to an acceptable level (Figs. 2.9—left), other than the fact that there is a need for a sequence of depth images, and therefore, the holes in a single depth image cannot be filled. Moreover, when the colour information does not correspond with the depth data, the results often contain invalid depth values.

The well-known KinectFusion approach of [75] takes advantage of the neighbouring frames to complete the missing depth during real-time 3D reconstruction. However, camera motion and a static scene are of utmost importance and despite being robust, the approach cannot be utilized for a static view of a scene without any camera motion. In [13], missing depth regions are grouped into one of two categories: the ones created as a result of occlusion by foreground objects, assumed to be in motion, and the holes created by reflective surfaces and other random factors. Subsequently, they use the deepest neighbouring values to fill pixels according to the groups they are placed in. Even though the assumptions might be true in many real-life scenarios, they are not universal, and static objects can be the cause of missing or invalid data in depth images captured via many consumer depth sensors.

The approach in [48] focuses on repairing the inconsistencies in depth videos. Depth values of certain objects in one frame sometimes vary from the values of the same objects in a neighbouring frame, while the planar existence of the object has not changed. An adaptive temporal filtering is thus proposed based on the correspondence between depth and RGB sequences. The authors of [130] note that the challenge in detecting and mending temporal inconsistencies in depth videos is due to the dynamic content and outliers. Consequently, they propose using the intrinsic static structure, which is initialized by taking the first frame and refined as more frames become available. The depth values are then enhanced by combining the input depth and the intrinsic static structure, the weight of which depends on the probability of the input value belonging to the structure. As can be seen in Fig. 2.13 (left), the method proposed in [130] does not introduce artefacts into the results due to motion delay because temporal consistency is only enforced on static regions, as opposed to [48], which applies temporal filtering to all regions.

Temporal-based methods generate reasonable results even when spatial-based approaches are unable to, and are necessary when depth consistency and homogeneity is important in a depth sequence, which it often is. On the other hand, the dependency on other frames is a hindrance that causes delays or renders the method only applicable as an offline approach. Moreover, there are many scenarios where a depth sequence is simply not available but a single depth image still needs to be completed. **Spatio-temporal** completion approaches, however, combine the elements of the spatial and temporal-based methods to fill holes in depth images [25, 137].

In [137], the process of depth completion is carried out in two stages. First, a *deepest depth image* is generated by combining the spatio-temporal information

Fig. 2.13 Left: example of the results of completion based on intrinsic static structure (ISS) [130] compared to adaptive temporal filtering (ATF) [48]; **right:** example of the results of spatio-temporal completion (STC) [25] compared to exemplar-based inpainting (EBI) [36] on still frames

in the depth and RGB images and used to fill the holes. Subsequently, the filled depth image is enhanced based on the joint information of geometry and colour. To preserve local features of the depth image, filters adapted to RGB image features are utilized. In another widely used method, the authors of [24] use an adaptive spatio-temporal approach to fill depth holes utilizing bilateral and Kalman filters. The approach is made up of three blocks: an adaptive joint bilateral filter that combines the depth and colour information is used, random fluctuations of pixel values are subsequently handled by applying an adaptive Kalman filter on each pixel, and finally, an interpolation system uses the stable values in the regions neighbouring the holes provided by the previous blocks, and by means of a 2D Gaussian kernel, fills the missing depth values.

In another method [25], scene depth is completed using a joint bilateral filter applied to neighbouring pixels, the weights of which are determined based on visual data, depth information and a temporal consistency map that is created to track the reliability of the depth values near the hole regions. The resulting values are taken into account when filtering successive frames, and iterative filtering can ensure increasing accuracy as new samples are acquired and filtered. As can be seen in Fig. 2.13 (right), the results are superior to the ones produced by the inpainting algorithm proposed in [36].

Improvements made to what can be obtained from a regular video camera alongside a time-of-flight camera are discussed in [122], and the main focus of the work is on depth upsampling and colour/depth alignment. However, one of the issues addressed is depth completion, which is performed via a multi-scale technique following the works in [57, 84]. The output undergoes joint bilateral filtering and spatio-temporal processing to remove noise by averaging values from several consecutive frames.

The approach presented in [74] uses a sequence of frames to locate outliers with respect to depth consistency within the frame, and utilizes an improved and more efficient regression technique using least median of squares (LMedS) [124] to fill holes and replace outliers with valid depth values. The approach is capable of hole filling and sharp depth refinement within a sequence of frames but can fail in the presence of invalid depth shared between frames or sudden changes in depth due to fast moving dynamic objects within the scene.

While depth completion can be a useful process for creating full dense depth for various vision-based application, learning-based monocular depth estimation techniques can be an invaluable tool that can provide hole-free scene depth in a cheap and efficient manner, completely removing the need for any depth completion in the process. In the next section, a brief outline of the advances made in the field of monocular depth estimation is presented.

2.4   Monocular Depth Estimation

Over the past few years, research into monocular depth estimation, i.e. predicting complete scene depth from a single RGB image, has significantly escalated [44, 50, 55, 87, 99, 143]. Using offline model training based on ground truth depth data, monocular depth prediction has been made possible [44, 45, 87, 99, 162] sometimes with results surpassing those of more classical depth estimation techniques. Ground truth depth, however, is extremely difficult and expensive to acquire, and when it is obtained it is often sparse and flawed, constraining the practical use of monocular depth estimation in real-world applications. Solutions to this problem of data scarcity include the possibility of using synthetic data containing sharp pixel-perfect scene depth [6] for training or completely dispensing with using ground truth depth, and instead utilizing a secondary supervisory signal during training which indirectly results in producing the desired depth [32, 50, 55, 143].

In the following, a brief description of monocular depth estimation techniques within three relevant areas is provided: approaches utilizing handcrafted features based on monocular cues within the RGB image, approaches based on graphical models and finally techniques using deep neural networks trained in various ways to estimate depth from a single image.

2.4.1   Handcrafted Features

While binocular vision is commonly associated with depth perception in humans and machines, estimating depth from a single image based on monocular cues and features is technically possible for both humans and machines, even if the results are not very accurate. Such monocular cues include size considering visual angles, grain and motion parallax. Monocular depth estimation techniques have utilized such features to estimate depth from a single RGB image.

Based on the assumption that the geometric information contained within a scene combined with motion extracted from a sequence can be valuable features for 3D reconstruction, the authors of [70] estimate depth based on temporal continuity and geometric perspective. In [153], different cues such as motion, colour and contrast are combined to extract the foreground layer, which is then used to estimate depth. Motion parameters and optical flow are calculated using structure from motion.

In [67, 68], an assumption of ground-vertical geometric structure is used as the basis to construct a basic 3D model from a single photograph. This is accomplished by labelling the image according to predefined geometric classes and subsequently creating a statistical model based on scene orientation. The authors of [81] propose a non-parametric approach based on SIFT Flow, where scene depth is reconstructed from an input RGB image by transferring the depth of multiple similar images and then applying warping and optimizing procedures. The work in [97] investigates using semantic scene segmentation results to guide the depth reconstruction process instead of directly predicting depth based on features present in the scene. The work in [87] also takes advantage of combining semantic object labels with depth features to aid in the depth estimation process.

It is important to note that predicting depth based on monocular cues within the scene is not robust enough to deal with complex and cluttered scenes even though approaches using such features have managed to produce promising results when it comes to scenes that contain clear predefined features and adhere to simple structural assumptions.

2.4.2 Graphical Models

Within the current literature on monocular depth estimation, there are approaches that take advantage of graphical models to recover scene depth. For instance, the authors of [40] introduce a dynamic Bayesian network model capable of reconstructing a 3D scene from a monocular image based on the assumption that all scenes contain a *floor-wall* geometry. The model distinguishes said floor-wall boundaries in each column of the image and using perspective geometry reconstructs a 3D representation of the scene. While the approach produces very promising results, the underlying assumption it is built on (indoor scenes framed by a floor-wall constraint) limits the capabilities of the approach.

The work in [127] utilizes a discriminatively trained Markov random field (MRF) and linear regression to estimate depth. The images are segmented into homogeneous regions and the produced patches are used as super-pixels instead of pixels during the depth estimation process. This extended version of the approach [128] utilizes the MRF in order to combine planes predicted by the linear model to describe the 3D position and orientation of segmented patches within RGB images. Since depth is predicted locally, the combined output lacks global coherence. Additionally, the model is manually tuned which is a detriment against achieving a learning-based system.

The method proposed in [62] presents cascaded classification models. The approach combines the tasks of scene categorization, object detection, multi-class image segmentation and, most relevant here, 3D reconstruction by coupling repeated instantiations of the sophisticated off-the-shelf classifiers in order to improve the overall performance at each level.

In [101], monocular depth estimation is formulated as an inference problem in a discrete/continuous conditional random field (CRF) model, in which continuous variables encode the depth information associated with super-pixels from the input RGB image, and the discrete ones represent the relationships between the neighbouring super-pixels. Using input images with available ground truth depth, the unary potentials are calculated within a graphical model, in which the discrete/continuous optimization problem is solved with the aid of particle belief propagation [71, 114].

To better exploit the global structure of the scene, [162] proposes a hierarchical representation of the scene based on a CRF, which is capable of modelling local depth information along with mid-level and global scene structures. Not unlike [101], the model attempts to solve monocular depth estimation as an inference problem in a graphical model in which the edges provide an encoding of the interactions within and across the different layers of the proposed scene hierarchy.

More recently, the authors of [142] attempt to perform monocular depth estimation using sparse manual labels for object sizes within a given scene. Utilizing these manually estimated object sizes and the geometric relationship between them, a coarse depth image is primarily created. This depth output is subsequently refined using a CRF that propagates the estimated depth values to generate the final depth image for the scene.

Monocular depth estimation techniques based on graphical models can produce impressive results but despite their excellent generalization capabilities, deep neural networks generate sharper and more accurate depth images, even though they can be prone to overfitting and require larger quantities of training data.

2.4.3 Deep Neural Networks

Recent monocular depth estimation techniques using deep convolutional neural networks *directly supervised* using data with ground truth depth images have revolutionized the field by producing highly accurate results. For instance, the approach in [45] utilizes a multi-scale network that estimates a coarse global depth image and a second network that locally refines the depth image produced by the first network. The approach is extended in [44] to perform semantic segmentation and surface normal estimation as well as depth prediction.

In the work by [90], a fully convolutional network is trained to estimate more accurate depth based on efficient feature upsampling within the network architecture. In the upsampling procedure, the outputs of four convolutional layers are fused by applying successive upsampling operations. On the other hand, the authors of [98] point to the past successes that CRF-based methods have achieved in monocular depth estimation and present a deep convolutional neural field model that takes advantage of the capabilities of a continuous CRF. The unary and pairwise potentials of the continuous CRF are learned in a deep network resulting in depth estimation for general scenes with no geometric priors.

The work in [26] trains a supervised model for estimation formulated as a pixel-wise classification task. This reformulation of the problem is made possible by transforming the continuous values in the ground truth depth images into class labels by discretizing the values into bins and labelling the bins based on their depth ranges. Solving depth estimation as a classification problem provides the possibility to obtain confidence values for predicted depth in the form of probability distributions. Using the obtained confidence values, an information gain loss is applied that enables selecting predictions that are close to ground truth values during training.

Similarly, the authors of [94] also present monocular depth estimation as a pixel-wise classification problem. Different side-outputs from the dilated convolutional neural network architecture are fused hierarchically to take advantage of multi-scale depth cues. Finally, soft-weighted-sum inference is used instead of the hard-max inference, which transforms the discretized depth score to continuous depth value. The authors of [69] attempt to solve the commonly found issue of blurring effects in the results of most monocular depth estimation techniques by fusing features extracted at different scales from a network architecture that includes a multi-scale feature fusion module and a refinement module trained via an objective function that measures errors in depth, gradients and surface normals.

While these approaches produce consistently more encouraging results than their predecessors, the main drawback of any directly supervised depth estimation model is its dependence on large quantities of dense ground truth depth images for training. To combat this issue, synthetic depth images have recently received attention in the literature. The authors of [6] take advantage of aligned nearly photorealistic RGB images and their corresponding synthetic depth extracted from a graphically rendered virtual environment primarily designed for gaming for training a monocular depth estimation model. Additionally, a cycle-consistent adversarially trained style transfer approach [161] is used to deal with the domain shift between the synthetic images used for training and the real-world images the model is intended for in practice. Figure 2.14 (EST) contains examples of the results of this approach, which are very sharp and with clear object boundaries due to the fact that pixel-perfect synthetic depth has been used as training data. Likewise, the authors of [159] propose a similar

Fig. 2.14 Qualitative comparison of depth and ego-motion from video (DEV) [160], estimation based on left/right consistency (LRC) [55]; **SSE:** semi-supervised depth estimation (SSE) [86], depth estimation via style transfer (EST) [6]

framework in which a separate network takes as its input both synthetic and real-world images and produces modified images which are then passed through a second network trained to perform monocular depth estimation.

While the use of synthetic training data can be a helpful solution to the issue of scarcity of ground truth depth, a new class of *indirectly supervised* monocular depth estimators have emerged that do not require ground truth depth, and calculate disparity by reconstructing the corresponding view within a stereo correspondence framework and thus use this view reconstruction as a secondary supervisory signal. For instance, the work in [143] proposes the Deep3D network, which learns to generate the right view from the left image used as the input, and in the process produces an intermediary disparity image. The model is trained on stereo pairs from a dataset of 3D movies to minimize the pixel-wise reconstruction loss of the generated right view compared to the ground truth right view. The desired output is a probabilistic disparity map that is used by a differentiable depth image-based rendering layer in the network architecture. While the results of the approach are very promising, the method is very memory intensive.

The approach in [50] follows a similar framework with a model very similar to an autoencoder, in which the encoder is trained to estimate depth for the input image (left) by explicitly creating an inverse warp of the output image (right) in the decoder using the estimated depth and the known inter-view displacement, to reconstruct the input image. The technique uses an objective function similar to [143] but is not fully differentiable.

On the other hand, the authors of [55] argue that a simple image reconstruction as done in [50, 143] does not produce depth with high enough quality and uses bilinear sampling [77] and a left/right consistency check between the disparities produced relative to both the left and right images incorporated into training to produce better results. Examples of the results of this approach can be seen in Fig. 2.14 (LRC). Even though the results are consistently impressive across different images, blurring effects within the depth image still persist.

In [152], the use of sequences of stereo image pairs is investigated for estimating depth and visual odometry. It is argued that utilizing stereo sequences as training data makes the model capable of considering both spatial (between left/right views) and temporal (forward/backward) warp error in its learning process, and can constrain scene depth and camera motion to remain within a reasonable scale.

While the approaches that benefit from view synthesis through learning the inter-view displacement and thus the disparity are capable of producing very accurate and consistent results and the required training data is abundant and easily obtainable, there are certain shortcomings. First, the training data must consist of temporally aligned and rectified stereo images, and more importantly, in the presence of occluded regions (i.e. groups of pixels that are seen in one image but not the other), disparity calculations fail and meaningless values are generated (as can be seen in Fig. 2.14 (LRC)).

On the other hand, the work in [160] estimates depth and camera motion from video by training depth and pose prediction networks, indirectly supervised via view synthesis. The results are favourable especially since they include ego-motion but

Table 2.3 Comparing the results of monocular depth estimation techniques over the KITTI dataset using the data split in [45]. S* denotes the synthetic data captured from a graphically rendered virtual environment

Method	Training data	Error metrics (lower, better)				Accuracy metrics (higher, better)		
		Abs. Rel.	Sq. Rel.	RMSE	RMSE log	$\delta <$ 1.25	$\delta <$ 1.25^2	$\delta <$ 1.25^3
Dataset mean [53]	[53]	0.403	0.530	8.709	0.403	0.593	0.776	0.878
Eigen et al. Coarse [44]	[53]	0.214	1.605	6.563	0.292	0.673	0.884	0.957
Eigen et al. Fine [44]	[53]	0.203	1.548	6.307	0.282	0.702	0.890	0.958
Liu et al. [99]	[53]	0.202	1.614	6.523	0.275	0.678	0.895	0.965
Zhou et al. [160]	[53]	0.208	1.768	6.856	0.283	0.678	0.885	0.957
Zhou et al. [160]	[53]+[34]	0.198	1.836	6.565	0.275	0.718	0.901	0.960
Garg et al. [50]	[53]	0.152	1.226	5.849	0.246	0.784	0.921	0.967
Godard et al. [55]	[53]	0.148	1.344	5.927	0.247	0.803	0.922	0.964
Godard et al. [55]	[53]+[34]	0.124	1.076	5.311	0.219	0.847	0.942	0.973
Zhan et al. [152]	[53]	0.144	1.391	5.869	0.241	0.803	0.928	0.969
Atapour et al. [6]	S*	**0.110**	0.929	4.726	0.194	**0.923**	**0.967**	0.984
Kuznietsov et al. [86]	[53]	0.113	**0.741**	**4.621**	**0.189**	0.862	0.960	**0.986**

the depth outputs are very blurry (as can be seen in Fig. 2.14 (DEV)), do not consider occlusions and are dependent on camera parameters. The training in the work of [86] is supervised by sparse ground truth depth and the model is then enforced within a stereo framework via an image alignment loss to output dense depth. This enables the model to take advantage of both direct and indirect training, leading to higher fidelity depth outputs than most other comparators, as demonstrated in Fig. 2.14 (SSE) and Table 2.3.

Within the literature, there are specific metrics that are commonly used to evaluate the performance of monocular depth estimation techniques. Given an estimated depth image d'_p and the corresponding ground truth depth d_p at pixel p with N being the total number of pixels for which valid ground truth and estimated depth exist, the following metrics are often used for performance evaluation in the literature:

- Absolute relative error (*Abs. Rel.*) [128]:

$$\frac{1}{N} \sum_p \frac{|d_p - d'_p|}{d_p}. \tag{2.2}$$

- Squared relative error (*Sq. Rel.*) [128]:

$$\frac{1}{N} \sum_p \frac{||d_p - d'_p||^2}{d_p}.$$ (2.3)

- Linear root mean square error (*RMSE*) [62]:

$$\sqrt{\frac{1}{N} \sum_p ||d_p - d'_p||^2}.$$ (2.4)

- Log scale invariant RMSE (*RMSE log*) [45]:

$$\sqrt{\frac{1}{N} \sum_p ||log(d_p) - log(d'_p)||^2}.$$ (2.5)

- Accuracy under a threshold [87]:

$$max\left(\frac{d'_p}{d_p}, \frac{d_p}{d'_p}\right) = \delta < threshold.$$ (2.6)

Table 2.3 provides a quantitative analysis of the state-of-the-art approaches proposed in [6, 44, 50, 55, 86, 99, 152, 160]. The experiment is carried out on the test split used in [45], which has now become a convention for evaluations within the monocular depth estimation literature.

2.5 Conclusions

The primary focus of this chapter has been on techniques specifically designed to complete, enhance and refine depth images. This is particularly important as there are still several issues blocking the path to a perfect depth image such as missing data, invalid depth values, low resolution and noise despite the significant efforts currently underway with regard to improving scene depth capture technologies.

The depth completion problem has been formulated in a variety of different ways, as has the related problem of RGB inpainting. Diffusion-based and energy minimization solutions to the problem are accurate with respect to structural continuity within the scene depth and can produce smooth surfaces within object boundaries, which can be a desirable trait for certain applications. However, these solutions are often inefficient, computationally expensive, and can bring forth implementation issues. Depth images can also be completed using an exemplar-based paradigm, which can accurately replicate object texture and relief as well as preserve the necessary geometric structures within the scene. There are, of course, a variety of other problem formulations, such as matrix completion, labelling, image-to-image mapping and alike, each focusing on certain traits within the desired scene depth.

Input requirements can also vary for different depth completion techniques. Depending on the acquisition method, depth is commonly obtained along with an aligned or easily alignable RGB image of the same scene. The information contained within this RGB image can be used to better guide the filling approach applied to the depth image. However, not all depth images are accompanied by a corresponding RGB image and processing the colour information can add to the computational requirements which may not be necessary depending on the application.

Within the depth completion literature, there are **spatial-based** methods that limit themselves to the information in the neighbouring regions adjacent to the holes in the depth image and possibly the accompanying RGB image. Some of these algorithms make use of *filtering* techniques, while some utilize *interpolation and extrapolation* approaches. The filtering, interpolation and extrapolation methods can provide fast and clean results but suffer from issues like smoothed boundaries and blurred edges. Some research has been focused on using *inpainting-based* techniques, which have been proven successful in completing RGB images post object removal. Despite their satisfactory results, these methods are not all efficient and can generate additional artefacts near target and object boundaries. There are also *Reconstruction methods* that can generate accurate results using techniques inspired by scene synthesis methods. However, they are mostly difficult to implement and some have a strict dependency on the corresponding RGB view.

Temporal-based depth completion techniques make use of the motion information and the depth in the neighbouring frames of a video to fill the hole regions in the current depth frame. Sometimes the information in a single depth image is not enough to complete that image, which is where spatial-based methods fall short. Temporal-based approaches, however, do not suffer from this issue and have a larger supply of information at their disposal. This class of methods is still not perfect, and the need to process other frames to complete a depth image makes them more suited for offline applications rather than real-time systems.

Additionally, various **spatio-temporal-based** methods have been proposed that use both the spatial information contained within the scene depth and the temporal continuity extracted from a sequence to perform depth completion. Although these methods can be more accurate than spatial-based techniques and more efficient than temporal-based approaches, they still suffer from the issues of both these categories.

Furthermore, while future avenues of research need to explicitly consider computational efficiency, within the contemporary application domains of consumer depth cameras and stereo-based depth recovery, it is also highly likely they will be able to exploit temporal aspects of a live depth stream. It is thus possible that both temporal and spatio-temporal techniques will become the primary areas of growth within this domain over the coming years. This trend will be heavily supported by aspects of machine learning as innovative solutions to the issue of acquiring high-quality ground truth depth data become increasingly widespread.

Of course, another innovative solution to the problem of obtaining accurate 3D scenes is to provide a cheap and efficient alternative to the current 3D capture technologies that can produce high-fidelity hole-free scene depth, entirely circumnavigating the need for depth completion as a necessary post-processing operation. Recent learning-based monocular depth estimation methods have made significant strides towards achieving this goal by providing accurate and plausible depth mostly in real time from a single RGB image.

References

1. Abrams A, Hawley C, Pless R (2012) Heliometric stereo: shape from sun position. In: European conference on computer vision, pp 357–370
2. Arias P, Facciolo G, Caselles V, Sapiro G (2011) A variational framework for exemplar-based image inpainting. Comput Vis 93(3):319–347
3. Atapour-Abarghouei A, Breckon T (2017) DepthComp: real-time depth image completion based on prior semantic scene segmentation. In: British machine vision conference. BMVA, pp 1–12
4. Atapour-Abarghouei A, Breckon T (2018) A comparative review of plausible hole filling strategies in the context of scene depth image completion. Comput Graph 72:39–58
5. Atapour-Abarghouei A, Breckon T (2018) Extended patch prioritization for depth filling within constrained exemplar-based RGB-D image completion. In: International conference on image analysis and recognition, pp 306–314
6. Atapour-Abarghouei A, Breckon T (2018) Real-time monocular depth estimation using synthetic data with domain adaptation via image style transfer. In: IEEE conference on computer vision and pattern recognition, pp 2800–2810
7. Atapour-Abarghouei A, Payen de La Garanderie G, Breckon TP (2016) Back to Butterworth – a Fourier basis for 3D surface relief hole filling within RGB-D imagery. In: International conference on pattern recognition. IEEE, pp 2813–2818
8. Badrinarayanan V, Kendall A, Cipolla R (2017) SegNet: a deep convolutional encoder-decoder architecture for image segmentation. IEEE Trans Pattern Anal Mach Intell 39(12):2481–2495
9. Baek SH, Choi I, Kim MH (2016) Multiview image completion with space structure propagation. In: IEEE conference on computer vision and pattern recognition, pp 488–496
10. Ballester C, Caselles V, Verdera J, Bertalmio M, Sapiro G (2001) A variational model for filling-in gray level and color images. In: International conference on computer vision, vol 1. IEEE, pp 10–16
11. Barbero A, Sra S (2011) Fast Newton-type methods for total variation regularization. In: International conference on machine learning, pp 313–320
12. Barnes C, Shechtman E, Finkelstein A, Goldman D (2009) Patchmatch: a randomized correspondence algorithm for structural image editing. ACM Trans Graph 28(3):24
13. Berdnikov Y, Vatolin D (2011) Real-time depth map occlusion filling and scene background restoration for projected-pattern based depth cameras. In: Graphic conference on IETP
14. Berger K, Ruhl K, Schroeder Y, Bruemmer C, Scholz A, Magnor MA (2011) Markerless motion capture using multiple color-depth sensors. In: Vision modeling and visualization, pp 317–324
15. Bertalmio M, Sapiro G, Caselles V, Ballester C (2000) Image inpainting. In: International conference on computer graphics and interactive techniques, pp 417–424
16. Bertalmio M, Vese L, Sapiro G, Osher S (2003) Simultaneous structure and texture image inpainting. IEEE Trans Image Process 12(8):882–889
17. Breckon T, Fisher R (2005) Plausible 3D colour surface completion using non-parametric techniques. Math Surf XI 3604:102–120
18. Breckon TP, Fisher R (2005) Non-parametric 3D surface completion. In: International conference on 3D digital imaging and modeling, pp 573–580

19. Breckon TP (2008) Fisher R (2008) 3D surface relief completion via non-parametric techniques. IEEE Trans Pattern Anal Mach Intell 30(12):2249–2255
20. Breckon TP, Fisher R (2012) A hierarchical extension to 3D non-parametric surface relief completion. Pattern Recogn 45:172–185
21. Buades A, Coll B, Morel JM (2005) A non-local algorithm for image denoising. In: International conference on computer vision and pattern recognition, vol 2. IEEE, pp 60–65
22. Bugeau A, Bertalmío M, Caselles V, Sapiro G (2010) A comprehensive framework for image inpainting. IEEE Trans Image Process 19(10):2634–2645
23. Butler A, Izadi S, Hilliges O, Molyneaux D, Hodges S, Kim D (2012) Shake'n'sense: reducing interference for overlapping structured light depth cameras. In: Conference human factors in computing systems, pp 1933–1936
24. Camplani M, Salgado L (2012) Adaptive spatiotemporal filter for low-cost camera depth maps. In: International conference on emerging signal processing applications. IEEE, pp 33–36
25. Camplani M, Salgado L (2012) Efficient spatiotemporal hole filling strategy for Kintect depth maps. In: IS&T/SPIE electronic imaging, pp 82,900E–82,900E
26. Cao Y, Wu Z, Shen C (2017) Estimating depth from monocular images as classification using deep fully convolutional residual networks. IEEE Trans Circuits Syst Video Technol 28(11):3174–3182
27. Cavestany P, Rodriguez A, Martinez-Barbera H, Breckon T (2015) Improved 3D sparse maps for high-performance structure from motion with low-cost omnidirectional robots. In: International conference on image processing, pp 4927–4931
28. Chan T, Shen J (2000) Mathematical models for local deterministic inpaintings. Technical report CAM TR 00-11, UCLA
29. Chang A, Dai A, Funkhouser T, Halber M, Nießner M, Savva M, Song S, Zeng A, Zhang Y (2017) Matterport3D: learning from RGB-D data in indoor environments. In: International conference on 3D vision
30. Chen C, Cai J, Zheng J, Cham TJ, Shi G (2013) A color-guided, region-adaptive and depth-selective unified framework for Kintect depth recovery. In: International workshop on multimedia signal processing. IEEE, pp 007–012
31. Chen C, Cai J, Zheng J, Cham TJ, Shi G (2015) Kinect depth recovery using a color-guided, region-adaptive, and depth-selective framework. ACM Trans Intell Syst Technol 6(2):12
32. Chen W, Fu Z, Yang D, Deng J (2016) Single-image depth perception in the wild. In: Advances in neural information processing systems, pp 730–738
33. Cong P, Xiong Z, Zhang Y, Zhao S, Wu F (2015) Accurate dynamic 3D sensing with fourier-assisted phase shifting. Sel Top Signal Process 9(3):396–408
34. Cordts M, Omran M, Ramos S, Rehfeld T, Enzweiler M, Benenson R, Franke U, Roth S, Schiele B (2016) The cityscapes dataset for semantic urban scene understanding. In: IEEE conference on computer vision and pattern recognition, pp 3213–3223
35. Crabb R, Tracey C, Puranik A, Davis J (2008) Real-time foreground segmentation via range and color imaging. In: IEEE conference on computer vision and pattern recognition workshops, pp 1–5
36. Criminisi A, Pérez P, Toyama K (2004) Region filling and object removal by exemplar-based image inpainting. IEEE Trans Image Process 13(9):1200–1212
37. Dabov K, Foi A, Katkovnik V, Egiazarian K (2007) Image denoising by sparse 3D transform-domain collaborative filtering. IEEE Trans Image Process 16(8):2080–2095
38. Darabi S, Shechtman E, Barnes C, Goldman DB, Sen P (2012) Image melding: combining inconsistent images using patch-based synthesis. ACM Trans Graph 31(4):82–1
39. Daribo I, Saito H (2011) A novel inpainting-based layered depth video for 3DTV. IEEE Trans Broadcast 57(2):533–541
40. Delage E, Lee H, Ng AY (2006) A dynamic Bayesian network model for autonomous 3D reconstruction from a single indoor image. In: IEEE conference on computer vision and pattern recognition, vol 2. IEEE, pp 2418–2428
41. Ding L, Sharma G (2017) Fusing structure from motion and lidar for dense accurate depth map estimation. In: International conference on acoustics, speech and signal processing. IEEE, pp 1283–1287

42. Efros AA, Freeman WT (2001) Image quilting for texture synthesis and transfer. In: Conference on computer graphics and interactive techniques. ACM, pp 341–346
43. Efros AA, Leung TK (1999) Texture synthesis by non-parametric sampling. In: International conference on computer vision, vol 2. IEEE, pp 1033–1038
44. Eigen D, Fergus R (2015) Predicting depth, surface normals and semantic labels with a common multi-scale convolutional architecture. In: International conference on computer vision, pp 2650–2658
45. Eigen D, Puhrsch C, Fergus R (2014) Depth map prediction from a single image using a multi-scale deep network. In: Advances in neural information processing systems, pp 2366–2374
46. El-laithy RA, Huang J, Yeh M (2012) Study on the use of microsoft Kinect for robotics applications. In: Position location and navigation symposium. IEEE, pp 1280–1288
47. Felzenszwalb PF, Huttenlocher DP (2004) Efficient graph-based image segmentation. Comput Vis 59(2):167–181
48. Fu D, Zhao Y, Yu L (2010) Temporal consistency enhancement on depth sequences. In: Picture coding symposium. IEEE, pp 342–345
49. Gangwal OP, Djapic B (2010) Real-time implementation of depth map post-processing for 3D-TV in dedicated hardware. In: International conference on consumer electronics. IEEE, pp 173–174
50. Garg R, Carneiro G, Reid I (2016) Unsupervised CNN for single view depth estimation: geometry to the rescue. In: European conference on computer vision. Springer, pp 740–756
51. Garro V, Mutto CD, Zanuttigh P, Cortelazzo GM (2009) A novel interpolation scheme for range data with side information. In: Conference on visual media production. IEEE, pp 52–60
52. Gatys LA, Ecker AS, Bethge M (2016) Image style transfer using convolutional neural networks. In: IEEE conference on computer vision and pattern recognition, pp 2414–2423
53. Geiger A, Lenz P, Stiller C, Urtasun R (2013) Vision meets robotics: the KITTI dataset. Robotics research, pp 1231–1237
54. Ghiasi G, Lee H, Kudlur M, Dumoulin V, Shlens J (2017) Exploring the structure of a real-time, arbitrary neural artistic stylization network. In: British machine vision conference, pp 1–12
55. Godard C, Mac Aodha O, Brostow GJ (2017) Unsupervised monocular depth estimation with left-right consistency. In: IEEE conference on computer vision and pattern recognition, pp 6602–6611
56. Goodfellow I, Pouget-Abadie J, Mirza M, Xu B, Warde-Farley D, Ozair S, Courville A, Bengio Y (2014) Generative adversarial nets. In: Advances in neural information processing systems, pp 2672–2680
57. Gortler SJ, Grzeszczuk R, Szeliski R, Cohen MF (1996) The lumigraph. In: Conference on computer graphics and interactive techniques. ACM, pp 43–54
58. Guillemot C, Le Meur O (2014) Image inpainting: overview and recent advances. Signal Process Mag 31(1):127–144
59. Hansard M, Lee S, Choi O, Horaud RP (2012) Time-of-flight cameras: principles, methods and applications. Springer Science & Business Media, Berlin
60. Hays J, Efros AA (2007) Scene completion using millions of photographs. ACM Trans Graph 26(3):4
61. He K, Sun J, Tang X (2010) Guided image filtering. In: European conference on computer vision. Springer, pp 1–14
62. Heitz G, Gould S, Saxena A, Koller D (2009) Cascaded classification models: combining models for holistic scene understanding. In: Advances in neural information processing systems, pp 641–648
63. Herrera D, Kannala J, Heikkilä J et al (2013) Depth map inpainting under a second-order smoothness prior. In: Scandinavian conference on image analysis. Springer, pp 555–566
64. Hervieu A, Papadakis N, Bugeau A, Gargallo P, Caselles V (2010) Stereoscopic image inpainting: distinct depth maps and images inpainting. In: International conference on pattern recognition, pp 4101–4104. IEEE (2010)

65. Hirschmuller H (2008) Stereo processing by semi-global matching and mutual information. IEEE Trans Pattern Anal Mach Intell 30:328–341
66. Hirschmuller H, Scharstein D (2007) Evaluation of cost functions for stereo matching. In: IEEE conference on computer vision and pattern recognition, pp 1–8
67. Hoiem D, Efros AA, Hebert M (2005) Automatic photo pop-up. ACM Trans Graph 24:577–584
68. Hoiem D, Efros AA, Hebert M (2005) Geometric context from a single image. In: International conference on computer vision, vol 1. IEEE, pp 654–661
69. Hu J, Ozay M, Zhang Y, Okatani T (2018) Revisiting single image depth estimation: toward higher resolution maps with accurate object boundaries. arXiv preprint arXiv:1803.08673
70. Huang X, Wang L, Huang J, Li D, Zhang M (2009) A depth extraction method based on motion and geometry for 2D to 3D conversion. In: Intelligent information technology application, vol 3. IEEE, pp 294–298
71. Ihler A, McAllester D (2009) Particle belief propagation. In: Artificial intelligence and statistics, pp 256–263
72. Ihrke I, Kutulakos KN, Lensch H, Magnor M, Heidrich W (2010) Transparent and specular object reconstruction. Computer graphics forum, vol 29. Wiley Online Library, New York, pp 2400–2426
73. Iizuka S, Simo-Serra E, Ishikawa H (2017) Globally and locally consistent image completion. ACM trans Graph 36(4):107
74. Islam AT, Scheel C, Pajarola R, Staadt O (2017) Robust enhancement of depth images from depth sensors. Comput Graph 68:53–65
75. Izadi S, Kim D, Hilliges O, Molyneaux D, Newcombe R, Kohli P, Shotton J, Hodges S, Freeman D, Davison A et al (2011) Kinectfusion: real-time 3D reconstruction and interaction using a moving depth camera. In: ACM symposium user interface software and technology, pp 559–568
76. Jackson PT, Atapour-Abarghouei A, Bonner S, Breckon T, Obara B (2018) Style augmentation: data augmentation via style randomization, pp 1–13. arXiv preprint arXiv:1809.05375
77. Jaderberg M, Simonyan K, Zisserman A, et al (2015) Spatial transformer networks. In: Advances in neural information processing systems, pp 2017–2025
78. Janarthanan V, Jananii G (2012) A detailed survey on various image inpainting techniques. Adv Image Process 2(2):1
79. Jia J, Tang CK (2003) Image repairing: robust image synthesis by adaptive n-d tensor voting. In: IEEE conference on computer vision and pattern recognition, vol 1, pp I–643
80. Johnson J, Alahi A, Fei-Fei L (2016) Perceptual losses for real-time style transfer and super-resolution. In: European conference on computer vision, pp 694–711
81. Karsch K, Liu C, Kang SB (2014) Depth transfer: depth extraction from video using non-parametric sampling. IEEE Trans Pattern Anal Mach Intell 36(11):2144–2158
82. Kim Y, Ham B, Oh C, Sohn K (2016) Structure selective depth superresolution for RGB-D cameras. IEEE Trans Image Process 25(11):5227–5238
83. Komodakis N, Tziritas G (2007) Image completion using efficient belief propagation via priority scheduling and dynamic pruning. IEEE Trans Image Process 16(11):2649–2661
84. Kopf J, Cohen MF, Lischinski D, Uyttendaele M (2007) Joint bilateral upsampling. ACM Trans Graph 26(3):96
85. Kumar V, Mukherjee J, Mandal SKD (2016) Image inpainting through metric labeling via guided patch mixing. IEEE Trans Image Process 25(11):5212–5226
86. Kuznietsov Y, Stückler J, Leibe B (2017) Semi-supervised deep learning for monocular depth map prediction. In: IEEE conference on computer vision and pattern recognition, pp 6647–6655
87. Ladicky L, Shi J, Pollefeys M (2014) Pulling things out of perspective. In: IEEE conference on computer vision and pattern recognition, pp 89–96
88. Lai K, Bo L, Ren X, Fox D (2011) A large-scale hierarchical multi-view RGB-D object dataset. In: International conference on robotics and automation. IEEE, pp 1817–1824

89. Lai P, Tian D, Lopez P (2010) Depth map processing with iterative joint multilateral filtering. In: Picture coding symposium. IEEE, pp 9–12
90. Laina I, Rupprecht C, Belagiannis V, Tombari F, Navab N (2016) Deeper depth prediction with fully convolutional residual networks. In: International conference on 3D vision. IEEE, pp 239–248
91. Lee JH, Choi I, Kim MH (2016) Laplacian patch-based image synthesis. In: IEEE conference on computer vision and pattern recognition, pp 2727–2735
92. Lee SB, Ho YS (2009) Discontinuity-adaptive depth map filtering for 3D view generation. In: International conference on immersive telecommunications. ICST, p 8
93. Levin A, Lischinski D, Weiss Y (2008) A closed-form solution to natural image matting. IEEE Trans Pattern Anal Mach Intell 30(2):228–242
94. Li B, Dai Y, He M (2018) Monocular depth estimation with hierarchical fusion of dilated CNNs and soft-weighted-sum inference. Pattern Recogn
95. Li C, Wand M (2016) Combining markov random fields and convolutional neural networks for image synthesis. In: IEEE conference on computer vision and pattern recognition, pp 2479–2486
96. Lindner M, Schiller I, Kolb A, Koch R (2010) Time-of-flight sensor calibration for accurate range sensing. Comput Vis Image Underst 114(12):1318–1328
97. Liu B, Gould S, Koller D (2010) Single image depth estimation from predicted semantic labels. In: IEEE conference on computer vision and pattern recognition. IEEE, pp 1253–1260
98. Liu F, Shen C, Lin G (2015) Deep convolutional neural fields for depth estimation from a single image. In: IEEE conference on computer vision and pattern recognition, pp 5162–5170
99. Liu F, Shen C, Lin G, Reid I (2016) Learning depth from single monocular images using deep convolutional neural fields. IEEE Trans Pattern Anal Mach Intell 38(10):2024–2039
100. Liu J, Gong X, Liu J (2012) Guided inpainting and filtering for Kinect depth maps. In: International conference on pattern recognition. IEEE, pp 2055–2058
101. Liu M, Salzmann M, He X (2014) Discrete-continuous depth estimation from a single image. In: IEEE conference on computer vision and pattern recognition, pp 716–723
102. Liu S, Lai P, Tian D, Gomila C, Chen CW (2010) Joint trilateral filtering for depth map compression. In: Visual communications and image processing. International Society for Optics and Photonics, pp 77,440F–77,440F
103. Liu S, Wang Y, Wang J, Wang H, Zhang J, Pan C (2013) Kinect depth restoration via energy minimization with TV 21 regularization. In: International conference on image processing. IEEE, pp 724–724
104. Lu S, Ren X, Liu F (2014) Depth enhancement via low-rank matrix completion. In: IEEE conference on computer vision and pattern recognition, pp 3390–3397
105. Ma Y, Worrall S, Kondoz AM (2008) Automatic video object segmentation using depth information and an active contour model. In: Workshop on multimedia signal processing. IEEE, pp 910–914
106. Matyunin S, Vatolin D, Berdnikov Y, Smirnov M (2011) Temporal filtering for depth maps generated by Kintect depth camera. In: 3DTV conference. IEEE, pp 1–4
107. Miao D, Fu J, Lu Y, Li S, Chen CW (2012) Texture-assisted Kinect depth inpainting. In: International symposium circuits and systems. IEEE, pp 604–607
108. Min D, Lu J, Do MN (2012) Depth video enhancement based on weighted mode filtering. IEEE Trans Image Process 21(3):1176–1190
109. Mueller M, Zilly F, Kauff P (2010) Adaptive cross-trilateral depth map filtering. In: 3DTV conference. IEEE, pp 1–4
110. Nguyen HT, Do MN (2005) Image-based rendering with depth information using the prop-agation algorithm. In: International conference on acoustics, speech, and signal processing, pp 589–592
111. Nguyen K, Fookes C, Sridharan S, Tistarelli M, Nixon M (2018) Super-resolution for bio-metrics: a comprehensive survey. Pattern Recogn 78:23–42
112. Nguyen QH, Do MN, Patel SJ (2009) Depth image-based rendering from multiple cameras with 3D propagation algorithm. In: International conference on immersive telecommunica-tions. ICST, p 6

113. Pathak D, Krahenbuhl P, Donahue J, Darrell T, Efros AA (2016) Context encoders: feature learning by inpainting. In: IEEE conference on computer vision and pattern recognition, pp 2536–2544
114. Peng J, Hazan T, McAllester D, Urtasun R (2011) Convex max-product algorithms for continuous MRFs with applications to protein folding. In: International conference on machine learning, pp 729–736
115. Perona P, Malik J (1990) Scale-space and edge detection using anisotropic diffusion. IEEE Trans Pattern Anal Mach Intell 12(7):629–639
116. Petschnigg G, Szeliski R, Agrawala M, Cohen M, Hoppe H, Toyama K (2004) Digital photography with flash and no-flash image pairs. ACM trans Graph 23:664–672
117. Po LM, Zhang S, Xu X, Zhu Y (2011) A new multi-directional extrapolation hole-filling method for depth-image-based rendering. In: International conference on image processing. IEEE, pp 2589–2592
118. Popat K, Picard RW (1993) Novel cluster-based probability model for texture synthesis, classification, and compression. In: Visual communications, pp 756–768
119. Pritch Y, Kav-Venaki E, Peleg S (2009) Shift-map image editing. Int Conf Comput Vis 9:151–158
120. Qi F, Han J, Wang P, Shi G, Li F (2013) Structure guided fusion for depth map inpainting. Pattern Recogn Lett 34(1):70–76
121. Richard MMOBB, Chang MYS (2001) Fast digital image inpainting. In: International conference on visualization, imaging and image processing, pp 106–107
122. Richardt C, Stoll C, Dodgson NA, Seidel HP, Theobalt C (2012) Coherent spatiotemporal filtering, upsampling and rendering of RGBZ videos. Computer graphics forum, vol 31. Wiley Online Library, New York, pp 247–256
123. Ringbeck T, Möller T, Hagebeuker B (2007) Multidimensional measurement by using 3D PMD sensors. Adv Radio Sci 5:135
124. Rousseeuw PJ (1984) Least median of squares regression. Am Stat Assoc 79(388):871–880
125. Sabov A, Krüger J (2008) Identification and correction of flying pixels in range camera data. In: Conference on computer graphics. ACM, pp 135–142
126. Sarbolandi H, Lefloch D, Kolb A (2015) Kinect range sensing: structured-light versus time-of-flight Kinect. Comput Vis Image Underst 139:1–20
127. Saxena A, Chung SH, Ng AY (2006) Learning depth from single monocular images. In: Advances in neural information processing systems, pp 1161–1168
128. Saxena A, Sun M, Ng AY (2009) Make3d: learning 3D scene structure from a single still image. IEEE Trans Pattern Anal Mach Intell 31(5):824–840
129. Scharstein D, Szeliski R (2002) A taxonomy and evaluation of dense two-frame stereo correspondence algorithms. Int J Comput Vis 47:7–42
130. Sheng L, Ngan KN, Li S (2014) Temporal depth video enhancement based on intrinsic static structure. In: International conference on image processing. IEEE, pp 2893–2897
131. Suthar R, Patel MKR (2014) A survey on various image inpainting techniques to restore image. Int J Eng Res Appl 4(2):85–88
132. Tao MW, Srinivasan PP, Malik J, Rusinkiewicz S, Ramamoorthi R (2015) Depth from shading, defocus, and correspondence using light-field angular coherence. In: IEEE conference on computer vision and pattern recognition, pp 1940–1948
133. Telea A (2004) An image inpainting technique based on the fast marching method. Graph Tools 9(1):23–34
134. Tippetts B, Lee DJ, Lillywhite K, Archibald J (2016) Review of stereo vision algorithms and their suitability for resource-limited systems. Real-Time Image Process 11(1):5–25
135. Tomasi C, Manduchi R (1998) Bilateral filtering for gray and color images. In: International conference on computer vision. IEEE, pp 839–846
136. Vijayanagar KR, Loghman M, Kim J (2014) Real-time refinement of Kinect depth maps using multi-resolution anisotropic diffusion. Mob Netw Appl 19(3):414–425
137. Wang J, An P, Zuo Y, You Z, Zhang Z (2014) High accuracy hole filling for Kintect depth maps. In: SPIE/COS photonics Asia, pp 92,732L–92,732L

138. Wang L, Huang Z, Gong Y, Pan C (2017) Ensemble based deep networks for image super-resolution. Pattern Recogn 68:191–198
139. Wei LY, Lefebvre S, Kwatra V, Turk G (2009) State of the art in example-based texture synthesis. In: Eurographics state of the art report, pp 93–117
140. Wexler Y, Shechtman E, Irani M (2007) Space-time completion of video. IEEE Trans Pattern Anal Mach Intell 29(3):463–476
141. Whyte O, Sivic J, Zisserman A (2009) Get out of my picture! internet-based inpainting. In: British machine vision conference, pp 1–11
142. Wu Y, Ying S, Zheng L (2018) Size-to-depth: a new perspective for single image depth estimation. arXiv preprint arXiv:1801.04461
143. Xie J, Girshick R, Farhadi A (2016) Deep3D: fully automatic 2D-to-3D video conversion with deep convolutional neural networks. In: European conference on computer vision. Springer, pp 842–857
144. Xu X, Po LM, Cheung CH, Feng L, Ng KH, Cheung KW (2013) Depth-aided exemplar-based hole filling for DIBR view synthesis. In: International symposium circuits and systems. IEEE, pp 2840–2843
145. Xue H, Zhang S, Cai D (2017) Depth image inpainting: improving low rank matrix completion with low gradient regularization. IEEE Trans Image Process 26(9):4311–4320
146. Yang C, Lu X, Lin Z, Shechtman E, Wang O, Li H (2017) High-resolution image inpainting using multi-scale neural patch synthesis. In: IEEE conference on computer vision and pattern recognition, pp 4076–4084
147. Yang J, Ye X, Li K, Hou C, Wang Y (2014) Color-guided depth recovery from RGB-D data using an adaptive autoregressive model. IEEE Trans Image Process 23(8):3443–3458
148. Yang NE, Kim YG, Park RH (2012) Depth hole filling using the depth distribution of neighboring regions of depth holes in the Kintect sensor. In: International conference on signal processing, communication and computing. IEEE, pp 658–661
149. Yang Q, Tan KH, Culbertson B, Apostolopoulos J (2010) Fusion of active and passive sensors for fast 3D capture. In: International workshop on multimedia signal processing. IEEE, pp 69–74
150. Yeh RA, Chen C, Yian Lim T, Schwing AG, Hasegawa-Johnson M, Do MN (2017) Semantic image inpainting with deep generative models. In: IEEE conference on computer vision and pattern recognition, pp 6882–6890
151. Yu J, Lin Z, Yang J, Shen X, Lu X, Huang TS (2018) Generative image inpainting with contextual attention. In: IEEE conference on computer vision and pattern recognition, pp 1–15
152. Zhan H, Garg R, Weerasekera CS, Li K, Agarwal H, Reid I (2018) Unsupervised learning of monocular depth estimation and visual odometry with deep feature reconstruction. In: IEEE conference on computer vision and pattern recognition, pp 340–349
153. Zhang G, Jia J, Hua W, Bao H (2011) Robust bilayer segmentation and motion/depth estimation with a handheld camera. IEEE Trans Pattern Anal Mach Intell 33(3):603–617
154. Zhang L, Shen P, Zhang S, Song J, Zhu G (2016) Depth enhancement with improved exemplar-based inpainting and joint trilateral guided filtering. In: International conference on image processing. IEEE, pp 4102–4106
155. Zhang L, Tam WJ, Wang D (2004) Stereoscopic image generation based on depth images. In: International conference on image processing, vol 5. IEEE, pp 2993–2996
156. Zhang R, Isola P, Efros AA (2016) Colorful image colorization. In: European conference on computer vision, pp 649–666
157. Zhang Y, Funkhouser T (2018) Deep depth completion of a single RGB-D image. In: IEEE conference on computer vision and pattern recognition, pp 175–185
158. Zhang Z (2012) Microsoft Kinect sensor and its effect. IEEE Multimedia 19(2):4–10
159. Zheng C, Cham TJ, Cai J (2018) T2net: synthetic-to-realistic translation for solving single-image depth estimation tasks. In: European conference on computer vision, pp 767–783
160. Zhou T, Brown M, Snavely N, Lowe DG (2017) Unsupervised learning of depth and ego-motion from video. In: IEEE conference on computer vision and pattern recognition, pp 6612–6619

161. Zhu JY, Park T, Isola P, Efros AA (2017) Unpaired image-to-image translation using cycle-consistent adversarial networks. International conference on computer vision, pp 2242–2251
162. Zhuo W, Salzmann M, He X, Liu M (2015) Indoor scene structure analysis for single image depth estimation. In: IEEE conference on computer vision and pattern recognition, pp 614–622

Chapter 3
Depth Super-Resolution with Color Guidance: A Review

Jingyu Yang, Zhongyu Jiang, Xinchen Ye and Kun Li

Abstract Depth super-resolution (SR) with color guidance is a classic vision problem to upsample low-resolution depth images. It has a wide range of applications in 3D reconstruction, automotive driver assistance and augmented reality. Due to the easy acquirement of the aligned high-resolution color images, there have been many depth SR approaches with color guidance in the past years. This chapter provides a comprehensive survey of the recent developments in this field. We divide these methods into three categories: regularization-based methods, filtering-based methods, and learning-based methods. Regularization-based methods make the ill-posed SR problem well constrained by utilizing regularization terms. Filtering-based methods upsample depth images via local filters with the instruction of guidance images. Learning-based methods can be further divided into traditional dictionary learning methods based on sparse representations and current popular deep learning methods. We survey the state-of-the-art methods, discuss their benefits and limitations, and point out some problems in this field.

This work was supported by the National Natural Science Foundation of China under Grant 61702078.

J. Yang (✉) · Z. Jiang · K. Li
Tianjin University, Tianjin 300072, China
e-mail: yjy@tju.edu.cn

Z. Jiang
email: jiang_zhongyu@tju.edu.cn

K. Li
e-mail: lik@tju.edu.cn

X. Ye
Dalian University of Technology, Dalian 116100, China
e-mail: yexch@dlut.edu.cn

3.1 Introduction

Despite the rapid progress of depth sensing technologies, there still exists a significant gap between depth cameras and color cameras, particularly in terms of spatial resolution. For example, the spatial resolution of off-the-shelf smartphone cameras can be as high as nearly 50 Megapixels; while those of commodity Time-of-Flight (ToF) depth cameras are at the level of 200 kilo pixels, or even lower for low-cost versions in mobile devices. Such a significant resolution gap has impeded their applications in many tasks, e.g., 3DTV, and 3D reconstruction, which requires depth maps should have the same (or at least similar) resolution as the associated color images. This raises the problem of depth super-resolution (SR), which is closely related to generic image super-resolution, but also involves many additional elements.

The depth SR problem has two unique characteristics: (1) piecewise smooth spatial distribution of depth map and (2) the available the auxiliary high-resolution color images. Depth images and color images are two descriptions of the same scene, and they often simultaneously present discontinuities at the same locations, which is referred to as structural correlation. Therefore, state-of-the-art depth SR schemes are carefully designed to exploit such structural correlation [14, 15, 29]. In practical applications, they have slight viewpoint difference and thus view warping is required before resolution enhancement. Moreover, structural inconsistency between RGB-D pairs also exists. Different depths may have similar colors, and areas with intensive color variation may have close depth values, which would seriously interfere with the depth SR. Early works paid more attention to the inconsistency of RGB-D pairs, while recent works tend to remedy or avoid texture-copying artifacts [19, 32, 33]. In the past decade, depth SR has evolved along with the development of generic image SR. Similarly, depth SR methods can be mainly divided into three categories: regularization-based methods, filtering-based methods, and learning-based methods. This chapter reviews depth SR methods with color guidance following this taxonomy.

This chapter is organized as follows: Sect. 3.2 formulates the general depth SR problem, summarizes the main challenges, and gives a taxonomy of the vast literature. Section 3.3 reviews regularization-based methods that super-resolve depth maps via solving an energy function. Section 3.4 overviews the category that interpolates missing pixels at the high-resolution grids via advanced filtering schemes. Section 3.5 first discusses depth SR methods with dictionary learning techniques, and then turns to more data-driven approaches using advanced deep learning paradigms. Finally, Sect. 3.6 draws conclusions.

3.2 Problem Statement, Challenges, and Taxonomy

3.2.1 Challenges

The captured depth image is a degraded version of the underlying high-quality depth image, due to the limitation of current depth capturing systems. There are mainly four types of degradations, namely random missing depths, structured missing depths, noise, and undersampling. Among the degradations, undersampling is a common and important one. The degradation model of undersampling, which is an ill-posed problem, can be described as

$$\mathbf{y} = \mathbf{Hx} + \mathbf{n}, \tag{3.1}$$

where $\mathbf{x}$ and $\mathbf{y}$ denote the vector forms of the underlying high-resolution depth map and the captured low-resolution one, respectively. $\mathbf{H}$ represents the composite operator of blurring and sampling and $\mathbf{n}$ is additive noise.

The low resolution of depth images has hindered their widespread use, and therefore, there are many works to recover high-resolution depth images. Despite great progress, there are still some problems in depth SR.

- Although there are many methods to remedy texture-copying artifacts, methods to solve the problem is less in deep learning methods.
- How to super-resolve different degradation types and sampling ratios in low-resolution (LR) depth images in a single model is an ongoing direction.
- Compared with a lot of color image datasets, there are less data to support deep learning of depth related tasks.
- Most methods upsample LR depth images from regular downsampling. It maybe better to adopt adaptive downsampling to generate LR depth images.

3.2.2 Taxonomy

There are usually three types of methods in depth SR: regularization-based methods, filtering-based methods, and learning-based methods. Among learning-based methods, they contain traditional dictionary learning methods and current popular deep learning methods. In the rest of the chapter, we will introduce representative methods in detail.

3.3 Regularization-Based Methods

In this category, the depth SR is formulated as an optimization problem, which includes various regularization terms to make the ill-posed SR problem well constrained.

Ferstl et al. [5] propose to use high order total variation regularization, named Total Generalized Variation (TGV), to upsample the depth image, which avoids the problem of surface flattening. Furthermore, they use an anisotropic diffusion tensor based on the intensity image (expressed as $\mathbf{T}$ in Eq. (3.2)), which utilizes the correspondence and depth pairs. The proposed tensor is claimed to not only weight the depth gradient but also orient the gradient direction during the optimization process. It is worth mentioning that they also propose real ToF datasets coupled with groundtruth measurements to promote the quantitative comparison of real depth map super-resolution.

$$\mathbf{T} = \exp(-\beta|\nabla\mathbf{I}_H|^\gamma)\mathbf{n}\mathbf{n}^T + \mathbf{n}^\perp\mathbf{n}^{\perp T}, \tag{3.2}$$

where $\mathbf{I}$ is the intensity image, $\mathbf{n}$ is the normalized direction of the image gradient $\mathbf{n} = \frac{\nabla I_H}{|\nabla I_H|}$, $n^\perp$ is the normal vector to the gradient, and the scalars β, γ adjust the magnitude and the sharpness of the tensor.

Yang et al. [29] propose an adaptive color-guided autoregressive (AR) model based on the tight fit between the AR model and depth maps. The regularization is constructed based on the AR prediction errors subject to measurement consistency. The AR weights are computed according to both local correlation and the nonlocal similarity. Among them, the color weight $a_{x,y}^I$ is designed in Eq. (3.3) to make use of the correlations of RGB-D pairs, which utilizes a bilateral kernel to weight the distance of local patches. Therefore, compared with the standard Non-Local Mean (NLM) filter, it can carry shape information of local image structures. Several depth enhancement problems are unified into an elegant depth recovery framework which produces state-of-the-art results.

$$a_{x,y}^I = \exp\left(-\frac{\sum_{i\in\mathscr{C}}\|\mathbf{B}_x \circ (P_x^i - P_y^i)\|_2^2}{2 \times 3 \times \sigma_2^2}\right), \tag{3.3}$$

where σ_2 controls the decay rate, $\circ$ is the element-wise operator. P_x^i denotes an operator which extracts a patch centered at x in color channel i. The bilateral filter kernel $\mathbf{B}_x$ is defined in the extracted patch:

$$\mathbf{B}_x(\mathbf{x}, \mathbf{y}) = \exp\left(-\frac{\|\mathbf{x} - \mathbf{y}\|_2^2}{2\sigma_3^2}\right)\exp\left(-\frac{\sum_{i\in\mathscr{C}}(\mathbf{I}_x^i - \mathbf{I}_y^i)}{2 \times 3 \times \sigma_4^2}\right), \tag{3.4}$$

where $\mathbf{I}$ is the color image. σ_3 and σ_4 are the parameters of the bilateral kernel, which balance the importance of the spatial distance and intensity difference, respectively.

Along this avenue, Dong et al. [3] exploit both local and nonlocal structural regularization. The local regularization term consists of two local constraints in the gradient domain and spatial domain, respectively. The nonlocal regularization involves a low-rank constraint to utilize global characterization of color-depth dependency. Liu et al. [20] also combine local and nonlocal manifolds into the regularization. The local manifold is a smoothness regularizer, which models the local neighboring relationship of pixels in depth. The nonlocal manifold takes advantages of self-similar

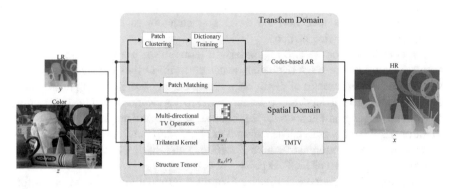

Fig. 3.1 The pipeline of paper [10]

structures to build highly data-adaptive orthogonal bases. Besides, they define a 3D thresholding operator on local and nonlocal manifolds to enforce the sparsity on the manifold spectral bases.

Jiang et al. [10] upsample the LR depth with both transform and spatial domain regularization. In the transform domain, the regularization actually belongs to an AR model, where each patch is sparsified with a PCA dictionary. In the spatial domain regularization, they extend the standard total variation to multidirectional total variation, which can better characterize the geometrical structures spatially orientated at arbitrary directions. The overall pipeline is shown in Fig. 3.1

The above methods mostly design effective weights. The works in [12, 18] propose robust penalty functions, which are nonconvex, as the smoothness regularization. The two penalty functions all have the similar essential form as presented in Eq. (3.5) They claimed that the penalty function is robust against the inconsistency of RGB-D pairs by adjusting gradient magnitude variation by rescaling of intensity gradients. Therefore, they significantly reduce texture-copying artifacts.

$$\omega(x^2) = \exp\left(-\frac{x^2}{\sigma}\right) \tag{3.5}$$

Compared with the previous methods, the works in [19, 32] explicitly deal with texture copying artifacts. The work in [19] adapts the bandwidth to the relative smoothness of patches, which can effectively suppress texture-copying artifacts and preserve depth discontinuities. The method, in general, can be used in many existing methods. The paper in [32] more explicitly considers the inconsistency between edges of RGB-D pairs by quantizing the inconsistency. The quantization inconsistency is embedded in the smoothness term. Experiments evaluated on multiple datasets demonstrate the ability to mitigate texture-copying artifacts.

Zuo et al. [33] compute guidance affinities of Markov Random Field regularization by multiple minimum spanning trees (MSTs). The method can preserve depth edges due to the paths of the MSTs. Edge inconsistency between RGB-D pairs is also considered and embedded into the weights of edges in each MST. Therefore, it mitigates texture-copying artifacts.

Liu et al. [20] propose two regularization terms in the graph domain. The first regularizer utilizes the graph Laplacian, which performs well in preserving the piecewise smooth characteristic of depth map. A specifically designed weight matrix is defined to make use of depth and color images. Besides the internal smoothness prior, an external graph gradient operator is proposed, which is the nonlocal version of the traditional gradient operator. The external gradient consistency regularizer enforces utilizing only the common structures of RGB-D pairs. In this way, they remedy the inconsistency problem of RGB-D pairs.

Gu et al. [6] introduce a task-driven learning formulation to obtain the different guidances to different enhancement tasks. Besides, dynamic depth guidance is learned along with the iterations due to the updating of the depth image.

Generally speaking, regularization-based methods often use hand designed functions to approximate image priors, such as nonlocal similarity, piecewise smoothness, local correlation, and so on. Despite the careful design in these regularization functions and their weights, they cannot completely describe real complex image priors. Moreover, methods of this category are typically time consuming to solve the optimization problem, which limits their applications in practical systems.

3.4   Filtering-Based Methods

Filtering-based methods aim to recover a depth map by performing weighted averaging of depth values from local pixels, and the weights are predicted by some weighting strategies derived from the color image. The representative filtering-based methods consist of the bilateral filter, Non-local Means (NL-Means) filter, guided filter, and others.

Eisemann et al. [4] proposed a joint bilateral filter (JBF) based on the classic bilateral filter (BF) with the help of an additional reference image (e.g., color image). The equation of JBF is expressed as

$$\tilde{I}_p = \frac{1}{k_p} \sum_{q \in \Omega} I_q f(||p - q||) g(||\hat{I}_p - \hat{I}_q||), \qquad (3.6)$$

where k_p is a normalization factor, and $\tilde{I}_p$, $\hat{I}_p$ are the filtered output and reference image at pixel index p, respectively. I_q is the input image at pixel index q. Ω is the spatial support of the filter kernel. $f(\cdot)$ and $g(\cdot)$ are two Gaussian kernels given by

$$f(p, q) = \exp\left(\frac{-||p - q||^2}{2\sigma_D^2}\right), \quad g(\hat{I}_p, \hat{I}_q) = \exp\left(\frac{-||\hat{I}_p - \hat{I}_q||^2}{2\sigma_R^2}\right), \qquad (3.7)$$

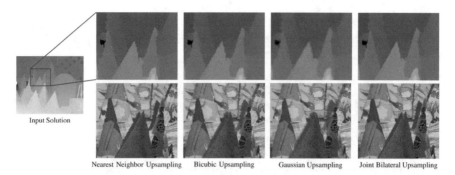

Input Solution

Nearest Neighbor Upsampling   Bicubic Upsampling   Gaussian Upsampling   Joint Bilateral Upsampling

Fig. 3.2 Examples of recovered depth maps from different methods. We also show corresponding 3D views from an offset camera using the upsampled depth map (figure originated from [13])

where σ_D and σ_R are the kernel bandwidth parameters. Inspired by JBF, Kopf et al. [13] proposed a joint bilateral upsampling (JBU), which considers recovering a high-resolution (HR) depth map $\tilde{S}$ from the low-resolution (LR) depth map S and corresponding high-resolution color image $\hat{I}$, see Fig. 3.2. Thus, the JBU has the following form:

$$\tilde{S}_p = \frac{1}{k_p} \sum_{q_\downarrow \in \Omega} S_{q_\downarrow} f(\|p_\downarrow - q_\downarrow\|) g(\|\hat{I}_p - \hat{I}_q\|), \tag{3.8}$$

where $\tilde{S}$ is the HR filtered output and $\hat{I}$ is the HR color image. p, q denote the indices in the HR image and $p_\downarrow, q_\downarrow$ denote the indices in the LR image.

Unlike JBF and JBU, Liu et al. [17] proposed to utilize geodesic distance instead of Euclidean distance in the filter kernels to avoid producing artifacts when the colors of the surfaces across the depth boundaries are similar. The geodesic distance is given by the length of the shortest path:

$$d_G(p, q) = \min_{k \in K} \sum_{i=2}^{|k|} (\frac{1}{r} \|p_k^{(i)} - p_k^{(i-1)}\| + \lambda \|\hat{I}(p_k^{(i)}) - \hat{I}(p_k^{(i-1)})\|), \tag{3.9}$$

where p and q are indices in the HR images. k is a path joining p and q, and $|k|$ is the number of nodes in path k, and K is the set of all the paths. r is the upsampling rate and λ is a weighting parameter. Thus, the method with geodesic distance is defined as

$$\tilde{S}_p = \frac{1}{k_p} \sum_{q_\downarrow \in \Omega} S_{q_\downarrow} g_G(p, q), \tag{3.10}$$

where $g_G(p, q)$ is

$$g_G(p, q) = \exp(\frac{-d_G^2(p, q)}{2\sigma^2}), \tag{3.11}$$

and σ is the kernel bandwidth parameter.

The NL-Means filter [2] shares a similar idea with the JBF method, but considers comparing patches surrounding both pixels instead of the single pixel values at position p and q, which is expressed as

$$\tilde{I}_p = \frac{1}{k_p} \sum_{q \in \Omega} I_q f(p,q) g(p,q). \tag{3.12}$$

The functions $f(p,q)$, $g(p,q)$ have the following form:

$$f(p,q) = \exp(-\frac{1}{h} \sum_{k \in N} G_\sigma(||k||_2)(I(p+k) - I(q+k))^2),$$
$$g(p,q) = \exp(-\frac{1}{h} \sum_{k \in N} G_\sigma(||k||_2)(\hat{I}(p+k) - \hat{I}(q+k))^2), \tag{3.13}$$

where h is a smoothing parameter and N is the number of pixels in patch Ω. The pixelwise distances are weighted according to their offsets k from the central pixel by a Gaussian kernel G_σ with standard deviation σ. Based on this, Huhle et al. [8] extended NL-Means by adding two terms $\xi_{pk}, \hat{\xi}_{pk}$ to $f(p,q)$, $g(p,q)$, respectively, where

$$\xi_{pk} = \exp(-\frac{(I(p) - I(p+k))^2}{h}), \quad \hat{\xi}_{pk} = \exp(-\frac{(\hat{I}(p) - \hat{I}(p+k))^2}{h}). \tag{3.14}$$

These two additional terms constrain the similarity comparison to regions of similar depths, using the same parameter h as in the computation of the inter-patch distances.

In contrast, He et al. [7] proposed another filtering method named guided filter under the assumption that there is a local linear model between the filtered output $\tilde{I}$ and the guidance image $\hat{I}$ (here the color image is used as guidance image). The guided filter has the following form:

$$\tilde{I}_p = \sum_{q \in \Omega} W_{p,q}(\hat{I}) I_q, \tag{3.15}$$

where $W_{p,q}(\cdot)$ is a function of the guidance image $\hat{I}$ and independent of the input image I. In particular, $W_{p,q}(\hat{I})$ is explicitly expressed by

$$W_{p,q}(\hat{I}) = \frac{1}{|\omega|^2} \sum_{q \in \Omega} \left(1 + \frac{(\hat{I}_p - \mu) - (\hat{I}_q - \mu)}{\sigma^2}\right), \tag{3.16}$$

where μ and σ are the mean and variance of $\hat{I}$ in Ω, and $|\omega|$ is the number of pixels in Ω. Compared with the guided filter that applies the linear regression to all pixels covered by a fixed-sized square window non-adaptively, Lu et al. [22] proposed a local multipoint filtering algorithm, which utilizes spatial adaptivity to define local support regions and weighted averaging to fuse multiple estimates.

Shen et al. [25] pointed out that there may be a completely different structure in the guided color image and the target one, and simply passing all patterns to the target could lead to significant errors. Thus, they proposed the concept of mutual structure, which refers to the structural information that is contained in both images. The mutual structure can be measured by the similarity $\mathscr{S}$

$$\mathscr{S}(\tilde{I}_p, \hat{I}_p) = \left(\sigma(\tilde{I}_p)^2 + \sigma(\hat{I}_p)^2\right)\left(1 - \rho(\tilde{I}_p, \hat{I}_p)^2\right)^2, \tag{3.17}$$

where $\sigma(\tilde{I}_p)$, $\sigma(\hat{I}_p)$ are the variance of patch Ω centered at p in $\tilde{I}$, $\hat{I}$, and $\rho(\cdot)$ is the normalized cross-correlation (NCC), expressed as

$$\rho(\tilde{I}_p, \hat{I}_p) = \frac{cov(\tilde{I}_p, \hat{I}_p)}{\sqrt{\sigma(\tilde{I}_p)\sigma(\hat{I}_p)}}, \tag{3.18}$$

where $cov(\tilde{I}_p, \hat{I}_p)$ is the covariance of patch Ω.

For other methods, Min et al. [24] proposed weighted mode filtering (WMF) based on the joint histogram. The weight based on a similarity measure between reference and neighboring pixels is used to construct the histogram, and a final solution is then determined by seeking a global mode on the histogram. Barron et al. [1] proposed the bilateral solver—a form of bilateral-space optimization (FBS), which solves a regularized least squares optimization problem to produce an output that is bilateral-smooth and close to the input. Lo et al. [21] proposed a joint trilateral filtering (JTF) which not only extracts spatial and range information of local pixels, but also integrates local gradient information of the depth image to alleviate the texture-copying artifacts. Yang et al. [28] proposed a global autoregressive depth recovery iteration algorithm, in which each iteration is equivalent to a nonlocal filtering process with a residue feedback, see Fig. 3.3.

The filtering-based methods enjoy simplicity in design and implementation, lower computational complexities. However, the short-sighted local judgement cannot pro-

(a)　　　　　(b)　　　　　(c)　　　　　(d)　　　　　(e)

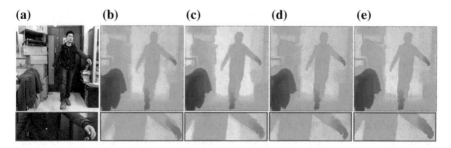

Fig. 3.3 Examples of depth recovery results from different methods: **a** color image, **b** FBS [1], **c** FGI [15], **d** GlobalAR [29], and **e** GAR [28] (figure originated from [28])

vide enough information to recover the global structure, and may introduce annoying artifacts in regions where the associated color image contains rich textures.

3.5 Learning-Based Methods

Methods of this category contain traditional dictionary learning methods and current popular deep learning methods. Dictionary learning methods attempt to find a suitable dictionary from image patches. Based on the dictionary, the densely expressed images in the real world can be converted into suitable sparse representations. Compared with dictionary learning methods, deep learning methods constantly update the network parameters until convergence in order to learn complex and nonlinear mapping functions.

3.5.1 Dictionary Learning Methods

Methods of this category design dictionaries to represent images. The core form of dictionary learning methods can be expressed as

$$\min_{\mathbf{B}, \boldsymbol{\alpha}_i} \sum_{i=1}^{m} \|\mathbf{x}_i - \mathbf{B}\boldsymbol{\alpha}_i\|_2^2 + \lambda \sum_{i=1}^{m} \|\boldsymbol{\alpha}_i\|_1, \tag{3.19}$$

where vector $\mathbf{x}_i$ is the ith signal, matrix $\mathbf{B}$ denotes the dictionary, $\boldsymbol{\alpha}_i$ is the sparse coefficients, λ represents the weight parameter to balance the two terms. Based on this basic form, there are many variants of this category.

Xie et al. [27] propose a coupled dictionary for the single depth image SR. Which contains two dictionaries for LR patches and HR ones respectively. They impose local constraints on the coupled dictionary learning and reconstruction process, which can reduce the prediction uncertainty and prevent the dictionary from over-fitting. The work in [31] proposes a dictionary selection method using basis pursuit to generate multiple dictionaries adaptively. The work [23] does not have an explicit dictionary. However, the external HR depth patches can be viewed as a dictionary and the sparse representation solution can be considered as seeking the most similar patch.

Li et al. [16] design three related dictionaries for LR depth patch, color patch, and HR depth patch respectively to build the SR mapping function. The method assumes that the LR depth image, the HR depth image, and the color image shared the same sparse coefficients under the respective dictionaries. Kiechle et al. [11] also jointly learn a pair of analysis operators to make the RGB-D pairs have a correlated co-support.

The dictionaries have either fixed bases or they are learnt from a limited number of patches, and therefore they have limited expressive ability. Moreover, the optimization process to find the optimal dictionary or sparse coefficients is computationally intensive.

3.5.2 Deep Learning Methods

Recent depth recovery techniques using deep convolutional neural networks directly supervised by ground truth depth images has revolutionized the field by highly accurate results.

The work in [9] (MSG-Net) proposed a gradual up-sampling framework with a multi-scale color guidance module, which further exploits the dependency between color texture and depth structure. Specifically, the rich hierarchical HR intensity features at different levels progressively resolve ambiguity in depth map up-sampling. The HR features in the intensity branch act as complements of the LR depth structures in depth branch, as shown in Fig. 3.4. The compared results can be seen in Fig. 3.5.

Similarly, [14] employed a two-path CNN to learn an end-to-end network to obtain the HR depth map from the LR depth map with the assistance of the corresponding HR color image. The architecture is designed based on the concept of joint filters, in which a fusion branch is added to jointly filter the informative feature maps from

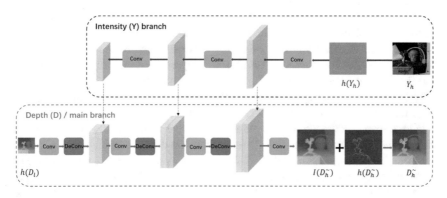

Fig. 3.4 The architecture of MSG-Net (adapted from [9])

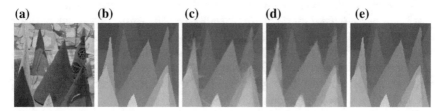

Fig. 3.5 Visual comparison of $8\times$ upsampling results. **a** Color image. **b** Ground truth. **c** Guided Filtering [7]. **d** Ferstl *et al.* [5]. **e** MSG-Net [9] (figure originated from [9])

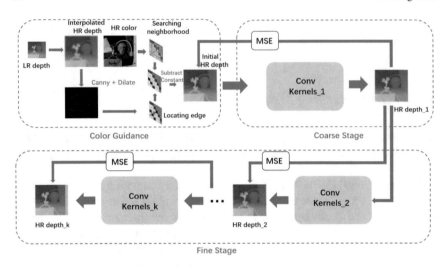

Fig. 3.6 The cascade coarse-to-fine network (adapted from [14])

both the depth and guidance branches. It can leverage the guidance image as a prior and transfer the structural details from the guidance image to the target image for suppressing noise and enhancing spatial resolution.

The above two methods [9, 14] directly use the information of the color image on the feature level and achieve satisfactory performance for depth map recovery. In contrast, other methods focus on extracting accurate depth boundaries to facilitate the process of depth recovery. Ye et al. [30] proposed a joint deep edge-inference and depth SR framework, which first learns a binary map of depth edges from the LR depth map and corresponding HR color image, and then takes advantage of the edge information to guide the reconstruction of the depth map. The color branch acts as a feature extractor to determine informative edge features from the color image. Then, the upsampling feature maps from the depth branch are concatenated with the feature maps extracted from the color branch at the same resolution. The convolutional layers are added to extract the final HR edge map. Finally, a depth filling module is designed to obtain a high-quality depth map with the help of the extracted depth edges.

The paper in [26] proposed a deep cascaded coarse-to-fine network as shown in Fig. 3.6. It aims to learn different sizes of filter kernels. At the coarse stage, larger filter kernels are learned by the CNN to obtain a coarse depth map. As to the fine stage, the coarse depth map is used as the input, and smaller filter kernels are learned to get more accurate results. The depth edge guidance strategy fuses color difference and spatial distance for depth image upsampling, which can alleviate texture-copying artifacts and preserve edge details effectively.

Deep learning methods usually have better performance than traditional methods and have real-time speed. As is well known, deep learning methods are driven by big data. However, there is less high-quality data available for depth SR compared with color SR.

3.6 Conclusion

In this chapter, we have reviewed some state-of-the-art methods in depth SR with color guidance. Due to the ill-posed nature, we first focused on regularization-based methods, which make the problem well constrained via various regularization terms. These regularization terms make use of depth image priors, such as nonlocal similarity, piecewise smoothing and so on. We then shifted the focus to filtering-based methods. Methods of this category upsample depth images via local filters, whose weights are dependent on RGB-D correlations. Compared with other traditional methods, filtering-based methods have low computational complexity. However, the local judgement of filtering-based methods cannot provide enough information to recover global structures. Finally, we review the learning-based methods, which contain traditional dictionary-based methods and deep learning-based methods. The core idea of dictionary-based methods is the sparse representation of images, especially depth images. Methods of this category learn a dictionary from limited data. On the contrary, deep learning based methods achieve much better performance due to their excellent learning ability. Moreover, the deep learning-based methods have real-time speed. Despite the success of deep learning, there is an urgent need for larger training data sets in the depth field, which are currently small when compared with the color field. This is more obvious in real depth image datasets captured by Kinect or ToF sensors.

References

1. Barron JT, Poole B (2016) The fast bilateral solver. In: European conference on computer vision. Springer, pp 617–632
2. Buades A, Coll B, Morel JM (2005) A non-local algorithm for image denoising. In: CVPR, vol 2. IEEE, New York, pp 60–65
3. Dong W, Shi G, Li X, Peng K, Wu J, Guo Z (2016) Color-guided depth recovery via joint local structural and nonlocal low-rank regularization. IEEE Trans Multimed 19(2):293–301
4. Eisemann E, Durand F (2004) Flash photography enhancement via intrinsic relighting. In: ACM transactions on graphics (TOG), vol 23. ACM, New York, pp 673–678
5. Ferstl D, Reinbacher C, Ranftl R, Rüther M, Bischof H (2013) Image guided depth upsampling using anisotropic total generalized variation. In: Proceedings of the IEEE international conference on computer vision, pp 993–1000
6. Gu S, Zuo W, Guo S, Chen Y, Chen C, Zhang L (2017) Learning dynamic guidance for depth image enhancement. In: Proceedings of the IEEE conference on computer vision and pattern recognition, pp 3769–3778
7. He K, Sun J, Tang X (2012) Guided image filtering. IEEE Trans Pattern Anal Mach Intell 35(6):1397–1409

8. Huhle B, Schairer T, Jenke P, Straser W (2010) Fusion of range and color images for denoising and resolution enhancement with a non-local filter. Comput Vis Image Underst 114(12):1336–1345

9. Hui T, Loy CC, Tang X (2016) Depth map super-resolution by deep multi-scale guidance. In: Computer vision - ECCV 2016 - 14th European conference, Amsterdam, The Netherlands, October 11–14, 2016, Proceedings, Part III, pp 353–369. https://doi.org/10.1007/978-3-319-46487-9_22

10. Jiang Z, Hou Y, Yue H, Yang J, Hou C (2018) Depth super-resolution from RGB-D pairs with transform and spatial domain regularization. IEEE Trans Image Process 27(5):2587–2602

11. Kiechle M, Hawe S, Kleinsteuber M (2013) A joint intensity and depth co-sparse analysis model for depth map super-resolution. In: Proceedings of the IEEE international conference on computer vision, pp 1545–1552

12. Kim Y, Ham B, Oh C, Sohn K (2016) Structure selective depth superresolution for RGB-D cameras. IEEE Trans Image Process Publ IEEE Signal Process Soc 25(11):5227–5238

13. Kopf J, Cohen MF, Lischinski D, Uyttendaele M (2007) Joint bilateral upsampling. In: ACM transactions on graphics (ToG), vol 26. ACM, New York, p 96

14. Li Y, Huang JB, Ahuja N, Yang MH (2016) Deep joint image filtering. In: European conference on computer vision. Springer, Berlin, pp 154–169

15. Li Y, Min D, Do MN, Lu J (2016) Fast guided global interpolation for depth and motion. In: European conference on computer vision. Springer, pp 717–733

16. Li Y, Xue T, Sun L, Liu J (2012) Joint example-based depth map super-resolution. In: 2012 IEEE international conference on multimedia and expo. IEEE, pp 152–157

17. Liu MY, Tuzel O, Taguchi Y (2013) Joint geodesic upsampling of depth images. In: Proceedings of the IEEE CVPR, pp 169–176

18. Liu W, Chen X, Yang J, Wu Q (2016) Robust color guided depth map restoration. IEEE Trans Image Process 26(1):315–327

19. Liu W, Chen X, Yang J, Wu Q (2016) Variable bandwidth weighting for texture copy artifact suppression in guided depth upsampling. IEEE Trans Circuits Syst Video Technol 27(10):2072–2085

20. Liu X, Zhai D, Chen R, Ji X, Zhao D, Gao W (2018) Depth restoration from RGB-D data via joint adaptive regularization and thresholding on manifolds. IEEE Trans Image Process 28(3):1068–1079

21. Lo KH, Wang YCF, Hua KL (2017) Edge-preserving depth map upsampling by joint trilateral filter. IEEE Trans Cybern 48(1):371–384

22. Lu J, Shi K, Min D, Lin L, Do MN (2012) Cross-based local multipoint filtering. In: Proceedings of the IEEE CVPR, pp 430–437

23. Mac Aodha O, Campbell ND, Nair A, Brostow GJ (2012) Patch based synthesis for single depth image super-resolution. In: Computer vision–ECCV 2012. Springer, Berlin, pp 71–84

24. Min D, Lu J, Do M (2011) Depth video enhancement based on joint global mode filtering. IEEE Trans Image Process 21(3):1176–1190

25. Shen X, Zhou C, Xu L, Jia J (2015) Mutual-structure for joint filtering. In: CVPR, pp 3406–3414

26. Wen Y, Sheng B, Li P, Lin W, Feng DD (2019) Deep color guided coarse-to-fine convolutional network cascade for depth image super-resolution. IEEE Trans Image Process 28(2):994–1006. https://doi.org/10.1109/TIP.2018.2874285

27. Xie J, Feris RS, Yu SS, Sun MT (2015) Joint super resolution and denoising from a single depth image. IEEE Trans Multimed 17(9):1525–1537

28. Yang J, Ye X, Frossard P (2018) Global auto-regressive depth recovery via iterative non-local filtering. IEEE Trans Broadcast 99:1–15

29. Yang J, Ye X, Li K, Hou C, Wang Y (2014) Color-guided depth recovery from RGB-D data using an adaptive autoregressive model. IEEE Trans Image Process 23(8):3443–3458

30. Ye X, Duan X, Li H (2018) Depth super-resolution with deep edge-inference network and edge-guided depth filling. In: 2018 IEEE international conference on acoustics, speech and signal processing, ICASSP 2018, Calgary, AB, Canada, April 15–20, pp 1398–1402 (2018). https://doi.org/10.1109/ICASSP.2018.8461357

31. Zheng H, Bouzerdoum A, Phung SL (2013) Depth image super-resolution using multi-dictionary sparse representation. In: 2013 IEEE international conference on image processing. IEEE, pp 957–961
32. Zuo Y, Wu Q, Zhang J, An P (2016) Explicit modeling on depth-color inconsistency for color-guided depth up-sampling. In: 2016 IEEE international conference on multimedia and expo (ICME). IEEE, pp 1–6
33. Zuo Y, Wu Q, Zhang J, An P (2018) Minimum spanning forest with embedded edge inconsistency measurement model for guided depth map enhancement. IEEE Trans Image Process 27(8):4145–4159

Chapter 4
RGB-D Sensors Data Quality Assessment and Improvement for Advanced Applications

Pablo Rodríguez-Gonzálvez and Gabriele Guidi

Abstract Since the advent of the first Kinect as a motion controller device for the Microsoft XBOX platform (November 2010), several similar active and low-cost range sensing devices, capable of capturing a digital RGB image and the corresponding Depth map (RGB-D), have been introduced in the market. Although initially designed for the video gaming market with the scope of capturing an approximated 3D image of a human body in order to create gesture-based interfaces, RGB-D sensors' low cost and their ability to gather streams of 3D data in real time with a frame rate of 15–30 fps, boosted their popularity for several other purposes, including 3D multimedia interaction, robot navigation, 3D body scanning for garment design and proximity sensors for automotive design. However, data quality is not the RGB-D sensors' strong point, and additional considerations are needed for maximizing the amount of information that can be extracted by the raw data, together with proper criteria for data validation and verification. The present chapter provides an overview of RGB-D sensors technology and an analysis of how random and systematic 3D measurement errors affect the global 3D data quality in the various technological implementations. Typical applications are also reported, with the aim of providing readers with the basic knowledge and understanding of the potentialities and challenges of this technology.

4.1 Introduction

Generating accurate and dense 3D information is an increasing requirement in a variety of scientific fields. Such a requirement is also the motivation to provide new tools and algorithms in a quick and economic way. High precision applications were

P. Rodríguez-Gonzálvez (✉)
Department of Mining Technology, Topography and Structures, Universidad de León, Ponferrada, Spain
e-mail: p.rodriguez@unileon.es

G. Guidi
Department of Mechanical Engineering, Politecnico di Milano, Milan, Italy
e-mail: gabriele.guidi@polimi.it

© Springer Nature Switzerland AG 2019
P. L. Rosin et al. (eds.), *RGB-D Image Analysis and Processing*,
Advances in Computer Vision and Pattern Recognition,
https://doi.org/10.1007/978-3-030-28603-3_4

limited to expensive sensors, such as triangulation-based laser scanners and pattern projection range devices for small volumes, or terrestrial laser scanners based on Time of Flight (ToF) or Phase Shift (PS) detection, being possible alternatives to the use of digital cameras and photogrammetry-based approaches [54]. For an in-depth taxonomy and data acquisition, please refer to Chap. 1. The development of the video game industry, as well as the massive size of the video game market favoured not only the appearance of RGB-D sensors, but also the mass production with a cost per-unit far lower than ToF and PS devices. Originally designed just for implementing gesture-based interfaces, RGB-D sensors offered new possibilities for the 3D digitization of complex objects of small to medium size, as well as real-time 3D acquisition [21]. As a result, RGB-D sensors have filled an application gap among the 3D sensing techniques available (Fig. 4.1). This figure shows different 3D sensing systems and methods, in terms of uncertainty and measurement range. According to the International Vocabulary of Metrology (VIM) [32], the measurement uncertainty of each measuring equipment or device represents the cumulative effect of the systematic errors, associated with the concept of accuracy, and unavoidable random errors, associated with the concept of precision. The former, once modelled, can be eliminated through a proper calibration; the latter, depending on unpredictable causes like electronic noise that can be only statistically characterized for making the end user aware of the measurement system's intrinsic limitations. Additional considerations about measurement precision, accuracy and trueness can be found in Sect. 4.2.

3D point cloud reliability is a key issue in some applications, especially in modelling complex objects. Thus, the characterization and later removal of the systematic errors that cause possible distortions, are required. The present chapter is devoted to identifying various error sources from their effect in the 3D point cloud, namely, random or systematic [22].

The first RGB-D sensors were designed for the entertainment industry in 2010 to capture human body poses for interaction with video games. They are characterized by the generation of a range image, or structured point cloud, where every pixel of the 2D image has been assigned a distance or depth value. Structured point clouds are a constrained representation where point cloud vertices adhere to an underlying structure, in this case, a grid with arbitrary sampling [3]. The resulting data are organized like an image, making it possible, during meshing operations, to find the nearest neighbours in a much more time-efficient way. On the contrary, the widespread active terrestrial laser systems used in Geomatics deliver 3D data in the form of an unstructured point cloud, expressed by an indefinite number of triplets representing the x, y, z values of the measured points over the scanned scene.

Due to the need for capturing not only static scenes but also body movements, RGB-D cameras are designed for generating a high frame rate 3D data acquisition. The main disadvantages are their low precision in distance measurement, and their low spatial resolution. At present, there is a trend to miniaturize RGB-D cameras, so they can be mounted on a smartphone or a tablet, enabling gesture recognition on non-gaming devices. In the case of sensors based on the principle of triangulation, the smaller baseline between the emitter and receiver constrains the achievable precision. Moreover, the mass production of RGB-D cameras at affordable prices makes

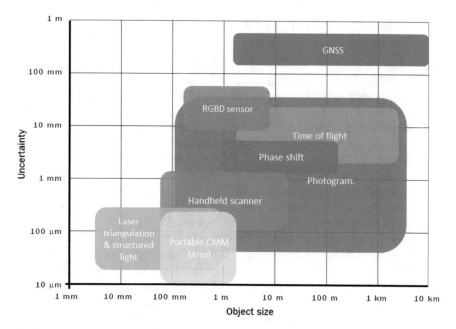

Fig. 4.1 Comparison among different 3D sensing systems and methods in terms of uncertainty and measurement range. Acronyms: GNSS (Global Navigation Satellite System), TLS (Terrestrial Laser Scanners), CMM (Coordinate Measurement Machine). Adapted from [53]

their individual calibration impossible, so the systematic error component becomes predominant over the random one [21]. Please note that this increased final error is still suitable for non-advanced applications.

Despite these drawbacks, RGB-D sensors are a low-cost alternative to other well-established active systems, such as laser triangulation devices, structured-light range devices, or even TLSs for small to medium size objects. Their autonomy, portability and high acquisition frame rate have revolutionized the field of 3D documentation with the Kinect Fusion project [46], further refined in the following years [26].

Typical application fields are dense 3D mapping of indoor environments [13, 27] and 'Simultaneous Localization And Mapping' (SLAM) tasks [56]. Other more specific applications have been developed in the field of pose recognition [59], activity detection [37], object recognition and placement [33], 3D scene labelling and indoor segmentation and support [60]. For additional applications please refer to Chaps. 8, 9 (object detection), 10 (foreground detection and segmentation) and 11 (pose estimation).

4.1.1 Historical Overview of RGB-D Sensing Technologies

The earliest paradigm of multimodal interaction with the environment came from Bolt's 'Put-That-There' system [5] developed at MIT from the late 70s. However, the study and implementation of low-cost 3D sensors for managing gesture-based interfaces has been more a research field rather than a real industrial interest in general purpose applications, mainly due to its relatively low social acceptance and to the high cost of the associated devices [50]. The first mass-produced gaming gesture device was the Nintendo 'Power Glove' in 1989. The device was based on ultrasound-based position detection and derived from the NASA funded 'Dataglove' project where the position was determined by magnetic tracking [14]. Despite its technical advances, it involved a physical contact with the user, who needed to wear it. The turning point could be dated to circa 2000, from the need for the video gaming industry to manage 3D interactions. As a result, it provided a boost in the development of human–machine interfaces, alternative to keyboard-driven cursors. In 1999, Richard Marks conceived a dedicated webcam embedding some gesture recognition based on 2D images. This was the core of the later Sony 'EyeToy' device [43]. Despite not being a 3D device, it works in complete absence of contact. In 2006, Nintendo presented the 'Wii', which is a handheld 3D motion sensing controller for their gaming consoles. The camera embedded in the Wii controller features an integrated multi-object tracking of up to four simultaneous infrared (IR) light sources. As a result, the 6 Degrees-Of-Freedom (DOF) of the player's hand holding the device are estimated, along with the corresponding acceleration components. This approach, enriched with gyroscopes and magnetometers, led to wearable technologies for delivering fitness related services [40]. This device represented a major step forward in the 3D user–machine interaction, and its low-cost (approx. $40), generated a significant boom for the manufacturer [47].

The extremely good results of Wii caused a reaction of the competitors, who began to search alternative ways for measuring the position and orientation of the player, without any device held by the end user. This led Microsoft to begin the 'Project Natal', whose purpose was to develop a device looking at the user (like Sony's earlier Eyetoy), but with a full 3D vision of the scene, on the basis of which it could generate gesture-based 3D input for a gaming console. In 2010 was produced the first device, named Microsoft 'Kinect'. Its 3D sensing technology, developed by Primesense and named 'Light coding technology,' is based on the triangulation principle. This approach, very similar to that employed by white light pattern projection devices, was implemented in an efficient way, packed in a single chip, coupled with a standard colour camera and a microphone, thus allowing the production of a small and inexpensive multimodal input unit (less than $200). The key element of such a device was to get a 3D input from the user's movements, able to extract from the body posture of the player a simplified skeleton whose nodes' relative positions could trigger specific actions of a virtual environment like a 3D video game [10].

The Primesense device is based on triangulation. It involves the projection of a speckle pattern of near-IR laser light constantly projected on the scene. The resulting

Table 4.1 Summary of technical specification of RGB-D sensors available. Adapted from [15]. Abbreviations employed: SL: Structured-Light; ToF: Time-of-Flight; AS: Active Stereoscopy; PS: Passive Stereoscopy

Device	Measurement principle	Range (m)	Spatial resolution (pixels)	Frame rate (fps)	Field of view (°)
ASUS Xtion	SL	0.8–4.0	640 × 480	30	57 × 43
Creative Senz 3D	ToF	0.15–1.0	320 × 240	60	74 × 58
Intel D415	AS	0.16–10	1280 × 720	90	63.4 × 40.4
Intel D435	AS	0.2–4.5	1280 × 720	90	85.2 × 58
Intel Euclid	AS	0.5–6.0	640 × 480	90	59 × 46
Intel R200	AS	0.5–6.0	640 × 480	90	59 × 46
Intel SR300	SL	0.2–1.5	640 × 480	90	71.5 × 55
Kinect v1	SL	0.8–4.0	640 × 480	30	57 × 43
Kinect v2	ToF	0.5–4.5	512 × 424	30	70 × 60
Occipital	SL	0.8–4.0	640 × 480	30	57 × 43
Orbbec Astra S	SL	0.4–2.0	640 × 480	30	60 × 49.5
Sense 3D scanner	SL	0.8–4.0	640 × 480	30	57 × 43
SoftKinectic DS325	ToF	0.15–1.0	320 × 240	60	74 × 58
StereoLab ZED	PS	0.5–20	4416 × 1242	100	110° (diag.)

image is affected by a parallax shift in the direction of the baseline between the laser projector and the perspective center of the infrared camera. This is why all the sensors using this type of technology are grouped in Table 4.1 under the category 'structured light.'

In 2014, Google presented project 'Tango' [23], with the aim of including a 3D scanner in a phone. This limited-run experimental phone has a Kinect-like vision to accurately annotate objects in the user's environment. In 2015, the Chinese company Orbbec released the 'Astra S', an RGB-D sensor composed of an IR camera, a coded pattern projector and an RGB camera. All these sensors represent a re-interpretation of the same Primesense concept, based on triangulation between an IR camera and a structured-light pattern projector.

In 2014, a technology competing with Primesense was introduced. To update the Kinect device, Microsoft developed a novel 3D sensor based on a flash camera that determines the distance to objects by measuring the roundtrip travel time of an amplitude-modulated light from the source to the target and back to the camera at each pixel. Each pixel of the receiving unit incorporates a ToF detector that operates using the 'Quantum Efficiency Modulation.'

In 2016, Intel proposed its version of a low-cost RGB-D sensor, by using again an IR pattern projection, but a double IR camera. In this case, the triangulation occurs on the two cameras and the pattern is used for generating identifiable features on the illuminated surface. For this reason, this approach is also known as 'Active Stereoscopy'.

Driven by the market, new RGB-D sensors are being developed. In Table 4.1 a summary of RGB-D sensors is shown.

4.1.2   State of the Art

The potential for the 3D mapping of objects and indoor environments of RGB-D sensors was recently discovered, opening new applications in several areas, from robotics to surveillance to forensics [36]. The first generation of RGB-D sensors (2010–2014) were all based on the triangulation principle and had a rapid diffusion in the market. The second generation of RGB-D sensors (2014–the present) features modifications in the acquisition system, changing from structured-light to ToF and active stereo, increasing the application possibilities.

The advancements encompass a wide range of options. However, they are closer to research than to commercial applications. The development that has had the most impact is gesture and action recognition. Human action recognition from RGB-D devices has attracted increasing attention since their appearance in 2010. This task is based on the skeleton tracking from depth maps. However, this only works when the human subject is facing the RGB-D sensors and in the absence of occlusions [63]. For advanced applications, such as nursing or surveillance, it is necessary to apply additional algorithms for a proper activity recognition [63].

Indoor scene reconstruction and mobile mapping have been another active research topic for RGB-D cameras [26, 46]. Their low cost presented an attractive opportunity, especially in the robotics field (see Chap. 13). The first approaches were based on the reconstruction of static environments. Then they evolved into real-time scanning and scan integration. The later developments allowed an operator to capture dense 3D geometry models of dynamic scenes and scene elements [64]. In this sense, RGB-D sensors have been proposed to track in real time a 3D elastic deformable object, which is of special interest for robot dynamic manipulation [48]. For a recent overview of surface tracking, please refer to [64].

RGB-D sensors are a powerful resource for security and surveillance systems. Presently, they are being used by some smartphone manufacturers as a part of their face recognition system. This approach is based on the development and improvement of specialized algorithms, and the computation of descriptors to perform a classification [30]. RGB-D sensors have also been used in forensic science for advanced applications, such as body measurements for gait recognition or anthropometric purposes [61]. Alternative advance applications in this field are real-time biometrics, such as face recognition and face analysis [6]. In these tasks, the active light source could cope with the illumination changes of RGB passive methods (which could disturb the final 3D model), making the RGB-D sensor an inexpensive way for real-time analysis.

Garment modelling and design from an RGB-D camera has been addressed. This has a twofold approach; the anthropometric measures, as mentioned in the forensic applications, and the garment modelling [8]. The last one involves the individual garment components and their design attributes from depth maps. In [49] a method to capture clothes in motion was presented, based on a 4D data acquisition. The garments of a person in motion can be estimated by segmenting the 4D data stream, obtaining the undressed body shape and tracking the clothing surface over time. As a result, it is possible to retarget the clothing to new body shapes.

For example, a Microsoft Kinect II has been employed to derive crop height models of a cornfield directly from the point clouds [24]. The results derived exclusively from the 3D data without prior or supplementary measurements show an underestimation of crop height and individual plant height. However, by combining multiple RGB-D point clouds, the difference from the ground truth provided by a TLS is reduced to a mean value of –6 cm (canopy height model and plant height).

Earth Science fields, such as glaciology, stream bathymetry, and geomorphology, have been proposed as advance application fields for RGB-D sensors, as stated in [42]. In [25] the applicability of Kinect fusion libraries using the Kinect sensor for capturing two common karst features in caves (stalagmites and flowstone walls) is investigated. The Kinect sensor was compared to a Terrestrial Laser Scanner, performing inside the nominal depth precision of the sensor at the given distances to the object. In spite of a systematic overestimation of the extension of the 3D survey, the authors stated that the ease-of-use, low-cost and real-time 3D point cloud generation offer additional benefits for applications in geosciences. Characterization of 2D free surface and temporal water depth field evolution was carried out with a Primesense Carmine 1.09 and Microsoft Kinect for Windows SDK 1.8 [44].

Drone application is another advanced field. In [29] a stripped-down Microsoft Kinect sensor was employed for an autonomous flight of a micro air vehicle in an indoor environment, combining visual odometry and autonomous flight and mapping. The mean position deviation was 6.2 cm, with a maximum deviation of 19 cm. In [58] an Intel Realsense R200 was attached to a drone. Applying a Visual SLAM approach and customized camera parameters for outdoor use, a 3D map of a construction site was generated in real time. It can monitor construction progress, compute earthmoving volumes and track the real-time locations and trajectories of on-site entities (e.g. labourers, equipment, materials) even in a Global Navigation Satellite System (GNSS) denied environment. Compared to photogrammetry, the average error is 3.3 cm; however, the presence of holes in the model due to the limited sensing range of IR sensors constrains the RGB-D applicability. Other reported problems are related to achieving effective memory management of an onboard computer.

The use of RGB-D sensors for automotive and autonomous vehicles has similar constraints. It requires the understanding of the environment in which the vehicle is moving, including objects in the surroundings, with a process called scene labelling [31]. For additional details please refer to Chap. 17.

The use of RGB-D cameras for advanced applications also requires the use of radiometry to obtain more complete derived products. The first radiometric calibration equation for the IR sensor for the Microsoft Kinect II is reported in [51]. It is a reflectance-based approach that allows us to convert the recorded digital levels into physical values. Experimental results confirm that the RGB-D sensor is valid for exploiting the radiometric possibilities ranging from pathological analysis to agricultural and forest resource evaluation. Parallel approaches are based on RGB-D vignetting calibration [1] to improve the visual appearance of final models, and even to improve the tracking performance of SLAM systems by optimizing a joint geometric and photometric cost function. More details about SLAM and RGB-D odometry can be found in Chap. 6.

4.2 Metrological Analysis of RGB-D Sensor Performance

In addition to random measurement errors typical of any 3D device, RGB-D sensors, due to their low-cost components, have significant systematic errors. The latter arise from the various components, e.g. IR emitter, lens distortions and aberrations, mechanical tolerances in the sensor assembly. These issues contribute to the higher percentage of the global error budget [21]. To employ an RGB-D sensor in advanced applications, the device has to be properly calibrated in order to eliminate, or at least greatly reduce, the systematic component of the error. As a result, the final error will be significantly decreased.

According to the VIM [32], verification is the provision of objective evidence that a given item fulfils specified requirements, whereas validation is the same as verification, where the specified requirements are adequate for an intended use. Measurement precision is the closeness of agreement between measured quantity values obtained by replicate measurements on the same or similar objects under specified conditions. On the contrary, measurement accuracy indicates the closeness of agreement between a measured quantity value and a true quantity value of an object being measured (i.e. a 'measurand'). Please note that the latter is more a theoretical concept than a measurable parameter. When the average of an infinite number of occurrences of the same measured quantity value is compared to a reference value, the closeness of the two is indicated as trueness instead of accuracy. This procedure becomes feasible in reality when the 'infinite' number of repeated measures is substituted by a number 'large enough' to approximate an asymptotic value within a predefined tolerance.

For practical purposes, true quantity, or ground truth, is provided by instruments and techniques with a higher precision than the tested one, also referred to as an 'independent check' [57]. This ratio should be five or more times the a priori precision of the system being tested. Under these conditions, the error deviation of the independent check from the ground truth can be dismissed [52].

Starting from a general approach for the metrological characterization of triangulation-based range devices [22], the metrological characterization of RGB-D sensors has been proposed by different authors since 2011 [35], testing different commercial sensors, calibration artefacts and configurations. However, the results obtained showed a high variability, related to the 3D results. As an example, the definition of the optimal range of work depends on the software choice. A Primesense-based Kinect obtained the best overall performance for a range of 1–3 m operating with the OpenKinect framework [36]. With the same sensor, [2] reported an optimal working range of 0.8–1.5 m operating with the SDK; and [45] provided a range of 0.7–2 m with the OpenNI framework.

All the studies showed that the RGB-D precision depends strongly on the distance of the measured object, and highlights that its main limitation is the short acquisition range. For the first generation of RGB-D sensors, based on triangulation, precision decreases quadratically with distance [16, 21].

The spatial resolution is influenced both by optical means, as in any other active range device, and by numeric means, given that any value in the range image is generated by an Analog-to-Digital (A/D) conversion of a measured value made with a fixed number of bits. The numerical representation of the measured values, therefore, gives a fixed number of levels, represented by 2n, with n number of bits of the converted value. For example, for an Intel RealSense device, such depth is 12 bits, so the available levels are $2^{12} = 4096$. Measuring in the range 0–1 m the granularity will be therefore dr $= 1000/4096 = 0.24$ mm, while in the range 0–5 m will be dr $= 5000/4096 = 1.22$ mm. A similar behaviour is confirmed also for the Microsoft Kinect, [36] where it has been verified that the distance measurements resolution decreases with distance and is approximately 2 mm at 1 m and about 7.5 mm at 5 m.

Other drawbacks are related to the limited measurement capacity of low reflectivity surfaces, excessive background illumination and acquisition of surfaces near parallel to the optical axis [11]. Moreover, shifts in the depth image due to the thermal changes induced by the Peltier element heating and cooling the IR projector to stabilize the wavelength, were also reported [42].

The high affordability of RGB-D sensors allows them to replace custom ToF cameras. Several studies compared them, in order to assess in which case this assumption is suitable. In [39] a Microsoft Kinect I was compared to two ToF cameras based on PMD. The authors reported a limited ability to measure on surfaces with low reflectivity. An angular resolution of 0.49° was reported, instead of the theoretical angular resolution 0.09° (0.12° in height). For the experimental setup, a Böhler Star was used [4] to determine the angular or lateral resolution of depth measurement devices.

The discrepancy was explained by the authors as due to the fact that multiple pixels are required to generate one depth value. Similarly, in [62] a Microsoft Kinect I was compared to three ToF devices (SwissRanger 4000, SICK LMS_200 and Fotonic B70). The authors stated that for smaller environments, a sphere of radius 3 m, the structured-light based RGB-D sensor provides a less precise substitute for a laser rangefinder. In a comparison of the Microsoft Kinect I and the SwissRanger 4000, the measurement accuracy decreases for angles larger than 60° [34]. Moreover, the structured-light sensor is affected by metallic surfaces (a typical factor in industrial environments), since the measurement accuracy depends much more on the distance of the camera to the objects than on the surface properties of the captured objects.

Another research topic is the comparison between the structured light and ToF RGB-D cameras. In [17] Kinect I and Kinect II are compared using a standard calibrated metrological artefact, involving the evaluation of accuracy and precision for different angles and distances. Both RGB-D sensors yielded a similar precision at 1 m range, but at 2 m range, Kinect II (ToF) improved the results of Kinect I (structured-light). In terms of accuracy, both devices showed a similar pattern. The decrease in precision with range for Kinect II is lower than the first-generation device. A dedicated study of ToF Microsoft Kinect II error source is addressed in [38]. The authors studied the preheating time, namely the delay required to provide a reliable range measurement. By repeatedly observing the measured distance of a planar surface from the sensor, the resulting values vary in the first 30 min up to 5 mm and eventually reduce to 1 mm. The authors also addressed the effects of different materials on distance measurements. They concluded that by using different light intensities for compensating the material's absorption, the lower the intensities, the longer the measured distances, with distance deviations up to 12 mm in black areas. Regarding the variation of the measurement error with the sensor-to-surface distance, the authors reported a degradation of its standard deviation, which is dependent on the object range according to an exponential function. Finally, the authors reported that RGB-D sensors, if compared to standard photogrammetry approaches, performed less accurately. In order to help users make a decision on which measurement principle to select (triangulation or ToF) depending on their application circumstances, in [55] a weight factor represented by the performance ratio between the two RGB-D sensors categories is proposed.

In the study [21] five different RGB-D sensors were analysed to assess the error components (systematic and random) using a flat target in a range from 0.55 to 1.45 m. The authors confirmed that the calibration of sensors is a critical issue. After having estimated the systematic and the random measurement errors for the five specimens tested, the random component was in fact significantly smaller than the total detected error. Primesense-based devices exhibited an uncertainty that ranged from 2 mm to 3.9 mm (Kinect 1), from 1.9 to 2.9 mm (Asus Xtion) and from 1.3 to 2.8 mm (Structure). Realsense devices increased the uncertainty ranges from 3 to 6.9 mm, while Kinect 2 yielded values from 1.4 to 2.7 mm.

There are many error sources to be accounted for an RGB-D sensor. According to [55] they can be summed up as follows:

1. Ambient background light.
2. Multi-device interference.
3. Temperature drift.
4. Systematic distance error.
5. Depth inhomogeneity at object boundaries (also called flying pixels).
6. Multi-path effects.
7. Intensity-related distance error (this bias is reported for ToF-based sensors).
8. Semi-transparent and scattering media.
9. Dynamic scenery.

In a 3D measurement process using a RGB-D camera, the causes for inaccuracies can be classified in two categories according to [34]:

- Inaccuracies in the RGB-D camera's pose estimation:

    - Inaccuracies of the pose estimation device.
    - Inaccurate relative transformation between depth camera and pose estimation device.

(a)   (b)

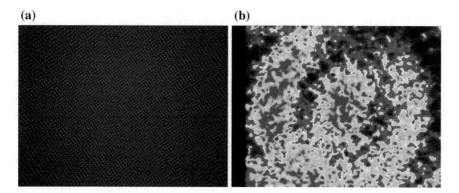

Fig. 4.2 Example of RGB-D uncertainty: **a** the infrared pattern used to generate the depth map; **b** colour-coded depth of a planar surface

- Inaccurate alignment of world coordinate system and 3D model coordinate system.
- Temporal offset between pose acquisition by the pose estimation device and depth image acquisition by depth camera.

• Inaccuracies of the RGB-D camera itself:

  - Random measurement errors.
  - Systematic measurement errors.
  - Motion blur effects.

In Fig. 4.2, the global uncertainty (random plus systematic components) is illustrated for the scan of a planar surface using a RealSense D415. The colour palette was set with very narrow thresholds around the nominal sensor-to-surface distance (approx. 910 mm), in order to make the errors more 'readable'.

The rest of the present section is focused on the random and systematic component discussion for an RGB-D advanced application.

4.2.1 Random Errors

Random error, mainly due to the sensor's electronic noise, affects the depth image either in its spatial component, as discrepancies of measured distance within a single frame, or in its temporal evolution, as discrepancies of measured distances between consecutive frames [41]. Due to the high frame rate of RGB-D cameras, the use of individual depth images to estimate the spatial random component, allows us to ignore the effects of temperature in time. These have been proved to influence the performances of this category of devices over a time span of several tens of minutes [12]. In addition, the spatial characterization provides more practical applications and statistically significant results, since it allows us to estimate the accuracy and precision of different RGB-D devices.

Random errors are largely caused by the thermal noise of the electronic stage capturing the IR images, and by the laser speckle produced by the material response to coherent light. All these effects are superimposed on the deterministic content of the probing pattern, whose image is used for estimating the parallaxes in the different points of the frame. According to [21], it is possible to assume, and therefore model, the global random contribution of each range image as due to 'Additive White Gaussian Noise' (AWGN), similar to the thermal noise affecting CCD and CMOS sensors. The fact that this contribution can be considered additive with good approximation is confirmed by the literature [28].

4.2.2 Systematic Errors

The classical systematic error of RGB-D cameras is the so called 'distance inhomogeneity' [7], namely, the set of possible errors coming out of acquisitions at different distances from the sensor.

Such errors change over a range image according to a pattern depending on the specific device exemplar and the sensor-to-target distance. But, unlike random errors, those are constant in time. In addition, the systematic errors are specific for each different depth measuring technology [9].

This error can be characterized by the data acquisition of a planar surface at different known distances. The parametric nature of such a surface allows us to evaluate the global uncertainty (random plus systematic components). This approach has been studied in the literature [7, 18, 21, 38]. In 2012, Khoshelham and Elberink [36] characterized the first generation of Microsoft Kinect in terms of precision and accuracy, concluding that the systematic error is directly dependent on object distance, and it increases at the periphery of the depth image.

To individualize the random and systematic components from the global uncertainty of the RGB-D camera, there are two different approaches.

On the one hand, the averaging of several depth images is proposed. In this approach, the number of depth images taken into account affects the results. Early tests with a pattern projection device and a laser radar estimated an optimal averaging level of 16, after which the averaging does not give further improvement. However, in order to obtain a trade-off between measurement quality improvement and processing time, an optimal number of averaged images for a pattern projection device turned out to be 4 [19]. For obtaining a real-time averaging with a laser radar [20], the value turned out to be further reduced to 2 without significantly affecting the measurement performance. In [38] it is reported that increasing from 10 to 100 consecutive frames does not improve the plane fit standard deviation, but a smoothing effect is observed in the corners. Various authors proposed samples between 10 and 50 frames for this approach.

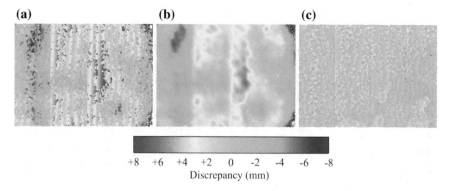

Fig. 4.3 Colour-coded error components: **a** Global uncertainty; **b** systematic component (low frequencies) decoupled from **a**, **c** random component (high frequencies) decoupled from **a**

On the other hand, in [21] a different approach based on an analysis in the frequency domain is proposed. The starting hypothesis is that the random errors, being essentially originated by AWGN, are characterized by high frequencies. Under this approach the RGB-D device can be considered as a black box whose specific behaviour affects the 3D cloud differently at different spatial frequencies. So, for the analysis of the distance errors with the flat plane, a λ-μ smoothing filter [19] was used [21]. The filter is basically a low-pass filter that removes high special frequency 3D point variations without further altering the point positions. The parameters should be set in compliance with the limits presented in [19], namely, $\lambda > 0$, $\mu < -\lambda$. This means considering three separate contributions for each depth sample collected by the sensor: (i) the actual measured value (Fig. 4.3a); (ii) the systematic error (Fig. 4.3b); (iii) the random error (Fig. 4.3c). The sum of the latter two defines the spatial measurement uncertainty. Figure 4.3 exemplifies the colour-coded deviation of each depth value from the fitting plane associated with a set of points, all nominally belonging to the same plane.

The low-pass filter applied in Fig. 4.3 has been computed in Meshlab, using $\lambda = 1$, $\mu = -0.53$ and 50 iterations.

4.2.3   Measurement Uncertainty

On the basis of the aforementioned approach it is possible to determine and compensate the systematic errors. In Fig. 4.4, an estimation of the global spatial uncertainty of different devices for a reference planar surface (σ_u), is represented. The same 3D cloud is low-pass filtered with the λ-μ smooth algorithm and meshed. The standard deviation between the raw 3D data and the filtered mesh represents an estimation of the spatial random error (σ_r). Once the random component is estimated, the differ-

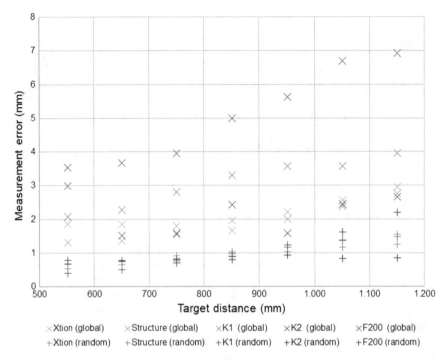

Fig. 4.4 Measurement uncertainty and random error component for five RGB-D sensors. Adapted from [21]

ence between σ_u and σ_r gives an estimation of the systematic component of the error (σ_s).

As expected, the trend of the global uncertainty σ_u generally follows a growing trend with distance for each triangulation-based device. However, this growth does not seem to be following a predictable behaviour, probably due to the poor (or absent) calibration of the camera in charge of collecting the IR image from which the distances are calculated. Unlike the triangulation-based devices, the Microsoft Kinect 2, the only ToF-based device represented in Figs. 4.4 and 4.5, exhibits a nearly constant value of the random error at the different distances. It shows a slow growth roughly linear, maintaining values always lower than 1 mm even at the maximum operating range. However, the apparently poor calibration of the optoelectronic device in charge of collecting the IR echoes from the scene tends to produce a global uncertainty much more erratic than the pure random error.

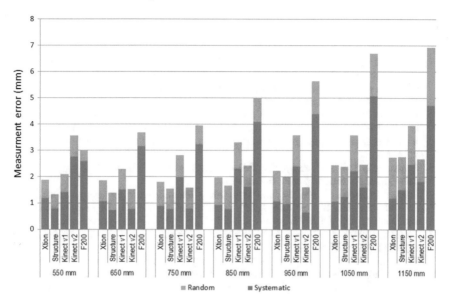

Fig. 4.5 Systematic and random error component for five RGB-D sensors. Adapted from [21]

In the following figure (Fig. 4.5) the error component decoupling for the selection of five RGB-D devices is explicitly provided. For further details about numerical results, please refer to [21].

4.3   Conclusions

In this chapter, an overview of RGB-D advanced applications and how random and systematic 3D measurement errors affect the global 3D data quality in the various technological implementations, has been presented.

The use of RGB-D sensors is somewhat hindered by their intrinsic characteristics such as low thermal stability, measurement uncertainty, repeatability and reproducibility. Therefore, they cannot be used without calibration for highly detailed 3D digitization works. However, the acquisition of shapes for determining volumes independently of the fine details, or the rough digitization of human bodies for the estimation of garment sizes is not critically affected by such details. In these cases, low-cost devices can be effectively used.

For some more advanced applications, a proper modelling of the optical system and an associated calibration process are required in order to enhance the RGB-D performance by reducing the strong systematic error component typically present in such devices.

References

1. Alexandrov SV, Prankl J, Zillich M, Vincze M (2016) Calibration and correction of vignetting effects with an application to 3D mapping. In: 2016 IEEE/RSJ international conference on intelligent robots and systems (IROS), 2016-November. IEEE, pp 4217–4223. https://doi.org/ 10.1109/IROS.2016.7759621, http://ieeexplore.ieee.org/document/7759621/
2. Alnowami M, Alnwaimi B, Tahavori F, Copland M, Wells K (2012) A quantitative assessment of using the Kinect for Xbox360 for respiratory surface motion tracking. In: Holmes III DR, Wong KH (eds) Proceedings of the SPIE, vol 8316, p. 83161T. https://doi.org/10.1117/12. 911463
3. Beraldin JA, Blais F, Cournoyer L, Godin G, Rioux M (2000) Active 3D sensing. Quaderni della Scuola Normale Superiore di Pisa 10:1–21
4. Boehler W, Bordas Vicent M, Marbs A (2003) Investigating laser scanner accuracy. Int Arch Photogramm, Remote Sens Spat Inf Sci **34**(Part 5), 696–701. http://cipa.icomos.org/ wp-content/uploads/2018/11/Boehler-e.a.-Investigating-laser-scanner-accuracy.pdf
5. Bolt RA (1980) Put-that-there. ACM SIGGRAPH Comput Graph 14(3):262–270. https://doi. org/10.1145/965105.807503
6. Boutellaa E, Hadid A, Bengherabi M, Ait-Aoudia S (2015) On the use of Kinect depth data for identity, gender and ethnicity classification from facial images. Pattern Recognit Lett 68:270–277. https://doi.org/10.1016/j.patrec.2015.06.027, https://linkinghub.elsevier. com/retrieve/pii/S0167865515001993
7. Carfagni M, Furferi R, Governi L, Servi M, Uccheddu F, Volpe Y (2017) On the performance of the intel SR300 depth camera: metrological and critical characterization. IEEE Sens J 17(14):4508–4519. https://doi.org/10.1109/JSEN.2017.2703829, http://ieeexplore.ieee.org/ document/7929364/
8. Chen X, Zhou B, Lu F, Wang L, Bi L, Tan P (2015) Garment modeling with a depth camera. ACM Trans Graph 34(6):1–12. https://doi.org/10.1145/2816795.2818059
9. Chow JCK, Ang KD, Lichti DD, Teskey WF (2012) Performance analysis of a low-cost triangulation-based 3D camera: Microsoft Kinect system. In: International archives of the photogrammetry, remote sensing and spatial information sciences - ISPRS archives, vol 39, pp 175–180. https://www.scopus.com/inward/record.uri?eid=2-s2.0-84876521082& partnerID=40&md5=6cc10b0385e613e15a0e17b7aa77f888
10. Chuan CH, Regina E, Guardino C (2014) American sign language recognition using leap motion sensor. In: 13th international conference on machine learning and applications. IEEE, pp 541–544. https://doi.org/10.1109/ICMLA.2014.110, http://ieeexplore.ieee.org/document/ 7033173/
11. Dal Mutto C, Zanuttigh P, Cortelazzo GM (2012) Time-of-flight cameras and microsoft kinect™. Springer briefs in electrical and computer engineering. Springer, Boston. https:// doi.org/10.1007/978-1-4614-3807-6
12. DiFilippo NM, Jouaneh MK (2015) Characterization of different Microsoft Kinect sensor models. IEEE Sens J 15(8):4554–4564. https://doi.org/10.1109/JSEN.2015.2422611, http:// ieeexplore.ieee.org/document/7084580/
13. Dong H, Figueroa N, El Saddik A (2014) Towards consistent reconstructions of indoor spaces based on 6D RGB-D odometry and KinectFusion. In: 2014 IEEE/RSJ international conference on intelligent robots and systems. IEEE, pp 1796–1803. https://doi.org/10.1109/IROS.2014. 6942798
14. Fisher SS (1987) Telepresence master glove controller for dexterous robotic end-effectors. In: Casasent DP (ed) Proceedings of SPIE - the international society for optical engineering, vol 726, p 396. https://doi.org/10.1117/12.937753
15. Giancola S, Valenti M, Sala R (2018) State-of-the-art devices comparison. Springer, Cham. https://doi.org/10.1007/978-3-319-91761-0_3

16. Gonzalez-Jorge H, Riveiro B, Vazquez-Fernandez E, Martínez-Sánchez J, Arias P (2013) Metrological evaluation of Microsoft Kinect and Asus Xtion sensors. Measurement 46(6):1800–1806. https://doi.org/10.1016/j.measurement.2013.01.011, https://linkinghub.elsevier.com/retrieve/pii/S0263224113000262
17. Gonzalez-Jorge H, Rodríguez-Gonzálvez P, Martínez-Sánchez J, González-Aguilera D, Arias P, Gesto M, Díaz-Vilariño L (2015) Metrological comparison between Kinect I and Kinect II sensors. Measurement 70:21–26. https://doi.org/10.1016/j.measurement.2015.03.042, https://linkinghub.elsevier.com/retrieve/pii/S0263224115001888
18. Guidi G (2013) Metrological characterization of 3D imaging devices. In: Remondino F, Shortis MR, Beyerer J, Puente León F (eds) Proceedings of SPIE - the international society for optical engineering, vol 8791, pp M1–M10. SPIE, Bellingham, WA 98227-0010 (2013). https://doi.org/10.1117/12.2021037, https://www.scopus.com/inward/record.uri?eid=2-s2.0-84880439273&doi=10.1117%2F12.2021037&partnerID=40&md5=32875bc13ad2c67c7eca834ff1f1613e, http://proceedings.spiedigitallibrary.org/proceeding.aspx?doi=10.1117/12.2021037, http://dx.medra.org/10.1117/12.2021
19. Guidi G, Beraldin JA, Atzeni C (2004) High-accuracy 3-D modeling of cultural heritage: the digitizing of Donatello's "Maddalena". IEEE Trans Image Process 13(3), 370–380 (2004). http://www.ncbi.nlm.nih.gov/pubmed/15376928
20. Guidi G, Frischer B, De Simone M, Cioci A, Spinetti A, Carosso L, Micoli LLL, Russo M, Grasso T (2005) Virtualizing ancient Rome: 3D acquisition and modeling of a Largeplaster-of-Paris model of imperial Rome. In: SPIE videometrics VIII, vol 5665. SPIE, Bellinghaam, WA, 98227-0010, pp 119–133. https://doi.org/10.1117/12.587355
21. Guidi G, Gonizzi S, Micoli L (2016) 3D capturing performances of low-cost range sensors for mass-market applications. In: ISPRS – international archives of the photogrammetry, remote sensing and spatial information sciences, vol XLI-B5, pp 33–40. https://doi.org/10.5194/isprsarchives-XLI-B5-33-2016, http://www.int-arch-photogramm-remote-sens-spatial-inf-sci.net/XLI-B5/33/2016/isprs-archives-XLI-B5-33-2016.pdf, https://www.scopus.com/inward/record.uri?eid=2-s2.0-84979243034&doi=10.5194%2Fisprsarchives-XLI-B5-33-2016&partnerID=40&md5=b89b0993755aed7358a
22. Guidi G, Russo M, Magrassi G, Bordegoni M (2010) Performance evaluation of triangulation based range sensors. Sensors 10(8):7192–7215. https://doi.org/10.3390/s100807192, http://www.mdpi.com/1424-8220/10/8/7192/
23. Gülch E (2016) Investigations on google tango development kit for personal indoor mapping. In: Sarjakoski T, Santos MY, Sarjakoski LT (eds) The 19th AGILE international conference on geographic information science. Helsinki, pp 1–3. https://agile-online.org/conference_paper/cds/agile_2016/posters/102_Paper_in_PDF.pdf
24. Hämmerle M, Höfle B (2016) Direct derivation of maize plant and crop height from low-cost time-of-flight camera measurements. Plant Methods 12(50):1–13. https://doi.org/10.1186/s13007-016-0150-6
25. Hammerle M, Hofle B, Fuchs J, Schroder-Ritzrau A, Vollweiler N, Frank N (2014) Comparison of Kinect and terrestrial LiDAR capturing natural karst cave 3-D objects. IEEE Geosci Remote Sens Lett 11(11):1896–1900. https://doi.org/10.1109/LGRS.2014.2313599, http://ieeexplore.ieee.org/document/6805129/
26. Henry P, Krainin M, Herbst E, Ren X, Fox D (2012) RGB-D mapping: using kinect-style depth cameras for dense 3D modeling of indoor environments. Int J Robot Res 31(5):647–663. https://doi.org/10.1177/0278364911434148, https://www.scopus.com/inward/record.uri?eid=2-s2.0-84860151074&doi=10.1177%2F0278364911434148&partnerID=40&md5=0644738abc2ed53e7c3ca98aab092cf2
27. Henry P, Krainin M, Herbst E, Ren X, Fox D (2014) RGB-D mapping: using depth cameras for dense 3D modeling of indoor environments. Springer tracts in advanced robotics, vol 79, pp 477–491. https://doi.org/10.1007/978-3-642-28572-1_33
28. Hirakawa K, Parks T (2006) Image denoising using total least squares. IEEE Trans Image Process 15(9):2730–2742. https://doi.org/10.1109/TIP.2006.877352, http://ieeexplore.ieee.org/document/1673453/

29. Huang AS, Bachrach A, Henry P, Krainin M, Maturana D, Fox D, Roy N (2017) Visual odometry and mapping for autonomous flight using an RGB-D camera. Springer tracts in advanced robotics, vol 100, pp 235–252. https://doi.org/10.1007/978-3-319-29363-9_14
30. Huynh T, Min R, Dugelay JL (2013) An efficient LBP-based descriptor for facial depth images applied to gender recognition using RGB-D face data. In: Park JI, Kim J (eds) Computer vision - ACCV 2012 workshops. Springer, Berlin, pp 133–145. https://doi.org/10.1007/978-3-642-37410-4_12
31. Jasch M, Weber T, Rätsch M (2017) Fast and robust RGB-D scene labeling for autonomous driving. J Comput 13(4):393–400. https://doi.org/10.17706/jcp.13.4.393-400
32. JCGM: The international vocabulary of metrology–basic and general concepts and associated terms (VIM), 3rd edn, pp 1–92. JCGM (Joint committee for guides in metrology). https://www.bipm.org/utils/common/documents/jcgm/JCGM_200_2012.pdf
33. Jiang Y, Lim M, Zheng C, Saxena A (2012) Learning to place new objects in a scene. Int J Robot Res 31(9):1021–1043. https://doi.org/10.1177/0278364912438781
34. Kahn S, Bockholt U, Kuijper A, Fellner DW (2013) Towards precise real-time 3D difference detection for industrial applications. Comput Ind 64(9):1115–1128. https://doi.org/10.1016/j.compind.2013.04.004, https://www.scopus.com/inward/record.uri?eid=2-s2.0-84894901168&doi=10.1016%2Fj.compind.2013.04.004&partnerID=40&md5=f2fe4cb5f2bac7f864ef9125481fafc8, https://linkinghub.elsevier.com/retrieve/pii/S0166361513000766
35. Khoshelham K (2012) Accuracy analysis of Kinect depth data. In: ISPRS - international archives of the photogrammetry, remote sensing and spatial information sciences, vol XXXVIII-5/, pp 133–138. https://doi.org/10.5194/isprsarchives-XXXVIII-5-W12-133-2011
36. Khoshelham K, Elberink SO (2012) Accuracy and resolution of Kinect depth data for indoor mapping applications. Sensors 12(2):1437–1454. https://doi.org/10.3390/s120201437, http://www.mdpi.com/1424-8220/12/2/1437
37. Koppula HS, Gupta R, Saxena A (2013) Learning human activities and object affordances from RGB-D videos. Int J Robot Res 32(8):951–970. https://doi.org/10.1177/0278364913478446
38. Lachat E, Macher H, Landes T, Grussenmeyer P (2015) Assessment and calibration of a RGB-D camera (Kinect v2 sensor) towards a potential use for close-range 3D modeling. Remote Sens 7(10):13070–13097. https://doi.org/10.3390/rs71013070, http://www.mdpi.com/2072-4292/7/10/13070
39. Langmann B, Hartmann K, Loffeld O (2012) Depth camera technology comparison and performance evaluation. In: ICPRAM 2012 - proceedings of the 1st international conference on pattern recognition applications and methods, vol 2, pp 438–444. https://www.scopus.com/inward/record.uri?eid=2-s2.0-84862218626&partnerID=40&md5=c83e57bc424e766df04598fa892293c2
40. Lightman K (2016) Silicon gets sporty. IEEE Spectr 53(3):48–53. https://doi.org/10.1109/MSPEC.2016.7420400
41. Mallick T, Das PP, Majumdar AK (2014) Characterizations of noise in Kinect depth images: a review. IEEE Sens J 14(6):1731–1740. https://doi.org/10.1109/JSEN.2014.2309987, https://www.scopus.com/inward/record.uri?eid=2-s2.0-84898974692&doi=10.1109%2FJSEN.2014.2309987&partnerID=40&md5=63ea250190e3e3c0576df168f2c031a9
42. Mankoff KD, Russo TA (2013) The Kinect: a low-cost, high-resolution, short-range 3D camera. Earth Surf Process Landf 38(9):926–936. https://doi.org/10.1002/esp.3332
43. Marks R (2011) 3D spatial interaction for entertainment. In,: (2011) IEEE symposium on 3D user interfaces (3DUI). IEEE. https://doi.org/10.1109/3DUI.2011.5759209
44. Martínez-Aranda S, Fernández-Pato J, Caviedes-Voullième D, García-Palacín I, García-Navarro P (2018) Towards transient experimental water surfaces: a new benchmark dataset for 2D shallow water solvers. Adv Water Resour 121:130–149. https://doi.org/10.1016/j.advwatres.2018.08.013, https://linkinghub.elsevier.com/retrieve/pii/S0309170818303658
45. Molnár B, Toth CK, Detrekői A (2012) Accuracy test of Microsoft Kinect for human morphologic measurements. ISPRS-Int Arch Photogramm, Remote Sens Spat Inf Sci **XXXIX-B3**, 543–547. https://doi.org/10.5194/isprsarchives-XXXIX-B3-543-2012

46. Newcombe RA, Izadi S, Hilliges O, Molyneaux D, Kim D, Davison AJ, Kohli P, Shotton J, Hodges S, Fitzgibbon A (2011) KinectFusion: real-time dense surface mapping and tracking. In: IEEE ISMAR. IEEE. http://research.microsoft.com/apps/pubs/default.aspx?id=155378
47. Nintendo: consolidated financial highlights (2008). www.nintendo.co.jp/ir/pdf/2008/080124e.pdf
48. Petit A, Lippiello V, Siciliano B (2015) Tracking fractures of deformable objects in real-time with an RGB-D sensor. In: 2015 international conference on 3D vision. IEEE, pp 632–639. https://doi.org/10.1109/3DV.2015.78, http://ieeexplore.ieee.org/document/7335534/
49. Pons-Moll G, Pujades S, Hu S, Black MJ (2017) Clothcap: seamless 4d clothing capture and retargeting. ACM Trans Graph 36(4):73:1–73:15. https://doi.org/10.1145/3072959.3073711
50. Rico J, Crossan A, Brewster S (2011) Gesture based interfaces: practical applications of gestures in real world mobile settings. In: England D (ed) Whole body interaction, Chap 14. Springer, London, pp 173–186. https://doi.org/10.1007/978-0-85729-433-3_14
51. Rodriguez-Gonzalvez P, Gonzalez-Aguilera D, Gonzalez-Jorge H, Hernandez-Lopez D (2016) Low-cost reflectance-based method for the radiometric calibration of kinect 2. IEEE Sens J 16(7):1975–1985. https://doi.org/10.1109/JSEN.2015.2508802, http://ieeexplore.ieee.org/document/7355312/
52. Rodríguez-Gonzálvez P, González-Aguilera D, Hernández-López D, González-Jorge H (2015) Accuracy assessment of airborne laser scanner dataset by means of parametric and non-parametric statistical methods. IET Sci, Meas Technol 9(4):505–513. https://doi.org/10.1049/iet-smt.2014.0053
53. Rodríguez-Gonzálvez P, Muñoz-Nieto ÁL, Zancajo-Blázquez S, González-Aguilera D (2016) Geomatics and forensic: progress and challenges. In: Forensic analysis - from death to justice. InTech, pp 3–25. https://doi.org/10.5772/63155, http://www.intechopen.com/books/forensic-analysis-from-death-to-justice/geomatics-and-forensic-progress-and-challenges
54. Rodríguez-Gonzálvez P, Rodríguez-Martín M, Ramos LF, González-Aguilera D (2017) 3D reconstruction methods and quality assessment for visual inspection of welds. Autom Constr 79:49–58. https://doi.org/10.1016/j.autcon.2017.03.002, https://www.scopus.com/inward/record.uri?eid=2-s2.0-85014686028&doi=10.1016%2Fj.autcon.2017.03.002&partnerID=40&md5=52443dfc1458f567799f89bcdb18ea8a
55. Sarbolandi H, Lefloch D, Kolb A (2015) Kinect range sensing: structured-light versus time-of-flight Kinect. Comput Vis Image Underst 139:1–20. https://doi.org/10.1016/j.cviu.2015.05.006, https://www.scopus.com/inward/record.uri?eid=2-s2.0-84939771517&doi=10.1016%2Fj.cviu.2015.05.006&partnerID=40&md5=fedadae1dc863b854951721e082d408d, https://linkinghub.elsevier.com/retrieve/pii/S1077314215001071
56. Scherer SA, Zell A (2013) Efficient onbard RGBD-SLAM for autonomous MAVs. In: 2013 IEEE/RSJ international conference on intelligent robots and systems. IEEE, Tokyo, pp 1062–1068. https://doi.org/10.1109/IROS.2013.6696482
57. Schofield W, Breach M (2007) Engineering surveying. Elsevier, New York. https://epdf.tips/engineering-surveying-sixth-edition.html
58. Shang Z, Shen Z (2018) Real-time 3D reconstruction on construction site using visual SLAM and UAV. In: Construction research congress 2018: construction information technology - selected papers from the construction research congress 2018, vol 2018-April, pp 305–315. https://doi.org/10.1061/9780784481264.030, https://www.scopus.com/inward/record.uri?eid=2-s2.0-85048697191&doi=10.1061%2F9780784481264.030&partnerID=40&md5=417f079c6ca456d09537d08fa4c3aea0
59. Shotton J, Girshick R, Fitzgibbon A, Sharp T, Cook M, Finocchio M, Moore R, Kohli P, Criminisi A, Kipman A, Blake A (2013) Efficient human pose estimation from single depth images. IEEE Trans Pattern Anal Mach Intell 35(12):2821–2840. https://doi.org/10.1109/TPAMI.2012.241, http://ieeexplore.ieee.org/document/6341759/
60. Silberman N, Hoiem D, Kohli P, Fergus R (2012) Indoor segmentation and support inference from RGBD images. Lecture notes in computer science (including subseries lecture notes in artificial intelligence and lecture notes in bioinformatics), vol 7576, LNCS(PART 5), pp 746–760. https://doi.org/10.1007/978-3-642-33715-4_54

61. Soileau L, Bautista D, Johnson C, Gao C, Zhang K, Li X, Heymsfield SB, Thomas D, Zheng J (2016) Automated anthropometric phenotyping with novel Kinect-based three-dimensional imaging method: comparison with a reference laser imaging system. Eur J Clin Nutr 70(4):475–481. https://doi.org/10.1038/ejcn.2015.132, http://www.nature.com/articles/ejcn2015132

62. Stoyanov T, Mojtahedzadeh R, Andreasson H, Lilienthal AJ (2013) Comparative evaluation of range sensor accuracy for indoor mobile robotics and automated logistics applications. Robot Auton Syst 61(10):1094–1105. https://doi.org/10.1016/j.robot.2012.08.011, https://linkinghub.elsevier.com/retrieve/pii/S0921889012001431

63. Zhao Y, Liu Z, Cheng H (2013) RGB-depth feature for 3D human activity recognition. China Commun 10(7):93–103. https://doi.org/10.1109/CC.2013.6571292

64. Zollhöfer M, Stotko P, Görlitz A, Theobalt C, Nießner M, Klein R, Kolb A (2018) State of the art on 3D reconstruction with RGB-D cameras. Comput Graph Forum 37(2):625–652. https://doi.org/10.1111/cgf.13386

Chapter 5
3D Reconstruction from RGB-D Data

Charles Malleson, Jean-Yves Guillemaut and Adrian Hilton

Abstract A key task in computer vision is that of generating virtual 3D models of real-world scenes by reconstructing the shape, appearance and, in the case of dynamic scenes, motion of the scene from visual sensors. Recently, low-cost video plus depth (RGB-D) sensors have become widely available and have been applied to 3D reconstruction of both static and dynamic scenes. RGB-D sensors contain an active depth sensor, which provides a stream of depth maps alongside standard colour video. The low cost and ease of use of RGB-D devices as well as their video rate capture of images along with depth make them well suited to 3D reconstruction. Use of active depth capture overcomes some of the limitations of passive monocular or multiple-view video-based approaches since reliable, metrically accurate estimates of the scene depth at each pixel can be obtained from a single view, even in scenes that lack distinctive texture. There are two key components to 3D reconstruction from RGB-D data: (1) spatial alignment of the surface over time and, (2) fusion of noisy, partial surface measurements into a more complete, consistent 3D model. In the case of static scenes, the sensor is typically moved around the scene and its pose is estimated over time. For dynamic scenes, there may be multiple rigid, articulated, or non-rigidly deforming surfaces to be tracked over time. The fusion component consists of integration of the aligned surface measurements, typically using an intermediate representation, such as the volumetric truncated signed distance field (TSDF). In this chapter, we discuss key recent approaches to 3D reconstruction from depth or RGB-D input, with an emphasis on real-time reconstruction of static scenes.

C. Malleson (✉) · J.-Y. Guillemaut · A. Hilton
Centre for Vision, Speech and Signal Processing & University of Surrey, Guildford
GU2 7XH, UK
e-mail: charles.malleson@surrey.ac.uk

J.-Y. Guillemaut
e-mail: j.guillemaut@surrey.ac.uk

A. Hilton
e-mail: a.hilton@surrey.ac.uk

© Springer Nature Switzerland AG 2019
P. L. Rosin et al. (eds.), *RGB-D Image Analysis and Processing*,
Advances in Computer Vision and Pattern Recognition,
https://doi.org/10.1007/978-3-030-28603-3_5

5.1 Introduction

The ability to model the real world in 3D is useful in various application areas from archaeology and cultural heritage preservation to digital media production and interactive entertainment, robotics and healthcare. A key task in computer vision is that of automatically generating virtual 3D models of real world scenes by reconstructing the shape, appearance and, in the case of dynamic scenes, motion of surfaces within the scene from images, video and other sensor input.

Traditionally, 3D reconstruction has been performed by photogrammetry from standard RGB cameras or using costly, specialized laser scanning equipment. Recently, low-cost video plus depth (RGB-D) sensors have become widely available and have been applied to 3D reconstruction of both static and dynamic scenes. RGB-D sensors contain an active depth sensor, which provides a stream of depth maps alongside standard colour video. Typical depth sensors are based on infrared structured light or time-of-flight principles (see Chap. 1 for an in depth overview of commodity depth capture devices). The low cost and ease of use of RGB-D devices as well as their video rate capture of images along with depth make them well suited to 3D reconstruction. Use of active depth capture overcomes some of the limitations of passive monocular or multiple-view video-based approaches since reliable, metrically accurate estimates of the scene depth at each pixel can be obtained from a single view, even in scenes that lack distinctive texture.

There are two key components to 3D reconstruction from RGB-D data:

- Spatial registration (alignment) of the surface over time
- Fusion of noisy, partial surface measurements into a more complete, consistent 3D model.

In the case of static scenes, the sensor is typically moved around the scene to obtain more complete coverage and the registration process amounts to estimating the sensor pose (ego motion) over time. For dynamic scenes, in addition to sensor motion, there may be multiple rigid, articulated, or non-rigidly deforming surfaces present, which need to be tracked over time in order to obtain a consistent surface model. The fusion component in 3D reconstruction consists of integration of the aligned surface measurements, typically using an intermediate representation, such as the volumetric truncated signed distance field (TSDF) before extracting an output mesh model.

In this chapter, we provide an overview of several approaches to static and dynamic 3D reconstruction from depth or RGB-D input, some of which operate online, often in real-time, and others which require offline or batch processing. A broad overview of recent static reconstruction approaches is presented in Sect. 5.2, followed in Sect. 5.3 by a more detailed description and evaluation of two real-time static scene reconstruction approaches, volumetric-based KinectFusion [44] and point-based surface fusion [33]. A brief overview of recent dynamic scene reconstruction approaches is presented in Sect. 5.4 and concluding remarks are provided in Sect. 5.5.

5.2   Overview of Rigid Reconstruction Approaches

Standard cameras produce images containing colour or intensity information. These images are inherently 2D and for general scenes, estimated correspondences between multiple disparate images are required in order to infer metrically accurate 3D geometry if camera poses are known (multiview stereo) or 3D geometry up to a scale factor if not (structure from motion [11, 45]). It is possible to estimate an approximate depth directly from a single monocular image, for instance using deep learning-based approaches, e.g. [18], however due to the ill-posed nature of the problem, such inferred depth is typically limited in terms of metric accuracy. Active depth sensors such as structured light or time-of-flight (ToF) cameras on the other hand, natively output either images of metrically accurate depth values, i.e. 2.5D depth maps which can be re-projected into 3D using the intrinsic camera calibration parameters; or in the case of some laser scanners may directly output a 3D 'point cloud', with or without a 2D image structure. Core approaches to registration and integration of surface measurements in are discussed below in Sects. 5.2.1 and 5.2.2, respectively.

5.2.1   Surface Registration

Much research has been done on tracking (finding the 6DOF pose of the sensor) and mapping (measurement integration) using multiple depth maps. If there is a large relative motion between the point clouds to be registered, a *coarse* registration needs to be performed in order to get them into approximate alignment and avoid local minima when subsequently performing *fine* registration (see [60] for a detailed review). Coarse registration is often performed using sparse feature matching, whereas accurate fine registration is usually performed using the full data set [44].

The Iterative Closest Point (ICP) algorithm introduced by Besl and McKay [2] forms the basis of most registration algorithms. In ICP data alignment is formulated as an iterative optimization of a 3D rigid body transform so as to minimize a cost function representing the distance between points on a 'source' (data) and their corresponding closest points on a 'target' (model) surface in alternation with updating the closest point correspondences. The translation is found directly from the centroids, and the rotation is found by constructing a cross-covariance matrix. In practice, because the ICP optimization converges monotonically to a local minimum, one either needs to try several initial rotations, or use a feature-based initial coarse alignment algorithm to increase the chance of finding the global minimum. The more complex the shape the more initial states are required (highly symmetrical shapes are most problematic and may result in the solution being under-constrained). Besl and McKay's method cannot directly handle non-overlapping data unless it is modified for robustness, for instance by using a maximum correspondence distance [60]. If, however the sensor is not moved significantly between frames (as is usually the case when using a handheld video rate sensor such as the Kinect [44]), the pose from the previous frame can be used as initialization, without performing a coarse registration step.

There exist many variants of the ICP algorithm which offer improved registration performance and or computational efficiency (see [55] for a detailed review). For instance, the point-to-plane method proposed by Chen and Medioni [9] minimizes the distance from the source point to the plane that is defined by the target point and its normal. This makes intuitive sense since the finite sample spacing means that samples in one image will generally not coincide with corresponding samples in the other. This has been shown to improve convergence and is preferred when surface normal estimates are available, as is the case when depth maps are used as input [44, 54]. A normal orientation test can be used to increase robustness by preventing matching of surfaces of opposite orientation (as could occur with thin objects). Luminance or colour image data has also been used in the ICP framework to help constrain the registration in cases where shape alone is ambiguous (for instance spheres). In [73], luminance information from a colour camera used in parallel with a depth sensor is used to establish point-to-point correspondences via a form of optical flow at each iteration.

Obtaining closest point associations for ICP is computationally expensive. When the points to be aligned come in a structured form (as with the 2D grid structure of depth images), significant speedups can be introduced by using the projective data association algorithm proposed by Blais and Levine [3]: using the intrinsic camera calibration information, transformed 3D points from the target image are projected into the source image to get the pixel index correspondences. Fitzgibbon [15] extends the ICP algorithm to perform robust registration using a Huber kernel and Levenberg–Marquardt (LM) non-linear optimization. This optimization approach yields a wider basin of convergence than standard ICP. The 'generalized ICP' proposed by Segal et al. [61] introduces a probabilistic framework and uses planar surface structure in both the data and the model (a plane-to-plane metric).

One way of increasing the speed of convergence of ICP is by performing early iterations on a subset of the available points for instance using a coarse-to-fine (multi-resolution) sampling of the depth map [44]. Other useful ways of subsampling include random subsampling and sampling based on colour information. Rusinkiewicz and Levoy [55] propose normal-space subsampling which bins points based on normals and samples uniformly across buckets, thus promoting correct registration of scenes containing no large distinctive features. ICP registration can also be extended to handle articulated point clouds [7, 13, 50] in which case pose parameters are iteratively determined for each bone in a skeletal model.

5.2.2 Surface Fusion

As stated in [23], the goal of 3D surface reconstruction is to estimate a manifold surface (with the correct topology) that accurately approximates an unknown object surface from a set of measured 3D sample points. When additional information (such as measurement uncertainty) is available it can aid reconstruction. There are two classes of technique for reconstructing 3D models from 2.5D images [23]. The first class uses prior models with an explicit parametric representation and fits the range data to them. The disadvantage of such methods is that they can only represent models of known object classes, for which the topological genus and modes of shape variation are known upfront (e.g. using a radial displacement map on a cylinder to model a human head [22]). The second class of techniques, which generate triangulated mesh representations is more generally applicable because it can represent arbitrary geometry and topology (which are often not known up front). The focus of this discussion will be on non-parametric approaches, in particular the widely used signed distance function.

5.2.2.1 Signed Distance Functions

To facilitate the generation of a 3D surface model by the fusion of aligned 2.5D depth maps it is common to use an intermediate non-parametric representation of volumetric occupancy. A representation widely used in computer vision graphics is the Signed Distance Function (SDF) introduced by Curless and Levoy [10]. The SDF is simply a field whose value at any given point contains the (signed) Euclidean distance between that point and the surface. Thus the SDF is zero at the surface interface, positive outside it (observed free space), and negative inside it (unobserved space). In practice, the SDF is represented in a discrete voxel grid defining the reconstructed volume and is truncated at a certain distance from the surface i.e. values more than a certain distance in front of a surface measurement receive a maximum value, and values more than a certain distance, μ, behind it receive no measurement (null). This truncation helps prevent surfaces from interfering with each other. Along with each Truncated Signed Distance Function (TSDF) value a weight is maintained which reflects the confidence in the TSDF value. These weights may depend on the confidence of a measurement (if available) or heuristics (for instance penalizing vertices whose estimated normal is close to perpendicular to the viewing direction or which are close to depth discontinuities [68]). A simple weighted running average update rule for the SDF and weight voxel grid can be used to incrementally incorporate measurements into the model, which adds any previously unobserved regions to the model, while averaging out noise in regions previously observed.

Obtaining the surface interface from the TSDF is simply a matter of extracting the zero crossings (an iso-surface at level zero). This is an advantage over probabilistic occupancy grids where one needs to seek the modes of the probability distribution in the grid [44]. If only a single view is required, one can perform a direct raycast [49] which is independent of scene complexity since areas outside the viewing frustum need not be visited. If, however, a complete polygonal mesh model is required a triangulation algorithm such as marching cubes is more suitable.

Originally proposed by Lorensen and Cline [36], the marching cubes algorithm is widely used for extracting triangle meshes from constant density surfaces (iso-surfaces) in volumetric datasets. The algorithm scans through a voxel grid and processes one $2 \times 2 \times 2$ cell at a time using lookup tables to determine the triangle topology within the cell and interpolation between vertices to find iso-surface inter-sections. This is efficient, but results in non-uniform triangle shape and size.

The 'marching triangles' algorithm proposed by Hilton et al. [24] performs the same task as marching cubes, but uses Delaunay triangulation and places vertices according to local surface geometry thus producing triangles with more uniform shape and size.

5.2.2.2 Other Surface Fusion Approaches

The point-based implicit surface reconstruction of Hoppe et al. [25] works with unor-ganized points and generates simplicial surfaces (i.e. triangle meshes) of arbitrary topology. It uses a signed distance function computed with the aid of normals esti-mated from k-nearest neighbour PCA with a graph optimization to get consistent orientations. When the source points come from (inherently organized) depth maps, normals may be estimated more efficiently using the image structure.

Turk and Levoy [68] create polygon meshes from multiple (ICP-registered) range images and then 'zipper' them together, that is they remove redundant triangles and connect ('clip') the meshes together. The mesh growing technique of Rutishauser et al. [57] merges depth maps incrementally with particular emphasis on the (anisotropic Gaussian) error model of their sensor and uses an explicit boundary representation to prevent filling surfaces in the model where no measurements have been made. Soucy and Laurendeau [63] estimate an integrated surface model piecewise from the canonical subset of the Venn diagram of the set of range views (here, a canonical subset contains a group of points exclusively visible in a particular combination of range views). This membership information is used in an averaging process, taking particular care at the intersections of subsets. The ball pivoting algorithm of Bernar-dini et al. [1] triangulates point clouds efficiently by beginning with a seed triangle and rotating a sphere around an edge until another point is reached, at which point another triangle is formed.

Hilton et al. [23] introduce a mesh-based geometric fusion algorithm based on a continuous implicit surface which (unlike previous algorithms employing discrete representations) can better reconstruct regions of complex geometry (holes, crease edges and thin objects). The algorithm also uses geometric constraints and statistical tests based on measurement uncertainty to guide reconstruction of complex geometry. While outperforming other integration strategies [10, 25, 57, 63, 68] in terms of complexity and the minimum feature size, minimum crease angle and minimum surface separation (thickness), this approach is relatively computationally expensive.

Radial Basis Functions (RBFs) have been used for interpolation of a surface from point samples. Globally supported RBFs are good at filling in missing data, but are computationally inefficient. Conversely, locally supported RBFs are less good at filling in missing data, but are more computationally efficient. Ohtake et al. [48] therefore propose to use compactly supported RBFs with a coarse-to-fine sampling of the points. The coarse levels fill in missing data and serve as carriers for the finer levels which add detail.

Kazhdan et al. [32] used oriented points to define an indicator function with value 1 inside the model and 0 outside it and cast the optimization as a Poisson problem. The resulting reconstructions are inherently watertight. Like Radial Basis Function (RBF) approaches, the method creates smooth surfaces. This can result in spurious protrusions from regions where no samples exist. The method is best suited to scenarios where the capture process has produced full surface coverage, such as single objects captured via a moving laser scanner or segmented performers in a multiview reconstruction setup, but is less well suited to partial coverage of larger scenes.

5.3   Real-Time Rigid Reconstruction

The first reported system that uses a low-cost depth sensor to perform real-time, online and metrically consistent 3D reconstruction of small to medium-sized scenes on a commodity PC is the 'KinectFusion' system of Newcombe et al. [29, 44], which is described in detail in the following subsections. Since KinectFusion was introduced, several variations on the theme of static scene reconstruction from depth maps have been proposed. Some of these have addressed handling of larger scenes within the limited GPU memory budget, for instance the moving volume approach of Roth and Vona [53], the 'Kintinuous' system of Whelan et al. [74], the hierarchical data structure of Chen et al. [8], and the spatial voxel hashing approach of Niessner et al. [46].

Keller et al. [33] propose a point-based alternative to (volumetric) KinectFusion. The unstructured 'surfel' (surface element) representation is more memory efficient than volumetric structures and manipulation (e.g. insertion/removal) of individual entities is easier than with structured representations such as meshes. The memory footprint of the surfel representation is significantly lower than for volumetric fusion, but mesh extraction is less straightforward. The dense planar SLAM system of [58] is based on the surfel fusion system of [33], but additionally detects planar regions, which can be stored in a compressed form and used for semantic understanding of the scene.

In SLAM++ [59], 3D models of known objects (such as chairs) are used in an object-level SLAM system which recognizes and tracks repeated instances of these objects in a cluttered indoor scene. The main benefits over standard approaches that use primitive-level tracking and mapping are increased representational efficiency and the native semantic structure of the output scene.

By allowing offline (post) processing, other recent works are able to produce higher quality models than currently possible with real-time methods. Zhou et al. [77] perform fusion of small fragments of a scene, which are each locally accurate, and then combine them via an elastic registration scheme to produce a complete surface with higher detail and reduced low-frequency distortion when compared to using a single grid for the whole scene. The method is off-line and requires hours to days of GPU processing time. Fuhrmann and Goesele's floating scale reconstruction approach [16] uses compactly supported basis functions for integration into an octree voxel grid structure and is formulated to take into account the fact that surface measurements represent finite sample areas rather than individual points, thus avoiding potential blurring of fine details by coarser samples that were captured from further away. In [78], Zollhofer et al. refine a model obtained by TSDF fusion of depth maps by using an offline shape-from-shading stage to enhance the level of reconstructed detail compared to depth-only fusion approaches.

The KinectFusion approach of Newcombe et al. [44], described in this section demonstrates the ability of low-cost depth sensors to quickly and cost-effectively produce compelling 3D models of small to medium-sized static indoor scenes by employing GPU acceleration of ICP sensor pose estimation and TSDF volumetric measurement fusion. Online real-time reconstruction of static scenes is achieved using a sequence of depth maps from a handheld Kinect sensor. The core components of the KinectFusion pipeline are model building by integration of captured depth maps into a volumetric TSDF representation (Sect. 5.3.3) and ICP registration of input depth maps to this model (Sect. 5.3.2). Outside the core registration and fusion loop, a textured mesh may be extracted using marching cubes and textured using projective texturing.

The parallelizable parts of the reconstruction pipeline may be implemented on the GPU by using, for instance, NVidia's CUDA toolkit [47]. Such GPU parallelization involves uploading input data from CPU memory to GPU memory; splitting it into parts, each of which is concurrently processed by a *kernel* function running in parallel *threads* across hundreds or thousands of GPU processing cores; and finally downloading the result back into CPU memory. How the work is split up depends on the application and performance considerations. For example a kernel may perform an operation on one or a small block of pixels or voxels.

Preliminaries of KinectFusion are presented below in Sect. 5.3.1, followed by details on ICP registration (Sect. 5.3.2), TSDF fusion (Sect. 5.3.3) and textured mesh extraction (Sect. 5.3.4). Finally, in Sect. 5.3.5, a related approach proposed by Keller et al. [33] is discussed, in which point-based fusion is used in place of volumetric TSDF fusion.

5.3.1 Preliminaries

The input from an RGB-D sensor consists of a video rate stream of RGB colour images, $C_i(t)$ and depth images, $D_i(t)$, containing Cartesian depth $d(\mathbf{u})$ for each pixel $\mathbf{u} = (col, row)$.

A standard pinhole camera model is used to characterise the RGB-D sensor. A fixed 3×3 intrinsic camera matrix $\mathbf{K}$ and a 4×4 camera pose matrix $\mathbf{T}$ (which varies over time) can be used to map between world and pixel coordinates. In practice, the RGB and depth cameras are usually not generated through the same lens aperture, and are thus offset from one another. For simplicity of processing, the depth map is often re-rendered from the RGB camera point of view in order to obtain direct pixel correspondence between them (this may be done on board the device or as a post-process). The camera matrix $\mathbf{K}$ is defined as

$$\mathbf{K} = \begin{bmatrix} f_x & 0 & c_x \\ 0 & f_y & c_y \\ 0 & 0 & 1 \end{bmatrix} \tag{5.1}$$

where f_x and f_y and c_x and c_y are the x and y focal lengths and principal point coordinates, respectively. A rigid body transformation matrix $\mathbf{T}$ contains a 3×3 orthonormal rotation matrix $\mathbf{R}$ (which has three degrees of freedom) and a 3D translation vector $\mathbf{t}$:

$$\mathbf{T} = \begin{bmatrix} \mathbf{R} & \mathbf{t} \\ \mathbf{0} & 1 \end{bmatrix} \tag{5.2}$$

The intrinsic parameters of the camera model can be estimated using, for instance, a checkerboard-based approach of Zhang et al. [75].

The following describes how the camera intrinsics and pose can be used to transform between 2D/2.5D image space, camera-local 3D space and global 3D space. Given the intrinsic camera calibration matrix, $\mathbf{K}$, an image-space depth measurement $d(\mathbf{u})$ can be converted to a camera-local 3D point, $\mathbf{p}_{cam}(\mathbf{u})$:

$$\mathbf{p}_{cam}(\mathbf{u}) = d(\mathbf{u}) \cdot \mathbf{K}^{-1}\dot{\mathbf{u}}, \tag{5.3}$$

where a dot on a vector denotes its homogeneous form, $\dot{\mathbf{u}} = [\mathbf{u}^T 1]^T$. This camera-local 3D point can be transformed to a global 3D point, $\mathbf{p}_{gbl}$, using the camera pose $\mathbf{T}$:

$$\mathbf{p}_{gbl}(\mathbf{u}) = \rho\left(\mathbf{T}\dot{\mathbf{p}}_{cam}\right), \tag{5.4}$$

where ρ is the de-homogenization operator, $\rho([\mathbf{a}^T \; w]^T) = \mathbf{a}/w$. Similarly, any global 3D point, $\mathbf{p}_{gbl}$ can be transformed into camera space:

$$\mathbf{p}_{cam} = \rho\left(\mathbf{T}^{-1}\dot{\mathbf{p}}_{gbl}\right), \tag{5.5}$$

and a camera-space 3D point can be projected into the depth map using the intrinsics as follows:

$$[x, y, z]^T = \mathbf{K} \cdot \mathbf{p}_{cam} \tag{5.6}$$

$$\mathbf{u} = [x/z, y/z]^T \tag{5.7}$$

$$d(\mathbf{u}) = z. \tag{5.8}$$

We now describe how the camera pose, $\mathbf{T}$ is estimated online for each incoming frame, thus allowing input depth frames to be registered for consistent surface integration.

5.3.2 Registration Using ICP

The camera pose estimation of KinectFusion is based on the ICP algorithm with fast projective data association [3] and the point-to-plane error metric [9] (see Sect. 5.2.1). The registration is done using the current depth map $D_i(t)$ as the source and a depth map synthesized from the current volumetric TSDF model of the scene as the target. This synthetic depth map is generated by ray-casting [49] the TSDF voxel grid from a prediction of the sensor pose for the current current frame. By assuming small frame-to-frame camera motion the pose of the target frame can be used as the pose from which to ray cast and also as the initial pose of the source in the ICP algorithm. Because any error in registration of the previous frame will have a relatively small effect on the model, the frame-to-model registration approach yields increased accuracy and significantly reduces the accumulation of drift that occurs in the raw frame-to-frame case, without requiring off-line optimization for loop closure.

The data association and error minimization stages of the ICP require normals $\mathbf{n}(\mathbf{u})$ for each pixel $\mathbf{u}$. Because the depth map is organized in a grid, adjacency is known and a given normal can be efficiently estimated using the point and its neighbours in the depth image (without the expensive neighbour finding computations required for general unorganized point clouds [25]). Because of their inherent noise however, the raw depth maps produce unacceptably poor normal maps, therefore a GPU-parallelized version of the bilateral filter [67] is applied to the depth map before using it in the registration algorithm, smoothing out noise while preserving depth discontinuities.

As with the normal estimation, the usually expensive data association component of ICP can be sped up significantly by employing the image structure of the depth images. Given global poses for both the source and target frames, each pixel index $\mathbf{u}$ in the source image is un-projected to form a 3D source point which is projected onto the target image plane to look up the target pixel index $\Omega(\mathbf{u})$. The target pixel at this index is then un-projected to get the target 3D point. This data association approach assumes that there is a small frame-to-frame transform between source and target. To remove false correspondences, any point pair separated by a (Euclidean) distance of more than t_d or whose normals have a dot product of less than t_a are rejected (see Fig. 5.1). If there is not a valid correspondence between source and target at $\mathbf{u}$ then $\Omega(\mathbf{u}) = \text{null}$. The association is implemented in parallel on the GPU with one thread per source pixel.

Let $\mathbf{p}_{ss}(\mathbf{u})$ be the 3D point produced by the pixel with index $\mathbf{u}$ in the source depth map (in its local coordinate system). Let $\mathbf{p}_{tg}(\phi(\mathbf{u}))$ be the global 3D point produced by the target depth map pixel associated with pixel $\mathbf{u}$ in the source image.

For any estimated global source frame pose $\mathbf{T}_{sg}$ the total point-to-plane error E is then given by

$$E(\mathbf{T}_{sg}) = \sum_{\Omega(\mathbf{u}) \neq \text{null}} \left| \left[\rho\left(\mathbf{T}_{sg}\dot{\mathbf{p}}_{ss}(\mathbf{u})\right) - \mathbf{p}_{tg}\left(\Omega(\mathbf{u})\right) \right]^T \mathbf{n}_{tg}\left(\Omega(\mathbf{u})\right) \right|. \qquad (5.9)$$

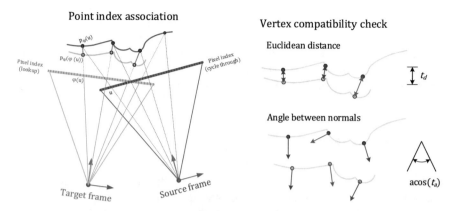

Fig. 5.1 Illustration of the fast projective data association technique. Left: each source image pixel is un-projected (producing a point in global 3D space) and then projected onto the target image plane to find its associated pixel index (2D coordinates) in the target image. The target image pixel at this index is then looked up and un-projected to produce the target 3D point. Right: the source and associated target points are checked for compatibility, rejecting inconsistent matches. Figure from [37]

The rigid body transform that minimizes E can be formulated by linearizing the rotation matrix (making use of a small angle assumption for incremental transforms) and writing the transform as a 6D parameter vector $\mathbf{x} = [\alpha, \beta, \gamma, t_x, t_y, t_z]^T$, where α, β and γ are the rotation angles (in radians) about the x, y and z-axes, respectively and t_x, t_y and t_z are the translation components.

As shown in [44], differentiating the linearised objective function and setting it to zero yields a 6×6 symmetric linear system

$$\sum_{\phi(\mathbf{u}) \neq \text{null}} \mathbf{a}^T \mathbf{a} \mathbf{x} = \sum \mathbf{a}^T b \tag{5.10}$$

where

$$\mathbf{a}^T = \left[[\mathbf{p}_{sg}]_\times \middle| \mathbf{I}_{3\times3} \right]^T \mathbf{n}_{tg}, \tag{5.11}$$

$$[\mathbf{p}]_\times := \begin{bmatrix} 0 & -p_z & p_y \\ p_z & 0 & -p_x \\ -p_y & p_x & 0 \end{bmatrix} \tag{5.12}$$

and

$$b = \mathbf{n}_{tg}^T [\mathbf{p}_{tg} - \mathbf{p}_{sg}]. \tag{5.13}$$

The summands of the normal system are computed in parallel on the GPU, summed using a parallel reduction, and finally solved on the CPU using a Cholesky decomposition followed by forward/backward substitution. At each iteration the solved incremental transform vector **x** is converted to a 4×4 rigid body transform matrix and composed onto the current pose estimate for use in the next iteration. To speed-up convergence of the ICP registration, a coarse-to-fine approach may be used, in which decimated versions of the depth maps are used for early iterations and finally using all points for a more precise registration.

5.3.3 Fusion Using TSDFs

Surface integration is performed using TSDF fusion [10], integrating incoming depth maps into the model in an online manner, integrating out noise and increasing scene coverage as more frames are added. The voxel grid $G = \{S, W\}$ consists of grids S and W which contain, for each voxel $\mathbf{v} = (x, y, z)$, the truncated signed distance function (TSDF) values $s(\mathbf{v})$ and weights $w(\mathbf{v})$, respectively. The voxel grid dimensions and leaf size as well as its location in global coordinates need to be chosen appropriately. The main constraint on the dimensions of the voxel grid is the limited size of the GPU memory. The leaf size (resolution) is implicitly calculated in terms of the physical volume and memory available. For example, a 2 m^3 cubic volume with 512^3 voxels would have leaves of side 4.0 mm and require approximately 1 GB of GPU memory using 32-bit floating point values. In the absence of constraints on memory, the voxel leaf size should be chosen on the order of the effective size of the input depth pixels in order to reconstruct all available detail.

For efficiency of implementation the projective signed distance function is used (Fig. 5.2). This allows each voxel site $\mathbf{v}$ to be visited in parallel and the distance along the ray used as an estimate of the TSDF $s(\mathbf{v})$. The model is updated incrementally as measurements from frame t are added using a weighted running average:

$$s_t(\mathbf{v}) = \frac{w_{t-1}(\mathbf{v})s_{t-1}(\mathbf{v}) + w_t^m(\mathbf{v})s_t^m(\mathbf{v})}{w_t(\mathbf{v})} \tag{5.14}$$

and

$$w_t(\mathbf{v}) = w_{t-1}(\mathbf{v}) + w_t^m(\mathbf{v}) \tag{5.15}$$

where s_t^m and w_t^m are the input TSDF and weight values for the current frame.

The truncation distance, μ, affects the minimum thickness of objects that can be reconstructed using the TSDF representation (surfaces thinner than μ can interfere with each other). This distance also affects the speed of reconstruction: larger values of μ allow bigger jumps when ray-casting (see below). If accuracy of fine detail is important, then μ should be made as small as possible whilst remaining larger than a few voxel leaf sides. It may also be made depth-dependent to account for the uncertainty in the depth measurement, which in the case of the Kinect v1 sensor increases quadratically with depth [34].

Using the pose from the last frame and the depth intrinsics, a synthetic depth image is generated by doing a per-pixel ray cast into the signed distance voxel grid S. Rays

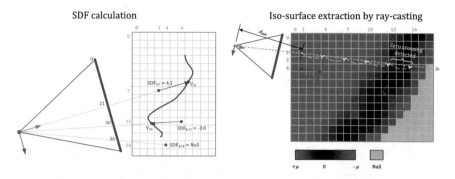

Fig. 5.2 Illustration of voxel grid model generation and extraction. Left: for a given frame, signed distance values are obtained for each voxel by projecting it onto the image plane and computing the distance between it and this un-projected pixel. Note that the truncation is not shown. Right: to extract a depth map, each pixel is un-projected along its ray starting at the minimum depth d_{min} and evaluating the tri-linearly interpolated voxel before skipping to the next. When a zero crossing is detected, ray-casting stops and the crossing is located more precisely. Figure from [37]

are marched from the minimum depth sensing range and in steps of $0.8\,\mu$ (slightly less than the minimum truncation distance) until the sign changes from positive to negative indicating a zero crossing (refer to Fig. 5.2). This skipping provides a speed-up whilst ensuring that a zero-crossing is not missed. When a zero crossing is detected, its location is found more precisely by tri-linear interpolation of the SDF before and after the sign change. If a negative-to-positive transition is found marching stops. Each of the pixels is ray cast by a single thread in parallel on the GPU.

5.3.4 Model Extraction and Texturing

The marching cubes algorithm [36] may be used to triangulate the TSDF model and generate an output mesh model of the scene. Each vertex of the resulting mesh is then projected into the input RGB images (using the previously estimated camera poses) and the corresponding pixel values looked up. A depth map is produced via an OpenGL rendering of the mesh from the point of view of the RGB camera. This depth map is used to check for occlusions of a given vertex with respect to the corresponding pixel in the RGB image and also to check the proximity of the test pixel to a depth discontinuity.

A simple weighting scheme is used to determine colours for each vertex by incremental update of a weight and colour frame by frame (analogous to Eq. 5.14). The weighting scheme weights contributions from different frame according to the proximity of vertex to depth discontinuities in the current frame as well as the angle between the vertex normal and the camera ray, down weighting contributions for pixels near depth edges and pixel corresponding to obliquely viewed surfaces. The aim of this weighting scheme is to reduce foreground/background texture contami-

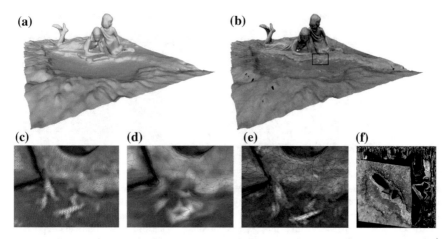

Fig. 5.3 Reconstruction of a statue using the Asus Xtion Pro Live RGB-D sensor. **a** Decimated mesh (35 k vertices). **b** Decimated mesh with texture map applied. **c** Raw mesh (per-vertex colour). **d** Decimated mesh (per-vertex colour). **e** Decimated mesh (texture map colour). **f** Texture map. Figure from [37], using their reimplementation of KinectFusion

nation and ghosting caused by any inaccuracies in the model or error in the intrinsic calibration and estimated pose of the camera. To avoid excessive ghosting of texture, a vertex colour is no longer updated once its colour weighting exceeds a threshold.

The mesh output by marching cubes is inherently densely sampled, with no triangles bigger than the voxel diagonal, even for flat, low curvature surface regions. This can lead to unnecessarily large mesh files which are inefficient to store, render and manipulate. Some regions with fine features or high curvature do benefit from having small triangles, however flatter surfaces can be decimated without losing any significant detail. The scan of a statue shown in Fig. 5.3 was produced using voxels of side 4.1 mm yielding a raw output mesh with 830 k vertices. Using quadric edge collapse decimation [17], the mesh can be reduced to 35 k vertices, with little loss of geometric detail, but resulting in loss of detail in the per-vertex colour due to lower resolution sampling. Using [69], a dense texture map may be generated, allowing the decimated mesh to represent the detailed appearance of the captured images while representing the shape more efficiently. Two further examples of scenes reconstructed with KinectFusion are shown in Fig. 5.4.

Due to the nature of typical sensors' depth map generation process (see Chap. 1), the size of reconstructed features is inherently limited. The depth maps produced typically also suffer from significant levels of quantization and random noise causing several mm of error in depth at typical indoor scene distances [34]. However, the fusion of hundreds of frames from slightly different viewpoints integrates this noise away to produce surface relief with submillimetre resolution, even when using TSDF voxels larger than 1 mm [39].

(a) Office scene. Three input depth frames (left) and meshed output model (right).

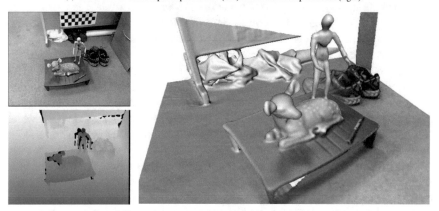

(b) Deer scene. Input RGB and depth frame (left) and reconstruction with/without texture (right).

Fig. 5.4 Sample input and volumetric reconstructions for two indoor scenes using the KinectFusion approach [44]. Figure from [37], using their reimplementation of KinectFusion

5.3.5 *Online Surfel-Based Fusion*

Keller et al. [33] propose an alternative approach to GPU-accelerated online rigid scene reconstruction similar in many respects to KinectFusion, but using a surface element (surfel) representation rather than a volumetric grid. Keller's method also contains a simple mechanism for detecting and removing dynamic outliers from the fused representation.

The representation used for fusion and the output model is a flat (unstructured) array of surface elements (surfels). Each surfel primitive consists of a position $\mathbf{p}$, normal $\mathbf{n}$, radius r, confidence c, timestamp t (last frame observed), and colour. A

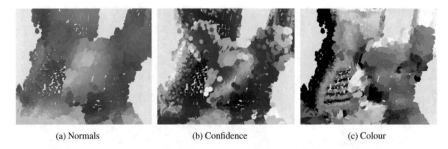

(a) Normals   (b) Confidence   (c) Colour

Fig. 5.5 Close up of surfel representation for 3D scene reconstruction from RGB-D video input. The representation consists of an unstructured set of points with additional properties including normal, radius, confidence, and colour. The points are rendered using hexagons. The confidence value is visualized using the following colour scale: 0 ▰▰▰▰▰ 30. Figure from [37], using their reimplementation of the approach of Keller et al. [33]

closeup of the surfel primitives is shown in Fig. 5.5 which illustrates these properties. The density of modelled surfels corresponds directly to the input depth sample density. Correspondences between incoming depth measurements and the surfel IDs are established by projection into a super-sampled lookup image for the current depth frame. The fusion technique is similar to TSDF fusion, in that it is based on a running weighted average of observations. As with KinectFusion, ICP registration is performed using a depth map synthesized from the current model. In this case, the depth map is synthesized by splat rendering the surfels using a graphics shader which outputs an oriented hexagon for each surfel (as opposed to the ray-casting used in the volumetric approach).

Upon commencement of reconstruction, new surface points are assigned zero confidence. As the corresponding surface point is re-observed in incoming frames, its position and normal are averaged with the incoming measurements and the confidence value increased. Surfels with a confidence below a threshold value c_{stable} are referred to as 'unstable'. The unstable points are excluded from the registration stage, so as to increase robustness to outliers and any dynamic elements in the scene.

An additional feature of the method of Keller et al. [33] is a simple online labelling of dynamic elements in the scene. This is performed by detecting model surfels which are outliers with respect to the current input frame, performing a region growing operation to expand the detected dynamic region, and demoting all these surfels to unstable status (with a weight just below the stability threshold c_{stable}). The demotion to unstable status aims to prevent dynamic objects from contaminating the (static scene) model by immediately removing them from the registration point set, but allows the points to be reintroduced, if the object stops moving (and the points attain stable status once again).

5.3.6   Evaluation

A 2000 frame synthetic dataset, *Tabletop*, was created by Malleson [37] to compare the performance of the volumetric [42] and surfel fusion [33] in terms of reconstructed geometry fidelity, camera pose estimation accuracy and functioning in the presence of dynamic content in the scene. The test scene, a tabletop 1.8 m across with various objects on it, is shown in Fig. 5.6. It contains thin and narrow structures as well as a toy car that moves across the table. The virtual RGB-D camera moves smoothly, around the scene as well as up and down.

The registration performance of volumetric and surfel-based fusion were evaluated for four variants of the *Tabletop* scene. The variants are the combinations of clean depth/simulated Kinect noisy depth (with noise simulated using [34]), and static geometry only/with the moving car. The absolute error in position and orientation with respect to ground truth is plotted in Fig. 5.7. Both the volumetric and surfel-based approaches produce good tracking on the clean data, with or without the moving car present. On the moving car variant the surfel-based registration fails when the car starts moving (at frame 400). A summary of the registration and reconstruction performance for each variant is presented in Table 5.1.

To directly compare the quality of the surface reconstruction between the volumetric and the surfel-based methods, tests were performed in which the two systems were fed the ground truth camera pose trajectories, with the version of the scene not containing the moving car. This factors out any differences resulting from error in ICP registration and handling of dynamic geometry. To make the reconstructed geometry of similar density between the methods, the voxel size for the volumetric tests was chosen such as to produce roughly the same number of vertices as surfels are produced by the surfel-based tests, roughly 1.5 M in each case. Figure 5.8 visualizes the Hausdorff distance between the ground truth geometry and the reconstructions with each method. The RMS error for the surfel fusion method is 1.1 mm, compared to 3.5 mm for the volumetric method. Qualitatively, the surfel fusion approach does not suffer from 'lipping' artefacts in reconstructions from TSDF fusion—the square edges of the cube are more faithfully reproduced. The TSDF fusion process also cannot handle very thin objects viewed from both sides because the opposing

Fig. 5.6   Three frames from the RGB-D rendering of the 2000 frame *Tabletop* test scene for assessing the performance of surfel-based fusion and volumetric fusion. Note the narrow and thin objects as well as the moving car (which is static for the first 400 frames of the sequence). Figure from [37]

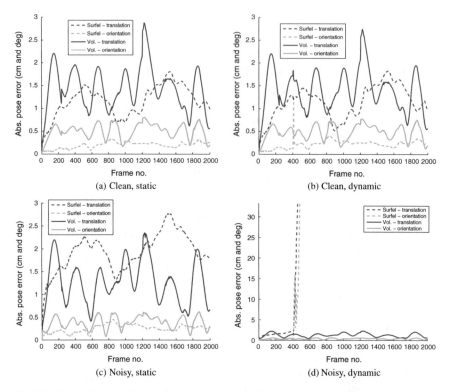

Fig. 5.7 Comparison of volumetric and surfel-based ICP registration performance on the four variants of the *Tabletop* sequence. **a** Clean depth, no moving objects. **b** Clean depth, with moving car. **c** Noisy depth, no moving objects. **d** Noisy depth, with moving car (note that the car moves from frame 400 onwards, which at which point the ICP loses track in this variant). Figure from [37]

Table 5.1 Registration and geometric accuracy for the *Tabletop* scene, using volumetric (Vol.) and surfel-based (Surf.) reconstruction approaches. The variants are as follows: fixed geometry only (F)/ with moving car (M); ground truth (GT)/ICP (ICP) camera registration; and clean (C)/noisy (N) depth maps

Variant			RMS position error (mm)		RMS orientation error (deg)		RMS recon error (mm)		Num model elements ($\times 10^6$)	
			Vol.	Surf.	Vol.	Surf.	Vol.	Surf.	Vol.	Surf.
F	GT	C	–	–	–	–	3.47	1.08	1.14	1.55
F	GT	N	–	–	–	–	3.73	1.04	1.07	1.58
F	ICP	C	9.54	12.17	0.27	0.21	4.09	3.12	1.20	1.59
F	ICP	N	8.05	19.77	0.20	0.27	4.18	3.28	1.20	1.67
M	GT	C	–	–	–	–	3.56	1.08	1.08	1.65
M	GT	N	–	–	–	–	3.78	1.04	1.11	1.67
M	ICP	C	8.87	11.99	0.23	0.23	4.19	3.76	1.23	1.68
M	ICP	N	7.69	2139.50	0.19	138.83	4.21	(failed)	–	–

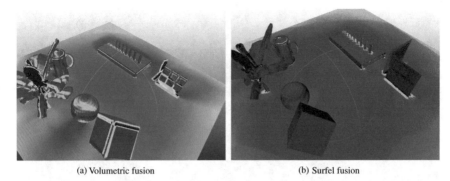

(a) Volumetric fusion   (b) Surfel fusion

Fig. 5.8 Hausdorff distance (0 ■■■■■ 5mm) between ground truth and reconstructed geometry for the two fusion approaches (using ground truth camera pose, no scene motion and clean depth maps). Note that the volumetric approach has lost the narrow and thin structures and that it exhibits lipping artefacts on corners of the cube. Figure from [37]

surfaces can 'cancel each other out' leading to artefacts. The surfel fusion method can handle thin surfaces without such artefacts, even for the zero-thickness sheet shown in the upper right of the scene in Fig. 5.8. The surfel method is also able to resolve the second smallest cylinder, which is not resolved by the volumetric method, since it is the same diameter as the size of a voxel (2.2 mm). (Neither of the methods can resolve the smallest cylinder which is a single pixel thick in some input depth frames, and not visible at all in others.)

The method proposed by Keller et al. [33] for segmenting out dynamic regions of the model is based on detecting inconsistencies between the incoming depth and the surfel model. The labelling is based on the value of the confidence field of the surfels, which begins at zero and increases as observations are added. This confidence field is analogous to the weight in the signed distance fusion in volumetric reconstruction. The progression of fusion is shown in Fig. 5.9, which shows surfel confidence via a colour coding. Surfels with confidence below a threshold are labelled as 'unstable'. Unstable points are excluded from the ICP registration. A 'dynamics map' is seeded with all registration outliers and a region growing approach based on position and normal similarity between neighbouring points is applied. Modelled points in the model marked in the dynamics map are demoted to unstable status. The region growing method used is fairly simplistic and does not work robustly in all scenarios. For example, as new model points are added at the edge of the frame (e.g. a floor or tabletop) as the camera pans, they will initially be unstable, and thus have no ICP correspondence, the dynamics depth map points in this region could then be expanded by the region growing to cover a large static area (e.g. the rest of the surface of the desk). In the test example of the *Tabletop* scene, the segmentation approach is not able to prevent the model from being corrupted when the car begins to move.

To evaluate drift on real-world data, a 900 frame time-mirrored sequence (450 frames played forward and then in reverse) was generated from the *Office* capture [37]. The difference between the estimated pose for the first and last frame of this

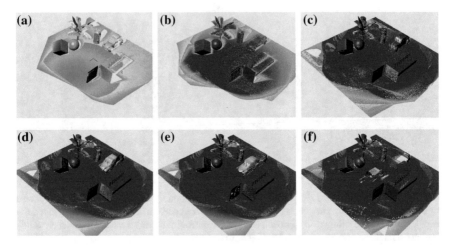

Fig. 5.9 Splat rendering showing progression of surfel-based fusion of the *Tabletop* sequence. The confidence value is visualized using the following colour scale: 0 ▮▬▬▬ 30, where the black line is the stability threshold. In **a**–**c** the car is stationary. In **d**–**f** the car is moving. Note the demotion of points on the car to unstable when it starts moving as well as the low confidence of new surfels on the moving car, each of which are not consistently observed for long enough to achieve stable status. Figure from [37]

sequence (which should be identical) gives an indication of the global pose estimation stability. The magnitude of the difference in estimated camera position and orientation at the start and end of the sequence were evaluated for both volumetric and surfel-based reconstruction methods and the results are shown in Fig. 5.10. Note that the surfel-based method proves less robust on this real data, with an accumulated drift of 5 cm compared to 1 cm for the volumetric method. The effect of this is demonstrated in Fig. 5.11 which shows the final reconstructed models and posed depth map for the first and last frames. The camera offset from the origin can be seen in the *last* frame, particularly for the surfel-based method. The gradual accumulation of drift in pose goes hand in hand with accumulated drift in the model. Therefore, the depth map in the *last* frame is consistent with the depth map, which means that the depth map and model are inconsistent with one another at the *first* frame. This mismatch is larger for the surfel-based method on account of the greater level of drift. The surfel-based reconstructed surface is also less complete than the volumetric surface, since some surface regions are only briefly observed in the input, meaning that they are treated as outliers by the fusion algorithm.

The flat array of surfels used in the surfel fusion approach has a memory footprint proportional to reconstructed surface area, whereas that of the fully allocated volumetric grids of KinectFusion is proportional to scene volume (regardless of occupied surface area). For a roughly equal sampling density, and typical scene content, the surfel representation is far more compact. For the example scene presented here, the $2\,m^2$ voxel grid containing 180 M voxels requires 1.4 GB to store, compared to just

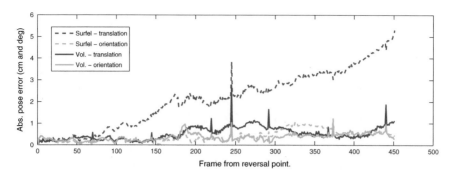

Fig. 5.10 Difference in pose between corresponding frames in time-mirrored image *Office* sequence as reconstructed using the volumetric and surfel-based approaches. Note the relatively large error for the surfel-based approach. Figure from [37]

(a) Volumetric fusion

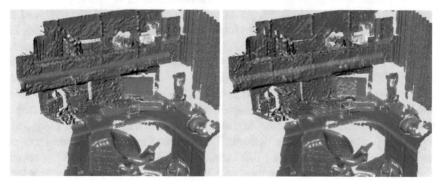

(b) Surfel fusion

Fig. 5.11 First (left) and last (right) frames in the time-mirrored *Office* sequence using **a** volumetric and **b** surfel-based reconstruction. The input depth map is shown projected into the reconstructed model. For the surfel-based reconstruction, note the significant pose offset from identity in the right-hand frame and misalignment of depth and model in the left-hand frame. Figure from [37]

72 MB for the comparably detailed 1.5 M surfel array (assuming 4 byte data types
are used throughout).

Note that the density of the surfels is directly set according to the local input
sample density, and it is not necessary to define a limited spacial extent for the
reconstruction up front as with a voxel grid.

One of the most prominent reconstruction artefacts manifested by the volumetric
method is 'lipping' at sharp corners (which results from the projective approximation to the true signed distance function [32]). This is particularly noticeable at the
edges of the cube in Fig. 5.8. The surfel-based approach does not suffer from this
type of artefact, thus given clean data and the simulated condition of ground truth
camera pose trajectories and clean depth, it produces cleaner geometry. However
under real-world conditions, i.e. using noisy Kinect depth and ICP for camera pose
estimation, registration and reconstruction were found to be more robust using the
volumetric fusion representation. This may be due to specific implementation details
(e.g. rounding behaviour), or perhaps qualitative differences in depth maps from
ray-casting versus hexagonal splat rendering.

5.4 Dynamic Scene Reconstruction

In the case of static scene reconstruction, surface registration is equivalent to finding the 6-DoF camera pose for each frame and a simple fixed TSDF voxel grid is
sufficient for measurement fusion (see Sect. 5.3). The core aspects of both static and
dynamic scene reconstruction are surface registration and surface fusion. Both these
aspects are, however, more challenging in the case of dynamic scenes, which may
contain multiple rigid, articulated, and non-rigidly deforming surfaces that need to
be tracked and consistently integrated into a surface model. This section provides a
brief summary of recent techniques for registration and fusion for dynamic scenes.

Multiple-view video has traditionally been used to capture full coverage of
dynamic 3D scenes for reconstruction (e.g. [6, 19, 64]). While high quality models can be obtained from them, adoption of multiview video reconstruction systems
has been limited by the cost and complexity of operation of multi-camera setups.
On the other hand, non-rigid structure from motion (NRSfM) approaches (e.g. [31,
35, 51, 56]) attempt to recover dynamic 3D shape and motion from a sequence of
images from a single, monocular RGB camera, making them usable with standard
video cameras and existing video footage. NRSfM is, however, a highly challenging,
under-constrained problem, since absolute depth is not known beforehand. Although
depth maps from commodity sensors tend to be noisy and incomplete, with a lower
resolution than current video cameras, their depth estimates are more robust than
those estimated from RGB images alone, particularly in low-textured or repetitively
textured regions. The availability of a reliable estimate of per-pixel depth for each
frame simplifies the reconstruction problem, however surface registration and temporally consistent fusion of dynamic scenes remains a challenging problem.

Depth maps are natively output by typical commodity RGB-D sensors (e.g. Microsoft Kinect v1/v2) and cover only the surface seen from a specific camera view. Certain low-level processing tasks can be performed using the depth maps directly, such as bilateral filtering [67], motion-compensated RGB-guided upsampling [52], depth-guided matting [70], and depth-aware video compositing. Tasks such as general dynamic scene editing can, however benefit from more complete 3D geometry preferably with '4D' temporal consistency, i.e. 3D surfaces which have known correspondences over time, which allows edits to appearance, shape and motion to be automatically propagated over a sequence (see [4, 5, 27]). In applications where a template scan of a non-rigid object of interest is able to be obtained beforehand (e.g. using a static reconstruction approach without the object deforming), this template model may be dynamically deformed to match RGB-D input of the object in a scene by using volumetric representations, either offline (e.g. [20]) or in real-time (e.g. [79]).

A core challenge in temporally consistent modelling is obtaining correspondences of surface points over time. Analogous to 2D *optical flow* between two RGB images (e.g. [65]), RGB-D *scene flow* estimates a per-pixel 3D translation (e.g. [14, 30, 71]) or translation and rotation (e.g. [26, 72]) between two RGB-D images. Frame-to-frame flow vectors can be propagated over time to form long-term feature tracks [65], which may use as an input to RGB-D-based dynamic scene modelling [38].

Surface meshes explicitly store oriented surfaces and are widely used in the manipulation of models in 3D graphics applications and media production. However, as is the case with static scene reconstruction approaches, intermediate representations such as volumetric and point-based, are often used to facilitate surface fusion. Fusion of non-rigid geometry using signed distance functions may be achieved, for instance, using a piecewise-rigid segmentation [41] or a warping field defined over a single reference volume [21, 43].

In DynamicFusion [43], Newcombe et al. perform real-time online tracking and reconstruction of dynamic objects from depth sensors without a template. Their approach is to warp each input frame back to a canonical frame using a per-frame volumetric warping field, and then perform TSDF fusion in this frame. For efficiency, only sparse warping field samples are estimated, and dense values are inferred by interpolation. The TSDF fusion weights take into account the confidence in the warping field, which decreases with distance from the warping field samples. The warping field is estimated by optimizing an energy consisting of an ICP data term and a regularization term that encourages smooth variation of the warping function (where the transformation nodes are connected with edges in a hierarchical deformation graph).

Similar to DynamicFusion, Innmann et al. [28] propose VolumeDeform, which incorporates sparse image features from the RGB images as well as dense depth constraints, which help in correct registration of scenes with low geometric variation.

In their Fusion4D approach, Dou et al. [12] perform online reconstruction from multiple depth sensors for improved scene coverage. Slavcheva et al. [62] propose KillingFusion, which performs real-time, non-rigid reconstruction using TSDF fusion without computing explicit point correspondences, instead directly optimizing a warping field between TSDFs. Because point correspondences are not computed, however, it does not support applications which require texture mapping (e.g. appearance editing).

In [40], a method for reconstruction of dynamic scenes from single-view RGB-D data based on a sparse set of temporally coherent surfels (tracked 3D points) which are explicitly connected using neighbourhood-based connectivity is proposed: simultaneous segmentation, shape and motion estimation of arbitrary scenes is performed without prior knowledge of the shape or non-rigid deformation of the scene. This surfel graph modelling is, however, limited in terms of the shape detail reproduced, and does not natively output a surface mesh. As a result, a subsequent dense surface reconstruction stage is required in order to obtain a detailed surface mesh. In their 'animation cartography' approach, Tevs et al. [66] employ surface 'charts' with shared, tracked landmarks in multiple graph structures. Probabilistic sparse matching is performed on the landmarks, and dense correspondence is then established for the remaining chart points by comparing landmark coordinates. They note that their system does not perform well on very noisy time-of-flight depth data and suggest using additional cues (e.g. colour) for such data.

A hybrid method for fusion and representation of dynamic scenes from RGB-D video has been proposed [38] which uses the complementary strengths of multiple representations at different stages of processing. *Depth maps* provide input 2.5D geometry and are used along with the corresponding RGB images to generate a graph of *sparse point tracks* for dense *volumetric* surface integration, while *residual depth maps* store differences between the final output 4D model and raw input. The intermediate *surfel graph* structure stores sparse, dynamic 3D geometry with neighbourhood-based connectivity, and is used for efficient segmentation and initial reconstruction of part shape and motion. The surfel graph representation drives a further intermediate TSDF *volumetric implicit surface* representation, which is used to integrate noisy input depth measurements into dense piecewise and global 3D geometry. The volumetric representation is finally extracted to an explicit, dense surface *mesh* suitable for dynamic scene rendering, as well as editing of shape, appearance and motion.

5.5 Conclusion

In this chapter, an overview of techniques for reconstruction from RGB-D input was presented and further detail provided on two approaches to real-time static scene reconstruction, namely KinectFusion [44] and surfel fusion [33]. Such volumetric and surfel-based reconstruction approaches are able to register and integrate hundreds or thousands of noisy depth maps in an online manner and produce metrically consistent models of static scenes with greater coverage and less noise than the individual input depth maps.

The frame-to-model ICP tracking approach proposed by Newcombe et al. [44] mitigates accumulation of error, which would be more severe with frame-to-frame tracking and thus helps maintain the level of detail in the reconstructed models. Assuming adequately small voxels (of the order of the depth pixel size), the main limiting factor in reconstruction resolution is the image (domain) resolution rather than the noise and quantization of depth values (range), which can be integrated away over time as frames are added. (The case is similar for the surfel-based representation, where the model resolution corresponds directly to the input sample density, rather than depending on a separately specified voxel size.) Higher quality, larger scale reconstructions can be achieved using offline reconstruction approaches such as that of Zhou et al. [76], which employs global optimization of the sensor pose and scene geometry.

Static scene reconstruction from RGB-D input is a well-developed field and current approaches are able to produce high quality results in real-time. Temporally consistent reconstruction of general dynamic scenes from RGB-D is a challenging open problem, however the field is fast moving and recent approaches such as DynamicFusion [43] and KillingFusion [62] have made significant progress towards reconstruction of dynamic, non-rigidly deforming objects through use of deforming volumetric representations for surface integration and tracking.

References

1. Bernardini F, Mittleman J (1999) The ball-pivoting algorithm for surface reconstruction. Trans Vis Comput Graph (TVCG)
2. Besl P, McKay N (1992) A method for registration of 3-D shapes. Trans Pattern Anal Mach Intell (PAMI) 14(2):239–256. https://doi.org/10.1109/34.121791
3. Blais G, Levine M (1995) Registering multiview range data to create 3D computer objects. Trans Pattern Anal Mach Intell (PAMI) 17(8):820–824. https://doi.org/10.1109/34.400574
4. Budd C, Huang P, Hilton A (2011) Hierarchical shape matching for temporally consistent 3D video. In: 3D imaging, modeling, processing, visualization and transmission (3DIMPVT), pp 172–179. https://doi.org/10.1109/3DIMPVT.2011.29
5. Budd C, Huang P, Klaudiny M, Hilton A (2013) Global non-rigid alignment of surface sequences. Int J Comput Vis (IJCV) 102(1–3):256–270. https://doi.org/10.1007/s11263-012-0553-4
6. Cagniart C, Boyer E, Ilic S (2010) Free-form mesh tracking: a patch-based approach. In: Computer vision and pattern recognition (CVPR), pp 1339–1346
7. Chang W, Zwicker M (2011) Global registration of dynamic range scans for articulated model reconstruction. ACM Trans Graph (TOG) 30
8. Chen J, Bautembach D, Izadi S (2013) Scalable real-time volumetric surface reconstruction. ACM Trans Graph (TOG)
9. Chen Y, Medioni G (1991) Object modeling by registration of multiple range images. In: International conference on robotics and automation, vol 3, pp 2724–2729. https://doi.org/10.1109/ROBOT.1991.132043
10. Curless B, Levoy M (1996) A volumetric method for building complex models from range images. In: Conference on computer graphics and interactive techniques, pp 303–312
11. Davison AJ (2003) Real-time simultaneous localisation and mapping with a single camera. In: International conference on computer vision (ICCV), vol 2, pp 1403–1410. https://doi.org/10.1109/ICCV.2003.1238654
12. Dou M, Khamis S, Degtyarev Y, Davidson P, Fanello SR, Kowdle A, Escolano SO, Rhemann C, Kim D, Taylor J, Kohli P, Tankovich V, Izadi S (2016) Fusion4d: real-time performance

capture of challenging scenes. ACM Trans Graph (TOG). https://doi.org/10.1145/2897824. 2925969

13. Fechteler P, Eisert P (2011) Recovering articulated pose of 3D point clouds. In: European conference on visual media production (CVMP), p 2011
14. Ferstl D, Riegler G, Rüether M, Bischof H (2014) CP-census: a novel model for dense variational scene flow from RGB-D data. In: British machine vision conference (BMVC), pp 18.1–18.11. https://doi.org/10.5244/C.28.18
15. Fitzgibbon A (2003) Robust registration of 2D and 3D point sets. Image Vis. Comput. 21(13–14):1145–1153. https://doi.org/10.1016/j.imavis.2003.09.004
16. Fuhrmann S, Goesele M (2014) Floating scale surface reconstruction. In: ASM SIGGRAPH
17. Garland M, Heckbert P (1998) Simplifying surfaces with color and texture using quadric error metrics. In: Conference on visualization. https://doi.org/10.1109/VISUAL.1998.745312
18. Godard C, Mac Aodha O, Brostow GJ (2017) Unsupervised monocular depth estimation with left-right consistency. In: CVPR
19. Guillemaut JY, Hilton A (2010) Joint multi-layer segmentation and reconstruction for free-viewpoint video applications. Int J Comput Vis (IJCV) 93(1):73–100. https://doi.org/10.1007/s11263-010-0413-z
20. Guo K, Xu F, Wang Y, Liu Y, Dai Q (2015) Robust non-rigid motion tracking and surface reconstruction using L0 regularization. In: International conference on computer vision (ICCV), vol 1. IEEE, pp 3083–3091. https://doi.org/10.1109/ICCV.2015.353
21. Guo K, Xu F, Yu T, Liu X, Dai Q, Liu Y (2017) Real-time geometry, albedo and motion reconstruction using a single RGBD camera. ACM Trans Graph (TOG)
22. Hernandez M, Choi J, Medioni G (2015) Near laser-scan quality 3-D face reconstruction from a low-quality depth stream. Image Vis Comput 36:61–69. https://doi.org/10.1016/j.imavis.2014.12.004
23. Hilton A, Stoddart A, Illingworth J, Windeatt T (1998) Implicit surface-based geometric fusion. Comput Vis Image Underst 69(3):273–291. https://doi.org/10.1006/cviu.1998.0664
24. Hilton A, Stoddart AJ, Illingworth J, Windeatt T (1996) Marching triangles: range image fusion for complex object modelling. In: International conference on image processing, vol 2, pp 381–384. https://doi.org/10.1109/ICIP.1996.560840
25. Hoppe H, DeRose T, Duchamp T, McDonald JA, Stuetzle W (1992) Surface reconstruction from unorganized points. In: ACM SIGGRAPH, pp 71–78
26. Hornáček M, Fitzgibbon A, Rother C (2014) SphereFlow: 6 DoF scene flow from RGB-D pairs. In: Computer Vision and Pattern Recognition (CVPR), pp 3526–3533 (2014). https://doi.org/10.1109/CVPR.2014.451
27. Huang P, Budd C, Hilton A (2011) Global temporal registration of multiple non-rigid surface sequences. In: Computer vision and pattern recognition (CVPR), pp 3473–3480. https://doi.org/10.1109/CVPR.2011.5995438
28. Innmann M, Zollhöfer M, Nießner M, Theobalt C, Stamminger M (2016) VolumeDeform: real-time volumetric non-rigid reconstruction. In: European conference on computer vision (ECCV), pp 362–379
29. Izadi S, Kim D, Hilliges O, Molyneaux D, Newcombe R, Kohli P, Shotton J, Hodges S, Freeman D, Davison A (2011) Others: KinectFusion: real-time 3D reconstruction and interaction using a moving depth camera. In: ACM symposium on user interface software and technology (UIST), pp. 559–568
30. Jaimez M, Souiai M, Gonzalez-Jimenez J, Cremers D (2015) A primal-dual framework for real-time dense RGB-D scene flow. In: International conference on robotics and automation (ICRA), vol 2015-June, pp 98–104. https://doi.org/10.1109/ICRA.2015.7138986
31. Ji P, Li H, Dai Y, Reid I (2017) 'Maximizing Rigidity' revisited: a convex programming approach for generic 3D shape reconstruction from multiple perspective views. In: International lion (ICCV), pp 929–937. https://doi.org/10.1109/ICCV.2017.106
32. Kazhdan M, Bolitho M, Hoppe H (2006) Poisson surface reconstruction. In: Proceedings of the fourth Eurographics symposium on Geometry processing, pp 61–70

33. Keller M, Lefloch D, Lambers M, Izadi S, Weyrich T, Kolb A (2013) Real-time 3D reconstruction in dynamic scenes using point-based fusion. In: International conference on 3D vision (3DV)
34. Khoshelham K, Elberink SO (2012) Accuracy and resolution of kinect depth data for indoor mapping applications. Sensors 12(2):1437–1454. https://doi.org/10.3390/s120201437
35. Kumar S, Dai Y, Li H (2017) Monocular dense 3D reconstruction of a complex dynamic scene from two perspective frames. In: International conference on computer vision (ICCV), pp 4659–4667. https://doi.org/10.1109/ICCV.2017.498
36. Lorensen W, Cline H (1987) Marching cubes: a high resolution 3D surface construction algorithm. In: ACM SIGGRAPH, vol 21. ACM, pp 163–169
37. Malleson C (2015) Dynamic scene modelling and representation from video and depth. PhD thesis, CVSSP, University of Surrey, Guildford, GU2 7XH, UK (2015)
38. Malleson C, Guillemaut J, Hilton A (2018) Hybrid modelling of non-rigid scenes from RGBD cameras. IEEE Trans Circuits Syst Video Technol 1–1. https://doi.org/10.1109/TCSVT.2018.2863027
39. Malleson C, Hilton A, Guillemaut JY (2012) Evaluation of kinect fusion for set modelling. In: European conference on visual media production (CVMP) (2012)
40. Malleson C, Klaudiny M, Guillemaut JY, Hilton A (2014) Structured representation of non-rigid surfaces from single view 3D point tracks. In: International conference on 3D vision (3DV), pp 625–632
41. Malleson C, Klaudiny M, Hilton A, Guillemaut JY (2013) Single-view RGBD-based reconstruction of dynamic human geometry. In: International conference on computer vision (ICCV) workshops, pp 307–314
42. Newcombe R, Davison A (2010) Live dense reconstruction with a single moving camera. In: Computer vision and pattern recognition (CVPR), pp 1498–1505. https://doi.org/10.1109/CVPR.2010.5539794
43. Newcombe R, Fox D, Seitz S (2015) DynamicFusion: reconstruction and tracking of non-rigid scenes in real-time. In: Computer vision and pattern recognition (CVPR)
44. Newcombe R, Izadi S, Hilliges O, Molyneaux D, Kim D, Davison A, Kohli P, Shotton J, Hodges S, Fitzgibbon A (2011) KinectFusion: real-time dense surface mapping and tracking. In: International symposium on mixed and augmented reality (ISMAR). IEEE, pp 127–136
45. Newcombe R, Lovegrove S, Davison A (2011) DTAM: Dense tracking and mapping in real-time. In: International conference on computer vision (ICCV), pp 2320–2327 (2011)
46. Nießner M, Zollhöfer M, Izadi S, Stamminger M (2013) Real-time 3D reconstruction at scale using voxel hashing. ACM Trans Graph **32**(6), 169:1—169:11 (2013). https://doi.org/10.1145/2508363.2508374
47. NVidia: CUDA. http://www.nvidia.com/cuda (2012). Accessed Feb 2012
48. Ohtake Y, Belyaev A, Seidel HP (2003) A multi-scale approach to 3D scattered data interpolation with compactly supported basis functions. In: Shape modeling international, SMI '03, pp 153–161
49. Parker S, Shirley P, Livnat Y, Hansen C, Sloan PP (1998) Interactive ray tracing for isosurface rendering. In: Conference on visualization, pp 233–238. https://doi.org/10.1109/VISUAL.1998.745713
50. Pellegrini S, Schindler K, Nardi D (2008) A generalisation of the ICP algorithm for articulated bodies. In: British machine vision conference (BMVC), Lm
51. Ranftl R, Vineet V, Chen Q, Koltun V (2016) Dense monocular depth estimation in complex dynamic scenes. In: Conference on computer vision and pattern recognition (CVPR), pp 4058–4066. https://doi.org/10.1109/CVPR.2016.440
52. Richardt C, Stoll C (2012) Coherent spatiotemporal filtering, upsampling and rendering of RGBZ videos. Comput Grap Forum 31(2)
53. Roth H, Marsette V (2012) Moving volume kinectfusion. In: British Machine Vision Conference (BMVC), pp 112.1—112.11. https://doi.org/10.5244/C.26.112
54. Rusinkiewicz S, Hall-Holt O, Levoy M (2002) Real-time 3D model acquisition. ACM Trans Graph (TOG) **21**(3) (2002). https://doi.org/10.1145/566654.566600

55. Rusinkiewicz S, Levoy M (2001) Efficient variants of the ICP algorithm. In: 3-D digital imaging and modeling, pp 145–152. IEEE (2001)
56. Russell C, Yu R, Agapito L (2014) Video pop-up: monocular 3D reconstruction of dynamic scenes. In: European conference on computer vision (ECCV), pp 583–598 (2014)
57. Rutishauser M, Stricker M, Trobina M (1994) Merging range images of arbitrarily shaped objects. In: Computer vision and pattern recognition (CVPR), pp 573–580 (1994). https://doi.org/10.1109/CVPR.1994.323797
58. Salas-Moreno R, Glocker B, Kelly P, Davison A (2014) Dense planar SLAM. In: International symposium on mixed and augmented reality (ISMAR)
59. Salas-Moreno RF, Newcombe RA, Strasdat H, Kelly PHJ, Davison AJ (2013) SLAM++: simultaneous localisation and mapping at the level of objects. In: Computer Vision and Pattern Recognition (CVPR), pp 1352–1359 (2013). https://doi.org/10.1109/CVPR.2013.178
60. Salvi J, Matabosch C, Fofi D, Forest J (2007) A review of recent range image registration methods with accuracy evaluation. Image Vis Comput 25(5):578–596. https://doi.org/10.1016/j.imavis.2006.05.012
61. Segal A, Haehnel D, Thrun S (2009) Generalized-ICP. In: Robotics, science and systems (2009)
62. Slavcheva M, Baust M, Cremers D, Ilic S (2017) KillingFusion: non-rigid 3D reconstruction without correspondences. In: Conference on computer vision and pattern recognition (CVPR), pp 5474–5483. https://doi.org/10.1109/CVPR.2017.581
63. Soucy M, Laurendeau D (1995) A general surface approach to the integration of a set of range views. Trans Pattern Anal Mach Intell (PAMI) 17(4):344–358. https://doi.org/10.1109/34.385982
64. Starck J, Hilton A (2007) Surface capture for performance-based animation. Comput Graph Appl 27(3):21–31
65. Sundaram N, Brox T, Keutzer K (2010) Dense point trajectories by GPU-accelerated large displacement optical flow. In: European conference on computer vision (ECCV)
66. Tevs A, Berner A, Wand M, Ihrke I, Bokeloh M, Kerber J, Seidel HP (2011) Animation cartography—intrinsic reconstruction of shape and motion. ACM Trans Graph (TOG) (2011)
67. Tomasi C, Manduchi R (1998) Bilateral filtering for gray and color images. In: International conference on computer vision (ICCV), pp 839–846
68. Turk G, Levoy M (1994) Zippered polygon meshes from range images. In: ACM SIGGRAPH, pp 311–318. https://doi.org/10.1145/192161.192241
69. Volino M, Hilton A (2013) Layered view-dependent texture maps. In: European conference on visual media production (CVMP)
70. Wang O, Finger J, Qingxiong Y, Davis J, Ruigang Y (2007) Automatic natural video matting with depth. In: Pacific Conference on Computer Graphics and Applications, pp 469–472 (2007). https://doi.org/10.1109/PG.2007.11
71. Wang P, Li W, Gao Z, Zhang Y, Tang C, Ogunbona P (2017) Scene flow to action map: a new representation for RGB-D based action recognition with convolutional neural networks. arXiv. https://doi.org/10.1109/CVPR.2017.52
72. Wang Y, Zhang J, Liu Z, Wu Q, Chou P, Zhang Z, Jia Y (2015) Completed dense scene flow in RGB-D space. In: Asian conference on computer vision (ACCV) workshops, vol 9009, pp 191–205 (2015). https://doi.org/10.1007/978-3-319-16631-5
73. Weik S (1997) Registration of 3-D partial surface models using luminance and depth information. In: International conference on recent advances in 3-D digital imaging and modeling. https://doi.org/10.1109/IM.1997.603853
74. Whelan T, Kaess M, Fallon M (2012) Kintinuous: spatially extended kinectfusion. RSS workshop on RGB-D: advanced reasoning with depth cameras
75. Zhang Z (1999) Flexible camera calibration by viewing a plane from unknown orientations. In: International conference on computer vision (ICCV), vol 00, pp 0–7
76. Zhou Q, Koltun V (2013) Dense scene reconstruction with points of interest. ACM Trans. Graph. (TOG) (2013)
77. Zhou Q, Miller S, Koltun V (2013) Elastic fragments for dense scene reconstruction. In: International conference on computer vision (ICCV), Figure 2 (2013). https://doi.org/10.1109/ICCV.2013.65

78. Zollhöfer M, Dai A, Innmann M, Wu C, Stamminger M, Theobalt C, Nießner M (2015) Shading-based refinement on volumetric signed distance functions. ACM Trans Graph (TOG) (2015)
79. Zollhöfer M, Nießner M, Izadi S, Rhemann C (2014) Real-time non-rigid reconstruction using an RGB-D camera. In: ACM SIGGRAPH (2014)

Chapter 6
RGB-D Odometry and SLAM

Javier Civera and Seong Hun Lee

Abstract The emergence of modern RGB-D sensors had a significant impact in many application fields, including robotics, augmented reality (AR), and 3D scanning. They are low-cost, low-power, and low-size alternatives to traditional range sensors such as LiDAR. Moreover, unlike RGB cameras, RGB-D sensors provide the additional depth information that removes the need of frame-by-frame triangulation for 3D scene reconstruction. These merits have made them very popular in mobile robotics and AR, where it is of great interest to estimate ego-motion and 3D scene structure. Such spatial understanding can enable robots to navigate autonomously without collisions and allow users to insert virtual entities consistent with the image stream. In this chapter, we review common formulations of odometry and Simultaneous Localization and Mapping (known by its acronym SLAM) using RGB-D stream input. The two topics are closely related, as the former aims to track the incremental camera motion with respect to a local map of the scene, and the latter to jointly estimate the camera trajectory and the global map with consistency. In both cases, the standard approaches minimize a cost function using nonlinear optimization techniques. This chapter consists of three main parts: In the first part, we introduce the basic concept of odometry and SLAM and motivate the use of RGB-D sensors. We also give mathematical preliminaries relevant to most odometry and SLAM algorithms. In the second part, we detail the three main components of SLAM systems: camera pose tracking, scene mapping, and loop closing. For each component, we describe different approaches proposed in the literature. In the final part, we provide a brief discussion on advanced research topics with the references to the state of the art.

J. Civera (✉) · S. H. Lee
I3A, Universidad de Zaragoza, Zaragoza, Spain
e-mail: jcivera@unizar.es

S. H. Lee
e-mail: seonghunlee@unizar.es

© Springer Nature Switzerland AG 2019
P. L. Rosin et al. (eds.), *RGB-D Image Analysis and Processing*,
Advances in Computer Vision and Pattern Recognition,
https://doi.org/10.1007/978-3-030-28603-3_6

6.1 Introduction: SLAM, Visual SLAM, and RGB-D Sensors

Visual Odometry and Visual Simultaneous Localization and Mapping—from here on referred to as their respective acronyms VO and VSLAM—are two tightly related topics that aim to extract 3D information from streams of visual data in real-time. Specifically, the goal of VO is to estimate the incremental motion (i.e., translation and rotation) of the camera as it moves. The goal of Visual SLAM is more ambitious: To estimate a globally consistent map of the scene and the camera trajectory with respect to it.

In the robotics research community, SLAM is considered as a fundamental capability for autonomous robots. See [4, 25] for an illustrative tutorial covering the earliest approaches, and [11] for a recent survey outlining the state of the art and the most relevant future directions. While the early pioneering works on SLAM mainly used laser scanners (e.g., [12]), the field rapidly pivoted to cameras for several reasons. Among them were the progress of computer vision algorithms and improved processors, as well as the camera's low cost, size, and power consumption.

Most visual SLAM methods have been traditionally based on low-level feature matching and multiple view geometry. This introduces several limitations to monocular SLAM. For example, a large-baseline motion is needed to generate sufficient parallax for reliable depth estimation; and the scale is unobservable. This can be partially alleviated by including additional sensors (e.g., stereo cameras [83], inertial measurement units (IMUs) [18], sonar [48]) or the prior knowledge of the system [66], or the scene [110]. Another challenge is the dense reconstruction of low texture areas [17]. Although recent approaches using deep learning (e.g., [9, 122]) have shown impressive results in this direction, more research is needed regarding their cost and dependence on the training data [29].

RGB-D sensors provide a practical hardware-based alternative to the challenges and limitations mentioned above. Their availability at low cost has facilitated many robotics and AR applications in the last decade. Intense research endeavors have produced numerous robust algorithms and real-time systems. Figure 6.1 shows several reconstruction examples from the state-of-the-art systems. Today, RGB-D cameras stand out as one of the preferred sensors for indoor applications in robotics and AR; and their future looks promising either on their own or in combination with additional sensors.

In this chapter, we will cover several state-of-the-art RGB-D odometry and SLAM algorithms. Our goal is to focus on the basic aspects of geometry and optimization, highlighting relevant aspects of the most used formulations and pointing to the most promising research directions. The reader should be aware that, as a consequence of condensing a vast array of works and presenting the basics in a homogeneous and easy-to-follow manner, some individual works might present slight variations from the formulation presented here. In general, we sacrificed extending ourselves over particular details in favor of a clearer overview of the field.

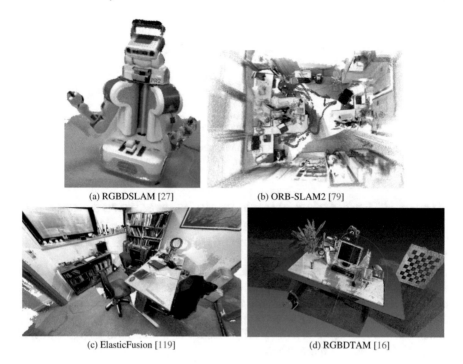

(a) RGBDSLAM [27]   (b) ORB-SLAM2 [79]

(c) ElasticFusion [119]   (d) RGBDTAM [16]

Fig. 6.1 State-of-the-art RGB-D SLAM systems

The rest of the chapter is organized as follows. Section 6.2 will give an overview on the most usual VO and VSLAM pipeline. Section 6.3 will introduce the notation used throughout the rest of the chapter. Section 6.4 will cover the algorithms for tracking the camera pose, Sect. 6.5 the algorithms for the estimation of the scene structure, and Sect. 6.6 the loop closure algorithms. Section 6.7 will refer to relevant scientific works and research lines that were not covered in the previous sections. Finally, Sect. 6.8 contains the conclusions and Sect. 6.9 provides links to some of the most relevant online resources, mainly the state-of-the-art open-source software and public benchmark datasets.

6.2 The Visual Odometry and SLAM Pipelines

The pipelines of RGB-D Odometry and SLAM have many components in common. Here, we will give a holistic view of the building blocks of standard implementations, highlighting their connections and introducing the terminology.

The seminal work of Klein and Murray [58] proposed the architecture that is used in most visual odometry and SLAM systems nowadays. Such architecture was later refined in papers like [28, 78, 105] among others. Basically, the idea is to partition

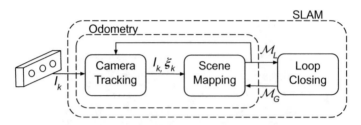

Fig. 6.2 High-level overview of VO and VSLAM systems. I_k: kth RGB-D image, ξ_k: kth camera pose, $\mathcal{M}_L$ and $\mathcal{M}_G$: the local and the global map

the processing into two (or more) parallel threads: one thread tracks the camera pose in real time at video rate, and the rest update several levels of scene representations at lower frequencies (in general, the larger and/or more complex the map, the lower the frequency of update).

Figure 6.2 illustrates a simple Tracking and Mapping architecture for RGB-D Odometry and SLAM that we will use in this chapter. The camera tracking thread estimates the camera motion ξ_k at time k given the current frame I_k and a local map $\mathcal{M}_L$. $\mathcal{M}_L$ is estimated from a set of keyframes summarizing the sequence. If SLAM is the aim, a globally consistent map $\mathcal{M}_G$ is estimated by means of loop closure and global optimization. In more detail:

- **Camera Tracking**: The camera tracking thread estimates the incremental camera motion. The most simple approach is to use the frame-to-frame constraints (e.g., [36, 54]). This is in fact inevitable when bootstrapping the system from the first two views. However, after initialization, it is quite usual to use more than two views in order to achieve higher accuracy. In this case, the standard approach is to estimate the camera motion using map-to-frame constraints with respect to a local map built from the past keyframes (see the next paragraph).
- **Scene Mapping**: Mapping approaches vary, depending on the application. Volumetric mapping discretizes the scene volume into voxels and integrates the information from the RGB-D views (e.g., [81, 117]). Point-based mapping performs a nonlinear optimization of camera poses and points (e.g., [79]). In the case of VO, the map is local and is estimated from a sliding window containing a selection of the last frames (e.g., [28, 115]). In the case of VSLAM, the map is estimated from a set of keyframes representative of the visited places.
- **Loop Closing**: In both odometry and SLAM drift is accumulated in purely exploratory trajectories. Such drift can be corrected if a place is revisited, using approaches denoted as loop closure. First, the place is recognized by its visual appearance (loop detection), and then the error of the global map is corrected (loop correction) [34, 79, 117].

6.3 Notation and Preliminaries

6.3.1 Geometry and Sensor Model

We denote an RGB-D input as $I : \Omega \mapsto \mathbb{R}^4$, where $\Omega \subset \mathbb{R}^2$ is the image plane of width w and height h. We represent the pixel coordinates as a 2D vector $\mathbf{p} = (u, v)^{\top}$ and the corresponding homogeneous coordinates as $\tilde{\mathbf{p}} = (\tilde{u}, \tilde{v}, \lambda)^{\top}$. Each pixel has RGB color and depth value, i.e., $I(u, v) = (r, g, b, d)^{\top}$. The depth channel is denoted as $D : \Omega \mapsto \mathbb{R}$, and the access to it as $D(u, v) = d$. The Euclidean coordinates of a 3D point k in some reference frame i (be it a camera or the world reference) are denoted by $\mathbf{P}_k^i = \left(X_k^i, Y_k^i, Z_k^i \right)^{\top}$ or $\tilde{\mathbf{P}}_k^i = \left(\lambda X_k^i, \lambda Y_k^i, \lambda Z_k^i, \lambda \right)^{\top}$ in homogeneous coordinates. These two coordinates are related by the dehomogenization operation: $\mathbf{P}_k^i = \pi_{3D}(\tilde{\mathbf{P}}_k^i)$. Inversely, the homogenization is denoted by $\pi_{3D}^{-1}(\mathbf{P}_k^i) := \left(X_k^i, Y_k^i, Z_k^i, 1 \right)^{\top}$.

The pose of camera j with respect to reference frame i is defined by the transformation $T_{ji} = \begin{bmatrix} R_{ji} & \mathbf{t}_{ji} \\ 0 & 1 \end{bmatrix} \in SE(3), R_{ji} \in SO(3), \mathbf{t}_{ji} \in \mathbb{R}^3$. The rotation matrix R_{ji} and translation vector $\mathbf{t}_{ji}$ are defined such that the transformation of point $\mathbf{P}_k^i$ in reference frame i to the jth camera reference frame is

$$\tilde{\mathbf{P}}_k^j = T_{ji} \tilde{\mathbf{P}}_k^i; \quad \mathbf{P}_k^j = R_{ji} \mathbf{P}_k^i + \mathbf{t}_{ji}. \tag{6.1}$$

Likewise, $\tilde{\mathbf{P}}_k^i$ can be obtained from $\tilde{\mathbf{P}}_k^j$ and T_{ji} with the inverse operation:

$$\tilde{\mathbf{P}}_k^i = T_{ji}^{-1} \tilde{\mathbf{P}}_k^j; \quad \mathbf{P}_k^i = R_{ji}^{\top} \left(\mathbf{P}_k^j - \mathbf{t}_{ji} \right). \tag{6.2}$$

As illustrated in Fig. 6.3, we adopt the standard pinhole model for the projection onto the image plane. First, the 3D point $\mathbf{P}_k^i$ is transformed to the camera frame j using Eq. 6.1. The homogeneous coordinates of the projection in the image space are given by

Fig. 6.3 The transformation of point k from reference frame i to camera reference frame j, and its projection onto the image plane using the pinhole camera model

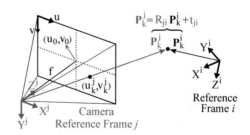

$$\tilde{\mathbf{p}}_k^j = (\tilde{u}_k^j, \tilde{v}_k^j, \lambda)^\top = \mathrm{K}\mathbf{P}_k^j = \mathrm{K}(\mathrm{R}_{ji}\mathbf{P}_k^i + \mathbf{t}_{ji}) \quad \text{with} \quad \mathrm{K} = \begin{bmatrix} f_x & 0 & u_0 \\ 0 & f_y & v_0 \\ 0 & 0 & 1 \end{bmatrix}, \quad (6.3)$$

where K is the calibration matrix containing the coordinates of the principal point $(u_0, v_0)^\top$ and the focal lengths $(f_x, f_y) = (fm_x, fm_y)$. Here, (m_x, m_y) denotes the number of pixels per unit distance in image coordinates in the x and y directions. The pixel coordinates are finally obtained by dehomogenization: $\mathbf{p}_k^j = (u_k^j, v_k^j)^\top = \pi_{2D}(\tilde{\mathbf{p}}_k^j) = (\tilde{u}_k^j/\lambda, \tilde{v}_k^j/\lambda)^\top$. The inverse operation (i.e., homogenization) is denoted by $\pi_{2D}^{-1}(\mathbf{p}_k^j) := (u_k^j, v_k^j, 1)^\top$.

Now, let reference frame i be another camera reference frame. Then, the *reprojection* of 2D point $\mathbf{p}_k^i$ in frame i to frame j is defined as the following three-step operation:

1. Backproject $\mathbf{p}_k^i$ with the measured depth d_k^i to estimate the 3D point $\mathbf{P}_k^i$ in frame i:

$$\mathbf{P}_k^{i\,\prime} = d_k^i \frac{\mathrm{K}^{-1}\pi_{2D}^{-1}(\mathbf{p}_k^i)}{\|\mathrm{K}^{-1}\pi_{2D}^{-1}(\mathbf{p}_k^i)\|}. \qquad (6.4)$$

2. Transform this estimate from frame i to frame j:

$$\mathbf{P}_k^{ji} = \pi_{3D}\left(\mathrm{T}_{ji}\pi_{3D}^{-1}\left(\mathbf{P}_k^{i\,\prime}\right)\right); \quad \mathbf{P}_k^{ji} = \mathrm{R}_{ji}\mathbf{P}_k^{i\,\prime} + \mathbf{t}_{ji} \qquad (6.5)$$

   (Notice that we use the superscript ji instead of j to distinguish the ground truth in frame j.)

3. Project the resulting 3D point to obtain its pixel coordinates in frame j.

$$\mathbf{p}_k^{ji} = \pi_{2D}\left(\mathrm{K}\mathbf{P}_k^{ji}\right). \qquad (6.6)$$

Altogether, the reprojection of point $\mathbf{p}_k^i$ to frame j is defined as follows:

$$\mathbf{p}_k^{ji}\left(\mathbf{p}_k^i, d_k^i, \mathrm{T}_{ji}\right) = \pi_{2D}\left(\mathrm{K}\left(\frac{d_k^i\mathrm{R}_{ji}\mathrm{K}^{-1}\pi_{2D}^{-1}(\mathbf{p}_k^i)}{\|\mathrm{K}^{-1}\pi_{2D}^{-1}(\mathbf{p}_k^i)\|} + \mathbf{t}_{ji}\right)\right). \qquad (6.7)$$

6.3.2 Nonlinear Optimization

Most state-of-the-art VO and VSLAM methods rely heavily on nonlinear optimization in order to estimate the state vector $\mathbf{x}$ (e.g., containing the camera poses and 3D map points) from a set of noisy measurements $\mathbf{z} = \{\mathbf{z}_1, \mathbf{z}_2, \ldots\}$ (e.g., image correspondences or pixel intensities).

According to Bayes' theorem, the following equation describes the conditional probability of the state $p(\mathbf{x}|\mathbf{z})$ given the measurement model $p(\mathbf{z}|\mathbf{x})$ and the prior over the state $p(\mathbf{x})$:

$$p(\mathbf{x}|\mathbf{z}) = \frac{p(\mathbf{z}|\mathbf{x})p(\mathbf{x})}{p(\mathbf{z})} \tag{6.8}$$

Our aim is then to find the state $\mathbf{x}$ that maximizes this probability. This is called the Maximum a Posteriori (MAP) problem, and the solution corresponds to the mode of the posterior distribution:

$$\mathbf{x}_{MAP} = \arg\max_{\mathbf{x}} p(\mathbf{x}|\mathbf{z}) = \arg\max_{\mathbf{x}} \frac{p(\mathbf{z}|\mathbf{x})p(\mathbf{x})}{p(\mathbf{z})} \tag{6.9}$$

Modern VSLAM and VO methods are based on smoothing and often assume a uniform prior $p(\mathbf{x})$. The normalization constant $p(\mathbf{z})$ does not depend on the state either. Therefore, we can drop $p(\mathbf{x})$ and $p(\mathbf{z})$ from (6.9), turning the problem into the Maximum Likelihood Estimation (MLE). Assuming the independence between the measurements, this means that (6.9) becomes

$$\mathbf{x}_{MAP} = \mathbf{x}_{MLE} = \arg\max_{\mathbf{x}} p(\mathbf{z}|\mathbf{x}) = \arg\max_{\mathbf{x}} \prod_k p(\mathbf{z}_k|\mathbf{x}). \tag{6.10}$$

Suppose that the measurement model is given by $\mathbf{z}_k = \mathbf{h}_k(\mathbf{x}) + \delta_k$, where $\delta_k \sim \mathcal{N}(\mathbf{0}, \Omega_k)$. The conditional distribution of the individual measurements is then $p(\mathbf{z}_k|\mathbf{x}) \sim \mathcal{N}(\mathbf{h}_k(\mathbf{x}), \Omega_k)$. Maximizing, for convenience, the log of the conditionals leads to

$$\mathbf{x}_{MAP} = \arg\max_{\mathbf{x}} \log(\prod_k p(\mathbf{z}_k|\mathbf{x})) = \arg\max_{\mathbf{x}} \sum_k \log(p(\mathbf{z}_k|\mathbf{x}))$$
$$= \arg\max_{\mathbf{x}} \sum_k \log(\exp(-\frac{1}{2}(\mathbf{z}_k - \mathbf{h}_k(\mathbf{x}))^\top \Omega_k^{-1}(\mathbf{z}_k - \mathbf{h}_k(\mathbf{x})))) = \arg\min_{\mathbf{x}} \sum_k ||\mathbf{r}_k(\mathbf{x})||^2_{\Omega_k}, \tag{6.11}$$

where $||\mathbf{r}_k(\mathbf{x})||_{\Omega_k} = \sqrt{(\mathbf{z}_k - \mathbf{h}_k(\mathbf{x}))^\top \Omega_k^{-1}(\mathbf{z}_k - \mathbf{h}_k(\mathbf{x}))}$ is called the *Mahalanobis* distance. As $\mathbf{h}_k(\mathbf{x})$ is typically nonlinear, we solve (6.11) using an iterative method. A standard approach is to use the Gauss–Newton algorithm described as follows:

1. Make an initial guess $\check{\mathbf{x}}$.
2. Linearize (6.11) using the Taylor approximation at $\check{\mathbf{x}}$.
3. Compute the optimal increment $\Delta\mathbf{x}^*$ that minimizes the linearized cost function.
4. Update the state: $\check{\mathbf{x}} \leftarrow \check{\mathbf{x}} + \Delta\mathbf{x}^*$.
5. Iterate the Step 2–4 until convergence.

The Taylor approximation in Step 2 gives

$$\mathbf{h}_k(\check{\mathbf{x}} + \Delta\mathbf{x}) \approx \mathbf{h}_k(\check{\mathbf{x}}) + \mathbf{J}_k \Delta\mathbf{x} \quad \text{with} \quad \mathbf{J}_k = \left.\frac{\partial \mathbf{h}_k(\mathbf{x})}{\partial \mathbf{x}}\right|_{\check{\mathbf{x}}}. \tag{6.12}$$

This allows us to approximate $||\mathbf{r}_k(\check{\mathbf{x}} + \Delta\mathbf{x})||^2_{\Omega_k}$ as

$$||\mathbf{r}_k(\check{\mathbf{x}} + \Delta\mathbf{x})||^2_{\Omega_k} = (\mathbf{z}_k - \mathbf{h}_k(\check{\mathbf{x}} + \Delta\mathbf{x}))^\top \Omega_k^{-1}(\mathbf{z}_k - \mathbf{h}_k(\check{\mathbf{x}} + \Delta\mathbf{x})) \tag{6.13}$$

$$\approx (\mathbf{z}_k - \mathbf{h}_k(\check{\mathbf{x}}) - \mathbf{J}_k\Delta\mathbf{x})^\top \Omega_k^{-1}(\mathbf{z}_k - \mathbf{h}_k(\check{\mathbf{x}}) - \mathbf{J}_k\Delta\mathbf{x}) \tag{6.14}$$

$$= \Delta\mathbf{x}^\top \mathbf{J}_k^\top \Omega_k^{-1}\mathbf{J}_k\Delta\mathbf{x} + (\mathbf{z}_k - \mathbf{h}_k(\check{\mathbf{x}}))^\top \Omega_k^{-1}(\mathbf{z}_k - \mathbf{h}_k(\check{\mathbf{x}}))$$

$$- 2(\mathbf{z}_k - \mathbf{h}_k(\check{\mathbf{x}}))^\top \Omega_k^{-1}\mathbf{J}_k\Delta\mathbf{x}. \tag{6.15}$$

Now, taking the derivative of $\sum_k ||\mathbf{r}_k(\check{\mathbf{x}} + \Delta\mathbf{x})||^2_{\Omega_k}$ with respect to $\Delta\mathbf{x}$ and setting it to zero, we obtain the optimal increment in the following form:

$$\Delta\mathbf{x}^* = -\underbrace{\left[\sum_k \mathbf{J}_k^\top \Omega_k^{-1}\mathbf{J}_k\right]^{-1}}_{\mathbf{H}^{-1}} \underbrace{\sum_k \mathbf{J}_k^\top \Omega_k^{-1}(\mathbf{h}_k(\check{\mathbf{x}}) - \mathbf{z}_k)}_{\mathbf{b}}. \tag{6.16}$$

The Levenberg–Marquardt algorithm, a variant of the Gauss–Newton method, includes a nonnegative damping factor λ in the update step:

$$\Delta\mathbf{x}^* = -(\mathbf{H} + \lambda\,\text{diag}(\mathbf{H}))^{-1}\mathbf{b}, \tag{6.17}$$

where λ is increased when the cost function reduces too slowly, and vice versa. For more details on the adjustment rule, see [74].

Since the least squares problems are very sensitive to outliers, a common practice is to adopt a robust weight function that downweights large errors:

$$\mathbf{x}_{\text{robust}} = \arg\min_{\mathbf{x}} \sum_k \omega\left(||\mathbf{r}_k(\mathbf{x})||_{\Omega_k}\right) ||\mathbf{r}_k(\mathbf{x})||^2_{\Omega_k}. \tag{6.18}$$

To solve this problem iteratively, it is usually assumed that the weights are dependent on the residual at the previous iteration, which turns the problem into a standard weighted least squares at each iteration. This technique is called the iteratively reweighted least squares (IRLS). The readers are referred to [47, 121] for more details on the robust cost functions and [5] for in-depth study of state estimation for robotics.

6.3.3 Lie Algebras

Standard optimization techniques assume that the state belongs to a Euclidean vector space. This does not hold for 3D rotation matrices R, belonging to the special orthogonal group SO(3), or for six degrees-of-freedom (DoF) rigid body motions T, belonging to the special Euclidean group SE(3). In both cases, state updates have to be done in the tangent space of SO(3) and SE(3) at the identity, which are denoted as $\mathfrak{so}(3)$ and $\mathfrak{se}(3)$. Elements of the tangent space $\mathfrak{so}(3)$ and $\mathfrak{se}(3)$ can be represented as vector $\boldsymbol{\omega} \in \mathbb{R}^3$ and $\boldsymbol{\xi} = [\boldsymbol{\omega}, \boldsymbol{v}]^\top \in \mathbb{R}^6$, respectively.

The *hat* operator $(\cdot)^\wedge$ converts $\boldsymbol{\omega} \in \mathbb{R}^3$ to the space of skew symmetric matrices of the Lie algebra and its inverse is denoted by the *vee* operator $(\cdot)^\vee$:

$$\boldsymbol{\omega}^\wedge = \begin{bmatrix} \omega_x \\ \omega_y \\ \omega_z \end{bmatrix}^\wedge = \begin{bmatrix} 0 & -\omega_z & \omega_y \\ \omega_z & 0 & -\omega_x \\ -\omega_y & \omega_x & 0 \end{bmatrix} \in \mathfrak{so}(3) \quad \text{and} \quad \left(\boldsymbol{\omega}^\wedge\right)^\vee = \boldsymbol{\omega} \in \mathbb{R}^3. \quad (6.19)$$

We denote the exponential and logarithmic mapping between $\mathfrak{se}(3)$ and SE(3) by $\exp_{SE(3)}(\boldsymbol{\xi})$ and $\log_{SE3}(T)$, respectively:

$$\exp_{SE(3)}(\boldsymbol{\xi}) := \begin{bmatrix} \exp(\boldsymbol{\omega}^\wedge) & V\boldsymbol{v} \\ 0 & 1 \end{bmatrix} = \begin{bmatrix} R & t \\ 0 & 1 \end{bmatrix} = T \in SE(3), \quad (6.20)$$

where

$$\exp(\boldsymbol{\omega}^\wedge) = I_{3\times3} + \frac{\sin(\|\boldsymbol{\omega}\|)}{\|\boldsymbol{\omega}\|} \boldsymbol{\omega}^\wedge + \frac{1 - \cos(\|\boldsymbol{\omega}\|)}{\|\boldsymbol{\omega}\|^2} \left(\boldsymbol{\omega}^\wedge\right)^2 \quad (6.21)$$

and

$$V = I_{3\times3} + \frac{1 - \cos\|\boldsymbol{\omega}\|}{\|\boldsymbol{\omega}\|^2} \boldsymbol{\omega}^\wedge + \frac{\|\boldsymbol{\omega}\| - \sin(\|\boldsymbol{\omega}\|)}{\|\boldsymbol{\omega}\|^3} \left(\boldsymbol{\omega}^\wedge\right)^2. \quad (6.22)$$

From (6.20), the logarithm map can be obtained:

$$\log_{SE(3)}(T) := \begin{bmatrix} (\log R)^\vee \\ V^{-1}t \end{bmatrix}, \quad (6.23)$$

where

$$\log R = \frac{\theta}{2\sin\theta} \left(R - R^\top\right) \quad \text{with} \quad \theta = \cos^{-1}\left(\frac{\text{trace}(R) - 1}{2}\right). \quad (6.24)$$

For optimization purposes, rigid body transformations can be conveniently represented as $\exp_{SE(3)}(\Delta\boldsymbol{\xi})T$, composed of the incremental motion $\Delta\boldsymbol{\xi} \in \mathfrak{se}(3)$ and the current estimate $T \in SE(3)$. This allows to optimize the incremental update $\Delta\boldsymbol{\xi}$ in the tangent space of the current estimate T. Once the optimal increment $\Delta\boldsymbol{\xi}^*$ is found, the transformation matrix T is updated as

$$\mathrm{T} \leftarrow \exp_{\mathrm{SE}(3)}(\Delta \boldsymbol{\xi}^*)\mathrm{T}. \qquad (6.25)$$

Note that we follow the *left-multiplication* convention to be consistent with [105, 119].

We refer the readers to [19] for a reference on the representation of 6 DoF pose in the 3D space, and to [101, 104] for introductions to Lie algebras for odometry and SLAM.

6.4 Camera Tracking

In this section, we detail the algorithms that are most commonly used for estimating the six DoF motion of an RGB-D camera. The methods will be divided attending to the type of residual they minimize:

- **Methods based on photometric alignment** (Sect. 6.4.1). The alignment results from the minimization of a photometric error over corresponding pixels in two frames.
- **Methods based on geometric alignment** (Sect. 6.4.2). While direct methods minimize a photometric error, we refer to geometric alignment methods to those that minimize geometric residuals either in the image or 3D domains.

Recent results suggest that direct methods present a higher accuracy than those based on geometric alignment, both in odometry [28] and mapping [126]. Most of the state-of-the-art systems are, because of this reason, based on dense frame alignment. Among the weaknesses of direct methods we can name their small basin of convergence, which can limit the accuracy in wide baselines cases, and their sensitivity to calibration errors, rolling shutter or unsynchronisation between the color and depth images [94].

6.4.1 Photometric Alignment

Assuming that the same scene point will have the same color in different images, photometric alignment aims to estimate the motion between two frames by minimizing the pixel intensity difference. This error criterion is called a *photometric reprojection* error. For each pixel $\mathbf{p}_k^i$ in the reference frame i, it is given by

$$r_{ph_k}(\Delta \boldsymbol{\xi}_{ji}) = I_i\left(\mathbf{p}_k^i\right) - I_j\left(\mathbf{p}_k^{ji}(\Delta \boldsymbol{\xi}_{ji})\right), \qquad (6.26)$$

where $\mathbf{p}_k^{ji}(\Delta \boldsymbol{\xi}_{ji})$ is the reprojection of $\mathbf{p}_k^i$ in frame j evaluated at the incrementally updated transformation $\exp_{\mathrm{SE}(3)}(\Delta \boldsymbol{\xi}_{ji})\mathrm{T}_{ji}$. Figure 6.4a illustrates this error. Notice that in (6.26) we omitted some of the variables in the reprojection function $\mathbf{p}_k^{ji}$ for

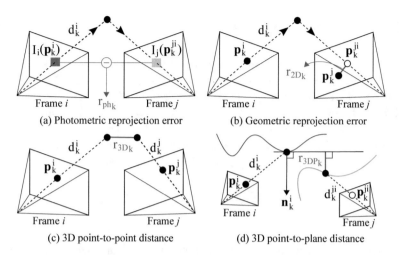

Fig. 6.4 Different types of error criteria frequently used in the literature: **a** A photometric reprojection error is the pixel intensity difference between a reference pixel in frame i and its reprojection in frame j. **b** Given a reference point in frame i, a geometric reprojection error is the image distance between its match and the reprojection in frame j. **c** A 3D point-to-point distance is the Euclidean distance between the backprojections of two matched points. **d** A 3D point-to-plane distance is the Euclidean distance between the tangent plane at the backprojected reference point in frame i and the backprojected reprojection of the point in frame j

readability. The full function is written as

$$\mathbf{p}_k^{ji}(\Delta\boldsymbol{\xi}_{ji}) \stackrel{(6.7)}{=} \mathbf{p}_k^{ji}\left(\mathbf{p}_k^i,\, d_k^i,\, \exp_{\mathrm{SE}(3)}(\Delta\boldsymbol{\xi}_{ji})\mathrm{T}_{ji}\right). \tag{6.27}$$

The total cost function to minimize, E_{ph}, is the weighted squared sum of the individual photometric errors for all considered pixels:

$$\Delta\boldsymbol{\xi}_{ji}^* = \arg\min_{\Delta\boldsymbol{\xi}_{ji}} E_{ph}(\Delta\boldsymbol{\xi}_{ji}) = \arg\min_{\Delta\boldsymbol{\xi}_{ji}} \sum_k \omega(r_{ph_k})\left(r_{ph_k}(\Delta\boldsymbol{\xi}_{ji})\right)^2 \tag{6.28}$$

with some weight function ω, e.g., constant for unweighted least squares, or robust weight function such as Huber's [47]. As discussed in Sect. 6.3.2, this problem can be solved using IRLS. Once the optimal increment is found, T_{ji} is updated using (6.25), and this optimization process is iterated until convergence.

Kerl et al. [54] proposes a similar photometric alignment between consecutive frames of a video, achieving very accurate odometry results. For study of different alignment strategies, we refer to [61]. The photometric alignment can also be done in a frame-to-map basis. For example, in [16], photometric and geometric errors are used to track the camera pose with respect to the closest keyframe in the map.

6.4.2 Geometric Alignment

In contrast to photometric alignment that directly uses raw pixel intensities, geometric alignment estimates the camera motion by minimizing the Euclidean distances between the two corresponding sets of geometric primitives in 2D or 3D.

2D Point-to-Point Alignment: A *geometric reprojection* error is the most representative type of 2D error used in VO and VSLAM. This error is illustrated in Fig. 6.4b. Given a point $\mathbf{p}_k^i$ in the reference frame i, it measures the image distance between its match $\mathbf{p}_k^j$ and the projection $\mathbf{p}_k^{ji}$ (6.27) in the current frame j:

$$r_{2D_k}(\Delta \boldsymbol{\xi}_{ji}) = \frac{\|\mathbf{p}_k^j - \mathbf{p}_k^{ji}(\Delta \boldsymbol{\xi}_{ji})\|}{\sigma_k^i} \quad \text{with} \quad \sigma_k^i = (\lambda_{\text{pyr}})^{L_{\text{pyr},\mathbf{p}_k^i}}, \qquad (6.29)$$

where σ_k^i is the standard deviation of the image point $\mathbf{p}_k^i$ that depends on the scale factor of the image pyramid $\lambda_{\text{pyr}}(> 1)$ and the level $L_{\text{pyr},\mathbf{p}_k^i}$ at which the point was detected.

Unlike photometric errors, geometric errors require data association. For sparse points, this can be done by matching feature descriptors (e.g., SIFT [68], SURF [6], ORB [89]) or extracting salient corners (e.g., Harris corner [39], FAST [88] or Shi-Tomasi [97] features) and tracking them [71]. Aggregating r_{2D_k} for every point k, we obtain the total cost function analogous to (6.28):

$$\Delta \boldsymbol{\xi}_{ji}^* = \underset{\Delta \boldsymbol{\xi}_{ji}}{\arg \min} \; E_{2D}(\Delta \boldsymbol{\xi}_{ji}) = \underset{\Delta \boldsymbol{\xi}_{ji}}{\arg \min} \sum_k \omega(r_{2D_k}) \left(r_{2D_k}(\Delta \boldsymbol{\xi}_{ji})\right)^2. \qquad (6.30)$$

Minimizing this cost function to estimate the camera motion is called *motion-only* bundle adjustment, and this method is used among others in ORB-SLAM2 [79] for tracking.

3D Point-to-Point Alignment: Instead of minimizing the reprojection error in 2D image space, one can also minimize the distance between the backprojected points in 3D space (see Fig. 6.4c). The 3D errors can be defined over dense point clouds or sparse ones. For the latter case, the first step should be the extraction and matching of the sparse salient points in the RGB channels. Henry et al. [41], for example, uses SIFT features [68], although others could be used.

Given two sets of correspondences in image i and j, the 3D geometric error is obtained as

$$r_{3D_k}(\Delta \boldsymbol{\xi}_{ji}) = \left\| \mathbf{P}_k^{j'} - \mathbf{P}_k^{ji}(\Delta \boldsymbol{\xi}_{ji}) \right\| \qquad (6.31)$$

$$\text{with} \quad \mathbf{P}_k^{ji}(\Delta \boldsymbol{\xi}_{ji}) := \pi_{3D}\left(\exp_{SE(3)}(\Delta \boldsymbol{\xi}_{ji}) \mathrm{T}_{ji} \pi_{3D}^{-1}\left(\mathbf{P}_k^{i'}\right)\right), \qquad (6.32)$$

where $\mathbf{P}_k^{i'}$ and $\mathbf{P}_k^{j'}$ are the 3D points backprojected from the 2D correspondence $\mathbf{p}_k^i$ and $\mathbf{p}_k^j$ using (6.4). Aggregating r_{2D_k} for every point k, we obtain the total cost function analogous to (6.28) and (6.30):

$$\Delta\xi_{ji}^* = \arg\min_{\Delta\xi_{ji}} E_{3D}(\Delta\xi_{ji}) = \arg\min_{\Delta\xi_{ji}} \sum_k \omega(r_{3D_k}) \left(r_{3D_k}(\Delta\xi_{ji})\right)^2. \qquad (6.33)$$

For the case of dense cloud alignment, the standard algorithm is *Iterative Closest Point (ICP)* [8]. ICP alternates the minimization of a geometric distance between points (the point-to-point distance in Eq. 6.31 or the point-to-plane one defined later in this section) and the search for correspondences (usually the nearest neighbors in the 3D space).

The strengths and limitations of sparse and dense cloud alignment are complementary for RGB-D data. Aligning dense point clouds can lead to more accurate motion estimation than aligning sparse ones, as they use more data. On the other hand, ICP might diverge if the initial estimate is not sufficiently close to the real motion. In practice, combining the two is a preferred approach: Sparse alignment, based on feature correspondences, can produce a robust and reliable initial seed. Afterward, dense alignment can refine such initial estimate using ICP.

3D Point-to-Plane Alignment: The point-to-plane distance, that minimizes the distance along the target point normal, is commonly used in dense RGB-D point cloud alignment [22, 41, 81, 118]. The residual is in this case

$$r_{3DP_k}(\Delta\xi_{ji}) = \left| \mathbf{n}_k^i \cdot \left(\mathbf{P}_k^{i\,'} - \left(\exp_{SE(3)}(\Delta\xi_{ji})\mathrm{T}_{ji}\right)^{-1} \left(d_k^{ji} \frac{\mathrm{K}^{-1}\pi_{2D}^{-1}\left(\mathbf{p}_k^{ji}(\Delta\xi_{ji})\right)}{\|\mathrm{K}^{-1}\pi_{2D}^{-1}\left(\mathbf{p}_k^{ji}(\Delta\xi_{ji})\right)\|} \right) \right) \right|,$$

$$(6.34)$$

where $\mathbf{P}_k^{i\,'}$ is the 3D backprojection of $\mathbf{p}_k^i$ using (6.4), $\mathbf{n}_k^i$ is the surface normal at $\mathbf{P}_k^{i\,'}$, $\mathbf{p}_k^{ji}(\Delta\xi_{ji})$ is the reprojection of $\mathbf{p}_k^i$ in frame j evaluated at the incrementally updated transformation $\exp_{SE(3)}(\Delta\xi_{ji})\mathrm{T}_{ji}$, which is given by (6.27) and (6.7), and d_k^{ji} is the measured depth at this reprojection in frame j. This error is illustrated in Fig. 6.4d. Aggregating r_{3DP_k} for every point k, we obtain the total cost function analogous to (6.28), (6.30) and (6.33):

$$\Delta\xi_{ji}^* = \arg\min_{\Delta\xi_{ji}} E_{3DP}(\Delta\xi_{ji}) = \arg\min_{\Delta\xi_{ji}} \sum_k \omega(r_{3DP_k}) \left(r_{3DP_k}(\Delta\xi_{ji})\right)^2. \qquad (6.35)$$

6.5 Scene Mapping

In this section, we briefly survey the main algorithms for estimating scene maps from several RGB-D views. There are two basic types of scene representations that are commonly used, and we will denote it as **point-based maps** (Sect. 6.5.1), and **volumetric maps** (Sect. 6.5.2).

6.5.1   Point-Based Mapping

Representing a scene as a set of points or surfels is one of the most common alternatives for estimating local maps of a scene. Bundle Adjustment [112], consisting on the joint optimization of a set of camera poses and points, is frequently used to obtain a globally consistent model of the scene [79]. However, there are also several recent VSLAM approaches that alternate the optimization between points and poses, reducing the computational cost with a small impact in the accuracy, given a sufficient number of points [84, 94, 120, 123].

In its most basic form, the map model consists of a set of n points and m RGB-D keyframes. Every point is represented by its 3D position in the world reference frame $\mathbf{P}_k^w$. For every keyframe i, we store its pose T_{iw} and its RGB-D image I_i.

Similarly to camera tracking in Sect. 6.4, map optimization algorithms are based on the photometric or geometric alignment between the keyframes. In this case, however, both the keyframe poses and point positions are optimized.

Photometric Bundle Adjustment: This method minimizes a cost function similar to (6.28), with the difference that it does not backproject the 2D points using the measured depths. Instead, it aims to find the 3D point that minimizes the photometric errors in all keyframes where it was visible. Let $\mathbf{P}_{\mathscr{M}} = (\mathbf{P}_1, \ldots, \mathbf{P}_k, \ldots, \mathbf{P}_n)^\top$ be the set of all map points and $\varDelta\boldsymbol{\xi}_{\mathscr{M}} = (\varDelta\boldsymbol{\xi}_{1w}, \ldots, \varDelta\boldsymbol{\xi}_{jw}, \ldots, \varDelta\boldsymbol{\xi}_{mw})^\top$ the set of incremental transformations to the current estimates of the keyframe poses. Then, the optimization problem is formulated as

$$\{\varDelta\boldsymbol{\xi}_{\mathscr{M}}^*, \mathbf{P}_{\mathscr{M}}^*\} = \underset{\varDelta\boldsymbol{\xi}_{\mathscr{M}}, \mathbf{P}_{\mathscr{M}}}{\arg\min} \ E_{ph}(\varDelta\boldsymbol{\xi}_{\mathscr{M}}, \mathbf{P}_{\mathscr{M}}) \tag{6.36}$$

$$= \underset{\varDelta\boldsymbol{\xi}_{jw}, \mathbf{P}_k^w}{\arg\min} \sum_j \sum_k \omega(r_{ph_k}) \left(r_{ph_k}(\varDelta\boldsymbol{\xi}_{jw}, \mathbf{P}_k^w) \right)^2 \tag{6.37}$$

with

$$r_{ph_k}(\varDelta\boldsymbol{\xi}_{jw}, \mathbf{P}_k^w)$$

$$= \begin{cases} 0 & \text{if } \mathbf{P}_k \text{ is not visible} \\ & \text{in frame } j, \\ I_i\left(\mathbf{p}_k^i\right) - I_j\left(\pi_{2\mathrm{D}}\left(\mathrm{K}\pi_{3\mathrm{D}}(\exp_{\mathrm{SE}(3)}(\varDelta\boldsymbol{\xi}_{jw})\mathrm{T}_{jw}\pi_{3\mathrm{D}}^{-1}(\mathbf{P}_k^w))) \right) & \text{otherwise,} \end{cases}$$

where $I_i\left(\mathbf{p}_k^i\right)$ is the pixel intensity at which $\mathbf{P}_k^w$ was detected in its reference keyframe i (i.e., the keyframe in which the point was first detected and parameterized).

Geometric Bundle Adjustment: This method minimizes a cost function similar to (6.30), with the difference that the reprojection with the measured depth is replaced by the projection of the current estimate of the 3D point. Using the same notation as for the photometric bundle adjustment, the optimization problem is formulated as

$$\{\Delta \boldsymbol{\xi}^*_{\mathcal{M}}, \mathbf{P}^*_{\mathcal{M}}\} = \underset{\Delta \boldsymbol{\xi}_{\mathcal{M}}, \mathbf{P}_{\mathcal{M}}}{\arg\min} \; E_{2D}(\Delta \boldsymbol{\xi}_{\mathcal{M}}, \mathbf{P}_{\mathcal{M}}) \tag{6.38}$$

$$= \underset{\Delta \boldsymbol{\xi}_{jw}, \mathbf{P}^w_k}{\arg\min} \sum_j \sum_k \omega(r_{2Dk}) \left(r_{2Dk}(\Delta \boldsymbol{\xi}_{jw}, \mathbf{P}^w_k)\right)^2 \tag{6.39}$$

with

$$r_{2Dk}(\Delta \boldsymbol{\xi}_{jw}, \mathbf{P}^w_k)$$

$$= \begin{cases} 0 & \text{if } \mathbf{P}_k \text{ is not detected} \\ & \text{in frame } j, \\[2ex] \dfrac{\left\| \mathbf{p}^j_k - \pi_{2D} \left(\mathrm{K} \pi_{3D} \left(\exp_{SE(3)} (\Delta \boldsymbol{\xi}_{jw}) \mathrm{T}_{jw} \pi_{3D}^{-1} (\mathbf{P}^w_k) \right) \right) \right\|}{\sigma^j_k} & \text{otherwise.} \end{cases}$$

Note that σ^j_k is defined in (6.29).

6.5.2 Volumetric Mapping

One of the main weaknesses of point-based representations for mapping is that they do not model the empty and occupied space. This can be a problem for applications such as robot navigation or occlusion modeling in AR. Volumetric mapping aims to overcome such problems by modeling the occupancy of the whole 3D scene volume.

The most usual model for volumetric maps is the Truncated Signed Distance Function [20], used for example in [59, 81, 116, 117]. In this representation, the 3D world is discretized into voxels and modeled as a volumetric signed distance field $\Phi : \mathbb{R}^3 \to \mathbb{R}$, where we assign to each cell the distance to the nearest object, which is defined positive if its center is outside the object and negative if it is inside it. Since only the surfaces and their surroundings are considered, the distances are usually truncated if larger than a threshold τ. Also, for every cell, a weight is stored that represents the confidence on the distance measurement. The algorithm for updating a TSDF with new depth measurements measurement was first presented in [20]. In a few words, it consists on a weighted running average on the distance measurements from the depth sensors.

TSDF is addressed in-depth in Chap. 5 of this book. For this reason, we do not extend further on it and refer the reader to this chapter, and the references there and in this section, for further detail on this topic.

6.6 Loop Closing

Loop closing algorithms correct the drift that has accumulated during exploratory trajectories, maintaining a consistent global representation of the environment. **Loop detection** (Sect. 6.6.1), is mainly based on the visual appearance between two keyframes of the map. When these two keyframes are imaging the same place and the loop closure has been detected, the geometric constraint between the two is added to the map, which is then updated according to it. This map update is known as **loop correction** (Sect. 6.6.2), and we detail the pose graph formulation as an efficient alternative for large map representations and loop closing correction.

6.6.1 Loop Detection

Due to the excellent performance of visual place recognition, many RGB-D SLAM systems use only the RGB channels for loop detection (e.g., [16, 34, 79]). The most used approaches are based on the bag of words model, first proposed in [100]. The implementation in [30] is particularly suited for visual SLAM, adding robustness to plain visual appearance by geometric and sequential consistency checks.

In the bag of words model the space of local descriptors is divided into discrete clusters using the k-means algorithm. Each cluster is referred to as a visual word, and the set of all visual words forms a visual dictionary. With such a partition, an image is described as the histogram of visual word occurrences. The place querying can be made very efficient by maintaining inverse indexes from the visual words to the database images in which they appear.

Bag-of-words descriptors have some limitations for RGB-D odometry and SLAM. They assume images of sufficient texture to extract salient point features, and they do not use the information of the depth channel from RGB-D images. Also, the extraction and description of local features has a considerable computational overhead.

There are several approaches in the literature that overcome such limitations. Gee and Mayol-Cuevas [32] proposes to find loop closure candidates without features, by the alignment of keyframes against synthetic views of the map. Shotton et al. [99] uses regression forests to predict correspondences between an RGB-D frame and the map, an approach that has been refined in [13, 37, 113] among others. Glocker et al. [33] proposed to encode each RGB-D image using randomized ferns.

6.6.2 Loop Correction

Once a loop is detected based on the appearance of two keyframes, a constraint between the poses of both can be computed by photometric and/or geometric alignment. When such constraint is added to the map optimization, the global map con-

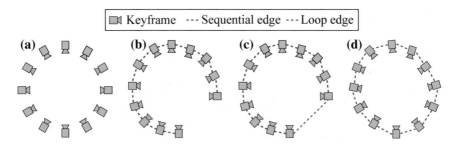

Fig. 6.5 An illustration of loop closure: **a** Ground truth. **b** Odometry result containing drift. **c** A loop detection followed by the computation of the loop constraint. **d** The keyframe trajectory after the pose graph optimization

sistency is achieved by accommodating this new constraint and correcting the accumulated drift. For computational reasons, this correction is frequently done by pose graph optimization. Figure 6.5 illustrates a loop closure process.

A pose graph is a compact map representation composed of the set of m keyframe poses summarizing the trajectory, i.e., $T_{kfs} = \{T_{1a}, T_{2a}, \ldots, T_{ma}\}$ where the reference frame a is chosen from one of the keyframes as the "anchor" to the rest. As this representation does not include map points, it is particularly useful for estimating globally consistent maps of large areas at a reasonable cost, and is used among others in [16, 26, 53].

Pose graph optimization aims to minimize the following cost:

$$\underset{T_{kfs}}{\arg\min}\ E_{graph} = \underset{T_{kfs}}{\arg\min} \sum_{(i,j)\in\varepsilon_{edge}} \mathbf{r}_{ij}^{\top}\Omega_{ij}^{-1}\mathbf{r}_{ij} \tag{6.40}$$

where ε_{edge} denotes the set of edges (i.e., relative pose constraints) in the pose graph, $\mathbf{r}_{ij}$ and Ω_{ij} are respectively the residual associated to the ith and jth camera poses and its uncertainty. Such residual is defined as

$$\mathbf{r}_{ij} = \log_{SE(3)}(T_{ij,0}T_{ja}T_{ia}^{-1}) \tag{6.41}$$

where $T_{ij,0}$ is the fixed transformation constraint from the alignment (Sect. 6.4) and $T_{ja}T_{ia}^{-1} = T_{ji}$ is the current estimate of the relative motion. For more details on the pose graph optimization method, the reader is referred to [62, 87].

6.7 Advanced Topics

In this section, we review some of the relevant approaches in RGB-D odometry and SLAM that, due to space reasons, were not covered in the main part of the chapter.

6.7.1 Hybrid Cost Function

In Sects. 6.4 and 6.5, we discussed different types of cost functions separately. Many state-of-the-art methods, however, minimize a weighted sum of multiple cost functions. This strategy allows for better utilization of RGB-D data, which can lead to performance gains [23, 53, 76, 77]. In [41], 3D point-to-point error was used for outlier rejection, and then the pose was refined by minimizing the combined 2D point-to-point cost and 3D point-to-plane cost. In [22, 118], the joint minimization of photometric and point-to-plane cost was used. Another popular method is to jointly minimize the photometric and (inverse) depth cost (which is not discussed here) [3, 16, 35, 53, 102].

6.7.2 Semantic Mapping

In recent years, there has been an impressive progress in the field of machine learning (specifically deep learning) for visual recognition and segmentation tasks. Building on them, there have appeared several visual SLAM algorithms that not only estimate geometric models, but also annotate them with high-level semantic information (see Fig. 6.6 for an illustration). The research on semantic mapping is not as mature as geometric mapping, with challenges related to robustness, accuracy and cost. The state-of-the-art systems, however, show promising results. Semantic mapping could improve the accuracy and robustness of current SLAM algorithms, and widen their applications. For example, [7] uses a combination of geometry and learning to remove dynamic objects and create lifelong maps, achieving better accuracy than geometric SLAM baselines. Similarly, [51] uses data association failures and region growing to segment and remove dynamic objects, improving the system robustness and accuracy.

One can differentiate between maps based on specific object instances and object categories. An approach like [92] adopts the map of the former type. It assumes that a database of relevant objects in the scene is available. The map is then modeled as a graph of keyframe and object poses, and it is optimized using the constraints from keyframe-to-keyframe point cloud alignment and keyframe-to-object using [24]. Object-based RGB-D SLAM has also been addressed in [108]

Most category-wise semantic mapping methods leverage 2D segmentation algorithms (e.g., [40]), differing on how they transfer the labels to the 3D maps. As a few examples, we refer to the following works for this area of research [42, 73, 75, 82, 106].

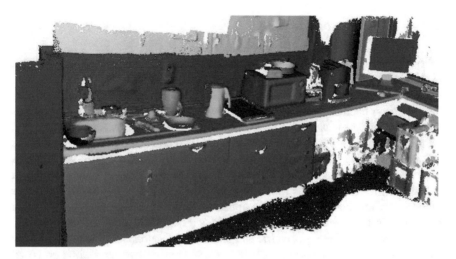

Fig. 6.6 Illustration of results from semantic RGB-D SLAM. Different colors indicate different object categories. Figures taken from [111]

6.7.3 Edge-Based Methods

While the majority of the existing methods consider each pixel as independent measurements, edge-based methods exploit the structural regularities of indoor scenes, modeling the scene geometry with lines or edges. This can provide an advantage over point-based methods, especially when the scene has weak texture but strong structural priors. One of the earliest works that demonstrated the advantage of edge-based registration in RGB-D SLAM is [15]. This method is based on an efficient edge detection for RGB-D point clouds and 3D registration of the edge points using the ICP algorithm. In [10], it is shown that the edge detection can be accelerated using the previous RGB-D frame. On the other hand, [70] proposes to model the straight lines only and incorporate their uncertainties in the pose estimation problem. Although this work is shown to outperform [15] under lighting variations, it fails when the scene contains few lines. To overcome this limitation, [69] uses both points and lines. In [63], direct edge alignment is proposed that minimizes the sum of squared distances between the reprojected and the nearest edge point using the distance transform of the edge map. Other works propose to jointly minimize this edge distance and other errors, e.g., a photometric error [114] and an ICP-based point-to-plane distance [93]. Later works such as [55, 124] take the image gradient direction also into account for the direct edge alignment. As in [54], these last two works estimate the camera pose using the iteratively reweighted least squares (IRLS) method with the t-distribution as a robust weight function.

6.7.4 Plane-Based Methods

Like edges, planes are abundant in man-made environments and can be modeled explicitly for tracking and mapping. In [109], an RGB-D SLAM system is proposed based on the 3D registration between the minimal set of point/plane primitives. This system is improved in [2] and [1] by incorporating the guided search of points/planes and triangulation of 2D-to-2D/3D point matches, respectively. Raposo et al. [86] proposes an odometry method that uses planes (and points if strictly necessary) and refines the relative pose using a direct method. In [91], a dense SLAM method is proposed based on dense ICP with a piecewise planar map. In both [45, 72], it is proposed to model planes in a global map, so that they are optimized together with the keyframe poses in the graph optimization for global consistency. The main difference is that the former uses direct image alignment in an EM framework, while the latter combines geometric and photometric methods for the fast odometry estimation. Besides, the latter adopts the minimal plane parameterization proposed in [50] and does not require GPU. A visual-inertial method based on [45] is proposed in [44]. In [31], it is proposed to use planar point features for tracking and mapping, as they are more accurate than the traditional point features and computationally inexpensive. Other works such as [56, 57, 65] use Manhattan world assumption, which simplifies the incorporation of the planes into a SLAM formulation. Finally, [85] shows that it can be beneficial to use points, lines and planes all together in a joint optimization framework.

6.7.5 Multisensor Fusion

The constraints coming from RGB-D data can be combined with other sources of information to increase the accuracy and robustness of the tracking and mapping processes. For example, [64] presents a tightly coupled formulation for RGB-D-inertial SLAM based on ElasticFusion [119]. In [60], RGB-D SLAM estimates the configuration space of an articulated arm. Houseago et al. [43] adds odometric and kinematic constraints from a wheeled robot with a manipulator, and [96] adds the kinematic constraints of a humanoid robot and inertial data.

6.7.6 Nonrigid Reconstructions

The 3D reconstruction of nonrigid environments is a very relevant and challenging area of research that has been frequently addressed using RGB-D sensors. Newcombe et al. [80] is one of the most representative systems, achieving impressive results for deformable surfaces. Rünz et al. [90] is a recent work that reconstructs a scene with multiple moving objects. Jaimez et al. [49] estimates very efficiently the odometry of an RGB-D camera and the flow of a scene that might contain static and dynamic parts. Scona et al. [95] classifies the scene parts into static and dynamic, fuses the static parts and discard the dynamic ones. A recent survey on 3D reconstruction from RGB-D camera, including dynamic scenes, is conducted in [125]. It places emphasis on high-quality offline reconstruction, which is complementary to the focus of this chapter on real-time online reconstruction and camera tracking.

6.8 Conclusions

Estimating the camera ego-motion and the 3D structure of the surrounding environment is a crucial component in many applications such as photogrammetry, AR and vision-based navigation. For this particular tasks, RGB-D cameras provide significant advantages over RGB cameras, as the additional depth measurements ease the process of metric scene reconstruction. Furthermore, they impose a relatively mild constraint on cost, size and power, making them a popular choice for mobile platforms. As a result, both academia and industry have shown an ever-increasing interest in RGB-D odometry and SLAM methods for the past decade.

In this chapter, we reviewed the general formulations of RGB-D odometry and SLAM. The standard pipeline of VSLAM systems consists of three main components: camera pose tracking, scene mapping and loop closing. For tracking and mapping, we discussed some of the widely used methods and highlighted the difference in their formulations (i.e., photometric vs. geometric alignment and point-based vs. volumetric mapping). For loop closing, we detailed the underlying principles of loop detection and drift correction, namely the appearance-based place recognition and pose graph optimization. Lastly, we presented a brief review of the advanced topics in the research field today.

6.9 Resources

There are a high number of available resources in the web related to RGB-D odometry and SLAM. We will refer here the most relevant open-source software and public databases.

Code

FOVIS [46] (https://fovis.github.io/)
Implementation of a feature-based RGB-D odometry.

DVO_SLAM [52–54, 103] (https://github.com/tum-vision/dvo_slam)
Implementation of a frame-to-frame RGB-D visual Odometry.
RGBDSLAM_v2 [27] (https://github.com/felixendres/rgbdslam_v2, http://wiki.ros.
org/rgbdslam, https://openslam-org.github.io/rgbdslam.html)
Implementation of an RGB-D SLAM system, with a feature-based camera tracking
and a pose graph as map model.
ElasticFusion [119] (https://github.com/mp3guy/ElasticFusion)
RGB-D scene-centered SLAM system that models the scene as a set of surfels that
are deformed to accommodate loop closures.
RGBDTAM [16] (https://github.com/alejocb/rgbdtam)
RGB-D SLAM system with a pose graph as map model and frame-to-frame tracking.
MaskFusion [90] (https://github.com/martinruenz/maskfusion)
A recent semantic (object-based) RGB-D SLAM system for dynamic scenes.
PlaneMatch [98] (https://github.com/yifeishi/PlaneMatch)
RGB-D SLAM algorithm that proposes a novel descriptor for planar surfaces and
exploits correspondences between them.

Databases

RGB-D SLAM Dataset and Benchmark (Also known as *the TUM dataset*) [107]
(https://vision.in.tum.de/data/datasets/rgbd-dataset).
It contains indoor recordings with ground truth camera pose in a wide variety of
conditions: rotation-only and general motion, static and dynamic environments and
small and mid-size scene coverage.
The ETH3D dataset [94] (https://www.eth3d.net/).
A benchmark dataset for RGB-D SLAM (among others), recorded with synchronized
global shutter cameras.
The Matterport dataset [14] (https://github.com/niessner/Matterport).
Annotated data captured throughout 90 properties with a Matterport Pro Camera.
Scannet [21] (http://www.scan-net.org/).
RGB-D video dataset annotated with 3D camera poses, reconstructions, and instance-
level semantic segmentations.
The ICL-NUIM dataset [38] (https://www.doc.ic.ac.uk/~ahanda/VaFRIC/iclnuim.
html).
This dataset contain RGB-D sequences on synthetic scenes; hence with camera pose
and scene ground truth.
InteriorNet [67] (https://interiornet.org/).
Dataset containing RGB-D-inertial streams for synthetic large scale interior scenes.

References

1. Ataer-Cansizoglu E, Taguchi Y, Ramalingam S (2016) Pinpoint SLAM: a hybrid of 2D and 3D simultaneous localization and mapping for RGB-D sensors. In: 2016 IEEE international conference on robotics and automation (ICRA), pp 1300–1307
2. Ataer-Cansizoglu E, Taguchi Y, Ramalingam S, Garaas T (2013) Tracking an RGB-D camera using points and planes. In: 2013 IEEE international conference on computer vision workshops, pp 51–58 (2013)
3. Babu BW, Kim S, Yan Z, Ren L (2016) σ-DVO: sensor noise model meets dense visual odometry. In: 2016 IEEE international symposium on mixed and augmented reality (ISMAR), pp 18–26
4. Bailey T, Durrant-Whyte H (2006) Simultaneous localization and mapping (SLAM): part II. IEEE Robot Autom Mag 13(3):108–117
5. Barfoot TD (2017) State estimation for robotics. Cambridge University Press
6. Bay H, Tuytelaars T, Van Gool L (2006) SURF: speeded up robust features. In: Proceedings of the European conference on computer vision (ECCV), pp 404–417
7. Bescós B, Fácil JM, Civera J, Neira J (2018) DynaSLAM: tracking, mapping, and inpainting in dynamic scenes. IEEE Robot Autom Lett 3(4):4076–4083
8. Besl PJ, McKay ND (1992) Method for registration of 3-D shapes. In: Sensor fusion IV: control paradigms and data structures, vol 1611. International Society for Optics and Photonics, pp 586–607
9. Bloesch M, Czarnowski J, Clark R, Leutenegger S, Davison AJ (2018) CodeSLAM—learning a compact, optimisable representation for dense visual SLAM. In: Proceedings of the IEEE conference on computer vision and pattern recognition, pp 2560–2568
10. Bose L, Richards A (2016) Fast depth edge detection and edge based RGB-D SLAM. In: 2016 IEEE international conference on robotics and automation (ICRA), pp 1323–1330
11. Cadena C, Carlone L, Carrillo H, Latif Y, Scaramuzza D, Neira J, Reid I, Leonard JJ (2016) Past, present, and future of simultaneous localization and mapping: towards the robust-perception age. IEEE Trans Robot 32(6):1309–1332
12. Castellanos JA, Montiel J, Neira J, Tardós JD (1999) The SPmap: a probabilistic framework for simultaneous localization and map building. IEEE Trans Robot Autom 15(5):948–952
13. Cavallari T, Golodetz S, Lord NA, Valentin J, Di Stefano L, Torr PH (2017) On-the-Fly adaptation of regression forests for online camera relocalisation. In: Proceedings of the IEEE conference on computer vision and pattern recognition, pp 4457–4466
14. Chang A, Dai A, Funkhouser T, Halber, M, Niessner M, Savva M, Song S, Zeng A, Zhang Y (2017) Matterport3D: learning from RGB-D data in indoor environments. In: International conference on 3D vision (3DV)
15. Choi C, Trevor AJB, Christensen HI (2013) RGB-D edge detection and edge-based registration. In: 2013 IEEE/RSJ international conference on intelligent robots and systems, pp 1568–1575
16. Concha A, Civera J (2017) RGBDTAM: a cost-effective and accurate RGB-D tracking and mapping system. In: 2017 IEEE/RSJ international conference on intelligent robots and systems (IROS). IEEE , pp 6756–6763
17. Concha A, Hussain MW, Montano L, Civera J (2014) Manhattan and piecewise-planar constraints for dense monocular mapping. In: Robotics: science and systems (2014)
18. Concha A, Loianno G, Kumar V, Civera J (2016) Visual-inertial direct SLAM. In: 2016 IEEE international conference on robotics and automation (ICRA), pp 1331–1338. IEEE
19. Corke P (2017) Robotics, vision and control: fundamental algorithms in MATLAB® second, completely revised, chap 1. Springer, pp 15–41
20. Curless B, Levoy M (1996) A volumetric method for building complex models from range images. In: Proceedings of the 23rd annual conference on Computer graphics and interactive techniques. ACM, pp 303–312

21. Dai A, Chang AX, Savva M, Halber M, Funkhouser T, Nießner M (2017) ScanNet: richly-annotated 3D reconstructions of indoor scenes. In: Proceedings of computer vision and pattern recognition (CVPR). IEEE (2017)
22. Dai A, Nießner M, Zollhöfer M, Izadi S, Theobalt C (2017) BundleFusion: real-time globally consistent 3D reconstruction using on-the-fly surface reintegration. ACM Trans Graph 36(3):24:1–24:18
23. Damen D, Gee A, Mayol-Cuevas W, Calway A (2012) Egocentric real-time workspace monitoring using an RGB-D camera. In: 2012 IEEE/RSJ international conference on intelligent robots and systems. IEEE, pp 1029–1036
24. Drost B, Ulrich M, Navab N, Ilic S (2010) Model globally, match locally: efficient and robust 3D object recognition. In: 2010 IEEE computer society conference on computer vision and pattern recognition. IEEE, pp 998–1005
25. Durrant-Whyte H, Bailey T (2006) Simultaneous localization and mapping: part I. IEEE Robot Autom Mag 13(2):99–110
26. Endres F, Hess J, Engelhard N, Sturm J, Cremers D, Burgard W (2012) An evaluation of the RGB-D SLAM system. In: 2012 IEEE international conference on robotics and automation (ICRA). IEEE, pp 1691–1696
27. Endres F, Hess J, Sturm J, Cremers D, Burgard W (2014) 3-D mapping with an RGB-D camera. IEEE Trans Robot 30(1):177–187
28. Engel J, Koltun V, Cremers D (2018) Direct sparse odometry. IEEE Trans Pattern Anal Mach Intell 40(3):611–625
29. Fácil, JM, Ummenhofer B, Zhou H, Montesano L, Brox T, Civera J (2019) CAM-Convs: camera-aware multi-scale convolutions for single-view depth. In: Proceedings of the IEEE conference on computer vision and pattern recognition
30. Gálvez-López D, Tardos JD (2012) Bags of binary words for fast place recognition in image sequences. IEEE Trans Robot 28(5):1188–1197
31. Gao X, Zhang T (2015) Robust RGB-D simultaneous localization and mapping using planar point features. Robot Auton Syst 72:1–14
32. Gee AP, Mayol-Cuevas WW (2012) 6D relocalisation for RGBD cameras using synthetic view regression. In: BMVC
33. Glocker B, Shotton J, Criminisi A, Izadi S (2015) Real-time RGB-D camera relocalization via randomized ferns for keyframe encoding. IEEE Trans Vis Comput Graph 21(5):571–583
34. Gutierrez-Gomez D, Guerrero JJ (2018) RGBiD-SLAM for accurate real-time localisation and 3D mapping. arXiv:1807.08271
35. Gutiérrez-Gómez D, Mayol-Cuevas W, Guerrero JJ (2015) Inverse depth for accurate photometric and geometric error minimisation in RGB-D dense visual odometry. In: 2015 IEEE international conference on robotics and automation (ICRA). IEEE, pp 83–89
36. Gutierrez-Gomez D, Mayol-Cuevas W, Guerrero JJ (2016) Dense RGB-D visual odometry using inverse depth. Robot Auton Syst 75:571–583
37. Guzman-Rivera A, Kohli P, Glocker B, Shotton J, Sharp T, Fitzgibbon A, Izadi S (2014) Multi-output learning for camera relocalization. In: Proceedings of the IEEE conference on computer vision and pattern recognition, pp 1114–1121
38. Handa A, Whelan T, McDonald J, Davison AJ (2014) A Benchmark for RGB-D visual odometry, 3D reconstruction and SLAM. In: 2014 IEEE international conference on robotics and automation (ICRA). IEEE, pp 1524–1531
39. Harris C, Stephens M (1988) A combined corner and edge detector. In: Proceedings of fourth alvey vision conference, pp 147–151
40. He K, Gkioxari G, Dollár P, Girshick R (2017) Mask R-CNN. In: Proceedings of the IEEE international conference on computer vision, pp 2961–2969
41. Henry P, Krainin M, Herbst E, Ren X, Fox D (2010) RGB-D mapping: using depth cameras for dense 3D modeling of indoor environments. In: The 12th international symposium on experimental robotics (ISER). Citeseer
42. Hermans A, Floros G, Leibe B (2014) Dense 3D semantic mapping of indoor scenes from RGB-D images. In: 2014 IEEE international conference on robotics and automation (ICRA). IEEE, pp 2631–2638

43. Houseago C, Bloesch M, Leutenegger S (2019) KO-Fusion: dense visual SLAM with tightly-coupled kinematic and odometric tracking. In: 2019 IEEE international conference on robotics and automation (ICRA). IEEE
44. Hsiao M, Westman E, Kaess M (2018) Dense planar-inertial SLAM with structural constraints. In: 2018 IEEE international conference on robotics and automation (ICRA). IEEE, pp 6521–6528
45. Hsiao M, Westman E, Zhang G, Kaess M (2017) Keyframe-Based dense planar SLAM. In: IEEE international conference on robotics and automation, ICRA
46. Huang AS, Bachrach A, Henry P, Krainin M, Maturana D, Fox D, Roy N (2011) Visual odometry and mapping for autonomous flight using an RGB-D camera. In: International symposium of robotics research. Springer (2011)
47. Huber PJ (2011) Robust statistics. Springer
48. Engel J, Sturm J, Cremers D (2014) Scale-Aware navigation of a low-cost quadrocopter with a monocular camera. Robot Auton Syst (RAS) 62(11):1646–1656
49. Jaimez M, Kerl C, Gonzalez-Jimenez J, Cremers D (2017) Fast odometry and scene flow from RGB-D cameras based on geometric clustering. In: 2017 IEEE international conference on robotics and automation (ICRA). IEEE, pp 3992–3999
50. Kaess M (2015) Simultaneous localization and mapping with infinite planes. In: IEEE international conference on robotics and automation, pp 4605–4611 (2015)
51. Keller M, Lefloch D, Lambers M, Izadi S, Weyrich T, Kolb A (2013) Real-time 3D reconstruction in dynamic scenes using point-based fusion. In: 2013 international conference on 3D vision-3DV 2013. IEEE, pp 1–8
52. Kerl C, Stuckler J, Cremers D (2015) Dense continuous-time tracking and mapping with rolling shutter RGB-D cameras. In: Proceedings of the IEEE international conference on computer vision, pp 2264–2272
53. Kerl C, Sturm J, Cremers D (2013) Dense visual SLAM for RGB-D cameras. In: Intelligent robots and systems (IROS). Citeseer, pp 2100–2106
54. Kerl C, Sturm J, Cremers D (2013) Robust odometry estimation for RGB-D cameras. In: 2013 IEEE international conference on robotics and automation (ICRA). IEEE, pp 3748–3754
55. Kim C, Kim P, Lee S, Kim HJ (2018) Edge-Based robust RGB-D visual odometry using 2-D edge divergence minimization. In: IEEE/RSJ international conference on intelligent robots and systems (IROS), pp 6887–6894
56. Kim P, Coltin B, Kim HJ (2018) Linear RGB-D SLAM for planar environments. Comput Vis—ECCV 2018:350–366
57. Kim P, Coltin B, Kim HJ (2018) Low-drift visual odometry in structured environments by decoupling rotational and translational motion. In: 2018 IEEE international conference on robotics and automation (ICRA), pp 7247–7253
58. Klein G, Murray D (2007) Parallel tracking and mapping for small AR workspaces. In: 6th IEEE and ACM international symposium on mixed and augmented reality, 2007. ISMAR 2007. IEEE, pp 225–234
59. Klingensmith M, Dryanovski I, Srinivasa S, Xiao J (2015) Chisel: real time large scale 3D reconstruction onboard a mobile device using spatially hashed signed distance fields. In: Robotics: science and systems, vol 4 (2015)
60. Klingensmith M, Sirinivasa SS, Kaess M (2016) Articulated robot motion for simultaneous localization and mapping (ARM-SLAM). IEEE Robot Autom Lett 1(2):1156–1163
61. Klose S, Heise P, Knoll A (2013) Efficient compositional approaches for real-time robust direct visual odometry from RGB-D data. In: 2013 IEEE/RSJ international conference on intelligent robots and systems (IROS). IEEE, pp 1100–1106
62. Kümmerle R, Grisetti G, Strasdat H, Konolige K, Burgard W (2011) g2o: a general framework for graph optimization. In: IEEE international conference on robotics and automation (ICRA), pp 3607–3613
63. Kuse M, Shaojie S (2016) Robust camera motion estimation using direct edge alignment and sub-gradient method. In: 2016 IEEE international conference on robotics and automation (ICRA), pp 573–579

64. Laidlow T, Bloesch M, Li W, Leutenegger S (2017) Dense RGB-D-Inertial SLAM with map deformations. In: 2017 IEEE/RSJ international conference on intelligent robots and systems (IROS). IEEE, pp 6741–6748
65. Le P, Košecka J (2017) Dense piecewise planar RGB-D SLAM for indoor environments. In: 2017 IEEE/RSJ international conference on intelligent robots and systems (IROS), pp 4944–4949
66. Lee SH, de Croon G (2018) Stability-based scale estimation for monocular SLAM. IEEE Robot Autom Lett 3(2):780–787
67. Li W, Saeedi S, McCormac J, Clark R, Tzoumanikas D, Ye Q, Huang Y, Tang R, Leutenegger S (2018) InteriorNet: mega-scale multi-sensor photo-realistic indoor scenes dataset. In: British machine vision conference (BMVC)
68. Lowe DG (2004) Distinctive image features from scale-invariant keypoints. Int J Comput Vis 60(2):91–110
69. Lu Y, Song D (2015) Robust RGB-D odometry using point and line features. In: 2015 IEEE international conference on computer vision (ICCV), pp 3934–3942
70. Lu Y, Song D (2015) Robustness to lighting variations: an RGB-D indoor visual odometry using line segments. In: 2015 IEEE/RSJ international conference on intelligent robots and systems (IROS), pp 688–694
71. Lucas BD, Kanade T (1981) An iterative image registration technique with an application to stereo vision. In: Proceedings of the 7th international joint conference on artificial intelligence, vol 2, pp 674–679
72. Ma L, Kerl C, Stückler J, Cremers D (2016) CPA-SLAM: consistent plane-model alignment for direct RGB-D SLAM. In: IEEE international conference on robotics and automation (ICRA), pp 1285–1291
73. Ma L, Stückler J, Kerl C, Cremers D (2017) Multi-view deep learning for consistent semantic mapping with RGB-D cameras. In: 2017 IEEE/RSJ international conference on intelligent robots and systems (IROS). IEEE, pp 598–605
74. Madsen K, Nielsen HB, Tingleff O (2004) Methods for non-linear least squares problems, 2nd edn, p 60
75. McCormac J, Handa A, Davison A, Leutenegger S (2017) SemanticFusion: dense 3D semantic mapping with convolutional neural networks. In: 2017 IEEE international conference on robotics and automation (ICRA). IEEE, pp 4628–4635
76. Meilland M, Comport AI (2013) On unifying key-frame and voxel-based dense visual SLAM at large scales. In: 2013 IEEE/RSJ international conference on intelligent robots and systems. IEEE, pp 3677–3683
77. Meilland M, Comport AI (2003) Super-Resolution 3D tracking and mapping. In: 2013 IEEE international conference on robotics and automation. IEEE, pp 5717–5723
78. Mur-Artal R, Montiel JMM, Tardós JD (2015) ORB-SLAM: a versatile and accurate monocular SLAM system. IEEE Trans Robot 31(5):1147–1163
79. Mur-Artal R, Tardós JD (2017) ORB-SLAM2: an open-source SLAM system for monocular, stereo, and RGB-D cameras. IEEE Trans Robot 33(5):1255–1262
80. Newcombe RA, Fox D, Seitz SM (2015) DynamicFusion: reconstruction and tracking of non-rigid scenes in real-time. In: Proceedings of the IEEE conference on computer vision and pattern recognition, pp 343–352
81. Newcombe RA, Izadi S, Hilliges O, Molyneaux D, Kim D, Davison AJ, Kohi P, Shotton J, Hodges S, Fitzgibbon A (2011) KinectFusion: real-time dense surface mapping and tracking. In: 2011 10th IEEE international symposium on mixed and augmented reality (ISMAR). IEEE, pp 127–136
82. Pham TT, Reid I, Latif Y, Gould S (2015) Hierarchical higher-order regression forest fields: an application to 3D indoor scene labelling. In: Proceedings of the IEEE international conference on computer vision, pp 2246–2254
83. Pire T, Fischer T, Castro G, De Cristóforis P, Civera J, Berlles JJ (2017) S-PTAM: stereo parallel tracking and mapping. Robot Auton Syst 93:27–42

84. Platinsky L, Davison AJ, Leutenegger S (2017) Monocular visual odometry: sparse joint optimisation or dense alternation? In: 2017 IEEE international conference on robotics and automation (ICRA). IEEE, pp 5126–5133
85. Proença PF, Gao Y (2018) Probabilistic RGB-D odometry based on points, lines and planes under depth uncertainty. Robot Auton Syst 104:25–39
86. Raposo C, Lourenço M, Antunes M, Barreto JP (2013) Plane-based odometry using an RGB-D camera. In: British machine vision conference (BMVC)
87. Rosen DM, Carlone L, Bandeira AS, Leonard JJ (2019) SE-Sync: a certifiably correct algorithm for synchronization over the special euclidean group. I J Robot Res 38(2–3)
88. Rosten E, Drummond T (2006) Machine learning for high-speed corner detection. In: European conference on computer vision. Springer, pp 430–443
89. Rublee E, Rabaud V, Konolige K, Bradski G (2011) ORB: an efficient alternative to SIFT or SURF. In: Proceedings of the IEEE international conference on computer vision, pp 2564–2571
90. Rünz M, Buffier M, Agapito L (2018) MaskFusion: real-time recognition, tracking and reconstruction of multiple moving objects. In: 2018 IEEE international symposium on mixed and augmented reality (ISMAR). IEEE, pp 10–20
91. Salas-Moreno RF, Glocker B, Kelly PHJ, Davison AJ (2014) Dense planar SLAM. In: IEEE international symposium on mixed and augmented reality, ISMAR, pp 157–164
92. Salas-Moreno RF, Newcombe RA, Strasdat H, Kelly PH, Davison AJ (2013) SLAM++: simultaneous localisation and mapping at the level of objects. In: Proceedings of the IEEE conference on computer vision and pattern recognition, pp 1352–1359
93. Schenk F, Fraundorfer F (2017) Combining edge images and depth maps for robust visual odometry. In: British machine vision conference
94. Schops T, Sattler T, Pollefeys M (2019) BAD SLAM: bundle adjusted direct RGB-D SLAM. In: Proceedings of the IEEE conference on computer vision and pattern recognition, pp 134–144
95. Scona R, Jaimez M, Petillot YR, Fallon M, Cremers D (2018) StaticFusion: background reconstruction for dense RGB-D SLAM in dynamic environments. In: 2018 IEEE international conference on robotics and automation (ICRA). IEEE, pp 1–9
96. Scona R, Nobili S, Petillot YR, Fallon M (2017) Direct visual SLAM fusing proprioception for a humanoid robot. In: 2017 IEEE/RSJ international conference on intelligent robots and systems (IROS). IEEE, pp 1419–1426
97. Shi J, Tomasi C (1994) Good features to track. In: 1994 proceedings of IEEE conference on computer vision and pattern recognition, pp 593–600
98. Shi Y, Xu K, Niessner M, Rusinkiewicz S, Funkhouser T (2018) PlaneMatch: patch coplanarity prediction for robust RGB-D reconstruction. arXiv:1803.08407
99. Shotton J, Glocker B, Zach C, Izadi S, Criminisi A, Fitzgibbon A (2013) Scene coordinate regression forests for camera relocalization in RGB-D images. In: Proceedings of the IEEE conference on computer vision and pattern recognition, pp 2930–2937
100. Sivic J, Zisserman A (2003) Video google: a text retrieval approach to object matching in videos. In: Proceedings of the ninth IEEE international conference on computer vision. IEEE, p 1470
101. Solà J, Deray J, Atchuthan D (2018) A micro lie theory for state estimation in robotics. arXiv:1812.01537
102. Steinbrucker F, Kerl C, Cremers D, Sturm J (2013) Large-Scale multi-resolution surface reconstruction from RGB-D sequences. In: 2013 IEEE international conference on computer vision, pp 3264–3271
103. Steinbrücker F, Sturm J, Cremers D (2011) Real-time visual odometry from dense RGB-D images. In: 2011 IEEE international conference on computer vision workshops (ICCV Workshops). IEEE, pp 719–722
104. Strasdat H (2012) Local accuracy and global consistency for efficient visual SLAM. PhD thesis, Department of Computing, Imperial College London

105. Strasdat H, Montiel J, Davison AJ (2010) Scale drift-aware large scale monocular SLAM. Robot Sci Syst VI 2(3):7
106. Stückler J, Waldvogel B, Schulz H, Behnke S (2015) Dense real-time mapping of object-class semantics from RGB-D video. J Real-Time Image Process 10(4):599–609
107. Sturm J, Engelhard N, Endres F, Burgard W, Cremers D (2012) A Benchmark for the evaluation of RGB-D SLAM systems. In: Proceedings of the international conference on intelligent robot systems (IROS)
108. Sünderhauf N, Pham TT, Latif Y, Milford M, Reid I (2017) Meaningful maps with object-oriented semantic mapping. In: 2017 IEEE/RSJ international conference on intelligent robots and systems (IROS). IEEE, pp 5079–5085
109. Taguchi Y, Jian Y, Ramalingam S, Feng C (2013) Point-Plane SLAM for hand-held 3D sensors. In: 2013 IEEE international conference on robotics and automation, pp 5182–5189
110. Tateno K, Tombari F, Laina I, Navab N (2017) CNN-SLAM: real-time dense monocular SLAM with learned depth prediction. In: IEEE computer society conference on computer vision and pattern recognition (CVPR)
111. Tateno K, Tombari F, Navab N (2015) Real-time and scalable incremental segmentation on dense SLAM. In: 2015 IEEE/RSJ international conference on intelligent robots and systems (IROS). IEEE, pp 4465–4472
112. Triggs B, McLauchlan PF, Hartley RI, Fitzgibbon AW (1999) Bundle adjustment—a modern synthesis. In: International workshop on vision algorithms. Springer, pp 298–372
113. Valentin J, Nießner M, Shotton J, Fitzgibbon A, Izadi S, Torr PH (2015) Exploiting uncertainty in regression forests for accurate camera relocalization. In: Proceedings of the IEEE conference on computer vision and pattern recognition, pp 4400–4408
114. Wang X, Dong W, Zhou M, Li R, Zha H (2016) Edge enhanced direct visual odometry. In: Proceedings of the british machine vision conference (BMVC), pp 35.1–35.11
115. Wang Y, Zhang Q, Zhou Y (2014) RGB-D mapping for indoor environment. In: 2014 9th IEEE conference on industrial electronics and applications, pp 1888–1892
116. Whelan T, Johannsson H, Kaess M, Leonard JJ, McDonald J (2013) Robust real-time visual odometry for dense RGB-D mapping. In: 2013 IEEE international conference on robotics and automation (ICRA). IEEE, pp 5724–5731
117. Whelan T, Kaess M, Johannsson H, Fallon M, Leonard JJ, McDonald J (2015) Real-Time large-scale dense RGB-D SLAM with volumetric fusion. Int J Robot Res 34(4–5):598–626
118. Whelan T, Leutenegger S, Salas-Moreno RF, Glocker B, Davison AJ (2015) ElasticFusion: dense SLAM without a pose graph. In: Robotics: science and systems (RSS)
119. Whelan T, Salas-Moreno RF, Glocker B, Davison AJ, Leutenegger S (2016) ElasticFusion: real-time dense SLAM and light source estimation. Int J Robot Res 35(14):1697–1716
120. Yokozuka M, Oishi S, Thompson S, Banno A (2019) VITAMIN-E: visual tracking and MappINg with extremely dense feature points. In: Proceedings of the IEEE conference on computer vision and pattern recognition, pp 9641–9650
121. Zhang Z (1997) Parameter estimation techniques: a tutorial with application to conic fitting. Image Vis Comput 15:59–76
122. Zhou H, Ummenhofer B, Brox T (2018) DeepTAM: deep tracking and mapping. In: Proceedings of the European conference on computer vision (ECCV), pp 822–838
123. Zhou QY, Koltun V (2014) Color map optimization for 3D reconstruction with consumer depth cameras. ACM Trans Graph (TOG) 33(4):155
124. Zhou Y, Li H, Kneip L (2019) Canny-VO: visual odometry with RGB-D cameras based on geometric 3-D-2-D edge alignment. IEEE Trans Robot 35(1):184–199
125. Zollhöfer M, Stotko P, Görlitz A, Theobalt C, Nießner M, Klein R, Kolb A (2018) State of the art on 3D reconstruction with RGB-D cameras. In: Computer graphics forum, vol 37. Wiley Online Library, pp 625–652
126. Zubizarreta J, Aguinaga I, Montiel J (2019) Direct sparse mapping. arXiv:1904.06577

Chapter 7
Enhancing 3D Capture with Multiple Depth Camera Systems: A State-of-the-Art Report

Oscar Meruvia-Pastor

Abstract Over the past decade, depth-sensing cameras rapidly found their way into consumer products and became a staple in computer vision, robotics, and 3D reconstruction systems. Under some circumstances, the use of multiple depth sensors brings unique advantages in facilitating model acquisition, such as capture from complementary points of view and higher sampling density, with the potential to reduce the effects of sensor noise. Typically, multiple camera systems allow users to obtain visual information that might be unavailable from a particular point of view in a single-camera setup. As a result of this characteristic, the use of multiple depth cameras has great potential for a number of applications. However, there are some challenges that arise when implementing multi-depth camera systems, including calibration, synchronization and registration. In this chapter, we survey how some of these challenges have been addressed and present the most comprehensive review to date of the techniques used to implement multiple depth-sensing camera systems. In addition, we present a wide array of applications supported by multiple depth camera systems (MDCs).

7.1 Introduction

The concept that multiple cameras should facilitate capture of the 3D environment is an intuitive one. After all, we avail of a visual system that relies on a dual-camera setup (our eyes) to help us collect essential information about our physical environment and support both 2D and 3D vision through mono- and stereoscopy. While the concept of using multiple depth-sensing cameras for filming or other applications is relatively new, the idea of using multiple cameras for capturing scenes from different viewpoints and combining the resulting images has been used widely in the film industry almost

O. Meruvia-Pastor (✉)
Department of Computer Science, Memorial University of Newfoundland, St. John's,
NL A1B 3X7, Canada
e-mail: oscar@mun.ca

© Springer Nature Switzerland AG 2019   145
P. L. Rosin et al. (eds.), *RGB-D Image Analysis and Processing*,
Advances in Computer Vision and Pattern Recognition,
https://doi.org/10.1007/978-3-030-28603-3_7

from the birth of motion pictures [78, 91, 105] and explored in computer graphics research for more than 25 years [13, 18, 33, 36, 54, 84, 90, 99, 103, 106].

In a way, most commercial RGB-D sensors are already multi-camera systems, as they are based on an internal configuration that consists of arrays of dual, usually infrared (IR) cameras, and a third, higher resolution RGB camera for color capture. Alternatively, some depth-sensing cameras such as the ZED [80, 95], obtain high-resolution RGB-D images in real-time using a pair of color cameras to obtain depth from regular stereoscopy (see Chap. 1 for more detailed overview of commodity depth capture devices). In this chapter, we explore how multiple RGB-D sensors are used to improve 3D capture. The assumption is that having more cameras will increase our capacity to provide a more complete picture of the environment [46]. Consumer-level depth-sensing cameras have been in the market for about a decade. With the introduction of the Kinect in 2010, Microsoft sparked an explosion of research involving RGB-D cameras. Intel was also an early promoter of the research and adoption of depth-sensing cameras, in particular portable ones. Its earlier portable depth-sensing cameras were the 2013 Creative Senz series [22], quickly followed by its RealSense series in 2016. Apart from the standalone cameras, other versions of these cameras have been integrated in laptops, tablets and mobile phones, and come with SDKs suitable for development by researchers and the general public [48].

Since having multiple cameras goes beyond the safety and commodity of a single, fully integrated depth sensor, new challenges, and opportunities arise that are not present in a single device setup, as illustrated in the video sequences published by Kreylos since 2010 [65]. For instance, the question comes up about whether a system must have the same type of camera or a variety of cameras and devices [19, 89, 104]. While the later would be a more flexible approach, it would be out of the scope of this chapter, as we focus on systems that rely on the use of a homogeneous set of cameras, which includes the vast majority of solutions involving multiple depth sensors. A typical MDCs configuration is shown in Fig. 7.1, but we will illustrate other configurations later in this chapter. Another issue is how to map the images captured

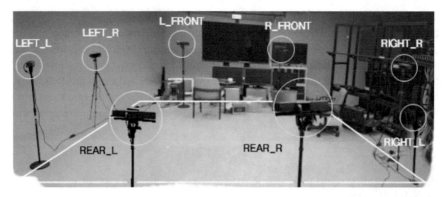

Fig. 7.1 A typical configuration of MDCs. This is a setup suitable for motion capture. Image reproduced with permission from [59]

(a)

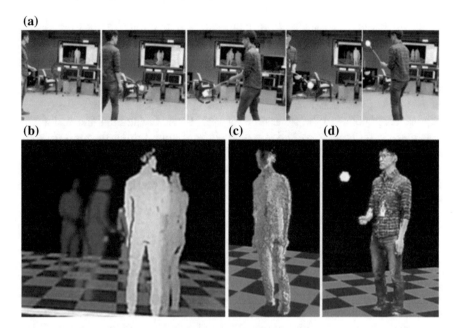

Fig. 7.2 3D capture process: **a** acquisition of input data points with a calibration tool, **b** depth images from different Kinect sensors, **c** unified point cloud after registration, and **d** unified point cloud with color mapping. Image reproduced with permission from [59]

from different cameras and combine them into a single scene. This encompasses the issues of calibration, synchronization and registration (see Fig. 7.2). Finally, an important question is which applications benefit the most from this type of systems. We will explore such applications later in this chapter.

Through the rest of this chapter we will use the term depth sensors and cameras interchangeably, and we will use the term MDCs (em-dee-cees), for Multiple Depth-sensing Camera systems, to describe system configurations that rely on multiple RGB-D cameras for visual capture. It is important to note that the literature sometimes refers to depth sensors as RGB-D cameras, and that, although most depth-sensing cameras capture RGB-D images, some depth sensors, such as the LeapMotion [67], do not capture RGB/color images along with the depth channel, as they rely purely on IR stereoscopy. However, for the sake of simplicity, we will use the terms depth sensors and RGB-D cameras interchangeably.

7.2 Implementation of MDCs

In most MDCs there are setup, calibration, and capture stages, with an optional segmentation/background removal stage and a registration, fusion, or merging stage, prior to some form of post- processing. The registration/fusion stage might happen online (in real-time, as the images are being recorded) or offline (as a post-processing stage), depending on whether or not the system supports real-time interactions. In terms of calibration, systems aim at reducing the calibration overhead and minimizing the amount of human intervention or expertise required to setup a system. Capture refers to the moment of recording, is normally straightforward, although in some cases, researchers place an emphasis in synchronization, to make sure all capture corresponds to the same time interval. Image registration and fusion will take place in different ways and it is here where solutions differ the most. In some cases, researchers also focus on aspects of post-processing, mainly considering issues of cleaning and analyzing the data, such as segmentation of foreground from background, identification of objects and/or individuals, and cognitive interpretation of the scene or events.

7.2.1 Setup and Calibration

In many cases, a multi-depth camera system requires a calibration step, which mainly consists in establishing a common frame of reference for all cameras recording the scene (see Fig. 7.2). This common frame of reference will be used to facilitate registration or fusion of the 3D scene. Depending on the application, other forms of integration, such as color matching [73, 114] and temporal synchronization or skeleton fusion (Fig. 7.3) might also be necessary.

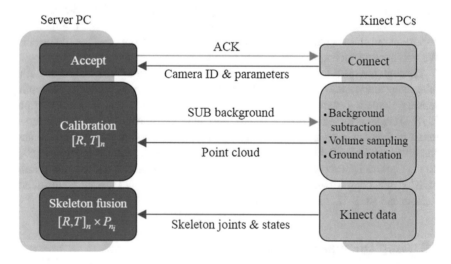

Fig. 7.3 A typical pipeline for MDCs, this client–server model illustrates initialization (connect), calibration, segmentation (background subtraction), registration (ground rotation), and postprocessing (skeleton fusion of joints and states). Image reproduced with permission from [59]

With regards to temporal synchronization, and especially for offline methods and methods utilizing one computer per sensor, it is essential that all cameras are synchronized at the beginning of the recording, because registration methods work under the assumption that the scenes to be registered are temporarily synchronized. Synchronization can be supported with dedicated hardware, for example, by having a hardware-controlled trigger that starts recording or capture for all cameras at the same time [44], or it can also be implemented with a client–server architecture where one server sends a synchronizing signal to all clients [63]. In some cases where recordings are not synchronized, it is possible to attempt to synchronize the inputs by software a posteriori (i.e., after the recording session) [1].

Success in providing an easy way to calibrate sensors is essential for adoption of the system. The most typical forms of calibration requires a user or a technician to calibrate the system. In most cases, the calibration task is supported by the use of a suitable prop or reference object used to create a common frame of reference for all cameras that can see the object within its field of view [97]. One of the most commonly used props for calibration is a calibration board imprinted with a chessboard pattern, which is commonly used for stereoscopic RGB camera setups, but cubes with identifiable patterns, and LED or Laser markers put on customized objects, are sometimes preferred, as they provide cues for all four RGB-D channels and are thus more suitable for RGB-D cameras [3, 66, 97]. Palasek et al. proposed a flexible calibration for a setup with three Kinects and a double-sided chessboard [82]. Classical chessboard patterns may not be viable when using pure IR depth cameras (which have no RGB channel), as the texture would vanish. In many cases, an initial calibration step can be performed once, allowing for continuous use of the system, provided the cameras are maintained in a fixed location. The time spent on calibrating a system can vary from little less than 5 min up to 45 min or more, depending on the complexity of the installation, the number of cameras, and the degree of knowledge required from a technician or user to setup a fully calibrated system. Thus, it is preferable to have a system that could either (a) perform automatic 3D calibration of a scene [100] or (b) forgo calibration as part of a model fusion or global registration process [53]. To make the MDC system user-friendly and accessible to a wider segment of the population, calibration should be done without requiring user expertise or hard-to-replicate calibration props. Another option is to perform self-calibration using a combination of projectors and depth sensors [53]. Finally, there are approaches such as [63, 71, 83, 112] that allow cameras to be moved around in the recording environment during the capture. These approaches usually implement algorithms to achieve registration of the scene on the fly (in real-time).

7.2.2 Sensor Interference

Most depth sensors were originally designed to be used as a single device to capture a portion of the environment. First-generation Kinects (V1) emitted structured infrared light into a scene and figured out depth from the patterns reflected from the infrared light. The p   lem of sensor interference appeared when multiple sensors covered overlapping   ions of the target subject. To deal with the interference problem, researchers hav roposed a variety of software- [87, 110] and hardware-based solutions, including   apting the sensors with vibrational components [14], modifying them for sele e scheduling of the IR projector subsystem [32], and time multiplexing [12, 87 While this issue was mostly present with the first generation of Kinects, sensor ir ference is not considered a major problem in the literature today, as most syster an simply cope with the level of occasional interference that is present in the curr sensors. Newer depth sensors such as the Kinect V2 (a.k.a. Kinect for Xbox One perate under a different principle (Time of flight, or TOF) to resolve the depth ima and interference can be solved by changing the signal shape [85], or by performir multi-view image fusion [60]. Furthermore, Intel reports that their MDCs suffer f n very little cross-talk when the sensors overlap in field of view [44], whereas s or interference is not an issue as more than 100 cameras are facing each other in crosoft's Mixed Reality capture system [20] (this system is discussed in more de l in Sect. 7.2.5). It is worth noting that depth sensors that use exclusively stereo R cameras inherently remove the need for using infrared light to resolve the depth formation and are thus free from multi-sensor interference [95]. Finally, a detail overview on the combination of multiple TOF depth sensors and color cameras is esented in [46].

7.2.3   Camera Registration and Model Fusion

When setting up an l C, the precise position and orientation of the depth cameras with respect to each her in the scene is usually unknown. As a result, the most significant challenge hen using multiple depth sensors is to find a set of affine transformations that 1 be used to combine the 3D samples captured from multiple viewpoints into a sin 3D scene. This is known as the registration problem. Morell-Gimenez et al. descr d the state of the art in 3D rigid registration methods up to 2014 [77], and Tam   al. surveyed 3D rigid and non rigid registration of multiple 3D datasets up to 20'   [98]. In general, most registration methods first approximate a coarse transformat using a subset of the available data points, and then refine it to find a more pre   e match of the scenes using the whole set of available data points or a significa larger dataset than what is used for coarse approximation. As noted in [77], a l e number of methods, such as [2, 51, 64, 94], use variations of RANSAC [34] fc oarse registration and Iterative Closest Point (ICP)[13, 18] for fine registration, ereas others use feature matching, image warping, or smooth fields of rigid transfo ations [25]. Other approaches use particle filtering and model-based approaches [l , 113]. After registration, the individual 3D meshes can be seamed together by u g a so-called "zippering" approach [2], or skeleton averaging [108]. Another popr approach in terms of image registration is the depth map fusion approach, whi was initially meant for scanning subjects with a single Kinect [79], but can also be d when using multiple Kinects [81].

7.2.4   Post-processing of MDCs' Resulting Data

The result of RGB-D recordings lends itself to further post-processing, benchmarking, and analysis. Several RGB-D datasets to evaluate model registration or depth map fusion approaches are publically available [4, 10, 15, 92]. For instance, Singh et al. [92] presented a system for quick generation of RGB-D images for a large-scale database of objects suitable for benchmarking, in a setup that would be a precursor to current volumetric capture systems (see Fig. 7.4). Many of these datasets were described in detail by Berger in 2014 [10], while an extensive list of RGB-D Datasets was summarized in 2017 by Cai et al. [15].

At some point in the data capture process, it is likely that some segmentation will be required. In many cases, the subjects of interest are the persons in the scene, or the objects in the foreground. They can be segmented out of each scene prior to attempting model fusion. Once the persons in a scene have been extracted from the background, a further post-processing task would be subject identification and pose estimation [8, 37]. Segmentation can also be of foreground from background objects in the scene, or it can be segmentation of static versus dynamic elements. Another typical element of post-processing is the classification of objects of interest in the scene, such as walls, furniture, and other obstacles. This is particularly relevant for robot vision [4].

Apart from static object analysis and classification, activity analysis using MDCs has also been proposed. For example, in the medical field, multiple efforts have been made to automatically classify the activity of patients to facilitate remote patient assessment and monitoring [23, 42], while in the area of smart systems, MDCs have been proposed to extract contextual information by combining several Kinect depth cameras, applying neural network algorithms to support context-aware interaction techniques, which allow users to share content and collaborate [109].

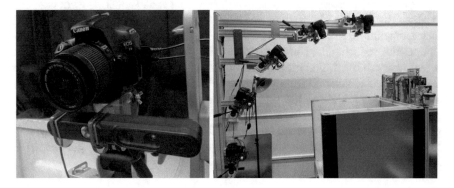

Fig. 7.4   Singh et al. presented a system for fast generation of RGB-D datasets. On the left: A Prime Sense Carmine depth sensor mounted together with a Canon T3 using RGBD Toolkit's mount. On the right: a side view of all Carmines mounted with their respective Canon T3s, pointed at a photo bench. (Image reproduced with permission from [92])

7.2.5 Volumetric Capture

Volumetric capture is a term that describes systems that cover the whole process of 3D capture with MDCs, with the result of producing a 3D reconstruction of a static scene or an animated sequence (sometimes referred to as a 4D movie, Free-Viewpoint Video, or 4D film). One of the first articles using the term volumetric 3D capture is the article by Maimone et al. [73], where five Kinects are used to capture an indoor scene in the context of a telepresence application. Today's volumetric capture studios are commercial enterprises that derive from the research on MDCs from the past fifteen years. In 2018, Intel introduced two major volumetric capture and filmmaking projects. First, a large-scale studio to support VR and AR video productions, using a very large array with hundreds of cameras, over a 10,000 sq. ft. (or 926 m^2) area [49], and supported by a massive neuromorphic computing microprocessor architecture [30]. Since such a large setup involves extremely high computational demands and overall costs, Intel's second initiative for independent filmmakers was a live studio proposition using four Intel RealSense cameras for volumetric capture in a regular room [50]. Intel has gone to great lengths to document how to setup and use its RealSense D400 series cameras for this second type of MDC [44].

Almost concurrently, Microsoft launched an intermediate-size competing studio solution supported by a large array of about a hundred cameras called Mixed Reality Capture Studios. The 3D objects captured in this platform (referred to as "holograms") can be used in combination with the HoloLens Mixed Reality system, which supports multiple users collaborating on the same VR environment [75, 76]. As opposed to having an array of RGB-D sensors, Microsoft's volumetric capture system relies on multiple RGB and IR cameras in combination with unstructured static IR laser light sources illuminating the capture volume, essentially breaking up an array of RGB-D cameras into its individual components (see Fig. 7.8). The Mixed Reality Capture studios are an implementation of a complete end-to-end solution for the capture of 4D video, based on the work by Collet et al. [20]. This work has been expanded by Dou et al. in an approach called "Motion2Fusion" to obtain a high speed fusion pipeline with a more robust response to changes in topology and more realistic results, reducing the Uncanny Valley effect from previous versions [27]. Other recent research on volumetric capture include the work of Satnik et al. [86], who used 3 inward looking Kinects V2 connected to a single PC to achieve volumetric reconstruction providing a low-cost hardware solution, while a portable volumetric capture system was presented in 2018 by Sterzentsenko et al. [96]. Their system relies on a group of four inward looking Intel RealSense D415 sensors mounted on tripods to capture a 360° view of their subjects for a low-cost and flexible MDC system.

7.3 Applications of MDCs

MDCs have been used to support a wide array of visual capture tasks. As can be appreciated from the literature below, the boundaries between one area of application and another are not well defined, as the sensors can be used to support more than one functional objective simultaneously. In fact, at the time of introduction in 2010, Microsoft's Kinect was promoted as a device that could be used both for gameplay and to operate the gaming console itself, potentially eliminating the need for hand-held controllers in gaming environments. In hindsight, this turned out not to be the case, but the devices still spurred significant advances in visual computing. Microsoft popularized the use of RGB-D sensors with the introduction of the Kinect Version 1. In 2013, a refined sensor called Kinect Version 2 was introduced, providing higher resolution, a wider field of view, and reduction in the interference effects when using multiple sensors. Microsoft stopped the distribution of Kinects after they eliminated it from the Xbox gaming platform in 2015, and completely discontinued the Kinect product line in 2017, integrating sophisticated depth-sensing capabilities in their HoloLens Head Mounted Displays (HMD's) and in their Mixer Reality Capture systems. Despite Microsoft's partial withdrawal from the market of commodity-grade depth sensors, Intel and other hardware manufacturers provide a wide range of alternatives to the original Kinects and continue to support the development of RGB-D sensors, which are now embedded in laptops, tablets and mobile phones. In the following sections, we will survey some of the most common applications of MDCs, going from 3D scanning of static models with fixed geometry, to capturing subjects with changeable geometry, but with fixed topology, all the way through capture of complex and dynamic scenes with changing geometry and topology that allow for real-time interaction.

7.3.1 Scene Reconstruction

A typical application of MDCs is to use them for scene reconstruction [1, 11]. In fact, one of the most well-publicized applications of the original Kinect is 3D model reconstruction of static subjects or rigid objects using KinectFusion [79]. Fundamental techniques for scene reconstruction from RGB-D images are presented in Chap. 5. Here, we focus on using MDCs for scene reconstruction. A key aspect of scene reconstruction lies on the arrangement of cameras, which can be divided in five common setups and is highly dependent on the goal of the application [9], as shown in Fig. 7.5. For instance, both [93] and [83] use two Kinects in a variety of arrangements to extend the field of view of the cameras. Later, Li et al. [68] use an outward-looking array of six sensors to create a 360° panoramic RGB-D scene, whereas Kainz et al. introduced the Omnikinect, an inward looking arrangement of eight fixed plus one movable Kinects suitable for motion capturing and reconstruction [56]. A system with similar functionality, but available as a general purpose 3D

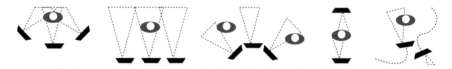

Fig. 7.5 Five typical capturing setups featuring MDCs. Multiple depth cameras are evenly placed in a virtual circle around the scene center (first on the left), multiple cameras are in line to capture a volume with a large side length (second), multiple cameras juxtaposed and facing away from each other, creating a panoramic view (third), and two cameras face each other, but are occluded by the scene content (fourth). Multiple uncalibrated moving cameras (fifth), with or without partial scene overlap in their viewing regions (Image reproduced with permission from [9])

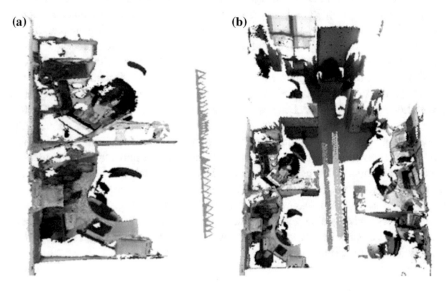

Fig. 7.6 Comparison of single-camera SLAM result and three-camera SLAM result. **a** is a single-camera SLAM result, the movement trajectory is in orange. **b** is a three-camera SLAM result with the same movement trajectory as **a**, different colors mean different camera trajectories. (Image reproduced with permission from [74])

scanning open source library for sets of second generation Kinects connected to individual PCs to support multiple cameras and stream synchronization is presented in [63]. Finally, one of the outstanding applications of MDCs is when they are used for simultaneous localization and mapping (SLAM) [11, 102, 104, 111], as shown in Fig. 7.6. Although not focused on MDCs, but in online 3D reconstruction using RGB-D sensors, a 2018 state of the art report [115] covers thoroughly the area of 3D reconstruction, whereas a 2017 comprehensive survey on the spatial arrangement of cameras in MDCs is presented by Wang et al. [103].

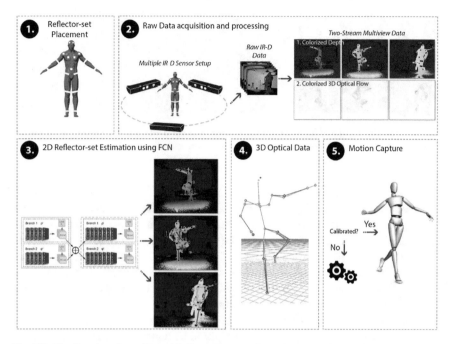

Fig. 7.7 Pipeline overview of DeepMoCap, a Retro-reflector based Motion Capture MDC system which uses a Fully Convolutional Network to learn reflector locations and their temporal dependency among sequential frames. Image reproduced without changes from [17], used under the Creative Commons Attribution License (CC BY 4.0) [21]

7.3.2 Gesture Capture and 3D Scanning of Individuals

One of the original applications of Microsoft's Kinect was to capture live action during gameplay with the goal of interpreting body motions and postures as commands to the gaming console. This was quickly extended to other contexts and sparked a large amount of research in gesture capture and interpretation, as well as 3D scanning of people. For instance, Rafighi et al. [83] introduced a dual-camera system to extend the field of view of the playing area so more people can play together while reducing the risk of inter-player collisions. While MDCs can be used for scanning individuals just as any other object, some MDCs have been proposed with the express intent to produce 3D scans of people to generate models or avatars that can be later used in games, fashion, or other applications. Such applications need to account for the variety of poses the human body can achieve [26, 57, 70, 101] and attempt to complete the missing parts of the body that might become evident as new angles and poses are tried by the subjects. For instance, the work of Wilson et al. [107] describes a system to capture moving subjects from multiple angles that aims at creating a complete coverage of the interaction from different points of view. Kilner et al. [57] proposed a system for scanning human subjects using eight Kinects placed within a

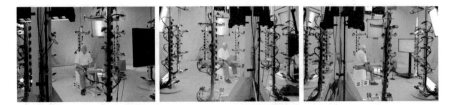

Fig. 7.8 Microsoft's Mixed Reality Capture studio in Redmond featuring the making of "Hold The World" with David Attenborough. Image used with permission from Factory 42 and Sky [31]

fixed frame surrounding a user, whereas [101] presented a system suitable for full body scanning at home using three Kinects. Dou et al. [28] proposed another system with eight Kinect sensors to capture a scan of a moving individual with the purpose of achieving a complete 3D reconstruction by integrating the missing elements of several scans over time, whereas Lin et al. [70] uses a system with 16 cameras to do a relatively fast scan of an individual within three seconds. Estimation of whole body poses in dynamic scenes using MDCs with and without markers is still an active area of research [17, 26, 45, 108]. For instance, Desai et al. use multiple scanners of freely moving subjects to perform a full body skeletal reconstruction [26], whereas Wu et al. present a system to track multiple individuals occluding each other or being occluded by other objects by averaging joint positions from complementary viewpoints [108].

7.3.3 Performance and Motion Capture for Entertainment and Health

Another application area of MDCs is as a motion capture (MoCap) platform for cinematic, gaming, and studio recording contexts, as discussed in Sect. 7.2.5. Typical setups for MoCap are shown in Figs. 7.1 and 7.8. Although one of the main advantages of RGB-D sensors and MDCs is to support marker-less motion capture [12], some recent approaches propose the use of fully convolutional neural networks for motion capture using retro-reflectors to obtain more robust tracking results [17] (see Fig. 7.7).

Originally, Microsoft's Kinect was introduced as a gaming console accessory, and some of the its most successful titles were dancing games. Accordingly, MDCs have been used by researchers for dance capture and analysis [7, 35]. MDCs can also be used for performance enhancement. In 2013, Fuhrman proposed a system of three Kinects to map a performer's motion to music [35] (see Fig. 7.9). While fixed camera approaches are standard for performance capture [59], some approaches allow for freely moving cameras to be used to capture a scene or performance [71, 112].

Apart from applications in entertainment, motion capture MDCs have also been proposed for use in the health case sector to study human kinetics [5], for gait analysis

Fig. 7.9 Fuhrmann et al. introduced an MDC system for live sound transformation using three sensors, with two of them placed at 90° from each other to extend the working volume of the trackers. Image reproduced with permission from [35], production: The XXth Century Ensemble Vienna—Peter Burwik

[6, 55], dance analysis [61], crowd behavior analysis [88], patient monitoring [40, 41], and medical assessment [24, 38, 69].

7.3.4 Telepresence, Teleconferencing, Augmented and Mixed Reality

An exciting proposition for the use of MDCs is for application in teleconferencing systems, as an additional depth channel allows for a more realistic experience and free-viewpoint vision for remote conferencing [3, 58, 73]. In 2012, Maimone et al. [73] proposed the use of MDCs for a telepresence application, while Alexiadis et al. [3] proposed a system to reconstruct 3D models of moving users in a setup of four Kinect cameras connected to a single PC to facilitate multiparty 3D tele-immersion. Mixed reality applications combine elements from the synthetic, computer-mediated imagery, with the real world. RoomAlive [53] was one of the first systems that mixed a hybrid capture and projector system to display computer imagery on the interior of a room for entertainment purposes using multiple projector and depth sensor pairs. The automotive industry has become interested in the concept of developing virtual training facilities, so researchers have proposed the use of MDCs for Mixed Reality Virtual Workshops [39]. In 3D telepresence, the goal is to provide a user with a virtual reconstruction of a remote scene in real time. This can be done by placing the user in an immersive digital world using VR HMD's or Mixed Reality systems, such as the Magic Leap [72], the HTC Vive [47], and the HoloLens [75]. All these devices need depth-sensing capabilities to provide compelling Mixed Reality experiences. Mixed and Augmented Reality MDCs have evolved to the point that the HMD integrates the depth-sensing capability. By having multiple users wearing Mixed Reality headsets, we have an ecosystem of MDCs where each user is wearing an RGB-D sensor that allows them to have a partial reconstruction of their environment and a shared Mixed

Fig. 7.10 Dou et al. presented an MDC system for real-time performance capture that is robust to many complex topology changes and fast motions. Image reproduced with permission from [29]

Reality experience. Furthermore, one of the most notable applications of MDCs for telepresence is the use of the HoloLens in combination with multiple depth sensors towards the implementation of a telepresence system introduced as Holoportation. In the Holoportation setup, an array of custom depth cameras surrounds users, some of which are wearing the HoloLens [81], to provide scene reconstruction within a room, with registration implemented using the Levenberg–Marquardt algorithm (LM) and Preconditioned Conjugate Gradient (PCG) in a fusion approach [29]. In a similar way, Joachmiczak et al. proposed an approach to combine the HoloLens with commodity depth sensors (Kinects), putting an emphasis on supporting mixed reality telepresence [52]. More recently, MDCs have been proposed to support mixed reality telepresence through open source platforms [62, 63] and interactive 3D tele-immersion [26], where one user can have the feeling of being at a remote location either by the use of VR HMDs or the HoloLens [62, 81]. One of the most impressive MDCs to date is the system presented by Dou et al., where an array of RGB-D cameras used to capture challenging scenes for immersive telepresence in real time. This system allows to capture not only fast changes in the geometry of the scene, but is robust to changes in topology [29]. For instance, a user can take off a piece of clothing and the system will produce separate meshes accordingly (see Fig. 7.10). Another recent approach for teleconferencing based on the use of high-resolution ZED camera arrays is presented in [43], it has the advantage that it does not require the user to wear any form of HMD, but at the expense of losing the immersive experience provided by HMD's.

7.4 Summary

Over the past decade, MDCs have rapidly evolved in many different directions, whereas initial systems were focused on 3D reconstruction of static scenarios, more recent systems focus on SLAM [74, 115]. Systems have also evolved from the capture of individuals to capture of scenes with multiple actors or players [83]. Increased flexibility comes from the possibility of obtaining scans from participants who are free to move and have their whole body captured and synthesized in a single textured model [28]. Improvements in communication technology and increased network bandwidth availability have brought forward the possibility of using MDCs for immersive telepresence [81]. In terms of scale, the proposed number of cameras has varied wildly, with Intel's large Volumetric Capture studio [49] being an example of massive enterprises aimed at full 3D reconstruction of scenes using large arrays of cameras, but also reflecting the vast amount of resources required to setup and maintain such a large-scale system. Recent research on MDCs focuses on the possibility of creating systems that are open source and accessible to a wider audience [52].

While we have witnessed how MDCs have been successfully proposed for many applications, and provide indeed more completed descriptions of the scene, there will always be a trade-off between completeness of view and computational demands, perhaps best illustrated by Intel's small versus large volumetric studio setups. Researchers and developers should estimate the number of ideal cameras for the application at hand, considering the resources available. In most cases, the principle of "less is more" will tend to hold true. One key characteristic of future MDCs will necessarily involve flexibility, which can refer to a number of aspects. The first would be flexibility in the number of cameras that a system supports. The second would refer to the placement of the sensors in the capture environment (fixed versus moveable). The third refers to the variety of sensors the system supports. The last one, but not least important, refers to the possibility of having systems that evolve over time, allowing for changes in configuration and scale as time goes by.

Acknowledgements The author would like to thank the anonymous reviewers for their kind revisions to improve the manuscript, Dr. Lourdes Peña-Castillo (Computer Science, Memorial University of Newfoundland) for her thorough proof reading of the manuscript, and the many authors who approved of the use of their images, including Dr. Kai Berger (Magic Leap Inc.) for contributing Fig. 7.5 and for his insightful comments on the draft.

References

1. Ahmed N, Junejo I (2014) Using multiple RGB-D cameras for 3D video acquisition and spatio-temporally coherent 3D animation reconstruction. Int J Comput Theory Eng 6. https://doi.org/10.7763/IJCTE.2014.V6.907, http://www.ijcte.org/papers/907-AC0002.pdf
2. Alexiadis DS, Zarpalas D, Daras P (2013) Real-time, full 3-d reconstruction of moving foreground objects from multiple consumer depth cameras. IEEE Trans Multimed 15(2):339–358. https://doi.org/10.1109/TMM.2012.2229264
3. Alexiadis S, Kordelas G, Apostolakis KC, Agapito JD, Vegas J, Izquierdo E, Daras P (2012) Reconstruction for 3D immersive virtual environments. In: 2012 13th international workshop on image analysis for multimedia interactive services (WIAMIS), pp 1–4. IEEE. https://doi.org/10.1109/WIAMIS.2012.6226760
4. Anand A, Koppula HS, Joachims T, Saxena A (2013) Contextually guided semantic labeling and search for three-dimensional point clouds. Int J Robot Res 32(1):19–34. https://doi.org/10.1177/0278364912461538

5. Asteriadis S, Chatzitofis A, Zarpalas D, Alexiadis DS, Daras P (2013) Estimating human motion from multiple Kinect sensors. In: Proceedings of the 6th international conference on computer vision/computer graphics collaboration techniques and applications, MIRAGE '13, pp 3:1–3:6. ACM, New York, NY, USA. https://doi.org/10.1145/2466715.2466727
6. Auvinet E, Meunier J, Multon F (2012) Multiple depth cameras calibration and body volume reconstruction for gait analysis. In: 2012 11th international conference on information science, signal processing and their applications (ISSPA), pp 478–483. https://doi.org/10.1109/ISSPA. 2012.6310598
7. Baek S, Kim M (2015) Dance experience system using multiple Kinects. Int J Future Comput Commun 4(1):45–49. https://doi.org/10.7763/IJFCC.2015.V4.353, http://www.ijfcc.org/vol4/353-N039.pdf
8. Baek S, Kim M (2017) User pose estimation based on multiple depth sensors. In: SIGGRAPH Asia 2017 Posters, SA '17, pp. 1:1–1:2. ACM, New York, NY, USA. https://doi.org/10.1145/3145690.3145709
9. Berger K (2013) A state of the art report on research in multiple RGB-D sensor setups. arXiv:1310.2050
10. Berger K (2014) A state of the art report on multiple RGB-D sensor research and on publicly available RGB-D datasets, pp 27–44. https://doi.org/10.1007/978-3-319-08651-4_2
11. Berger K, Meister S, Nair R, Kondermann D (2013) A state of the art report on kinect sensor setups in computer vision, pp 257–272. Springer, Berlin. https://doi.org/10.1007/978-3-642-44964-2_12, http://www.grk1564.uni-siegen.de/sites/www.grk1564.uni-siegen.de/files/inm2013/kinect-star.pdf
12. Berger K, Ruhl K, Schroeder Y, Bruemmer C, Scholz A, Magnor M (2011) Markerless Motion Capture using multiple Color-Depth Sensors. In: Eisert P, Hornegger J, Polthier K (eds) Vision, Modeling, and Visualization. The Eurographics Association. https://doi.org/10.2312/PE/VMV/VMV11/317-324, https://graphics.tu-bs.de/upload/publications/multikinectsMocap.pdf
13. Besl PJ, McKay ND (1992) A method for registration of 3-d shapes. IEEE Trans Pattern Anal Mach Intell 14(2):239–256. https://doi.org/10.1109/34.12179110.1109/34.121791
14. Butler DA, Izadi S, Hilliges O, Molyneaux D, Hodges S, Kim D (2012) Shake'n'sense: reducing interference for overlapping structured light depth cameras. In: Proceedings of the SIGCHI conference on human factors in computing systems, CHI '12, pp 1933–1936. ACM, New York, NY, USA. https://doi.org/10.1145/2207676.2208335
15. Cai Z, Han J, Liu L, Shao L (2017) RGB-D datasets using Microsoft Kinect or similar sensors: a survey. Multimed Tools Appl 76(3):4313–4355. https://doi.org/10.1007/s11042-016-3374-6
16. Calderita L, Bandera J, Bustos P, Skiadopoulos A (2013) Model-based reinforcement of Kinect depth data for human motion capture applications. Sensors 13(7):8835–8855. https://doi.org/10.3390/s130708835
17. Chatzitofis A, Zarpalas D, Kollias S, Daras P (2019) DeepMoCap: Deep optical motion capture using multiple depth sensors and retro-reflectors. Sensors 19:282. https://doi.org/10.3390/s19020282
18. Chen Y, Medioni G (1991) Object modeling by registration of multiple range images. In: Proceedings. 1991 IEEE international conference on robotics and automation, vol 3, pp 2724–2729. https://doi.org/10.1109/ROBOT.1991.132043
19. Cippitelli E, Gasparrini S, Gambi E, Spinsante S, Wåhslény J, Orhany I, Lindhy T (2015) Time synchronization and data fusion for RGB-Depth cameras and inertial sensors in aal applications. In: 2015 IEEE international conference on communication workshop (ICCW), pp 265–270. https://doi.org/10.1109/ICCW.2015.7247189
20. Collet A, Chuang M, Sweeney P, Gillett D, Evseev D, Calabrese D, Hoppe H, Kirk A, Sullivan S (2015) High-quality streamable free-viewpoint video. ACM Trans Graph 34(4):69:1–69:13. https://doi.org/10.1145/2766945
21. Creative Commons: Creative commons attribution license (cc by 4.0). https://creativecommons.org/licenses/by/4.0/ (2019). Accessed: 2019-06-25

22. Creative, Corp.: Creative senz3d. https://us.creative.com/p/peripherals/blasterx-senz3d (2013). Accessed 14 June 2019
23. Crispim-Junior CF, Gomez Uria A, Strumia C, Koperski M, Koenig A, Negin F, Cosar S, Nghiem AT, Chau DP, Charpiat G, Bremond F (2017) Online recognition of daily activities by color-depth sensing and knowledge models. Sens J, MDPI 17(7):2118. https://www.ncbi.nlm.nih.gov/pubmed/28661440
24. Czarnuch S, Ploughman M (2014) Automated gait analysis in people with multiple sclerosis using two unreferenced depth imaging sensors: preliminary steps. In: NECEC 2014, newfoundland electrical and computer engineering conference. https://doi.org/10.13140/2.1.2187.6481
25. Deng T, Bazin JC, Martin T, Kuster C, Cai J, Popa T, Gross M (2014) Registration of multiple RGBD cameras via local rigid transformations. https://doi.org/10.1109/ICME.2014.6890122, http://www.cs.utah.edu/~martin/calibration.pdf
26. Desai K, Prabhakaran B, Raghuraman S (2018) Combining skeletal poses for 3D human model generation using multiple Kinects. In: Proceedings of the 9th ACM multimedia systems conference, MMSys '18. ACM, New York, NY, USA, pp 40–51. https://doi.org/10.1145/3204949.3204958
27. Dou M, Davidson P, Fanello SR, Khamis S, Kowdle A, Rhemann C, Tankovich V, Izadi S (2017) Motion2Fusion: real-time volumetric performance capture. ACM Trans Graph 36(6):246:1–246:16. https://doi.org/10.1145/3130800.3130801
28. Dou M, Fuchs H, Frahm J (2013) Scanning and tracking dynamic objects with commodity depth cameras. In: 2013 IEEE international symposium on mixed and augmented Reality (ISMAR), pp 99–106. https://doi.org/10.1109/ISMAR.2013.6671769
29. Dou M, Khamis S, Degtyarev Y, Davidson PL, Fanello SR, Kowdle A, Orts S, Rhemann C, Kim D, Taylor J, Kohli P, Tankovich V, Izadi S (2016) Fusion4d: real-time performance capture of challenging scenes. ACM Trans Graph 35:114:1–114:13. https://www.samehkhamis.com/dou-siggraph2016.pdf
30. Esser SK, Merolla PA, Arthur JV, Cassidy AS, Appuswamy R, Andreopoulos A, Berg DJ, McKinstry JL, Melano T, Barch DR, di Nolfo C, Datta P, Amir A, Taba B, Flickner MD, Modha DS (2016) Convolutional networks for fast, energy-efficient neuromorphic computing. Proc Natl Acad Sci. https://doi.org/10.1073/pnas.1604850113
31. Factory 42: "Hold the World" with David Attenborough (2019). https://www.factory42.uk/. Accessed 28 June 2019
32. Faion F, Friedberger S, Zea A, Hanebeck UD (2012) Intelligent sensor-scheduling for multi-kinect-tracking. In: 2012 IEEE/RSJ international conference on intelligent robots and systems, pp. 3993–3999. https://doi.org/10.1109/IROS.2012.6386007
33. Fehrman B, McGough J (2014) Depth mapping using a low-cost camera array. In: 2014 Southwest symposium on image analysis and interpretation, pp 101–104. https://doi.org/10.1109/SSIAI.2014.6806039
34. Fischler MA, Bolles RC (1981) Random sample consensus: a paradigm for model fitting with applications to image analysis and automated cartography. Commun ACM 24(6):381–395. https://doi.org/10.1145/358669.358692
35. Fuhrmann A, Kretz J, Burwik P (2013) Multi sensor tracking for live sound transformation. In: Proceedings of the international conference on new interfaces for musical expression, pp 358–362. Graduate School of Culture Technology, KAIST, Daejeon, Republic of Korea. http://nime.org/proceedings/2013/nime2013_44.pdf
36. Gavrila D, Davis LS (1996) 3-d model-based tracking of humans in action: a multi-view approach. In: CVPR. https://doi.org/10.1109/CVPR.1996.517056
37. Ge S, Fan G (2015) Articulated non-rigid point set registration for human pose estimation from 3D sensors. pp. 15,218–15,245. MDPI AG. https://doi.org/10.3390/s150715218
38. Geerse DJ, Coolen B, Roerdink M (2015) Kinematic validation of a multi-Kinect v2 in-strumented 10-meter walkway for quantitative gait assessments. PLoS One 10:e0139,913. https://doi.org/10.1371/journal.pone.0139913, https://www.ncbi.nlm.nih.gov/pmc/articles/PMC4603795/. Accessed 01 Feb 2019

39. Geiselhart F, Otto M, Rukzio E (2016) On the use of multi-depth-camera based motion tracking systems in production planning environments. Procedia CIRP 41:759–764. https://doi.org/10.1016/j.procir.2015.12.088, http://www.sciencedirect.com/science/article/pii/S2212827115011671. Research and Innovation in Manufacturing: Key Enabling Technologies for the Factories of the Future - Proceedings of the 48th CIRP Conference on Manufacturing Systems
40. Ghose A, Chakravarty K, Agrawal AK, Ahmed N (2013) Unobtrusive indoor surveillance of patients at home using multiple Kinect sensors. In: Proceedings of the 11th ACM conference on embedded networked sensor systems, SenSys '13. ACM, New York, NY, USA, pp 40:1–40:2. https://doi.org/10.1145/2517351.2517412
41. Ghose A, Sinha P, Bhaumik C, Sinha A, Agrawal A, Dutta Choudhury A (2013) Ubiheld: ubiquitous healthcare monitoring system for elderly and chronic patients. In: Proceedings of the 2013 ACM conference on pervasive and ubiquitous computing adjunct publication, UbiComp '13 Adjunct. ACM, New York, NY, USA, pp 1255–1264. https://doi.org/10.1145/2494091.2497331
42. Gonzalez-Ortega D, Diaz-Pernas F, Martinez-Zarzuela M, Anton-Rodriguez M (2014) A Kinect-based system for cognitive rehabilitation exercises monitoring. Comput Methods Prog Biomed 113(2):620–631. https://doi.org/10.1016/j.cmpb.2013.10.014, http://www.sciencedirect.com/science/article/pii/S0169260713003568
43. Gotsch D, Zhang X, Merritt T, Vertegaal R (2018) Telehuman2: a cylindrical light field teleconferencing system for life-size 3D human telepresence. In: Proceedings of the 2018 CHI conference on human factors in computing systems, CHI '18. ACM, New York, NY, USA, pp 522:1–522:10. https://doi.org/10.1145/3173574.3174096
44. Grunnet-Jepsen A, Winer P, Takagi A, Sweetser J, Zhao K, Khuong T, Nie D, Woodfill J (2019) Using the realsense d4xx depth sensors in multi-camera configurations. White Paper. https://www.intel.ca/content/www/ca/en/support/articles/000028140/emerging-technologies/intel-realsense-technology.html/. Accessed 01 July 2019
45. Hong S, Kim Y (2018) Dynamic pose estimation using multiple RGB-D cameras. Sensors 18(11). https://doi.org/10.3390/s18113865, http://www.mdpi.com/1424-8220/18/11/3865
46. Horaud R, Hansard M, Evangelidis G, Ménier C (2016) An overview of depth cameras and range scanners based on time-of-flight technologies. Mach Vis Appl 27(7):1005–1020. https://doi.org/10.1007/s00138-016-0784-4, https://hal.inria.fr/hal-01325045
47. HTC Corp.: HTC Vive Wireless Adapter (2019) https://www.vive.com/us/wireless-adapter//. Accessed 14 June 2019
48. Intel Corp.: Intel realsense (2017). https://realsense.intel.com/. Accessed 21 Jan 2019
49. Intel Corp.: Intel volumetric content studio large (2019) https://newsroom.intel.com/wp-content/uploads/sites/11/2018/01/intel-studios-fact-sheet.pdf. Accessed 21 Jan 2019
50. Intel Corp.: Intel volumetric content studio small (2019). https://realsense.intel.com/intel-realsense-volumetric-capture/ (2019). Accessed 21 Jan 2019
51. Izadi S, Kim D, Hilliges O, Molyneaux D, Newcombe R, Kohli P, Shotton J, Hodges S, Freeman D, Davison A, Fitzgibbon A (2011) KinectFusion: real-time 3D reconstruction and interaction using a moving depth camera. In: Proceedings of the 24th annual ACM symposium on user interface software and technology, UIST '11. ACM, New York, NY, USA, pp 559–568. https://doi.org/10.1145/2047196.2047270
52. Joachimczak M, Liu J, Ando H (2017) Real-time mixed-reality telepresence via 3D reconstruction with hololens and commodity depth sensors. In: Proceedings of the 19th ACM international conference on multimodal interaction, ICMI 2017. ACM, New York, NY, USA, pp 514–515. https://doi.org/10.1145/3136755.3143031
53. Jones B, Sodhi R, Murdock M, Mehra R, Benko H, Wilson A, Ofek E, MacIntyre B, Raghuvanshi N, Shapira L (2014) Roomalive: magical experiences enabled by scalable, adaptive projector-camera units. In: Proceedings of the 27th annual ACM symposium on user interface software and technology, UIST '14. ACM, New York, NY, USA, pp 637–644. https://doi.org/10.1145/2642918.2647383

54. Joo H, Simon T, Li X, Liu H, Tan L, Gui L, Banerjee S, Godisart T, Nabbe B, Matthews I, Kanade T, Nobuhara S, Sheikh Y (2017) Panoptic studio: a massively multiview system for social interaction capture. IEEE Trans Pattern Anal Mach Intell 41(1):190–204. https://doi.org/10.1109/TPAMI.2017.2782743
55. Kaenchan S, Mongkolnam P, Watanapa B, Sathienpong S (2013) Automatic multiple Kinect cameras setting for simple walking posture analysis. In: 2013 international computer science and engineering conference (ICSEC), pp 245–249. https://doi.org/10.1109/ICSEC.2013.6694787
56. Kainz B, Hauswiesner S, Reitmayr G, Steinberger M, Grasset R, Gruber L, Veas E, Kalkofen D, Seichter H, Schmalstieg D (2012) OmniKinect: real-time dense volumetric data acquisition and applications. In: Proceedings of the 18th ACM symposium on virtual reality software and technology, VRST '12. ACM, New York, NY, USA, pp 25–32. https://doi.org/10.1145/2407336.2407342
57. Kilner J, Neophytou A, Hilton A (2012) 3D scanning with multiple depth sensors. In: Proceedings of 3rd international conference on 3D body scanning technologies, pp 295–301 (2012). https://doi.org/10.15221/12.295
58. Kim K, Bolton J, Girouard A, Cooperstock J, Vertegaal R (2012) TeleHuman: Effects of 3D perspective on gaze and pose estimation with a life-size cylindrical telepresence pod. In: Proceedings of the SIGCHI conference on human factors in computing systems, CHI '12. ACM, New York, NY, USA, pp 2531–2540. https://doi.org/10.1145/2207676.2208640
59. Kim Y, Baek S, Bae BC (2017) Motion capture of the human body using multiple depth sensors. ETRI J 39(2):181–190. https://doi.org/10.4218/etrij.17.2816.0045
60. Kim YM, Theobalt C, Diebel J, Kosecka J, Miscusik B, Thrun S (2009) Multi-view image and tof sensor fusion for dense 3D reconstruction. In: 2009 IEEE 12th international conference on computer vision workshops, ICCV workshops, pp 1542–1549. https://doi.org/10.1109/ICCVW.2009.5457430
61. Kitsikidis A, Dimitropoulos K, Douka S, Grammalidis N (2014) Dance analysis using multiple Kinect sensors. In: 2014 international conference on computer vision theory and applications (VISAPP) vol 2, pp 789–795 (2014). https://ieeexplore.ieee.org/document/7295020
62. Kolkmeier J, Harmsen E, Giesselink S, Reidsma D, Theune M, Heylen D (2018) With a little help from a holographic friend: The OpenIMPRESS mixed reality telepresence toolkit for remote collaboration systems. In: Proceedings of the 24th ACM symposium on virtual reality software and technology, VRST '18. ACM, New York, NY, USA, pp 26:1–26:11. https://doi.org/10.1145/3281505.3281542
63. Kowalski M, Naruniec J, Daniluk M (2015) Livescan3d: a fast and inexpensive 3D data acquisition system for multiple Kinect v2 sensors. In: 2015 international conference on 3D vision, pp 318–325. https://doi.org/10.1109/3DV.2015.43
64. Kramer J, Burrus N, Echtler F, Daniel HC, Parker M (2012) Object modeling and detection. Apress, Berkeley, CA, pp 173–206. https://doi.org/10.1007/978-1-4302-3868-3_9
65. Kreylos O (2010) Movies - 2 Kinects 1 box (2010). http://idav.ucdavis.edu/~okreylos/ResDev/Kinect/Movies.html. Accessed 22 June 2019
66. Kurillo G, Bajcsy R (2008) Wide-area external multi-camera calibration using vision graphs and virtual calibration object. In: 2008 Second ACM/IEEE international conference on distributed smart cameras, pp 1–9 (2008). https://doi.org/10.1109/ICDSC.2008.4635695
67. Leap Motion Inc. (2019) Leap motion technology. https://www.leapmotion.com/technology/. Accessed 14 June 2019
68. Li H, Liu H, Cao N, Peng Y, Xie S, Luo J, Sun Y (2017) Real-time RGB-D image stitching using multiple Kinects for improved field of view. Int J Adv Robot Syst 14(2):1729881417695,560. https://doi.org/10.1177/1729881417695560
69. Li S, Pathirana PN, Caelli T (2014) Multi-kinect skeleton fusion for physical rehabilitation monitoring. In: 2014 36th Annual international conference of the IEEE engineering in medicine and biology society, pp 5060–5063. https://doi.org/10.1109/EMBC.2014.6944762
70. Lin S, Chen Y, Lai YK, Martin RR, Cheng ZQ (2016) Fast capture of textured full-body avatar with RGB-D cameras. Vis Comput 32(6):681–691. https://doi.org/10.1007/s00371-016-1245-9

71. Liu Y, Ye G, Wang Y, Dai Q, Theobalt C (2014) Human performance capture using multiple Handheld Kinects, pp. 91–108. Springer International Publishing, Cham. https://doi.org/10.1007/978-3-319-08651-4_5

72. Magic Leap Inc (2019) Introducing Spatiate to Magic Leap One. https://www.magicleap.com/news/product-updates/spatiate-on-magic-leap-one/, https://youtu.be/ePQ5w8oQxWM. Accessed 14 June 2019

73. Maimone A, Fuchs H (2012) Real-time volumetric 3D capture of room-sized scenes for telepresence. In: 2012 3DTV-conference: the true vision - capture, transmission and display of 3D video (3DTV-CON), pp 1–4. https://doi.org/10.1109/3DTV.2012.6365430

74. Meng X, Gao W, Hu Z (2018) Dense RGB-D SLAM with multiple cameras. Sensors 18(7) (2018). https://doi.org/10.3390/s18072118, https://www.mdpi.com/1424-8220/18/7/2118

75. Microsoft Corp (2019) Microsoft hololens - mixed reality technology for business. https://www.microsoft.com/en-us/hololens. Accessed 14 June 2019

76. Microsoft Corp (2019) Mixed reality capture studios. https://www.microsoft.com/en-us/mixed-reality/capture-studios. Accessed 27 June 2019

77. Morell-Gimenez V, Saval-Calvo M, Villena Martinez V, Azorin-Lopez J, Rodriguez J, Cazorla M, Orts S, Guilló A (2018) A survey of 3D rigid registration methods for RGB-D cameras, pp 74–98 (2018). https://www.researchgate.net/publication/325194952_A_survey_of_3d_rigid_registration_methods_for_RGB-D_cameras

78. Muybridge E, Wikipedia E (1878) Sallie gardner at a gallop. https://en.wikipedia.org/wiki/Sallie_Gardner_at_a_Gallop. Accessed 21 Jan 2019

79. Newcombe RA, Davison AJ, Izadi S, Kohli P, Hilliges O, Shotton J, Molyneaux D, Hodges S, Kim D, Fitzgibbon A (2011) KinectFusion: real-time dense surface mapping and tracking. In: 2011 10th IEEE international symposium on mixed and augmented reality (ISMAR). IEEE, pp 127–136. https://doi.org/10.1109/ISMAR.2011.6092378

80. Ortiz L, Cabrera E, Gonçalves L (2018) Depth data error modeling of the ZED 3D vision sensor from stereolabs. Electron Lett Comput Vis Image Anal 17. https://doi.org/10.5565/rev/elcvia.1084

81. Orts-Escolano S, Rhemann C, Fanello S, Chang W, Kowdle A, Degtyarev Y, Kim D, Davidson PL, Khamis S, Dou M, Tankovich V, Loop C, Cai Q, Chou PA, Mennicken S, Valentin J, Pradeep V, Wang S, Kang SB, Kohli P, Lutchyn Y, Keskin C, Izadi S (2016) Holoportation: virtual 3D teleportation in real-time. In: Proceedings of the 29th annual symposium on user interface software and technology, UIST '16. ACM, New York, NY, USA, pp 741–754. https://doi.org/10.1145/2984511.2984517

82. Palasek P, Yang H, Xu Z, Hajimirza N, Izquierdo E, Patras I (2015) A flexible calibration method of multiple Kinects for 3D human reconstruction. In: 2015 IEEE international conference on multimedia expo workshops (ICMEW), pp 1–4. https://doi.org/10.1109/ICMEW.2015.7169829

83. Rafighi A, Seifi S, Meruvia-Pastor O (2015) Automatic and adaptable registration of live RGBD video streams. In: Proceedings of the 8th international conference on motion in games. ACM. https://doi.org/10.1145/2984511.2984517

84. Rander P, Narayanan PJ, Kanade T (1997) Virtualized reality: constructing time-varying virtual worlds from real world events. In: Proceedings. Visualization '97 (Cat. No. 97CB36155), pp 277–283. https://doi.org/10.1109/VISUAL.1997.663893

85. Sarbolandi H, Lefloch D, Kolb A (2015) Kinect range sensing: structured-light versus time-of-flight Kinect. Comput Vis Image Underst 139:1–20. https://doi.org/10.1016/j.cviu.2015.05.006, http://www.sciencedirect.com/science/article/pii/S1077314215001071

86. Satnik, A., Izquierdo, E.: Real-time multi-view volumetric reconstruction of dynamic scenes using Kinect v2. In: 2018 - 3DTV-conference: the true vision - capture, transmission and display of 3D video (3DTV-CON), pp 1–4 (2018). https://doi.org/10.1109/3DTV.2018.8478536

87. Schröder Y, Scholz A, Berger K, Ruhl K, Guthe S, Magnor M (2011) Multiple Kinect studies. Technical Report - Computer Graphics Lab, TU Braunschweig **2011-09-15**. http://www.digibib.tu-bs.de/?docid=00041359

88. Seer S, Brändle N, Ratti C (2012) Kinects and human kinetics: a new approach for studying crowd behavior. arXiv:1210.28388
89. Shi Z, Sun Y, Xiong L, Hu Y, Yin B (2015) A multisource heterogeneous data fusion method for pedestrian tracking. Math Prob Eng 150541:1–10. https://doi.org/10.1155/2015/150541
90. Si L, Wang Q, Xiao Z (2014) Matching cost fusion in dense depth recovery for camera-array via global optimization. In: 2014 international conference on virtual reality and visualization, pp 180–185. https://doi.org/10.1109/ICVRV.2014.67
91. Silberman S (2003) Matrix2. https://www.wired.com/2003/05/matrix2/. Accessed 25 June 2019
92. Singh A, Sha J, Narayan KS, Achim T, Abbeel P (2014) BigBIRD: a large-scale 3D database of object instances. In: 2014 IEEE international conference on robotics and automation (ICRA), pp 509–516. https://doi.org/10.1109/ICRA.2014.6906903
93. Song W, Yun S, Jung SW, Won CS (2016) Rotated top-bottom dual-Kinect for improved field of view. Multimed Tools Appl 75(14):8569–8593. https://doi.org/10.1007/s11042-015-2772-5
94. Steinbruecker F, Sturm J, Cremers D (2011) Real-time visual odometry from dense RGB-D images. In: Workshop on live dense reconstruction with moving cameras at the international conference on computer vision (ICCV). https://vision.in.tum.de/data/software/dvo
95. Stereolabs Inc (2019) ZED camera and SDK overview. https://www.stereolabs.com/zed/docs/ZED_Datasheet_2016.pdf. Accessed 21 Jan 2019
96. Sterzentsenko V, Karakottas A, Papachristou A, Zioulis N, Doumanoglou A, Zarpalas D, Daras P (2018) A low-cost, flexible and portable volumetric capturing system. In: 2018 14th international conference on signal-image technology internet-based systems (SITIS), pp 200–207 (2018). https://doi.org/10.1109/SITIS.2018.00038
97. Svoboda T, Martinec D, Pajdla T (2005) A convenient multicamera self-calibration for virtual environments. Presence 14(4):407–422. https://doi.org/10.1162/105474605774785325, http://citeseerx.ist.psu.edu/viewdoc/download?doi=10.1.1.83.9884&rep=rep1&type=pdf
98. Tam GKL, Cheng ZQ, Lai YK, Langbein FC, Liu Y, Marshall AD, Martin RR, Sun X, Rosin PL (2013) Registration of 3D point clouds and meshes: a survey from rigid to nonrigid. IEEE Trans Vis Comput Graph 19:1199–1217. https://doi.org/10.1109/TVCG.2012.310
99. Taylor D (1996) Virtual camera movement: the way of the future? Am Cinematogr 77(9):93–100 (1996). https://www.digitalair.com/pdfs/Virtual_Camera_Movement_1996.pdf
100. Toldo R, Beinat A, Crosilla F (2010) Global registration of multiple point clouds embedding the generalized procrustes analysis into an ICP framework (2010). https://www.researchgate.net/publication/228959196_Global_registration_of_multiple_point_clouds_embedding_the_Generalized_Procrustes_Analysis_into_an_ICP_framework
101. Tong J, Zhou J, Liu L, Pan Z, Yan H (2012) Scanning 3D full human bodies using Kinects. IEEE Trans Vis Comput Graph 18(4):643–650. https://doi.org/10.1109/TVCG.2012.56
102. Walas K, Nowicki M, Ferstl D, Skrzypczynski P (2016) Depth data fusion for simultaneous localization and mapping – RGB-DD SLAM. In: 2016 IEEE international conference on multisensor fusion and integration for intelligent systems (MFI), pp 9–14. https://doi.org/10.1109/MFI.2016.7849459
103. Wang D, Pan Q, Zhao C, Hu J, Xu Z, Yang F, Zhou Y (2017) A study on camera array and its applications. IFAC-PapersOnLine 50(1), 10,323–10,328. https://doi.org/10.1016/j.ifacol.2017.08.1662. 20th IFAC World Congress
104. Wen C, Qin L, Zhu Q, Wang C, Li J (2014) Three-dimensional indoor mobile mapping with fusion of two-dimensional laser scanner and rgb-d camera data. IEEE Geosci Remote Sens Lett 11(4):843–847. https://doi.org/10.1109/LGRS.2013.2279872
105. Wikipedia (2019) Multiple-camera setup. https://en.wikipedia.org/wiki/Multiple-camera_setup. Accessed 25 June 2019
106. Wilburn B, Joshi N, Vaish V, Talvala EV, Antunez E, Barth A, Adams A, Horowitz M, Levoy M (2005) High performance imaging using large camera arrays. ACM Trans Graph 24(3):765–776. https://doi.org/10.1145/1073204.1073259

107. Wilson AD, Benko H (2010) Combining multiple depth cameras and projectors for interactions on, above and between surfaces. In: Proceedings of the 23rd annual ACM symposium on user interface software and technology, UIST '10. ACM, New York, NY, USA, pp 273–282. https://doi.org/10.1145/1866029.1866073

108. Wu CJ, Quigley A, Harris-Birtill D (2017) Out of sight: A toolkit for tracking occluded human joint positions. Pers Ubiquitous Comput 21(1):125–135. https://doi.org/10.1007/s00779-016-0997-6

109. Wu, X., Yu, C., Shi, Y.: Multi-depth-camera sensing and interaction in smart space. In: 2018 IEEE smartworld, ubiquitous intelligence computing, Advanced trusted computing, scalable computing communications, Cloud big data computing, Internet of people and smart city innovation (SmartWorld/SCALCOM/UIC/ATC/CBDCom/IOP/SCI), pp 718–725. https://doi.org/10.1109/SmartWorld.2018.00139

110. Xiang S, Yu L, Yang Y, Liu Q, Zhou J (2015) Interfered depth map recovery with texture guidance for multiple structured light depth cameras. Image Commun 31(C):34–46. https://doi.org/10.1016/j.image.2014.11.004

111. Yang S, Yi X, Wang Z, Wang Y, Yang X (2015) Visual SLAM using multiple RGB-D cameras. In: 2015 IEEE International conference on robotics and biomimetics (ROBIO), pp 1389–1395. https://doi.org/10.1109/ROBIO.2015.7418965

112. Ye G, Liu Y, Deng Y, Hasler N, Ji X, Dai Q, Theobalt C (2013) Free-viewpoint video of human actors using multiple handheld Kinects. IEEE Trans Cybern 43(5):1370–1382. https://doi.org/10.1109/TCYB.2013.2272321

113. Zhang L, Sturm J, Cremers D, Lee D (2012) Real-time human motion tracking using multiple depth cameras. 2012 IEEE/RSJ international conference on intelligent robots and systems, pp 2389–2395. https://doi.org/10.1109/IROS.2012.6385968

114. Zhou QY, Koltun V (2014) Color map optimization for 3D reconstruction with consumer depth cameras. ACM Trans Graph 33(4):155:1–155:10. https://doi.org/10.1145/2601097.2601134, http://vladlen.info/papers/color-mapping.pdf

115. Zollhöfer M, Stotko P, Görlitz A, Theobalt C, Nießner M, Klein R, Kolb A (2018) State of the art on 3D reconstruction with RGB-D cameras. Comput Graph Forum (Eurographics State of the Art Reports (2018) 37(2). https://doi.org/10.1111/cgf.13386, https://web.stanford.edu/~zollhoef/papers/EG18_RecoSTAR/paper.pdf

Part II
RGB-D Data Analysis

Part I of this book described how RGB-D data is acquired, cleaned and enhanced. Part II focuses on RGB-D data analysis. This level aims to understand the object-level semantics in the scene. Once the images have been acquired, then major tasks are segmentation, object detection, object pose estimation and semantic modelling. The challenge is to cope with viewpoint variability, occlusion, clutter and similar looking distractors. These provide the basis for numerous applications, some of which are described in Part III.

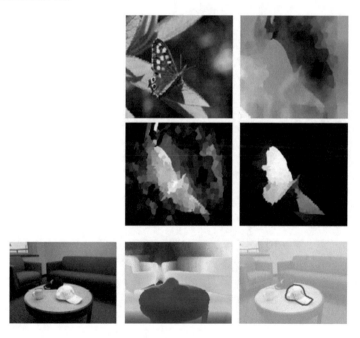

RGB-D enables better estimation of saliency compared to colour alone. The first row shows colour and depth, while the second row shows the saliency map using only colour and followed by the saliency map using colour and depth (Chap. 9). The bottom row shows an RGB and heatmapped depth image followed by the result of foreground segmentation (Chap. 10).

Chapter 8
RGB-D Image-Based Object Detection: From Traditional Methods to Deep Learning Techniques

Isaac Ronald Ward, Hamid Laga and Mohammed Bennamoun

Abstract Object detection from RGB images is a long-standing problem in image processing and computer vision. It has applications in various domains including robotics, surveillance, human–computer interaction, and medical diagnosis. With the availability of low- cost 3D scanners, a large number of RGB-D object detection approaches have been proposed in the past years. This chapter provides a comprehensive survey of the recent developments in this field. We structure the chapter into two parts; the focus of the first part is on techniques that are based on hand-crafted features combined with machine learning algorithms. The focus of the second part is on the more recent work, which is based on deep learning. Deep learning techniques, coupled with the availability of large training datasets, have now revolutionized the field of computer vision, including RGB-D object detection, achieving an unprecedented level of performance. We survey the key contributions, summarize the most commonly used pipelines, discuss their benefits and limitations and highlight some important directions for future research.

8.1 Introduction

Humans are able to efficiently and effortlessly detect objects, estimate their sizes and orientations in the 3D space, and recognize their classes. This capability has long been studied by cognitive scientists. It has, over the past two decades, attracted a

I. R. Ward (✉) · M. Bennamoun
University of Western Australia, Crawley, WA, Australia
e-mail: isaacronaldward@gmail.com

M. Bennamoun
e-mail: mohammed.bennamoun@uwa.edu.au

H. Laga
Murdoch University, Perth, WA, Australia
e-mail: H.Laga@murdoch.edu.au

The Phenomics and Bioinformatics Research Centre, University of South Australia, Adelaide, SA, Australia

© Springer Nature Switzerland AG 2019
P. L. Rosin et al. (eds.), *RGB-D Image Analysis and Processing*,
Advances in Computer Vision and Pattern Recognition,
https://doi.org/10.1007/978-3-030-28603-3_8

lot of interest from the computer vision and machine learning communities mainly because of the wide range of applications that can benefit from it. For instance, robots, autonomous vehicles, and surveillance and security systems rely on accurate detection of 3D objects to enable efficient object recognition, grasping, manipulation, obstacle avoidance, scene understanding and accurate navigation.

Traditionally, object detection algorithms operate on images captured with RGB cameras. However, in the recent years, we have seen the emergence of low-cost 3D sensors, hereinafter referred to as *RGB-D sensors*, that are able to capture depth information in addition to RGB images. Consequently, numerous approaches for object detection from RGB-D images have been proposed. Some of these methods have been specifically designed to detect specific types of objects, e.g. humans, faces and cars. Others are more generic and aim to detect objects that may belong to one of many different classes. This chapter, which focuses on generic object detection from RGB-D images, provides a comprehensive survey of the recent developments in this field. We will first review the traditional methods, which are mainly based on hand-crafted features combined with machine learning techniques. In the second part of the chapter, we will focus on the more recent developments, which are mainly based on deep learning.

The chapter is organized as follows; Sect. 8.2 formalizes the object detection problem, discusses the main challenges, and outlines a taxonomy of the different types of algorithms. Section 8.3 reviews the traditional methods, which are based on hand-crafted features and traditional machine learning techniques. Section 8.4 focuses on approaches that use deep learning techniques. Section 8.5 discusses some RGB-D-based object detection pipelines and compares their performances on publicly available datasets, using well-defined performance evaluation metrics. Finally, Sect. 8.6 summarizes the main findings of this survey and discusses some potential challenges for future research.

8.2 Problem Statement, Challenges, and Taxonomy

Object detection from RGB-D images can be formulated as follows; given an RGB-D image, we seek to find the location, size and orientation of objects of interest, e.g. cars, humans and chairs. The position and orientation of an object is collectively referred to as the *pose*, where the orientation is provided in the form of Euler angles, quaternion coefficients or some similar encoding. The location can be in the form of a 3D bounding box around the visible and/or non-visible parts of each instance of the objects of interest. It can also be an accurate 2D/3D segmentation, i.e. the complete shape and orientation even if only part of the instance is visible. In general, we are more interested in detecting the whole objects, even if parts of them are not visible due to clutter, self-occlusions, and occlusion with other objects. This is referred to as *amodal* object detection. In this section, we discuss the most important challenges in this field (Sect. 8.2.1) and then lay down a taxonomy for the state of the art (Sect. 8.2.2).

8.2.1 Challenges

Though RGB-D object detection has been extensively investigated, there are a number of challenges that efficient solutions should address. Below, we classify these challenges into whether they are due to intrinsic or extrinsic factors. Extrinsic factors refer to all the *external* factors that might affect object detection (see Fig. 8.1). Extrinsic challenges include:

- **Occlusions and background clutter** . The task of object detection algorithms is to not only localize objects in the 3D world, but also to estimate their physical sizes and poses, even if only parts of them are visible in the RGB-D image. In real-life situations, such occlusions can occur at anytime, especially when dealing with dynamic scenes. Clutter can occur in the case of indoor and outdoor scenes. While biological vision systems excel at detecting objects under such challenging situations, occlusions and background clutter can significantly affect object detection algorithms.
- **Incomplete and sparse data**. Data generated by RGB-D sensors can be incomplete and even sparse in some regions, especially along the $z-$, i.e. depth, direction. Efficient algorithms should be able to detect the full extent of the object(s) of interest even when significant parts of it are missing.
- **Illumination**. RGB-D object detection pipelines should be robust to changes in lighting conditions. In fact, significant variations in lighting can be encountered in indoor and outdoor environments. For example, autonomously driving drones and domestic indoor robots are required to operate over a full day–night cycle and are likely to encounter extremes in environmental illumination. As such, the

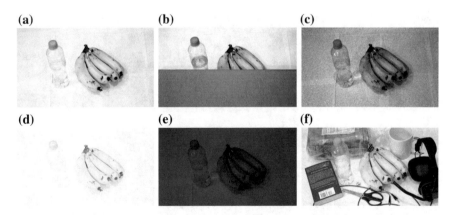

(a)   (b)   (c)

(d)   (e)   (f)

Fig. 8.1 Illustration of some extrinsic challenges in object detection. **a** Objects of interest are clearly separated from each other and from the uniform background. **b** Two objects partially occluded by a cardboard box. **c** Sensor noise that might affect images. **d** An overexposed image. **e** An underexposed image. **f** A cluttered image, which hinders the detection of smaller and occluded objects

appearance of objects can be significantly affected not only in the RGB image but also in the depth map, depending on the type of 3D sensors used for the acquisition.

- **Sensor limitations**. Though sensor limitations classically refer to colour image noise that occurs on imaging sensors, RGB-D images are also prone to other unique sensor limitations. Examples include spatial and depth resolution. The latter limits the size of the objects that can be detected. Depth sensor range limitations are particularly noticeable, e.g. the Microsoft Kinect, which is only sufficiently accurate to a range of approximately 4.5 m [79]. This prevents the sensor from adequately providing RGB-D inputs in outdoor contexts where more expensive devices, e.g. laser scanners, may have to be used [56].

- **Computation time**. Many applications, e.g. autonomous driving, require real-time object detection. Despite hardware acceleration, using GPUs, RGB-D-based detection algorithms can be slower when compared to their 2D counterparts. In fact, adding an extra spatial dimension increases, relatively, the size of the data. As such, techniques such as sliding windows and convolution operations, which are very efficient on RGB images, become significantly more expensive in terms of computation time and memory storage.

- **Training data**. Despite the widespread use of RGB-D sensors, obtaining large *labelled* RGB-D datasets to train detection algorithms is more challenging when compared to obtaining purely RGB datasets. This is due to the price and complexity of RGB-D sensors. Although low-cost sensors are currently available, e.g. the Microsoft Kinect, these are usually more efficient in indoor setups. As such, we witnessed a large proliferation of indoor datasets, whereas outdoor datasets are fewer and typically smaller in size.

Fig. 8.2 Illustration of some intrinsic challenges in object detection. **a–c** Intra-class variations where objects of the same class (chair) appear significantly different. **d–f** Inter-class similarities where objects belonging to different classes (cat, cougar and lion) appear similar

Intrinsic factors, on the other hand, refer to factors such as deformations, intra-class variations, and inter-class similarities, which are properties of the objects themselves (see Fig. 8.2):

- **Deformations**. Objects can deform in a rigid and non-rigid way. As such, detection algorithms should be invariant to such shape-preserving deformations.
- **Intra-class variations and inter-class similarities**. Object detection algorithms are often required to distinguish between many objects belonging to many classes. Such objects, especially when imaged under uncontrolled settings, display large intra-class variations. Also, natural and man-made objects from different classes may have strong similarities. Such intra-class variations and inter-class similarities can significantly affect the performance of the detection algorithms, especially if the number of RGB-D images used for training is small.

This chapter discusses how the state-of-the-art algorithms addressed some of these challenges.

8.2.2   Taxonomy

Figure 8.3 illustrates the taxonomy that we will follow for reviewing the state-of-the-art techniques. In particular, both traditional (Sect. 8.3) and deep learning-based (Sect. 8.4) techniques operate in a pipeline of two or three stages. **The first** stage takes the input RGB-D image(s) and generates a set of region proposals. **The second** stage then refines that selection using some accurate recognition techniques. It also estimates the accurate locations (i.e. centres) of the detected objects, their sizes and their pose. This is referred to as the object's bounding box. This is usually sufficient for applications such as object recognition and autonomous navigation. Other applications, e.g. object grasping and manipulation, may require an accurate segmentation of the detected objects. This is usually performed either within the second stage of the pipeline or separately with an additional segmentation module, which only takes as input the region within the detected bounding box.

Note that, in most of the state-of-the-art techniques, the different modules of the pipeline operate in an independent manner. For instance, the region proposal module can use traditional techniques based on hand-crafted features, while the recognition and localization module can use deep learning techniques.

Another important point in our taxonomy is the way the input is represented and fed into the pipeline. For instance, some methods treat the depth map as a one-channel image where each pixel encodes depth. The main advantage of this representation is that depth can be processed in the same way as images, i.e. using 2D operations, and thus there is a significant gain in the computation performance and memory requirements. Other techniques use 3D representations by converting the depth map into either a point cloud or a volumetric grid. These methods, however, require 3D operations and thus can be significantly expensive compared to their 2D counterparts.

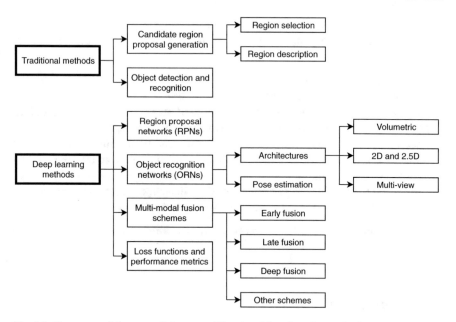

Fig. 8.3 Taxonomy of the state-of-the-art traditional and deep learning methods

The last important point in our taxonomy is the fusion scheme used to merge multimodal information. In fact, the RGB and D channels of an RGB-D image carry overlapping as well as complementary information. The RGB image mainly provides information about the colour and texture of objects. The depth map, on the other hand, carries information about the geometry (e.g. size, shape) of objects, although some of this information can also be inferred from the RGB image. Existing state-of-the-art techniques combine this complementary information at different stages of the pipeline (see Fig. 8.3).

8.3 Traditional Methods

The first generation of algorithms that aim to detect the location and pose of objects in RGB-D images relies on hand-crafted features[1] combined with machine learning techniques. They operate in two steps: (1) candidate region selection and (2) detection refinement.

---

[1]Here, we defined hand-crafted or hand-*engineered* features as those which have been calculated over input images using operations which have been explicitly defined by a human designer (i.e. *hand-crafted*), as a opposed to learned features which are extracted through optimization procedures in learning pipelines.

8.3.1   Candidate Region Proposals Generation

The first step of an object detection algorithm is to generate a set of candidate regions, also referred to as hypotheses, from image and depth cues. The set will form the potential object candidates and should cover the majority of the true object locations. This step can be seen as a coarse recognition step in which regions are roughly classified into whether they contain the objects of interest or not. While the classification is not required to be accurate, it should achieve a high recall so that object regions will not be missed.

8.3.1.1   Region Selection

The initial set of candidate regions can be generated by using (1) bottom-up clustering-and-fitting, (2) sliding windows or (3) segmentation algorithms.

Bottom-up clustering-and-fitting methods start at the pixel and point level, and iteratively cluster such data into basic geometric primitives such as cuboids. These primitives can be further grouped together to form a set of complex object proposals. In the second stage, an optimal subset is selected using some geometric, structural, and/or semantic cues. Jiang and Xiao [35] constructed a set of cuboid candidates using pairs of superpixels in an RGB-D image. Their method starts by partitioning the depth map, using both colour and surface normals, into superpixels forming piecewise planar patches. Optimal cuboids are then fit to pairs of adjacent planar patches. Cuboids with high fitting accuracy are then considered as potential candidate hypotheses. Representing objects using cuboids has also been used in [8, 39, 51]. Khan et al. [39] used a similar approach to fit cuboids to pairs of adjacent planar patches and also to individual planar patches. The approach also distinguishes between scene bounding cuboids and object cuboids.

These methods tend, in general, to represent a scene with many small components, especially if it contains objects with complex shapes. To overcome this issue, Jiang [34] used approximate convex shapes, arguing that they are better than cuboids in approximating generic objects.

Another approach is to use a **sliding window method** [15, 80, 81] where detection is performed by sliding, or *convolving*, a window over the image. At each window location, the region of the image contained in the window is extracted, and these regions are then classified as potential candidates or not depending on the similarity of that region to the objects of interest. Nakahara et al. [57] extended this process by using multi-scale windows to make the method robust to variations in the size of objects that can be detected. Since the goal of this step is to extract candidate regions, the classifier is not required to be accurate. It is only required to have a high recall to ensure that the selected candidates cover the majority of the true object locations. Thus, these types of methods are generally fast and often generate a large set of candidates.

Finally, **segmentation-based region selection methods** [6, 9] extract candidate regions by segmenting the RGB-D image into meaningful objects and then considering segmented regions separately. These methods are usually computationally expensive and may suffer in the presence of occlusions and clutter.

8.3.1.2 Region Description

Once candidate regions have been identified, the next step is to describe these regions with features that characterize their geometry and appearance. These descriptors can be used to refine the candidate region selection, either by using some supervised recognition techniques, e.g. Support Vector Machines [80], AdaBoost [16] and hierarchical cascaded forests [6], or by using unsupervised procedures.

In principle, any type of features which can be computed from the RGB image can be used. Examples include colour statistics, Histogram of Oriented Gradients (HOG) descriptor [13], Scale-Invariant Feature Transform (SIFT) [14], the Chamfer distance [7] and Local Binary Patterns (LBPs) [31]. Some of these descriptors can be used to describe the geometry if computed from the depth map, by treating depth as a grayscale image. Other examples of 3D features include:

- **3D normal features**. These are used to describe the orientation of an object's surface. To compute 3D normals, one can pick n nearest neighbours for each point, and estimate the surface normal at that point using principal component analysis (PCA). This is equivalent to fitting a plane and choosing the normal vector to the surface to be the normal vector to that plane, see [41].
- **Point density features** [80]. It is computed by subdividing each 3D cell into $n \times n \times n$ voxels and building a histogram of the number of points in each voxel. Song et al. [80] also applied a 3D Gaussian kernel to assign a weight to each point, cancelling the bias of the voxel discretization. After obtaining the histogram inside the cell, Song et al. [80] randomly pick 1000 pairs of entries and compute the difference within each pair, obtaining what is called the stick feature [76]. The stick feature is then concatenated with the original count histogram to form the point density feature. This descriptor captures both the first order (point count) and second order (count difference) statistics of the point cloud [80].
- **Depth statistics**. This can include the first and second order statistics as well as the histogram of depth.
- **Truncated Signed Distance Function (TSDF)** [59]. For a region divided into $n \times n \times n$ voxels, the TSDF value of each voxel is defined as the signed distance between the voxel centre and the nearest object point on the line of sight from the camera. The distance is clipped to be between -1 and 1. The sign indicates whether the voxel is in front of or behind a surface, with respect to the camera's line of sight.
- **Global depth contrast (GP-D)** [67]. This descriptor measures the saliency of a superpixel by considering its depth contrast with respect to all other superpixels.

Chaps. 9 and 10 present additional hand-crafted features which are used in RGB-D saliency detection pipelines.

- **Local Background Enclosure (LBE) descriptor** [22]. This descriptor, which is also used to detect salient objects, is designed based on the observation that salient objects tend to be located in front of their surrounding regions. Thus, the descriptor can be computed by creating patches, via superpixel segmentation [2], and considering the angular density of the surrounding patches which have a significant depth difference to the centre patch (a difference beyond a given threshold). Feng et al. [22] found that LBE features outperform depth-based features such as anisotropic Center-Surround Difference (ACSD) [36], multi-scale depth contrast (LMH-D) [60], and global depth contrast (GP-D) [67], when evaluated on the RGBD1000 [60] and NJUDS2000 [36] RGB-D benchmarks.
- **Cloud of Oriented Gradients (COG) descriptor** [70]. It extends the HOG descriptor, which was originally designed for 2D images [10, 24], to 3D data.
- **Histogram of Control Points (HOCP) descriptor** [73, 74]. A volumetric descriptor calculated over patches of point clouds featuring occluded objects. The descriptor is derived from the Implicit B-Splines (IBS) feature.

In general, these hand-crafted features are computed at the pixel, superpixel, point, or patch level. They can also be used to characterize an entire region by aggregating the features computed at different locations on the region using histogram and/or Bag-of-Words techniques, see [41]. For instance, Song et al. [80] aggregate the 3D normal features by dividing, uniformly, the half-sphere into 24 bins along the azimuth and elevation angles. Each bin encodes the frequency of the normal vectors whose orientation falls within that bin. Alternatively, one can use a Bag-of-Words learned from training data to represent each patch using a histogram which encodes the frequency of occurrences of each code word in the patch [80].

8.3.2   Object Detection and Recognition

Given a set of candidate objects, one can train, using the features described in Sect. 8.3.1, a classifier that takes these candidates and classifies them into either true or false detections. Different types of classifiers have been used in the literature. Song and Xiao [80] use Support Vector Machines. Asif et al. [6] use hierarchical cascade forests. In general, any type of classifiers, e.g. AdaBoost, can be used to complete this task. However, in many cases, this approach is not sufficient and may lead to excessive false positives and/or false negatives. Instead, given a set of candidates, other approaches select a subset of shapes that best describes the RGB-D data whilst satisfying some geometrical, structural and semantic constraints. This has been formulated as the problem of optimizing an objective function of the form [34, 35]

$$E(x) = E_d(x) + E_r(x), \tag{8.1}$$

where x is the indicator vector of the candidate shapes, i.e. $x(i) = 1$ means that the ith shape is selected for the final subset. Khan et al. [39] extended this formulation to classify RGB-D superpixels as cluttered or non-cluttered, in addition to object detection. As such, another variable y is introduced. It is a binary indicator vector whose ith entry indicates whether the ith superpixel is cluttered or not. This has also been formulated as the problem of optimizing an objective function of the form

$$U(x, y) = E(x) + U(y) + U_c(x, y). \qquad (8.2)$$

Here, $E(x)$ is given by Eq. (8.1). $U(y)$ also consists of two potentials:

$$U(y) = U_d(y) + U_r(y), \qquad (8.3)$$

where the unary term U_d is the data likelihood of a superpixel's label, and the pairwise potential U_r encodes the spatial smoothness between neighbouring superpixels. The third term of Eq. (8.2) encodes compatibility constraints, e.g. enforcing the consistency of the cuboid labelling and the superpixel labelling.

The data likelihood term E_d. This term measures the cost of matching the candidate shape to the data. For instance, Jiang et al. [35] used cuboids for detection, and defined this term as the cost of matching a cuboid to the candidate shape. On the other hand, Jiang [34] used convex shapes, and defined E_d as a measure of concavity of the candidate shape. Several other papers take a learning approach. For instance, Khan et al. [39] computed seven types of cuboid features (volumetric occupancy, colour consistency, normal consistency, tightness feature, support feature, geometric plausibility feature and cuboid size feature), and then predicted the local matching quality using machine learning approaches.

The data likelihood term U_d. Khan et al. [39] used a unary potential that captures, on each superpixel, the appearance and texture properties of cluttered and non-cluttered regions. This is done by extracting several cues including image and depth gradient, colour, surface normals, LBP features and self-similarity features. Then, a Random Forest classifier was trained to predict the probability of a region being a clutter or a non-clutter.

The regularization terms E_r **and** U_r. The second terms of Eqs. (8.1) and (8.3) are regularization terms, which incorporate various types of constraints. Jian [34] define this term as

$$E_r(x) = \alpha N(x) + \beta I(x) - \lambda A(x), \qquad (8.4)$$

where α, β and λ are weights that set the importance of each term. $N(x)$ is the number of selected candidates, $I(x)$ measures the amount of intersection (or overlap) between two neighbouring candidate shapes, and $A(x)$ is the amount of area covered by the candidate shapes projected onto the image plane. Jiang and Xiao [35], and later Khan et al. [39], used the same formulation but added a fourth term, $O(x)$, which penalizes occlusions.

For the superpixel pairwise term of Eq. (8.3), Khan et al. [39] defined a contrast-sensitive Potts model on spatially neighbouring superpixels, which encouraged the smoothness of cluttered and non-cluttered regions.

The compatibility term U_c. Khan et al. [39] introduced the compatibility term to link the labelling of the superpixels to the cuboid selection task. This ensures consistency between the lower level and the higher level of the scene representation. It consists of two terms: a superpixel membership potential and a superpixel-cuboid occlusion potential. The former ensures that a superpixel is associated with at least one cuboid if it is not a cluttered region. The latter ensures that a cuboid should not appear in front of a superpixel which is classified as clutter, i.e. a detected cuboid cannot completely occlude a superpixel on the 2D plane which takes a clutter label.

Optimization. The final step of the process is to solve the optimization problem of Eqs. (8.1) or (8.3). Jian [34] showed that the energy function of Eq. (8.1) can be linearized and optimized using efficient algorithms such as the branch-and-bound method. Khan et al. [39], on the other hand, transformed the minimization problem into a Mixed Integer Linear Program (MILP) with linear constraints, which can be solved using the branch-and-bound method.

8.4 Deep Learning Methods

Despite the extensive research, the performance of traditional methods is still far from the performance of the human visual system, especially when it comes to detecting objects in challenging situations, e.g. highly cluttered scenes and scenes with high occlusions. In fact, while traditional methods perform well in detecting and producing bounding boxes on visible parts, it is often desirable to capture the full extent of the objects regardless of occlusions and clutter. Deep learning-based techniques aim to overcome these limitations. They generally operate following the same pipeline as the traditional techniques (see Sect. 8.3), i.e. region proposals extraction, object recognition and 3D bounding box location and pose estimation. However, they replace some or all of these building blocks with deep learning networks. This section reviews the different deep learning architectures that have been proposed to solve these problems. Note that these techniques can be combined with traditional techniques; e.g. one can use traditional techniques for region proposals and deep learning networks for object recognition, bounding box location and pose refinement.

8.4.1 Region Proposal Networks

In this section, we are interested in amodal detection, i.e. the inference of the full 3D bounding box beyond the visible parts. This critical step in an object detection pipeline is very challenging since different object categories can have very different object sizes in 3D. Region Proposal Networks (RPNs) are central to this task since they reduce the search space considered by the remainder of the object detection pipeline.

We classify existing RPNs into three different categories. **Methods in the first category** perform the detection on the RGB image and then, using the known camera projection matrix, lift the 2D region to a 3D frustum that defines a 3D search space for the object. In general, any 2D object detector, e.g. [53], can be used for this task. However, using deep CNNs allows the extraction of rich features at varying degrees of complexity and dimensionality, which is beneficial for the purpose of RGB-D object detection tasks. In fact, the success of the recent object detection pipelines can be largely attributed to the automatic feature learning aspect of convolutional neural networks. For instance, Qi et al. [62] used the Feature Pyramid Networks (FPN) [52], which operate on RGB images, to detect region proposals. Lahoud and Ghanem [45], on the other hand, use the 2D Faster R-CNN [69] and VGG-16 [77], pre-trained on the 2D ImageNet database [72], to position 2D bounding boxes around possible objects with high accuracy and efficiency. These methods have been applied for indoor and outdoor scenes captured by RGB-D cameras, and for scenes captured using LIDAR sensors [12].

The rational behind these methods is that the resolution of data produced by most 3D sensors is still lower than the resolution of RGB images, and that 2D object detectors are mature and quite efficient. RGB-based detection methods, however, do not benefit from the additional information encoded in the depth map.

The second class of methods aim to address these limitations. They treat depth as an image and perform the detection of region proposals on the RGB-D image either by using traditional techniques or by using 2D convolutional networks. For instance, Gupta et al. [29], and later Deng and Latecki [15], computed an improved contour image from an input RGB-D image. An improved contour image is defined as the contour image but augmented with additional features such as the gradient, normals, the geocentric pose and appearance features such as the soft edge map produced by running the contour detector on the RGB image. They then generalize the multi-scale combinatorial grouping (MCG) algorithm [5, 61] to RGB-D images for region proposal and ranking. Note that both the hand-crafted features as well as the region recognition and ranking algorithms can be replaced with deep learning techniques, as in [62].

Chen et al. [12] took the point cloud (produced by LIDAR sensors) and the RGB image, and produced two types of feature maps: the bird's eye view features and the front view features. The bird's eye view representation is encoded by height, intensity, and density. First, the point cloud is projected and discretized into a 2D grid with a fixed resolution. For each cell in the grid, the height feature is computed as the maximum height of the points in that cell. To encode more detailed height information, the point cloud is divided equally into m slices. A height map is computed for each slice, thus obtaining m height maps. The intensity feature is defined as the reflectance value of the point which has the highest height in each cell. Finally, a network that is similar to the region proposal network of [68] was used to generate region proposals from the bird's eye view map.

These methods require the fusion of the RGB and depth data. This can be done by simply concatenating the depth data with the RGB data and using this as input to the RPN. However, depth data encodes geometric information, which is distinct from the spatial and colour information provided by monocular RGB images. As such, Alexandre et al. [3] found that fusing amodal networks with a majority voting scheme produced better results in object recognition tasks, with an improvement of 29% when compared to using simple RGB and depth frame concatenation. Note that, instead of performing fusion at the very early stage, e.g. by concatenating the input modalities, fusion can be performed at a later stage by concatenating features computed from the RGB and D maps, or progressively using the complementarity-aware fusion network of Chen et al. [11], see Sect. 8.4.3.

The third class of methods take a 3D approach. For instance, Song and Xia [81] projected both the depth map and the RGB image into the 3D space forming a volumetric scene. The 3D scene is then processed with a fully 3D convolutional network, called a *3D Amodal Region Proposal Network*, which generates region proposals in the form of 3D bounding boxes at two different scales. Multi-scale RPNs allow the detection of objects of different sizes. It performs a 3D sliding-window search with varying window sizes, and produces an objectness score for each of the non-empty proposal boxes [4]. Finally, redundant proposals are removed using non-maximum suppression with an IoU threshold of 0.35 in 3D. Also, the approach ranks the proposals based on their objectness score and only selects the top 2000 boxes to be used as input to the object recognition network.

3D detection can be very expensive since it involves 3D convolutional operations. In fact, it can be more than 30 times slower than its 2D counterpart. Also, the solution space is very large since it includes three dimensions for the location and two dimensions for the orientation of the bounding boxes. However, 3D voxel grids produced from depth maps are generally sparse as they only contain information near the shape surfaces. To leverage this sparsity, Engelcke et al. [18] extended the approach of Song et al. [80] by replacing the SVM ensemble with a 3D CNN, which operates on voxelized 3D grids. The key advantage of this approach is that it leverages the sparsity encountered in point clouds to prevent huge computational cost that occurs with 3D CNNs. In this approach, the computational cost is only proportional to the number of occupied grid cells rather than to the total number of cells in the discretized 3D grid as in [84].

8.4.2   Object Recognition Networks

Once region proposals have been generated, the next step is to classify these regions into whether they correspond to the objects we want to detect or not, and subsequently refine the detection by estimating the accurate location, extent, and pose (position and orientation) of each object's bounding box. The former is a classification problem, which has been well solved using Object Recognition Networks (ORNs) [6, 17, 75]. An ORN takes a candidate region, and assigns to it a class label, which can be binary, i.e. 1 or 0, to indicate whether it is an object of interest or not, or multi-label where the network recognizes the class of the detected objects.

There are several ORN architectures that have been proposed in the literature [12, 15, 28, 55, 81]. In this section, we will discuss some of them based on **(1)** whether they operate on 2D or 3D (and subsequently whether they are using 2D or 3D convolutions), and **(2)** how the accurate 3D location and size of the bounding boxes are estimated.

8.4.2.1 Network Architectures for Object Recognition

(1) Volumetric approaches. The first class of methods are volumetric. The idea is to lift the information in the detected regions into 3D volumes and process them using 3D convolutional networks. For instance, Maturana et al. [55] used only the depth information to recognize and accurately detect the objects of interest. Their method first converts the point cloud within each 3D region of interest into a $32 \times 32 \times 32$ occupancy grid, with the z axis approximately aligned with gravity. The point cloud is then fed into a 3D convolutional network, termed *VoxNet*, which outputs the class label of the region.

Song and Xia [81] followed a similar volumetric approach but they jointly learned the object categories and the 3D box regression from both depth and colour information. Their approach operates as follows. For each 3D proposal, the 3D volume from depth is fed to a 3D ConvNet, and the 2D colour patch (the 2D projection of the 3D proposal) is fed to a 2D ConvNet (based on VGG and pre-trained on ImageNet). The two latent representations learned by the two networks are then concatenated and further processed with one fully connected layer. The network then splits into two branches, each composed of one fully connected layer. The first branch is a classification branch as it produces the class label. The second branch estimates the location and size of the 3D amodal bounding box of the detected object. This approach has two important features; **first**, it combines both colour and geometry (through depth) information to perform recognition and regress the amodal bounding box. These two types of information are complementary and thus combining them can improve performance. The **second** important feature is that it does not directly estimate the location and size of the bounding box but instead it estimates the residual. That is, it first takes an initial estimate of the size of the bounding box (using some prior knowledge about the class of shapes of interest). The network is then trained to learn the correction that one needs to apply to the initial estimate in order to obtain an accurate location and size of the bounding box.

(2) 2D and 2.5D approaches. In the context of object detection, 2D approaches operate over the two spatial dimensions in the input (i.e. an RGB image), without exploiting the data encoded in depth images. 2.5D inputs refer to inputs with attached depth images, but importantly, these depth images are treated similarly to how colour images are (without exploiting 3D spatial relationships, i.e. using the depth frames as 2D maps where each pixel encodes the depth value). Finally, 3D approaches use the rich spatial data encoded in volumetric or point cloud representations of data (or any other representation which represents the data over three spatial dimensions).

These 2D and 2.5D approaches are mainly motivated by the performance of the human visual system in detecting and recognizing objects just from partial 2D information. In fact, when the majority of an object area on the depth map is not visible, the depth map only carries partial information. However, information encoded in the 2D image is rich, and humans can still perceive the objects and estimate their 3D locations and sizes from such images [15]. 2D and 2.5D approaches try to mimic the human perception and leverage the 2.5D image features directly using current deep learning techniques.

In particular, Deng and Latecki [15] followed the same approach as Song and Xia [81] but operate on 2D maps using 2D convolutional filters. The main idea is to regress the 3D bounding box just from the RGB and depth map of the detected 2D regions of interests. Their approach replaces the 3D ConvNet of Song and Xia [81] with a 2D ConvNet that processes the depth map. Thus, it is computationally more efficient than the approaches which operate on 3D volumes, e.g. [15].

(3) **Multi-view approaches**. The 2D and 2.5D approaches described above can be extended to operate on multi-view inputs. In fact, many practical systems, e.g. autonomous driving, acquire RGB-D data from multiple viewpoints. Central to multi-view techniques is the fusion mechanism used to aggregate information from different views (see also Sect. 8.4.3), which can be multiple images and/or depth maps captured from multiple viewpoints. Some of the challenges which need to be addressed include catering for images gathered at varying resolutions.

Chen et al. [12] proposed a Multi-View 3D network (MV3D), a region-based fusion network, which combines features from multiple views. The network jointly classifies region proposals and regresses 3D bounding box orientations. The pipeline operates in two stages: multi-view ROI pooling and deep fusion. The former is used to obtain feature vectors of the same length, since features from different views/modalities usually have different resolutions. The deep fusion network fuses multi-view features hierarchically to enable more interactions among features of the intermediate layers from different views.

8.4.2.2 Pose Estimation

One of the main challenges in amodal object detection from RGB-D images is how to accurately estimate the pose of the bounding box of the detected object, even if parts of the objects are occluded. Early works such as Song and Xia [81] do not estimate orientation but use the major directions of the room in order to orient all proposals. This simple heuristic works fine for indoor scenes, e.g. rooms. However, it cannot be easily extended to outdoor scenes or scenes where no prior knowledge of their structure is known.

Another approach is to perform an exhaustive search of the best orientations over the discretized space of all possible orientations. For example, Maturana et al. [55] performed an exhaustive search over $n = 12$ orientations around the z axis and selected the one with the largest activation. At training time, Maturana et al. [55] augmented the dataset by creating $n = 12$ to $n = 18$ copies of each input instance, each rotated $360°/n$ intervals around the z-axis (assuming that the z axis is known). At testing time, the activations of the output layer over all the n copies are aggregated by pooling. This approach, which can be seen as a voting scheme, has been also used to detect landing zones from LIDAR data [54].

Gupta et al. [28] considered the problem of fitting a complete 3D object model to the detected objects, instead of just estimating the location, orientation, and size of the object's bounding box. They first detect and segment object instances in the scene and then use a convolutional neural network (CNN) to predict the coarse pose of the object. Gupta et al. [28] then use the detected region (segmentation mask) to create a 3D representation of the object by projecting points from the depth map. The Iterative Closest Point (ICP) algorithm [71] is then used to align 3D CAD models to these 3D points.

Finally, some recent approaches regress pose in the same way as they perform recognition, i.e. using CNNs. This is usually achieved using a region recognition network, which has two branches of fully connected layers; one for recognition and another one for bounding box regression [12, 15]. Existing methods differ in the way the bounding boxes are parameterized. For instance, Cheng et al. [12] represent a bounding box using its eight corners. This is a redundant representation as a cuboid can be described with less information. Deng and Latecki [15] used a seven-entry vector $[x_{cam}, y_{cam}, z_{cam}, l, w, h, \theta]$ where $[x_{cam}, y_{cam}, z_{cam}]$ corresponds to the coordinates of the bounding box's centroid under the camera coordinate system. $[l, w, h]$ represents its 3D size, and θ is the angle between the principal axis and its orientation vector under the tilt coordinate system. Note that these methods do not directly regress the pose of the bounding box. Instead, starting from an initial estimate provided by the Region Proposal Network, the regression network estimates the offset vector, which is then applied to the initial estimate to obtain the final pose of the bounding box.

8.4.3 Fusion Schemes

In the context of RGB-D object detection, we aim to exploit the multiple modalities that are present in RGB-D images, which carry complementary information (colour and depth data). This, however, requires efficient fusion mechanisms. In this section, we discuss some of the strategies that have been used in the literature.

(1) Early fusion. In this scheme, the RGB image and the depth map are concatenated to form a four-channel image [30]. This happens at the earliest point in the network, i.e. before any major computational layers process the image. The concatenated image is then processed with 2D or 3D convolutional filters. This scheme was adopted in [32] for the purpose of saliency detection.

(2) Late fusion. In this scheme, the RGB image and the depth map are processed separately, e.g. using two different networks, to produce various types of features.

These features are then fused together, either by concatenation or by further processing using convolutional networks. Eitel et al. [17], for example, used two networks, one for depth and one for the RGB image, with each network separately trained on ImageNet [40]. The feature maps output by the two networks are then concatenated and presented to a final fusion network, which produces object class predictions. This approach achieved an overall accuracy of $91.3\% \pm 1.4\%$ on the Washington RGB-D Object Dataset, see Table 8.3 for more details regarding pipeline performance.

Note that, Chen et al. [12] showed that early and late fusion approaches perform similarly when tested on the hard category of the KITTI dataset, scoring an average precision of 87.23% and 86.88%.

(3) Deep fusion. Early and late fusion schemes are limited in that they only allow the final joint predictions to operate on early or deep representations, so useful information can be discarded. Chen et al. [12] introduced a deep learning fusion scheme, which fuses features extracted from multiple representations of the input. The fusion pipeline uses element-wise mean pooling operations instead of simple concatenations (as in early or late fusion). Chen et al. [12] showed that this fusion mechanism improved performance by about 1% compared to early and late fusion.

(4) Sharable features learning and complementarity-aware fusion. The fusion methods described above either learn features from colour and depth modalities separately, or simply treat RGB-D as a four-channel data. Wang et al. [83] speculate that different modalities should contain not only some modal-specific patterns but also some shared common patterns. They then propose a multimodal feature learning framework for RGB-D object recognition. First, two deep CNN layers are constructed, one for colour and another for depth. They are then connected with multimodal layers, which fuse colour and depth information by enforcing a common part to be shared by features of different modalities. This produces features reflecting shared properties as well as modal-specific properties from different modalities.

Cheng et al. [11] proposed a fusion mechanism, termed *complementarity-aware (CA) fusion*, which encourages the determination of complementary information from the different modalities at different abstraction levels. They introduced a CA-Fuse module, which enables cross-modal, cross-level connections and modal/level-wise supervisions, explicitly encouraging the capture of complementary information from the counterpart, thus reducing fusion ambiguity and increasing fusion efficiency.

8.4.4 Loss Functions

In general, the region proposal network (RPN) and the object recognition network (ORN) operate separately. The RPN first detects candidate regions. The ORN then refines the detection by discarding regions that do not correspond to the objects of interest. The ORN then further refines the location, size, and orientation of the bounding boxes. As such, most of the state-of-the-art techniques train these networks separately using separate loss functions.

Loss functions inform the network on how poorly it completed its designated task over each training batch using a scalar metric (referred to as the loss, cost or inverse fitness). The calculation of the loss should incorporate error that the algorithm accumulated during the completion of its task, as the network will change its weights in order to reduce the loss, and thus the error. For example, in object classification networks, the loss might be defined as the mean squared error between the one-hot encoded ground truth labels, and the network's output logits. For object detection networks, the IoU (see Fig. 8.4) of the detected region and the ground truth region may be incorporated. In this way the loss function design is task-dependant, and performance increases have been observed to be contingent on the loss function's design [85]. Typically, loss functions are hand-crafted, though weightings between terms can be learned [37]. Naturally, numerous loss functions have been devised to train networks to accomplish various tasks [38].

A common loss function that has been used for classification (in the RPN as well as in the ORN) is the softmax regression loss. Let $\boldsymbol{\theta}$ be the parameters of the network, m the number of training samples, n_c the number of classes, and $y_i \in \{1, \ldots, n_c\}$ the output of the network for the training sample x_i. The softmax regression loss is defined as

$$L(\boldsymbol{\theta}) = -\sum_{i=1}^{m}\sum_{k=1}^{n_c} \mathbf{1}(y_i = k) \log\left(p(y^i = k|x^i; \boldsymbol{\theta})\right). \tag{8.5}$$

Here, $\mathbf{1}(s)$ is equal to 1 if the statement s is true and 0 otherwise. This loss function has been used by Gupta et al. [28] to train their region proposal network, which also provides a coarse estimation of each object's pose.

Song and Xia [81], on the other hand, trained their multi-scale region proposal network using a loss function that is a weighted sum of two terms: an objectness term and a box regression term:

$$L(p, p^*, \mathbf{t}, \mathbf{t}^*) = L_{cls}(p, p^*) + \lambda p L_{1\_smooth}(\mathbf{t}, \mathbf{t}^*), \tag{8.6}$$

where p^* is the predicted probability of this region being an object and p is the ground truth, L_{cls} is the log loss over the two categories (object vs. non-object) [26], and $\mathbf{t}$ is a 6-element vector, which defines the location and scale of the bounding box of the region. The second term, which is the box regression loss term, is defined using the smooth L_1 function as follows:

$$L_{1\_smooth}(x) = \begin{cases} 0.5x^2 \text{ if } |x| < 1, \\ |x| - 0.5, \text{ otherwise.} \end{cases} \tag{8.7}$$

Song and Xia [81] also used a similar loss function to train their ORN. The only difference is in the second term, which is set to zero when the ground truth probability p is zero. This is because there is no notion of a ground truth bounding box for background RoIs. Hence, the box regression term is ignored. Finally, Maturana et al. [55]

used the multinomial negative log-likelihood plus 0.001 times the L_2 weight norm for regularization.

8.5 Discussion and Comparison of Some Pipelines

In this section, we discuss some pipelines for object detection from RGB-D data and compare their performance on standard benchmarks. We will first review examples of the datasets that have been used for training and testing the techniques (Sect. 8.5.1), discuss different performance evaluation metrics (Sect. 8.5.1), and finally compare and discuss the performance of some of the key RGB-D-based object detection pipelines (Sect. 8.5.3).

8.5.1 Datasets

Many of the state-of-the-art algorithms rely on large datasets to train their models and evaluate their performance. Both traditional machine learning and advanced deep learning approaches require labelled datasets in the form of RGB-D images and their corresponding ground truth labels. The labels can be in the form of 2D bounding boxes highlighting the object regions in the RGB image and/or the depth map, oriented 3D bounding boxes (3DBBX) delineating the 3D regions of the objects, and/or exact segmentations (in the form of segmentation masks) of the objects of interest.

Table 8.1 summarizes the main datasets and benchmarks that are currently available in the literature. Note that several types of 3D sensors have been used for the acquisition of these datasets. For instance, the SUN RGB-D dataset was constructed using four different sensors: the Intel RealSense 3D Camera, the Asus Xtion LIVE PRO, and Microsoft Kinect v1 and v2. Intel Asus and Microsoft Kinect v1 sensors use infrared (IR) light patterns to generate quantized depth maps, an approach known as *structured light*, whereas Microsoft Kinect v2 uses time-of-flight ranging. These sensors are suitable for indoor scenes since their depth range is limited to a few metres. On the other hand, The KITTI dataset, which includes outdoor scene categories, has been captured using a Velodyne HDL-64E rotation 3D laser scanner.

Note that some datasets, such as the PASCAL3D+, are particularly suitable for testing the robustness of various algorithms to occlusions, since an emphasis was placed on gathering data with occlusions.

Table 8.1 Examples of datasets used for training and evaluating object detection pipelines from RGB-D images

Name	Description	Size
KITTI 2015 [56]	Cluttered driving scenarios recorded in and around Karlsruhe in Germany	400 annotated dynamic scenes from the raw KITTI dataset
KITTI 2012 [23]	As above	389 image pairs and more than 200,000 3D object annotations
SUN RGB-D [79]	Indoor houses and universities in North America and Asia	10, 335 images, 800 object categories, and 47 scene categories annotated with 58,657 bounding boxes (3D)
NYUDv2 [58]	Diverse indoor scenes taken from three cities	1,449 RGB-D images over 464 scenes
PASCAL3D+ [89]	Vehicular and indoor objects (augments the PASCAL VOC dataset [19])	12 object categories with 3,000 instances per category
ObjectNet3D [88]	Indoor and outdoor scenes	90,127 images sorted into 100 categories. 201,888 objects in these images and 44,147 3D shapes
RGBD1000 [60]	Indoor and outdoor scenes captured with a Microsoft Kinect	1, 000 RGB-D images
NJUDS2000 [36]	Indoor and outdoor scenes	2,000 RGB-D images
LFSD [50]	Indoor (60) and outdoor (40) scenes captured with a Lytro camera	100 light fields each composed from raw light field data, a focal slice, an all-focus image and a rough depth map
Cornell Grasping [1]	Several images and point clouds of typical graspable indoor objects taken at different poses	1,035 images of 280 different objects
ModelNet10 [87]	Object aligned 3D CAD models for the 10 most common object categories found in the SUN2012 database [90]	9,798 total instances split amongst 10 object categories, each with their own test/train split
ModelNet40 [87]	Object aligned 3D CAD models for 40 common household objects	12,311 total instances split amongst 40 object categories, each with their own test/train split
Caltech-101 [20]	Single class object centric images with little or no clutter. Most objects are presented in a stereotypical pose	9,144 images sorted into 101 categories, with 40 to 800 images per category
Caltech-256 [27]	Single class images with some clutter	30,607 images sorted into 256 categories with an average of 119 images per category
Washington RGB-D [46]	Turntable video sequences at varying heights of common household objects	300 objects organized into 51 categories. Three video sequences per object

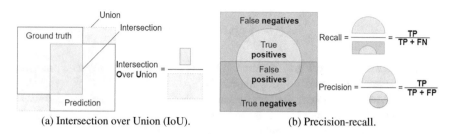

(a) Intersection over Union (IoU).   (b) Precision-recall.

Fig. 8.4 **a** Illustration of the Intersection over Union (IoU) metric in 2D. **b** Illustration of how precision and recall are calculated from a model's test results. Recall is the ratio of correct predictions to total objects in the dataset. It measures how complete the predictions are. Precision is the ratio of correct predictions to total predictions made, i.e. how correct the predictions are

8.5.2 Performance Criteria and Metrics

Object detection usually involves two tasks; the first is to assess whether the object exists in the RGB-D image (classification) and the second is to exactly localize the object in the image (localization). Various metrics have been proposed to evaluate the performance of these tasks. Below, we discuss the most commonly used ones, see also [42].

Computation time. Object detection algorithms operate in two phases; the training phase and the testing phase. While, in general, algorithms can afford having a slow training phase, the computation time at runtime is a very important performance criterion. Various applications may have different requirements. For instance, time-critical applications such as autonomous driving and surveillance systems should operate in real time. Other applications, e.g. offline indexing of RGB-D images and videos, can afford slower detection times. However, given the large amount of information they generally need to process, real-time detection is desirable. Note that, there is often a trade-off between computation time at runtime and performance.

Intersection over Union (IoU). It measures the overlap between a ground truth label and a prediction as a proportion of the union of the two regions, see Fig. 8.4. IoU is a useful metric for measuring the predictive power of a 2D/3D object detector. IoU thresholds are applied to sets of detections in order to precisely define what constitutes a positive detection. For example, an IoU > 0.5 might be referred to as a positive detection. Such thresholds are referred to as *overlap criterion*.

Precision–recall curves. Precision and recall are calculated based on a model's test results, see Fig. 8.4. The precision–recall curve is generated by varying the threshold which determines what is counted as a positive detection of the class. The model's precision at varying recall values are then plotted to produce the curve.

Average Precision (AP). It is defined as the average value of precision over the interval from recall $r = 0$ to $r = 1$, which is equivalent to measuring the area under the precision–recall curve (r here is the recall):

$$AP = \int_0^1 \text{precision}(r)dr. \tag{8.8}$$

Mean Average Precision (mAP) score. It is defined as the mean average precision over all classes and/or over all IoU thresholds.

F- and E-Measures. These are two measures which combine precision and recall into a single number to evaluate the retrieval performance. The F-measure is the weighted harmonic mean of precision and recall. It is defined as

$$F_\alpha = \frac{(1+\alpha) \times \text{precision} \times \text{recall}}{\alpha \times \text{precision} + \text{recall}}, \tag{8.9}$$

where α is a weight. When $\alpha = 1$ then

$$F_1 \equiv F = 2 \times \frac{\text{precision} \times \text{recall}}{\text{precision} + \text{recall}}. \tag{8.10}$$

The E-Measure is defined as $E = 1 - F$, which is equivalent to

$$E = 2 \left(\frac{1}{\text{precision}} + \frac{1}{\text{recall}} \right)^{-1}. \tag{8.11}$$

Note that the maximum value of the E-measure is 1.0 and the higher the E-measure is, the better is the detection algorithm. The main property of the E-measure is that it quantifies how good are the results retrieved in the top of the ranked list. This is very important since, in general, the user of a search engine is more interested in the first page of the query results than in the later pages.

Localization performance. The localization task is typically evaluated using the Intersection over Union threshold (IoU) as discussed above.

8.5.3 Discussion and Performance Comparison

Tables 8.2 and 8.3 summarize the performance, on various datasets and using various performance metrics, of some traditional and deep learning-based RGB-D object detection pipelines. Below, we discuss the pipelines whose performances are highlighted in bold in Table 8.3, with a focus on analysing the operational steps which allow them to offer increased performance.

The Deep Sliding Shapes model for amodal 3D object detection in RGB-D images [81] extends its predecessor [80], which used hand-crafted features and SVMs. The network begins by replacing the 3D exhaustive search with a 3D multiscale RPN, which produces 3D RoIs. Non-maximum suppression with an IoU constraint of less than 0.35 is enforced on the RPN output to reduce the number of RoIs. Each RoI is then projected to 2D and fed to a VGG-19-based deep feature extrac-

Table 8.2 Performance of some traditional RGB-D-based object detection methods across multiple datasets and performance metrics. All values taken directly from the cited publications. *Class.* refers to classification accuracy, *Reco.* to recognition accuracy and *mAP* to mean Average Precision. All metrics are measured in percentages except F-score, which is in the range [0, 1]

Method	Dataset	Detection rate		Recall IoU > 0.5	Class.	Reco.	mAP IoU > 0.25	F-score
		IoU > 0.7	IoU > 0.75					
Linear cuboid matching [35]	NYUDv2	75.0						
Extended CPMC [51]	NYUDv2			42.8	60.5			0.36
Convex shapes [34]	NYUDv2		78.2					
Sliding shapes [80]	NYUDv2[a]						39.6	
DSS [81]	NYUDv2[a]						72.3	
DSS [81]	NYUDv2[b]						36.3	
Amodal detection [15]	NYUDv2[b]						40.9	
DSS [81]	SUN RGB-D						29.6	
CoG [70]	SUN RGB-D[c]						47.6	
Separating objects/clutter [39]	RMRC 2013	38.0						
Sliding shapes [80]	RMRC 2013						62.4	
M-HMP [9]	Caltech Bird-200					30.3		
M-HMP [9]	Caltech-256				58.0			
M-HMP [9]	MIT Scene-67				51.2			

(continued)

Table 8.2 (continued)

Method	Dataset	Detection rate		Recall IoU > 0.5	Class.	Reco.	mAPIoU > 0.25	F-score
		IoU > 0.7	IoU > 0.75					
STEM-CaRFs [6]	Washington					97.6		
STEM-CaRFs [6]	Cornell grasping					94.1		
GP [67]	NLPR							0.72
GP [67]	NJUDS400							0.76
LBE [22]	NJUDS2000							0.72
LBE [22]	RGBD1000							0.73
3DHoG [10]	i-LIDS[d]				92.1			

[a]Considering only 5 categories from the NYUDv2 dataset
[b]3D annotations for the NYUDv2 dataset were improved in [15] and this improved dataset was used to calculate performance
[c]Considering only 10 categories from the SUN RGB-D dataset
[d]Scenario 1 of the i-LIDS dataset

tor [77], which produces the class labels as well as the 3D bounding boxes of the detected objects.

Sun et al. [82] proposed an object detection framework for a mobile manipulation platform. The framework is composed of an RPN, an ORN and a Scene Recognition Network (SRN). Its main feature is that the convolutional operations of the three modules are shared, subsequently reducing the computational cost. The ORN, which achieved a mean average precision (mAP) of 52.4% on the SUN RGB-D dataset, outperformed Faster R-CNN [69], RGB-D RCNN [29] and DPM [21].

Another example is the object detection pipeline of Qi et al. [62], which produces the full extents of an object's bounding box in 3D from RGB-D images by using four subnetworks, namely:

- **A joint 2D RPN/ORN**. It generates 2D region proposals from the RGB image, and classifies them into one of the n_c object categories.
- **A PointNet-based network**. It performs 3D instance segmentation of the point clouds within 3D frustums extended from the proposed regions.
- **A lightweight regression PointNet (T-Net)**. It estimates the true centre of the complete object and then transforms the coordinates such that the predicted centre becomes the origin.
- **A box estimation network**. It predicts, for each object, its amodal bounding box for the entire object even if parts of it are occluded.

The approach simultaneously trains the 3D instance segmentation PointNet, the T-Net and the amodal box estimation PointNet, using a loss function that is defined as a weighted sum of the losses of the individual subnetworks. Note that Qi et al. [62]'s network architecture is similar to the architecture of the object classification network of [63, 65] but it outputs the object class scores as well as the detected object's bounding box. The work also shares some similarities to [45], which used hand-crafted features.

8.6 Summary and Perspectives

In this chapter, we have reviewed some of the recent advances in object detection from RGB-D images. Initially we focused on traditional methods, which are based on hand-crafted features combined with machine learning techniques. We then shifted our attention to more recent techniques, which are based on deep learning networks. In terms of performance, deep learning-based techniques significantly outperform traditional methods. However, these methods require large datasets for efficient training. We expect that in the near future, this will become less of an issue since RGB-D sensors are becoming cheaper and annotated RGB-D datasets will thus become widely available.

Although they achieve remarkable performance compared to traditional methods, deep learning techniques are still in their infancy. For instance, amodal object detection, i.e. estimating the entire 3D bounding box of an object, especially when parts

Table 8.3 Performance of some deep learning-based object detection methods across multiple datasets and performance metrics. All values taken directly from the original publications. *mAP* refers to mean Average Precision, *Class* refers to classification accuracy, *Valid* to validation set and *Seg* to instance segmentation. All metrics are measured in percentages except F-score, which is in the range [0, 1]

Method	Dataset	Detection mAP			mAP[a]	Seg.	Class.	F-score $\alpha^2 = 0.3$
		IoU > 0.25	IoU > 0.5	IoU > 0.7				
Rich Features [29]	NYUDv2					37.3		
RGB-D DPM [29]	NYUDv2					23.9		
RGB R-CNN [29]	NYUDv2					22.5		
Amodal 3D [15]	NYUDv2	40.9						
DSS [81]	NYUDv2	**36.3**						
VoxNet [55]	NYUDv2						71.0	
ShapeNet [87]	NYUDv2						58.0	
Frustrum PointNets [62]	SUN RGB-D[b]	**54.0**						
DSS [81]	SUN RGB-D[b]	**42.1**						
COG [70]	SUN RGB-D[b]	47.6						
2D-driven [45]	SUN RGB-D[b]	45.1						
Faster R-CNN [69]	SUN RGB-D		50.8					
Unified CNN [82]	SUN RGB-D		**52.4**					
Frustrum PointNets [62]	KITTI (valid)[c]			63.7				
MV3D [12]	KITTI (valid)[c]			55.1				
MV3D [12]	KITTI (test)[c]				79.8			

(continued)

Table 8.3 (continued)

Method	Dataset	Detection mAP			mAP[a]	Seg.	Class.	F-score $\alpha^2 = 0.3$
		IoU > 0.25	IoU > 0.5	IoU > 0.7				
3D FCN [48]	KITTI (test)[c]				68.3			
Vote3Deep [18]	KITTI (test)[c]				63.2			
Vote3D [84]	KITTI (test)[c]				42.6			
VeloFCN [49]	KITTI (test)[c]				46.9			
Complement-Aware [11]	NLPR							0.85
Salient Deep Fusion [66]	NLPR							0.78
LMH [60]	NLPR							0.65
GP [67]	NLPR							0.72
ACSD [36]	NLPR							0.54
PointNet [63]	ModelNet40						89.2	
PointNet++ [65]	ModelNet40						91.9	
VoxNet [65]	ModelNet40						85.9	
3D ShapeNets [86]	ModelNet40						84.7	
Subvolumes [64]	ModelNet40						89.2	
VoxNet [55]	ModelNet40						83.0	
ShapeNet [87]	ModelNet40						77.0	
Faster R-CNN [69][d,e]	PASCAL 2012[f]				76.4			
ION [30]	PASCAL 2012[f]				74.6			

(continued)

Table 8.3 (continued)

Method	Dataset	Detection mAP			mAP[a]	Seg.	Class.	F-score $\alpha^2 = 0.3$
		IoU > 0.25	IoU > 0.5	IoU > 0.7				
SSD512 [30]	PASCAL 2012[f]				76.8			
Short Conns [32]	PASCAL 2010[f]							0.82
MMDL [17]	Washington						91.3	
STEM-CaRFs [6]	Washington						88.1	
CNN Features [75]	Washington						89.4	
VoxNet [55]	ModelNet10						92.0	
ShapeNet [87]	ModelNet10						84.0	
Faster R-CNN on FPN [52]	COCO test-dev				36.2			
AttractioNet [25]	COCO test-dev				35.7			
Complement-Aware [11]	NJUDS							0.86
Short Conns [32]	MSRA-B							0.92
MMDL [17]	Scenes						82.1	

[a]Values in this column use unspecified IoU thresholds
[b]Using only 10 categories from the SUN RGB-D dataset
[c]Using the hard, cars subset of the KITTI dataset
[d]Results taken from [30]
[e]Uses ResNet-101
[f]Using the PASCAL Visual Object Classes (VOC) evaluation

of the object are occluded, still remains challenging especially in highly cluttered scenes. Self-occluding objects also challenge deep learning-based pipelines, especially when dealing with dynamic objects that deform in a non-rigid way [33, 44]. Similarly, object detection performance for objects at various scales, particularly at small scales, is still relatively low. In fact, the performance comparison of Table 8.3 does not consider the robustness of the methods to scale variation.

Existing techniques focus mainly on the detection of the bounding boxes of the objects of interest. However, many situations, e.g. robust grasping, image editing, and accurate robot navigation, require the accurate detection of object boundaries. Several works have attempted to achieve this using, for example, template matching. This, however, remains an open problem.

Another important avenue for future research is how to incorporate spatial relationships and relationships between semantic classes in deep learning-based RGB-D object detection pipelines. These relationships are important cues for recognition and it has been already shown in many papers that they can significantly boost the performance of traditional techniques [43]. Yet, this knowledge is not efficiently exploited in deep learning techniques.

Finally, there are many aspects of object detection from RGB-D images that have not been covered in this chapter. Examples include saliency detection [11, 47, 66, 78], which aims to detect salient regions in an RGB-D image. Additionally, we have focused in this chapter on generic objects in indoor and outdoor scenes. There is, however, a rich literature on specialized detectors which focus on specific classes of objects, e.g. humans and human body parts such as faces and hands (see Chaps. 9 and 10).

Acknowledgements This work is supported by ARC DP 150100294 and ARC DP 150104251.

References

1. Cornell grasping dataset (2018). http://pr.cs.cornell.edu/grasping/rect_data/data.php. Accessed 13 Dec 2018
2. Achanta R, Shaji A, Smith K, Lucchi A, Fua P, Süsstrunk S (2012) SLIC superpixels compared to state-of-the-art superpixel methods. IEEE Trans Pattern Anal Mach Intell 34(11):2274–2282. https://doi.org/10.1109/TPAMI.2012.120
3. Alexandre LA (2014) 3D object recognition using convolutional neural networks with transfer learning between input channels. In: IAS
4. Alexe B, Deselaers T, Ferrari V (2010) What is an object? In: 2010 IEEE computer society conference on computer vision and pattern recognition, pp 73–80. https://doi.org/10.1109/CVPR.2010.5540226
5. Arbeláez P, Pont-Tuset J, Barron J, Marques F, Malik J (2014) Multiscale combinatorial grouping. In: Computer vision and pattern recognition
6. Asif U, Bennamoun M, Sohel FA (2017) RGB-D object recognition and grasp detection using hierarchical cascaded forests. IEEE Trans Robot 33(3):547–564. https://doi.org/10.1109/TRO.2016.2638453
7. Barrow HG, Tenenbaum JM, Bolles RC, Wolf HC (1977) Parametric correspondence and chamfer matching: two new techniques for image matching. In: Proceedings of the 5th International

joint conference on artificial intelligence - volume 2, IJCAI'77, . Morgan Kaufmann Publishers Inc., San Francisco, CA, USA, pp 659–663. http://dl.acm.org/citation.cfm?id=1622943. 1622971

8. Bleyer M, Rhemann C, Rother C (2012) Extracting 3D scene-consistent object proposals and depth from stereo images. In: European conference on computer vision. Springer, pp 467–481

9. Bo L, Ren X, Fox D (2014) Learning hierarchical sparse features for RGB-(D) object recognition. Int J Robot Res 33(4):581–599

10. Buch NE, Orwell J, Velastin SA (2009) 3D extended histogram of oriented gradients (3DHOG) for classification of road users in urban scenes. In: BMVC

11. Chen H, Li Y (2018) Progressively complementarity-aware fusion network for RGB-D salient object detection. In: The IEEE conference on computer vision and pattern recognition (CVPR)

12. Chen X, Ma H, Wan J, Li B, Xia T (2017) Multi-view 3D object detection network for autonomous driving. In: IEEE CVPR, vol 1, p 3

13. Dalal N, Triggs B (2005) Histograms of oriented gradients for human detection. In: 2005 IEEE computer society conference on computer vision and pattern recognition (CVPR'05), vol 1, pp 886–893. https://doi.org/10.1109/CVPR.2005.177

14. Lowe DG (2004) Distinctive image features from scale-invariant keypoints. Int J Comput Vision (IJCV)

15. Deng Z, Latecki LJ (2017) Amodal detection of 3D objects: inferring 3D bounding boxes from 2D ones in RGB-depth images. In: Conference on computer vision and pattern recognition (CVPR), vol 2, p 2

16. Schapire RE (2013) Explaining adaboost, pp 37–52. https://doi.org/10.1007/978-3-642-41136-6-5

17. Eitel A, Springenberg JT, Spinello L, Riedmiller MA, Burgard W (2015) Multimodal deep learning for robust RGB-D object recognition. arXiv:1507.06821

18. Engelcke M, Rao D, Wang DZ, Tong CH, Posner I (2017) Vote3deep: Fast object detection in 3D point clouds using efficient convolutional neural networks. In: 2017 IEEE international conference on robotics and automation (ICRA). IEEE, pp 1355–1361

19. Everingham M, Van Gool L, Williams C, Winn J, Zisserman A (2010) The PASCAL visual object classes (VOC) challenge. In: 2010 IEEE Conference on computer vision and pattern recognition (CVPR)

20. Fei-Fei L, Fergus R, Perona P (2004) Learning generative visual models from few training examples: an incremental bayesian approach tested on 101 object categories. In: 2004 conference on computer vision and pattern recognition workshop, pp. 178–178

21. Felzenszwalb PF, Girshick RB, McAllester D, Ramanan D (2010) Object detection with discriminatively trained part-based models. IEEE Trans Pattern Anal Mach Intell 32(9):1627–1645

22. Feng D, Barnes N, You S, McCarthy C (2016) Local background enclosure for RGB-D salient object detection. In: 2016 IEEE conference on computer vision and pattern recognition (CVPR), pp. 2343–2350. https://doi.org/10.1109/CVPR.2016.257

23. Geiger A, Lenz P, Urtasun R (2012) Are we ready for autonomous driving? the KITTI vision benchmark suite. In: Conference on computer vision and pattern recognition (CVPR)

24. Getto R, Fellner DW (2015) 3D object retrieval with parametric templates. In: Proceedings of the 2015 Eurographics workshop on 3D object retrieval, 3DOR '15. Eurographics Association, Goslar Germany, Germany, pp 47–54. https://doi.org/10.2312/3dor.20151054

25. Gidaris S, Komodakis N (2016) Attend refine repeat: active box proposal generation via in-out localization. CoRR arXiv:1606.04446

26. Girshick RB (2015) Fast R-CNN. CoRR arXiv:1504.08083

27. Griffin G, Holub A, Perona P (2007) Caltech-256 object category dataset. Technical Report 7694, California Institute of Technology. http://authors.library.caltech.edu/7694

28. Gupta S, Arbeláez P, Girshick R, Malik J (2015) Aligning 3D models to RGB-D images of cluttered scenes. In: Proceedings of the IEEE conference on computer vision and pattern recognition, pp 4731–4740

29. Gupta S, Girshick RB, Arbeláez P, Malik J (2014) Learning rich features from RGB-D images for object detection and segmentation. CoRR arXiv:1407.5736

30. Han J, Zhang D, Cheng G, Liu N, Xu D (2018) Advanced deep-learning techniques for salient and category-specific object detection: a survey. IEEE Signal Process Mag 35(1):84–100. https://doi.org/10.1109/MSP.2017.2749125
31. He D, Wang L (1990) Texture unit, texture spectrum, and texture analysis. IEEE Trans Geosci Remote Sens 28(4):509–512. https://doi.org/10.1109/TGRS.1990.572934
32. Hou Q, Cheng M, Hu X, Borji A, Tu Z, Torr PHS (2016) Deeply supervised salient object detection with short connections. CoRR arXiv:1611.04849
33. Jermyn IH, Kurtek S, Laga H, Srivastava A (2017) Elastic shape analysis of three-dimensional objects. Synth Lect Comput Vis 12(1):1–185
34. Jiang H (2014) Finding approximate convex shapes in RGBD images. In: European conference on computer vision. Springer, pp 582–596
35. Jiang H, Xiao J (2013) A linear approach to matching cuboids in RGBD images. In: Proceedings of the IEEE conference on computer vision and pattern recognition, pp 2171–2178
36. Ju R, Ge L, Geng W, Ren T, Wu G (2014) Depth saliency based on anisotropic center-surround difference. In: 2014 IEEE international conference on image processing (ICIP), pp 1115–1119. https://doi.org/10.1109/ICIP.2014.7025222
37. Kendall A, Cipolla R (2017) Geometric loss functions for camera pose regression with deep learning. CoRR arXiv:1704.00390
38. Khan S, Rahmani H, Shah SAA, Bennamoun M (2018) A guide to convolutional neural networks for computer vision. Morgan and Claypool Publishers
39. Khan SH, He X, Bennamoun M, Sohel F, Togneri R (2015) Separating objects and clutter in indoor scenes. In: Proceedings of the IEEE conference on computer vision and pattern recognition, pp 4603–4611
40. Krizhevsky A, Sutskever I, Hinton GE (2012) Imagenet classification with deep convolutional neural networks. In: Proceedings of the 25th international conference on neural information processing systems - volume 1, NIPS'12. Curran Associates Inc., USA, pp 1097–1105. http://dl.acm.org/citation.cfm?id=2999134.2999257
41. Laga H, Guo Y, Tabia H, Fisher RB, Bennamoun M (2018) 3D shape analysis: fundamentals, theory, and applications. Wiley
42. Laga H, Guo Y, Tabia H, Fisher RB, Bennamoun M (2019) 3D shape analysis: fundamentals, theory, and applications. Wiley
43. Laga H, Mortara M, Spagnuolo M (2013) Geometry and context for semantic correspondences and functionality recognition in man-made 3D shapes. ACM Trans Graph (TOG) 32(5):150
44. Laga H, Xie Q, Jermyn IH, Srivastava A (2017) Numerical inversion of SRNF maps for elastic shape analysis of genus-zero surfaces. IEEE Trans Pattern Anal Mach Intell 39(12):2451–2464
45. Lahoud J, Ghanem B (2017) 2D-driven 3D object detection in RGB-D images. In: The IEEE international conference on computer vision (ICCV)
46. Lai K, Bo L, Ren X, Fox D (2013) RGB-D object recognition: features, algorithms, and a large scale benchmark. In: Consumer depth cameras for computer vision. Springer, pp 167–192
47. Lei Z, Chai W, Zhao S, Song H, Li F (2017) Saliency detection for RGB-D images using optimization. In: 2017 12th international conference on computer science and education (ICCSE), pp 440–443. https://doi.org/10.1109/ICCSE.2017.8085532
48. Li B (2016) 3D fully convolutional network for vehicle detection in point cloud. CoRR arXiv:1611.08069
49. Li B, Zhang T, Xia T (2016) Vehicle detection from 3D lidar using fully convolutional network. arXiv:1608.07916
50. Li N, Ye J, Ji Y, Ling H, Yu J (2017) Saliency detection on light field. IEEE Trans Pattern Anal Mach Intell 39(8):1605–1616. https://doi.org/10.1109/TPAMI.2016.2610425
51. Lin D, Fidler S, Urtasun R (2013) Holistic scene understanding for 3D object detection with RGBD cameras. In: Proceedings of the IEEE international conference on computer vision, pp 1417–1424
52. Lin TY, Dollár P, Girshick RB, He K, Hariharan B, Belongie SJ (2017) Feature pyramid networks for object detection. In: CVPR, vol 1, p 4

53. Long J, Shelhamer E, Darrell T (2014) Fully convolutional networks for semantic segmentation. CoRR arXiv:1411.4038
54. Maturana, D., Scherer, S.: 3D convolutional neural networks for landing zone detection from LiDAR. In: 2015 IEEE international conference on robotics and automation (ICRA), pp 3471–3478. https://doi.org/10.1109/ICRA.2015.7139679
55. Maturana D, Scherer S (2015) VoxNet: a 3D convolutional neural network for real-time object recognition. In: IEEE/RSJ international conference on intelligent robots and systems, pp 922–928
56. Menze M, Geiger A (2015) Object scene flow for autonomous vehicles. In: Conference on computer vision and pattern recognition (CVPR)
57. Nakahara H, Yonekawa H, Sato S (2017) An object detector based on multiscale sliding window search using a fully pipelined binarized CNN on an FPGA. In: 2017 international conference on field programmable technology (ICFPT), pp 168–175. https://doi.org/10.1109/FPT.2017.8280135
58. Nathan Silberman Derek Hoiem, P.K., Fergus, R.: Indoor segmentation and support inference from RGB-D images. In: ECCV (2012)
59. Newcombe RA, Izadi S, Hilliges O, Molyneaux D, Kim D, Davison AJ, Kohi P, Shotton J, Hodges S, Fitzgibbon A (2011) Kinectfusion: Real-time dense surface mapping and tracking. In: 2011 10th ieee international symposium on mixed and augmented reality, pp 127–136. https://doi.org/10.1109/ISMAR.2011.6092378
60. Peng H, Li B, Xiong W, Hu W, Ji R (2014) RGB-D salient object detection: a benchmark and algorithms. In: ECCV
61. Pont-Tuset J, Arbeláez P, Barron J, Marques F, Malik J (2015) Multiscale combinatorial grouping for image segmentation and object proposal generation. arXiv:1503.00848
62. Qi CR, Liu W, Wu, C, Su H, Guibas LJ (2018) Frustum pointnets for 3D object detection from RGB-D data. In: The IEEE conference on computer vision and pattern recognition (CVPR)
63. Qi CR, Su H, Mo K, Guibas LJ (2017) Pointnet: Deep learning on point sets for 3D classification and segmentation. In: Proceedings of computer vision and pattern recognition (CVPR), vol 1(2). IEEE, p 4
64. Qi CR, Su H, Nießner M, Dai A, Yan M, Guibas LJ (2016) Volumetric and multi-view CNNs for object classification on 3D data. CoRR arXiv:1604.03265
65. Qi CR, Yi L, Su H, Guibas LJ (2017) Pointnet++: deep hierarchical feature learning on point sets in a metric space. In: Advances in neural information processing systems, pp 5099–5108
66. Qu L, He S, Zhang J, Tian J, Tang Y, Yang Q (2017) RGB-D salient object detection via deep fusion. IEEE Trans Image Process 26(5):2274–2285. https://doi.org/10.1109/TIP.2017.2682981
67. Ren J, Gong X, Yu L, Zhou W, Yang MY (2015) Exploiting global priors for RGB-D saliency detection. In: 2015 IEEE conference on computer vision and pattern recognition workshops (CVPRW), pp 25–32. https://doi.org/10.1109/CVPRW.2015.7301391
68. Ren S, He K, Girshick R, Sun J (2015) Faster r-cnn: towards real-time object detection with region proposal networks. In: Advances in neural information processing systems, pp 91–99
69. Ren S, He K, Girshick RB, Sun J (2015) Faster R-CNN: towards real-time object detection with region proposal networks. CoRR arXiv:1506.01497
70. Ren Z, Sudderth EB (2016) Three-dimensional object detection and layout prediction using clouds of oriented gradients. In: 2016 IEEE conference on computer vision and pattern recognition (CVPR), pp 1525–1533. https://doi.org/10.1109/CVPR.2016.169
71. Rusinkiewicz S, Levoy M (2001) Efficient variants of the ICP algorithm. In: Proceedings Third international conference on 3-d digital imaging and modeling, pp 145–152. https://doi.org/10.1109/IM.2001.924423
72. Russakovsky O, Deng J, Su H, Krause J, Satheesh S, Ma S, Huang Z, Karpathy A, Khosla A, Bernstein M, Berg AC, Fei-Fei L (2015) ImageNet large scale visual recognition challenge. Int J Comput Vis (IJCV) 115(3):211–252. https://doi.org/10.1007/s11263-015-0816-y
73. Sahin C, Kouskouridas R, Kim T (2016) Iterative hough forest with histogram of control points for 6 dof object registration from depth images. CoRR arXiv:1603.02617

74. Sahin C, Kouskouridas R, Kim T (2017) A learning-based variable size part extraction archi- tecture for 6d object pose recovery in depth. CoRR arXiv:1701.02166
75. Schwarz M, Schulz H, Behnke S (2015) RGB-D object recognition and pose estimation based on pre-trained convolutional neural network features. In: 2015 IEEE international conference on robotics and automation (ICRA), pp 1329–1335. https://doi.org/10.1109/ICRA.2015.7139363
76. Shotton J, Girshick R, Fitzgibbon A, Sharp T, Cook M, Finocchio M, Moore R, Kohli P, Criminisi A, Kipman A et al (2013) Efficient human pose estimation from single depth images. IEEE Trans Pattern Anal Mach Intell 35(12):2821–2840
77. Simonyan K, Zisserman A (2014) Very deep convolutional networks for large-scale image recognition. arXiv:1409.1556
78. Song H, Liu Z, Xie Y, Wu L, Huang M (2016) RGBD co-saliency detection via bagging-based clustering. IEEE Signal Processing Lett 23(12):1722–1726
79. Song S, Lichtenberg SP, Xiao J (2015) Sun RGB-D: a RGB-D scene understanding benchmark suite. In: 2015 IEEE conference on computer vision and pattern recognition (CVPR). IEEE, pp 567–576
80. Song S, Xiao J (2014) Sliding shapes for 3D object detection in depth images. In: European conference on computer vision. Springer, pp 634–651
81. Song S, Xiao J (2016) Deep sliding shapes for a modal 3D object detection in rgb-d images. In: CVPR
82. Sun H, Meng Z, Tao PY, Ang MH (2018) Scene recognition and object detection in a unified convolutional neural network on a mobile manipulator. In: 2018 IEEE international conference on robotics and automation (ICRA), pp 1–5. https://doi.org/10.1109/ICRA.2018.8460535
83. Wang A, Cai J, Lu J, Cham TJ MMSS: multi-modal sharable and specific feature learning for RGB-D object recognition. In: Proceedings of the IEEE international conference on computer vision, pp 1125–1133
84. Wang DZ, Posner I (2015) Voting for voting in online point cloud object detection. In: Robotics: science and systems
85. Ward IR, Jalwana MAAK, Bennamoun M (2019) Improving image-based localization with deep learning: the impact of the loss function. CoRR arXiv:1905.03692
86. Wu Z, Song S, Khosla A, Tang X, Xiao J (2014) 3D shapenets for 2.5d object recognition and next-best-view prediction. CoRR
87. Wu Z, Song S, Khosla A, Yu F, Zhang L, Tang X, Xiao J (2015) 3D shapenets: a deep rep- resentation for volumetric shapes. In: 2015 IEEE conference on computer vision and pattern recognition (CVPR), pp 1912–1920. https://doi.org/10.1109/CVPR.2015.7298801
88. Xiang Y, Kim W, Chen W, Ji J, Choy C, Su H, Mottaghi R, Guibas L, Savarese S (2016) ObjectNet3D: a large scale database for 3D object recognition. In: European conference on computer vision. Springer, pp 160–176
89. Xiang Y, Mottaghi R, Savarese S (2014) Beyond pascal: a benchmark for 3D object detection in the wild. In: 2014 IEEE winter conference on applications of computer vision (WACV). IEEE, pp 75–82
90. Xiao J, Hays J, Ehinger KA, Oliva A, Torralba A (2010) SUN database: large-scale scene recognition from abbey to zoo. In: 2010 IEEE computer society conference on computer vision and pattern recognition, pp 3485–3492. https://doi.org/10.1109/CVPR.2010.5539970

Chapter 9
RGB-D Salient Object Detection: A Review

Tongwei Ren and Ao Zhang

Abstract Salient object detection focuses on extracting attractive objects from the scene, which serves as a foundation of various vision tasks. Benefiting from the progress in acquisition devices, the depth cue is convenient to obtain, and is used in salient object detection in RGB-D images in combination with the color cue. In this chapter, we comprehensively review the advances in RGB-D salient object detection. We first introduce the task and key concepts in RGB-D salient object detection. Then, we briefly review the evolution of salient object detection technology, especially those for RGB images, since many RGB-D salient object detection methods derive from the existing RGB ones. Next, we present the typical RGB-D salient object detection methods, evaluate their performance on public datasets, and summarize their issues. Finally, we discuss some open problems and suggestions for future research.

9.1 Introduction

When introducing salient object detection from a cognitive perspective, it refers to finding objects, which attract more attention than the surrounding regions when the human visual system perceives the scene. The task of salient object detection in computer vision is inspired by early tasks, which try to simulate human attention [13, 17], a concept that has been studied in cognitive psychology for many years [27]. Because of the complexity of human visual system, the criterion of judging whether an object is salient cannot be explicitly listed with a couple of simple standards. There are many factors that can influence the judgement of salient objects, for example, salient objects are context dependent. The change of scene or even the change of location in the same scene may cause a difference in the saliency rank of objects.

T. Ren (✉) · A. Zhang
Software Institute, Nanjing University, Nanjing 210093, China
e-mail: rentw@nju.edu.cn

A. Zhang
e-mail: zhanga@smail.nju.edu.cn

© Springer Nature Switzerland AG 2019   203
P. L. Rosin et al. (eds.), *RGB-D Image Analysis and Processing*,
Advances in Computer Vision and Pattern Recognition,
https://doi.org/10.1007/978-3-030-28603-3_9

(a)   (b)   (c)

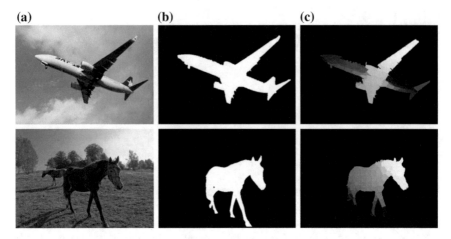

Fig. 9.1 Examples of salient object detection. **a** Original images. **b** Groundtruths of salient object detection. **c** Saliency maps. The saliency maps are generated by Guo et al. [11]

Both local contrast and global contrast with other objects in the same context should be taken into consideration.

When introducing the salient object from a precise and computational perspective, it refers to segmenting the entire objects, which are the most attention-grabbing compared to surrounding regions, rather than only parts of the objects [2]. Referring to some popular salient object detection dataset construction [1, 4, 5, 33], the concrete way of judging whether an object is salient, is to ask a couple of annotators to choose the most attention-grabbing object in the scene. Figure 9.1 shows an example of salient object detection.

Saliency analysis technology mainly includes fixation prediction and salient object detection. Different from fixation prediction, salient object detection aims to extract the entire attractive objects rather than presenting the gaze points by highlighting a few spots on heat maps, which is more useful to serve as a foundation of various vision tasks, such as object detection, information retrieval, and video analysis.

In recent years, benefiting from the progress of acquisition devices, depth cues can be conveniently obtained by depth cameras and binocular cameras, and its potential in salient object detection is explored. In reality, the human visual system perceives both color and depth information from the scene, and uses them together in distinguishing salient objects. Depth cues help to distinguish salient objects from the background, especially when the objects have complex structure or texture. Figure 9.2 shows a comparison between saliency maps using color cue and saliency maps using both color and depth cues. Thus, it is useful to combine depth cues with color cues in salient object detection on RGB-D images.

However, due to the performance limitation of current acquisition devices, the depth maps are usually of low quality, low resolution and accuracy in particular, which brings serious noise and can mislead salient object detection. How to handle

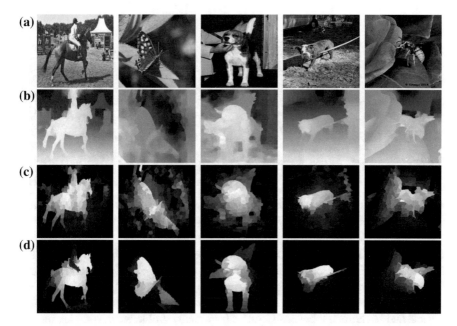

Fig. 9.2 Examples of comparison between saliency maps using only color cue and saliency maps using both color cue and depth cue. **a** Original images. **b** Depth maps. **c** Saliency maps using only color cue. **d** Saliency maps using both color cue and depth cue. The saliency maps are generated by Guo et al. [11]

the low quality of depth maps in salient object detection has not yet been solved. Moreover, color cues and depth cues play complementary roles in salient object detection, but they conflict with each other sometimes. How to combine color cues and depth cues while handling their inconsistency still needs further investigation.

In this chapter, we comprehensively review the advances in RGB-D salient object detection, and the rest of the chapter is organized as follows. In Sect. 9.2, we briefly review the evaluation of salient object detection, especially those on RGB images, since many RGB-D salient object detection methods derive from the existing RGB ones. In Sect. 9.3, we present the typical RGB-D salient object detection methods, evaluate their performance on public datasets, and summarize their issues. In Sect. 9.6, we discuss some open problems and suggestions for future research.

9.2   Salient Object Detection Evolution

In the past decades, great progress has been made in salient object detection on RGB images. A large number of RGB salient object detection methods are proposed, and they achieve significant performance. These methods explore the effectiveness of color cues in salient object detection, while providing the useful inspiration for

Fig. 9.3 Examples of co-saliency object detection. **a** Image series. **b** Saliency maps. **c** Groundtruths of co-saliency object detection. The saliency maps are generated by Cong et al. [6]

depth cue in RGB-D salient object detection. The early RGB salient object detection methods are mainly based on handcrafted features of global or local contrast, while there are many corresponding RGB-D methods [8, 9, 14–16, 18, 22, 25, 28, 31]. These methods perform well on images which have simple and high-contrast salient objects and background, but easily suffer from many problems on complex images, such as incomplete objects. To improve the completeness of the detected salient objects, graph-based models are used to propagate the saliency among adjacent and similar regions, which can effectively enhance the missing parts in the salient objects while suppressing the residual saliency on the background. Graph-based methods also inspire some RGB-D salient object detection methods [11, 22]. Recently, deep learning-based methods show their remarkable abilities in salient object detection, including deep neural networks, multi-context deep networks, multi-scale deep networks, symmetrical networks, and weakly supervised deep networks [3, 12, 23].

Beyond extracting salient objects from a single image, co-saliency detection focuses on detecting common salient objects from several related images [6, 7, 10, 26]. By exploring the inter-image correspondence among images, co-saliency can extract the salient objects with similar appearances from multiple images effectively. Compared to RGB-D salient object detection, the multiple images used in co-saliency detection have the same modality, i.e., color cue, but not different ones. Moreover, co-saliency detection requires that the objects should be salient in all the images, but the objects are usually only present in the color cue or the depth cue in RGB-D salient object detection. Figure 9.3 shows an example of co-saliency object detection. Recently, some research works combine co-saliency detection and RGB-D salient object detection, and extracts common salient objects from multiple RGB-D images.

Video salient object detection aims to extract salient objects from video sequences [29, 30]. From a certain perspective, video salient object detection can be treated as a special co-saliency detection, in which all the adjacent video frames contain the common salient objects with similar appearances. Figure 9.4 shows an example of video salient object detection. Nevertheless, video salient object detection is usually

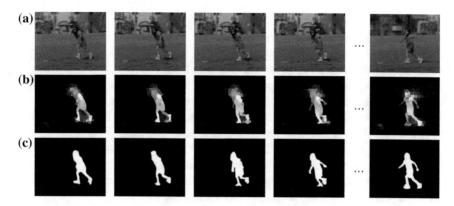

Fig. 9.4 Examples of video salient object detection. **a** Video frames. **b** Saliency maps. **c** Groundtruths of video salient object detection. The saliency maps are generated by Wang et al. [30]

conducted in a different way. In one aspect, the adjacent video frames are similar in both objects and background. And it follows that inter-frame analysis can provide little additional information compared to single frame analysis. From another perspective, the motion cues that can be estimated from the adjacent frames usually plays a key role in salient object detection, because the moving objects are easy to attract human attention. The exploration [29, 30] of motion cues has some similar characteristics to that of depth cues, for example, the estimated object motion is usually inaccurate and the detection results on color cues and motion cues conflict each other sometimes. Thus, the studies on video salient object detection, especially on the fusion of color cues and motion cues, may provide useful inspiration to RGB-D salient object detection.

9.3 RGB-D Salient Object Detection

Based on the numbers of modalities and images used in salient object detection, RGB-D salient object detection can be roughly classified into three categories: depth-based salient object detection, depth- and color-based salient object detection, and RGB-D co-saliency detection.

9.3.1 Depth-Based Salient Object Detection

Depth-based salient object detection aims to explore the effectiveness of depth cues in salient object detection directly and independently, i.e., extracting salient objects from depth maps without considering color cues.

Based on the assumption that depth is intrinsic in biological vision, Ouerhani et al. [21] investigated the power of depth in saliency analysis, and pointed out that depth cue is beneficial in predicting human gazes. Ju et al. [15, 16] proposed the first depth-based salient object detection method with the assumption that salient objects stand out from their surroundings in depth. The method is based on anisotropic center-surround difference, and refines its results by integrating the 3D spatial prior. However, they used fixed weights to combine depth contrast from different directions to predict pixel level saliency, which might lead to low quality on some specific directions of the saliency map. There is also another disadvantage that the area chosen to generate depth contrast in each direction for a single pixel was fixed, which may lead to a vague saliency map under some condition, especially when the salient object takes up a big portion of the whole image.

In order to detect salient objects easier and more accurate, Sheng et al. [24] enhanced the depth comparison between salient objects and the background instead of extracting features from depth maps directly, based on the fact that contrast between pixels in many depth maps is not obvious due to various view points used to capture depth maps.

The depth cue is simpler than the color cue in saliency analysis because it only contains one channel rather than three. However, it suffers from the problems of low quality, which tends to hamper the accurate salient object detection. Moreover, the depth maps of natural images are usually connected, which prevents segmenting the salient objects from the background without the assistance of color cue [31].

9.3.2   Depth- and Color-Based Salient Object Detection

As compared to only using depth cues, it is a common and better solution to combine depth cues and color cues in salient object detection. Early works usually directly treat the depth cue as a complement channel of the color cue [14] or mix the features from depth cues with those from color, luminance and texture [8], which ignores the differences among different modalities in saliency representation.

To study whether and how depth information influences visual saliency, Lang et al. [18] built a 3D eye fixation dataset using Kinect to study the power of depth in attention prediction. They drew a set of conclusions based on their observations, including (i) Humans are likely to fixate on areas with closer depth. (ii) The majority of fixation consists of only a few interesting objects both in 2D and 3D. (iii) There is a nonlinear relationship between depth and saliency and the relationship is different under different scenes with different depth ranges. (iv) The incorporation of depth cues will cause a huge difference between fixation distribution of 2D version and fixation distribution of 3D version, especially in complex scenes. Based on the above observations, they integrated depth into 2D methods as a probabilistic prior and found that the predictive power could be increased by 6–7%. However, they combine the depth prior through simple summation or multiplication, which are not efficient enough and suffer when there are conflicts between color cues and depth cues.

Based on the observations that there are obvious depth gaps between salient objects and background and some domain knowledge of stereoscopic photography, Niu et al. [20] proposed to compute the saliency based on the global disparity contrast, and leverage domain knowledge of stereoscopic photography in salient object detection. However, there are drawbacks that they considered the depth cue as the fourth channel of color cue that ignores the differences among different modalities in saliency representation, and there are some certain salient objects whose depth comparison between background are consistent rather than abrupt which is conflicted with their basic assumption.

Peng et al. [22] built a RGB-D dataset using Kinect and combined depth and existing 2D models for improvement. They proposed a multi-level saliency map combination method. For low level saliency maps, a multi-contextual feature combining local, global and background contrast to measure pixel-wise saliency is employed. The feature performs a fixed, passive measurement of depth contrast. For mid level saliency maps, a graph-based propagation method is adopted, which are helpful in reducing the saliency value in the background area. Notably, most of the contrast-based methods without further optimization would suffer from the problem of high saliency in the background, while graph-based methods show a better performance on this problem. For high-level saliency maps, some spatial priors are incorporated. Because of the fact that most of the salient objects occur in the central area of the scene, spatial priors could contribute to eliminating some interference from background objects with high contrast for color cue or depth cue. Finally, they combine three levels' saliency maps by adding the first two levels' saliency maps and then multiplying high level saliency maps. Despite the delicate process of multi-contextual features in low level and diverse feature extraction in different levels, the combination method consists of simply summation and multiplication, which cannot make an effective combination of different saliency maps.

To eliminate the regions with high depth contrast in the background, Feng et al. [9] computed a local background enclosure feature, then applied the priors on depth, spatial, and background, and refined the boundaries of salient objects with Grabcut segmentation. There are several improvements compared to Ju et al. [15, 16] on how to take advantage of depth cues, including (i) Incorporation of angular information could be considered as a kind of contrast with adaptive weights which ameliorated the problem brought by fixed weights of contrast in different directions in [15, 16]. (ii) The area of contrast for each pixel was reduced compared to Ju et al. [15, 16], which only drew attention to distinguishing salient objects from local background.

Guo et al. [11] further proposed a salient object detection method based on saliency evolution, which generated accurate but incomplete salient objects by fusing the saliency analysis results on color cues and depth cues, and refined the saliency maps by propagating saliency among adjacent and similar regions in super-pixel level. The main contribution of Guo et al. [11] was that they proposed an effective method to combine color cue and depth cue. To be more specific, the saliency evolution strategy implemented with a single-layer cellular automata can reduce the high saliency regions in the background and improve the completeness of salient objects. However, if some parts of the salient object are very thin compared to the main part, like a tentacle of an alien, the final saliency map would be vague in these thin parts, due to the fact that evolution strategy tends to assign higher saliency value when most of its surrounding area has high saliency value, while the surrounding of the thin parts do not have high saliency value.

Wang and Wang [28] proposed a multistage salient object detection method, which generated color cue and depth cue-based saliency maps, weighted them with depth bias and 3D spatial prior, and fused all the saliency maps by multilayer cellular automata. Different from Guo et al. [11] which utilized a single-layer cellular automata on the multiplication of different saliency maps, they use a multilayer cellular automata to fuse all saliency maps directly, which shows superior performance.

Song et al. [25] exploited different features on multiple levels and generated several multi-scale saliency maps by performing a discriminative saliency fusion on hundreds of corresponding regional saliency results. To be more specific, the discriminative saliency fusion employed a random forest regressor to find the most discriminative ones, which would be used in generating multi-scale saliency maps. Different from many other proposed fusion methods that use weighted summation or multiplication, the discriminative fusion is nonlinear which will not suffer when the amount of salient results exceed one hundred. Based on several generated multi-scale saliency maps, a further fusion is needed to generate a final saliency map. Bootstrap learning was employed to combine these saliency maps, which performed salient objects segmentation at the same time. Evidently, the segmentation contributed to both reducing the saliency value in the background and refining the boundary of saliency objects.

In recent years, similar to that in many other vision tasks, deep learning shows its power in salient object detection. However, recent deep learning methods mainly pay their attention to color cue, while there are few of them taking advantage of both color cue and depth cue. In the following part, we introduce two RGB-D salient object detection methods which are deep learning based.

Qu et al. [23] designed a Convolutional Neural Network (CNN) to fuse different low level saliency cues into hierarchical features for automatic detection of salient objects. They adopted well-designed saliency feature vectors as the input instead of directly feeding raw images to the network, which could take advantage of the knowledge in the previous advances in salient object detection and reduced learning ambiguity to detect the salient object more effectively. Moreover, it integrates Laplacian propagation with the learned CNN to extract a spatially consistent saliency map. Thanks to the superiority of CNN in fusing different feature vectors, the performance is improved compared to other non-deep learning-based methods, but they ignored the strong power of CNN in feature extraction.

Han et al. [12] transferred the structure of the RGB-based deep neural network to be applicable for depth cue, and fused the deep representations of both color and depth views automatically to obtain the final saliency map. Different from Qu et al. [23], CNN is used in all of stages including feature extraction and feature fusion.

Chen and Li [3] designed a complementarity-aware fusion module and explored the complement across all levels in order to obtain sufficient fusion results. There is a difference between Han et al. [12] and Chen and Li [3] that Han et al. [12] combined depth cue and color cue after feature extraction, Chen and Li [3] fused two cues from the beginning of the feature extraction and performed fusion in every stage of the process.

9.3.3 RGB-D Co-saliency Detection

RGB-D co-saliency detection aims to further explore the inter-image correspondence and to perform better in salient object detection.

Fu et al. [10] utilized the depth cue to enhance identification of similar foreground objects via a proposed RGB-D co-saliency map, as well as to improve detection of object-like regions and provide depth-based local features for region comparison. Moreover, they formulated co-segmentation in a fully connected graph structure together with mutual exclusion constraints to deal with the images where the common object appears more than or less than once.

Song et al. [26] proposed a RGB-D co-saliency method via bagging-based clustering, which generates the saliency maps on single images, clusters them into weak co-saliency maps, and integrates the weak co-saliency maps adaptively into the final saliency map based on a clustering quality criterion.

Cong et al. [7] proposed an iterative RGB-D co-saliency method, which utilizes the existing single saliency maps as the initialization, and generates the final RGB-D co-saliency map by using a refinement cycle model.

Another method proposed by Cong et al. [6] utilized the depth cue to enhance identification of co-saliency. It calculated the intra saliency maps on each single image and the inter saliency maps based on the multi-constraint feature matching, refined the saliency maps with cross label propagation, and integrated all the original and optimized saliency maps to the final co-saliency result.

9.4 Evaluation

9.4.1 Datasets

There are many datasets for RGB salient object detection, such as MSRA10K [5] and XPIE [32], but the datasets for RGB-D salient object detection are quite scarce.

For depth- and color-based salient object detection, also for depth- based salient object detection, there are two existing datasets: RGBD1000 [22] and NJU2000 [16]. Specifically, RGBD1000 dataset consists of 1000 RGB-D images with the maximum resolution of 640×640, which are captured by Kinect. RGBD1000 also provides two versions of depth cues, including raw depth map and smoothed depth map. Figure 9.5 shows an overview of RGBD1000. NJU2000 dataset consists of 2000 RGB-D images

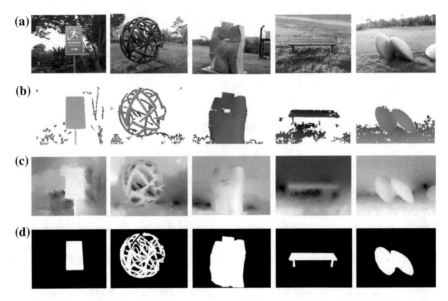

Fig. 9.5 Overview of RGB1000. **a** Original images. **b** Raw depth maps. **c** Smoothed depth maps. **d** Groundtruths of salient object detection

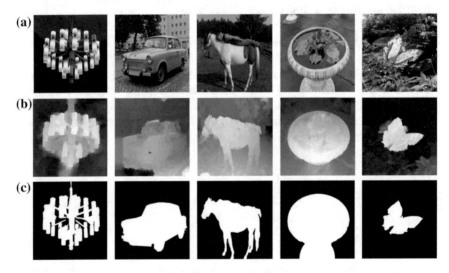

Fig. 9.6 Overview of NJU2000. **a** Original images. **b** Depth maps. **c** Groundtruths of salient object detection

with the maximum resolution of 600×600, whose depth cues are generated by a depth estimation algorithm. Figure 9.6 shows an overview of NJU2000.

For RGB-D co-saliency detection, there are two typical datasets: RGBD Coseg183 [10] and RGBD Cosal150 [6]. Specifically, RGBD Coseg183 dataset consists of 183

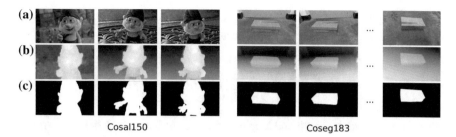

Fig. 9.7 Overview of NJU1000. **a** Original images. **b** Depth maps. **c** Groundtruths of co-saliency object detection

RGB-D images captured by Kinect, which are divided into 16 groups and each group contains 12–36 images, and the maximum resolution of the images is 640×480; RGBD Cosal150 dataset consists of 150 RGB-D images with the estimated depth cues, which are divided into 21 groups and each group contains 2–20 images, and the maximum resolution of the images is 600×600. Figure 9.7 shows an overview of Coseg183 [10] and RGBD Cosal150 [6].

9.4.2 Metrics

The evaluation of RGB-D salient object detection performance uses the same metrics as other salient object detection tasks. By comparing the generated saliency map to the manually labeled groundtruth, several evaluation metrics can be calculated for quantitative evaluation, including Area Under the Curve (AUC), F-measure, and Mean Absolute Error (MAE). Specifically, AUC metric calculates the area under Receiver Operating Characteristic (ROC) curve, which is better if larger. F-measure calculates a weighted harmonic mean of precision P and recall R, which is defined as follows:

$$F_\beta = \frac{(1 + \beta^2) P \times R}{\beta^2 \times P + R},$$ (9.1)

where β^2 is usually set to 0.3 to emphasize the precision. A larger F_β score means better performance.

Weighted F-measure calculates the F-measure with weighted precision P^w and recall R^w, which is defined as follows:

$$F_\beta^w = \frac{(1 + \beta^2) P^w \times R^w}{\beta^2 \times P^w + R^w}.$$ (9.2)

It will be lower than normal F-measure. The specific calculation of weighted precision P^w and recall R^w can be referred in [19].

MAE is calculated based on the difference between the salient object detection result S and the groundtruth G, which is defined as follows:

$$MAE = \frac{1}{w \times h} \sum_{i=1}^{w} \sum_{j=1}^{h} |S(i, j) - G(i, j)|, \qquad (9.3)$$

where w and h are the width and height of the image. A smaller MAE score means better performance.

9.4.3 Comparison Analysis

We compared the performance of typical RGB-D salient object detection methods. All the results are provided by the authors or generated by their source codes. For depth-based salient object detection, we compared Ju et al. [16] and Sheng et al. [24]; for depth- and color-based salient object detection, we compared Lang et al. [18], Niu et al. [20], Peng et al. [22], Guo et al. [11], Qu et al. [23], and Chen and Li [3]; for RGB-D co-saliency detection, we compared Song et al. [26] and Cong et al. [6].

Tables 9.1, 9.2 and 9.3 show the performance of the compared methods in depth-based salient object detection, depth- and color-based salient object detection, and RGB-D co-saliency detection, respectively.

We can see that

(i) As shown in Table 9.1, Sheng et al. [24] is slightly better than Ju et al. [16] in all three metrics. A possible explanation would be discussed as follows. They both employed depth cue as the basic cue to generate saliency maps. However, Ju et al. [16] only emphasized the depth contrast on the origin depth map, and they fixed the weights of depth contrast from different directions rather than using adaptive weights, which may lead to low quality on some specific direction of the saliency map. Ju et al. [16] also used the weighted summation of the biggest contrast values among a relatively large area from different directions in depth maps to calculate pixel level salient value, which would lead to a vague saliency map, especially when the salient object takes up a big portion of the whole image. As shown in Fig. 9.1, prediction of a small salient object is relatively more accurate than that of a big salient object. By contrast, Sheng et al. [24] developed a new preprocessing method to enhance the depth contrast on depth maps and then used the preprocessed depth map to generate saliency maps.

(ii) By comparing methods of Lang et al. [18], Niu et al. [20], Peng et al. [22] and Guo et al. [11] in Table 9.2, which used both color cues and depth cues without deep learning modules, we find that Guo et al. [11] outperform other methods and Peng et al. [22] take the second place. A possible explanation would be discussed as follows. Lang et al. [18] and Niu et al. [20] combined color cues and depth cues simply by adding or multiplying saliency maps generated with different cues. Similarly, Peng

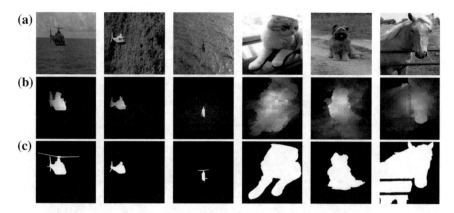

Fig. 9.8 Examples of Ju et at. [16]. **a** Original images. **b** Saliency maps. **c** Groundtruths of salient object detection

et al. [22] calculated the final saliency map by adding the first two levels' saliency maps and multiplying the third level's saliency maps (Fig. 9.8).

In spite of the similarity between the fusion methods of Peng et al. [22], Lang et al. [18] and Niu et al. [20], Peng et al. [22] incorporated different levels' depth contrast, e.g., local contrast, global contrast, and background contrast. Notably, Peng et al. [22] also employed graph-based method to generate saliency maps of the second level, which contributed to reducing high saliency maps in the background. All the above works of Peng et al. [22] helped to generate saliency maps with high quality. By contrast, Guo et al. [11] proposed a new method to combine depth cue and color cue in salient object detection. They generated saliency maps using color cue and saliency maps using depth separately, which are both of low quality. After multiplying two saliency maps, Guo et al. [11] conducted a refinement step by employing a single-layer cellular automaton that boosted the final performance. Figure 9.9 shows a comparison between the above methods. To conclude, simply calculating summation and multiplication are not efficient ways to fuse different saliency maps. There is still a demand for exploiting other efficient fusing strategies.

(iii) By comparing two deep learning-based methods, Qu et al. [23] and Chen and Li [3], we find that Chen's method is better than Qu's method. A possible explanation would be discussed as follows. Qu et al. [23] only used the deep learning module to fuse two saliency maps generated independently with depth cue and color cue. By contrast, Qu et al. [23] employed Convolutional Neural Network (CNN) both to extract features from RGB images and depth maps and fuse saliency maps, which utilized the power of CNN in feature extraction. Thus, Qu et al. [23] can make a better performance.

(iv) Table 9.2 shows that the deep learning-based methods, e.g., Qu et al. [23] and Chen and Li [3], outperform other methods, which shows the power of deep learning in saliency feature representation.

(a)   (b)   (c)   (d)   (e)   (f)

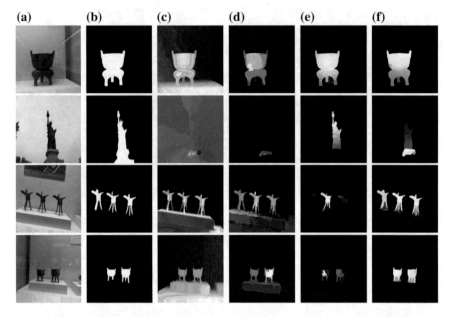

Fig. 9.9 Examples of saliency maps using both color cue and depth cue without deep learning modules. **a** Original images. **b** Groundtruths. **c** Results of Lang et al. [18]. **d** Results of Niu et al. [20]. **e** Results of Peng et al. [22]. **f** Results of Guo et al. [11]

Table 9.1 Evaluation of different depth-based salient object detection methods on RGBD1000 and NJU2000 datasets

	RGBD1000			NJU2000		
	AUC	F_β	MAE	AUC	F_β	MAE
Ju et al. [16]	0.92	0.67	0.16	0.93	0.75	0.19
Sheng et al. [24]	0.95	0.68	0.15	0.95	0.78	0.16

(v) By comparing Tables 9.1 and 9.2, the depth-based methods are not inferior to many methods based on color and depth. It shows that the effective combination of color cue and depth cue is not yet achieved. Simply multiplying or adding saliency maps generated with different cues are not efficient.

(vi) By comparing Tables 9.1 and 9.3, the performance of RGB-D co-saliency detection is better than that on single images. It shows that the analysis of inter-image correspondence is beneficial to salient object detection.

Table 9.2 Evaluation of different depth- and color-based salient object detection methods on RGBD1000 and NJU2000 datasets

	RGBD1000				NJU2000			
	AUC	F_β	F_β^w	MAE	AUC	F_β	F_β^w	MAE
Lang et al. [18]			0.16	0.33			0.31	0.29
Niu et al. [20]	0.80	0.47	0.23	0.18	0.81	0.61	0.35	0.22
Peng et al. [22]			0.46	0.11			0.34	0.21
Guo et al. [11]		0.55	0.55	0.10		0.43	0.60	0.20
Qu et al. [23]	0.88	0.64		0.12	0.83	0.64		0.20
Chen and Li [3]		0.82				0.83		

Table 9.3 Evaluation of different RGB-D co-saliency detection methods on RGBD Coseg183 and RGBD Cosal150 datasets

	RGBD Cosal183		
	AUC	F_β	MAE
Song et al. [26]	0.97	0.83	0.05
Cong et al. [6]	0.96	0.84	0.14

9.5 Discussion

By analyzing all above methods, we summarize three main points related to the effect of depth cue in salient object detection, which may give some inspiration for future RGB-D salient object detection models' design:

The first point is about feature extraction. In the past few years, there are mainly two ways to extract features in depth maps, including various contrast-based methods and deep learning-based methods. It should be noted that graph-based methods are not ways to extract features. They are used to make refinement or generate final saliency maps. For contrast-based methods, a bunch of different contrasts are developed to make a better performance, while there are relatively less deep learning-based methods paying attention to depth feature extraction.

The second point is about saliency map fusion. With the incorporation of depth cue, there is often a need to fuse several candidate saliency maps, or some intermediate results. The amount of saliency maps or intermediate results required to fuse are quite different in various proposed models from two to three hundred. Especially when the amount is as high as three hundred, the effectiveness of fusion strategy will matter a lot for the final results. The simplest strategies are weighted summation and point-wise multiplication, while there are many other more effective ones, like evolution-based fusion [11], multilayer cellular-based fusion [28], random forest regressor selection-based fusion [25], bootstrap-based fusion [25], and deep learning-based fusion [3, 12, 23].

The third point is about refinement of saliency maps, which includes two aspects: eliminate saliency in the background and make better segmentation in the foreground. Most of contrast-based methods without further refinement will suffer from high saliency in the background, due to the fact that there are many objects in the background that have strong contrast with surrounding areas for either color cue or depth cue. To avoid the high saliency in the background, graph-based methods are proposed which propagate saliency based on some specific seed points instead of generating saliency value directly on the whole image or depth map. For the second aspect, there is often an incompleteness of salient objects or vagueness in some specific areas, because many parts are not obviously distinct from the background or big enough to be detected by some proposed models. In this condition, refinement like using Grabcut [9] and bootstrap-based segmentation [25] can help to make a better segmentation of foreground objects.

9.6   Conclusion

In this chapter, we comprehensively reviewed the advances in RGB-D salient object detection, including depth-based salient object detection, depth- and color-based salient object detection and RGB-D co-saliency. We first introduced the evolution of salient object detection, and analyzed the relationship between RGB-D salient object detection and salient object detection on other media, e.g., RGB images, multiple images for co-saliency detection and videos. Furthermore, we presented the typical methods of these three categories, and evaluated their performance on four public datasets.

Though many RGB-D salient object detection methods have been proposed, there are still many unsolved issues. The low quality of depth maps may influence the performance of RGB-D salient image detection methods. How to enhance depth maps or improve the robustness to depth noise will be a critical issue for RGB-D salient object detection. Moreover, compared to the datasets for RGB salient object detection, the datasets for RGB-D salient object detection are scarce and their sizes are smaller. It would be a significant benefit to construct a large-scale datasets for RGB-D salient object detection.

Acknowledgements This work is supported by the National Science Foundation of China (61202320, 61321491) and Collaborative Innovation Center of Novel Software Technology and Industrialization.

References

1. Borji A (2014) What is a salient object? A dataset and a baseline model for salient object detection. IEEE Trans Image Process 24(2):742–756
2. Borji A, Cheng MM, Jiang H, Li J (2015) Salient object detection: a benchmark. IEEE Trans Image Process 24(12):5706–5722

3. Chen H, Li Y (2018) Progressively complementarity-aware fusion network for RGB-D salient object detection. In: Proceedings of the IEEE conference on computer vision and pattern recognition, pp 3051–3060
4. Cheng MM, Mitra NJ, Huang X, Hu SM (2014) Salientshape: group saliency in image collections. Vis Comput 30(4):443–453
5. Cheng MM, Mitra NJ, Huang X, Torr PH, Hu SM (2014) Global contrast based salient region detection. IEEE Trans Pattern Anal Mach Intell 37(3):569–582
6. Cong R, Lei J, Fu H, Huang Q, Cao X, Hou C (2017) Co-saliency detection for RGBD images based on multi-constraint feature matching and cross label propagation. IEEE Trans Image Process 27(2):568–579
7. Cong R, Lei J, Fu H, Lin W, Huang Q, Cao X, Hou C (2017) An iterative co-saliency framework for RGBD images. IEEE Trans Cybern 99:1–14
8. Fang Y, Wang J, Narwaria M, Le Callet P, Lin W (2014) Saliency detection for stereoscopic images. IEEE Trans Image Process 23(6):2625–2636
9. Feng D, Barnes N, You S, McCarthy C (2016) Local background enclosure for RGB-D salient object detection. In: Proceedings of the IEEE conference on computer vision and pattern recognition, pp 2343–2350
10. Fu H, Xu D, Lin S, Liu J (2015) Object-based RGBD image co-segmentation with mutex constraint. In: Proceedings of the IEEE conference on computer vision and pattern recognition, pp 4428–4436
11. Guo J, Ren T, Bei J (2016) Salient object detection for RGB-D image via saliency evolution. In: 2016 IEEE international conference on multimedia and expo (ICME). IEEE, pp 1–6
12. Han J, Chen H, Liu N, Yan C, Li X (2017) CNNs-based RGB-D saliency detection via cross-view transfer and multiview fusion. IEEE Trans Cybern 99:1–13
13. Itti L, Koch C, Niebur E (1998) A model of saliency-based visual attention for rapid scene analysis. IEEE Trans Pattern Anal Mach Intell 11:1254–1259
14. Jeong S, Ban SW, Lee M (2008) Stereo saliency map considering affective factors and selective motion analysis in a dynamic environment. Neural Netw 21(10):1420–1430
15. Ju R, Ge L, Geng W, Ren T, Wu G (2014) Depth saliency based on anisotropic center-surround difference. In: 2014 IEEE international conference on image processing (ICIP). IEEE, pp 1115–1119
16. Ju R, Liu Y, Ren T, Ge L, Wu G (2015) Depth-aware salient object detection using anisotropic center-surround difference. Signal Process Image Commun 38:115–126
17. Koch C, Ullman S (1987) Shifts in selective visual attention: towards the underlying neural circuitry. In: Matters of intelligence. Springer, pp 115–141
18. Lang C, Nguyen TV, Katti H, Yadati K, Kankanhalli M, Yan S (2012) Depth matters: influence of depth cues on visual saliency. In: European conference on computer vision. Springer, pp 101–115
19. Margolin R, Zelnik-Manor L, Tal A (2014) How to evaluate foreground maps? In: Proceedings of the IEEE conference on computer vision and pattern recognition, pp 248–255
20. Niu Y, Geng Y, Li X, Liu F (2012) Leveraging stereopsis for saliency analysis. In: 2012 IEEE conference on computer vision and pattern recognition. IEEE, pp 454–461
21. Ouerhani N, Hugli H (2000) Computing visual attention from scene depth. In: Proceedings 15th international conference on pattern recognition. ICPR-2000, vol 1. IEEE, pp 375–378
22. Peng H, Li B, Xiong W, Hu W, Ji R (2014) RGBD salient object detection: a benchmark and algorithms. In: European conference on computer vision. Springer, pp 92–109
23. Qu L, He S, Zhang J, Tian J, Tang Y, Yang Q (2017) RGBD salient object detection via deep fusion. IEEE Trans Image Process 26(5):2274–2285
24. Sheng H, Liu X, Zhang S (2016) Saliency analysis based on depth contrast increased. In: 2016 IEEE international conference on acoustics, speech and signal processing (ICASSP). IEEE, pp 1347–1351
25. Song H, Liu Z, Du H, Sun G, Le Meur O, Ren T (2017) Depth-aware salient object detection and segmentation via multiscale discriminative saliency fusion and bootstrap learning. IEEE Trans Image Process 26(9):4204–4216

26. Song H, Liu Z, Xie Y, Wu L, Huang M (2016) RGBD co-saliency detection via bagging-based clustering. IEEE Signal Process Lett 23(12):1722–1726
27. Treisman AM, Gelade G (1980) A feature-integration theory of attention. Cogn Psychol 12(1):97–136
28. Wang A, Wang M (2017) RGB-D salient object detection via minimum barrier distance transform and saliency fusion. IEEE Signal Process Lett 24(5):663–667
29. Wang W, Shen J, Porikli F (2015) Saliency-aware geodesic video object segmentation. In: Proceedings of the IEEE conference on computer vision and pattern recognition, pp 3395–3402
30. Wang W, Shen J, Yang R, Porikli F (2017) Saliency-aware video object segmentation. IEEE Trans Pattern Anal Mach Intell 40(1):20–33
31. Wang Y, Ren T, Hua Zhong S, Liu Y, Wu G (2018) Adaptive saliency cuts. Multim Tools Appl 77:22213–22230
32. Xia C, Li J, Chen X, Zheng A, Zhang Y (2017) What is and what is not a salient object? Learning salient object detector by ensembling linear exemplar regressors. In: Proceedings of the IEEE conference on computer vision and pattern recognition, pp 4142–4150
33. Yan Q, Xu L, Shi J, Jia J (2013) Hierarchical saliency detection. In: Proceedings of the IEEE conference on computer vision and pattern recognition, pp 1155–1162

Chapter 10
Foreground Detection and Segmentation in RGB-D Images

Runmin Cong, Hao Chen, Hongyuan Zhu and Huazhu Fu

Abstract Depth information available in RGB-D images facilitate many computer vision tasks. As a newly emerging and significant topic in the computer vision community, foreground detection and segmentation for RGB-D images have gained a lot of research interest in the past years. In this chapter, an overview of some foreground-based tasks in RGB-D images is provided, including saliency detection, co-saliency detection, foreground segmentation, and co-segmentation. We aim at providing comprehensive literature of the introduction, summaries, and challenges in these areas. We expect this review to be beneficial to the researchers in this field and hopefully, encourage more future works in this direction.

10.1 Introduction

As a traditional task in computer vision, foreground detection and segmentation have gained more attention from academia and industry. In general, the foreground object is defined as the salient target in an image. As we all know, the human visual system has the ability to allocate more attention to attractive parts or objects for further processing. Thus, the visual saliency detection task expects the computer to also

R. Cong
Beijing Key Laboratory of Advanced Information Science and Network Technology, Institute of Information Science, Beijing Jiaotong University, Beijing 100044, China
e-mail: rmcong@bjtu.edu.cn

H. Chen
Department of Mechanical Engineering, City University of Hong Kong, Hong Kong SAR, China
e-mail: hchen47-c@my.cityu.edu.hk

H. Zhu
Institute for Infocomm Research, Agency for Science, Technology and Research, Singapore, Singapore
e-mail: zhuh@i2r.a-star.edu.sg

H. Fu (✉)
Inception Institute of Artificial Intelligence, Abu Dhabi, United Arab Emirates
e-mail: hzfu@ieee.org

© Springer Nature Switzerland AG 2019 221
P. L. Rosin et al. (eds.), *RGB-D Image Analysis and Processing*,
Advances in Computer Vision and Pattern Recognition,
https://doi.org/10.1007/978-3-030-28603-3_10

have the ability to automatically identify salient regions from the input data [13, 73, 80], which has been applied in retrieval [66], retargeting [41], compression [30], enhancement [25, 43, 47], coding [40], foreground annotation [5], quality assessment [24], thumbnail creation [75], action recognition [77], and video summarization [35]. Image segmentation is also a fundamental problem in image processing and computer vision, which plays a significant role in object detection [12], object recognition [69], object tracking [1], and so on. It is essentially a technology to group image pixels into a set of regions with certain foreground labels.

When faced with a scene , the human visual system can not only perceive the appearance of the target but also capture the depth information of the scene. The development of imaging devices and sensors has made the acquisition of depth map simple and convenient, laying the data foundation for the task of RGB-D foreground detection and segmentation. From the depth map, we can capture many useful attributes for foreground extraction from the complex background, such as shape representation, contour information, internal consistency, and surface normal. In this chapter, we will review and summarize some depth-guided saliency detection and segmentation tasks, including

- **RGB-D saliency detection**. This task aims at making full use of depth cue to enhance the identification of the salient objects from a given image.
- **RGB-D co-saliency detection**. This task aims at detecting the common and salient regions from an RGB-D image group containing multiple related images.
- **RGB-D semantic segmentation**. This task aims at classifying each pixel in an image to a predefined category to support higher level reasoning with the help of the depth information.
- **RGB-D co-segmentation**. This task aims at extracting similar foreground objects from among a set of related images by combining the depth information and multiple image corresponding constraint.

10.2   RGB-D Saliency Detection

Salient object detection aims at identifying the most human-attractive object/objects in a scene. It has been a fundamental task in computer vision and serves as an important auxiliary stage for a large range of computer/robotic vision tasks. The traditional salient object detection is based on RGB inputs to measure the distinctiveness of the object appearance. However, when salient object and background share a similar color or the scenario is under weak illumination, the previous RGB-induced saliency detection methods will encounter challenges to distinguish the salient object.

Fortunately, the synchronized depth information, equipped by the off-the-shelf sensors such as Kinect or RealSense, provides additional geometry cues to assist the inference of the salient object. Figure 10.1 illustrates some examples predicted by state-of-the-art RGB and RGB-D saliency detection models [7, 33], respectively. The comparison in Fig. 10.1 well verifies the complementary of the depth modality in

RGB   Depth   GT   RGB_Sal   RGBD_Sal

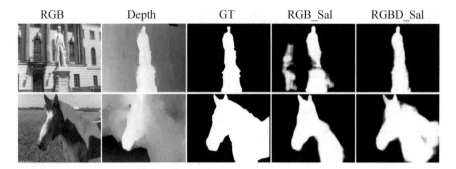

Fig. 10.1 Saliency examples to show the cross-modal complementarity. RGB_Sal and RGBD_Sal denote the saliency map inferred by Hou et al. [33] and Chen and Li [7] using the RGB image and the RGB-D image pair, respectively

saliency inference. Specifically, it is hard to localize the salient object adequately and highlight the salient regions uniformly simply with the RGB channels, especially in the cases of the similar appearance between salient object and background, complex background, and the intra-variable salient regions. In contrast, the RGB-D saliency detection model is able to leverage the synchronized RGB and depth images to collaboratively localize the salient object and refine the salient details. It is also easy to note that in some cases, only one modality carries discriminative saliency cues. Thus, it is the key question that how to combine the two modalities for desired complementary and collaborative decision.

10.2.1   Methods Based on Handcrafted Features

Early efforts on RGB-D salient object detection are mainly based on handcrafted features. Table 10.1 shows the comparison of these works in terms of feature designing, saliency inference, and the multi-modal fusion schemes. The main difference among these RGB-D salient object detection models is the design of depth-induced saliency features. Most of the previous works [17, 19, 48, 50, 82] directly use the raw depth value as the feature and a popular assumption is that the closer object is more likely to be salient due to photographic habits, which is adopted in [19, 48]. However, in a considerable of scenes, some background regions also hold small depth values due to the geometry structure. Desingh et al. [18] used the surface normal as the feature to measure the distinctiveness of the segmented 3D surfaces/regions. Considering the scene structure of the depth, Ju et al. [37] replaced the absolute depth with relative depth for contrast and proposed to evaluate the center-surround difference in diverse directions. Feng et al. [20] estimated the proportion of the object distinguishing from the background and designed a saliency cue named "local background enclosure". To further improve the representative ability for the objects with different scales, Song

Table 10.1 Comparison of the RGB-D salient object detection models based on handcrafted features

Methods	Year	Depth feature	Inference scheme	Fusion scheme
LSSA [48]	2012	Original depth values	Global contrast + local contrast	/
DRM [18]	2013	Surface normals (superpixels)	Global contrast	Result fusion (SVM)
NLPR [50]	2014	Original depth values (superpixels)	Global contrast + local contrast + background-prior	Feature fusion + result fusion
SRDS [19]	2014	Original depth values	Global contrast	Result fusion
ACSD [37]	2014	Anisotropic Center-Surround Difference (superpixels)	Local contrast	/
DCMC [17]	2016	Original depth values (superpixels)	Global contrast	Feature fusion
LBE [20]	2016	Local Background Enclosure (superpixels)	Local contrast	Feature fusion
SE [26]	2016	Anisotropic Center-Surround Difference (superpixels)	Global contrast + local contrast	Feature fusion + result fusion
MDSF [62]	2017	Average depth values + histogram (multi-scale superpixels)	Global contrast	Feature fusion
MBP [82]	2018	Original depth values	Global contrast	Result fusion

et al. [62] segmented the RGB-D image pair into different numbers of superpixels to form the multi-scale representation.

Another focus is the inference system for the depth-induced saliency. Inspired by the previous RGB-induced saliency detection frameworks, most of the inference systems for depth-induced saliency propose that the regions with distinguished depth values in its local or global contexts will be more salient. Desingh et al. [18] leveraged the global contrast method [10] widely used in RGB saliency detection to compute the saliency score of each region. The similar global contrast framework is also used in [17, 26, 50] to consider the depth structure globally. Instead of measuring the feature discrepancy with all other regions in the image, the works [20, 37] contrasted the feature discrepancy in a local context. Regarding the advantages of the global- and local contrast solutions, some works [26, 48, 50] resorted to a hybrid scheme that comparing the feature difference in multiple contexts jointly by combining the global contrast, local contrast and the background-prior contrast strategies.

Finally, the multi-modal fusion problem is typically solved by concatenating RGB and depth features as joint inputs such as in [17, 20, 62], or separately contrasting the RGB and depth cues and combining the inference from two modalities by multiplication [19], summation [82], or other designs [18], which are termed as "feature fusion" and "result fusion" schemes respectively. Besides, some works [26, 50] combine the two fusion strategies to use the cross-modal information in both feature design and saliency inference stages.

10.2.2   Methods Based on Deep Learning Techniques

Recent efforts resort to the convolutional neural network (CNN) to learn more powerful RGB-D representations. Among these CNN-based solutions, the "two-stream" architecture is the most typical one, which means each of the RGB and depth data is separately processed by a stream and then fused for joint prediction. Table 10.2 compares the CNN-based RGB-D salient object detection models in terms of network patterns and training schemes. Due to the insufficiency of the training samples, a promising scheme for training the depth stream is to use the models well trained in the RGB modality such as the VGG net [60] as initialization. To this end, the three-channel HHA [28] (horizontal disparity, **h**eight above ground and the **a**ngle of the local surface normal) representations encoded from the single-channel depth values are widely used as inputs of the depth modality. Besides, the stage-wise training scheme is also adopted in some works to facilitate better fusion results.

According to the convergence point of two modalities, the two-stream architecture can be categorized into three patterns:

Table 10.2 Comparison of the RGB-D salient object detection models based on convolutional neural networks

Method	Year	Input of the depth stream	Training scheme of the depth stream	Fusion scheme	End-to-end or stage-wise training
DF [54]	2017	Handcrafted features	Train from scratch	Early fusion	Stage-wise
CTMF [29]	2017	HHA	Fine-tune RGB CNN	Late fusion	Stage-wise
MMCI [9]	2018	HHA	Fine-tune RGB CNN	Multi-level fusion	Stage-wise
PCA-Net [7]	2018	HHA	Original VGG	Multi-level fusion	End-to-end
TA-Net [8]	2019	HHA	Original VGG	Multi-level fusion	End-to-end

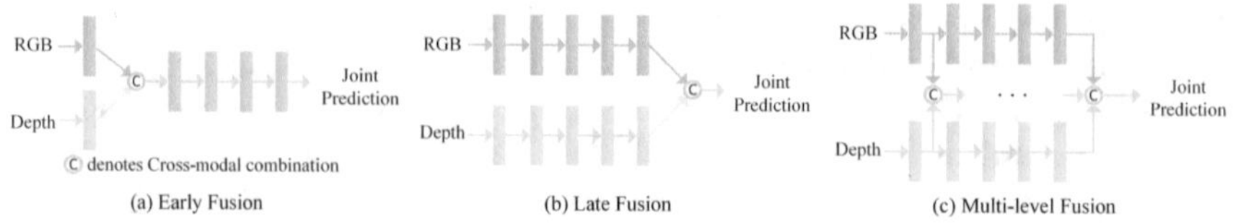

Fig. 10.2 The comparison of different two-stream multi-modal fusion patterns

Early fusion. As shown in Fig. 10.2a, the "early fusion" scheme combines the cross-modal features in a shallow point. The combined features are then forwarded to learn high-level multi-modal representations and joint decision via the following shared stream. For example, in [54], low-level features are first crafted from RGB and depth images using the contrasting paradigms in multiple contexts separately. The contrasting results from each modality, serving as feature vectors, are then concatenated as joint inputs to train a CNN from scratch. The motivation for the early fusion scheme is to enable the output of each subsequent layer to be a heterogeneous multi-modal representation. However, due to the cross-modal discrepancy, it is hard to train a shared deep network which can well extract representations from both modalities, especially when the training samples are insufficient. Also, the early fusion scheme makes it hard to inherit the well-trained networks such as the VGG model as initialization, while training the cross-modal network from scratch may decrease the performance. As a result, the "early fusion" results show similar characteristics as the ones generated by the methods with handcrafted features, denoting its failure in learning and combining high-level cross-modal representations.

Late fusion. Another pipeline follows the late fusion pattern shown in Fig. 10.2b, which means that each of the RGB and depth data is separately learned by a respective model-specific stream and the high-level features from two streams are combined for joint prediction. Compared to the early fusion pattern, the late fusion one eases the training of each modality due to the availability of readily fine-tuning existing well-trained models. In [29], two fully connected layers at the end of each stream were combined by mapping into another shared fully connected layer to learn joint representations. This multi-modal fusion architecture achieves promising high-level cross-modal combination and impressive performance in jointly localizing the salient object. Besides, accounting for the insufficiency of the training samples, this work also proposes two transfer learning strategies to facilitate the learning of the depth stream. They argue that it allows better training of the depth stream if initialize it with the trained RGB saliency detection network rather than the original model trained with the ImageNet. The reason lies in that the former initialization strategy enjoys smaller cross-task discrepancy and endows the depth stream with pre-understanding on saliency detection. The original VGG model is learned for the image classification task, which naturally differs from the pixel-wise one (i.e., saliency detection). Another strategy is to introduce deep supervisions in the intermediate layer of the depth stream to enhance the update of the parameters in its shallow layers.

Multi-level fusion. It has been acknowledged that different layers in a CNN contribute to saliency detection in a level-specific manner. Concretely, the deeper layers carry more global contexts and are more responsible for localizing the salient object, while the shallower layers provide more spatial details for refining the object boundaries. Despite the effectiveness of the early or late fusion pattern in exploring multi-modal representations and collaborative inference, it is hard to take the cross-modal complementarity residing in multiple layers into account simultaneously with performing multi-modal fusion only in an early or late point.

To exploit the cross-modal complementarity in multiple levels, recent works focus on designing a multi-level fusion pattern (Fig. 10.2c), in which the cross-modal fusion is implemented in multiple layers to generate multi-level multi-modal representations for inference. In [9], two cross-modal fusion paths were designed for collaborative localization and refinement of the salient object respectively. The stream for each modality contains a global reasoning branch equipped by a fully connected layer and a local capturing branch performed by dilated convolutional layers. The predictions from global and local branches in each modality are then combined respectively and then summed as the final inference. More recently, Chen and Li [7] proposed a progressive top-down cross-level cross-modal fusion path, in which the cross-modal complements are densely combined in each level and the saliency map is progressively enhanced from coarse to fine. Apart from the design on how to combine cross-modal residing multiple levels sufficiently, this work innovatively proposed to model the cross-modal complementarity as a residual function and recast the problem of incorporating cross-modal complements into approximating the residual. This reformulation reveals the cross-modal complementarity explicitly and eases the cross-modal fusion effectively. To solve the multi-modal fusion problem in both the bottom-up and top-down processes simultaneously, Chen and Li [8] designed another stream to distil cross-modal cues in the encoding path. The cross-modal cues are then selected and combined by an attention-aware top-down path.

10.3   RGB-D Co-saliency Detection

With the explosive growth of data volume, multiple relevant images with common objects need to be processed collaboratively. Co-saliency detection aims at detecting the common and salient regions from an image group containing multiple related images [13, 80, 81], which has been applied in object co-detection [27], foreground co-segmentation [6], and image matching [68]. This task is more challenging due to the fact that the categories, locations, and intrinsic attributes are entirely unknown. For the co-salient object in an image group, there are two properties that should be satisfied, i.e., (a) the object should be salient with respect to the background in each individual image and (b) the object should be similar in appearance and repeated occurrence among multiple images. Figure 10.3 provides some examples of co-saliency detection task. As shown, all the cows should be detected as the salient objects in each individual image. However, only the brown cow is the common

Fig. 10.3 Illustration of the co-saliency detection. The first row presents the input images and the second row shows the co-salient objects

object in the whole image group. Therefore, the inter-image correspondence among multiple images plays an important role in representing the common attribute and discriminating the salient objects.

As mentioned earlier, a depth map can provide many useful attributes (e.g., shape, contour, and surface normal), and the superiority has been demonstrated in many computer vision tasks, including scene understanding, object detection, image enhancement, and saliency detection. Considering the depth cue with the inter-image correspondence jointly, we can achieve RGB-D co-saliency detection. At present, there are two commonly used datasets for this task, i.e., RGB-D Coseg183 dataset [22] and RGB-D Cosal150 dataset [14]. The RGB-D Coseg183 dataset[1] contains 183 RGB-D images with corresponding pixel-wise ground truth in total that distributed in 16 image groups. The RGB-D Cosal150 dataset[2] includes 21 image groups containing a total of 150 RGB-D images, and the pixel-wise ground truth for each image is provided. Due to the challenging nature of this task and limited data sources, only a few methods have been proposed to achieve RGB-D co-saliency detection. In the following introduction, we will focus on how to capture the inter-image correspondence and utilize the depth cue in different models.

Song et al. [63] proposed an RGB-D co-saliency detection method via bagging-based clustering and adaptive fusion. First, some candidate object regions were generated based on RGB-D single saliency maps through the gPb-owt-ucm [2] segmentation technique. Then, in order to make regional clustering more robust to different image sets, the inter-image correspondence was explored via feature bagging and regional clustering. Note that, three depth cues, including average depth value, depth range, and the Histogram of Oriented Gradient (HOG) on the depth map, were extracted to represent the depth attributes of each region in this paper. For each clustering group, the corresponding cluster-level weak co-saliency maps were obtained. Finally, considering the quality of clustering result, a clustering quality (CQ) criterion was devised to adaptively combine the weak co-saliency maps into

---

[1] http://hzfu.github.io/proj_rgbdseg.html.

[2] https://rmcong.github.io/proj_RGBD_cosal.html.

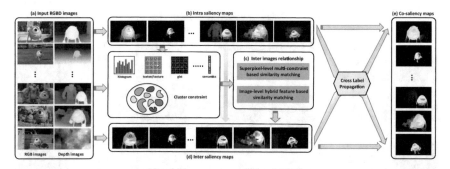

Fig. 10.4 Framework of the method [14]. **a** The input RGB-D images. **b** The intra-saliency maps produced by existing single saliency method collaborating with depth information. **c** The inter-image corresponding relationship by combining the superpixel-level multi-constraint-based similarity matching and image-level hybrid feature-based similarity matching. **d** The inter- saliency maps by integrating the corresponding relationships and intra-saliency maps. **e** The co-saliency maps with cross-label propagation

the final co-saliency map for each image in a discriminative way. In this paper, the inter-image correspondence was formulated as a clustering process, and the depth feature was used as a supplement to color feature in an explicit way. However, the clustering method may be sensitive to the noise and degenerate the accuracy of the algorithm.

Taking the depth cue as an additional feature, Cong et al. [14] proposed a co-saliency detection method for RGB-D images by using the multi-constraint feature matching and cross-label propagation. The framework is shown in Fig. 10.4. The main contributions of this paper lie in two aspects, i.e., (a) the inter-image relationship was modeled at two scales including multi-constraint- based superpixel-level similarity matching and hybrid feature-based image-level similarity matching and (b) the cross-label propagation scheme was designed to refine the intra- and inter-saliency maps in a crossway and generate the final co-saliency map. In this paper, the inter-saliency of a superpixel was computed as the weighted sum of the intra-saliency of corresponding superpixels in other images, where the superpixel-level feature matching result provides the corresponding relationship between the super-pixels among different images, and the weighted coefficient is calculated by the image-level similarity measurement.

In [15], a co-saliency detection method for RGB-D images was proposed that integrates the intra-saliency detection, hierarchical inter-saliency detection based on global and pairwise sparsity reconstructions, and energy function refinement. The hierarchical sparsity representation was first used to capture the inter-image correspondence in co-saliency detection. The framework is shown in Fig. 10.5. In this paper, the depth cue was used as an additional feature, and the corresponding relationship among multiple images was simulated as a hierarchical sparsity framework considering the global and pairwise sparsity reconstructions. The global inter-saliency reconstruction model described the inter-image correspondence from

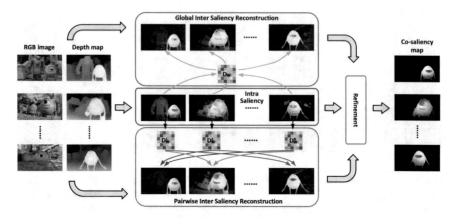

Fig. 10.5 Framework of the method [15] that integrates the intra-saliency detection, hierarchical inter-saliency detection based on global and pairwise sparsity reconstructions, and energy function refinement

the perspective of the whole image group via a common reconstruction dictionary, while the pairwise inter-saliency reconstruction model utilized a set of foreground dictionaries produced by other images to capture local inter-image information. In addition, an energy function refinement model, including the unary data term, spatial smooth term, and holistic consistency term, was proposed to improve the intra-image smoothness and inter-image consistency and to generate the final co-saliency map.

For co-saliency detection, more attention should be paid to inter-image formulation rather than the intra-saliency calculation. In other words, we can directly use the existing single-image saliency model as initialization in co-saliency detection. However, the existing co-saliency detection methods mainly rely on the designed cues or initialization and lack the refinement cycle. Therefore, Cong et al. [16] proposed an iterative co-saliency detection framework for RGB-D images, which can effectively exploit any existing 2D saliency model to work well in RGB-D co-saliency scenarios by making full use of the depth information and inter-image correspondence. The framework is shown in Fig. 10.6, which integrates the addition scheme, deletion scheme, and iteration scheme. The addition scheme aimed at introducing the depth information into the 2D saliency model and improving the performance of single saliency map. The deletion scheme focused on capturing the inter-image correspondence via a designed common probability function. The iterative scheme was served as an optimization process through a refinement cycle to further improve the performance.

Generally, the depth map has the following three properties, i.e., (a) the depth value of the salient object is larger than the background, (b) the high-quality depth map can provide sharp and explicit boundary of the object, and (c) the interior depth value of the object appears smoothness and consistency. Inspired by these observations, a novel depth descriptor, named Depth Shape Prior (DSP), was designed based on depth propagation and region grow, which aims to exploit the shape attribute from

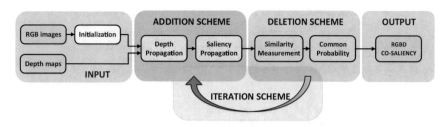

Fig. 10.6 Framework of the method [16], which integrates the addition scheme, deletion scheme, and iteration scheme

(a) Dog   (b) Sculpture

Fig. 10.7 Illustration of DSP descriptor. From the left to right in a group are the RGB image, depth map, and DSP map

the depth map and convert the RGB saliency into RGB-D saliency. Several identified superpixels are selected as the root seeds first, and then the DSP map can be calculated via depth smoothness and depth consistency. Figure 10.7 provides an illustration of the DSP descriptor, which effectively captures the shape of the salient object from the depth map. Note that, any RGB saliency map can be converted to an RGB-D saliency map by introducing the DSP descriptor.

In [16], the deletion scheme was designed to capture the corresponding relationship among multiple images, suppress the common and non-common backgrounds, and enhance the common salient regions from the perspective of multiple images. As we all know, the common object is defined as the object with repeated occurrence in most of the images. Based on this definition, a common probability function was used to evaluate the likelihood that a superpixel belongs to the common regions, and it was defined as the sum of maximum matching probability among different images.

10.4 RGB-D Semantic Segmentation

The ambition of achieving artificial intelligence cannot be achieved without the help of semantic understanding. Semantic segmentation/scene labeling is such an important component which aims to classify each pixel in an image to a predefined category to support higher level reasoning. Most scene labeling work deals with outdoor scenarios. On the other hand, indoor scenes are more challenging given poor lighting condition, cluttered object distribution and large object variations among different scene types.

Fig. 10.8 A typical pipeline of recent RGB-D semantic segmentation system

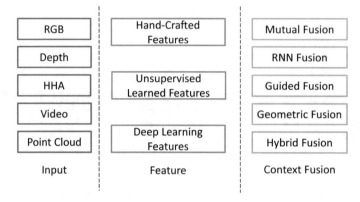

Fig. 10.9 Existing methods could be classified according to their inputs, features and context fusion methods. More details please refer to Sects. 10.4.1–10.4.3

Since the introduction of Kinect-V1, the rapid development of semiconductor has significantly reduced the cost and size of RGB-D cameras, which makes its large-scale application possible in the coming few years. RGB-D cameras have an additional depth sensor which makes higher level scene understanding more robust and accurate. Indoor RGB-D scene labeling has wide applications, such as human–computer interaction, augmented reality and robotics. To leverage the complementary information between RGB and depth channels, researchers have spent tremendous efforts in terms of effective representation learning to efficient scene parsing inference. Although much progress has been achieved in the past few years, indoor scene labeling is still challenging due to the large intra-object variation, spatial layout changes, occluded objects, and low-light conditions.

A typical RGB-D semantic segmentation system consists of following components with a typical pipeline shown in Fig. 10.8: (1) **Data**: typical inputs includes RGB and Depth Images/Frames; (2) **Feature Representation**: the input will be transformed to discriminative representations for further learning modules; (3) **Inference**: together with the labeled annotations, the incoming features will be used to train the classifier to output; with the classifier responses, some methods may use graphical model or other statistical models to perform further inference. Recent methods could be categories according to the differences in these three stages, as shown in Fig. 10.9.

10.4.1 Input: From Raw Pixel to Point Cloud

The input to the existing system is quite diverse. Besides **RGB** and **Depth** image, **HHA encoding** [28] is another measure which is recently become popular whose channels represents horizontal disparity, height above ground, and norm angle respectively.

Moreover, the input is not limited to static images, the sequential **RGB-D video frames** [31] have also been applied to solve video indoor scene labeling problem. Alternatively, **3D point clouds** and volumetric representation [51–53, 76] are also becoming popular though at a higher computational cost.

10.4.2 Feature: From Handcrafted to Data-Driven

Given diverse inputs, many descriptors have been proposed for representing the scenes. Handcrafted features were used in several previous works on RGB-D scene labeling, including SIFT [59], KDES [55] and other sophisticated features [42]. However, these low-level features require a lot of hand-crafting and combinations, which is hard to generalize to new tasks and modalities.

To avoid the limitations of hand-craft features, the unsupervised feature learning has been proposed, such as multi-modal learning [49], deep autoencoders [71], and convolutional deep belief networks [61]. Although these methods achieve promising performance, the learning process does not consider the supervised information, hence the learned features are redundant and less discriminative.

With the advances of 2D CNN and the availability of depth sensors enable progress in RGB-D segmentation. Several works [44, 72] encoded depth to HHA image, and then RGB image and HHA image were fed into two separate networks, and the two predictions were summed up in the last layer.

10.4.3 Context Fusion: From Local to Global

Achieving satisfactory RGB-D semantic segmentation requires integration of contexts from various scales and various modalities. The contexts from local regions convey rich details for visually pleasing results; on the other hand, the contexts from a larger receptive field make the method easier to differentiate between ambiguous categories. Moreover, complementary information from RGB and depth channels should also be leveraged to learn more discriminative features. To balance the information from local and global contexts, and effectively leverage the contexts from complementary modalities, different methods have been proposed.

- **Mutual Fusion**: Cheng et al. [11] proposed a locality-sensitive deconvolution network by building a feature affinity matrix to perform weighted average pooling and unpooling with gated fusion. Wang et al. [72] divided the features into the sharable and non-sharable part to learned discriminative features for fully convolutional networks. Wang et al. [71] proposed to use multiple layer's encoder–decoder structure to learn complementary features.

- **RNN Fusion**: Li et al. [44] developed a novel Long Short-Term Memorized Context Fusion (LSTM-CF) Model that captures and fuses contextual information from multiple channels of photometric and depth data, and incorporates this model into deep convolutional neural networks (CNNs) for end-to-end training.

- **Guidance Fusion**: Some recent research argued that depth information is more important than the RGB counterparts, hence they proposed to use depth as a guide to help learn better features from RGB modalities. For example, Lin et al. [45] discretized depth into different layers, and then a context-aware receptive field was introduced to allow better focus on the contextual information from each layer, and the adjacent features were fused together. Kong and Fowlkes [39] proposed a depth-aware gating module that adaptively selects the pooling field size in a convolutional network architecture in a recurrent fashion such that the fine-grained details are preserved for distant objects while larger receptive fields are used for those nearby. Wang and Neumann [74] presented Depth-aware CNN by leveraging depth similarity between pixels in the process of information propagation without introducing any additional networks and achieved faster and better indoor scene labeling accuracy.

- **Geometric Fusion**: 3D CNNs [64, 65] on volumetric representations have been proposed to solve the RGB-D object detection problem, however, suffers from the high memory and computational cost. Recently, many deep learning frameworks [51–53, 76] have been proposed to overcome the limitations of 3D volumes by leveraging point clouds. Qi et al. [53] built a k-nearest neighbor graph on top of 3D point cloud with the node corresponds to a set of points associated with a feature extracted by a unary CNN from 2D images. The PointNet [51, 52] was proposed by representing each point with three coordinates (x, y, z) with additional dimensions from surface normals or other local or global features, which significantly reduce the computational costs. Wang et al. [76] used PointNet with an output of a similarity matrix yielding point-wise group proposals, a confidence map which was used to prune the proposals, and a semantic segmentation map to assign the class label for each group.

- **Hybrid Fusion**: Actually, existing fusion methods can also be adopted in a hybrid manner. For example, He et al. [31] used spatiotemporal correspondences across frames to aggregate information over space and time. In [34], the RNN fusion in [44] was extended to point cloud semantic segmentation with a novel slice pooling layer to project unordered points' features to an ordered sequence of feature vectors so that RNN fusion could be further applied.

10.4.4   Future Directions

Our survey only covers a small fraction of the existing literature, including

- **Beyond full supervision**: most state-of-the-art methods are based on full supervision, which requires access to dense pixel-wise annotation. However, collecting such dense annotation is time consuming and expensive [58]. Recently, Shun et al. [67] proposed to use weak supervision for RGB-D object detection and instance segmentation, which is an area less explored in the community.
- **Beyond class segmentation**: most segmentation methods still produce class segmentation, e.g., all pixels of the same category are assigned the same label. On the other hand, people are also interested in knowing "what, where, and how many" of the objects in the scene, which could facilitate higher level tasks, such as visual navigation and robot object manipulation [57]. With the recent advents in deep learning object detection and RGB-D instance segmentation dataset [3, 79], we envision the instance-level RGB-D segmentation will have further development.

10.5   RGB-D Image Co-segmentation

As an interesting extension of single RGB-D image segmentation, the multiple RGB-D image applications are also studied. In this section, we introduce two branches of multiple RGB-D image applications, RGB-D image co-segmentation, and RGB-D video segmentation.

10.5.1   RGB-D Image Co-segmentation

RGB-D image co-segmentation aims at extracting similar foreground objects from among a set of related images by combining the depth information and multiple image corresponding constraint [23, 36, 38, 56]. In contrast to the foreground from the single image, co-segmentation makes use of the information in multiple images to infer the primary objects to extract. Existing methods operate on RGB images and utilize descriptors such as color histograms, texture to perform co-segmentation. However, color-based features have limitations, as they cannot distinguish foreground from a similarly colored background, and are sensitive to illumination differences among multiple images. These issues are illustrated in Fig. 10.10c, where the common foreground object is merged with a background object of similar color in the second row, and illumination change causes the target to be missed in the third row.

To address this problem, the depth cue is introduced into co-segmentation, which can help to reduce ambiguities with color descriptors. How to effectively utilize depth information in co-segmentation is not straightforward. In single RGB-D image segmentation, depth can be treated as an additional color channel, since the depth over a

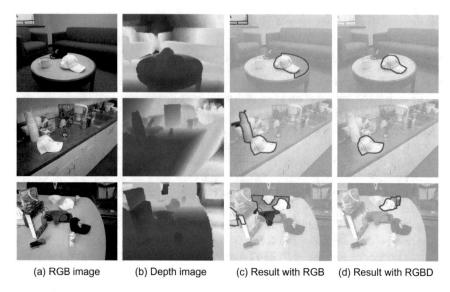

(a) RGB image   (b) Depth image   (c) Result with RGB   (d) Result with RGBD

Fig. 10.10 The example of co-segmentation on RGB and RGB-D images. Given a set of RGB images (**a**) and the corresponding depth maps (**b**). Co-segmentation on RGB images (**c**) may exhibit errors on the similarly colored background objects (second row) or illumination change (third row). By contrast, the co-segmentation on RGB-D images notably improves the result

foreground object is generally consistent yet distinct from the background [46]. However, in co-segmentation where commonalities among images are exploited, different depth values for the same object in different images can create matching problems. Fu et al. [22] presented an object-based RGB-D image co-segmentation method based on RGB-D co-saliency maps, which capitalizes on depth cues to enhance identification of common foreground objects among images. Depth was utilized to provide additional local features for region comparison and to improve the selection of object-like regions [28]. Objectness has been used in co-segmentation to overcome limitations of low-level features in separating complex foregrounds and backgrounds [70], but such methods have been formulated with an assumption that exactly one common object exists in all of the images. This RGB-D co-segmentation method [22] first generated a foreground candidate pool for each image by using RGB-D-based object proposal generator [28]. For each candidate region, an RGB-D co-saliency score was computed and added to the RGB-D objectness score calculated in candidate generation to measure the likelihood that the candidate belongs to the foreground. With the candidates and their likelihood scores, a candidate selection graph was built, with each node representing a candidate in an image, and pairwise edges added to connect all pairs of candidates among all of the images. Mutual exclusion constraints were also introduced between nodes to restrict candidate selection within the same image. The graph was formulated as a binary integer quadratic program (IQP) problem, which is optimized by using the fixed-point iteration technique.

10.5.2 Extension: RGB-D Video Segmentation

Video could be considered as multiple images with temporal constraint. The goal of video foreground segmentation is to detect and separate the primary objects from the background in a video [4]. This task has importance for many vision applications such as activity recognition and video retrieval.

RGB-D video segmentation has attracted much interest because of the wide availability of affordable RGB-D sensors. While these uses of depth are suitable for precise region extraction in image segmentation, the video segmentation task addressed is instead driven by relationships among regions in different frames. For example, Hickson et al. [32] proposed an efficient and scalable algorithm for segmenting 3D RGB-D point clouds by combining depth, color, and temporal information using a multistage, hierarchical graph-based approach. The study shows that the multistage segmentation with depth then color yields better results than a linear combination of depth and color. In [78], a spatiotemporal RGB-D video segmentation framework was proposed to automatically segment and track objects with continuity and consistency over time in a long RGB-D video. The method could automatically extract multiple objects of interest and track them without any user input hint.

Besides the general RGB-D video segmentation, the foreground extraction is also proposed. In [21], an RGB-D video foreground segmentation method was given, which takes advantage of depth data and can extract multiple foregrounds in the scene. This video segmentation was addressed as an object proposal selection problem formulated in a fully connected graph where a flexible number of foregrounds may be chosen. In the graph, each node represented a proposal, and the edges modeled intra-frame and inter-frame constraints on the solution. The proposals were generated based on an RGB-D video saliency map in which depth-based features are utilized to enhance identification of foregrounds.

10.6 Conclusions

The development of imaging devices and sensors has made the acquisition of depth map simple and convenient, laying the data foundation for the task of RGB-D foreground detection and segmentation. From the depth map, we can capture many useful attributes for foreground extraction from the complex background, such as shape representation, contour information, internal consistency, and surface normal. In this chapter, deriving from depth cue, we review different types of foreground detection and segmentation algorithms, summarize the existing methods, and discuss the challenges and future works. At present, how to effectively exploit the depth information to enhance the identification and segmentation has not yet reached a consensus. In the future, combining the explicit and implicit depth information to obtain a more comprehensive depth representation is a meaningful attempt for depth-guided visual tasks.

References

1. Almomani R, Dong M (2013) Segtrack: a novel tracking system with improved object segmentation. In: ICIP, pp 3939–3943
2. Arbelaez P, Maire M, Fowlkes C, Malik J (2009) From contours to regions: an empirical evaluation. In: CVPR. IEEE, pp 2294–2301
3. Armeni I, Sax A, Zamir AR, Savarese S (2017) Joint 2D-3D-semantic data for indoor scene understanding. arXiv:1702.01105
4. Cao X, Wang F, Zhang B, Fu H, Li C (2016) Unsupervised pixel-level video foreground object segmentation via shortest path algorithm. Neurocomputing 172:235–243
5. Cao X, Zhang C, Fu H, Guo X, Tian Q (2016) Saliency-aware nonparametric foreground annotation based on weakly labeled data. IEEE Trans Neural Netw Learn Syst 27(6):1253–1265
6. Chang K, Liu T, Lai S (2011) From co-saliency to co-segmentation: an efficient and fully unsupervised energy minimization model. In: CVPR, pp 2129–2136
7. Chen H, Li Y (2018) Progressively complementarity-aware fusion network for RGB-D salient object detection. In: CVPR, pp 3051–3060
8. Chen H, Li Y (2019) Three-stream attention-aware network for RGB-D salient object detection. IEEE Trans Image Process PP(99):1–12
9. Chen H, Li Y, Su D (2019) Multi-modal fusion network with multi-scale multi-path and cross-modal interactions for RGB-D salient object detection. Pattern Recognit 86:376–385
10. Cheng MM, Mitra NJ, Huang X, Torr PH, Hu SM (2015) Global contrast based salient region detection. IEEE Trans Pattern Anal Mach Intell 37(3):569–582
11. Cheng Y, Cai R, Li Z, Zhao X, Huang K (2017) Locality-sensitive deconvolution networks with gated fusion for RGBD indoor semantic segmentation. In: CVPR, pp 1475–1483
12. Cinbis RG, Verbeek J, Schmid C (2013) Segmentation driven object detection with fisher vectors. In: ICCV, pp 2968–2975
13. Cong R, Lei J, Fu H, Cheng MM, Lin W, Huang Q (2018) Review of visual saliency detection with comprehensive information. IEEE Trans Circuits Syst Video Technol PP(99):1–19
14. Cong R, Lei J, Fu H, Huang Q, Cao X, Hou C (2018) Co-saliency detection for RGBD images based on multi-constraint feature matching and cross label propagation. IEEE Trans Image Process 27(2):568–579
15. Cong R, Lei J, Fu H, Huang Q, Cao X, Ling N (2019) HSCS: hierarchical sparsity based co-saliency detection for RGBD images. IEEE Trans Multimed 21(7):1660–1671
16. Cong R, Lei J, Fu H, Lin W, Huang Q, Cao X, Hou C (2019) An iterative co-saliency framework for RGBD images. IEEE Trans Cybern 49(1):233–246
17. Cong R, Lei J, Zhang C, Huang Q, Cao X, Hou C (2016) Saliency detection for stereoscopic images based on depth confidence analysis and multiple cues fusion. IEEE Signal Process Lett 23(6):819–823
18. Desingh K, Krishna KM, Rajan D, Jawahar C (2013) Depth really matters: improving visual salient region detection with depth. In: BMVC
19. Fan X, Liu Z, Sun G (2014) Salient region detection for stereoscopic images. In: ICDSP, pp 454–458
20. Feng D, Barnes N, You S, McCarthy C (2016) Local background enclosure for RGB-D salient object detection. In: CVPR, pp 2343–2350
21. Fu H, Xu D, Lin S (2017) Object-based multiple foreground segmentation in RGBD video. IEEE Trans Image Process 26(3):1418–1427
22. Fu H, Xu D, Lin S, Liu J (2015) Object-based RGBD image co-segmentation with mutex constraint. In: CVPR, pp 4428–4436
23. Fu H, Xu D, Zhang B, Lin S, Ward R (2015) Object-based multiple foreground video co-segmentation via multi-state selection graph. IEEE Trans Image Process 24(11):3415–3424
24. Gu K, Wang S, Yang H, Lin W, Zhai G, Yang X, Zhang W (2016) Saliency-guided quality assessment of screen content images. IEEE Trans Multimed 18(6):1098–1110

25. Guo C, Li C, Guo J, Cong R, Fu H, Han P (2019) Hierarchical features driven residual learning for depth map super-resolution. IEEE Trans Image Process 28(5):2545–2557

26. Guo J, Ren T, Bei J (2016) Salient object detection for RGB-D image via saliency evolution. In: ICME, pp 1–6

27. Guo X, Liu D, Jou B, Zhu M, Cai A, Chang SF (2013) Robust object co-detection. In: CVPR, pp 3206–3213

28. Gupta S, Girshick R, Arbeláez P, Malik J (2014) Learning rich features from RGB-D images for object detection and segmentation. In: ECCV, pp 345–360

29. Han J, Chen H, Liu N, Yan C, Li X (2018) CNNs-based RGB-D saliency detection via cross-view transfer and multiview fusion. IEEE Trans Cybern 48(11):3171–3183

30. Han S, Vasconcelos N (2006) Image compression using object-based regions of interest. In: ICIP, pp 3097–3100

31. He Y, Chiu W, Keuper M, Fritz M (2017) STD2P: RGBD semantic segmentation using spatio-temporal data-driven pooling. In: CVPR, pp 7158–7167

32. Hickson S, Birchfield S, Essa I, Christensen H (2014) Efficient hierarchical graph-based segmentation of RGBD videos. In: CVPR, pp 344–351

33. Hou Q, Cheng MM, Hu X, Borji A, Tu Z, Torr P (2017) Deeply supervised salient object detection with short connections. In: CVPR, pp 5300–5309

34. Huang Q, Wang W, Neumann U (2018) Recurrent slice networks for 3D segmentation on point clouds. In: CVPR, pp 2626–2635

35. Jacob H, Padua F, Lacerda A, Pereira A (2017) Video summarization approach based on the emulation of bottom-up mechanisms of visual attention. J Intell Inf Syst 49(2):193–211

36. Joulin A, Bach F, Ponce J (2010) Discriminative clustering for image co-segmentation. In: CVPR, pp 1943–1950

37. Ju R, Ge L, Geng W, Ren T, Wu G (2014) Depth saliency based on anisotropic center-surround difference. In: ICIP, pp 1115–1119

38. Kim G, Xing E, Fei-Fei L, Kanade T (2011) Distributed cosegmentation via submodular optimization on anisotropic diffusion. In: ICCV, pp 169–176

39. Kong S, Fowlkes C (2018) Recurrent scene parsing with perspective understanding in the loop. In: CVPR, pp 956–965

40. Lei J, Duan J, Wu F, Ling N, Hou C (2018) Fast mode decision based on grayscale similarity and inter-view correlation for depth map coding in 3D-HEVC. IEEE Trans Circuits Syst Video Technol 28(3):706–718

41. Lei J, Wu M, Zhang C, Wu F, Ling N, Hou C (2017) Depth-preserving stereo image retargeting based on pixel fusion. IEEE Trans Multimed 19(7):1442–1453

42. Lerma C, Kosecká J (2015) Semantic parsing for priming object detection in indoors RGB-D scenes. Int J Robot Res 34:582–597

43. Li C, Guo J, Cong R, Pang Y, Wang B (2016) Underwater image enhancement by dehazing with minimum information loss and histogram distribution prior. IEEE Trans Image Process 25(12):5664–5677

44. Li Z, Gan Y, Liang X, Yu Y, Cheng H, Lin L (2016) LSTM-CF: unifying context modeling and fusion with LSTMs for RGB-D scene labeling. In: ECCV, pp 541–557

45. Lin D, Chen G, Cohen-Or D, Heng P, Huang H (2017) Cascaded feature network for semantic segmentation of RGB-D images. In: ICCV, pp 1320–1328

46. Mishra A, Shrivastava A, Aloimonos Y (2012) Segmenting "simple" objects using RGB-D. In: ICRA, pp 4406–4413

47. Ni M, Lei J, Cong R, Zheng K, Peng B, Fan X (2017) Color-guided depth map super resolution using convolutional neural network. IEEE Access 2:26666–26672

48. Niu Y, Geng Y, Li X, Liu F (2012) Leveraging stereopsis for saliency analysis. In: CVPR, pp 454–461

49. Pei D, Liu H, Liu Y, Sun F (2013) Unsupervised multimodal feature learning for semantic image segmentation. In: IJCNN, pp 1–6

50. Peng H, Li B, Xiong W, Hu W, Ji R (2014) RGBD salient object detection: a benchmark and algorithms. In: ECCV, pp 92–109

51. Qi C, Su H, Mo K, Guibas L (2017) PointNet: deep learning on point sets for 3D classification and segmentation. In: CVPR, pp 77–85
52. Qi C, Yi L, Su H, Guibas L (2017) PointNet++: deep hierarchical feature learning on point sets in a metric space. In: NIPS, pp 5099–5108
53. Qi X, Liao R, Jia J, Fidler S, Urtasun R (2017) 3D graph neural networks for RGBD semantic segmentation. In: ICCV, pp 5209–5218
54. Qu L, He S, Zhang J, Tian J, Tang Y, Yang Q (2017) RGBD salient object detection via deep fusion. IEEE Trans Image Process 26(5):2274–2285
55. Ren X, Bo L, Fox D (2012) RGB-(D) scene labeling: features and algorithms. In: CVPR, pp 2759–2766
56. Rother C, Minka T, Blake A, Kolmogorov V (2006) Cosegmentation of image pairs by histogram matching-incorporating a global constraint into MRFs. In: CVPR, pp 993–1000
57. Sahin C, Kim TK (2019) Recovering 6D object pose: a review and multi-modal analysis. In: ECCV workshops, pp 15–31
58. Sahin C, Kouskouiras R, Kim TK (2016) Iterative hough forest with histogram of control points. In: IROS, pp 4113–4118
59. Silberman N, Fergus R (2011) Indoor scene segmentation using a structured light sensor. In: ICCV workshops, pp 601–608
60. Simonyan K, Zisserman A (2014) Very deep convolutional networks for large-scale image recognition. arXiv:1409.1556
61. Socher R, Huval B, Bath B, Manning C, Ng AY (2012) Convolutional-recursive deep learning for 3D object classification. In: NIPS, pp 665–673
62. Song H, Liu Z, Du H, Sun G, Le Meur O, Ren T (2017) Depth-aware salient object detection and segmentation via multiscale discriminative saliency fusion and bootstrap learning. IEEE Trans Image Process 26(9):4204–4216
63. Song H, Liu Z, Xie Y, Wu L, Huang M (2016) RGBD co-saliency detection via bagging-based clustering. IEEE Signal Process Lett 23(12):1722–1726
64. Song S, Xiao J (2016) Deep sliding shapes for amodal 3D object detection in RGB-D images. In: CVPR, pp 808–816
65. Song S, Yu F, Zeng A, Chang A, Savva M, Funkhouser T (2017) Semantic scene completion from a single depth image. In: CVPR, pp 190–198
66. Sun J, Liu X, Wan W, Li J, Zhao D, Zhang H (2015) Database saliency for fast image retrieval. IEEE Trans Multimed 17(3):359–369
67. Sun L, Zhao C, Stolkin R (2017) Weakly-supervised DCNN for RGB-D object recognition in real-world applications which lack large-scale annotated training data. arXiv:1703.06370
68. Toshev A, Shi J, Daniilidis K (2007) Image matching via saliency region correspondences. In: CVPR, pp 1–8
69. Uijlings JRR, van de Sande KEA, Gevers T, Smeulders AWM (2013) Selective search for object recognition. Int J Comput Vis 104(2):154–171
70. Vicente S, Rother C, Kolmogorov V (2011) Object cosegmentation. In: CVPR, pp 2217–2224
71. Wang A, Lu J, Wang G, Cai J, Cham T (2014) Multi-modal unsupervised feature learning for RGB-D scene labeling. In: ECCV, pp 453–467
72. Wang J, Wang Z, Tao D, See S, Wang G (2016) Learning common and specific features for RGB-D semantic segmentation with deconvolutional networks. In: ECCV, pp 664–679
73. Wang W, Lai Q, Fu H, Shen J, Ling H (2019) Salient object detection in the deep learning era: an in-depth survey. arXiv:1904.09146
74. Wang W, Neumann U (2018) Depth-aware CNN for RGB-D segmentation. In: ECCV, pp 144–161
75. Wang W, Shen J, Yu Y, Ma KL (2017) Stereoscopic thumbnail creation via efficient stereo saliency detection. IEEE Trans Vis Comput Graph 23(8):2014–2027
76. Wang W, Yu R, Huang Q, Neumann U (2018) SGPN: similarity group proposal network for 3D point cloud instance segmentation. In: CVPR, pp 2569–2578
77. Wang X, Gao L, Song J, Shen H (2017) Beyond frame-level CNN: saliency-aware 3-D CNN with LSTM for video action recognition. IEEE Signal Process Lett 24(4):510–514

78. Xie Q, Remil O, Guo Y, Wang M, Wei M, Wang J (2018) Object detection and tracking under occlusion for object-level RGB-D video segmentation. IEEE Trans Multimed 20(3):580–592
79. Yi L, Kim VG, Ceylan D, Shen IC, Yan M, Su H, Lu C, Huang Q, Sheffer A, Guibas L (2016) A scalable active framework for region annotation in 3D shape collections. ACM Trans Graph 210:1–12
80. Zhang D, Fu H, Han J, Borji A, Li X (2018) A review of co-saliency detection algorithms: fundamentals, applications, and challenges. ACM Trans Intell Syst Technol 9(4):1–31
81. Zhang Y, Li L, Cong R, Guo X, Xu H, Zhang J (2018) Co-saliency detection via hierarchical consistency measure. In: ICME, pp 1–6
82. Zhu C, Li G (2018) A multilayer backpropagation saliency detection algorithm and its applications. Multimed Tools Appl 77:25181–25197

Chapter 11
Instance- and Category-Level 6D Object Pose Estimation

Caner Sahin, Guillermo Garcia-Hernando, Juil Sock and Tae-Kyun Kim

Abstract Interest in estimating the 6D pose, i.e. 3D locations and rotations, of an object of interest has emerged since its promising applications in fields such as robotics and augmented reality. To recover poses from objects that have been seen in advance, instance-level methods have been presented to overcome challenges such as occlusion, clutter and similarly looking distractors. The problem has recently been addressed at the category level, where poses of object instances from a given category that have not been seen a priori are estimated, introducing new challenges such as distribution shifts and intra-class variations. In this chapter, the 6D object pose estimation problem at the levels of both instances and categories is presented, discussed, and analysed by following the available literature on the topic. First, the problem and its associated challenges are formulated and presented. To continue, instance-level methods are dissected depending on their architectures and category-level methods are examined according to their search space dimension. Popular datasets, benchmarks and evaluation metrics on the problem are presented and studied with respect to the challenges that they present. Quantitative results of experiments available in the literature are analysed to determine how methods perform when presented with different challenges. The analyses are further extended to compare three methods by using our own implementations aiming to solidify already published results. To conclude, the current state of the field is summarised and potential future research directions are identified.

C. Sahin (✉) · G. Garcia-Hernando · J. Sock · T.-K. Kim
Department of Electrical-Electronic Engineering, Imperial Computer Vision
and Learning Lab (ICVL), Imperial College, London SW7 2AZ, UK
e-mail: c.sahin14@imperial.ac.uk

G. Garcia-Hernando
e-mail: g.garcia-hernando@imperial.ac.uk

J. Sock
e-mail: ju-il.sock08@imperial.ac.uk

T.-K. Kim
e-mail: tk.kim@imperial.ac.uk

© Springer Nature Switzerland AG 2019
P. L. Rosin et al. (eds.), *RGB-D Image Analysis and Processing*,
Advances in Computer Vision and Pattern Recognition,
https://doi.org/10.1007/978-3-030-28603-3_11

243

11.1 Introduction

6D object pose estimation is an important problem in the realm of computer vision that aims to infer the 3D position and 3D orientation of an object in camera-centred coordinates [56]. It has extensively been studied in the past decade given its importance in many rapidly evolving technological areas such as robotics and augmented reality. Particularly, increasing ubiquity of Kinect-like RGB-D sensors and low-cost availability of depth data facilitate object pose estimation scenarios related to the above-mentioned areas.

Robotic manipulators that pick and place the goods from conveyors, shelves, pallets, etc., facilitate several processes comprised within logistics systems, e.g. warehousing, material handling, packaging [11, 31, 42, 61]. The Amazon Picking Challenge (APC) [18] is an important example demonstrating the promising role of robotic manipulation for the completion of such tasks. APC integrates many tasks, such as mapping, motion planning, grasping, object manipulation, with the goal of autonomously moving items by robotic systems from a warehouse shelf into a tote. Regarding the automated handling of items by robots, accurate object detection and 6D pose estimation is an important task that when successfully performed improves the autonomy of the manipulation. Household robotics is another field where the ability to recognize objects and accurately estimating their poses is a key element. This capability is needed for such robots, since they should be able to navigate in unconstrained human environments, calculating grasping and avoidance strategies. In this scenario, unlike industrial applications, the workspace is completely unknown, and thus making indispensable the existence of 6D pose estimators, which are highly robust to changing, dynamic environments. Aerial images are required to be automatically analysed to recognise abnormal behaviours in target terrains [1]. Unmanned aerial vehicles perform surveillance and reconnaissance functions to ensure high-level security detecting and estimating 6D poses of interested objects [4, 16, 41]. Virtual reality (VR) and augmented reality (AR) systems need to know accurate positions, poses, and geometric relations of objects to place virtual objects in the real world [6, 25, 38].

11.2 Problem Formulation

6D object pose estimation is addressed in the literature at the level of both instances and categories. Instance-level 6D object pose estimation tasks require the same statistical distribution on both source data, from which a classifier is learnt, and target data, on which the classifiers will be tested. Hence, instance-based methods estimate 6D poses of *seen* objects, mainly aiming to report improved results in overcoming instances' challenges such as viewpoint variability, occlusion, clutter and similar-looking distractors. However, instance-based methods cannot easily be generalised for category-level 6D object pose estimation tasks, which inherently involve the challenges such as distribution shift among source and target domains, high intra-class variations and shape discrepancies between objects.

We formulate instance-level 6D object pose estimation as a prediction problem as follows: Given an RGB-D image I where an instance S of the interested object O exists, the 6D object pose estimation is casted as a joint probability estimation problem and formulated it as given below:

$$(\mathbf{x}, \theta)^* = \arg \max_{\mathbf{x}, \theta} p(\mathbf{x}, \theta | I, S) \tag{11.1}$$

where $\mathbf{x} = (x, y, z)$ is the 3D translation and $\theta = (r, p, y)$ is the 3D rotation of the instance S. (r, p, y) depicts the Euler angles, roll, pitch and yaw, respectively. According to Eq. 11.1, methods for the 6D object pose estimation problem target to maximise the joint posterior density of the 3D translation $\mathbf{x}$ and 3D rotation θ. This formulation assumes that there only exists one instance of the interested object in the RGB-D image I, and hence, producing the pair of pose parameters $(\mathbf{x}, \theta)$, which is of the instance S. Note that this existence is known a priori by any 6D object pose estimation method.

When the image I involves multiple instances $\mathscr{S} = \{S_i | i = 1, \dots, n\}$ of the object of interest, the problem formulation becomes

$$(\mathbf{x}_i, \theta_i)^* = \arg \max_{\mathbf{x}_i, \theta_i} p(\mathbf{x}_i, \theta_i | I, \mathscr{S}), \quad i = 1, \dots, n. \tag{11.2}$$

Note that the number of instances n is known a priori by the method. Given an instance C of a category of interest c, the 6D object pose estimation problem is formulated at the level of categories by transforming Eq. 11.1 into the following form:

$$(\mathbf{x}, \theta)^* = \arg \max_{\mathbf{x}, \theta} p(\mathbf{x}, \theta | I, C, c). \tag{11.3}$$

Note that Eq. 11.3 assumes that there is only one instance of the category of interest in the RGB-D image I (known a priori by any 6D object pose estimation approach), and hence, producing the pair of object pose parameters $(\mathbf{x}, \theta)$, which is of the instance C. When the image I involves multiple instances $\mathscr{C} = \{C_i | i = 1, \dots, n\}$ of the category of interest, Eq. 11.2 takes the following form, where the number of instances n is known in advance:

$$(\mathbf{x}_i, \theta_i)^* = \arg \max_{\mathbf{x}_i, \theta_i} p(\mathbf{x}_i, \theta_i | I, \mathscr{C}, c), \quad i = 1, \dots, n. \tag{11.4}$$

11.3 Challenges of the Problem

Any method engineered for 6D object pose estimation has to cope with the challenges of the problem in order to work robustly in a generalised fashion. These challenges can be categorised according to the level at which they are observed: challenges of instances and challenges of categories. Note that instances' challenges can also be observed at the level of categories, but not the other way round.

11.3.1 Challenges of Instances

The challenges mainly encountered at the level of instances are viewpoint variability, texture-less objects, occlusion, clutter and similar-looking distractors.

Viewpoint variability. Testing scenes, where target objects are located, can be sampled to produce sequences that are widely distributed in the pose space by $[0° - 360°]$, $[-180° - 180°]$, $[-180° - 180°]$ in the roll, pitch and yaw angles, respectively. As the pose space gets wider, the amount of data required for training a 6D estimator increases in order to capture reasonable viewpoint coverage of the target object.

Texture-less objects. Texture is an important information for RGB cameras, which can capture and represent a scene by 3 basic colours (channels): red, green and blue. An object of interest can easily be distinguished from the background or any other instances available in the scene, if it is sufficiently textured. This is mainly because the texture on the surface defines discriminative features which represent the object of interest. However, when objects are texture-less, this discriminative property disappears, and thus making methods strongly dependent on the depth channel in order to estimate 6D poses of objects.

Occlusion. As being one of the most common challenges observed in 6D object pose estimation, occlusion occurs when an object of interest is partly or completely blocked by other objects existing in the scene. Naive occlusion is handled by either modelling it during an off-line training phase or engineering a part-based approach that infers the 6D pose of the object of interest from its unoccluded (occlusion-free) parts. However, the existence of severe occlusion gives rise to false positive estimations, degrading methods' performance.

Clutter. Clutter is a challenge mainly associated with complicated backgrounds of images in which existing objects of interest even cannot be detected by the naked eye. Several methods handle this challenge by training the algorithms with cluttered background images. However, utilising background images diminishes the generalisation capability of methods, making those data dependent.

Similar-Looking Distractors. Similar-looking distractors along with similar-looking object classes, is one of the main challenges in 6D object pose recovery. When the similarity is in the depth channel, 6D pose estimators become strongly confused due to the lack of discriminative selection of shape features. This deficiency is compensated by RGB in case there is no colour similarity.

11.3.2   Challenges of Categories

The challenges mainly encountered at category-level 6D object pose estimation are intra-class variation and distribution shift.

Intra-class variation. Despite the fact that instances from the same category typically have similar physical properties, they are not exactly the same. While texture and colour variations are seen in the RGB channel, geometry and shape discrepancies are observed in depth channel. Geometric dissimilarities are related to scale and dimensions of the instances, and shape-wise, they appear different in case they physically have extra parts out of the common ones. Category-level 6D object pose estimators handle intra-class variations during training by using the data of the instances belonging to the source domain.

Distribution shift. Any 6D pose estimator working at the level of categories is tested on the instances in the target domain. Since the objects in the target domain are different than those of the source domain, there is a shift between the marginal probability distributions of these two domains. Additionally, this distribution shift itself also changes as the instances in the target domain are unseen by the 6D pose estimator.

11.4   Methods

In this section, we analyse instance-level object pose estimation methods architecture wise, and category-level object pose estimators according to their search space dimension.

11.4.1   Instance-Based Methods

This family involves template-based, point-to-point, conventional learning-based, and deep learning methods.

Template-based. Template-based methods involve an off-line template generation phase. Using the 3D model M of an interested object O, a set of RGB-D templates are synthetically rendered from different camera viewpoints. Each pair of RGB and depth images is annotated with 6D pose and is represented with feature descriptors. The 3D model M can either be a CAD or a reconstructed model. A template-based method takes an RGB-D image I as input on which it runs a sliding window during an on-line test phase. Each of the windows is represented with feature descriptors and is compared with the templates stored in a memory. The distances between each window and the template set are computed. The 6D pose of a template is assigned to the window that has the closest distance with that template [26, 29, 39, 46].

Point-to-point. These methods simultaneously estimate object location and pose by establishing for each scene point a spatial correspondence to a model point, and then rotationally aligning the scene to model point cloud. To this end, point pair features (PPF) are used along with a voting scheme. Both models and scenes are represented with point pair features. During an on-line stage, a set of point pair features are computed from the input depth image I_D. Created point pairs are compared with the ones stored in the global model representation. This comparison is employed in the feature space, and a set of potential matches, and the corresponding 6D pose are obtained [10, 11, 14, 15, 27, 34].

Conventional Learning-based. Conventional learning-based can be divided into two depending on their off-line step: (i) holistic-based and (ii) part-based. In holistic learning, the process of generating holistic training data is the same as the template generation phase of 'template-based methods'. In part-based learning, a set of patches is extracted from each pair of RGB and depth images available in the holistic training data. Each of the extracted patches is annotated with 6D pose and is represented with features. The holistic and part-based training data are separately used to train a regressor, which can be a random forest, a nearest neighbour classifier or an SVM. Further, during an on-line inference stage, an RGB-D image I is taken as input by a conventional learning-based method. If the method is holistic, bounding boxes are extracted from I by running a sliding window over the image and fed into a holistic regressor [5, 51]. When the method is based on parts, extracted patches are sent to a part-based regressor [7, 8, 35, 40, 48, 49, 54]. Both types of regressors output 6D pose parameters $(\mathbf{x}, \theta)$. Several conventional learning-based methods employ a final pose refinement step in order to further improve the 6D pose [35]. As ICP-like algorithms are used to further refine the pose, classifier/regressor itself can be also engineered so that this refinement included architecture wise [48, 49, 54].

Deep learning. The current paradigm in the community is to learn deep discriminative feature representations. Wohlhart et al. [57] utilise a convolutional neural network (CNN) structure to learn discriminative descriptors and then pass them to a nearest neighbour classifier in order to find the closest object pose. However, this approach has one main limitation, which is the requirement of background images during training along with the holistic ones belonging to the object, thus making its performance dataset specific. The studies in [13, 33] learn deep representation of parts in an unsupervised fashion only from foreground images using auto-encoder architectures. The features extracted during the inference stage are fed into a Hough forest in [13], and into a codebook of pre-computed synthetic local object patches in [33] to get pose hypotheses. While Wohlhart and Lepetit [57] focus on learning feature embeddings based on metric learning with triplet comparisons, Balntas et al. [3] further examine the effects of using object poses as guidance to learning robust features for 3D object pose estimation in order to handle symmetry issue.

Recent methods adopt CNNs for 6D object pose estimation by just taking RGB images as inputs without a depth channel [58]. BB8 [45] and Tekin et al. [55] perform corner-point regression followed by PnP for 6D pose estimation. A computationally expensive post-processing step is typically used, examples being iterative closest point (ICP) [7] or a verification network [32].

11.4.2 Category-Based Methods

There have been a large number of methods addressing object detection and pose estimation at the level of categories. However, none of these methods are engineered to estimate the full 6D poses of the instances of a given category as formulated in Sect. 11.2, out of the architecture presented in [47]. Our classification for category-level methods is based on the dimension concerned.

2D. One line of methods is based on visual perception of the RGB channel. Deformable part models [2, 19, 43] are designed to work in RGB, detecting objects of the category of interest in 2D. A more recent paradigm is to learn generic feature representations on which fine-tuning will be applied afterwards. CNN-based approaches [21] have been developed for this purpose, however, they require large-scale annotated images to provide the generalisation on feature representations [12]. Since these approaches work in the context of RGB modality, the success of such methods is limited to coarse/discrete solutions in 2D. Several studies exploit 3D geometry by fusing depth channel with RGB [24, 30]. They mainly use CNN architectures in order to learn representations, which are subsequently fed into SVM classifiers. Even though performance improvement is achieved, they are not generalised well to go beyond 2D applications.

3D. Methods engineered for 3D object detection focus on finding the bounding volume of objects and do not predict the 6D pose of the objects [17, 23, 37, 59]. While Zhou and Tuzel [60] directly detect objects in 3D space taking 3D volumetric data as input, the studies in [9, 36, 44] first produce 2D object proposals in 2D images and then project these proposals into 3D space to further refine the final 3D bounding box location.

4D. SVM-based sliding shapes (SS) [52] method detects objects in the context of depth modality naturally tackling the variations of texture, illumination and viewpoint. The detection performance of this method is further improved in deep sliding shapes (Deep SS) [53], where more powerful representations encoding geometric shapes are learnt with CNNs. These two methods run sliding windows in the 3D space, mainly concerning 3D object detection of bounding boxes aligned around the gravity direction rather than full 6D pose estimation. The system in [22], inspired by Song and Xiao [52], estimates detected and segmented objects' rotation around the gravity axis using a CNN. It combines individual detection/segmentation and pose estimation frameworks. The ways the methods above [22, 52, 53] address the challenges of categories are relatively naive. Both SS and the method in [22] rely on the availability of large-scale 3D models in order to cover the shape variance of objects in the real world. Deep SS performs slightly better with respect to the categories' challenges, however, its effort is limited to the capability of CNNs.

6D. The study in [47] presents 'Intrinsic Structure Adaptors (ISA)', a part-based random forest architecture, for full 6D object pose estimation at the level of categories in depth images. To this end, *3D skeleton structures* are derived as shape-invariant features, and are used as privileged information during the training phase of the architecture.

11.5 Datasets

Every dataset used in this study is composed of several object classes, for each of which a set of RGB-D test images are provided with ground truth object poses.

11.5.1 Datasets of Instances

The collected datasets of instances mainly differ from the point of the challenges that they involve (see Table 11.1).

Viewpoint (VP) + Clutter (C). Every dataset involves the test scenes in which objects of interest are located at *varying viewpoints* and *cluttered backgrounds*.

VP + C + Texture-less (TL). Test scenes in the LINEMOD [26] dataset involve *texture-less* objects at varying viewpoints with cluttered backgrounds. There are 15 objects, for each of which more than 1100 real images are recorded. The sequences provide views from 0° to 360° around the object, 0–90° tilt rotation, ∓45° in-plane rotation, and 650–1150 mm object distance.

Table 11.1 Datasets collected: each dataset shows different characteristics mainly from the challenge point of view (VP: viewpoint, O: occlusion, C: clutter, SO: severe occlusion, SC: severe clutter, MI: multiple instance, SLD: similar-looking distractors, BP: bin picking)

Dataset	Challenge	# Obj. classes	Modality	# Total frame	Obj. dist. (mm)
LINEMOD	VP + C + TL	15	RGB-D	15,770	600–1200
MULT-I	VP + C + TL + O + MI	6	RGB-D	2067	600–1200
OCC	VP + C + TL + SO	8	RGB-D	9209	600–1200
BIN-P	VP + SC + SO + MI + BP	2	RGB-D	180	600–1200
T-LESS	VP + C + TL + O + MI + SLD	30	RGB-D	10,080	600–1200

VP + C + TL + Occlusion (O) + Multiple Instance (MI). Occlusion is one of the main challenges that make the datasets more difficult for the task of object detection and 6D pose estimation. In addition to close and far range 2D and 3D clutter, testing sequences of the Multiple-Instance (MULT-I) dataset [54] contain *foreground occlusions* and *multiple object instances*. In total, there are approximately 2000 real images of 6 different objects, which are located at the range of 600–1200 mm. The testing images are sampled to produce sequences that are uniformly distributed in the pose space by $[0° - 360°]$, $[-80° - 80°]$, and $[-70° - 70°]$ in the yaw, roll, and pitch angles, respectively.

VP + C + TL + Severe Occlusion (SO). Occlusion, clutter, texture-less objects, and change in viewpoint are the most well-known challenges that could successfully be dealt with the state-of-the-art 6D object detectors. However, *heavy existence* of these challenges severely degrades the performance of 6D object detectors. Occlusion (OCC) dataset [7] is one of the most challenging datasets in which one can observe up to 70–80% occluded objects. OCC includes the extended ground truth annotations of LINEMOD: in each test scene of the LINEMOD [26] dataset, various objects are present, but only ground truth poses for one object are given. Brachmann et al. [7] form OCC considering the images of one scene (bench wise) and annotating the poses of 8 additional objects.

VP + SC + SO + MI + Bin Picking (BP). In *bin-picking* scenarios, multiple instances of the objects of interest are arbitrarily stocked in a bin, and hence the objects are inherently subjected to severe occlusion and severe clutter. Bin-Picking (BIN-P) dataset [13] is created to reflect such challenges found in industrial settings. It includes 183 test images of 2 textured objects under varying viewpoints.

VP + C + TL + O + MI + Similar-Looking Distractors (SLD). *Similar-looking distractor(s)* along with similar-looking object classes involved in the datasets strongly confuse recognition systems causing a lack of discriminative selection of shape features. Unlike the above-mentioned datasets and their corresponding challenges, the T-LESS [28] dataset particularly focuses on this problem. The RGB-D images of the objects located on a table are captured at different viewpoints covering 360° rotation, and various object arrangements generate occlusion. Out-of-training objects, similar-looking distractors (planar surfaces), and similar-looking objects cause 6 DoF methods to produce many false positives, particularly affecting the depth modality features. T-LESS has 30 texture-less industry-relevant objects, and 20 different test scenes, each of which consists of 504 test images.

11.6   Evaluation Metrics

Several evaluation metrics have been proposed to determine whether an estimated 6D pose is correct. The multi-modal analyses of instance-level methods presented in Sect. 11.7 are based on the Average Distance (AD) metric [26], and the multi-modal analyses of category-level methods are based on 3D Intersection over Union (IoU) [52]. These two metrics are detailed in this section.

Average Distance (AD). This is one of the most widely used metrics in the literature [26]. Given the ground truth $(\bar{\mathbf{x}}, \bar{\theta})$ and estimated $(\mathbf{x}, \theta)$ poses of an object of interest O, this metric outputs ω_{AD}, the score of the average distance between $(\bar{\mathbf{x}}, \bar{\theta})$ and $(\mathbf{x}, \theta)$. It is calculated over all points $\mathbf{s}$ of the 3D model M of the object of interest:

$$\omega_{AD} = \underset{\mathbf{s} \in M}{\text{avg}} ||(\bar{R}\mathbf{s} + \bar{T}) - (R\mathbf{s} + T)|| \tag{11.5}$$

where $\bar{R}$ and $\bar{T}$ depict rotation and translation matrices of the ground truth pose $(\bar{\mathbf{x}}, \bar{\theta})$, while R and T represent rotation and translation matrices of the estimated pose $(\mathbf{x}, \theta)$. Hypotheses ensuring the following inequality are considered as correct:

$$\omega_{AD} \leq z_\omega \Phi \tag{11.6}$$

where Φ is the diameter of the 3D model M, and z_ω is a constant that determines the coarseness of a hypothesis which is assigned as correct. Note that, Eq. 11.5 is valid for objects whose models are not ambiguous or do not have any subset of views under which they appear to be ambiguous. In case the model M of an object of interest has indistinguishable views, Eq. 11.5 transforms into the following form:

$$\omega_{AD} = \underset{\mathbf{s}_1 \in M, \mathbf{s}_2 \in M}{\text{avg min}} ||(\bar{R}\mathbf{s}_1 + \bar{T}) - (R\mathbf{s}_2 + T)|| \tag{11.7}$$

where ω_{AD} is calculated as the average distance to the closest model point. This function employs many-to-one point matching and significantly promotes symmetric and occluded objects, generating lower ω_{AD} scores.

Intersection over Union. This metric is originally presented to evaluate the performance of the methods working in 2D space. Given the estimated and ground truth bounding boxes B and $\bar{B}$ and assuming that they are aligned with image axes, it determines the area of intersection $B \cap \bar{B}$, and the area of union $B \cup \bar{B}$, and then comparing these two, outputs the overlapping ratio ω_{IoU}:

$$\omega_{IoU} = \frac{B \cap \bar{B}}{B \cup \bar{B}} \tag{11.8}$$

According to Eq. 11.8, a predicted box is considered to be correct if the overlapping ratio ω_{IoU} is more than the threshold $\tau_{IoU} = 0.5$. This metric is further extended to work with 3D volumes calculating overlapping ratio $\omega_{IoU_{3D}}$ over 3D bounding boxes [52]. The extended version assumes that 3D bounding boxes are aligned with gravity direction, but makes no assumption on the other two axes.

In this study, we employ a twofold evaluation strategy for the instance-level 6D object detectors using the AD metric: (i) Recall. The hypotheses on the test images of every object are ranked, and the hypothesis with the highest weight is selected as the estimated 6D pose. Recall value is calculated comparing the number of correctly estimated poses and the number of the test images of the interested object. (ii) F1 scores. Unlike recall, all hypotheses are taken into account, and F1 score, the harmonic mean of precision and recall values are presented. For evaluating the category-level detectors, the 3D IoU metric is utilised, and Average Precision (AP) results are provided.

11.7 Multi-modal Analyses

At the level of instances, we analyse ten baselines on the datasets with respect to both challenges and the architectures. Two of the baselines [26, 54] are our own implementations. The first implementation is of Linemod [26]. Since it is one of the methods been at the forefront of 6D object pose estimation research, we choose this method for implementation to enhance our analyses on the challenges. It is based on templates, and frequently been compared by the state of the art. We compute the colour gradients and surface normal features using the built-in functions and classes provided by OpenCV. Our second implementation is a latent-class Hough forest (LCHF) [54]. There are a high number of learning-based 6D object pose estimation methods in the literature, using random forests as regressors. We have implemented LCHF, since it demonstrates the characteristics of such regressors. The features in LCHF are the part-based version of the features introduced in [26]. Hence, we inherit the classes given by OpenCV in order to generate part-based features used in LCHF. We train each method for the objects of interest by ourselves and using the learnt classifiers, we test those on all datasets. Note that the approaches use only foreground samples during training/template generation. In this section, 'LINEMOD' refers to the dataset, whilst 'Linemod' is used to indicate the method itself.

At the level of categories, we analyse four baselines [22, 47, 52, 53], one of which is our own implementation [47]. The architecture presented in [47] is a part-based random forest architecture. Its learning scheme is privileged. The challenges of the categories are learnt during training in which 3D skeleton structures are derived as shape-invariant features. In the test stage, there is no skeleton data, and the depth pixels are directly used as features in order to vote the 6D pose of an instance, given the category of interest.

11.7.1 Analyses at the Level of Instances

Utilising the AD metric, we compare the chosen baselines along with the challenges, (i) regarding the recall values that each baseline generates on every dataset, (ii) regarding the F1 scores. The coefficient z_ω is 0.10, and in case we use different thresholds, we will specifically indicate in the related parts.

Table 11.2 Methods' performance are depicted object-wise based on recall values computed using the average distance (AD) evaluation protocol

Method	ch.	ape	bvise	cam	can	cat	dril	duck	box	glue	hpunch	iron	lamp	phone	**AVER**
Kehl et al. [33]	RGB-D	96.9	94.1	97.7	95.2	97.4	96.2	97.3	99.9	78.6	96.8	98.7	96.2	92.8	95.2
LCHF [54]	RGB-D	84	95	72	74	91	92	91	48	55	89	72	90	69	78.6
Linemod [26]	RGB-D	95.8	98.7	97.5	95.4	99.3	93.6	95.9	99.8	91.8	95.9	97.5	97.7	93.3	96.3
Drost et al. [15]	D	86.5	70.7	78.6	80.2	85.4	87.3	46	97	57.2	77.4	84.9	93.3	80.7	78.9
Kehl et al. [32]	RGB	65	80	78	86	70	73	66	100	100	49	78	73	79	76.7

(a) LINEMOD dataset

Method	ch.	camera	cup	joystick	juice	milk	shampoo	**AVER**
LCHF [54]	RGB-D	52.5	99.8	98.3	99.3	92.7	97.2	90
Linemod [26]	RGB-D	18.3	99.2	85	51.6	72.2	53.1	63.2

(b) MULT-I dataset

Method	ch.	ape	can	cat	drill	duck	box	glue	hpunch	**AVER**
Xiang et al. [58]	RGB-D	76.2	87.4	52.2	90.3	77.7	72.2	76.7	91.4	78
LCHF [54]	RGB-D	48.0	79.0	38.0	83.0	64.0	11.0	32.0	69.0	53
Hinters et al. [27]	RGB-D	81.4	94.7	55.2	86.0	79.7	65.5	52.1	95.5	76.3
Linemod [26]	RGB-D	21.0	31.0	14.0	37.0	42.0	21.0	5.0	35.0	25.8
Xiang et al. [58]	RGB	9.6	45.2	0.93	41.4	19.6	22.0	38.5	22.1	25

(c) OCC dataset

Method	ch.	cup	juice	AVER
LCHF [54]	RGB-D	90.0	89.0	90
Brachmann et al. [7]	RGB-D	89.4	87.6	89
Linemod [26]	RGB-D	88.0	40.0	64

(d) BIN-P dataset

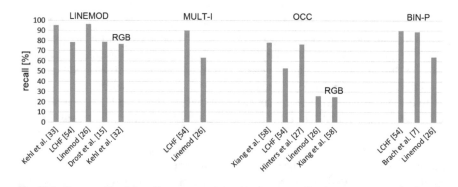

Fig. 11.1 Success of each baseline on every dataset is shown, recall values are computed using the average distance (AD) metric

Recall-only Discussions: Recall-only discussions are based on the numbers provided in Table 11.2, and Fig. 11.1.

Clutter, Viewpoint, Texture-less objects. Highest recall values are obtained on the LINEMOD dataset (see Fig. 11.1), meaning that the state-of-the-art methods for 6D object pose estimation can successfully handle the challenges, clutter, varying viewpoint and texture-less objects. LCHF, detecting more than half of the objects with over 80% accuracy 'box' and 'glue' being the most difficult ones (see Table 11.2a),

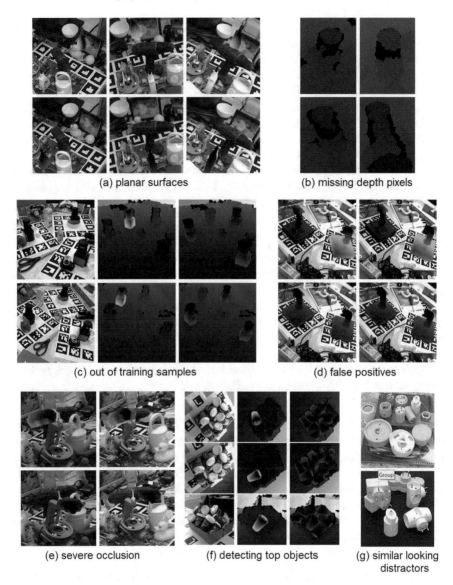

Fig. 11.2 **a–g** Challenges encountered during test are exemplified (green renderings are hypotheses, and the red ones are ground truths)

since these objects have planar surfaces, confusing the features extracted in the depth channel (example images are given in Fig. 11.2a).

Occlusion. In addition to the challenges of LINEMOD dataset, occlusion is introduced in MULT-I. Linemod's performance decreases since occlusion affects holistic feature representations in both colour and depth channels. LCHF performs better on this dataset than Linemod. Since LCHF is trained using the parts coming from positive training images, it can easily handle occlusion by using the information acquired from occlusion-free parts of the target objects. However, LCHF performance degrades on 'camera'. In comparison with the other objects in the dataset, 'camera' has relatively smaller dimensions. In most of the test images, there are non-negligible amounts of missing depth pixels (Fig. 11.2b) along the borders of this object, and thus confusing the features extracted in depth channel. In such cases, LCHF is prone to detect similar-looking out of training objects and generate many false positives (see Fig. 11.2c). The hypotheses produced by LCHF for 'joystick' are all considered as false positives (Fig. 11.2d). When the recall that LCHF produces is evaluated on the 'joystick' object setting z_ω to the value of 0.15, an 89% accuracy is observed.

Severe Occlusion. OCC involves challenging test images where the objects of interest are cluttered and severely occluded. The best performance on this dataset is caught by Xiang et al. [58], and there is still room for improvement in order to fully handle this challenge. Despite the fact that the distinctive feature of this benchmark is the existence of 'severe occlusion', there are occlusion-free target objects in several test images. In case the test images of a target object include unoccluded and/or naively occluded samples (with the occlusion ratio up to 40–50% of the object dimensions) in addition to severely occluded samples, methods produce relatively higher recall values (e.g. 'can, driller, duck, holepuncher', Table 11.2c). On the other hand, when the target object has additionally other challenges such as planar surfaces, methods' performance (LCHF and Linemod) decreases (e.g. 'box', Fig. 11.2e).

Severe Clutter. In addition to the challenges discussed above, BIN-P inherently involves severe clutter, since it is designed for bin-picking scenarios, where objects are arbitrarily stacked in a pile. According to the recall values presented in Table 11.2d, LCHF and Brachmann et al. [7] perform 25% better than Linemod. Despite having severely occluded target objects in this dataset, there are unoccluded/relatively less occluded objects at the top of the bin. Since our current analyses are based on the top hypothesis of each method, the produced success rates show that the methods can recognise the objects located on top of the bin with reasonable accuracy (Fig. 11.2f).

Similar-Looking Distractors. We test both Linemod and LCHF on the T-LESS dataset. Since most of the time the algorithms fail, we do not report quantitative analyses, instead we discuss our observations from the experiments. The dataset involves various object classes with strong shape and colour similarities. When the background colour is different than that of the objects of interest, colour gradient features are successfully extracted. However, the scenes involve multiple instances, multiple objects similar in shape and colour, and hence the features queried exist in the scene at multiple locations. The features extracted in depth channel are also severely affected by the lack of discriminative selection of shape information. When the objects of interest have planar surfaces, the detectors cannot easily discriminate foreground and background in depth channel, since these objects in the dataset are relatively smaller in dimension (see Fig. 11.2g).

Part-based versus Holistic approaches. Holistic methods [15, 26, 27, 32, 58] formulate the detection problem globally. Linemod [26] represents the windows extracted from RGB and depth images by the surface normals and colour gradient features. Distortions along the object borders arising from occlusion and clutter, i.e. the distortions of the colour gradient and surface normal information in the test processes, mainly degrade the performance of this detector. Part-based methods [7, 8, 13, 33, 54] extract parts in the given image. Despite the fact that LCHF uses the same kinds of features as in Linemod, LCHF detects objects extracting parts, thus making the method more robust to occlusion and clutter. As illustrated in Table 11.2, the part-based method LCHF consistently overperforms the holistic method Linemod on all datasets.

Template based versus Random forest based. Template-based methods, i.e. Linemod, match the features extracted during test to a set of templates, and hence they cannot easily be generalised well to unseen ground truth annotations. Methods based on random forests [7, 8, 13, 54] efficiently benefit the randomisation embedded in this learning tool, consequently providing good generalisation performance on new unseen samples. Table 11.2 clearly depicts that methods based on random forests [7, 8, 13, 54] generate higher recall values than template-based Linemod.

RGB-D versus Depth. Methods utilising both RGB and depth channels demonstrate higher recall values than methods that are of using only depth, since RGB provides extra clues to ease the detection. This is depicted in Table 11.2a where learning- and template-based methods of RGB-D perform much better than point-to-point technique [15] of depth channel.

RGB-D versus RGB (CNN structures). More recent paradigm is to adopt CNNs to solve 6D object pose estimation problem taking RGB images as inputs. In Table 11.2, the methods [32, 58] are based on CNN structures. According to Table 11.2a, SSD-6D, the deep approach of Kehl et al. [32] produces 76.7% recall value. Despite the fact that it shows the minimum performance on the LINEMOD dataset, it is important to consider that the method is trained and tested only on RGB channel, while the rest of methods additionally use the depth data. The method of Xiang et al. [58] is evaluated on OCC dataset in both RGB-D and RGB channels. The best performance on the OCC dataset is demonstrated by the deep method of Xiang et al. [58], in case it is trained and is evaluated in RGB-D channel. However, its performance degrades when trained only using RGB data.

Robotic manipulators that pick and place the items from conveyors, shelves, pallets, etc., need to know the pose of one item per RGB-D image, even though there might be multiple items in its workspace. Hence, our recall-only analyses mainly target to solve the problems that could be encountered in such cases. Based on the analyses currently made, one can make important conclusions, particularly from the point of the performances of the detectors. On the other hand, recall-based analyses are not enough to illustrate which dataset is more challenging than the others. This is especially true in cluttered scenarios where multiple instances of target objects are severely occluded. Therefore, in the next part, we discuss the performance of the baselines from another perspective, regarding precision–recall curves and F1 scores, where the 6D detectors are investigated sorting all detection scores across all images.

Precision–Recall Discussions: Our precision–recall discussions are based on the F1 scores provided in Table 11.3, and Fig. 11.3a.

We first analyse the performance of the methods [26, 32, 33, 54] on the LINEMOD dataset. On average, Kehl et al. [33] outperform other methods proving the benefit of learning deep features. Despite estimating 6D in RGB images, SSD-6D [32] exhibits the advantages of using CNN structures for 6D object pose estimation. LCHF and Linemod demonstrate lower performance, since the features used by these methods are manually crafted. The comparison between Figs. 11.1 and 11.3a reveals that the results produced by the methods have approximately the same characteristics on the LINEMOD dataset with respect to recall and F1 scores.

The methods tested on the MULT-I dataset [15, 26, 32, 33, 54] utilise the geometry information inherently provided by depth images. Despite this, SSD-6D [32], estimating 6D pose only from RGB images, outperforms other methods, showing the superiority of CNNs for the 6D problem over other frameworks.

Table 11.3 Methods' performance are depicted object-wise based on F1 scores computed using the average distance (AD) evaluation protocol

Method	ch.	ape	bvise	cam	can	cat	dril	duck	box	glue	hpunch	iron	lamp	phone	**AVER**
Kehl et al. [33]	RGB-D	0.98	0.95	0.93	0.83	0.98	0.97	0.98	1	0.74	0.98	0.91	0.98	0.85	0.93
LCHF [54]	RGB-D	0.86	0.96	0.72	0.71	0.89	0.91	0.91	0.74	0.68	0.88	0.74	0.92	0.73	0.82
Linemod [26]	RGB-D	0.53	0.85	0.64	0.51	0.66	0.69	0.58	0.86	0.44	0.52	0.68	0.68	0.56	0.63
Kehl et al. [32]	RGB	0.76	0.97	0.92	0.93	0.89	0.97	0.80	0.94	0.76	0.72	0.98	0.93	0.92	0.88

(a) LINEMOD dataset

Method	ch.	camera	cup	joystick	juice	milk	shampoo	**AVER**
Kehl et al. [33]	RGB-D	0.38	0.97	0.89	0.87	0.46	0.91	0.75
LCHF [54]	RGB-D	0.39	0.89	0.55	0.88	0.40	0.79	0.65
Drost et al. [15]	D	0.41	0.87	0.28	0.60	0.26	0.65	0.51
Linemod [26]	RGB-D	0.37	0.58	0.15	0.44	0.49	0.55	0.43
Kehl et al. [32]	RGB	0.74	0.98	0.99	0.92	0.78	0.89	0.88

(b) MULT-I dataset

Method	ch.	ape	can	cat	dril	duck	box	glue	hpunch	**AVER**
LCHF [54]	RGB-D	0.51	0.77	0.44	0.82	0.66	0.13	0.25	0.64	0.53
Linemod [26]	RGB-D	0.23	0.31	0.17	0.37	0.43	0.19	0.05	0.30	0.26
Brachmann et al. [8]	RGB	-	-	-	-	-	-	-	-	0.51
Kehl et al. [32]	RGB	-	-	-	-	-	-	-	-	0.38

(c) OCC dataset

Method	ch.	cup	juice	**AVER**
LCHF [54]	RGB-D	0.48	0.29	0.39
Doumanoglou et al. [13]	RGB-D	0.36	0.29	0.33
Linemod [26]	RGB-D	0.48	0.20	0.34

(d) BIN-P dataset

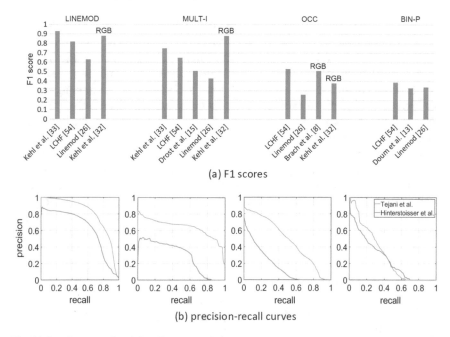

(a) F1 scores

(b) precision-recall curves

Fig. 11.3 **a** Success of each baseline on every dataset is shown, F1 scores are computed using the average distance (AD) metric. **b** Precision–recall curves of averaged F1 scores for Tejani et al. [54] and Hinterstoisser et al. [26] are shown: from left to right, LINEMOD, MULT-I, OCC, BIN-P

LCHF [54] and Brachmann et al. [8] best perform on OCC with respect to F1 scores. As this dataset involves test images where highly occluded objects are located, the reported results depict the importance of designing part-based solutions.

The most important difference is observed on the BIN-P dataset. While the success rates of the detectors on this dataset are higher than 60% with respect to the recall values (see Fig. 11.1), according to the presented F1 scores, their performance is less than 40%. Taking into account all the hypotheses and challenges of this dataset, i.e. severe occlusion and severe clutter, we observe strong degradation in the accuracy of the detectors.

In Fig. 11.3b, we lastly report precision–recall curves of LCHF and Linemod. Regarding these curves, one can observe that as the datasets are getting more difficult, from the point of challenges involved, the methods produce less accurate results.

11.7.2 Analyses at the Level of Categories

Our analyses at the level of categories are based on Table 11.4 and Fig. 11.4. Table 11.4 depicts the test results of the methods [22, 47, 52, 53] on the RMRC dataset [50] evaluated using the metric in [52]. A short analysis on the table reveals

ISA demonstrates 50% average precision. The highest value ISA reaches is on the *toilet* category, mainly because of the limited deviation in shape in between the instances. ISA next best performs on *bed*, with 52% mean precision. The accuracy on both the categories *bed* and *table* are approximately the same. Despite the fact that all forests used in the experiments undergo a relatively a naive training process, the highest number of the instances during training are used for the chair category. However, ISA performs worse on this category since the images in the test dataset poses strong challenges of the instances, such as occlusion, clutter, and high diversity from the shape point of view. On average, Deep SS [53] outperforms other methods including ISA. In the real experiments, the use of the forest trained on less number of data and ground truth information degrades the performance of ISA across the problem's challenges. Sample results are lastly presented in Fig. 11.4. In these figures, the leftmost images are the inputs of ISA, and the 2nd and the 3rd columns demonstrate the estimations of the forests, whose training is based on $Q_1 \& Q_2 \& Q_3$

Table 11.4 3D object detection comparison on the RMRC dataset [50] using the evaluation metric in [52]

Method	Input channel	Bed	Chair	Table	Toilet	Mean
Sliding shapes [52]	Depth	33.5	29	34.5	67.3	41.075
[22] on instance seg.	Depth	71	18.2	30.4	63.4	45.75
[22] on estimated model	Depth	72.7	47.5	40.6	72.7	58.375
Deep sliding shapes [53]	Depth	83.0	58.8	68.6	79.2	72.40
ISA [47]	Depth	52.0	36.0	46.5	67.7	50.55

Fig. 11.4 Sample results generated by ISA on real data: (for each triplet) each row is for per scene. First column depicts depth images of scenes. Estimations in the middle belong to ISAs trained using $Q_1 \& Q_2 \& Q_3$ (using 3D skeleton representation as privileged data), and hypotheses on the right are of ISAs trained on Q_1 only (no 3D skeleton information)

Fig. 11.5 Sample unsuccessful results generated by ISA on real data: (first row) the category of interest is *table*. (second row) the interested category is *chair*. All hypotheses are of ISAs trained using $Q_1 \& Q_2 \& Q_3$ (using 3D skeleton representation as privileged data)

and Q_1, respectively. Training the forest using the quality function $Q_1 \& Q_2 \& Q_3$ stands for utilising 3D skeleton representation as privileged data for training. However, in case the forest is trained using the quality function Q_1, ISA does not use any skeleton information during training. For further details, check the architecture of ISA [47]. Figure 11.5 demonstrates several failed results. Since ISA is designed to work on the depth channel, planar surfaces confuse the features extracted from the test images with the features learnt during training, consequently resulting in unsuccessful estimations.

11.8 Discussions and Conclusions

We outline our key observations which provide guidance for future research.

At the level of instances reasonably accurate results have been obtained on textured objects at varying viewpoints with cluttered backgrounds. In cases where occlusion is introduced in the test scenes, depending on the architecture of the baseline, good performance is demonstrated. Part-based solutions can handle the occlusion problem better than the ones global, using the information acquired from occlusion-free parts of the target objects. However, heavy existence of occlusion and clutter severely affects the detectors. It is possible that modelling occlusion during training can improve the performance of a detector across severe occlusion. But when occlusion is modelled, the baseline could be data-dependent. In order to maintain the generalisation capability of the baseline, contextual information can additionally be utilised during the modelling. Currently, similar-looking distractors along with similar looking object classes seem the biggest challenge in recovering instances' 6D, since the lack of discriminative selection of shape features strongly confuse recognition systems. One possible solution could be considering the instances that have strong similarity in shape in the same category. In such a case, detectors trained using the data coming from the instances involved in the same category can report better detection results.

Architecture-wise, template-based methods matching model features to the scene and random forest based learning algorithms, along with their good generalisation performance across unseen samples, underlie object detection and 6D pose estimation. The recent paradigm in the community is to learn deep discriminative feature representations. Several methods address 6D pose estimation with the use of deep features [13, 33]. Depending on the availability of large-scale 6D annotated depth datasets, feature representations can be learnt on these datasets that can be customised for the 6D problem.

These implications are related to automation in robotic systems. The implications can provide guidance for robotic manipulators that pick and place the items from conveyors, shelves, pallets, *etc*. Accurately detecting objects and estimating their fine pose under uncontrolled conditions improves the grasping capability of the manipulators. Beyond accuracy, the baselines are expected to show real-time performance. Although the detectors we have tested cannot perform in real-time, their run-time could be improved with parallelisation.

At the level of categories, DPMs [2, 19, 21, 43], being at the forefront of the category-level detection research, mainly present RGB-based discrete solutions in 2D. Several studies [24, 30] combine depth data with RGB. Although promising, they are not capable enough for the applications beyond 2D. More recent methods working at the level of categories are engineered to work in 3D [9, 17, 36, 59] and 4D [22, 52, 53]. The ways the methods [9, 17, 22, 36, 52, 53, 59] address the challenges of categories are relatively simple. They rely on the availability of large-scale 3D models in order to cover the shape variance of objects in the real world. Unlike the 3D/4D methods, ISA [47] is a dedicated architecture that directly tackles the challenges of the categories, intra-class variations, distribution shifts, while estimating objects' 6D pose. The recent introduction of new datasets with 6D object pose annotations, e.g., [20] is likely to lead to the development of new approaches for 6D object pose estimation in the presence of new challenges such as human–object and robot–object interaction.

References

1. Amer K, Samy M, ElHakim R, Shaker M, ElHelw M (2017) Convolutional neural network-based deep urban signatures with application to drone localization. In: 2017 IEEE international conference on computer vision workshop (ICCVW). IEEE, pp 2138–2145
2. Azizpour H, Laptev I (2012) Object detection using strongly-supervised deformable part models. In: European conference on computer vision. Springer, pp 836–849
3. Balntas V, Doumanoglou A, Sahin C, Sock J, Kouskouridas R, Kim TK (2017) Pose guided RGBD feature learning for 3D object pose estimation. In: Proceedings of the IEEE international conference on computer vision, pp 3856–3864
4. Blösch M, Weiss S, Scaramuzza D, Siegwart R (2010) Vision based MAV navigation in unknown and unstructured environments. In: 2010 IEEE international conference on robotics and automation (ICRA). IEEE, pp 21–28

5. Bonde U, Badrinarayanan V, Cipolla R (2014) Robust instance recognition in presence of occlusion and clutter. In: European conference on computer vision. Springer, pp 520–535
6. Born F, Masuch M (2017) Increasing presence in a mixed reality application by integrating a real time tracked full body representation. In: International conference on advances in computer entertainment. Springer, pp 46–60
7. Brachmann E, Krull A, Michel F, Gumhold S, Shotton J, Rother C (2014) Learning 6D object pose estimation using 3D object coordinates. In: European conference on computer vision. Springer, pp 536–551
8. Brachmann E, Michel F, Krull A, Ying Yang M, Gumhold S, et al (2016) Uncertainty-driven 6D pose estimation of objects and scenes from a single RGB image. In: Proceedings of the IEEE conference on computer vision and pattern recognition, pp 3364–3372
9. Chen X, Ma H, Wan J, Li B, Xia T (2017) Multi-view 3D object detection network for autonomous driving. In: IEEE CVPR, vol 1, p 3
10. Choi C, Christensen HI (2012) 3D pose estimation of daily objects using an RGB-D camera. In: 2012 IEEE/RSJ international conference on intelligent robots and systems (IROS). IEEE, pp 3342–3349
11. Choi C, Taguchi Y, Tuzel O, Liu MY, Ramalingam S (2012) Voting-based pose estimation for robotic assembly using a 3D sensor. In: ICRA. Citeseer, pp 1724–1731
12. Deng J, Dong W, Socher R, Li LJ, Li K, Fei-Fei L (2009) Imagenet: a large-scale hierarchical image database. In: IEEE conference on computer vision and pattern recognition, 2009. CVPR 2009. IEEE, pp 248–255
13. Doumanoglou A, Kouskouridas R, Malassiotis S, Kim TK (2016) Recovering 6D object pose and predicting next-best-view in the crowd. In: Proceedings of the IEEE conference on computer vision and pattern recognition, pp 3583–3592
14. Drost B, Ilic S (2012) 3D object detection and localization using multimodal point pair features. In: 2012 second international conference on 3D imaging, modeling, processing, visualization & transmission. IEEE, pp 9–16
15. Drost B, Ulrich M, Navab N, Ilic S (2010) Model globally, match locally: efficient and robust 3D object recognition. In: 2010 IEEE conference on computer vision and pattern recognition (CVPR). IEEE, pp 998–1005
16. Dryanovski I, Morris W, Xiao J (2011) An open-source pose estimation system for micro-air vehicles. In: 2011 IEEE international conference on robotics and automation (ICRA). IEEE, pp 4449–4454
17. Engelcke M, Rao D, Wang DZ, Tong CH, Posner I (2017) Vote3deep: fast object detection in 3D point clouds using efficient convolutional neural networks. In: 2017 IEEE international conference on robotics and automation (ICRA). IEEE, pp 1355–1361
18. Eppner C, Höfer S, Jonschkowski R, Martín-Martín R, Sieverling A, Wall V, Brock O (2016) Lessons from the Amazon Picking Challenge: four aspects of building robotic systems. In: Robotics: science and systems
19. Felzenszwalb PF, Girshick RB, McAllester D, Ramanan D (2010) Object detection with discriminatively trained part-based models. IEEE Trans Pattern Anal Mach Intell 32(9):1627–1645
20. Garcia-Hernando G, Yuan S, Baek S, Kim TK (2018) First-person hand action benchmark with RGB-D videos and 3D hand pose annotations. In: Proceedings of the IEEE conference on computer vision and pattern recognition, pp 409–419
21. Girshick R, Donahue J, Darrell T, Malik J (2014) Rich feature hierarchies for accurate object detection and semantic segmentation. In: Proceedings of the IEEE conference on computer vision and pattern recognition, pp 580–587
22. Gupta S, Arbeláez P, Girshick R, Malik J (2015) Aligning 3D models to RGB-D images of cluttered scenes. In: Proceedings of the IEEE conference on computer vision and pattern recognition, pp 4731–4740
23. Gupta S, Arbelaez P, Malik J (2013) Perceptual organization and recognition of indoor scenes from RGB-D images. In: Proceedings of the IEEE conference on computer vision and pattern recognition, pp 564–571

24. Gupta S, Girshick R, Arbeláez P, Malik J (2014) Learning rich features from RGB-D images for object detection and segmentation. In: European conference on computer vision. Springer, pp 345–360
25. Hettiarachchi A, Wigdor D (2016) Annexing reality: enabling opportunistic use of everyday objects as tangible proxies in augmented reality. In: Proceedings of the 2016 CHI conference on human factors in computing systems. ACM, pp 1957–1967
26. Hinterstoisser S, Lepetit V, Ilic S, Holzer S, Bradski G, Konolige K, Navab N (2012) Model based training, detection and pose estimation of texture-less 3D objects in heavily cluttered scenes. In: Asian conference on computer vision. Springer, pp 548–562
27. Hinterstoisser S, Lepetit V, Rajkumar N, Konolige K (2016) Going further with point pair features. In: European conference on computer vision. Springer, pp 834–848
28. Hodan T, Haluza P, Obdržálek, Š, Matas J, Lourakis M, Zabulis X (2017) T-LESS: an RGB-D dataset for 6D pose estimation of texture-less objects. In: 2017 IEEE winter conference on applications of computer vision (WACV). IEEE, pp 880–888
29. Hodaň T, Zabulis X, Lourakis M, Obdržálek, Š, Matas J (2015) Detection and fine 3D pose estimation of texture-less objects in RGB-D images. In: 2015 IEEE/RSJ international conference on intelligent robots and systems (IROS). IEEE, pp 4421–4428
30. Hoffman J, Gupta S, Leong J, Guadarrama S, Darrell T (2016) Cross-modal adaptation for RGB-D detection. In: 2016 IEEE international conference on robotics and automation (ICRA). IEEE, pp 5032–5039
31. Huang J, Cakmak M (2017) Code3: a system for end-to-end programming of mobile manipulator robots for novices and experts. In: Proceedings of the 2017 ACM/IEEE international conference on human–robot interaction. ACM, pp 453–462
32. Kehl W, Manhardt F, Tombari F, Ilic S, Navab N (2017) SSD-6D: making RGB-based 3D detection and 6D pose estimation great again. In: Proceedings of the international conference on computer vision (ICCV 2017), Venice, Italy, pp 22–29
33. Kehl W, Milletari F, Tombari F, Ilic S, Navab N (2016) Deep learning of local RGB-D patches for 3D object detection and 6D pose estimation. In: European conference on computer vision. Springer, pp 205–220
34. Kim E, Medioni G (2011) 3D object recognition in range images using visibility context. In: 2011 IEEE/RSJ international conference on intelligent robots and systems (IROS). IEEE, pp 3800–3807
35. Krull A, Brachmann E, Michel F, Ying Yang M, Gumhold S, Rother C (2015) Learning analysis-by-synthesis for 6D pose estimation in RGB-D images. In: Proceedings of the IEEE international conference on computer vision, pp 954–962
36. Lahoud J, Ghanem B (2017) 2D-driven 3D object detection in RGB-D images. In: 2017 IEEE international conference on computer vision (ICCV). IEEE, pp 4632–4640
37. Lin D, Fidler S, Urtasun R (2013) Holistic scene understanding for 3D object detection with RGBD cameras. In: Proceedings of the IEEE international conference on computer vision, pp 1417–1424
38. Lindlbauer D, Mueller J, Alexa M (2017) Changing the appearance of real-world objects by modifying their surroundings. In: Proceedings of the 2017 CHI conference on human factors in computing systems. ACM, pp 3954–3965
39. Liu MY, Tuzel O, Veeraraghavan A, Taguchi Y, Marks TK, Chellappa R (2012) Fast object localization and pose estimation in heavy clutter for robotic bin picking. Int J Robot Res 31(8):951–973
40. Michel F, Kirillov A, Brachmann E, Krull A, Gumhold S, Savchynskyy B, Rother C (2017) Global hypothesis generation for 6D object pose estimation. In: IEEE conference on computer vision and pattern recognition (CVPR)
41. Mondragón IF, Campoy P, Martinez C, Olivares-Méndez MA (2010) 3D pose estimation based on planar object tracking for UAVs control. In: 2010 IEEE international conference on robotics and automation (ICRA). IEEE, pp 35–41
42. Patel R, Curtis R, Romero B, Correll N (2016) Improving grasp performance using in-hand proximity and contact sensing. In: Robotic grasping and manipulation challenge. Springer, pp 146–160

43. Pepik B, Stark M, Gehler P, Schiele B (2012) Teaching 3D geometry to deformable part models. In: 2012 IEEE conference on computer vision and pattern recognition (CVPR). IEEE, pp 3362–3369
44. Qi CR, Liu W, Wu C, Su H, Guibas LJ (2018) Frustum pointnets for 3D object detection from RGB-D data. In: Proceedings of the IEEE conference on computer vision and pattern recognition, pp 918–927
45. Rad M, Lepetit V (2017) BB8: a scalable, accurate, robust to partial occlusion method for predicting the 3D poses of challenging objects without using depth. In: 2017 IEEE international conference on computer vision (ICCV). IEEE, pp 3848–3856
46. Rios-Cabrera R, Tuytelaars T (2013) Discriminatively trained templates for 3D object detection: a real time scalable approach. In: Proceedings of the IEEE international conference on computer vision, pp 2048–2055
47. Sahin C, Kim TK (2018) Category-level 6D object pose recovery in depth images. In: 2018 IEEE European conference on computer vision workshop (ECCVW)
48. Sahin C, Kouskouridas R, Kim TK (2016) Iterative Hough forest with histogram of control points for 6 DoF object registration from depth images. In: 2016 IEEE/RSJ international conference on intelligent robots and systems (IROS). IEEE, pp 4113–4118
49. Sahin C, Kouskouridas R, Kim TK (2017) A learning-based variable size part extraction architecture for 6D object pose recovery in depth images. Image Vis Comput 63:38–50
50. Silberman N, Hoiem D, Kohli P, Fergus R (2012) Indoor segmentation and support inference from RGBD images. In: European conference on computer vision. Springer, pp 746–760
51. Sock J, Kasaei SH, Lopes LS, Kim TK (2017) Multi-view 6D object pose estimation and camera motion planning using RGBD images. In: 2017 IEEE international conference on computer vision workshop (ICCVW). IEEE, pp 2228–2235
52. Song S, Xiao J (2014) Sliding shapes for 3D object detection in depth images. In: European conference on computer vision. Springer, pp 634–651
53. Song S, Xiao J (2016) Deep sliding shapes for amodal 3D object detection in RGB-D images. In: Proceedings of the IEEE conference on computer vision and pattern recognition, pp 808–816
54. Tejani A, Tang D, Kouskouridas R, Kim TK (2014) Latent-class Hough forests for 3D object detection and pose estimation. In: European conference on computer vision. Springer, pp 462–477
55. Tekin B, Sinha SN, Fua P (2018) Real-time seamless single shot 6D object pose prediction. In: Proceedings of the IEEE conference on computer vision and pattern recognition, pp 292–301
56. Uenohara M, Kanade T (1995) Vision-based object registration for real-time image overlay. In: Computer vision, virtual reality and robotics in medicine. Springer, pp 13–22
57. Wohlhart P, Lepetit V (2015) Learning descriptors for object recognition and 3D pose estimation. In: Proceedings of the IEEE conference on computer vision and pattern recognition, pp 3109–3118
58. Xiang Y, Schmidt T, Narayanan V, Fox D (2017) PoseCNN: a convolutional neural network for 6D object pose estimation in cluttered scenes. arXiv:1711.00199
59. Zhang Y, Bai M, Kohli P, Izadi S, Xiao J (2017) Deepcontext: context-encoding neural pathways for 3D holistic scene understanding. In: Proceedings of the IEEE international conference on computer vision, pp 1192–1201
60. Zhou Y, Tuzel O (2018) Voxelnet: end-to-end learning for point cloud based 3D object detection. In: Proceedings of the IEEE conference on computer vision and pattern recognition, pp 4490–4499
61. Zhu M, Derpanis KG, Yang Y, Brahmbhatt S, Zhang M, Phillips C, Lecce M, Daniilidis K (2014) Single image 3D object detection and pose estimation for grasping. In: 2014 IEEE international conference on robotics and automation (ICRA). IEEE, pp 3936–3943

Chapter 12
Geometric and Semantic Modeling from RGB-D Data

Song-Hai Zhang and Yu-Kun Lai

Abstract With the increasing availability of RGB-D cameras, using RGB-D data for geometric and semantic modeling has received significant interest in recent years. Geometric modeling aims to build an accurate geometric representation for 3D objects or scenes, whereas semantic modeling focuses on analyzing and understanding semantic objects in the captured scenes. They have many applications ranging from robotic navigation to VR/AR. In this chapter, we will overview recent efforts on this research topic, in particular, research using advanced machine learning techniques, exploiting the complementary characteristics of geometry and image information in RGB-D data, and incorporating prior knowledge.

12.1 Introduction

Geometric and semantic modeling produces digital- and object-level representations of real-world scenes, which is key to a wide range of applications, including 3D environment understanding, mixed reality, as well as the next generation of robotics. Geometric modeling aims to build an accurate geometric representation for 3D objects or scenes, whereas semantic modeling focuses on analyzing and understanding semantic objects in the captured scenes.

Currently, consumer-level color and depth (RGB-D) cameras (e.g., Microsoft Kinect and Intel RealSense) are now widely available and are affordable to the general public. Ordinary people can now easily obtain 3D data of their real-world environments. Meanwhile, other booming 3D technologies in areas such as augmented reality, stereoscopic movies, and 3D printing are also becoming common in

S.-H. Zhang (✉)
Department of Computer Science and Technology, Tsinghua University,
Beijing 100084, China
e-mail: shz@tsinghua.edu.cn

Y.-K. Lai
School of Computer Science and Informatics, Cardiff University, Cardiff CF24 3AA, UK
e-mail: LaiY4@cardiff.ac.uk

© Springer Nature Switzerland AG 2019

P. L. Rosin et al. (eds.), *RGB-D Image Analysis and Processing*,
Advances in Computer Vision and Pattern Recognition,
https://doi.org/10.1007/978-3-030-28603-3_12

our daily life. There is an ever-increasing need for ordinary people to digitize their living environments. Helping ordinary people quickly and easily acquire 3D digital representations of their living surroundings is an urging yet still challenging problem in the research field. In recent decades, we have seen a massive increase in digital images available on the Internet. Benefiting from such data, research on 2D images has been significantly boosted, by mining and exploiting the huge amount of 2D image data. In contrast, while the growth of 3D digital models has been accelerating over the past few years, the growth remains slow in comparison, mainly because making 3D models is a demanding job which requires expertise and is time consuming. Fortunately, the prevalence of low-cost RGB-D cameras along with recent advances in modeling techniques offers a great opportunity to change this situation. In the longer term, big 3D data has the potential to change the landscape of 3D visual data processing.

This chapter focuses on digitizing real-world scenes, which has received significant interest in recent years. It has many applications which may fundamentally change our daily life. With such techniques, furniture stores can offer 3D models of their products online so that customers can better view the products and choose the furniture they would buy. People without interior design experience can give digital representations of their homes to experts or expert systems [34, 65] for advice on better furniture arrangement. Anyone with Internet access can virtually visit digitized museums all over the world [60]. Moreover, the modeled indoor scenes can be used for augmented reality [26] and serve as a training basis for intelligent robots to better understand real-world environments [43].

Nevertheless, high-fidelity scene modeling is still a challenging problem, especially from RGB-D data. The difficulties mainly come from two aspects [10]: First, objects often have complicated 3D geometry, non-convex structures, often with messy surroundings and substantial variation between parts. Second, depth information captured by consumer-level scanning devices is often noisy, may be distorted, and can have large gaps. To address these challenges, various methods have been proposed in the past few years and this is still an active research area in both the computer graphics and computer vision communities.

Benefiting from the increasing amount of public RGB-D datasets, learning-based methods such as 2D and 3D convolutional neural networks (CNNs), achieve impressive results to tackle both geometric and semantic modeling problems from RGB-D data, including gap filling of 3D shapes [6], object detection [21, 51], and semantic segmentation [39]. Meanwhile, unlike treating geometric and semantic modeling separately, semantic SLAM (Simultaneous Localization and Mapping) [5] shows another trend for scene modeling that integrates metric information, semantic information, and data associations into a single optimization framework and thus improves localization performance and loop closure, as well as semantic segmentation (see Chap. 6 for more discussions on RGB-D SLAM techniques).

This chapter significantly extends our earlier survey paper [9] and includes key developments in recent years. The rest of the chapter will be organized as follows. We first briefly introduce in Sect. 12.2 different types of RGB-D data and publicly available RGB-D datasets. After that, in Sects. 12.3 and 12.4, we systematically categorize existing geometric modeling and semantic modeling methods respectively, overview each technique and examine their advantages and disadvantages. Finally, in Sect. 12.5, we summarize the current state of the art and elaborate on future research directions.

12.2   RGB-D Data and Public Datasets

The depth image along with an aligned RGB image forms an RGB-D image frame, which depicts a single view of the target scene, including both the color and the shape. Such RGB-D image frames can be reprojected to 3D space to form a colored 3D point cloud. RGB-D images and colored point clouds are the two most common representations of RGB-D data. RGB-D images are mostly used by the computer vision community as they bear the same topology as images, while in the computer graphics community, RGB-D data is more commonly viewed as point clouds. Point clouds obtained from a projective camera are organized (a.k.a. structured or ordered) point clouds because there is a one-to-one correspondence between points in the 3D space and pixels in the image space. This correspondence contains adjacency information between 3D points which is useful in certain applications, e.g., to simplify algorithms or make algorithms more efficient as neighboring points can be easily obtained. With the correct camera parameters, organized colored point clouds and the corresponding RGB-D images can be transformed into each other. If such an equivalent RGB-D image does not exist for a colored point cloud, then the point cloud is unorganized (a.k.a. unstructured or unordered). To fully depict a target scene, multiple RGB-D image frames captured from different views are typically needed. As scannerless cameras are usually used, scene RGB-D data captured is essentially RGB-D image streams (sequences) which can later be stitched into a whole scene point cloud using 3D registration techniques.

Depending on the operation mechanism, there is a fundamental limitation of all active (e.g., laser-based) RGB-D scanning systems, that they cannot capture depth information on surfaces with highly absorptive or reflective materials. However, these kinds of materials, such as mirrors, window glass, and shiny steels, are very common in real-world scenes. Apart from this common limitation, consumer-level RGB-D cameras have some other drawbacks caused by their low cost. First, the spatial resolution of such cameras is generally low (512×484 pixels in the latest Kinect). Second, the depth information is noisy and often has significant camera distortions. Third, even for scenes without absorptive or reflective materials, the depth images may still involve small gaps around object borders. In general, the depth information obtained by cheap scanning devices is not entirely reliable, which practical scene modeling algorithms must take into consideration. See Chaps. 2 and 3 for detailed discussion of techniques to address incompleteness and low resolution of RGB-D images.

The popularity of RGB-D cameras and the abundance of research on RGB-D data analysis have resulted in a number of public RGB-D datasets as well as 3D

Object/Scene datasets in recent years. The wider availability of large-scale RGB-D repositories stimulates the development of data-driven approaches for scene modeling. Although most of these datasets are built and labeled for specific applications, such as scene reconstruction, object detection and recognition, scene understanding and segmentation, as long as they provide full RGB-D image streams of scenes, they can be used as training data and benchmarks for scene modeling including geometric modeling and semantic modeling. Here, we briefly describe some popular ones, which are summarized in Table 12.1.

ScanNet [15]: This dataset is an RGB-D video dataset containing 2.5 million views (RGB-D images) of real-world environments in 1513 scans acquired in 707 distinct locations. The data is annotated with estimated calibration parameters, camera poses, 3D surface reconstructions, textured meshes, dense object-level semantic segmentation, and aligned CAD models. This dataset is the largest one so far.

SceneNN [25]: This is an RGB-D scene dataset consisting of 100 scenes, all of which are reconstructed into triangle meshes and have per-vertex and per-pixel annotation of object labels. The data is also annotated with axis-aligned bounding boxes, oriented bounding boxes, and object poses.

PiGraphs [44]: Savva et al. released an RGB-D dataset on their research of relations between human poses and arrangements of object geometry in the scene. This dataset consists of 26 scans captured with Kinect v1 devices and reconstructed with the VoxelHashing. This dataset has more complete and clean semantic labels, including object parts and object instances.

Cornell RGB-D Dataset [2, 29]: This dataset contains RGB-D data of 24 office scenes and 28 home scenes, all of which are captured by Kinect. RGB-D images of each scene are stitched into scene point clouds using an RGB-D SLAM algorithm. Object-level labels are given on the stitched scene point clouds.

Washington RGB-D Scenes Dataset [30]: This dataset consists of 14 indoor scenes containing objects in 9 categories (chair, coffee table, sofa, table, bowls, caps, cereal boxes, coffee mugs, and soda cans). Each scene is a point cloud created by aligning a set of Kinect RGB-D image frames using Patch Volumes Mapping. Labels of background and the 9 object classes are given on the stitched scene point clouds.

NYU Depth Dataset [47, 48]: This dataset contains 528 different indoor scenes (64 in the first version [47] and 464 in the second [48]) captured from large US cities with Kinect. The captured scenes mainly consist of residential apartments, including living rooms, bedrooms, bathrooms, and kitchens. Dense labeling of objects at the class and instance levels is provided for 1449 selected frames. This dataset does not contain camera pose information because it is mainly built for segmentation and object recognition in single frames. To get full 3D scene point clouds, users may need to estimate camera poses from the original RGB-D streams.

Sun RGB-D Dataset [50]: This dataset is captured by four different sensors and contains 10,335 RGB-D images, at a similar scale as PASCAL VOC. The whole dataset is densely annotated and includes 146,617 2D polygons and 64,595 3D bounding boxes with accurate object orientations, as well as a 3D room layout and scene category for each image.

Table 12.1 Some popular RGB-D datasets

Dataset	Year	Size	Labels	Annotation	Reconstruction	URL
ScanNet v2	2018	1513 scans, 2.49 M frames	All	Per-pixel, per-vertex, instance-level semantic segmentation	Dense 3D	http://www.scan-net.org/
SceneNN	2016	100 scans, 2.47 M frames	All	Per-pixel, per-vertex, instance-level semantic segmentation	Dense 3D	http://www.scenenn.net/
PiGraphs	2016	26 scans	All	Per-vertex, instance-level semantic segmentation	Dense 3D	http://graphics.stanford.edu/projects/pigraphs/
Sun RGB-D	2016	10 K frames	All	2D polygons, bounding boxes, object orientation	Aligned poses	http://RGB-D.cs.princeton.edu/
Sun 3D	2013	415 scans	8 scans	2D polygons	Aligned poses	http://sun3d.cs.princeton.edu/
NYU v2	2012	464 scans, 408 K frames	1449 frames	Per-pixel, instance-level semantic segmentation	None	https://cs.nyu.edu/~silberman/datasets/nyu_depth_v2.html
SunCG & House3D	2017	45 K Scenes	All	Object level annotation	Rendering	http://suncg.cs.princeton.edu/
Washington v2	2014	14 scans	All	Per-vertex	Dense 3D	http://RGB-D-dataset.cs.washington.edu/

SUN 3D Dataset [61]: This dataset contains 415 RGB-D image sequences captured by Kinect from 254 different indoor scenes, in 41 different buildings across North America, Europe, and Asia. Polygons of semantic class and instance labels are given on frames and propagated through the whole sequences. Camera pose for each frame is also provided for registration.

SUNCG Dataset & House3D [52]: SUNCG dataset is a richly annotated, large-scale dataset of 3D scenes, which contains over 45K different scenes with manually created realistic room and furniture layouts. All of the scenes are semantically annotated at the object level. Sourced from the SUNCG dataset, House3D [59] is built as a virtual 3D environment consisting of over 45K indoor 3D scenes, ranging from studios to multi-storey houses with swimming pools and fitness rooms. All 3D objects are fully annotated with category labels. Agents in the environment have access to observations of multiple modalities, including RGB images, depth, segmentation masks, and top-down 2D map views. In particular, SUNCG dataset and House3D environment have also received a lot of attention in the community of scene modeling.

12.3   Geometric Modeling

The main objective of geometric modeling is to fully recover 3D geometry of 3D objects or scenes. Geometric modeling from RGB-D data is a fundamental problem in computer graphics. Ever since the 1990s, researchers have investigated methods for digitizing the shapes of 3D objects using laser scanners, although 3D scanners were hardly accessible to ordinary people until recently. Early works typically start by registering a set of RGB-D images captured by laser sensors (i.e., transforming RGB-D images into a global coordinate system) using iterative closest point registration (ICP) [4, 11], and fuse the aligned RGB-D frames into a single point cloud or a volumetric representation [14] which can be further converted into 3D mesh models. Different from expensive and accurate laser scanners, the prevalence of consumer-level RGB-D cameras poses challenges to traditional registration and fusion algorithms of geometric modeling. The limitations of RGB-D data have been explained in Sect. 12.2. Benefiting from the robotics community, a series of vision-based SLAM techniques and systems are proposed to cope with low-quality of RGB-D data captured by consumer-level RGB-D cameras, and achieve real-time performance.

A well-known technique is the KinectFusion system [26] which provides model creation using a moving Kinect camera. Similar to traditional schemes, KinectFusion adopts a volumetric representation of the acquired scene by maintaining a signed distance value for each grid voxel. Each frame is registered to the whole constructed scene model rather than the previous frames using a coarse-to-fine iterative ICP algorithm. This frame-to-model registration scheme has more resistance to noise and camera distortions, and can perform efficiently to allow real-time applications. The system is easy to use and achieves real-time performance with GPU acceleration. However, it also has some drawbacks. RGB information has been neglected by the system. And the volumetric representation based mechanism significantly limits its usage for large and complex scenes, as memory consumption is in proportion to the voxel number of the volumetric representation. Reconstructing large-scale scenes even with a moderate resolution to depict necessary details requires extensive amount of memory, which easily exceeds the memory capacity of ordinary computers. Moreover, the acquisition and registration errors inevitably exist, and can be significant for consumer-level scanning devices. Although using frame-to-model registration is more robust than frame-to-frame registration, it is still not a global optimization technique. Errors will keep accumulating over the long acquisition process, when scanning larger scenes with longer moving trajectories. Error accumulation can result in the loop closure problem which generates misalignment when reconstructing large rooms using KinectFusion when the camera trajectory forms a closed loop.

ElasticFusion [58] is another type of visual SLAM method that uses "surfels", a point-based representation of 3D scenes, rather than a volume representation. Beyond KinectFusion, it estimates camera poses not only by the ICP algorithm for the depth information, but also with RGB information for correspondences under the color consistency assumption. The fused model is represented as a surfel set. Each surfel is composed of center position, radius, normal, color (RGB), and a timestamp. ElasticFusion also includes loop closure detection by utilizing the randomized fern encoding approach. Ferns encode an RGB-D image as a string of code made up of the values of binary tests on each of the RGB-D channels in a set of fixed pixel locations. Attempts are made to find a matching predicted view for each frame in the fern encoding database. If a match is detected, the method attempts to register the views together and check if the registration is globally consistent with the model's geometry. If so, it reflects this registration in the map with a nonrigid deformation, which brings the surface into global alignment.

Various state-of-the-art RGB-D SLAM algorithms have been proposed in recent years [1]. They can be divided into two types: sparse mapping and dense mapping. For sparse mapping, only some sparsely selected keyframes are used for reconstruction which can quickly provide rough structure of the target scene, while for dense mapping, the whole RGB-D stream is used which can give detailed reconstruction as long as sufficient data is available. In both cases, the key technique is feature point matching, which is the basis for both transform estimation and loop closure detection. Due to the poor quality of depth images obtained by low-cost scanning devices, most sparse mapping systems mainly rely on distinctive feature descriptors detected from RGB images (e.g., SIFT [32], SURF [3] or ORB [40]) to find corresponding point pairs. As real-world scenes usually contain large textureless areas, e.g., walls with uniform colors, or repeated patterns, e.g., tiled floors, even state-of-the-art feature descriptors may easily generate falsely matched point correspondences. To reduce the impact of falsely detected point correspondences on reconstruction, the RANSAC (RANdom SAmple Consensus) algorithm [20] is often adopted to determine a subset of correspondences which conforms to a consistent rigid transform. RANSAC is an iterative, randomized approach to estimating parameters of a mathematical model (in this case a rigid transform) that fits observed data (in this case sample points) which is robust to outliers that often occur in low-quality RGB-D data [55]. However, this may still fail in challenging cases. In practice, manual correction of some falsely estimated transforms is often needed in sparse mapping applications [10]. In contrast, with the help of dense depth streams, a frame-to-frame ICP registration algorithm can provide stronger cues for inferring camera poses. Thus, dense mapping RGB-D SLAM systems [18, 23] currently provide more automatic and robust solutions to modeling scenes with consumer-level RGB-D sensors.

Although the geometry of 3D scenes or models are generated by fusing RGB-D data from different views, data missing still often occurs due to RGB-D sensor visibility. The increasingly available public RGB-D datasets make it possible to reconstruct and complete 3D shapes using learning-based methods, which provides nice solutions to this ill-posed problem. Deep learning on 3D shapes has made significant progress in recent years, achieving state-of-the-art performance for typical tasks such as 3D object classification and semantic segmentation [7, 13, 37]. For 3D shape reconstruction and completion, most methods utilize a volumetric representation to allow flexible topological changes, and reconstruct 3D scenes either from RGB images [12, 27, 49, 54, 62] or depth images [19, 53, 63]. For shape completion, representative methods [46, 57] are also based on volumetric representations, and thus have similar drawbacks of limited resolution.

Some recent effort [6, 16, 22] was made to address this limitation. The basic idea of these methods is to use a coarse-to-fine strategy, where initially a coarse 3D shape is reconstructed, which is then refined using detailed information. Specifically, Dai et al. [16] proposed a 3D-Encoder-Predictor Network (3D-EPN) that predicts an initial coarse yet complete volume representation, which is refined using an iterative synthesis process whereby similar voxels to the predicted patch are used to augment the patch detail. This was extended by [22] by introducing a dedicated local 3D CNN for patch refinement. These methods still require expensive processing during patch refinement. A more efficient solution was proposed in [6] based on a 3D cascaded fully convolutional network (3D-CFCN) architecture, which is end-to-end trainable, and produces iteratively refined geometry through the network. As a result, the method is able to efficiently generate high-resolution volumetric representation of shapes in a single pass.

12.4 Semantic Modeling

The main objective of geometric modeling of scenes is to fully recover 3D geometry. These methods take the target scene as a whole regardless of what contents are presented therein, and thus cannot provide a semantic representation of the modeled scene. Semantic modeling is a type of modeling algorithms which focuses on reconstructing scenes down to the level of specific objects. Typically, RGB-D data of each semantic region is separated from the surrounding environment and fitted using either existing object models, part models or even geometric primitives (e.g., planes or cylinders).

Semantic modeling produces a semantically meaningful representation of the modeled scene (e.g., knowing the scene contains a table and four chairs), and the scene understanding results are beneficial for many higher level applications, or even necessary to make them possible, such as furniture rearrangement of indoor scenes [66]. Furthermore, semantic information can be used to improve geometric modeling results. In cluttered real-world scenes, it is not practically possible to capture every single corner of the scene due to occlusion. Nevertheless, the occluded structure can be inferred with simple semantic knowledge such as desk surfaces being horizontal planes or chairs being plane symmetric. As the basic shapes of most interior objects are already known from prior knowledge, semantic modeling systems typically only require sparse RGB-D images, so that the modeling process is much simpler compared with traditional geometric modeling in terms of the effort for data acquisition.

In general, semantic modeling is processed on the sparse or dense geometric information (e.g., a point cloud) modeled from the input RGB-D data, and is essentially a semantic segmentation of the scene geometry. However, automatically separating a scene into different levels of semantic regions is still a challenging problem. On the one hand, to understand what objects are present in the scene, each object must be separated from its surroundings. On the other hand, recognizing the type and shape of an object is ultimately important for determining whether an adjacent region belongs to the object or not, and hence helps with effective segmentation. This is an intricate chicken-and-egg problem. To break the inter-dependency, human prior knowledge is often adopted in the form of semantic or contextual rules. As there is no universal definition of semantics, there are significant differences for modeling algorithms in taken the advantages of semantic or contextual information. Therefore, based on the level of semantic information being processed or produced, we classify semantic modeling methods into two categories: primitive-based methods (Sect. 12.4.1) and model-based methods (Sect. 12.4.2).

12.4.1   Primitive-Based Methods

The core of primitive-based methods is finding best-fitting primitives for the input RGB-D data. Due to the robustness to outliers, existing work [20] utilizes random sample consensus (RANSAC) as the primitive fitting algorithm to distinguish between inliers and outliers. However, RANSAC needs to solve many constraints and can run into instability when these constraints contain an excessive amount of noise. As a one-model approach, RANSAC can only estimate multiple model instances one by one [36, 60]. In the case when multiple models exist, the Hough transform [17] is used for robust estimation of models by determining instances of objects within a certain class of shapes. The most obvious disadvantage of the Hough transform is the huge time complexity in estimating complex models from large-scale input scans. Thus, Hough transform is typically used when the problem can be converted into a 2D parameter space [36, 60]. It is very common to see duplicated primitives because of the noisy and incomplete data. A consistent scene representation is necessary for global consolidation. Based on different applications, different types of global consolidation methods are used with different a priori assumptions.

For large-scale interior architectural modeling, the box assumption is the foundation of the state-of-the-art architectural modeling approach [60]. Based on this assumption, the method segments the input point cloud into a set of horizontal 2D slices, and projects the points in each slice onto a 2D plane. Then, the line segments detected in the 2D space are merged into 2D rectangles and combined with other slices to form 3D cuboids. As each planar primitive may form general polygonal shapes other than rectangles, convex hull or alpha-shape algorithms are needed to determine the space extent [42]. In the large-scale scenes, primitive-based methods have been extended to model interior furniture. This is because the furniture in the scene normally comes from a small number of prototypes and repeats multiple times. A supervised method is proposed in [28] which contains two stages. Each object of interest is pre-scanned and represented as a set of stable primitives along with necessary inter-part junction attributes in the learning stage, and the whole scene is segmented and each segment is fitted with primitives in the modeling stage. Then all repeated furniture can be modeled through hierarchical matching. The main advantage of this method is that variation between furniture parts can be handled by specifying the degree-of-freedom of each stable primitive in the pre-scanned object. Differently, Mattausch et al. [33] proposed an unsupervised method for modeling also by detecting repeated objects. In this work, the scene point cloud is converted into a collection of near planar patch primitives first. Then, the patches can be clustered in a Euclidean embedding space based on spatial configurations of neighboring patches and their geometric similarity. Thus, the repeated objects can be modeled. The merit of this approach is that the primitives become semantic abstraction of objects, not just meaningless generic geometric shapes, and the repeated objects can be robustly recovered from noisy and incomplete data due to the repeated occurrences of instances in the training data.

Convex decomposition is another method for shape composition. Ren et al. [67] proposed an approach to decomposing arbitrary 2D and 3D shapes into a minimum number of near-convex parts. However, this type of decomposition cannot guarantee the models are formed by primitive shapes. A lot of CAD models are designed by a combination of primitive shapes. As a result, these objects can be modeled by using primitive-based approaches. Li et al. [31] introduced an iterative constrained optimization scheme to globally consolidate locally fitted primitives by considering the mutual relations between orientation, equality, and placement. Recently, Tulsiani et al. [56] learned to assemble objects using volumetric primitives. They used a deep neural network to estimate the parameters of primitives such as the number, size, and orientation, and the obtained reconstruction allows an interpretable representation for the input object. However, this is an unsupervised method, and therefore the fitted primitives may not correspond to semantic parts. The method is also only able to obtain an approximate reconstruction due to the use of a relatively small number of primitives.

12.4.2   Model-Based Methods

Despite attempts with certain levels of success as we described in the previous sub-section, primitive-based methods have fundamental limitations in modeling interior objects. For example, both [28, 33] only tackle large-scale public or office buildings with many repeated objects, but in outer scenes and typical home environments many objects only occur once (e.g., a television or a bed). Moreover, many objects (e.g., keyboards, desk lamps and various types of chairs) are too complex to be depicted in detail using a set of simple primitives. Thus, primitive-based methods can only offer an approximation to the target scene.

3D repositories of objects offer the possibility for object-level semantic modeling. Each object is regarded as a sample in the object feature space. Along with the samples growing, the semantic modeling tends to build an implicit description of the feature of a certain semantic object. Model-based approaches thus take advantages of such information to semantically segment 3D scenes into objects. Many existing data-driven methods show that if we have sufficient 3D objects, the results tend to be reasonable. The growing availability of accessible 3D models online (e.g., in the Trimble 3D Warehouse) has made it possible. Model-based methods thus represent a new trend in the scene modeling.

Nan et al. [35] use a search-classify strategy and a region growing method to find independent point clouds from high-quality laser scans and assign a semantic label for each meaningful object. They first train classifiers with Randomized Decision Forests (RDF) for individual predefined object categories. In the online stage, they first over-segment the input point cloud. Starting from a seed region in the over-segmentation, the point cloud of an individual object is detected and separated from the background by iteratively adding regions which helps to increase classification confidence. After that, a deform-to-fit technique is used to adapt 3D models in the training set to fit the segmented and classified point cloud objects. Their method relies on high-quality scans, to make the problem more tractable.

Shao et al. [45] present an interactive approach to semantic modeling of indoor scenes from sparse sets of low-quality Kinect scans. To avoid problems brought in by poor-quality depth images, they rely on user interaction to reliably segment RGB-D images into regions with semantic labels manually assigned. Then an automatic algorithm is used to find the best-matched model for each object and arranged them to reconstruct the target scene. For complex scenes with many object instances, Shao's method [45] requires extensive user assistance for segmentation and labeling to resolve ambiguity due to noise and occlusion. Neighboring objects normally have strong contextual relationships (e.g., monitors are found on desks, and chairs are arranged around tables). Such relationships provide strong cues to determine semantic categories of each object, and has been used in a number of recognition and retrieval tasks, delivering significant improvements in precision. By utilizing such information, Chen et al. [10] propose an automatic solution to this problem. They exploit co-occurrence contextual information in a 3D scene database, and use this information to constrain modeling, ensuring semantic compatibility between matched models.

Hu et al. [24] propose an automatic learning-based approach to semantic labeling (that assigns object labels to individual points), and instance segmentation (that decomposes the input point cloud into a set of disjoint subsets each corresponding to an individual object). To facilitate feature extraction, point clouds are first split into a set of patches, using an improved dynamic region growing strategy. Then the main idea of this method is to exploit patch clusters as an intermediate representation to bridge the gap between low-level patches and high-level object semantics. Through patch clusters, patch contextual information is learned from the training set and used in the test stage to improve patch classification performance. Segmenting a point cloud into patches is not trivial, and both under-segmentation and over-segmentation can result in poor patches and overall degradation of performance. This paper further develops a multi-scale approach to selecting locally suitable scales with the guidance of learned contextual information.

The performance of model-based methods relies heavily on the quality, diversity and the number of existing 3D models as well as scenes that represent plausible combinations of models. Novel scenes or scene items without representation in the existing 3D model database are likely to lead to poor results. CNN based methods relieve the problem to some extent by better capturing the implicit features of semantic objects. CNNs have already shown their success in representing implicit features in images. We can regard pixels as 2D regular grid. It is intuitive to extend CNNs to 3D regular grids, i.e., VoxelNet [68], to cope with semantic segmentation of the scene. However, the volume representation is required as input, which needs voxelization from point clouds or RGB-D data. The volume with high resolution to preserve details of complex scenes leads to heavy complexity of CNNs on 3D. PointNet [8] and PointNet++ [38] made a good attempt to learn CNNs directly on point clouds. They achieve input order invariance by using a symmetric function over inputs.

12.5 Conclusion

In this chapter, we present an extensive survey of indoor scene modeling from RGB-D data. We first briefly introduce some public datasets in this area. We divide methods into two categories: geometric modeling and semantic modeling, and overview various indoor scene modeling techniques along with their advantages and limitations in each category. However, from the reviewed methods we can see that robust modeling of real-world complex, cluttered or large-scale indoor scenes remains an open problem because of numerous challenges. Generally, researchers in this area have reached a consensus that utilizing prior knowledge is the right direction to improve modeling algorithms, especially when the data is incomplete and noisy. In fact, with simple prior knowledge, even traditional geometric modeling methods can benefit significantly. Zhou et al. [41] use an observation that scene parts which have been scanned particularly thoroughly tend to be points of interest (POI). By detecting POI from the scanning trajectory and protecting local geometry in POI, they can significantly improve reconstruction results of complex scenes. Yang et al. [64] extend the classic SLAM framework to object level using the prior knowledge by semantic object detection in RGB channels. Therefore, where to get more human prior knowledge and how to make better use of human prior knowledge have become a focus of current indoor scene modeling research. We hope this survey gives valuable insights into this important topic and encourages new research in this area.

References

1. OpenSLAM. http://openslam.org/
2. Anand A, Koppula HS, Joachims T, Saxena A (2011) Contextually guided semantic labeling and search for 3D point clouds. CoRR. http://arxiv.org/abs/1111.5358
3. Bay H, Ess A, Tuytelaars T, Van Gool L (2008) Speeded-up robust features (SURF). Comput Vis Image Underst 110(3):346–359
4. Besl PJ, McKay ND (1992) A method for registration of 3-D shapes. IEEE Trans PAMI 14(2):239–256
5. Bowman SL, Atanasov N, Daniilidis K, Pappas GJ (2017) Probabilistic data association for semantic slam. In: 2017 IEEE international conference on robotics and automation (ICRA), pp 1722–1729. https://doi.org/10.1109/ICRA.2017.7989203
6. Cao YP, Liu ZN, Kuang ZF, Kobbelt L, Hu SM (2018) Learning to reconstruct high-quality 3D shapes with cascaded fully convolutional networks. In: The European conference on computer vision (ECCV)
7. Chang AX, Funkhouser TA, Guibas LJ, Hanrahan P, Huang Q, Li Z, Savarese S, Savva M, Song S, Su H, Xiao J, Yi L, Yu F (2015) ShapeNet: an information-rich 3D model repository. CoRR. http://arxiv.org/abs/1512.03012
8. Charles RQ, Su H, Kaichun M, Guibas LJ (2017) PointNet: deep learning on point sets for 3D classification and segmentation. In: IEEE conference on computer vision and pattern recognition (CVPR), pp 77–85. https://doi.org/10.1109/CVPR.2017.16
9. Chen K, Lai Y, Hu S (2015) 3D indoor scene modeling from RGB-D data: a survey. Comput Vis Media 1(4):267–278
10. Chen K, Lai YK, Wu YX, Martin R, Hu SM (2014) Automatic semantic modeling of indoor scenes from low-quality RGB-D data using contextual information. ACM Trans Graph 33(6):208:1–208:12). https://doi.org/10.1145/2661229.2661239
11. Chen Y, Medioni G (1992) Object modelling by registration of multiple range images. Image Vis Comput 10(3):145–155
12. Choy CB, Xu D, Gwak J, Chen K, Savarese S (2016) 3D-R2N2: a unified approach for single and multi-view 3D object reconstruction. In: Leibe B, Matas J, Sebe N, Welling M (eds.) Computer vision – ECCV 2016, pp 628–644. Springer International Publishing
13. Çiçek Ö, Abdulkadir A, Lienkamp SS, Brox T, Ronneberger O (2016) 3D U-Net: learning dense volumetric segmentation from sparse annotation. In: Ourselin S, Joskowicz L, Sabuncu MR, Unal G, Wells W (eds) Medical image computing and computer-assisted intervention – MICCAI 2016, pp 424–432. Springer International Publishing
14. Curless B, Levoy M (1996) A volumetric method for building complex models from range images
15. Dai A, Chang AX, Savva, M., Halber, M., Funkhouser, T., Nießner, M.: ScanNet: Richly-annotated 3D reconstructions of indoor scenes. In: Proceedings of the computer vision and pattern recognition (CVPR), IEEE (2017)
16. Dai A, Ruizhongtai Qi C, Niessner M (2017) Shape completion using 3D-encoder-predictor CNNs and shape synthesis. In: IEEE conference on computer vision and pattern recognition (CVPR)

17. Duda RO, Hart PE (1972) Use of the Hough transformation to detect lines and curves in pictures. Commun ACM 15(1):11–15. https://doi.org/10.1145/361237.361242
18. Endres F, Hess J, Engelhard N, Sturm J, Burgard W (2012) An evaluation of the RGB-D SLAM system
19. Firman M, Mac Aodha O, Julier S, Brostow GJ (2016) Structured prediction of unobserved voxels from a single depth image. In: IEEE conference on computer vision and pattern recognition (CVPR)
20. Fischler MA, Bolles RC (1981) Random sample consensus: a paradigm for model fitting with applications to image analysis and automated cartography. Commun ACM 24(6):381–395
21. Gupta S, Girshick R, Arbeláez P, Malik J (2014) Learning rich features from RGB-D images for object detection and segmentation. In: Fleet D, Pajdla T, Schiele B, Tuytelaars T (eds) Computer vision - ECCV 2014. Springer International Publishing, Cham, pp 345–360
22. Han X, Li Z, Huang H, Kalogerakis E, Yu Y (2017) High-resolution shape completion using deep neural networks for global structure and local geometry inference. In: IEEE international conference on computer vision (ICCV) (2017)
23. Henry P, Krainin M, Herbst E, Ren X, Fox D (2010) RGB-D mapping: using depth cameras for dense 3D modeling of indoor environments. In: Proceedings of the international symposium experimental robotics, pp 22–25
24. Hu SM, Cai JX, Lai YK (2019) Semantic labeling and instance segmentation of 3D point clouds using patch context analysis and multiscale processing. IEEE Trans Vis Comput Graph 1. https://doi.org/10.1109/TVCG.2018.2889944
25. Hua BS, Pham QH, Nguyen DT, Tran MK, Yu LF, Yeung SK (2016) SceneNN: a scene meshes dataset with aNNotations. In: International conference on 3D vision (3DV)
26. Izadi S, Kim D, Hilliges O, Molyneaux D, Newcombe R, Kohli P, Shotton J, Hodges S, Freeman D, Davison A, Fitzgibbon A (2011) KinectFusion: real-time 3D reconstruction and interaction using a moving depth camera. In: Proceedings of the ACM symposium on user interface software and technology, pp 559–568
27. Ji M, Gall J, Zheng H, Liu Y, Fang L (2017) SurfaceNet: An end-to-end 3D neural network for multiview stereopsis. In: IEEE international conference on computer vision (ICCV)
28. Kim YM, Mitra NJ, Yan DM, Guibas L (2012) Acquiring 3D indoor environments with variability and repetition. ACM Trans Graph 31(6):138:1–138:11
29. Koppula HS, Anand A, Joachims T, Saxena A (2011) Semantic labeling of 3D point clouds for indoor scenes. In: Shawe-Taylor J, Zemel RS, Bartlett PL, Pereira FCN, Weinberger KQ (eds) NIPS, pp 244–252
30. Lai K, Bo L, Fox D (2014) Unsupervised feature learning for 3D scene labeling. In: Proceedings of the ICRA
31. Li Y, Wu X, Chrysathou Y, Sharf A, Cohen-Or D, Mitra NJ (2011) GlobFit: consistently fitting primitives by discovering global relations. ACM Trans Graph 30(4):52:1–52:12. https://doi.org/10.1145/2010324.1964947
32. Lowe DG (1999) Object recognition from local scale-invariant features. In: Proceedings of the ICCV, vol. 2, pp 1150–1157
33. Mattausch O, Panozzo D, Mura C, Sorkine-Hornung O, Pajarola R (2014) Object detection and classification from large-scale cluttered indoor scans. Comput Graph Forum 33(2):11–21
34. Merrell P, Schkufza E, Li Z, Agrawala M, Koltun V (2011) Interactive furniture layout using interior design guidelines. ACM Trans Graph 30(4):87:1–87:10
35. Nan L, Xie, K., Sharf, A.: A search-classify approach for cluttered indoor scene understanding. ACM Trans Graph 31(6):137:1–137:10
36. Oesau S, Lafarge F, Alliez P (2014) Indoor scene reconstruction using feature sensitive primitive extraction and graph-cut. ISPRS J Photogramm Remote Sens 90:68–82. https://doi.org/10.1016/j.isprsjprs.2014.02.004, https://hal.inria.fr/hal-00980804
37. Qi CR, Su H, Mo K, Guibas LJ (2017) PointNet: deep learning on point sets for 3D classification and segmentation. In: IEEE conference on computer vision and pattern recognition (CVPR)
38. Qi CR, Yi L, Su H, Guibas LJ (2017) PointNet++: deep hierarchical feature learning on point sets in a metric space. In: Guyon I, Luxburg UV, Bengio S, Wallach H, Fergus R, Vishwanathan S, Garnett R (eds) Advances in neural information processing systems, pp 5099–5108

39. Qi X, Liao R, Jia J, Fidler S, Urtasun R (2018) 3D graph neural networks for RGBD semantic segmentation. In: 2017 IEEE international conference on computer vision (ICCV), vol 00, pp 5209–5218. https://doi.org/10.1109/ICCV.2017.556, http://doi.ieeecomputersociety.org/10.1109/ICCV.2017.556

40. Rublee E, Rabaud V, Konolige K, Bradski G (2011) ORB: an efficient alternative to SIFT or SURF. In: International conference on computer vision. Barcelona

41. Salas-Moreno RF, Newcombe RA, Strasdat H, Kelly PH, Davison AJ (2013) SLAM++: simultaneous localisation and mapping at the level of objects. In: Proceedings of the CVPR, pp 1352–1359. http://doi.ieeecomputersociety.org/10.1109/CVPR.2013.178

42. Sanchez V, Zakhor A (2012) Planar 3D modeling of building interiors from point cloud data. In: Proceedings of the international conference on image processing (ICIP), pp 1777–1780

43. Savva M, Chang AX, Hanrahan P, Fisher M, Nießner M (2014) SceneGrok: inferring action maps in 3D environments. ACM Trans Graph (TOG) 33(6)

44. Savva M, Chang AX, Hanrahan P, Fisher M, Nießner M (2016) PiGraphs: learning interaction snapshots from observations. ACM Trans Graph (TOG) 35(4)

45. Shao T, Xu W, Zhou K, Wang J, Li D, Guo B (2012) An interactive approach to semantic modeling of indoor scenes with an RGBD camera. ACM Trans Graph 31(6):136:1–136:11

46. Sharma A, Grau O, Fritz M (2016) VConv-DAE: deep volumetric shape learning without object labels. In: Hua G, Jégou H (eds) Computer vision – ECCV 2016 Workshops, pp 236–250. Springer International Publishing

47. Silberman N, Fergus R (2011) Indoor scene segmentation using a structured light sensor. In: Proceedings of the International conference on computer vision - workshop on 3D representation and recognition

48. Silberman N, Hoiem D, Kohli P, Fergus R (20102) Indoor segmentation and support inference from RGBD images. In: Proceedings of the ECCV, pp 746–760

49. Sinha A, Unmesh A, Huang Q, Ramani K (2017) SurfNet: generating 3D shape surfaces using deep residual networks. In: IEEE conference on computer vision and pattern recognition (CVPR)

50. Song S, Lichtenberg SP, Xiao J (2015) SUN RGB-D: A RGB-D scene understanding benchmark suite. In: 2015 IEEE conference on computer vision and pattern recognition (CVPR), pp 567–576. https://doi.org/10.1109/CVPR.2015.7298655

51. Song S, Xiao J (2016) Deep sliding shapes for amodal 3D object detection in RGB-D images. In: 2016 IEEE conference on computer vision and pattern recognition (CVPR), pp 808–816. https://doi.org/10.1109/CVPR.2016.94

52. Song S, Yu F, Zeng A, Chang AX, Savva M, Funkhouser T (2017) Semantic scene completion from a single depth image. In: IEEE conference on computer vision and pattern recognition

53. Song S, Yu F, Zeng A, Chang AX, Savva M, Funkhouser T (2017) Semantic scene completion from a single depth image. In: IEEE conference on computer vision and pattern recognition (CVPR)

54. Tatarchenko M, Dosovitskiy A, Brox T (2016) Multi-view 3D models from single images with a convolutional network. In: Leibe B, Matas J, Sebe N, Welling M (eds) Computer vision – ECCV 2016, pp 322–337. Springer International Publishing

55. Tsai C, Wang C, Wang W (2013) Design and implementation of a RANSAC RGB-D mapping algorithm for multi-view point cloud registration. In: 2013 CACS international automatic control conference (CACS), pp 367–370. https://doi.org/10.1109/CACS.2013.6734162

56. Tulsiani S, Su H, Guibas LJ, Efros AA, Malik J (2017) Learning shape abstractions by assembling volumetric primitives. In: IEEE conference on computer vision and pattern recognition (CVPR)

57. Wang W, Huang Q, You S, Yang C, Neumann U (2017) Shape inpainting using 3D generative adversarial network and recurrent convolutional networks. In: IEEE international conference on computer vision (ICCV)

58. Whelan T, Salas-Moreno RF, Glocker B, Davison AJ, Leutenegger S (2016) ElasticFusion: real-time dense SLAM and light source estimation. Int J Robot Res 35(14):1697–1716. https://doi.org/10.1177/0278364916669237

59. Wu Y, Wu Y, Gkioxari G, Tian Y (2018) Building generalizable agents with a realistic and rich 3D environment. arXiv:1801.02209
60. Xiao J, Furukawa Y (2012) Reconstructing the world's museums. In: Proceedings of the 12th European conference on computer vision, ECCV '12
61. Xiao J, Owens A, Torralba A (2013) SUN3D: a database of big spaces reconstructed using SfM and object labels. In: The IEEE international conference on computer vision (ICCV)
62. Yan X, Yang J, Yumer E, Guo Y, Lee H (2016) Perspective transformer nets: learning single-view 3D object reconstruction without 3D supervision. In: Lee DD, Sugiyama M, Luxburg UV, Guyon I, Garnett R (eds) Advances in neural information processing systems, pp 1696–1704
63. Yang B, Wen H, Wang S, Clark R, Markham A, Trigoni N (2017) 3D object reconstruction from a single depth view with adversarial learning. In: The IEEE international conference on computer vision (ICCV) Workshops
64. Yang S, Kuang ZF, Cao YP, Lai YK, Hu SM (2019) Probabilistic projective association and semantic guided relocalization for dense reconstruction. In: IEEE International Conference Robotics and Automation (ICRA)
65. Yu LF, Yeung SK, Tang CK, Terzopoulos D, Chan TF, Osher SJ (2011) Make it home: automatic optimization of furniture arrangement. ACM Trans Graph 30(4):86:1–86:12
66. Zhang SH, Zhang SK, Liang Y, Hall P (2019) A survey of 3D indoor scene synthesis. J Comput Sci Technol 34(3):594–608. https://doi.org/10.1007/s11390-019-1929-5
67. Zhou R, Yuan J, Li C, Liu W (2011) Minimum near-convex decomposition for robust shape representation. In: IEEE international conference on computer vision (ICCV)
68. Zhou Y, Tuzel O (2018) VoxelNet: End-to-end learning for point cloud based 3D object detection. In: The IEEE conference on computer vision and pattern recognition (CVPR)

Part III
RGB-D Applications

Part III of this book focuses on RGB-D data applications. Since low-cost RGB-D sensors were brought to the market a decade ago, a plethora of applications have taken advantage of them. There is enormous scope for RGB-D sensors to drive natural user interfaces, e.g. using the user's hand or full body as a controller. Another big user of RGB-D has been for health care; two examples are included here: monitoring and therapy. Robots are increasingly entering both the home and workplace, and also find use in health care, e.g. for elderly care, as well as in manufacturing. Another emerging technology is for the development of self-driving cars, which require a bank of sensors—often including RGB-D—to enable navigation.

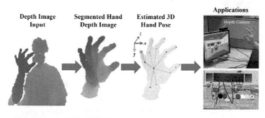

Some examples of applications using RGB-D imagery: 'Cosero' (a service robot), see Chap. 13, hand pose estimation, see Chap. 16, visualisation of the LIDAR depth map used for autonomous driving, see Chap. 17.

Chapter 13
Semantic RGB-D Perception for Cognitive Service Robots

Max Schwarz and Sven Behnke

Abstract Cognitive robots need to understand their surroundings not only in terms of geometry, but they also need to categorize surfaces, detect objects, estimate their pose, etc. Due to their nature, RGB-D sensors are ideally suited to many of these problems, which is why we developed efficient RGB-D methods to address these tasks. In this chapter, we outline the continuous development and usage of RGB-D methods, spanning three applications: Our cognitive service robot Cosero, which participated with great success in the international RoboCup@Home competitions, an industrial kitting application, and cluttered bin picking for warehouse automation. We learn semantic segmentation using convolutional neural networks and random forests and aggregate the surface category in 3D by RGB-D SLAM. We use deep learning methods to categorize surfaces, to recognize objects and to estimate their pose. Efficient RGB-D registration methods are the basis for the manipulation of known objects. They have been extended to non-rigid registration, which allows for transferring manipulation skills to novel objects.

13.1 Introduction

The need for truly *cognitive* robots, i.e. robots that can react to and reason about their environment, has been made very clear in recent years. Applications like personal service robots, elderly care, guiding robots, all require higher levels of cognition than what is available today. But also classical domains of robotics, like industrial automation, will benefit greatly from smarter robots which truly relieve the load of their human coworkers.

M. Schwarz (✉) · S. Behnke
Autonomous Intelligent Systems, Computer Science Institute VI University of Bonn,
Bonn, Germany
e-mail: schwarz@ais.uni-bonn.de
URL: http://www.ais.uni-bonn.de

S. Behnke
e-mail: behnke@cs.uni-bonn.de

© Springer Nature Switzerland AG 2019
P. L. Rosin et al. (eds.), *RGB-D Image Analysis and Processing*,
Advances in Computer Vision and Pattern Recognition,
https://doi.org/10.1007/978-3-030-28603-3_13

A key stepping stone towards higher cognitive function is environment perception. The ready availability of affordable RGB-D sensors, starting with the Microsoft Kinect, now encompassing a multitude of sensors with different properties, has sparked the development of many new perception approaches. Especially in the robotics community, which is not only interested with *perceiving* the environment, but also especially *interacting* with it, the direct combination of color information with geometry offers large advantages over classical sensors which capture the modalities separately.

The interest in our group in RGB-D sensors started with our work in the field of cognitive service robots. An increasing number of research groups worldwide are working on complex robots for domestic service applications. Autonomous service robots require versatile mobile manipulation and human-robot interaction skills in order to really become useful. For example, they should fetch objects, serve drinks and meals, and help with cleaning. The everyday tasks that we perform in our households are highly challenging to achieve with a robotic system, though, because the environment is complex, dynamic, and structured for human rather than robotic needs.

We have developed cognitive service robots since 2008, according to the requirements of the annual international RoboCup@Home competitions [72]. These competitions benchmark integrated robot systems in predefined test procedures and in open demonstrations within which teams can show the best of their research. Benchmarked skills comprise mobility in dynamic indoor environments, object retrieval and placement, person perception, complex speech understanding, and gesture recognition.

Starting from the methods developed for our Cognitive service robot Cosero, described in Sect. 13.3, we will show how proven RGB-D methods and key ideas were carried over to subsequent robotic systems in other applications, susch as industrial kitting (Sect. 13.4) and cluttered bin picking for warehouse automation (Sect. 13.5).

13.2   Related Work

Service Robots Prominent examples of service robots include Armar [1], developed at KIT, that has demonstrated mobile manipulation in a kitchen environment [68]. The Personal Robot 2 (PR2 [39]), developed by Willow Garage, popularized the Robot Operating System (ROS [46]) that is used by many research groups. It is equipped with two 7-DOF compliant arms on a liftable torso. For mobility, the robot drives on four individually steerable wheels, similar to our Cosero robot. PR2 perceives its environment using 2D and 3D laser scanners, and a structured light RGB-D sensor in the head. Bohren et al. [9] demonstrated fetching drinks from a refrigerator and delivering them to users with the PR2 platform. Beetz et al. [6] used a PR2 and a custom-built robot to cooperatively prepare pancakes.

Another example is Rollin' Justin [10], developed at DLR. Similarly, it is equipped with two compliant arms and a four-wheeled mobile base. The robot demonstrated several dexterous manipulation skills such as making coffee by operating a pad machine [5] and cleaning windows [35]. Further examples are HoLLie [22], developed at FZI Karlsruhe, and Care-O-Bot 4 [30], recently introduced by Fraunhofer IPA.

The RoboCup Federation holds annual competitions in its @Home league [27], which serve as a general benchmark for service robots. Since research labs usually focus on narrow tasks, this competition is especially important for guiding and evaluating the research on service robotics in a more holistic perspective. Systems competing in the 2017 edition, which was held in Nagoya, Japan, are described in the corresponding team description papers [40, 67, 69]. Most of these custom-designed robots consist of a wheeled mobile base with LiDAR and RGB-D sensors and a single manipulator arm, although humanoid shapes with two arms are becoming more common. Notably, RGB-D sensors play a large role in the competition, since they offer highly semantic environment understanding (see [27, 67]) at very low cost.

Mapping In order to act in complex indoor environments, service robots must perceive the room structure, obstacles, persons, objects, etc. Frequently, they are equipped with 2D or 3D laser scanners to measure distances to surfaces. Registering the laser measurements in a globally consistent way yields environment maps. Graph optimization methods [66] are often used to solve the simultaneous localization and mapping (SLAM) problem. Efficient software libraries are available to minimize the registration error [28, 33]. 2D maps represent walls and obstacles only at the height of a horizontal scan plane [37]. If 3D laser scanners are used [54, 74], the full 3D environment structure can be modeled.

In recent years, RGB-D cameras (see Chap. 1) became available to measure geometry and colored texture of surfaces in smaller indoor environments. Registering these measurements yields colored 3D environment models (see Chap. 5, [14, 29, 70, 71]).

Semantic Perception In addition to modelling the environment geometry and appearance, semantic perception is needed for many tasks. This involves the categorization of surfaces, the detection and recognition of objects and the estimation of their pose. Surface categorization is also known as object-class segmentation. The task is to assign a class label to every pixel or surface element. For example, Hermans et al. [23] train random decision forests to categorize pixels in RGB-D frames. They estimate camera motion and accumulate pixel decisions in a 3D semantic map. Spatial consistency is enforced by a pairwise Conditional Random Field (CRF).

In contrast, Eigen et al. [13] process single frames at multiple resolutions. They train convolutional neural networks (CNN) to predict depth, surface normals, and semantic labels. The network is initialized with pre-trained features [31]. Long et al. [36] combined upsampled predictions from intermediate layers with a final full-resolution layer which leads to more refined results. A whole-image classification network was adapted to a fully convolutional network and finetuned for semantic segmentation. Another example of a convolutional architecture for semantic segmentation is the work of Badrinarayanan et al. [3]. They use a multi-stage encoder-decoder architecture that first reduces spatial resolution through maximum pooling and later uses the indices of the local pooling maxima for non-linear upsampling to produce class labels at the original resolution.

For the detection of objects, e.g., implicit shape models [34] and Hough forests [17] have been proposed. In recent years, CNNs have also been successfully used for the detection of objects in complex scenes. Girshick et al. [20], for example, use a bottom-up method for generating category-independent region proposals and train a CNN to categorize size-normalized regions. To accelerate detection, all regions are processed with a single forward pass of the CNN [19]. Another line of research is to directly train CNNs to regress object bounding boxes [15, 53]. Ren et al. [47] developed a region proposal network (RPN) that regresses from anchors to regions of interest. More methods are discussed in Chap. 8.

For estimating the pose of objects in 3D data, often voting schemes are used. Drost et al. [12] and Papazov et al. [44] proposed point pair features, defined by two points on surfaces and their normals, which vote for possible object poses. This approach has been recently extended by Choi et al. [11] to incorporate color information from RGB-D sensors. In recent years, CNNs also have been trained to estimate object pose [4, 65]. 3D convolutional neural networks have been used for modeling, detection, and completion of 3D shapes [73]. For an in-depth review of 6D pose estimation methods, we refer to Chap. 11.

13.3   Cognitive Service Robot Cosero

Since 2008, the Autonomous Intelligent Systems group at University of Bonn has been developing cognitive service robots for domestic service tasks [61]. According to the requirements of the RoboCup@Home competitions, we developed the cognitive service robot *Cosero*, shown in Fig. 13.1, that balances the aspects of robust mobility, human-like manipulation, and intuitive human-robot-interaction. The robot is equipped with an anthropomorphic torso and two 7 DoF arms that provide adult-like reach and support a payload of 1.5 kg each. The grippers consist of two pairs of Festo FinGripper fingers on rotary joints, which conform to grasped objects. Cosero's torso can be twisted around and lifted along the vertical axis to extend its workspace, allowing the robot to grasp objects from a wide range of heights—even from the floor. Its narrow base moves on four pairs of steerable wheels that provide omnidirectional driving. For perceiving its environment, Cosero is equipped with multimodal sensors. Four laser range scanners on the ground, on top of the mobile base, and in the torso (rollable and pitchable) measure distances to objects, persons, or obstacles for navigation purposes. The head is mounted on a pan-tilt joint and features a Microsoft Kinect RGB-D camera for object and person perception in 3D and a directed microphone for speech recognition. A camera in the torso provides a lateral view onto objects in typical manipulation height. Cosero is controlled by a high-performance Intel Core-i7 quad-core notebook, located on the rear part of the base.

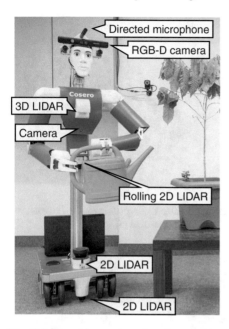

Directed microphone

RGB-D camera

3D LIDAR

Camera

Rolling 2D LIDAR

2D LIDAR

2D LIDAR

- Environment Perception

  - 2D/3D Laser-based Mapping and Localization
  - RGB-D SLAM
  - Motion Segmentation
  - Semantic Segmentation

- Object Perception

  - Object Segmentation
  - Object Recognition
  - Object Detection and Pose Estimation
  - Primitive-based Object Detection
  - Object Tracking
  - Non-rigid Object Registration

- Perception of Persons

  - Person Detection and Tracking
  - Person Identification
  - Gesture Recognition
  - Speech Recognition

Fig. 13.1 Cognitive service robot *Cosero* with sensors marked and perceptional modules

13.3.1 Environment Perception

RGB-D SLAM For modelling 3D geometry and appearance of objects, we developed an efficient RGB-D-SLAM method, based on Multi-Resolution Surfel Maps (MRSMaps [59]). The key idea is to represent the distribution of points in voxels and their color using a Gaussian. For registering RGB-D views, local multiresolution is used, i.e., the vicinity of the sensor is modeled in more detail than further-away parts of the environment. Graph optimization [33] is used to globally minimize registration error between key views. Figure 13.2a shows a resulting map of an indoor scene. To reduce the need for sensor motion and to avoid looking only into free space, we constructed a sensor head with four RGB-D cameras that view four orthogonal directions [55]. Figure 13.2b shows a map of a room that has been created by moving this multi-sensor in a loop.

Motion Segmentation RGB-D SLAM assumes static scenes. By modeling multiple rigid bodies as MRSMap and estimating their relative motion by expectation-maximization (EM), a dense 3D segmentation of the dynamic scene is obtained [60]. Figure 13.3a shows an example. From common and separate motion, a hierarchy of moving segments can be inferred [56], as shown in Fig. 13.3b.

Semantic Segmentation We developed several approaches for object-class segmentation. One method is using random forests (RF) to label RGB-D pixels [50] based on rectangular image regions that are normalized in size and position by depth

(a)   **(b)**

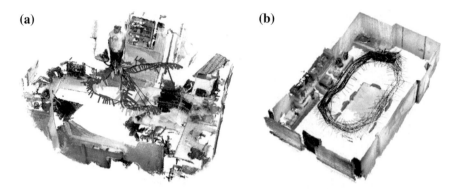

Fig. 13.2 RGB-D SLAM: **a** Multi-resolution surfel map obtained by registering RGB-D views [59]; **b** RGB-D map of a room obtained from four moving RGB-D cameras [55]

(a)   **(b)**

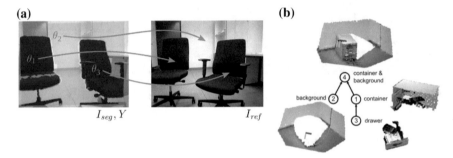

Fig. 13.3 Motion segmentation: **a** Three rigid bodies and their motion modeled as MRSMap [60]; **b** Motion hierarchy inferred from common/separate motions [56]

and computed efficiently from integral images. Both training and recall have been accelerated by GPU. To obtain a 3D semantic map, we estimate camera motion by RGB-D SLAM and accumulate categorizations in voxels [64].

We developed a method to smooth the noisy RF pixel labels that is illustrated in Fig. 13.4a. It over-segments the scene in RGB-D superpixels and learns relations between them that are modeled as a Conditional Random Field (CRF), based on pair-wise features such as color contrast and normal differences. We also proposed CNN-based methods for semantic segmentation [24, 26, 48], with innovations, such as additional input features derived from depth, like height above ground [49] or distance from wall [26] (Fig. 13.4b), and size-normalization of covering windows from depth [49].

For temporal integration, we directly trained the Neural Abstraction Pyramid [7]— a hierarchical, recurrent, convolutional architecture for learning image interpretation (Fig. 13.5a)—for object class segmentation of RGB-D video sequences [45]. It learns to recursively integrate semantic decisions over time. Figure 13.5b shows an example result.

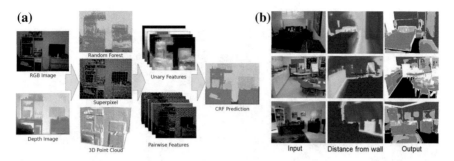

Fig. 13.4 Semantic segmentation: **a** Random forest labeling is refined by a superpixel-CRF [41]; **b** CNN segmentation based on semantic and geometric features [26].

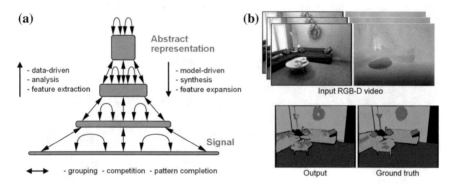

Fig. 13.5 Recurrent temporal integration for semantic segmentation: **a** Neural Abstraction Pyramid (NAP) architecture [7]; **b** NAP-based semantic segmentation [45]

13.3.2   Object Perception

When attempting manipulation, our robot captures the scene geometry and appearance with its RGB-D camera. In many situations, objects are located well separated on horizontal support surfaces, such as tables, shelves, or the floor. To ensure good visibility, the camera is placed at an appropriate height above and distance from the surface, pointing downwards with an angle of approximately 45°. To this end, the robot aligns itself with tables or shelves using the rollable laser scanner in its hip in its vertical scan plane position. Figure 13.6a shows a scene.

Object Segmentation An initial step for the perception of objects in these simple scenes is to segment the captured RGB-D images into support planes and objects on these surfaces. Our plane segmentation algorithm rapidly estimates normals from the depth images of the RGB-D camera and fits a horizontal plane through the points with roughly vertical normals by RANSAC [63]. The points above the detected support plane are grouped to object candidates based on Euclidean distance. All points

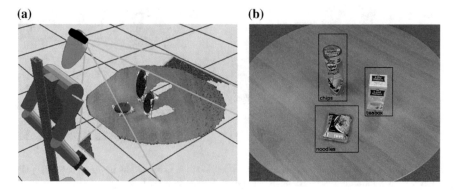

Fig. 13.6 Object perception: **a** RGB-D view of a tabletop scene. Detected objects are represented by a fitted red ellipse; **b** Recognized objects

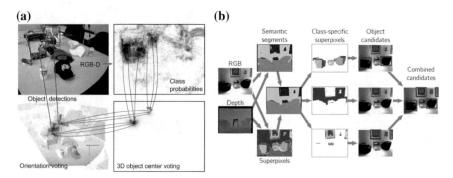

Fig. 13.7 3D Object detection: **a** 6D object detection using Hough forest [2]; **b** Generating object proposals separately in semantic channels [18]

within a range threshold form a segment that is analyzed separately. In Fig. 13.6a, the detected segments are shown.

Object Detection and Pose Estimation For the detection and pose estimation of objects in complex RGB-D scenes, we developed a Hough Forest [17] based approach [2] that is illustrated in Fig. 13.7a. Decision trees do not only learn to categorize pixels, but also vote for object centers in 3D. Each detected object votes for object orientations, which yields detection of objects with the full 3D pose. Figure 13.7b illustrates an extension of a saliency-based object discovery method [18], which groups RGB-D superpixels based on semantic segmentation [26] and detects objects per class. This improves the generated object proposals.

For categorizing objects, recognizing known instances, and estimating object pose, we developed an approach that analyzes an object which has been isolated using table-top segmentation. The RGB-D region of interest is preprocessed by fading out the background of the RGB image (see Fig. 13.8 top left). The depth measurements are converted to an RGB image as well by rendering a view from a canonical eleva-

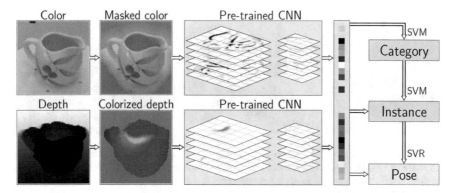

Fig. 13.8 Object categorization, instance recognition, and pose estimation based on features extracted by a CNN [52]. Depth is converted to a color image by rendering a canonical view and encoding distance from the object vertical axis

Fig. 13.9 Object detection based on geometric primitives [43]: **a** Point cloud captured by Cosero's Kinect camera; **b** Detected cylinders; **c** Detected objects

tion and encoding distance from the estimated object vertical axis by color, as shown in Fig. 13.8 bottom left. Both RGB images are presented to a convolutional neural network, which has been pretrained on the ImageNet data set for categorization of natural images. This produces semantic higher-layer features, which are concatenated and used to recognize object category, object instance, and to estimate the azimuth viewing angle onto the object using support vector machines and support vector regression, respectively. This transfer learning approach has been evaluated on the Washington RGB-D Object data set and improved the state-of-the-art [52].

Primitive-Based Object Detection   Objects are not always located on horizontal support surfaces. For a bin picking demonstration, we developed an approach to detect known objects which are on top of a pile, in an arbitrary pose in transport boxes. The objects are described by a graph of shape primitives. Figure 13.9 illustrates the object detection process. First, individual primitives, like cylinders of appropriate diameter are detected using RANSAC. The relations between these are checked. If they match the graph describing the object model, an object instance is instantiated, verified and registered to the supporting 3D points. This yields object pose estimates in 6D. Based on this, mobile bin picking has been demonstrated with Cosero [43].

(a)   (b)   (c)

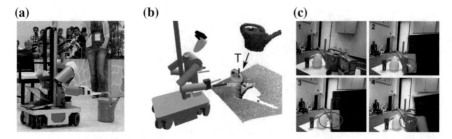

Fig. 13.10 Object tracking: **a** Cosero approaching a watering can; **b** A multi-view 3D model of the watering can (MRSMap, upper right) is registered with the current RGB-D frame to estimate its relative pose T, which is used to approach and grasp it; **c** Joint object detection and tracking using a particle filter, despite occlusion

The method has been extended to the detection of object models that combine 2D and 3D shape primitives [8].

Object Tracking Cosero tracks the pose of known objects using models represented as multi-resolution surfel maps (MRSMaps, [59]), which we learn from moving an RGB-D sensor around the object and performing SLAM. Our method estimates the camera poses by efficiently registering RGB-D key frames. After loop closing and globally minimizing the registration error, the RGB-D measurements are represented in a multiresolution surfel grid, stored as an octree. Each volume element represents the local shape of its points as well as their color distribution by a Gaussian. Our MRSMaps also come with an efficient RGB-D registration method which we use for tracking the pose of objects in RGB-D images. The object pose can be initialized using our planar segmentation approach. Figure 13.10a,b illustrates the tracking with an example. To handle difficult situations, like occlusions, we extended this approach to joint detection and tracking of objects modeled as MRSMaps using a particle filter [38] (see Fig. 13.10c).

Non-rigid Object Registration To be able to manipulate not only known objects, but also objects of the same category that differ in shape and appearance, we extended the coherent point drift method (CPD) [42] to efficiently perform deformable registration between dense RGB-D point clouds (see Fig. 13.11a). Instead of processing the dense point clouds of the RGB-D images directly with CPD, we utilize MRSMaps to perform deformable registration on a compressed measurement representation [58]. The method recovers a smooth displacement field which maps the surface points between both point clouds. It can be used to establish shape correspondences between a partial view on an object in a current image and a MRSMap object model. From the displacement field, the local frame transformation (i.e., 6D rotation and translation) at a point on the deformed surface can be estimated. By this, we can determine how poses such as grasps or tool end-effectors change by the deformation between objects (Fig. 13.11b).

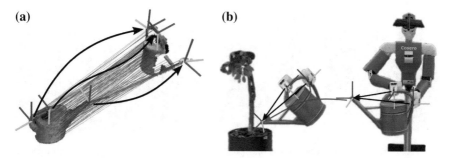

Fig. 13.11 Object manipulation skill transfer: **a** An object manipulation skill is described by grasp poses and motions of the tool tip relative to the affected object; **b** Once these poses are known for a new instance of the tool, the skill can be transferred

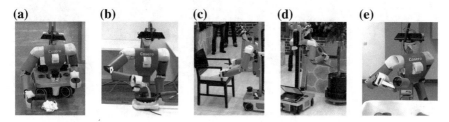

Fig. 13.12 Mobile manipulation demonstrations: **a** Picking laundry from the floor; **b** Cooking an omelette; **c** Pushing a chair; **d** Watering a plant; **e** Bin picking

13.3.3   Robot Demonstrations at RoboCup Competitions

The developed perceptual components for the robot environment and workspace objects were the basis for many demonstrations of in RoboCup@Home league competitions [72], the top venue for benchmarking domestic service robots.

Mobile Manipulation Several predefined tests in RoboCup@Home include object retrieval and placement. We often used open challenges to demonstrate further object manipulation capabilities. For example, in the RoboCup 2011 *Demo Challenge*, Cosero was instructed where to stow different kinds of laundry, picked white laundry from the floor (Fig. 13.12a), and put it into a basket. In the final round, our robot demonstrated a cooking task. It moved to a cooking plate to switch it on. For this, we applied our real-time object tracking method (Sect. 13.3.2) in order to approach the cooking plate and to estimate the switch grasping pose. Then, Cosero drove to the location of the dough and grasped it. Back at the cooking plate, it opened the bottle by unscrewing its lid and poured its contents into the pan (Fig. 13.12b).

In the RoboCup 2012 final, Cosero demonstrated the approaching, bi-manual grasping, and moving of a chair to a target pose (Fig. 13.12c). It also approached and grasped a watering can with both hands and watered a plant (Fig. 13.12d). Both were realized through registration of learned 3D models of the objects (Sect. 13.3.2). The

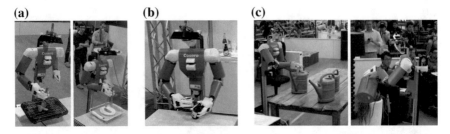

Fig. 13.13 Tool use demonstrations: **a** Grasping sausages with a pair of tongs. **b** Bottle opening; **c** Plant watering skill transfer to unknown watering can

Fig. 13.14 Human-robot interaction and tool use: **a** Following a guide through a crowd; **b** Recognizing pointing gestures; **c** Using a dustpan and a swab; **d** Using a muddler

robot also demonstrated our bin picking approach, which is based on primitive-based object detection and pose estimation (Fig. 13.12e).

Tool Use In the RoboCup 2013 *Open Challenge*, Cosero demonstrated tool-use skill transfer based on our deformable registration method (Sect. 13.3.2). The jury chose one of two unknown cans. The watering skill was trained for a third instance of cans before. Cosero successfully transferred the tool-use skill and executed it (Fig. 13.13c). In the final, Cosero demonstrated grasping of sausages with a pair of tongs (Fig. 13.13a). The robot received the tongs through object hand-over from a team member. It coarsely drove behind the barbecue that was placed on a table by navigating in the environment map and tracked the 6-DoF pose of the barbecue using MRSMaps (Sect. 13.3.2) to accurately position itself relative to the barbecue. It picked one of two raw sausages from a plate next to the barbecue with the tongs and placed it on the barbecue. While the sausage was grilled, Cosero handed the tongs back to a human and went to fetch and open a beer. It picked the bottle opener from a shelf and the beer bottle with its other hand from a table. Then it executed a bottle opening skill [57] (Fig. 13.13b).

In the RoboCup 2014 final, Cosero grasped a dustpan and a swab in order to clean some dirt from the floor (Fig. 13.14c). After pouring out the contents of the dustpan into the dustbin, it placed the tools back on a table and started to make caipirinha. For this, it used a muddler to muddle lime pieces (Fig. 13.14d).

Cosero also demonstrated awareness and interaction with humans (Fig. 13.14). Since the methods for these capabilities mainly use LIDAR tracking and RGB computer vision techniques and are thus out of scope for this chapter, we refer to [62] for details.

Competition Results We participated in four international RoboCup@Home and four RoboCup German Open @Home competitions 2011–2014. Our robot systems performed consistently well in the predefined tests and our open demonstrations convinced the juries which consisted of team leaders, members of the executive committee, and representatives of the media, science, and industry. Our team NimbRo won three international competitions 2011–2013 and four German Open competitions 2011–2014 in a row and came in third at RoboCup 2014 in Brazil.

13.4   Kitting-Type Picking in the STAMINA Project

Techniques that were developed for the Cosero system are applicable to a much wider range of problems. As a first application, we investigated industrial bin picking in the STAMINA project [25]. The project targeted shop floor automation, in particular the automation of kitting tasks, where a robotic system needs to collect objects from different sources according to a kitting order. The completed *kit* is then delivered to the manufacturing line.

13.4.1   System Description

Figure 13.15 shows the STAMINA robot during a typical kitting task. The system consists of a movable base equipped with an industrial arm, carrying a 4-DoF endeffector for grasping a wide variety of items. The system carries three ASUS Xtion Pro RGB-D cameras for perceiving the workspace, and a PrimeSense Carmine RGB-D camera at the wrist for close-range object perception.

The main difficulty lies in detection and pose estimation of the parts to be collected. We employ a two-stage work flow for this purpose (see Fig. 13.16). Here, methods developed for the Cosero system are re-used. In the first stage, a segmentation of the scene into individual parts is performed, following the RGB-D tabletop segmentation method described in Sect. 13.3.2.

After identifying a possible target part, the wrist camera is positioned above it and the part is recognized and its pose is estimated. Here, we employ the RGB-D registration method described in Sect. 13.3.2. A key advantage is that we can use the quality of the registration (measured using observation likelihoods for each matched surfel pair) for judging whether we actually (a) have identified a part of the correct type and (b) the registration was successful. Figure 13.17 shows a typical object perception process.

Fig. 13.15 The STAMINA cognitive robot performing an industrial kitting task in the experimental kitting zone at PSA Peugeot Citroën

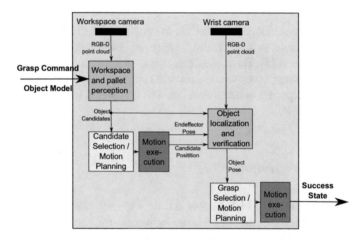

Fig. 13.16 Flow diagram of the two-staged perception pipeline

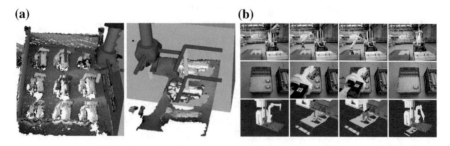

Fig. 13.17 RGB-D registration in a bin picking context: **a** Detected objects with selected grasp target and fine registration using wrist-mounted RGB-D camera; **b** Pick-and-place process with outside, top, and 3D visualization views

Table 13.1 Bin picking results. The replanning column gives the number of times replanning of the arm trajectory was necessary. This condition was detected automatically. Taken from [32]

Task	Trials	Replanning	Success rate	Time [s]
5 parts	4	1	4/4	856 ± 105
4 parts	6	3	6/6	723 ± 96
3 parts	3	1	3/3	593 ± 106
2 parts	3	1	3/3	325 ± 16
1 part	14	4	14/14	234 ± 105

13.4.2 Evaluation

The STAMINA system was evaluated in realistic trials performed at PSA Peugeot Citroën, conducted in a 1,200 m² logistics kitting zone. The tests ranged from isolated "baseline" tests showcasing the robustness of the perception and motion planning methods (see Table 13.1 for brief results) to larger system-level and integrated tests, which proved overall robustness to a wide variety of possible situations and failures. We refer to [32] for full details on the evaluation.

13.5 Cluttered Bin Picking in the Amazon Robotics Challenge

The Amazon Picking Challenge (APC) 2016 and the subsequent Amazon Robotics Challenge 2017 were further opportunities to continue development of the so-far established object perception methods and to test them in realistic situations. The challenge required participants to pick requested items out of highly cluttered, unsorted arrangements in narrow shelf bins or crowded shipment totes.

In contrast to the STAMINA application discussed in Sect. 13.4, the highly cluttered arrangements of different object require *semantic* segmentation of the scene into single objects, as geometry alone is insufficient for separation. Since a vacuum gripper is used to grasp the objects, requirements on pose estimation can be relaxed, though, since suitable vacuuming spots can be found on the live RGB-D input.

13.5.1 System Description

Figure 13.18 shows an overview of the system at APC 2016. It consists of a Universal Robots UR10 6-DoF robotic arm equipped with a custom 2-DoF endeffector. The endeffector consists of a linear joint for reaching into the narrow shelf bins, and a vacuum suction cup on a rotary joint, which allows to apply suction from above or

Fig. 13.18 Our system at the Amazon Picking Challenge 2016. Left: Full system including robotic arm, endeffector, shelf, and red tote. Right: Custom-built endeffector with linear and rotatory joints, two Intel RealSense SR300 RGB-D cameras, and lighting

(a) RGB frame   (b) Upper depth   (c) Lower depth   (d) Stereo depth   (e) Fused result

Fig. 13.19 RGB-D fusion from two sensors. Note the corruption in the left wall in the lower depth frame, which is corrected in the fused result

from the front. The endeffector carries two Intel RealSense SR300 RGB-D cameras and illuminates the scene using own LED lighting to stay independent of outside lighting effects.

The RGB-D streams are interpreted by a separate vision computer. It carries four NVIDIA Titan X GPUs for on-site retraining of the deep learning models.

13.5.1.1 RGB-D Preprocessing

The decision to include two RGB-D cameras was made because of the difficult measurement situation inside the shelf bin. We observed that the nature of the sensors resulted in asymmetric effects, such as corruption of depth measurements on one of the bin walls (see Fig. 13.19). Depth completion alone (e.g. as presented in Chap. 2 did not yield sufficient results, as complete areas were missing. The second camera, mounted with 180° angle with respect to the first camera, had the measurement problems on the other side and thus can be used to correct for these effects. For breaking the tie between the two depth sources, an additional depth stream can be computed using stereo information from the two RGB cameras. For details on the RGB-D fusion strategy, we refer to [51].

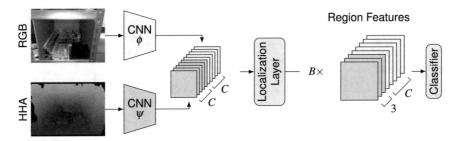

Fig. 13.20 Two-stream architecture for RGB-D object detection [51]. Input images in both modalities are processed individually using CNNs ϕ and ψ. The concatenated feature maps are then used in the classical Fast R-CNN pipeline using RoI pooling and a classification network

13.5.1.2 Object Perception

For separating the objects in these cluttered situations, we designed an RGB-D object detection method. We followed up on research begun with the depth colorization method described in Sect. 13.3.2 and further investigated means of leveraging the depth modalities in deep-learning settings. For a modern object detection approach based on Faster R-CNN [47], we benchmarked different methods of incorporating depth in [51], such as a depth-based region proposal generator, a geometry-based encoding called HHA (horizontal disparity, height above ground, angle to gravity) either downsampled and provided to the classifier component, or processed in parallel to the RGB stream in a two-stream architecture. The best-performing method was to learn a separate depth feature extractor using a self-supervised approach called Cross Modal Distillation [21]. Here, the depth CNN is trained to imitate the output of a pre-trained RGB CNN on RGB-D frames. In this way, expensive annotation of RGB-D frames can be avoided. The trained depth CNN is then used in parallel with the pre-trained RGB CNN in a two-stream architecture (see Fig. 13.20). We also obtained small but consistent gains by combining the object detection results with the semantic segmentation approach described in Sect. 13.3.1.

13.5.2 Evaluation

The system was evaluated during the Amazon Picking Challenge 2016, where it performed highly successfully and reached a second place in the Stow competition (tote → shelf) and third place in the Pick competition (shelf → tote). Our system actually performed the highest number of correct grasps during the pick competition (see Table 13.2), highlighting the robustness, speed, and precision of the presented RGB-D perception methods, but dropped three items while moving them, with the subsequent penalties leading to the third place.

Table 13.2 Picking run at APC 2016

Bin	Item	Pick	Drop	Report	Bin	Item	Pick	Drop	Report
A	Duct tape	×	×	×	G	Scissors	×	×	×
B	Bunny book	✓	✓	$\times^b$	H	Plush bear	✓	×	✓
C	Squeaky eggs	✓	×	✓	I	Curtain	✓	×	✓
D	*Crayons*[a]	✓	×	✓	J	Tissue box	✓	×	✓
E	Coffee	✓	✓	$\times^2$	K	Sippy cup	✓	×	✓
F	Hooks	✓	×	✓	L	Pencil cup	✓	✓	$\times^2$
						Sum	10	3	7

The table shows the individual picks (A-L) executed during the official picking run
[a]Misrecognized, corrected on second attempt
[b]Incorrect report, resulting in penalty

Fig. 13.21 Object detection in scenes with cluttered background. The frames are part of a publicly released RGB-D dataset of 129 frames, captured in a cluttered workshop environment. See http://centauro-project.eu/data_multimedia/tools_data for details

In addition to the system-level evaluation during the APC 2016, we also evaluated our methods on in-house datasets. These consists of a 333-frame bin picking dataset, and a 129-frame RGB-D dataset with tools in front of highly cluttered background, captured for the CENTAURO disaster response project[1] (see Fig. 13.21). Here it demonstrated highly robust detection with 97% mAP score (see Table 13.3). The combination of the RGB-D object detector with semantic segmentation was also investigated and yielded small but consistent improvements (see Table 13.3). We refer to [51] for details.

---

[1]https://www.centauro-project.eu.

Table 13.3 Object detection results on the APC and CENTAURO tools datasets. *Det+Seg F1* is the semantic segmentation network boosted with object detection results

Dataset	Object detection		Semantic segmentation	
	Mean AP	F1	Seg F1	Det+Seg F1
APC shelf	0.912	0.798	0.813	0.827
APC tote	0.887	0.779	0.839	0.853
CENTAURO tools	0.973	0.866	0.805	–

13.6 Conclusion

In this chapter, we described semantic RGB-D perception approaches developed for our cognitive service robot Cosero, industrial kitting in the STAMINA project, and cluttered bin picking for the Amazon Picking Challenge 2016.

We developed several object perception methods to implement the variety of manipulation skills of our robot. We segment scenes at high frame-rate into support surfaces and objects. In order to align to objects for grasping, we register RGB-D measurements on the object with a 3D model using multi-resolution surfel maps (MRSMaps). Through deformable registration of MRSMaps, we transfer object manipulation skills to differently shaped instances of the same object category. Tool-use is one of the most complex manipulation skills for humans and robots in daily life. We implemented several tool-use strategies using our perception and control methods.

The outstanding results achieved at multiple national and international Robo-Cup@Home competitions clearly demonstrate the versatility and robustness of the introduced methods. The development and benchmarking of the system gave us many insights into the requirements for complex personal service robots in scenarios such as cleaning the home or assisting the elderly. Challenges like RoboCup@Home show that a successful system not only consists of valid solutions to isolated problems—the proper integration of the overall system is equally important.

We also successfully demonstrated applicability of the developed methods for object detection, semantic segmentation, and RGB-D registration on other systems and in other domains, such as bin picking and disaster response.

Despite a large number of successful demonstrations, our systems are limited to short tasks in partially controlled environments. In order to scale towards real application in domestic service scenarios, we need to address open issues—and many of these are related to RGB-D perception. Object recognition and handling that scales to the large variety of objects in our daily homes is still an open research problem. Significant progress has been made, e.g. through deep learning methods, but occlusions and material properties like transparency or highly reflective surfaces make it still challenging to analyze typical household scenes. Similarly, perceiving people and understanding their actions in the many situations possible in everyday environments is a challenge.

One promising approach to address these challenges is transfer learning which leverages the feature hierarchies from the large RGB data sets to the small robotic data sets at hand, requiring only few annotated training examples. Another line of research is to instrument the environment with a multitude of sensors in order to track all objects continuously with high accuracy [16].

Acknowledgements The authors thank the numerous people involved in development and operation of the mentioned robotic systems: Nikita Araslanov, Ishrat Badami, David Droeschel, Germán Martín García, Kathrin Gräve, Dirk Holz, Jochen Kläß, Christian Lenz, Manus McElhone, Anton Milan, Aura Munoz, Matthias Nieuwenhuisen, Arul Selvam Periyasamy, Michael Schreiber, Sebastian Schüller, David Schwarz, Ricarda Steffens, Jörg Stückler, and Angeliki Topalidou-Kyniazopoulou.

References

1. Asfour T, Regenstein K, Azad P, Schroder J, Bierbaum A, Vahrenkamp N, Dillmann R (2006) Armar-III: an integrated humanoid platform for sensory-motor control. In: IEEE-RAS international conference on humanoid robots (humanoids)
2. Badami I, Stückler J, Behnke S (2013) Depth-enhanced Hough forests for object-class detection and continuous pose estimation. In: ICRA workshop on semantic perception, mapping and exploration (SPME)
3. Badrinarayanan V, Kendall A, Cipolla R (2015) SegNet: a deep convolutional encoder-decoder architecture for image segmentation. arXiv:1511.00561
4. Bansal A, Russell B, Gupta A (2016) Marr revisited: 2D-3D alignment via surface normal prediction. arXiv:1604.01347
5. Bäuml B, Schmidt F, Wimböck T, Birbach O, Dietrich A, Fuchs M, Friedl W, Frese U, Borst C, Grebenstein M, Eiberger O, Hirzinger G (2011) Catching flying balls and preparing coffee: Humanoid Rollin'Justin performs dynamic and sensitive tasks. In: IEEE international conference on robotics and automation (ICRA)
6. Beetz M, Klank U, Kresse I, Maldonado A, Mösenlechner L, Pangercic D, Rühr T, Tenorth M (2011) Robotic roommates making pancakes. In: IEEE-RAS international conference on humanoid robots (Humanoids), pp 529–536
7. Behnke S (2003) Hierarchical neural networks for image interpretation. Lecture notes in computer science. Springer
8. Berner A, Li J, Holz D, Stückler J, Behnke S, Klein R (2013) Combining contour and shape primitives for object detection and pose estimation of prefabricated parts. In: IEEE international conference on image processing (ICIP)
9. Bohren J, Rusu R, Jones E, Marder-Eppstein E, Pantofaru C, Wise M, Mösenlechner L, Meeussen W, Holzer S (2011) Towards autonomous robotic butlers: lessons learned with the PR2. In: IEEE international conference on robotics and automation (ICRA)
10. Borst C, Wimböck T, Schmidt F, Fuchs M, Brunner B, Zacharias F, Giordano PR, Konietschke R, Sepp W, Fuchs S, et al (2009) Rollin'Justin–mobile platform with variable base. In: IEEE international conference robotics and automation (ICRA)
11. Choi C, Christensen HI (2016) RGB-D object pose estimation in unstructured environments. Robot Auton Syst 75:595–613
12. Drost B, Ulrich M, Navab N, Ilic S (2010) Model globally, match locally: efficient and robust 3D object recognition. In: IEEE conference on computer vision and pattern recognition (CVPR)

13. Eigen D, Fergus R (2015) Predicting depth, surface normals and semantic labels with a common multi-scale convolutional architecture. In: ICCV
14. Endres F, Hess J, Sturm J, Cremers D, Burgard W (2014) 3-D mapping with an RGB-D camera. IEEE Trans Robot 30(1):177–187
15. Erhan D, Szegedy C, Toshev A, Anguelov D (2014) Scalable object detection using deep neural networks. In: IEEE conference on computer vision and pattern recognition (CVPR)
16. Fox D (2016) The 100-100 tracking challenge. In: Keynote at ICRA conference
17. Gall J, Lempitsky VS (2009) Class-specific Hough forests for object detection. In: IEEE conference on computer vision and pattern recognition (CVPR)
18. Garcia GM, Husain F, Schulz H, Frintrop S, Torras C, Behnke S (2016) Semantic segmentation priors for object discovery. In: International conference on pattern recognition (ICPR)
19. Girshick RB (2015) Fast R-CNN. In: IEEE international conference on computer vision (ICCV)
20. Girshick RB, Donahue J, Darrell T, Malik J (2016) Region-based convolutional networks for accurate object detection and segmentation. IEEE Trans Pattern Anal Mach Intell 38(1):142–158
21. Gupta S, Hoffman J, Malik J (2016) Cross modal distillation for supervision transfer. In: Proceedings of the IEEE conference on computer vision and pattern recognition, pp 2827–2836
22. Hermann A, Sun J, Xue Z, Rühl SW, Oberländer J, Roennau A, Zöllner JM, Dillmann R (2013) Hardware and software architecture of the bimanual mobile manipulation robot HoLLiE and its actuated upper body. In: IEEE/ASME international conference on advanced intelligent mechatronics (AIM)
23. Hermans A, Floros G, Leibe B (2014) Dense 3D semantic mapping of indoor scenes from RGB-D images. In: ICRA
24. Höft N, Schulz H, Behnke S (2014) Fast semantic segmentation of RGB-D scenes with GPU-accelerated deep neural networks. In: German conference on AI
25. Holz D, Topalidou-Kyniazopoulou A, Stückler J, Behnke S (2015) Real-time object detection, localization and verification for fast robotic depalletizing. In: 2015 IEEE/RSJ international conference on intelligent robots and systems (IROS), pp 1459–1466
26. Husain F, Schulz H, Dellen B, Torras C, Behnke S (2016) Combining semantic and geometric features for object class segmentation of indoor scenes. IEEE Robot Autom Lett 2(1):49–55
27. Iocchi L, Holz D, Ruiz-del Solar J, Sugiura K, van der Zant T (2015) RoboCup@Home: analysis and results of evolving competitions for domestic and service robots. Artif Intell 229:258–281
28. Kaess M, Johannsson H, Roberts R, Ila V, Leonard JJ, Dellaert F (2012) iSAM2: incremental smoothing and mapping using the Bayes tree. Int J Robot Res 31(2):216–235
29. Kerl C, Sturm J, Cremers D (2013) Robust odometry estimation for RGB-D cameras. In: IEEE international conference on robotics and automation (ICRA)
30. Kittmann R, Fröhlich T, Schäfer J, Reiser U, Weißhardt F, Haug A (2015) Let me introduce myself: I am Care-O-bot 4. In: Mensch und computer
31. Krizhevsky A, Sutskever I, Hinton GE (2012) ImageNet classification with deep convolutional neural networks. In: NIPS, pp 1097–1105
32. Krueger V, Rovida F, Grossmann B, Petrick R, Crosby M, Charzoule A, Garcia GM, Behnke S, Toscano C, Veiga G (2018) Testing the vertical and cyber-physical integration of cognitive robots in manufacturing. Robot Comput Integr Manufact 57:213–229
33. Kümmerle R, Grisetti G, Strasdat H, Konolige K, Burgard W (2011) G^2o: a general framework for graph optimization. In: IEEE international conference on robotics and automation (ICRA), pp 3607–3613
34. Leibe B, Leonardis A, Schiele B (2008) Robust object detection with interleaved categorization and segmentation. Int J Comput Vis 77(1–3):259–289
35. Leidner D, Dietrich A, Schmidt F, Borst C, Albu-Schäffer A (2014) Object-centered hybrid reasoning for whole-body mobile manipulation. In: IEEE international conference on robotics and automation (ICRA)
36. Long J, Shelhamer E, Darrell T (2015) Fully convolutional networks for semantic segmentation. In: CVPR

37. Mazuran M, Burgard W, Tipaldi GD (2016) Nonlinear factor recovery for long-term SLAM. Int J Robot Res 35(1–3):50–72
38. McElhone M, Stückler J, Behnke S (2013) Joint detection and pose tracking of multi-resolution surfel models in RGB-D. In: European conference on mobile robots
39. Meeussen W, Wise M, Glaser S, Chitta S, McGann, C, Mihelich P, Marder-Eppstein E, Muja M, Eruhimov V, Foote T, Hsu J, Rusu RB, Marthi B, Bradski G, Konolige K, Gerkey BP, Berger E (2010) Autonomous door opening and plugging in with a personal robot. In: IEEE International conference on robotics and automation (ICRA), pp 729–736
40. Memmesheimer R, Seib V, Paulus D (2017) homer@UniKoblenz: winning team of the RoboCup@Home open platform league 2017. In: Robot world cup. Springer, pp 509–520
41. Müller AC, Behnke S (2014) Learning depth-sensitive conditional random fields for semantic segmentation of RGB-D images. In: ICRA, pp 6232–6237
42. Myronenko A, Song X (2010) Point set registration: coherent point drift. IEEE Trans Pattern Anal Mach Intell (PAMI) 32(12):2262–2275
43. Nieuwenhuisen M, Droeschel D, Holz D, Stückler J, Berner A, Li J, Klein R, Behnke S (2013) Mobile bin picking with an anthropomorphic service robot. In: IEEE international conference on robotics and automation (ICRA)
44. Papazov C, Haddadin S, Parusel S, Krieger K, Burschka D (2012) Rigid 3D geometry matching for grasping of known objects in cluttered scenes. Int J Robot Res 31(4):538–553
45. Pavel MS, Schulz H, Behnke S (2015) Recurrent convolutional neural networks for object-class segmentation of RGB-D video. In: International joint conference on neural networks (IJCNN)
46. Quigley M, Gerkey B, Conley K, Faust J, Foote T, Leibs J, Berger E, Wheeler R, Ng A (2009) ROS: an open-source robot operating system. In: IEEE international conference on robotics and automation (ICRA)
47. Ren S, He K, Girshick RB, Sun J (2015) Faster R-CNN: towards real-time object detection with region proposal networks. In: Advances in neural information processing systems (NIPS), pp 91–99
48. Schulz H, Behnke S (2012) Learning object-class segmentation with convolutional neural networks. In: European symposium on artificial neural networks
49. Schulz H, Höft N, Behnke S (2015) Depth and height aware semantic RGB-D perception with convolutional neural networks. In: ESANN
50. Schulz H, Waldvogel B, Sheikh R, Behnke S (2015) CURFIL: random forests for image labeling on GPU. In: International conference on computer vision theory and applications (VISAPP), pp 156–164
51. Schwarz M, Milan A, Periyasamy AS, Behnke S (2018) RGB-D object detection and semantic segmentation for autonomous manipulation in clutter. Int J Robot Res 37(4–5):437–451
52. Schwarz M, Schulz H, Behnke S (2015) RGB-D object recognition and pose estimation based on pre-trained convolutional neural network features. In: IEEE international conference on robotics and automation (ICRA), pp 1329–1335
53. Sermanet P, Eigen D, Zhang X, Mathieu M, Fergus R, LeCun Y (2013) OverFeat: integrated recognition, localization and detection using convolutional networks. arXiv:1312.6229
54. Stoyanov T, Magnusson M, Andreasson H, Lilienthal AJ (2012) Fast and accurate scan registration through minimization of the distance between compact 3D NDT representations. Int J Robot Res 31(12):1377–1393
55. Stroucken S (2013) Graph-basierte 3D-kartierung von innenräumen mit einem RGBD-multikamera-system. Diplomarbeit, Universität Bonn, Computer Science VI
56. Stückler J, Behnke S (2013) Hierarchical object discovery and dense modelling from motion cues in RGB-D video. In: International conference artificial intelligence (IJCAI)
57. Stückler J, Behnke S (2014) Adaptive tool-use strategies for anthropomorphic service robots. In: IEEE-RAS International conference on humanoid robots (Humanoids)
58. Stückler J, Behnke S (2014) Efficient deformable registration of multi-resolution surfel maps for object manipulation skill transfer. In: IEEE international conference on robotics and automation (ICRA)

59. Stückler J, Behnke S (2014) Multi-resolution surfel maps for efficient dense 3D modeling and tracking. J Vis Commun Image Represent 25(1):137–147
60. Stückler J, Behnke S (2015) Efficient dense rigid-body motion segmentation and estimation in RGB-D video. Int J Comput Vis 113(3):233–245
61. Stückler J, Droeschel D, Gräve K, Holz D, Schreiber M, Topalidou-Kyniazopoulou A, Schwarz M, Behnke S (2014) Increasing flexibility of mobile manipulation and intuitive human-robot interaction in RoboCup@Home. In: RoboCup 2013: robot world cup XVII. Springer, pp 135–146
62. Stückler J, Schwarz M, Behnke S (2016) Mobile manipulation, tool use, and intuitive interaction for cognitive service robot cosero. Front Robot AI 3:58
63. Stückler J, Steffens R, Holz D, Behnke S (2013) Efficient 3D object perception and grasp planning for mobile manipulation in domestic environments. Robot Auton Syst 61(10):1106–1115
64. Stückler J, Waldvogel B, Schulz H, Behnke S (2015) Dense real-time mapping of object-class semantics from RGB-D video. J R Time Image Proc 10(4):599–609
65. Su H, Qi CR, Li Y, Guibas LJ (2015) Render for CNN: viewpoint estimation in images using CNNs trained with rendered 3D model views. In: IEEE international conference on computer vision (ICCV)
66. Thrun S, Montemerlo M (2006) The graph SLAM algorithm with applications to large-scale mapping of urban structures. Int J Robot Res 25(5–6):403–429
67. van der Burgh M, Lunenburg J, Appeldoorn R, Wijnands R, Clephas T, Baeten M, van Beek L, Ottervanger R, van Rooy H, van de Molengraft M (2017) Tech United Eindhoven @Home 2017 team description paper. University of Technology Eindhoven
68. Vahrenkamp N, Asfour T, Dillmann R (2012) Simultaneous grasp and motion planning: humanoid robot ARMAR-III. Robot Autom Mag
69. Wachsmuth S, Lier F, Meyer zu Borgsen S, Kummert J, Lach L, Sixt D (2017) ToBI-team of bielefeld a human-robot interaction system for RoboCup@ home 2017
70. Whelan T, Kaess M, Johannsson H, Fallon MF, Leonard JJ, McDonald J (2015) Real-time large-scale dense RGB-D SLAM with volumetric fusion. Int J Robot Res 34(4–5):598–626
71. Whelan T, Leutenegger S, Salas-Moreno R, Glocker B, Davison AJ (2015) ElasticFusion: dense SLAM without a pose graph. In: Robotics: science and systems
72. Wisspeintner T, van der Zant T, Iocchi L, Schiffer S (2009) RoboCup@Home: scientific competition and benchmarking for domestic service robots. Interact Stud 10(3):392–426
73. Wu Z, Song S, Khosla A, Yu F, Zhang L, Tang X, Xiao J (2015) 3D ShapeNets: a deep representation for volumetric shapes. In: IEEE conference on computer vision and pattern recognition (CVPR)
74. Zhang J, Singh S (2014) Loam: lidar odometry and mapping in real-time. In: Robotics: science and systems conference (RSS), pp 109–111

Chapter 14
RGB-D Sensors and Signal Processing for Fall Detection

Susanna Spinsante

Abstract Globally, falls are a major public health problem, and an important cause of morbidity and mortality in the older population. As such, fall detection is one of the most important application areas within the framework of Ambient-Assisted Living (AAL) solutions. Studies report that the majority of falls occur at home, as a person's living environment is filled with potential hazards, predominantly in the living room and in the bedroom. In addition, recent studies report that fall kinematics varies depending on the weight and size of the falling person, and that most people fall in the evening or during the night. All these features may be captured by RGB-D sensors properly installed in the environment, and detected by suitable processing of the signals generated by the sensors themselves. Fall detection based on RGB-D signal processing has gained momentum in the past years, thanks to the availability of easy-to-use sensors that are able to provide not only raw RGB-D signals but also preprocessed data like joints and skeleton spatial coordinates; additionally, depth signal processing allows to maintain adequate privacy in human monitoring, especially at the levels deemed acceptable by monitored subjects in their own home premises. This chapter will first provide an overview of the RGB-D sensors mostly used in fall detection applications, by discussing their main properties and the modalities by which they have been used and installed. Then, the most relevant signal processing approaches aimed at fall detection will be presented and analyzed, together with an overview of their performances, advantages and limitations, as discussed and presented in the most relevant and up-to-date literature. The aim of the chapter is to provide the reader with a basic understanding of what is reasonably expectable, in terms of detection capability, from RGB-D sensors, applied to fall detection; what are the main depth signal processing approaches according to the sensor usage, and what type of information can be extracted from them.

S. Spinsante (✉)
Dipartimento di Ingegneria dell'Informazione, Università Politecnica delle Marche,
Via Brecce Bianche 12, 60131 Ancona, Italy
e-mail: s.spinsante@staff.univpm.it

© Springer Nature Switzerland AG 2019
P. L. Rosin et al. (eds.), *RGB-D Image Analysis and Processing*,
Advances in Computer Vision and Pattern Recognition,
https://doi.org/10.1007/978-3-030-28603-3_14

14.1 Depth Sensing for Real-World Knowledge

Traditional video cameras and imaging sensors, commonly referred to as RGB sensors, provide the user with a two-dimensional (2D) knowledge of the physical world, thus missing the third dimension, i.e., *depth*, which is fundamental to capture and understand the complexity of the objects surrounding each of us in our real-world experience, see Chaps. 13 and 17. This limitation becomes even more critical when thinking about some of the recent technological developments that are expected to disrupt our common habits like autonomous driving and robot-based manufacturing [19, 27]. Driven by the needs posed by new consumer applications in a variety of fields, and supported by the ever-increasing availability of computational resources, even onboard mobile devices, the research, development and commercialization of imaging technologies able to sense the *third dimension* have advanced tremendously in just a few years, thus making it possible to easily find high-resolution and high-speed sensors at affordable costs. Before the invention of the Microsoft Kinect sensor, depth cameras, mainly based on the Time Of Flight (TOF) technique, were exploited in a restricted set of computer vision domains, due to the high price of such devices, often joint with poor quality (see Chap. 1). The low-cost but high-resolution depth and visual (RGB) sensing made available for widespread use with the introduction of Kinect as an off-the-shelf technology has opened up new opportunities to explore fundamental problems in computer vision including object and activity recognition, people tracking, 3D mapping and localization.

Based on the definition provided by Geng in [25], *surface imaging deals with measurement of the* (x, y, z) *coordinates of points on the surface of an object*. Typically, real-world objects have a nonplanar surface, that has to be described in a three-dimensional space. For this reason, surface imaging is also known as *3D surface imaging*. By the measurement, a map of the depth (or range) coordinate (z) is obtained, as a function of the position (x, y) in a Cartesian coordinate system. This process is also known as depth mapping.

Two main approaches have been traditionally applied in range sensing, namely, triangulation and TOF. The former may be implemented as a passive approach through the use of stereovision, or as an active one, by resorting to structured light. Stereovision emulates humans' vision principle, retrieving depth information by processing of the same scene from two different points of view. This way, depth is computed starting from the disparity information of the identical pixels between two images taken at different positions. Depth is inversely proportional to disparity and depends on hardware parameters related to the cameras (typically RGB ones) used. As such, stereovision requires knowledge of the geometry of the cameras that constitute the entire system, and calibration has to be performed every time the system configuration changes. The active approach for triangulation relies on structured light, in which cameras project an infrared light pattern onto the scene and estimate the disparity given by the perspective distortion of the pattern, due to the varying object's depth [5].

On the other hand, TOF cameras as well as LIght Detection And Ranging (LIDAR) scanners measure the time that light emitted by an illumination unit requires to hit an object surface and travel back to a detector. Different from LIDARs, that require mechanical components to scan the surrounding environment [26], distance computation in TOF cameras is performed by integrated circuits, using standard CMOS or CCD technologies. In fact, the distance is measured indirectly, from the phase shift of the modulated optical signal emitted by a LED or laser switched on and off very quickly, reflected by an object and captured back by the camera lens. The correlation between the transmitted and the received signals is calculated, and the result represents the delay associated with the round-trip path of the emitted and reflected signal. By repeating the computation for each pixel, its depth is obtained from the delay value. Finally, the whole depth frame is generated.

Most of the mass-market RGB-D cameras rely on structured light or TOF approaches [41]. These RGB-D cameras often suffer from very specific noise characteristics and sometimes very challenging data distortions, which, in most cases, have to be taken into account with respect to the requirements of the application one wants to address, and tackled by properly designed processing algorithms. Additionally, structured light based RGB-D cameras, such as the first version of Kinect (V1), and TOF cameras like the second one (V2) feature several functional differences, related to the camera's resilience against background light, which is critical for outdoor applications, the quality of depth data, and the robustness in dealing with semi-transparent media and the so-called multi-path effect, resulting from indirect paths taken by the active light [49]. Finally, structured light based solutions require a baseline between the illumination unit and the sensor, which is not required by TOF devices. Stereo-based systems are typically much cheaper and smaller than other solutions, as they allow to obtain 3D information of the scene just from a couple of RGB cameras. However, the easiness of adoption comes at the expense of a quite demanding preprocessing step finalized to solve the so-called correspondence problem. Additionally, to improve the accuracy in the disparity estimation process, a stereo system needs a minimum amount of baseline length, which directly affects its physical size. TOF devices exhibit a lower software complexity, but require fast hardware, such as the pulse width modulation (PWM) drivers used for waveforms generation, which increases the cost of the final system. Nevertheless, the depth resolution provided by TOF devices is better than the others, and can go down to a few millimeters [28]. Another benefit is the possibility of use a TOF camera in outdoor scenarios, which is not directly possible for structured-light systems like the Kinect V1 sensor, because solar light strongly affects infrared cameras [24]. In such cases, suitable countermeasures should be taken.

For a long time, the detection and identification of objects and humans *in the wild*, i.e., in real-world settings, have been hot research issues and complex tasks to tackle. In fact, despite the great amount of algorithms developed within the computer vision realm to process video and image signals and extract the information of interest, RGB-based object segmentation and tracking algorithms are not always reliable in uncontrolled environments, where clutter or sudden changes in the illumination conditions may occur frequently. By effectively combining depth and RGB data, light-invariant object segmentation based on depth information is obtained (at least at medium–low ambient light levels) as well as surface texture invariance. Object tracking and identification accuracy can be increased exploiting the depth, motion and appearance information of an object [50]. Last but not least, the inherent privacy-preserving capability of depth cameras increases acceptance by the monitored subjects, thus allowing to take computer vision out of the lab, into real environments (e.g., people's homes) [47]. Human Action Recognition (HAR) is at the foundation of many different applications related to behavioral analysis, surveillance, and safety, and it has been a very active research area in the past years. The release of inexpensive RGB-D sensors fostered researchers working in this field: indoor applications for Active and Assisted Living (AAL), which do not require very high depth resolution and precision, have been easily implemented using both structured light sensors, as Kinect V1, and TOF devices, like Kinect V2, in particular. Such devices represented a very good compromise between cost, performance, and usability, and allowed implementation of unobtrusive and privacy-preserving solutions, with respect to classic video-based analysis.

As of today, manufacturing of the Kinect sensor and adapter has been discontinued, but the Kinect technology continues to live on in other commercial products. Above all, the wealth of depth-based algorithms and processing approaches whose development was incredibly pushed by the availability of the Kinect technology, remains and continues to be effectively applicable, thanks to new devices that have appeared in the market to replace the previous ones.

14.2 Consumer RGB-D Sensors

In November 2010, Microsoft released the Kinect RGB-D sensor as a new Natural User Interface (NUI) for its XBOX 360 gaming platform. The Kinect, like other RGB-D sensors, provided color information as well as the estimated depth for each pixel in a captured frame, being an order of magnitude cheaper than similar sensors that had existed before it.

The availability of Kinect as a low-cost tool that could be easily interfaced to a computer, and whose signals could be manipulated by using programming languages common within the academic research practice, like MATLAB or Visual Studio, made it possible to kickstart an incredible amount of research projects and activities related not only to fall detection, but also to the more general domain of human action recognition.

Kinect has been discontinued, but alternative sensors appear in the market, a couple of which are briefly outlined in the following sections.

14.2.1 Microsoft® Kinect™ Sensor

The per-pixel depth sensing technology based on the structured light approach [25] and used in Kinect V1 was developed by PrimeSense and covered as United States Patent US7433024 [20]. For this reason, the depth measurement performed by the sensor was not known in detail. The infrared projector onboard the device emitted a single beam, which was transformed in a pattern of speckles using a transparency, on which the image of the pattern was impressed. A specific scheme of speckles may help in the process of image correlation computation: for example, the use of a quasi-periodic pattern may improve the knowledge of the spatial frequency spectrum. This way, an infrared speckle pattern was projected by the sensor, then captured by an integrated infrared camera, and compared part-by-part to reference patterns stored in the device, previously captured at *known* depths. The comparison process was performed through a correlation algorithm between a group of speckles inside the captured image, and the same group inside the reference image. The sensor then estimated the per-pixel depth, based on which reference patterns the projected one matched best. The depth data provided by the infrared sensor was then correlated to a calibrated RGB camera to obtain an RGB image and the depth value associated with each pixel of the frame. A popular unified representation of this data is the so-called *point cloud*, i.e., a collection of points in the 3D space.

Originally, Kinect was officially launched as a camera-based controller for games. Almost immediately, hackers and independent developers started to create open-source drivers for this sensor, to use it in different ways and applications. Kinect V1 and Kinect V2, two versions of the sensor, succeeded over the years, with the second one based on the TOF approach. Table 14.1 reports the main characteristics of both, whereas Fig. 14.1 shows the Kinect V2 device.

Table 14.1 Main features of Kinect V1 and Kinect V2 (manufacturer's specification)

Feature	Kinect v1	Kinect v2
Depth sensing technology	Structured light	Time of flight
RGB image resolution	640×480 @15/30 fps	1920×1080 @30 fps
	1280×960 @12 fps	(15 fps with low light)
IR image resolution	640×480 @30 fps	512×424 @30 fps
Depth sensing resolution	640×480 @30 fps	512×424 @30 fps
	320×240 @30 fps	
	80×60 @30 fps	
Depth sensing range	[0.4, 3] m (near mode)	[0.5, 4.5] m
	[0.8, 4] m (normal mode)	
Field of view	57° horizontal	70° horizontal
	43° vertical	60° vertical
Skeleton tracking	Skeleton with 20 joints	Skeleton with 25 joints
	Up to 2 subjects	Up to 6 subjects
Audio	Multi-array microphone	Multi-array microphone

Fig. 14.1 The Kinect V2
device and its onboard
sensors

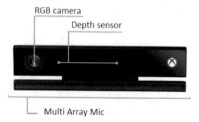

While it is quite easy-to-use depth or RGB data from a Kinect sensor apart, the infrared and RGB cameras onboard the device have different fields of view and different reference systems with different origins, so a specific area in a depth frame does not correspond to the same area inside the corresponding RGB frame. Coordinates mapping between video and depth frames has to be implemented if the two types of data have to be used jointly in a given application. As a consequence, it is necessary to calibrate both the infrared (IR) and RGB cameras, in order to use their information jointly. The following parameters can be computed by a calibration procedure:

- *intrinsic parameters*: coefficients that allow conversion between image coordinates and 3D coordinates, and depend on the camera lens;
- *distortion coefficients*: parameters that depend on lens distortion;
- *extrinsic parameters*: coefficients required to convert the systems of coordinates of different cameras, and depend on the mutual position of the cameras.

Some libraries available at those time, like the ones included in the SDK by Microsoft and OpenNI, provided built-in functionalities but were not very accurate. As a consequence, in [14], the built-in methods mentioned above are compared against a calibration-based solution based on the open-source RGBDemo toolkit, and on the approach presented by Zhang in [56]. Starting from a pixel belonging to the depth frame, to obtain the corresponding pixel inside the RGB frame the following steps need to be implemented:

- transformation between the depth frame coordinate space and the 3D depth camera coordinate space, based on the intrinsic parameters of the depth camera;
- conversion between the 3D depth camera coordinate space and the 3D RGB camera coordinate space based on the extrinsic parameters of both the cameras;
- conversion between the 3D RGB camera coordinate space and the 2D RGB image coordinate space, based on the intrinsic parameters of the RGB camera;
- removal of the lens distortion exploiting the distortion coefficients.

The mathematical relations between the different coordinate systems is defined by the pinhole camera model. The different coordinate systems are the depth camera coordinate system $[X_d\ Y_d\ Z_d]^T$, the depth frame coordinate system $[x_d\ y_d\ 1]^T$, the RGB camera coordinate system $\left[X_{rgb}\ Y_{rgb}\ Z_{rgb}\right]^T$, and the RGB frame coordinate system $\left[x_{rgb}\ y_{rgb}\ 1\right]^T$. The relationship between the camera coordinate system, and the image one is defined by [29] as

$$\begin{bmatrix} x_d \\ y_d \\ 1 \end{bmatrix} = K_d \begin{bmatrix} X_d \\ Y_d \\ Z_d \end{bmatrix} \qquad (14.1)$$

where K_d is the matrix that contains the intrinsic parameters of the IR camera, and:

$$K_d = \begin{bmatrix} f_x & 0 & c_x \\ 0 & f_y & c_y \\ 0 & 0 & 1 \end{bmatrix} \qquad (14.2)$$

In the above equation, f is the focal length, and $f_x = a_x f$, $f_y = a_y f$ are used to differentiate the focal length along both the directions. The parameters c_x and c_y take into account the translation between the coordinates $[X_d \ Y_d \ Z_d]^T$ and $[x_d \ y_d \ 1]^T$. The conversion between the depth camera coordinates $[X_d \ Y_d \ Z_d]^T$ and the RGB camera coordinates $\begin{bmatrix} X_{rgb} \ Y_{rgb} \ Z_{rgb} \end{bmatrix}^T$ needs a rotation matrix R, and a translation vector $t = [t_1 \ t_2 \ t_3]^T$. Together, they define the mutual positions of both the systems:

$$\begin{bmatrix} X_{rgb} \\ Y_{rgb} \\ Z_{rgb} \end{bmatrix} = R \begin{bmatrix} X_d \\ Y_d \\ Z_d \end{bmatrix} + \begin{bmatrix} t_1 \\ t_2 \\ t_3 \end{bmatrix} \qquad (14.3)$$

Finally, the coordinates in the RGB frame, can be retrieved based on Eq. (14.1), by using the intrinsic parameters of the RGB camera:

$$\begin{bmatrix} x_{rgb} \\ y_{rgb} \\ 1 \end{bmatrix} = K_{rgb} \begin{bmatrix} X_{rgb} \\ Y_{rgb} \\ Z_{rgb} \end{bmatrix} \qquad (14.4)$$

The pixel coordinates $\begin{bmatrix} x_{rgb} \ y_{rgb} \end{bmatrix}^T$ inside the RGB frame correspond to the pixel $[x_d \ y_d]^T$ inside the depth frame.

The image distortion introduced by the lenses can be removed by exploiting the distortion coefficients, as described in [30]. Although specific distortion models have been proposed for the depth camera of the Kinect sensor, the RGB distortion model can be applied to the depth frame too. The official Microsoft SDK and the OpenNI SDK provided methods that, taking as an input the coordinates of a pixel in the depth frame, were able to output the corresponding coordinates of the pixel in the RGB frame that corresponded to the same 3D point. These solutions did not require any calibration procedure and were very easy to use, but not so accurate. The RGBDemo tool required the calibration parameters of the device and provided solutions to compute them, based on some OpenCV primitives.

The approach detailed above follows one of the RGBDemo tool, but does not require any additional library, so it can be integrated into different solutions without dependencies. The intrinsic, extrinsic and distortion coefficients used as calibration parameters are evaluated with the same tool provided by RGBDemo, because each Kinect device has its own lenses, and its own intrinsic/extrinsic parameters. The good news is that they do not depend on the position or setup configuration, therefore the calibration step needs to be performed just once.

14.2.2 Intel® RealSense™ Depth Cameras

In 2015, Intel announced a family of stereoscopic and highly portable consumer RGB-D sensors, that included subpixel disparity accuracy, assisted illumination, and were able to operate well even in outdoor settings. Keselman et al. in [34] provided a comprehensive overview of these imaging systems called Intel RealSense cameras. The general relationship between disparity d and depth z is described by

$$z = \frac{f \cdot B}{d} \tag{14.5}$$

where the focal length of the imaging sensor f is in pixels, while the baseline between the camera pair B is in the desired depth units (typically m or mm). Errors in the disparity space are usually constant for a stereo system, and due to imaging properties and quality of the matching algorithm. As the active texture projector available on the Intel RealSense modules generates a texture which makes image matching unambiguous, the disparity errors are strongly reduced. Devices belonging to the Intel R200 family share similar (or identical) images, projectors, and imaging processor, thus providing very similar performance in terms of depth estimation accuracy. Each unit is individually calibrated in the factory, down to a subpixel-accurate camera model for all the three lenses on the board. Undistortion and rectification are done in hardware for the left-right pair of imagers, and performed on the host for the color camera.

Figure 14.2 shows a RealSense device belonging to the R200 family, which obtains higher accuracy results in passive, well-illuminated conditions. The minimum distance the R200 can detect is a function of its fixed disparity search range. This is a hard limit in real-world space, of around half a meter at 480×360 resolution. At lower resolutions, the minimum distance moves closer to the camera, as the fixed

Fig. 14.2 The RealSense R200 sensor by Intel (from https://www.intel.it/)

range covers a larger fraction of the field of view. For example, it is roughly one third of a meter at 320×240.

The R400 family is a follow up of the R200 one, featuring basic improvements in the stereoscopic matching algorithm, that has been expanded to include various new techniques. The correlation cost function has been expanded too, integrating other matching measures beyond the simple Census correlation available in the R200 series. Optimizations in ASIC design allow the RS400 family to exhibit a lower power consumption than the R200, when running on the same input image resolutions.

14.2.3 Orbbec® Depth Cameras

In 2017, a new depth sensor was launched in the market, called camera-computer Orbbec Persee (http://orbbec3d.com/product-astra/). The innovative feature of this device is the incorporated ARM processor aimed at replacing the traditional configuration based on the use of a laptop or PC, connected by cable to the sensor. Additionally, the all-in-one camera-computer is shipped at a quite affordable cost, compared to Kinect or RealSense devices.

Similar to Kinect, the Orbbec device includes an RGB camera, a depth camera, an IR projector, and two microphones. Several SDKs are compatible with the device, for software development. Among them is the Astra SDK, supported by the same company that manufactures the sensor, and the OpenNI framework for 3D natural interaction sensors. Table 14.2 summarizes the main technical features of the Persee camera. From the same manufacturer, other devices are also available, like the Orbbec Astra S, with a depth range of [0.4, 2] m, and the Astra Mini, a "naked" version of the sensor with no enclosure featuring a very small form factor. They are all shown in Fig. 14.3.

Coroiu et al. in [15] show that it is possible to safely exchange the Kinect sensor with the Orbbec sensor. In some conditions, it is even possible to mix the training and testing data generated by the two different devices. According to the authors' experiments over 16 classifiers used in pose recognition algorithms, the choice of the sensor does not affect the accuracy of the process. However, for other 7 classifiers,

Table 14.2 Main features of the Orbbec Persee camera (manufacturer's specification)

Feature	Orbbec persee
Depth sensing technology	Structured light
RGB image resolution	1280×720 @30 fps
Depth sensing resolution	640×480 @30 fps
Depth sensing range	[0.6, 8.0] m (optimal [0.6, 5.0] m)
Field of view	60° horizontal, 49.5° vertical (73° diagonal)
Audio	2 microphones

(a)   **(b)**   **(c)**

Fig. 14.3 The Orbbec devices: **a** Persee camera-computer, **b** Astra S, and **c** Astra mini

mixing the data generated from the two sensors resulted in a major drop in accuracy. From these outcomes, it is possible to say that the even if the sensors are equivalent from the point of view of their performances in-depth acquisition, mixing the data generated from them can result in a loss of accuracy, in some cases. While it is not clear what is the physical resolution of the depth sensor of the Persee camera-computer, the camera can produce a point cloud with a resolution of up to 1280×1024 at 5 Hz. By limiting the requested resolution to 640×480, the frame rate increases up to 30 Hz, as reported in Table 14.2.

14.2.4 Depth Measurement Accuracy

Since its appearance in the market, the Kinect sensor raised a great interest among researchers, for the possibility to exploit such a low cost and easy-to-use tool in even complex applications, like contactless measurement systems based on the availability of the depth information. In mapping and navigation, that are typical applications in the robotic domain, a prior knowledge of the depth error estimation is critical. Even in fall detection, where distance measurements are collected to understand the relative position of the subject's center of mass with respect to the floor, the depth measurement accuracy may affect the reliability of the processing algorithms used to detect and classify a fall event.

As already mentioned, Kinect V1 adopted a structured-light method, projecting patterns of many stripes at once, for the acquisition of a multitude of samples simultaneously. In Kinect V2, the better quality TOF technology with active sensors was used, to measure the distance of a surface by calculating the round-trip time of an emitted pulse of light.

According to He et al. [28], the errors that may occur in TOF depth measurements can be of two types: systematic and non-systematic. Systematic errors are caused by the intrinsic properties and the imaging conditions of the camera system; they can be identified and corrected in the calibration process. Non-systematic errors are caused by unpredictable features of the environment [7] and by imperfections of the sensor. Non-systematic errors vary randomly, and it is difficult to determine a general mathematical model for describing their exact behavior. They might not be corrected, but an upper bound can be estimated in specific, restricted ambient conditions. When the environment does not substantially change, estimated error bounds obtained with significant statistics can be used with a great probability of success.

Lachat et al. [37] analyzed photometric and depth data, to determine the depth error considering the average value of a window of 10×10 central pixels of the depth image of a wall. The variation between the real distance of the sensor to the wall (measured by tachometry) and the values of the depth maps were assumed as the sensor error. Yang et al. in [53] evaluated the Kinect V2's depth accuracy, and also proposed a method to improve it, by applying the trilateration principle and using multiple devices. According to the results of this work, where the depth accuracy was assessed using a planar surface and measuring distances with an AGPtek Handheld Digital Laser Point Distance Meter (measuring range: 40 m, accuracy: ± 2 mm, laser class: class II, laser type: 635 nm), the accuracy error distribution of Kinect V2 satisfies an elliptical cone with 60-degree angle in vertical direction and 70-degree angle in the horizontal direction. As Kinect V2 is not able to measure the depth within a range of 0.5 m, the resolution in such a range is set to 0. The mean depth resolution and max resolution increase with distance, so a coarser depth image is generated when the range at which the sensor is used increases; a larger tilt angle leads to a lower depth resolution and a larger standard deviation; when the distance is larger than 2 m, the max resolution and standard deviation increase faster. More details can be found in [53].

In [10], the errors computed by capturing images of a checkerboard at several distances from the RGB-D sensor under test, are the basis for generating a parametric model of polynomial or exponential type, representing the Root Mean Square (RMS) depth error throughout the sensor's operating range. Using curve fittings methods, an equation is obtained that generalizes the RMS error as a function of the distance between the sensor and the checkerboard pattern, without the need to model geometrically the sensor's data capture method, as it was done in many previous works.

A quantitative comparison of calibration methods for RGB-D sensors using different technologies is presented in [51]. Three calibration algorithms have been compared by applying their results to three different RGB-D sensors. The obtained parameters for each camera have been tested in different situations, and applied in 3D reconstruction of objects, which is a quite demanding application. In general, consumer RGB-D sensors exhibit acceptable accuracy for many applications, but in some cases, they work at the limit of their sensitivity, near to the minimum feature size that can be perceived. In these cases, calibration processes are critical in order to increase the sensor's accuracy and enable it to meet the requirements of such kinds of applications.

14.3 Processing of RGB-D Signals for Fall Detection

Fall detection is a widely investigated field of research, in which many different solutions have been proposed over the years, by resorting to a wide range of different technologies. In recent times, the additional challenge of fall prevention has gained interest, with the aim of designing solutions that can help to prevent and hopefully to avoid falls, and not only automatically detect them.

In the literature, the first approaches to fall detection tried to use wearable devices. In [8], tri-axial accelerometers are placed on the trunk and the thigh of 10 volunteers that perform Activities of Daily Living (ADL) and simulate falls. Kangas et al. [31] used a tri-axial accelerometer attached to belt at the waist, involving elderly people in a test campaign to perform ADLs. Alternative research approaches used cameras as a source of information to detect risky activities [2, 4, 18, 48]. Compared to wearable-based solutions, the camera approach overcomes the problem of invasiveness of the sensing devices, but at the same time it suffers from ambient illumination variations and introduces issues related to the limited covered area.

The availability of cheap depth sensors enabled an improvement of the robustness in camera-based approaches for fall detection solutions. In particular, the Kinect sensor has been used in different implementations [23, 43, 44, 46].

14.3.1 The Importance of Fall Detection

A fall is defined by the World Health Organization (WHO) as an *event*, which results in *a person coming to rest inadvertently on the ground or floor or other lower level*. This problem affects particularly the aged population: approximately 28–35% of people aged 65 and over fall each year, increasing to 32–42% of those over 70 years old.[1] These numbers are confirmed in developed countries, like the EU28 group, where approximately 100,000 older people die from consequences of a fall each year. Both intrinsic (older age, neurodegenerative disorders, Parkinson's disease, impairment in muscle strength, balance, and vision) and extrinsic factors (effects of medications, loose carpets, slippery floors, poor lighting, clutter and obstacles on stairways) influence the occurrence of a fall event [6]. Even the fear of falling represents another traumatic consequence for elderly, because it can reduce their autonomy. If the intrinsic factors can be reduced, the extrinsic ones are more difficult to control and avoid.

Besides the direct consequences correlated to a fall (like superficial cuts, broken or fractured bones, and abrasions or tissue damage), the so-called long-life, defined as involuntarily remaining on the ground for an hour or more following a fall, represents a serious risk for the health. As stated in [8], half of elderly people who experience a long-life die within 6 months. Taking into account all these aspects, reliable and secure systems for automatic fall detection and notification (like those exploiting inertial sensors, infrared, vibration, acoustic, and magnetic sensors, video cameras, RGB-D, and radar sensors) can provide a valuable support to alleviate the impact of falls on elderly's quality of life, and are strongly recommended. They should ensure an adequate robustness against false alarms, being not invasive at the same time. The proportion of elderly people is increasing worldwide, and many of them

---

[1]https://www.who.int/ageing/projects/falls_prevention_older_age/en/.

prefer living at home rather than in nursing homes. For this reason, a wide range of technology-based applications have been developed to assist the elderly in their own premises.

Within the domain of non-wearable approaches to fall detection and, in a broader sense, home monitoring, proposals adopting depth cameras (RGB-D sensors) gained interest in recent years, as they enable event detection without infringing the monitored subject's privacy. However, RGB-D sensors suffer from the limited detection range. Additionally, depth sensors using the structured light approach (like the recent Orbbec Astra Mini device[2]) are prone to light changing conditions and possible destructive interference, in multiple sensors configuration [42]. However, this last limitation can be overcome resorting to TOF sensors, like Kinect V2.

Reliable monitoring systems can be beneficial not only to tackle fall detection issues, but also to comprehensively evaluate the pattern of life of an individual. Irregularities in the pattern of life of a monitored subject can be used for early detection of deteriorating health conditions (e.g., initial symptoms of dementia), and can even provide the opportunity for timely and more effective treatment [16, 21].

14.3.2   Approaches to Fall Detection Based on RGB-D Signals

Fall detection approaches based on computer vision have the advantage of being less intrusive than those exploiting wearable sensors, even if capturing videos or images may be perceived as a privacy infringement by the monitored subject. In recent years, many researchers focused on designing fall detection systems exploiting depth image information, to both improve the detection accuracy and keep a higher level of preserved privacy. In fact, the availability of depth information allows to implement simpler identification procedures to detect human subjects. Additionally, the advantages of this technology, with respect to classical video-based ones, are: the reduced susceptibility to variations in light intensity; the provision of 3D information by a single camera (while a stereoscopic system is necessary in the RGB domain to achieve the same goal); better privacy retention, as it is far more difficult than with videos to recognize the facial details of the people captured by the depth camera.

In fall detection systems based on the use of depth sensors, two main configurations have been investigated: the one adopting the sensor in front or almost-front view, and the one in which the sensor is installed on the ceiling, and top-view depth frames are acquired and processed by the system. The most relevant difference between the above-mentioned configurations is that the latter cannot rely on the skeleton joints coordinates that are usually available, automatically or through proper elaboration, when the depth sensor is used in front view. As a consequence, in the top-view configuration, additional processing steps need to be performed on the raw depth data

[2]https://orbbec3d.com/astra-mini/.

provided by the sensor, to detect and segment a human subject's blob over which fall detection or action recognition is then carried out.

14.3.2.1 Front-View Approaches

Yun et al. in [55] propose a system to analyze pose and motion dynamics, which is focused on measuring the intensity and temporal variation of pose change and pose motion in single camera views, instead of relying on bounding boxes. Since it is a broadly accepted intuition that a falling person usually undergoes large physical movement and displacement in a short-time interval, features allowing for a more accurate detection could be obtained by studying the intensity and temporal variations of pose change and body movement. Among the measures that can be used to characterize pose and motion dynamics, centroid velocity, head-to-centroid distance, histogram of oriented gradients, and optical flow are used, thus studying the statistics of the change or difference between pose and motion descriptors. This approach aims for a simple and effective solution avoiding the need to combine multiple cameras. By the proposed approach, the authors show how to characterize pose and motion dynamics, based on the aforementioned measures; how to extract compact features based on the mean and variance of the pose and motion dynamics; and finally how to detect a human by combining depth information and background mixture models. The proposed fall detection scheme obtains a high detection rate along with a low false positive rate when experimented on a dataset including 1008 RGB videos and 1008 depth videos captured in front view, 50% of which, approximately, contain human falls and the remaining ones contain lying down activities.

In [35], a features-fusion approach is shown to be effective in obtaining high detection rate with small false alarms, in experiments on an RGB-D video dataset, captured in front view. In the proposed scheme, foreground human detection is performed by differencing RGB frames, then Speeded-Up Robust Features (SURF) keypoints are used to mark the blob boundary, thus identifying the target bounding box. Local shape and motion features are extracted from target contours, instead of structural features from rigid bounding boxes. Histogram of Oriented Gradients (HOG) and Histogram of Oriented Optical Flow (HOOF)-based features are then computed and used to encode global shape and motion. The main contribution of this work consists of forming contours of target persons in depth images based on morphological skeleton; extracting local shape and motion features from target contours; encoding global shape and motion in HOG and HOOF features from RGB images, and combining various shape and motion features for enhanced fall detection.

Panahi et al. in [45] select two models to be used for fall detection. The former one, that relies on previous works such as [54], only considers abnormalities associated with the subject detected to lie on the floor, neglecting the speed of falling. This is based on the idea that an elderly tends to use a bed or a sofa to rest, due to myasthenia and problems in sitting and standing, and the falling of an elderly is not necessarily realized at high speed. In the second model, similar to [36], slowly lying down on the ground is recognized as a normal activity, and retaining time in an abnormal pose is considered, to take a final decision. A silhouette of fitted cubes using 3D momentum, as well as joint tracking, are exploited for feature extraction. The proposed methods are tested over a database including 30 videos of fall positions along with 40 videos captured from different routine activities such as sitting, bending, grabbing objects from under table, performed by five different persons. The use of the subject's centroid distance from the floor efficiently contributes to improving the results. This research outperforms similar works where color images or devices like accelerometers are used, attaining 100% and 97.5% sensitivity and specificity, respectively.

In [22], the joint use of an RGB-D camera-based system and wearable devices is investigated, to check the effectiveness of a data fusion approach to tackling fall detection, mainly addressing the associate synchronization issues. The datasets created in a lab settings to test and validate the proposed algorithm are available too [12, 13].

The work by Abobakr et al. [1] proposes an end-to-end deep learning architecture composed of convolutional and recurrent neural networks to detect fall events from front-view depth frames. The deep convolutional network (ConvNet) analyses the human body and extracts visual features from the input frames. By modeling complex temporal dependencies between subsequent frame features, using Long-Short-Term Memory (LSTM) recurrent neural networks, fall events are detected. Both models are combined and jointly trained in an end-to-end ConvLSTM architecture. This way the model learns visual representations and complex temporal dynamics of fall motions simultaneously.

Fall detection solutions based on processing RGB-D signals captured from sensors in front view may suffer from occlusions and other environmental factors (such as passing subjects or pets) that can prevent from a correct identification of falls. For these reasons, alternative approaches based on the use of depth sensors mounted on the ceiling have been considered. Such a placement of the sensor has advantages and can lead to simplification of the algorithms devoted to distinguishing the accidental falls from ADLs.

14.3.2.2 Top-View Approaches

In 2014, the work by Kepski et al. [33] demonstrated how to achieve a reliable fall detection with a low computational cost and a very low level of false positive alarms, by exploiting the joint use of a body-worn tri-axial accelerometer, and a ceiling-mounted RGB-D camera. The former was used to detect a potential fall by identifying the impact shock. The generated fall hypothesis was then verified using the distance to the ground of the topmost points of the subject's blob captured by the top-view depth frames. This sensor-fusion approach allowed the authors to ignore a lot of false positive alarms, which would be generated by the use of the accelerometer alone.

Many other approaches aimed at fall detection and based on the fusion of RGB-D and other sensor types followed, as extensively reported in [11], where systems based on radar and RGB-D sensors are reviewed. Both radar and RGB-D sensors enable contactless and nonintrusive monitoring, which is an advantage for practical deployment and users' acceptance and compliance, compared with other sensor technologies like video cameras or wearables.

In Chap. 18, the use of depth sensors alone, in top-view configuration, is thoroughly addressed, to show how this specific modality may achieve high performances even in crowded environments, by minimizing occlusions and being the most privacy-compliant approach at the same time. As presented in the same chapter, the first step in people detection and tracking from top-view captured depth frames is the segmentation, to retrieve the monitored subject's silhouette [38]. To this aim, several methods can be used, ranging from classical handcraft features based approaches, to deep learning techniques [39, 40].

In [32], the depth images from a ceiling-mounted Kinect camera are processed. Human silhouettes are obtained after background subtraction, and shape-based features are extracted. A binary Support Vector Machine (SVM) classifier fed with the obtained features is used to classify the fall events from non-fall events. The method proposed by the authors, tested on a publicly available dataset [36], classifies falls from other actions with an accuracy of 93.04%. In the dataset, 10 videos over 1000 depth frames containing falls and other actions, like standing, walking and sudden falls, are considered. A total of 782 non-fall sequences and 422 fall, and a fixed background sequence, are used in the simulation. Two classes of fall and non-fall frames categories are labeled manually; half of the sequences are used for training and other half for testing. The method works offline, on previously captured depth sequences of predetermined length.

The approach proposed by Gasparrini et al. in [23] relies exclusively on the use of the Kinect depth sensor, in a top-view configuration, and on low-complexity depth frame processing, being aimed at a real-time implementation to be effectively used out of lab settings. Four main steps maybe identified, namely: preprocessing and segmentation, object distinguishing algorithm, identification of human subject, and people tracking and fall detection. Figure 14.4 provides a graphic summary of the main steps included in the original algorithm, the details of which can be found in [23].

All the elements captured in the depth scene are recognized by means of an ad hoc segmentation algorithm, which analyzes the raw depth data directly provided by the sensor. The system extracts the elements, and implements a solution to classify all the blobs in the scene. Anthropometric relationships and features are exploited to recognize one or more human subjects among the blobs. Once a person is detected, tracking algorithm follows the silhouette between different frames. The use of a reference depth frame, containing the static surrounding background of the scene, allows to extract a human subject even during interaction with other objects, such as chairs or desks. In addition, the problem of blob fusion is taken into account and efficiently solved through an inter-frame processing algorithm. A fall is identified when the distance between the depth sensor and the blob centroid associated with the person becomes comparable with the floor distance. This implies that in some situations, where the blob is on the ground but its central point is not sufficiently

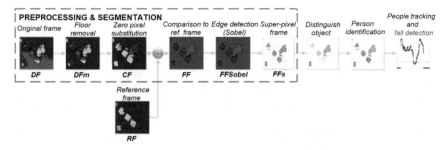

Fig. 14.4 Diagram summarizing the main steps of the algorithm proposed in [23]

close to the floor, the fall is not detected. These conditions may occur in cases of falls on the knees, or when the person falls but ends sitting on the ground, and the central point of the blob is dislocated within the shoulders or in the head area.

Experimental tests showed the effectiveness of the proposed solution, even in complex scenarios. A MATLAB implementation of the algorithm, working offline, was tested over a dataset acquired in a laboratory setting. The data collection protocol took into account the sensor setup (ceiling-mounted in top-view configuration), and the expected performances, summarized as follows:

- ability to detect falls in which the person ends lying on the ground;
- ability to detect falls in which the person ends sitting on the ground;
- ability to detect falls in which the person is lying on the ground on the knees, possibly interacting with objects present in the environment while falling;
- ability to manage the *recovery* of the person, that is to differentiate a fall in which the subject remains on the ground, from one in which the person is able to get up after the fall.

The data acquisition protocol included 32 types of falls, and 8 ADLs that can be confused with a fall, like picking up objects from the ground, bending, squatting, sitting down on a chair or sofa. These actions were performed by 20 subjects (5 females, 15 males) of age in 21–55, thus resulting in 800 sequences of depth frames (320×240 @ 30 fps), collected with the associated sequences of RGB frames (640×480 @ 30 fps) used as ground truth to evaluate the performance of the algorithm.

Following the offline and prototype implementation in MATLAB, a C++ version of the proposed algorithm was implemented and tested for real-time execution, on a desktop PC featuring Windows 7 O.S., Intel i5 processor, and 4GB RAM. The algorithm is natively adaptable to several depth sensors, once a 320×240 resolution and a 30 fps frame rate are set, as it only requires raw depth data as input. An embedded real-time implementation was also realized on a development platform, featuring Ubuntu Linaro 12.11 O.S., ARM Cortex-A9 Quad Core architecture processor, and 2GB RAM. In this case, the frame rate supported by the board was slightly lower than 30 fps, but the system still worked properly.

14.3.3 A Sample Real-Time Implementation

The algorithm designed in [23] and briefly discussed in the previous section has been further tested in a lab setting, and finally translated into a real-time software, ready to be used in pilots involving experiments in real settings. The original MATLAB version was converted into a Python one, which required some changes in the functional workflow.

The basic physical unit that needs to be installed is composed of a commercial depth sensor (a Kinect V1 device in the project herein discussed), and a mini-computer interfacing the sensor over a USB connection, running the real-time fall detection algorithm, and connected to the home Wi-Fi network. Then, based on the total area of the apartment to be monitored, and on the arrangement of the rooms within the apartment, the amount of units needed (sensor + mini-computer) may vary. For example, if the height of the apartment ceiling is limited (i.e., <3 m) and the area covered by a single Kinect is not enough to include the whole subject's shape when fallen, it is possible to install two sensors in such a way as to make the corresponding covered areas adjacent, thus obtaining a wider field of view. In order to limit as much as possible the hardware requirements of the system, each mini-computer is configured in such a way as to be able to run up to three independent instances of the real-time fall-detection algorithm, processing the input depth signals generated by up to three different Kinect devices.

Before moving to the pilot installation in a real setting, the Python code was tested again over the same dataset used for the MATLAB one, in order to check if the unavoidable implementation constraints had changed the expected performances. Considering the *warning* case as a distinct class of the dataset from *fall* and *ADL*, 3 classes are identified and 800 sequences overall, out of which 160 are classified as *ADL*, 319 are classified as *fall*, and 320 are classified as *warning*. By this approach, the resulting accuracy is 95.5%, taking into account that one sequence of the dataset has not been classified because the person's blob was not segmented at all. On the other hand, assuming to have two possible outputs, and therefore considering *fall* and *warning* within the same class, the system is characterized by the following performance: TP (true positive) = 629, TN (true negative) = 159, FP (false positive) = 1, FN (false negative) = 10, and therefore an accuracy of 98.5%. The confusion matrix resulting from the tests on the complete dataset is shown in Fig. 14.5.

Fig. 14.5 Confusion matrix obtained by testing the MATLAB implementation of the algorithm on the complete dataset

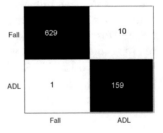

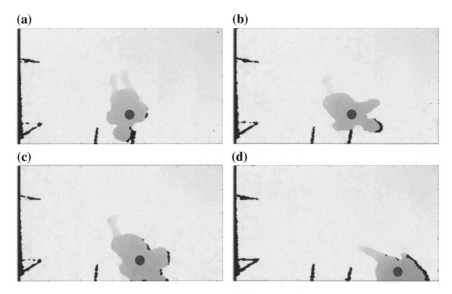

Fig. 14.6 In this sample sequence from **a** to **d**, the algorithm cannot correctly locate the central point of the blob within the head area. The subject recovers from a fall on the knees, then leaves the area covered by the sensor. The incorrect tracking of the subject makes it not possible for the algorithm to correctly classify the fall

Most of the errors from the algorithm consist of classifying as a *fall* a depth sequence that is labeled as a *warning*. Other errors are somehow related to the choice of the time thresholds. This occurs, for example, when the subject falls on his knees, but remains on this position for less time than the threshold. This way, the *fall* is actually recognized as an *ADL*. In other cases, the algorithm cannot correctly locate the head of the subject, thus failing to track the subject when recovering after a fall. One example is shown in Fig. 14.6.

The tracking of the subject may be lost when the blob falls at the boundaries of the area covered by the sensor, as shown in Fig. 14.7. In this condition, the fall detection algorithm does not work.

In order to limit the impact of tracking loss on the fall detection algorithm outcomes, the performance of the subject identification function and the blob tracking function have been improved during the implementation of the Python version. This way, blobs are identified at each frame and tracked correctly even when a blob fusion takes place. A comparison among the original frame acquired from the depth sensor and the blob map obtained from the algorithm is shown in Fig. 14.8a and b, respectively. The improvement of this function also allowed to reduce the overall computational burden of the algorithm, by providing a better quality information to the following processing steps. In order to avoid the loss of the subject's tracking due to unexpected situations, an additional check on the user's position has been added,

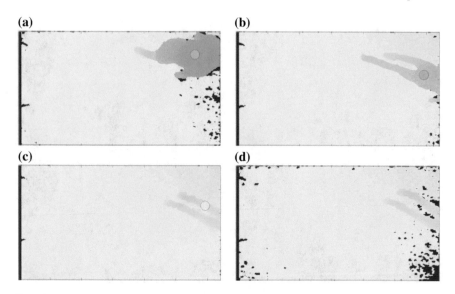

Fig. 14.7 In the sample sequence from **a** to **d** the blob of the subject is located at the boundaries of the area covered by the sensor and the tracking is lost

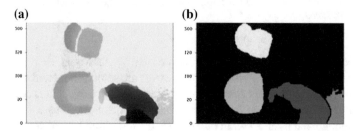

Fig. 14.8 a Original depth frame acquired from the sensor. **b** Blob map generated by the algorithm in the Python implementation

opting for reporting the possible loss of tracking, and documenting the situation with the acquisition of a video, or a frame, of the last known position of the subject.

Following the additional changes described above, the performance of the Python code has been tested for the second time on the same dataset used to check the original MATLAB version. Figure 14.9 shows the confusion matrix obtained. The overall accuracy goes down to 93.27%: despite the 5% reduction, the performance is still acceptable, and traded off with a truly real-time behavior. In fact, several execution optimizations have been integrated into the Python implementation; this way, small deviations in the processed data, with respect to the original routines, have been inevitably introduced in terms of accuracy.

As discussed by Debard et al. in [17], in camera-based fall detection systems, real-life data poses significant challenges, typically resulting in higher false alarm rates than those obtained in controlled lab environments. By analyzing the outcomes of the

Fig. 14.9 Confusion matrix obtained by testing the Python implementation of the algorithm on the complete dataset

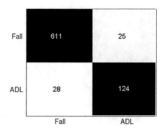

Python algorithm on the lab recorded dataset, we found that the degradation is mostly due to the incorrect detection of *ADL* that are classified as *fall*. Considering that we are working on a system focused on fall detection, this means we are probably going to receive an increased amount of false alarms, but this is practically more acceptable than an increased probability of missing true fall events.

About the real-time behavior of the algorithm, the following results were obtained: the MATLAB version running on a notebook equipped with Intel i7-7700HQ CPU @ 2.80 GHz and 16 GB RAM featured a processing time for single frame that varies from 50 to 100 ms; the Python version, tested on the pilot configuration (i.e., Intel NUC i3-7100U, 8GB RAM DDR4, and 128 GB NVMe SSD) provided 12–22 ms processing time per frame. As such, the requirement of a real-time frame processing has been fulfilled.

During the experimentation of the system in the real setting of the lady's apartment, some issues emerged. The most relevant one is due to the presence of a door on the wardrobe, the position of which may affect the proper detection of the subject within the depth frames captured by the sensor covering that area. In fact, when the door is open, a shaded area appears in the depth frame, over which the algorithm is not able to identify the person or maintain the correct tracking. This effect depends on the projection of the IR pattern on the door surface: as shown in the sequence of depth frames in Fig. 14.10, the black area appearing in the bottom-right side of the frame, when the door is open, corresponds to null depth values. As a consequence, the routines executed by the algorithm raise exceptions and the person's blob detection and tracking fail. Correspondingly, the system generates a number of fall notifications that are not correct.

Another critical situation emerges when the person moves near to the boundaries of the area covered by the sensor. In this case, as shown in the sequence of depth frames in Fig. 14.11, the tracking is not lost, but the central point of the blob (highlighted by the circle in the leftmost frame) gets misplaced and close to the floor, as the head is not detected. This way, a fall notification is raised, which is not correct.

The problems highlighted above are related to the physical displacement of the sensors, that cannot be arbitrarily chosen as it happens, on the contrary, in a lab setting. When dealing with a pilot installation in a real environment, many constraints are to be faced and traded off, to ensure the least obtrusiveness and the most acceptable performance. In any case, the issues presented can be quite efficiently

Fig. 14.10 Sequence of depth frames captured by the Kinect located over the wardrobe (from left to right). When the wardrobe door is open, the depth sensing fails (black area in the frames) and the algorithm raises errors

Fig. 14.11 Sequence of depth frames captured by the Kinect located over the living area (from left to right). When the person moves near to the boundaries, tracking is not lost but the incorrect placement of the blob central point causes an error fall notification

addressed through additional checks on the position of the subject, or the position of the wardrobe door, within the algorithm.

14.4 Future Perspectives

Despite the remarkable corpus of knowledge generated on the topic of automatic fall detection systems, as stated in the recent survey by Xu et al. [52], the domain of solutions based on RGB-D sensors still confronts challenges on theories and practice. Some of the open challenges are related to intrinsic limitations of the sensors, like the finite Field Of View (FOV), which need to be overcome by the use of systems including multiple devices, joint with proper algorithmic solutions able to synchronize the signals generated from the different sensors, and process them as a single, composite view of the monitored environment. This carries an unavoidable increase in complexity and computational requirements for the hardware (HW) platforms that should support a real-time execution of the software. Alternative approaches do not require to merge the views of each sensor into a single one, but then require to ensure person re-identification, in order to avoid losing continuity in the monitoring.

Another big and still mostly unsolved challenge is related to the availability of data captured in real-world settings, to train the classifiers used in automatic fall detection systems. The use of laboratory simulated falls has been an accepted approach in the research and academic community for a long time, due to the relevant difficulties associated with recording real-world falls. Just to mention one of the main issues, the rarity of falls means that recording them is both costly and time consuming. In 2012, Bagalà et al. [3] estimated that to collect 100 falls, 100,000 days of activity would need to be recorded, assuming a fall incidence of one fall per person every three years. The authors highlight the importance of testing fall-detection algorithms in real-life conditions in order to produce more effective automated alarm systems with higher acceptance. A large, shared real-world fall database could, potentially, provide an enhanced understanding of the fall process and the information needed to design and evaluate high-performance fall detectors.

Despite this challenge, the focus is now moving to real-world fall data due to the external validity issues inherent in simulated fall based testing, as presented in Sect. 14.3.3. Real-world data, by its very nature provides high ecological validity and therefore contributes to higher external validity. As highlighted in [9], to increase robustness and make results comparable, larger standardized datasets are needed containing data from a range of participant groups. Measures that depend on the definition and identification of non-falls should be avoided, keeping the focus on sensitivity, precision, and F-measure, as the most suitable robust measures for evaluating the real-world performance of a fall detection system.

References

1. Abobakr A, Hossny M, Abdelkader H, Nahavandi S (2018) RGB-D fall detection via deep residual convolutional LSTM networks. In: 2018 digital image computing: techniques and applications (DICTA), pp 1–7. https://doi.org/10.1109/DICTA.2018.8615759
2. Auvinet E, Multon F, Saint-Arnaud A, Rousseau J, Meunier J (2011) Fall detection with multiple cameras: an occlusion-resistant method based on 3-D silhouette vertical distribution. IEEE Trans Inf Technol Biomed 15(2):290–300. https://doi.org/10.1109/TITB.2010.2087385
3. Bagalà F, Becker C, Cappello A, Chiari L, Aminian K, Hausdorff J, Zijlstra W, Klenk J (2012) Evaluation of accelerometer-based fall detection algorithms on real-world falls. PLoS ONE 7(5). https://doi.org/10.1371/journal.pone.0037062
4. Banerjee T, Keller JM, Skubic M, Stone E (2014) Day or night activity recognition from video using fuzzy clustering techniques. IEEE Trans Fuzzy Syst 22(3):483–493. https://doi.org/10.1109/TFUZZ.2013.2260756
5. Bell T, Li B, Zhang S (2016) Structured light techniques and applications. American Cancer Society, New York, pp 1–24. https://doi.org/10.1002/047134608X.W8298
6. Bianchi F, Redmond SJ, Narayanan MR, Cerutti S, Lovell NH (2010) Barometric pressure and triaxial accelerometry-based falls event detection. IEEE Trans Neural Syst Rehabil Eng 18(6):619–627. https://doi.org/10.1109/TNSRE.2010.2070807
7. Borenstein J, Feng L (1996) Measurement and correction of systematic odometry errors in mobile robots. IEEE Trans Robot Autom 12(6):869–880. https://doi.org/10.1109/70.544770
8. Bourke A, O'Brien J, Lyons G (2007) Evaluation of a threshold-based tri-axial accelerometer fall detection algorithm. Gait Posture 26(2):194–199

9. Broadley R, Klenk J, Thies S, Kenney L, Granat M (2018) Methods for the real-world evaluation of fall detection technology: a scoping review. Sensors 18(7). https://doi.org/10.3390/s18072060, http://www.mdpi.com/1424-8220/18/7/2060

10. Cabrera E, Ortiz L, da Silva B, Clua E, Gonçalves L (2018) A versatile method for depth data error estimation in RGB-D sensors. Sensors 18(9). https://doi.org/10.3390/s18093122, http://www.mdpi.com/1424-8220/18/9/3122

11. Cippitelli E, Fioranelli F, Gambi E, Spinsante S (2017) Radar and RGB-depth sensors for fall detection: a review. IEEE Sens J 17(12):3585–3604. https://doi.org/10.1109/JSEN.2017.2697077

12. Cippitelli E, Gambi E, Gasparrini S, Spinsante S (2016) TST fall detection dataset v1. In: IEEE Dataport, IEEE. https://doi.org/10.21227/H2VC7J

13. Cippitelli, E., Gambi, E., Gasparrini, S., Spinsante, S.: TST Fall detection dataset v2. In: IEEE Dataport, IEEE (2016). https://doi.org/10.21227/H2QP48

14. Cippitelli E, Gasparrini S, Santis AD, Montanini L, Raffaeli L, Gambi E, Spinsante S (2015) Comparison of RGB-D mapping solutions for application to food intake monitoring. Springer International Publishing, Cham, pp 295–305. https://doi.org/10.1007/978-3-319-18374-9_28

15. Coroiu ADCA, Coroiu A (2018) Interchangeability of Kinect and Orbbec sensors for gesture recognition. In: 2018 IEEE 14th international conference on intelligent computer communication and processing (ICCP), pp 309–315. https://doi.org/10.1109/ICCP.2018.8516586

16. Daponte P, DeMarco J, DeVito L, Pavic B, Zolli S (2011) Electronic measurements in rehabilitation. In: 2011 IEEE international symposium on medical measurements and applications, pp 274–279. https://doi.org/10.1109/MeMeA.2011.5966782

17. Debard G, Mertens M, Goedemé T, Tuytelaars T, Vanrumste B (2017) Three ways to improve the performance of real-life camera-based fall detection systems. J Sens 2017. https://doi.org/10.1155/2017/8241910

18. Demiröz BE, Salah AA, Akarun L (2014) Coupling fall detection and tracking in omnidirectional cameras. In: Park HS, Salah AA, Lee YJ, Morency LP, Sheikh Y, Cucchiara R (eds) Human behavior understanding. Springer International Publishing, Cham, pp 73–85

19. Eric N, Jang JW (2017) Kinect depth sensor for computer vision applications in autonomous vehicles. In: International conference on ubiquitous and future networks, ICUFN, pp 531–535. https://doi.org/10.1109/ICUFN.2017.7993842

20. Freedman B, Shpunt A, Machlin M, Arieli Y (2012) Depth mapping using projected patterns. US8150142B2 Patent

21. Garcia NM, Garcia NC, Sousa P, Oliveira D, Alexandre C, Felizardo V (2014) TICE.Healthy: a perspective on medical information integration. In: IEEE-EMBS international conference on biomedical and health informatics (BHI), pp 464–467. https://doi.org/10.1109/BHI.2014.6864403

22. Gasparrini S, Cippitelli E, Gambi E, Spinsante S, Wåhslén J, Orhan I, Lindh T (2016) Proposal and experimental evaluation of fall detection solution based on wearable and depth data fusion. In: Loshkovska S, Koceski S (eds) ICT innovations 2015. Springer International Publishing, Cham, pp 99–108

23. Gasparrini S, Cippitelli E, Spinsante S, Gambi E (2014) A depth-based fall detection system using a kinect®. Sensor. Sensors 14(2):2756–2775. https://doi.org/10.3390/s140202756, http://www.mdpi.com/1424-8220/14/2/2756

24. Gasparrini S, Cippitelli E, Spinsante S, Gambi E (2015) Depth cameras in AAL environments: technology and real-world applications, vol 2–4. IGI Global. https://doi.org/10.4018/978-1-4666-8200-9.ch053

25. Geng J (2011) Structured-light 3D surface imaging: a tutorial. Adv Opt Photon 3(2):128–160. https://doi.org/10.1364/AOP.3.000128

26. Gokturk SB, Yalcin H, Bamji C (2004) A time-of-flight depth sensor - system description, issues and solutions. In: 2004 conference on computer vision and pattern recognition workshop, p 35. https://doi.org/10.1109/CVPR.2004.291

27. Halme RJ, Lanz M, Kämäräinen J, Pieters R, Latokartano J, Hietanen A (2018) Review of vision-based safety systems for human-robot collaboration. Procedia CIRP 72:111–116. https://doi.org/10.1016/j.procir.2018.03.043

28. He Y, Liang B, Zou Y, He J, Yang J (2017) Depth errors analysis and correction for Time-of-Flight (ToF) cameras. Sensors 17(1). https://doi.org/10.3390/s17010092
29. Heikkilä J (2000) Geometric camera calibration using circular control points. IEEE Trans Pattern Anal Mach Intell 22(10):1066–1077. https://doi.org/10.1109/34.879788
30. Herrera D, Kannala J, Heikkilä J (2012) Joint depth and color camera calibration with distortion correction. IEEE Trans Pattern Anal Mach Intell 34(10):2058–2064. https://doi.org/10.1109/TPAMI.2012.125
31. Kangas M, Vikman I, Wiklander J, Lindgren P, Nyberg L, Jämsä T (2009) Sensitivity and specificity of fall detection in people aged 40 years and over. Gait Posture 29(4):571–574
32. Kasturi S, Jo K (2017) Human fall classification system for ceiling-mounted Kinect depth images. In: 2017 17th international conference on control, automation and systems (ICCAS), pp 1346–1349. https://doi.org/10.23919/ICCAS.2017.8204202
33. Kepski M, Kwolek B (2014) Fall detection using ceiling-mounted 3D depth camera. In: 2014 international conference on computer vision theory and applications (VISAPP), vol 2, pp 640–647
34. Keselman L, Woodfill JI, Grunnet-Jepsen A, Bhowmik A (2017) Intel® RealSense™ stereoscopic depth cameras. In: 2017 IEEE conference on computer vision and pattern recognition workshops (CVPRW), pp 1267–1276. https://doi.org/10.1109/CVPRW.2017.167
35. Kumar DP, Yun Y, Gu YH (2016) Fall detection in RGB-D videos by combining shape and motion features. In: 2016 IEEE international conference on acoustics, speech and signal processing (ICASSP), pp 1337–1341. https://doi.org/10.1109/ICASSP.2016.7471894
36. Kwolek B, Kepski M (2014) Human fall detection on embedded platform using depth maps and wireless accelerometer. Comput Methods Programs Biomed 117(3):489–501. https://doi.org/10.1016/j.cmpb.2014.09.005
37. Lachat E, Macher H, Landes T, Grussenmeyer P (2015) Assessment and calibration of a RGB-D camera (Kinect v2 Sensor) towards a potential use for close-range 3D modeling. Remote Sens 7(10):13070–13097. https://doi.org/10.3390/rs71013070. http://www.mdpi.com/2072-4292/7/10/13070
38. Liciotti D, Massi G, Frontoni E, Mancini A, Zingaretti P (2015) Human activity analysis for in-home fall risk assessment. In: 2015 IEEE international conference on communication workshop (ICCW), pp 284–289. https://doi.org/10.1109/ICCW.2015.7247192
39. Liciotti D, Paolanti M, Frontoni E, Zingaretti P (2017) People detection and tracking from an RGB-D camera in top-view configuration: review of challenges and applications. Lecture notes in computer science (including subseries Lecture notes in artificial intelligence and lecture notes in bioinformatics) vol 10590 LNCS, pp 207–218. https://doi.org/10.1007/978-3-319-70742-6_20
40. Liciotti D, Paolanti M, Pietrini R, Frontoni E, Zingaretti P (2018) Convolutional networks for semantic heads segmentation using top-view depth data in crowded environment. In: Proceedings of the international conference on pattern recognition, vol 2018-August, pp 1384–1389. https://doi.org/10.1109/ICPR.2018.8545397
41. Magnor M, Grau O, Sorkine-Hornung O, Theobalt C (2015) Digital representations of the real world: how to capture, model, and render visual reality. A. K. Peters Ltd, Natick, MA, USA
42. Martín RM, Lorbach M, Brock O (2014) Deterioration of depth measurements due to interference of multiple RGB-D sensors. In: 2014 IEEE/RSJ international conference on intelligent robots and systems, pp 4205–4212. https://doi.org/10.1109/IROS.2014.6943155
43. Marzahl C, Penndorf P, Bruder I, Staemmler M (2012) Unobtrusive fall detection using 3D images of a gaming console: concept and first results. Springer, Berlin Heidelberg, Berlin, pp 135–146
44. Mastorakis G, Makris D (2014) Fall detection system using Kinect's infrared sensor. J R Time Image Process 9(4):635–646. https://doi.org/10.1007/s11554-012-0246-9
45. Panahi L, Ghods V (2018) Human fall detection using machine vision techniques on RGB-D images. Biomed Signal Process Control 44:146–153
46. Planinc R, Kampel M (2013) Introducing the use of depth data for fall detection. Pers Ubiquitous Comput 17(6):1063–1072. https://doi.org/10.1007/s00779-012-0552-z

47. Ricciuti M, Spinsante S, Gambi E (2018) Accurate fall detection in a top view privacy preserving configuration. Sensors (Switzerland) 18(6). https://doi.org/10.3390/s18061754
48. Rougier C, Meunier J, St-Arnaud A, Rousseau J (2011) Robust video surveillance for fall detection based on human shape deformation. IEEE Trans Circuits Syst Video Technol 21(5):611–622. https://doi.org/10.1109/TCSVT.2011.2129370
49. Sarbolandi H, Lefloch D, Kolb A (2015) Kinect range sensing: structured-light versus Time-of-Flight kinect. Comput Vis Image Underst. https://doi.org/10.1016/j.cviu.2015.05.006
50. Shao L, Han J, Xu D, Shotton J (2013) Computer vision for RGB-D sensors: Kinect and its applications [special issue intro.]. IEEE Trans Cybern 43(5):1314–1317. https://doi.org/10.1109/TCYB.2013.2276144
51. Villena-Martínez V, Fuster-Guilló A, Azorín-López J, Saval-Calvo M, Mora-Pascual J, Garcia-Rodriguez J, Garcia-Garcia A (2017) A quantitative comparison of calibration methods for RGB-D sensors using different technologies. Sensors 17(2). https://doi.org/10.3390/s17020243, http://www.mdpi.com/1424-8220/17/2/243
52. Xu T, Zhou Y, Zhu J (2018) New advances and challenges of fall detection systems: a survey. Appl Sci 8(3). https://doi.org/10.3390/app8030418, http://www.mdpi.com/2076-3417/8/3/418
53. Yang L, Zhang L, Dong H, Alelaiwi A, Saddik AE (2015) Evaluating and improving the depth accuracy of kinect for windows v2. IEEE Sens J 15(8):4275–4285. https://doi.org/10.1109/JSEN.2015.2416651
54. Yu M, Yu Y, Rhuma A, Naqvi S, Wang L, Chambers J (2013) An online one class support vector machine-based person-specific fall detection system for monitoring an elderly individual in a room environment. IEEE J Biomed Health Inform 17(6):1002–1014. https://doi.org/10.1109/JBHI.2013.2274479
55. Yun Y, Innocenti C, Nero G, Lindén H, Gu IYH (2015) Fall detection in RGB-D videos for elderly care. In: 2015 17th international conference on E-health networking, application services (HealthCom), pp 422–427. https://doi.org/10.1109/HealthCom.2015.7454537
56. Zhang Z (2000) A flexible new technique for camera calibration. IEEE Trans Pattern Anal Mach Intell 22(11):1330–1334. https://doi.org/10.1109/34.888718

Chapter 15
RGB-D Interactive Systems on Serious Games for Motor Rehabilitation Therapy and Therapeutic Measurements

Gabriel Moyà-Alcover, Ines Ayed, Javier Varona and Antoni Jaume-i-Capó

Abstract Serious games are games designed for a primary purpose different from that of pure entertainment, and the cognitive and motor activities required by these games attract the attention of users. In this chapter, we systematically review the use of RGB-D serious games in motor rehabilitation programs and survey the state of the art. The chapter then focuses on the design of serious games for motor rehabilitation therapy and where we present a development framework and implementation guidelines for RGB-D interactive systems for motor rehabilitation therapy and therapeutic measurements. In RGB-D-based interactive systems, users stand in front of the screen and interact with the video game using their body movements. We describe a RGB-D nonparametric approach for background subtraction, that uses both depth and color information in a unified way, to segment the patient. Finally, we show three different case studies where we applied the presented method. The first one consists of an interactive system based on a RGB-D sensor to calculate the Functional Reach Test (FRT). The second one consists on a RGB-D interactive system to improve the balance and postural control of adults with cerebral palsy. The last one consists of three serious games to improve the balance and postural control in elderly people. With conducted experiments and clinical studies, we demonstrate the validity of these systems.

G. Moyà-Alcover (✉) · J. Varona · A. Jaume-i-Capó
Departament de Ciències Matemàtiques i Informàtica, Universitat de les Illes Balears,
Cra. de Valldemossa, km 7.5, Palma (Illes Balears), Spain
e-mail: gabriel.moya@uib.es

J. Varona
e-mail: xavi.varona@uib.es

A. Jaume-i-Capó
e-mail: antoni.jaume@uib.es

I. Ayed
Departament de Ciències Matemàtiques i Informàtica, GresCom Lab, Ecole Supèrieure des
Communications de Tunis, Universitè de Carthage, tunis, Tunisia
e-mail: ines.ayed91@gmail.com

© Springer Nature Switzerland AG 2019
P. L. Rosin et al. (eds.), *RGB-D Image Analysis and Processing*,
Advances in Computer Vision and Pattern Recognition,
https://doi.org/10.1007/978-3-030-28603-3_15

15.1 Introduction

RGB-D-based interfaces have become very popular in rehabilitation settings, there are many applications of RGB-D in health care, see Chap. 14. With the emergence of low-cost, vision-based interfaces, see Chap. 1, both engineers and healthcare practitioners were increasingly attracted to the development and deployment of vision-based interactive systems for motor rehabilitation. Among RGB-D interfaces available in the market, Microsoft Kinect drew the most interest. RGB-D sensors provide color and depth data enabling full body tracking and gesture recognition. In addition, they offer a natural human–computer interaction, without the need to hold a physical controller, which reinforced its acceptance among therapists and patients. Therefore, it has been widely used and validated by researchers in different interactive applications.

On one hand, several research studies investigated the use of RGB-D sensors in motor rehabilitation therapy such as gait retraining [9], analysis of activities of daily living [10], guidance and movement correction [12], training static balance [29], and balance and postural control [22]. Many researchers largely focused on turning an existing set of physical therapy exercises into serious games or deploying existing commercial games and studying their effectiveness. Serious games are computer games designed to reach a specific goal in an engaging and entertaining way rather than pure entertainment. In health care, for instance, serious games are developed with the ultimate purpose of treatment, recovery, and rehabilitation. As we are only considering motor rehabilitation in this work, serious games have been demonstrated to be highly promising in this area [41] as they help motivating patients along therapy sessions [34]. As a matter of fact, motivation is very important especially in long-term therapies and among chronic patients who receive repetitive activities that become boring with time [7, 18]. Furthermore, it has been shown that rehabilitation results were better with motivated patients [34].

On the other hand, researchers conducted studies to validate the use of RGB-D interfaces for therapeutic measurements in order to measure the effectiveness of a therapy, for instance, measurement of Shoulder Range of Motion for the evaluation and diagnosis of adhesive capsulitis instead of using a goniometer [31], gait assessment by providing spatiotemporal and kinematic variables [37], balance tests such as Functional reach test [20] and Timed Up and Go test [8], and so forth. Developing such systems may help in quantifying the therapeutic evolution of patients at their homes thus avoiding unnecessary displacements to the hospital or rehabilitation center. In fact, patients usually perform rehabilitation exercises independently at home and receive, from time to time, a visit from a physiotherapist in order to check their performance and measure the effectiveness of the treatment [27, 32, 36]. To ensure an effective therapy, it is very important to measure its clinical outcomes by means of reliable and valid tests. Many tools and tests exist that serve for this purpose, however there are only few mechanisms that could be used at home without the facilities and equipment provided at hospitals or rehabilitation centers [16, 21]. For this reason,

RGB-D interfaces based on low- cost, vision-based systems represent an affordable alternative to be deployed at home.

That said, developing such interfaces for a target population that present some motor limitations or physical disabilities with the aim of rehabilitation requires a framework and some design guidelines; many problems were identified because of using non-tailored games such as commercial video game for rehabilitation [2]. This need for a common framework has become obvious with the popular increase of vision-based interactive serious games and measurements. Furthermore, some techniques have been shown to be motivating for patients such as background subtraction and mirror feedback, where the background is removed to minimize distractions and users can see themselves on the screen all the time, hence allowing them to immerse themselves in the virtual environment.

Therefore in this work, we summarize our contribution to this area of research. The remainder of this paper is organized as follows. In Sect. 15.2, we present the state of the art of vision-based games used for balance rehabilitation. In Sect. 15.3, we detail the method deployed to develop and implement RGB-D interactive systems for motor rehabilitation. Next, we present three case studies illustrating the method presented in the previous section. The last section is devoted to conclusions and proposed further work.

15.2   State of the Art

Many researchers have investigated the effectiveness of serious games using RGB-D input devices for motor rehabilitation. We conducted a systematic literature research in the Web of Science electronic database using Kitchenham guidelines [28]. Searches were undertaken using a combination of keywords such as "Kinect", "virtual reality", "serious games", "RGB-D", and "motor rehabilitation", for publications between 2007 and 2018. We identified 92 results using the aforementioned keywords, and an examination of both title and abstract yielded a final set of 49 studies. 46 articles used Microsoft Kinect and the other 3 used PrimeSense as the input RGB-D device for interaction. To these studies, we performed quality assessment using the Downs and Black checklist [14] and selected the first 10 having the highest scores to analyze. Rehabilitation after stroke had the biggest share of publications focusing mainly on upper extremity recovery.

For instance, Sin and Lee [44] studied the effects of additional training using Xbox commercial games on upper extremity function of post-stroke patients. Participants were randomized into two groups, where the experimental group had a 30-min conventional therapy plus 30 min of Virtual Reality (VR) training whereas the control group had only 30 min of conventional training. The VR training consisted of games from Kinect sports (Boxing and Bowling) and Kinect adventure (Rally Ball, 20,000 Leaks, and Space Pop). The authors reported significant improvements in the range of motion of the upper extremity, Fugl-Meyer Assessment, and the Box and Block Test scores of both groups comparing to the baseline, with significant differences between the experimental and control group at the end of the 6-week intervention. Similarly, Turkbey et al. [45] conducted a randomized controlled trial of sub-acute stroke patients, where experimental group had 20 sessions of Xbox Kinect training (playing Bowling and Mouse Mayhem Kinect games) in addition to the same conventional therapy training received by controls. Results showed that the experimental group had significantly greater improvements than the control group in Box and Blocks Test, Wolf Motor Function Test, and Brunnstrom motor recovery stages. Despite both studies reported better results in favor of the experimental group, these results could be biased due to the total intervention time given that the experimental group had additional VR training in comparison to the control group. This limitation was overcome by the study conducted by Lee et al. [30], where both experimental and control groups received the same training duration. Participants in the experimental group had 45-min VR training plus 45 min of standard therapy while the subjects in control group had 90 min of standard therapy. Games from Kinect Sports (Darts, Golf, Table Tennis, and Bowling), Kinect Adventures (Space pop, Rally Ball, and River rush), and Your Shape Fitness Evolved (Virtual smash and Light race) packages were selected for the VR training. Both groups improved over time and maintained this improvement at the 3-month follow-up, however there were no significant differences between the two groups. The experimental group exhibited higher pleasure than the control group.

The VR training of the above studies included Xbox Kinect Commercial games such as Kinect sports like Bowling, Boxing, and Darts, and Kinect adventures games like Rally Ball, 20,000 Leaks, Space Pop, etc. These games have not been designed specifically for rehabilitation. Hence in other studies, the authors used prototype games specific for rehabilitation. For example, Askin et al. [3] deployed two games of KineLabs developed by a research team of Hong Kong Polytechnic University for stroke rehabilitation (Good View Hunting to clean or delete dirty spots and Hong Kong Chef for making food). They randomized chronic stroke patients into two groups; the first group underwent 20 sessions of physical therapy (PT) plus 20 sessions of Kinect-based VR training and the second group received only 20 sessions of PT. Results indicated that both groups had benefited from the intervention training, however there were greater improvements in the group who received the additional VR training. Again, these results may bear some bias due to the nonequivalent amount of rehabilitation. Furthermore, in the randomized controlled trial conducted by Shin et al. [43], chronic hemiparetic stroke of experimental group underwent conventional occupational therapy (OT) plus VR rehabilitation using PrimeSense sensor. The VR training consists of a "rehabilitation training" module that asks the participant to imitate specific motions that are performed by an avatar and "Rehabilitation games" that facilitate rehabilitation exercises using gaming concepts. For the same amount of rehabilitation, the experimental group performed conventional OT only for 20 sessions over 4 weeks. As a result, the group who combined the conventional therapy with the VR training showed significant improvements in some items of SF-36 evaluating the Health-related quality of life; participants had significant improvement in role limitation due to emotional problems compared to baseline, and exhibited significant improvement in role limitation due to physical problems compared to the group having OT alone. In addition, both groups exhibited significant improvements in Hamilton Depression Rating Scale (HAMD) and upper extremity Fugl-Meyer Assessment (FMA) compared to baseline, although no inter-group differences were observed. In the same way, many researchers examined the feasibility and effectiveness of using RGB-D devices for postural stability and balance in people with Parkinson's disease [42], rehabilitation of patients with Multiple Sclerosis [33], balance, mobility skills, and fear of falling in women with fibromyalgia [11], balance, functional mobility and quality of life in geriatric individuals [26], and improving upper limb motor outcomes in children with Cerebral Palsy [49] by deploying either commercial or prototype games. To sum up, most studies suggest that deploying video games using RGB-D device input for rehabilitation is feasible, motivating, and exhibits promising results, however these results cannot be generalized due to the small sample sizes of participants recruited and the restriction of patients profiles, hence more research is needed to include a higher number of participants and tackle long-term effects.

15.3 Methodology

In this section, we present a method for implementing RGB-D serious games for rehabilitation. First, we describe the PROGame framework in order to guarantee that products are developed and validated by following a coherent and systematic method that leads to high-quality serious games. Then, we present a set of detailed guidelines for the specific case of vision-based interactive systems for motor rehabilitation therapy. From guidelines, we deduced that it is important for the user to delete the background in order to avoid distractors, for this reason we present a background subtraction method. Finally, we present 3 different study cases where we used the method to implement different vision-based systems for rehabilitation purposes.

15.3.1 PROGame Framework

Given the interdisciplinary nature of serious games development and based on similarities between serious game development requirements and web application requirements [25], and similarities between serious game for motor rehabilitation implementation and the clinical trial involving new drugs [19], we proposed a new framework for the development of serious games for motor rehabilitation therapy (PROGame) [1]. This framework is a two-dimensional process flow, where the basic development activities (planning and control, modeling, construction, and validation) are structured into three increments. The final activity of the model is a clinical study aimed at demonstrating the suitability of the serious game for the target therapy (see Fig. 15.1).

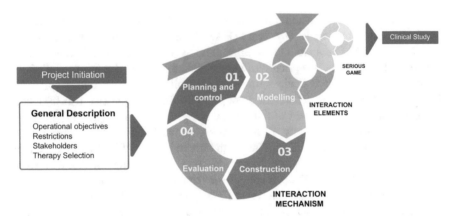

Fig. 15.1 Process flow for serious game development [1]

The first dimension includes three main activities. First in project initiation activity, a detailed specification of the game's requirements and constraints are defined. Then, four basic development activities are performed, adapted from the web application development model. These activities are: planning and control, modeling, construction, and evaluation. Finally, a clinical study is performed to quantify the improvement of a rehabilitation therapy based on types of functional exercises. A successful clinical study requires a definition of the experiment, participants, and measurements according to the final goals and type of the therapy suggested.

1. Project initiation activity: It is an entry point of the project where context, operational objectives, and restrictions for the serious game are identified by engineers and physiotherapists together, resulting in a detailed specification of the game's requirements and constraints.
2. Iterative flow: It contains the following four basic development activities:

    - Planning and control: It aims to achieve incremental project management for the development of serious games.
    - Modeling: It permits the development of models that enable the development team a better understanding of the requirements and design of the serious game.
    - Construction: It consists in producing executable software units mirroring the conceived design. This activity includes the production and testing of the software units that are part of an increment.
    - Evaluation: It aims to find and correct the errors of the serious game before making it available to the patients. It can be done by playing the game, while considering some aspects such as possible and safe interaction, effective therapy, and engaging game.

3. A final clinical study: The objective of a clinical study is quantifying the improvement of a rehabilitation therapy based on types of functional exercises. A successful clinical study requires a definition of the experiment, participants, and measurements according to the final goals and type of the therapy suggested.

The second dimension deals with the incremental development. The three core phases of the clinical trial already described are supported within this dimension. These phases have been included as three different increments: interaction mechanism, interaction elements, and serious game; where interaction mechanism aims to design an interaction mechanism to capture the selected therapy while considering existing technology, and interaction elements are designed in a way that pushes the patients to perform the therapy correctly. Finally, the aim of the final increment (serious game) is to design a serious game that encourages the patient to perform the therapy regularly.

15.3.2 Guidelines for Developing Motor Rehabilitation Serious Games

To ensure a successful serious games development, we were able, through our experience in implementing vision-based serious games for motor rehabilitation, to identify 7 main design issues [23]. These design issues detailed how to define the dimensions of PROGame framework, and in our case the dimensions of vision-based interactive systems for motor rehabilitation therapy and therapeutic measurements:

1. Development Paradigm: Usually engineers and physiotherapists find difficulty when it comes to clearly defining the objectives of serious games and therapy because they use different jargon. Opting for a prototype development paradigm may help in overcoming this problem and ensuring a good communication between the two teams [40].
2. Interaction Mechanism: When transferring an existing therapy to a serious game, the selected rehabilitation therapy becomes the means of interaction with the serious game. As many patients have difficulty in holding a physical device, vision- based interfaces can be used as an input device. These interfaces play a key role in adapting to the users' capabilities and enhancing their perception to the game [46]. An example of vision-based interaction which can be implemented by detecting the users' silhouette, the skin color, or the hand motion is depicted in Fig. 15.2.
3. Interaction Elements: Selecting interaction elements must ensure an optimal level of motivation for the users. It is demonstrated that patients can perform rehabilitation activities faster when the interaction objects are related to themes of their interest [22].
4. Feedback: Feedback is very important in serious games because it allows the users to understand the game, feel in control, and be aware of their current state

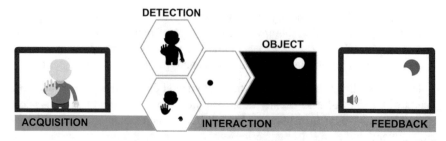

Fig. 15.2 Vision-based interaction which can be implemented by detecting the users' silhouette, the skin color or the hand motion

Fig. 15.3 Visual feedback in a serious game

(see Fig. 15.3). In vision-based systems, the user has no interaction device of reference, hence providing visual and audible feedback is critical [7, 24].

5. Adaptability: Serious game users have different capabilities and characteristics. A good serious game should be adaptable to the skills and evolution of each user by defining a set of configuration parameters that can be customized and adapted to each user. Such parameters include size and position of interaction objects, maximum playing time, mirror effect, contact time, and user distance from the RGB-D sensor.

6. Monitoring: In order to monitor the progress of each user, the system should save user's information, configuration parameters, and patient's performance along the therapy sessions. For example, an xml file for each user can be created and maintained by the game where data like date of the session, level pattern, playing time, user distance from monitor device, and contact time are saved, hence simplifying the monitoring task performed by the therapists. Thus, the system is best designed to be accessed by two different types of users: the patient and the specialist; where each one has different objectives when interacting with the system.

7. Clinical evaluation: A clinical evaluation is conducted in order to see the effectiveness of rehabilitation on the patients. Optimally, a clinical evaluation should

Fig. 15.4   Design intervention using pre and post assessments [1]

define the experiment, the participants, and the measurements according to the goals and type of the therapy. It is recommended to include a pre-assessment and post-assessment of every measurement as presented in Fig. 15.4, a control group, and a larger number of measurements.

15.3.3   Background Subtraction

In this kind of applications, the user can be easily distracted by the scene background as there can be moving elements such as the physiotherapists, or moving objects through a window. Another source of problems are background objects that can be mislead with the interaction objects due to similar colors or shapes. In order to avoid these problems, a background subtraction process based on a Kernel Density Estimation (KDE) model is applied [38] and the background is substituted with a predefined image, see Fig. 15.6.

Low-cost RGB-D devices that are able to capture depth and color images simultaneously at a frame rate up to 30 fps are available off the shelf. Depth information can help to overcome typical problems of color-based algorithms, adding physical information to the background model.

Adding a depth channel to KDE background model is not an obvious process because the depth channel differs in its characteristics from the color channels. In particular, the depth channel has a significant amount of missing information, where the sensor is unable to estimate the depth at certain pixels.

In order to select the regions that belong to the foreground, that is, where the user lies in an image sequence, we use a nonparametric algorithm that is capable to mix the color and depth information in a low-level way using the previous information as the reference to segment the current frame.

The scene modeling consists on a Kernel Density Estimation (KDE) process. Given the last n observations of a pixel, denoted by $\mathbf{x}_i$, $i = 1, \ldots, n$ in the d-dimensional observation space $\mathbf{R}^d$, which enclose the sensor data values, it is possible to estimate the probability density function (pdf) of each pixel with respect to all previously observed values [17].

$$P(\mathbf{x}) = \frac{1}{n}|\mathbf{H}|^{-\frac{1}{2}} \sum_{i=1}^{n} K\left(\mathbf{H}^{-\frac{1}{2}}(\mathbf{x} - \mathbf{x}_i)\right), \qquad (15.1)$$

where K is a multivariate kernel, satisfying $\int K(x)dx = 1$ and $K(u) \geq 0$. $\mathbf{H}$ is the bandwidth matrix, which is a symmetric positive $d \times d$-matrix.

Diagonal matrix bandwidth kernels allow different amounts of smoothing in each of the dimensions and are the most widespread due to computational reasons [47]. The most commonly used kernel density function is the Normal function and in our approach $N(0, \mathbf{H})$ is selected

$$
\mathbf{H} = \begin{pmatrix} \sigma_1^2 & 0 & \cdots & 0 \\ 0 & \sigma_2^2 & \cdots & 0 \\ \vdots & \vdots & \ddots & \vdots \\ 0 & 0 & \cdots & \sigma_d^2 \end{pmatrix}
$$

The final probability density function can be written as

$$
P(\mathbf{x}) = \frac{1}{n} \sum_{i=1}^{n} \prod_{j=1}^{d} \frac{1}{\sqrt{2\pi\sigma_j^2}} e^{-\frac{1}{2}\frac{(x_j - x_{ij})^2}{\sigma_j^2}}. \tag{15.2}
$$

Given this estimate at each pixel, a pixel is considered foreground if its probability is under a certain threshold.

In order to use the previously described scene model with color and depth information in a unified way, we need to perform a special treatment to sensor Absent Depth Observation (ADO). In our approach, we maintain a statistical model to differentiate the ones caused by the scene physical configuration from the other ones caused by the foreground objects.

15.4 Case Studies

PROGame framework is a two-dimensional process flow, where the basic development activities (planning and control, modeling, construction, and validation) are structured into three increments. The final activity of the model is a clinical study aimed at demonstrating the suitability of the serious game for the target therapy. Guidelines for serious games development are more specific defining 7 main issues: development paradigm, interaction mechanism, interaction elements, feedback, adaptability, monitoring, and clinical evaluation. Within this framework and following the guidelines defined, we present the following case studies. Background subtraction was applied so the user can see himself/herself on the screen all the time and interact with the system without distractions.

15.4.1 Functional Reach Test

In order to measure the evolution of a therapy program and be able to adjust it, it is important to measure its clinical outcomes using reliable and valid tests. The functional reach test [15] is one of the most common clinical measures used in measuring balance of an individual by measuring his limits of stability while standing. The test also detects limitations in daily activities and is helpful in detecting the risk of falls. In this test, the user is instructed to stand close to a wall and reach as far as he can, while raising his hand at 90° of shoulder flexion with a closed fist and without taking a step or touching the wall. The result of the test is the distance of reach. The test is performed three times and the average of the last two is considered as the final result. As the use of vision-based interactive applications for rehabilitation is growing, the same RGB-D device used by the patient for rehabilitation can also be used by the physiotherapist for clinical measurements.

15.4.1.1   Proposed System

We transferred the FRT into our experimental system as an interaction mechanism using Microsoft Kinect, thus the maximum distance that a user can reach forward can be measured automatically [4]. Using skeletal tracking information provided by Kinect, the system can measure the FRT in three steps. First, the physiotherapist asks the user to stand close to the wall facing the sensor with the right posture as to perform the FRT. When the physiotherapist confirms that the position performed is correct, the initial position is indicated to the system which stores the users' hand coordinates in that position. Second, the user is asked to reach forward as far as he can; the final position is then validated by the physiotherapist and stored by the system. Third, the system computes the difference between the initial position and the end position, hence the FRT result. The user can see himself and text messages on the screen to inform him about his movement execution (see Fig. 15.5).

15.4.1.2   Experiment

14 healthy adults (11 men; aged between 22 and 48 years) accepted to perform the FRT using the system on one hand and on the standard way on the other hand in order to validate the confidence of the measurements obtained by the system comparing to those obtained by the physiotherapist manually. Each participant used

Fig. 15.5 Screenshot of the experimental system. Left image depicts initial position, right image depicts final position

the experimental system three times and performed the FRT in the standard way three times. To avoid pre-learning effect, the order of the trials was randomly chosen, for example, one can perform the test on the standard way (FRT1), using the experimental system (ES1), ES2, FRT2, ES3, and FRT3. Consequently, a within-subjects design was used with the standard FRT as a control group. A demonstration of how the system works was done before the beginning of the experiment. The measurement used was the distance in cm between the final position and last position for both the experimental system and the standard FRT.

15.4.1.3   Results and Conclusions

The comparison between measures obtained from the experimental system and the standard FRT yielded an average absolute difference of 2.84 cm (± 2.62), and statistically significant differences were found applying a paired t-student test for the data. These preliminary results suggest that Microsoft Kinect is reliable and adequate in calculating the standard Functional Reach test (FRT).

15.4.2   Games for Patients with Cerebral Palsy

Cerebral palsy is the most common motor disability in children characterized by poor coordination and muscle weakness. Many children and adults with CP attend physiotherapy treatment to improve balance and postural control with the ultimate goal of improving their quality of life. In fact, balance control is very important in the performance of the majority of functional tasks. The treatment consists mainly of postural orientation exercises, exercises to strengthen the neck, back, and upper limb musculature, and coordination exercises. As these types of exercises must be repeated weekly and for a long period, both children and adults who are attending the program usually get demotivated and abandon the therapy. Therefore, we designed a serious game that aims to improve balance, increase motivation in users, and achieve high adherence to this long-term therapy [22].

15.4.2.1   Serious Game

The game consists in erasing motivational elements appearing on the screen by changing the user gravity center. We used the Continuously Adaptive Mean Shift (camshift) [6] algorithm to track an object based on color as a fundamental property, then we defined an appropriate mask for each interaction screen and applied the computer vision techniques to determine whether there is any interaction. A pointer was projected on the user's hand, so when the user touches the item displayed on the screen, the part of the interaction object that intersects with the pointer is erased. The contact duration with an element to completely erase it can be customized by

Fig. 15.6 Performance of the system in the ASPACE rehabilitation room

the therapist. Maximum playing time, mirror effect, and user distance can also be customized and adapted to different users.

15.4.2.2   Clinical Study

In order to quantify the rehabilitation improvement using the serious game, we conducted a clinical study in the rehabilitation center of ASPACE in Spain (see Fig. 15.6). Nine adults with CP (range 27–57 years) agreed to undergo the 24-week study. In the study, the participants played the serious game for at least 20 min each session, with an average of one session per week. Repetitions were set according to participants' tolerance for fatigue and physiotherapist's recommendations. All participants were pre- and post-assessed before and after the 24-week study period using Berg Balance Scale (BBS), Functional Reach Test (FRT), and Balance Tinetti Test.

15.4.2.3   Results and Conclusions

Upon completion of the clinical study, significant improvements in balance and gait were noted. There was a significant difference between pre- (29.5 ± 3.9) and post-assessment ($34.1\,\text{cm} \pm 2.2$) results of BBS. In FRT, scores had improved significantly for both hands; right upper limb (pre- ($8.6\,\text{cm} \pm 1.4$) and post-assessment ($10.1\,\text{cm} \pm 2.0$), $p = 0.007$) and left upper limb (pre- ($8.3\,\text{cm} \pm 2.0$ 2.0) and post-assessment ($10.1\,\text{cm} \pm 3.7$), $p = 0.052$). Furthermore, results of both Tinetti Balance section (TBS) and Tinetti gait section (TGS) were promising, resulting in a significant difference between pre- ($16.0\,\mathrm{cm} \pm 4.0$) and post-assessment ($21.0\,\mathrm{cm} \pm 2.8$) measures of Total Tinetti Score (TTS). Results showed also that motivation and adherence improved, and users were interested in continuing the rehabilitation with games after the end of the study.

In conclusion, results indicate that it is feasible to use interactive serious games in therapy programs for adults with cerebral palsy to improve motivation and thereby enhance balance and gait motor performance.

15.4.3   Fall Prevention Games for Elderly People

Elderly people are prone to falls. However, it has been demonstrated that exercising and physical activity help in reducing the risk of falls. The existing therapy exercises for fall prevention include reaching in different directions, small and large lateral steps, weight shifting to both sides, neck movements (flexion, extension, lateral flexion, and rotation), shoulder movements (flexion, extension, adduction and abduction), trunk movements (flexion, extension, lateral flexion, and rotation), knee movements (flexion and extension), and hip movements (flexion, extension, rotation, adduction, and abduction) [39, 48]. Based on the framework and guidelines detailed above, we transferred these exercises into a set of vision-based serious games for elderly people [5].

15.4.3.1   Serious Games

As presented in Fig. 15.7, we designed and developed three serious games using Unity and Microsoft Kinect for older adults to train their balance and postural control, thus minimizing their risk of falls:

- Reach game: The user has to move his centre of mass (COM) in order to reach with his hands one of the five balls located on his user plan, two symmetric items are added on the level of hips that can be eliminated by doing weight shifting movements. Once the user touches a ball, it disappears and reappears after a determined time set by the physiotherapist according to the user's speed.
- HitIt: Soccer balls fall randomly within the same plan of the user. To hit them, the user needs to make lateral steps, and touch them with his head when they are at his level. The game can be also played in a seated position. The user has to make lateral movements of the trunk to be able to touch the elements with his head.
- WatchOut: In contrast to HitIt game, here the user has to move laterally in order to escape falling eggs instead of catching them. Falling items fall randomly within the same plan of the user with adaptable falling rate and speed.

Fig. 15.7 Three examples of fall prevention games. Top image depicts the WatchOut game. Left image illustrates the Reach game, right image details the HitIt game

15.4.3.2   Case Study

Two participants (age: 78 and 72 years) were recruited from elderly house of Manouba in Tunisia. Along a period of 5 weeks, each participant underwent one 30-min session per day at a rate of 3 days a week. The rehabilitation program was divided between the three games, where the duration of each game was set by the therapist according to its understanding and its acceptability by the participants. Participants could have a break time between 3 and 6 min each 5 min of play according to their fatigue level. Balance was assessed using the Tinetti balance test as a pre-assessment and post-assessment test. Other measurements such as adherence, game scores, and adverse events were noted along the intervention. Gaming was assisted by an occupational therapist and monitored by the research team.

15.4.3.3   Results and Conclusions

The two participants attended 86.6% of the sessions with an average 30-min length each of which ensured a very high adherence. Plus, they both reported enjoyment during the playtime. For Tinetti scores, they showed a similar trend; there was an improvement of 4 points in the balance section score, while almost no difference was noted in the gait section. In fact, one participant moved from high risk for falls range to the risk for falls range, while the other participant stayed at high risk for falls range [13, 35]. Regarding the game score, it improved over time although there were no significant differences between the two participants nor between the scores at the beginning and end of the intervention. Finally, no adverse effects were registered during the sessions.

These findings, despite the small sample size, suggest that game-based rehabilitation can be useful to improve balance in elderly people and can be incorporated in fall prevention programs under the supervision of physiotherapists.

15.5   Conclusion

In this chapter, we presented an overall overview of the use of RGB-D-based interactive systems in serious games for motor rehabilitation and therapeutic measures.

First, we performed a systematic review from 2007 onwards where we identified 49 articles which we quality assessed using Downs and Black [14] and analyzed the top 10 for this chapter.

Next, we focused on the design of RGB-D-based serious games for health purposes. We presented the PROGame framework, a two-dimensional incremental process flow for serious game development for motor rehabilitation therapy. Then, we developed specific guidelines to ensure a successful RGB-D therapeutic serious games development, consisting of 7 main design issues.

After that, we described a background subtraction process based on a Kernel Density Estimation, to avoid the patient being distracted by the scene background as there can be moving elements such as the physiotherapists, or moving objects through a window.

Finally, we presented three different case studies where we applied the presented method. First, we presented an interactive system based on RGB-D to calculate the Functional Reach Test (FRT), one of the most widely used balance clinical measurements. We conducted a validation experiment in which results showed that there are no statistically significant differences with manual FRT. Second, we described an RGB-D interactive system to improve the balance and postural control of adults with cerebral palsy. We conducted a 24-week physiotherapy intervention program after which patients moved from high fall risk to moderate fall risk according to the Tinetti Balance Test. Third, we showed three RGB-D serious games to improve the balance and postural control in elderly people. We conducted a 5-week physiotherapy intervention program and the patients showed an improvement of 4 points in the total score of Tinetti Balance Test over the study period.

About future research directions of serious games for motor rehabilitation, we want to remark that the studies often discuss the results of a clinical trial, but most of them do not conduct follow-ups. The fact of avoiding to study a long-term effectiveness could delay their implementation on real environments.

Acknowledgements The authors acknowledge the Ministerio de Economía, Industria y Competitividad (MINECO), the Agencia Estatal de Investigación (AEI), and the European Regional Development Funds (ERDF) for their support to the project TIN2016-81143-R (MINECO/AEI/ERDF, EU). Ines Ayed benefited from the fellowship FPI/2039/2017 from the Vicepresidència i Conselleria d'Innovació, Recerca i Turisme del Govern de les Illes Balears.

References

1. Alcover EA, Jaume-i Capó A, Moyà-Alcover B (2018) PROGame: a process framework for serious game development for motor rehabilitation therapy. PloS One 13(5):e0197,383
2. Anderson F, Annett M, Bischof WF (2010) Lean on Wii: physical rehabilitation with virtual reality Wii peripherals. Stud Health Technol Inform 154(154):229–234
3. Aşkın A, Atar E, Koçyiğit H, Tosun A (2018) Effects of Kinect-based virtual reality game training on upper extremity motor recovery in chronic stroke. Somatosens Mot Res 35(1):25–32
4. Ayed I, Moyà-Alcover B, Martínez-Bueso P, Varona J, Ghazel A, Jaume-i Capó A (2017) Validación de dispositivos RGBD para medir terapéuticamente el equilibrio: el test de alcance funcional con Microsoft Kinect. Revista Iberoamericana de Automática e Informática Industrial RIAI 14(1):115–120
5. Ayed I, Ghazel A, Jaume-i Capó A, Moya-Alcover G, Varona J, Martínez-Bueso P (2018) Feasibility of Kinect-based games for balance rehabilitation: a case study. J Healthc Eng
6. Bradski GR (1998) Computer vision face tracking for use in a perceptual user interface
7. Burke JW, McNeill M, Charles DK, Morrow PJ, Crosbie JH, McDonough SM (2009) Optimising engagement for stroke rehabilitation using serious games. Vis Comput 25(12):1085
8. Cippitelli E, Gasparrini S, Gambi E, Spinsante S (2014) A depth-based joints estimation algorithm for get up and go test using Kinect. In: 2014 IEEE international conference on consumer electronics (ICCE), pp 226–227. IEEE
9. Clark RA, Pua YH, Bryant AL, Hunt MA (2013) Validity of the Microsoft Kinect for providing lateral trunk lean feedback during gait retraining. Gait Posture 38(4):1064–1066
10. Cogollor JM, Hughes C, Ferre M, Rojo J, Hermsdörfer J, Wing A, Campo S (2012) Handmade task tracking applied to cognitive rehabilitation. Sensors 12(10):14214–14231
11. Collado-Mateo D, Dominguez-Muñoz FJ, Adsuar JC, Merellano-Navarro E, Gusi N (2017) Exergames for women with fibromyalgia: a randomised controlled trial to evaluate the effects on mobility skills, balance and fear of falling. PeerJ 5:e3211
12. Da Gama A, Chaves T, Figueiredo L, Teichrieb V (2012) Guidance and movement correction based on therapeutics movements for motor rehabilitation support systems. In: 2012 14th symposium on virtual and augmented reality, pp 191–200. IEEE
13. del Nogal ML, González-Ramírez A, Palomo-Iloro A (2005) Evaluación del riesgo de caídas. protocolos de valoración clínica. Revista Española de Geriatría y Gerontología 40:54–63
14. Downs SH, Black N (1998) The feasibility of creating a checklist for the assessment of the methodological quality both of randomised and non-randomised studies of health care interventions. J Epidemiol Community Health 52(6):377–384
15. Duncan PW, Weiner DK, Chandler J, Studenski S (1990) Functional reach: a new clinical measure of balance. J Gerontol 45(6):M192–M197
16. Durfee WK, Savard L, Weinstein S (2007) Technical feasibility of teleassessments for rehabilitation. IEEE Trans Neural Syst Rehabil Eng 15(1):23–29
17. Elgammal A, Harwood D, Davis L (2000) Non-parametric model for background subtraction. In: European conference on computer vision, pp 751–767. Springer
18. Flores E, Tobon G, Cavallaro E, Cavallaro FI, Perry JC, Keller T (2008) Improving patient motivation in game development for motor deficit rehabilitation. In: Proceedings of the 2008 international conference on advances in computer entertainment technology, pp 381–384. ACM

19. Friedman LM, Furberg C, DeMets DL, Reboussin D, Granger CB (1998) Fundamentals of clinical trials, vol 3. Springer, Berlin
20. Galen SS, Pardo V, Wyatt D, Diamond A, Brodith V, Pavlov A (2015) Validity of an interactive functional reach test. Games Health J 4(4):278–284
21. Hailey D, Roine R, Ohinmaa A, Dennett L (2011) Evidence of benefit from telerehabilitation in routine care: a systematic review. J Telemed Telecare 17(6):281–287
22. Jaume-i Capó A, Martínez-Bueso P, Moya-Alcover B, Varona J (2014) Interactive rehabilitation system for improvement of balance therapies in people with cerebral palsy. IEEE Trans Neural Syst Rehabil Eng 22(2):419–427
23. Jaume-i Capó A, Moyà-Alcover B, Varona J (2014) Design issues for vision-based motor-rehabilitation serious games. Technologies of inclusive well-being, pp 13–24. Springer, Berlin
24. Jung Y, Yeh SC, Stewart J (2006) Tailoring virtual reality technology for stroke rehabilitation: a human factors design. In: CHI'06 extended abstracts on human factors in computing systems, pp 929–934. ACM
25. Kappel G, Pröll B, Reich S, Retschitzegger W (2006) Web engineering. Wiley, New York
26. Karahan AY, Tok F, Taskin H, Küçüksaraç S, Basaran A, Yildirim P (2015) Effects of exergames on balance, functional mobility, and quality of life of geriatrics versus home exercise programme: randomized controlled study. Cent Eur J Public Health 23:S14
27. Keays S, Bullock-Saxton J, Newcombe P, Bullock M (2006) The effectiveness of a pre-operative home-based physiotherapy programme for chronic anterior cruciate ligament deficiency. Physiother Res Int 11(4):204–218
28. Kitchenham B (2004) Procedures for performing systematic reviews. Keele, UK, Keele University vol 33, pp 1–26
29. Lange B, Koenig S, McConnell E, Chang CY, Juang R, Suma E, Bolas M, Rizzo A (2012) Interactive game-based rehabilitation using the Microsoft Kinect. In: Virtual reality short papers and posters (VRW), 2012 IEEE, pp 171–172. IEEE
30. Lee HC, Huang CL, Ho SH, Sung WH (2017) The effect of a virtual reality game intervention on balance for patients with stroke: a randomized controlled trial. Games Health J 6(5):303–311
31. Lee SH, Yoon C, Chung SG, Kim HC, Kwak Y, Park HW, Kim K (2015) Measurement of shoulder range of motion in patients with adhesive capsulitis using a Kinect. PloS One 10(6):e0129,398
32. Lourido BP, Gelabert SV (2008) La perspectiva comunitaria en la fisioterapia domiciliaria: una revisión. Fisioterapia 30(5):231–237
33. Lozano-Quilis JA, Gil-Gómez H, Gil-Gómez JA, Albiol-Pérez S, Palacios-Navarro G, Fardoun HM, Mashat AS (2014) Virtual rehabilitation for multiple sclerosis using a Kinect-based system: randomized controlled trial. JMIR Serious Games 2(2)
34. Maclean N, Pound P, Wolfe C, Rudd A (2002) The concept of patient motivation: a qualitative analysis of stroke professionals' attitudes. Stroke 33(2):444–448
35. Maki BE, Sibley KM, Jaglal SB, Bayley M, Brooks D, Fernie GR, Flint AJ, Gage W, Liu BA, McIlroy WE et al (2011) Reducing fall risk by improving balance control: development, evaluation and knowledge-translation of new approaches. J Saf Res 42(6):473–485
36. Mehta SP, Roy JS (2011) Systematic review of home physiotherapy after hip fracture surgery. J Rehabil Med 43(6):477–480
37. Mentiplay BF, Perraton LG, Bower KJ, Pua YH, McGaw R, Heywood S, Clark RA (2015) Gait assessment using the Microsoft Xbox one Kinect: concurrent validity and inter-day reliability of spatiotemporal and kinematic variables. J Biomech 48(10):2166–2170
38. Moya-Alcover G, Elgammal A, Jaume-i-Capó A, Varona J (2017) Modeling depth for nonparametric foreground segmentation using RGBD devices. Pattern Recognit Lett 96:76–85
39. Neumann DA (2013) Kinesiology of the musculoskeletal system-e-book: foundations for rehabilitation. Elsevier Health Sciences
40. Overmyer SP (1991) Revolutionary vs. evolutionary rapid prototyping: balancing software productivity and HCI design concerns. Center of excellence in command, control, communications and intelligence (C3I), vol 4400. George Mason University

41. Sandlund M, McDonough S, Häger-Ross C (2009) Interactive computer play in rehabilitation of children with sensorimotor disorders: a systematic review. Dev Med Child Neurol 51(3):173–179
42. Shih MC, Wang RY, Cheng SJ, Yang YR (2016) Effects of a balance-based exergaming intervention using the Kinect sensor on posture stability in individuals with parkinson's disease: a single-blinded randomized controlled trial. J Neuroeng Rehabil 13(1):78
43. Shin JH, Park SB, Jang SH (2015) Effects of game-based virtual reality on health-related quality of life in chronic stroke patients: a randomized, controlled study. Comput Biol Med 63:92–98
44. Sin H, Lee G (2013) Additional virtual reality training using Xbox Kinect in stroke survivors with hemiplegia. Am J Phys Med Rehabil 92(10):871–880
45. Türkbey TA, Kutlay Ş, Gök H (2017) Clinical feasibility of Xbox KinectTM training for stroke rehabilitation: a single-blind randomized controlled pilot study. J Rehabil Med 49(1):22–29
46. Varona J, Jaume-i Capó A, Gonzèlez J, Perales FJ (2008) Toward natural interaction through visual recognition of body gestures in real-time. Interact Comput 21(1–2):3–10
47. Wand MP, Jones MC (1993) Comparison of smoothing parameterizations in bivariate kernel density estimation. J Am Stat Assoc 88(422):520–528. https://doi.org/10.1080/01621459.1993.10476303
48. Zhang M, Fan Y (2014) Computational biomechanics of the musculoskeletal system. CRC Press, Boca Raton
49. Zoccolillo L, Morelli D, Cincotti F, Muzzioli L, Gobbetti T, Paolucci S, Iosa M (2015) Videogame based therapy performed by children with cerebral palsy: a cross-over randomized controlled trial and a cross-sectional quantitative measure of physical activity. Eur J Phys Rehabil Med 51(6):669–676

Chapter 16
Real-Time Hand Pose Estimation Using Depth Camera

Liuhao Ge, Junsong Yuan and Nadia Magnenat Thalmann

Abstract In recent years, we have witnessed a steady growth of the research in real-time 3D hand pose estimation with depth cameras, since this technology plays an important role in various human–computer interaction applications. In this chapter, we first review existing techniques and systems for real-time 3D hand pose estimation. Then, we will discuss two point-set-based methods for 3D hand pose estimation from depth images: (1) point-set-based holistic regression method that directly regresses holistic 3D hand pose; (2) point-set-based point-wise regression method that generates dense outputs for robust 3D hand pose estimation. Extensive experiments are conducted to evaluate the effectiveness of these two methods. We will also discuss the limitations and advantages of the proposed methods.

16.1 Introduction

In recent years, we have witnessed a rapid growth in virtual reality (VR) and augmented reality (AR) applications. Traditional mechanical devices, such as keyboards, mice, and joysticks, are cumbersome and unsuitable for immersive interactions in VR/AR applications. Can users directly use their bare hands to naturally interact with the virtual objects in the VR/AR environment? Thanks to the development of camera techniques and computer vision, vision-based hand pose estimation has become an important and promising technology for human–computer interaction [1, 2].

L. Ge · N. Magnenat Thalmann
Institute for Media Innovation, Nanyang Technological University Singapore,
Singapore 637553, Singapore
e-mail: ge0001ao@e.ntu.edu.sg

N. Magnenat Thalmann
e-mail: nadiathalmann@ntu.edu.sg

J. Yuan (✉)
Department of Computer Science and Engineering, State University
of New York at Buffalo, Buffalo, NY 14260-2500, USA
e-mail: jsyuan@buffalo.edu

© Springer Nature Switzerland AG 2019   355
P. L. Rosin et al. (eds.), *RGB-D Image Analysis and Processing*,
Advances in Computer Vision and Pattern Recognition,
https://doi.org/10.1007/978-3-030-28603-3_16

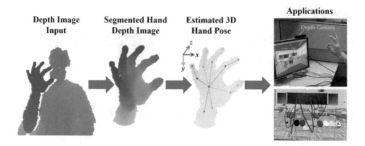

Fig. 16.1 Overview of 3D hand pose estimation from depth images. The input is a depth image; human hand is segmented from the depth image for hand pose estimation; the output is a set of 3D hand joint locations representing the 3D hand pose. The estimated 3D hand pose can be applied in various applications. The two snapshots of applications on the left are from our self-built systems

With the emergence of commercial depth cameras in the past 10 years, e.g., Microsoft Kinetic, Intel RealSense, Primesense Carmine, many research works have focused on 3D hand pose estimation from depth images [20, 25, 27, 42, 53, 58, 68, 72, 73], in which the 3D locations of hand joints are estimated. Compared with traditional cameras that capture intensity or color in the scene, depth cameras are robust in low-light environment, can capture 3D spatial information of the object and are invariant to color and texture. These properties make depth camera suitable for robust 3D hand pose estimation.

In this chapter, we investigate the problem of 3D hand pose estimation from depth images. As presented in Fig. 16.1, the input is a depth image capturing the hand gesture. Human hand is segmented from the input depth image for hand pose estimation. The output is a set of 3D hand joint locations representing the 3D hand pose. The estimated 3D hand pose can be used for various applications such as virtual object manipulation, virtual 3D drawing, virtual keyboard, etc.

Although 3D hand pose estimation from depth images has aroused a lot of research attention in recent years, it is still challenging to achieve efficient and robust hand pose estimation performance. First, estimating 3D hand pose from depth images is a high-dimensional and nonlinear regression problem. Second, hand pose in single depth images often suffers from severe self-occlusion problem. Third, the depth images captured from range sensors are usually noisy and may have data missing. In this chapter, we aim at solving these challenges for robust 3D hand pose estimation from single depth images. Convolutional Neural Networks (CNNs)-based methods for 3D hand pose estimation with depth cameras usually take 2D depth images as input, which cannot fully utilize the 3D spatial information in the depth image. To better leverage the depth information, we propose to directly take the 3D point cloud as input to the neural network for 3D hand pose estimation.

The major contributions of this chapter include the following:

- A point-set-based holistic regression method for 3D hand pose estimation is presented. The 3D point cloud extracted from the depth image is directly taken as network input to holistically regress 3D hand joint locations. To handle variations of hand global orientations, the hand point cloud is normalized with more consistent global orientations.

- A point-set-based point-wise regression method for 3D hand pose estimation is presented. The point-wise regression network directly takes the 3D point cloud as input and generates heat-maps as well as unit vector fields on the input point cloud. A post-processing method is proposed to infer 3D hand joint locations from the estimated heat-maps and unit vector fields.
- We conduct comprehensive experiments on three challenging hand pose datasets [47, 50, 58] to evaluate our methods. Experimental results show that our methods can achieve superior accuracy performance in real time.

The remainder of this chapter is organized as follows. Section 16.2 presents a literature review on hand pose estimation methods and related datasets. The point-set-based holistic regression method is presented in Sect. 16.3. Section 16.4 presents our point-set-based point-wise regression method. Section 16.5 presents extensive experiments to evaluate the effectiveness of our methods. The conclusions are drawn in Sect. 16.6.

16.2 Literature Review

Since directly using hand as an interface for human–computer interaction is very attractive but challenging, a lot of research works have focused on hand pose estimation in the past 30 years [7, 8, 11, 28, 31, 35, 58, 64, 66, 67, 72]. Methods for 3D hand pose estimation from depth images can be categorized into model-driven approaches, data-driven approaches, and hybrid approaches [48].

Model-driven approaches fit an explicit deformable hand model to depth images by minimizing a handcrafted cost function. The commonly used optimization methods are Particle Swarm Optimization (PSO) [28], Iterative Closest Point (ICP) [49, 75], and their combination [34]. Many hand models have been proposed. Oikonomidis et al. [29] propose a polygonal mesh hand model using geometric primitives. Qian et al. [34] approximate the 3D hand model using 48 spheres. Sridhar et al. [45] propose a Gaussian mixture model of hand which is also applied in [46, 70]. Melax et al. [21] propose to use a rigid-body representation of the hand model. Taylor et al. [53] create the hand model based on linear blend skinning and approximate loop subdivision, which is also applied in [16, 59]. Tkach et al. [55] propose to use sphere-meshes as the 3D hand model. Romero et al. [40] propose a realistic hand model which can capture nonrigid shape of hand pose and is learned from 3D scans of hands. Joo et al. [14] use a rigged hand mesh as the hand model for total capture of human.

However, there are some shortcomings for the model-driven methods. For instance, some model-driven methods usually need to explicitly define the anatomical size and hand motion constraints of the hand to match to the input depth image. Also, due to the high-dimensional hand pose parameters, they can be sensitive to initialization for the iterative model-fitting procedure to converge to the optimal pose.

In contrast to model-driven methods, the data-driven methods do not need the explicit specification of the hand size and motion constraints. Rather, such information is automatically encoded in the training data. Therefore, many recent methods are built upon such a scheme [5, 27, 47, 51, 52, 68].

Data-driven approaches learn a mapping from depth image to hand pose from training data. Some early works [38, 39, 41] focus on example-based method that searches the most similar images in a dataset to the input hand image, but cannot work well in high- dimensional space. Inspired by the pioneering work [43] of human pose estimation, [15, 18, 19, 47, 50, 63, 68] apply random forests and their variants as a discriminative model. In [68], the authors propose to use the random forest to directly regress for the hand joint angles from depth images, in which a set of spatial-voting pixels cast their votes for hand pose independently and their votes are clustered into a set of candidates. The optimal one is determined by a verification stage with a hand model. A similar method is presented in [52], which further adopts transfer learning to make up for the inconsistency between synthesis and real-world data. As the estimations from random forest can be ambiguous for complex hand postures, pre-learned hand pose priors are sometimes utilized to better fuse independently predicted hand joint distributions [17, 20]. In [47], the cascaded pose regression algorithm [6] is adapted to the problem of hand pose estimation. Particularly, the authors propose to first predict the root joints of the hand skeleton, based on which the rest joints are updated. In this way, the hand pose constraints can be well preserved during pose regression.

Limited by the handcrafted features, data-driven methods based on random forests are difficult to outperform current CNN-based methods in hand pose estimation. With the success of deep neural networks in various computer vision tasks and the emergence of large hand pose datasets [47, 50, 58, 72, 73], many of the recent 3D hand pose estimation methods are based on CNNs [3, 4, 9, 10, 12, 24, 27, 58, 61, 71]. However, deep learning based methods require large amount of training data to train the deep neural network. In addition, it is not easy to explicitly utilize the hand model as a prior in the neural networks.

Tompson et al. [58] first propose to apply CNNs in 3D hand pose estimation. They use CNNs to generate heat-maps representing the 2D probability distributions of hand joints in the depth image, and recover 3D hand pose from estimated heat-maps and corresponding depth values using model-based inverse kinematics. Oberweger et al. [24, 26] instead directly regress 3D coordinates of hand joints or a lower dimensional embedding of 3D pose from depth images. They also propose a feedback loop network [27] to iteratively refine the 3D hand pose. Zhou et al. [74] propose to directly regress hand model parameters from depth images. Sinha et al. [44] extract activation features from CNNs to synchronize hand poses in nearest neighbors by using the matrix completion algorithm. Ye et al. [71] propose a spatial attention network with a hierarchical hybrid method for hand pose estimation. Guo et al. [12] propose a region ensemble network that directly regresses 3D hand pose from depth images. Chen et al. [3] improve [12] through iterative refinement. Wan et al. [62] propose a dense pixel-wise estimation method that applies an hourglass network to generate 2D and 3D heat-maps as well as 3D unit vector fields, from which the 3D hand joint locations can be inferred. Moon et al. [22] propose a voxel-to-voxel prediction method that estimates per-voxel probability in a 3D volume of each hand joint using a 3D CNN. Rad et al. [36] consider the problem of transfer learning between synthetic images and real images. They map the real image features to the feature space of synthetic images. This method can leverage the large synthetic hand pose dataset and limited real data with hand pose annotation.

16.3   Point-Set-Based Holistic Regression for 3D Hand Pose Estimation

16.3.1   Overview

In this chapter, we propose a point-set-based holistic regression method for 3D hand pose estimation from single depth images, as illustrated in Fig. 16.2. Specifically, we first detect hand region from the original input depth image, then crop the hand from the original image. The cropped hand depth image is converted to a set of 3D points; the 3D point cloud of the hand is downsampled and normalized in an oriented bounding box to make our method robust to various hand orientations. The hierarchical PointNet [33] takes the 3D coordinates of normalized points attached to the estimated surface normals as the input, and holistically regresses a low-dimensional representation of the 3D hand joint locations which are then recovered in the camera coordinate system. We estimate the surface normals by performing PCA on the nearest neighboring points of the query point in the sampled point cloud to fit a local

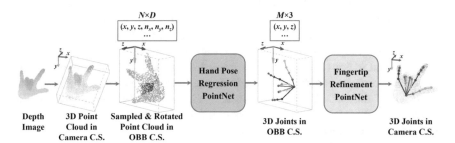

Fig. 16.2 Overview of our proposed Hand PointNet-based method with holistic regression for 3D hand pose estimation in single depth images. We normalize the 3D point cloud in an oriented bounding box (OBB) to make the network input robust to global hand rotation. The 3D coordinates of sampled and normalized points attached with estimated surface normals are fed into a hierarchical PointNet [33], which is trained in an end-to-end manner, to extract hand features and regress 3D joint locations. The fingertip refinement PointNet can further improve the estimation accuracy of fingertip locations

plane [13]. The fingertip locations are further refined by a basic PointNet, which takes the neighboring points of the estimated fingertip location as input.

16.3.2 PointNet Revisited

Basic PointNet: PointNet [32] is a type of neural network that directly takes a set of points as the input and is able to extract discriminative features of the point cloud. Each input point $x_i \in \mathbb{R}^D$ $(i = 1, \ldots, N)$ is mapped into a C-dimensional feature vector through multi-layer perceptron (MLP) networks, of which the weights across different points are shared. A vector max operator is applied to aggregate N point feature vectors into a global feature vector that is invariant to permutations of input points. Finally, the C-dimensional global feature vector is mapped into an F-dimensional output vector using MLP networks. It has been proved in [32] that PointNet has the ability to approximate arbitrary continuous set functions, given enough neurons in the network. Mathematically, given a set of input points $X = \{x_i\}_{i=1}^N \in \mathcal{X}$, a continuous set function $f : \mathcal{X} \to \mathbb{R}^F$ can be arbitrarily approximated by the PointNet, as proved in [32].

$$f(x_1, x_2, \ldots, x_N) \approx \gamma \left(\underset{i=1,\ldots,N}{\mathrm{MAX}} \{h(x_i)\} \right), \tag{16.1}$$

where γ and h are MLP networks, MAX is a vector max operator.

Hierarchical PointNet: The main limitation of the basic PointNet is that it cannot capture local structures of the point cloud in a hierarchical way. To address this problem, Qi et al. [33] proposed a hierarchical PointNet which has better generalization ability due to its hierarchical feature extraction architecture. In this work, we exploit the hierarchical PointNet for 3D hand pose estimation. The hierarchical PointNet consists of L point set abstraction levels. At the lth level $(l = 1, \ldots, L - 1)$, N_l points are selected as centroids of local regions; the k-nearest neighbors of the centroid point are grouped as a local region; a basic PointNet with shared weights across different local regions is applied to extract a C_l-dimensional feature of each local region, which represents the geometry information of the local region; N_l centroid points with d-dimensional coordinates and C_l-dimensional features are fed into the next level. At the last level, a global point cloud feature is abstracted from the whole input points of this level by using a basic PointNet.

16.3.3 Point Cloud Normalization

The hand depth image is first converted to a set of 3D points using the depth camera's intrinsic parameters. The 3D point set is then downsampled to N points.

One challenge of 3D hand pose estimation is the large variation in global orientation of the hand. To make our method robust to various hand orientations, we normalize the hand point cloud. The objective for hand point cloud normalization is to transform the original hand point cloud into a canonical coordinate system in which the global orientations of the transformed hand point clouds are as consistent as possible. This normalization step ensures that our method is robust to variations in hand global orientations.

In this work, we propose a simple yet effective method to normalize the 3D hand point cloud in OBB, instead of applying any additional networks to estimate the hand global orientation or transform the hand point cloud. OBB is a tightly fitting bounding box of the input point cloud [60]. The orientation of OBB is determined by performing principal component analysis (PCA) on the 3D coordinates of input points. The x, y, z axes of the OBB coordinate system (C.S.) are aligned with the eigenvectors of input points' covariance matrix, which correspond to eigenvalues from largest to smallest, respectively. The original points in camera C.S. are first transformed into OBB C.S., then these points are shifted to have zero mean and scaled to a unit size:

$$
\begin{aligned}
\boldsymbol{p}^{obb} &= \left(\boldsymbol{R}_{obb}^{cam}\right)^{T} \cdot \boldsymbol{p}^{cam}, \\
\boldsymbol{p}^{nor} &= \left(\boldsymbol{p}^{obb} - \bar{\boldsymbol{p}}^{obb}\right)\big/ L_{obb},
\end{aligned}
\tag{16.2}
$$

where $\boldsymbol{R}_{obb}^{cam}$ is the rotation matrix of the OBB in camera C.S.; $\boldsymbol{p}^{cam}$ and $\boldsymbol{p}^{obb}$ are 3D coordinates of point $\boldsymbol{p}$ in camera C.S. and OBB C.S., respectively; $\bar{\boldsymbol{p}}^{obb}$ is the centroid of point cloud $\left\{\boldsymbol{p}_i^{obb}\right\}_{i=1}^{N}$; L_{obb} is the maximum edge length of OBB; $\boldsymbol{p}^{nor}$ is the normalized 3D coordinate of point $\boldsymbol{p}$ in the normalized OBB C.S.

During training, the ground truth 3D joint locations in camera C.S. also apply the transformation in Eq. 16.2 to obtain the 3D joint locations in the normalized OBB C.S. During testing, the estimated 3D joint locations in the normalized OBB C.S. $\hat{\boldsymbol{\phi}}_m^{nor}$ are transformed back to those in camera C.S. $\hat{\boldsymbol{\phi}}_m^{cam}$ ($m = 1, \ldots, M$):

$$
\hat{\boldsymbol{\phi}}_m^{cam} = \boldsymbol{R}_{obb}^{cam} \cdot \left(L_{obb} \cdot \hat{\boldsymbol{\phi}}_m^{nor} + \bar{\boldsymbol{p}}^{obb}\right).
\tag{16.3}
$$

16.3.4 Holistic Regression Network

We design a 3D hand pose regression network which can be trained in an end-to-end manner. The input of the hand pose regression network is a set of normalized points $\boldsymbol{X}^{nor} = \left\{\boldsymbol{x}_i^{nor}\right\}_{i=1}^{N} = \left\{\left(\boldsymbol{p}_i^{nor}, \boldsymbol{n}_i^{nor}\right)\right\}_{i=1}^{N}$, where $\boldsymbol{p}_i^{nor}$ is the 3D coordinate of the normalized point, and $\boldsymbol{n}_i^{nor}$ is the corresponding 3D surface normal, which is approximated by performing PCA on the nearest neighboring points of the query point in the sampled point cloud to fit a local plane [13]. These N points are then fed into a hierarchical PointNet [33], which has three point set abstraction levels. The first two levels group input points into $N_1 = 512$ and $N_2 = 128$ local regions, respectively. Each local region contains $k = 64$ points. These two levels extract $C_1 = 1280$- and $C_2 = 256$-dimensional features for each local region, respectively. The last level extracts a 1024-dimensional global feature vector which is mapped to an F-dimensional output vector by three fully connected layers. Each MLP network is composed of several fully connected layers. All fully connected layers are followed by batch normalization and ReLU except for the last layer of the last MLP network. We do not use dropout layer in our implementation.

Since the degree of freedom of human hand is usually lower than the dimension of 3D hand joint locations $(3 \times M)$, the PointNet is designed to output an F-dimensional $(F < 3 \times M)$ representation of hand pose to enforce hand pose constraint and alleviate infeasible hand pose estimations, which is similar to [26]. In the training phase, given T training samples with the normalized point cloud and the corresponding ground truth 3D joint locations $\left\{\left(X_t^{nor}, \boldsymbol{\Phi}_t^{nor}\right)\right\}_{t=1}^{T}$, we minimize the following objective function:

$$w^* = \arg \min_{w} \sum_{t=1}^{T} \left\| \boldsymbol{\alpha}_t - \mathcal{F}\left(X_t^{nor}, w\right) \right\|^2 + \lambda \|w\|^2 \qquad (16.4)$$

where w denotes network parameters; $\mathcal{F}$ represents the hand pose regression Point-Net; λ is the regularization strength; $\boldsymbol{\alpha}_t$ is an F-dimensional projection of $\boldsymbol{\Phi}_t^{nor}$. By performing PCA on the ground truth 3D joint locations in the training dataset, we can obtain $\boldsymbol{\alpha}_t = E^T \cdot \left(\boldsymbol{\Phi}_t^{nor} - u\right)$, where E denotes the principal components, and u is the empirical mean. During testing, the estimated 3D joint locations are reconstructed from the network outputs:

$$\hat{\boldsymbol{\Phi}}^{nor} = E \cdot \mathcal{F}\left(X^{nor}, w^*\right) + u. \qquad (16.5)$$

16.3.5 Fingertip Refinement Network

To further improve the estimation accuracy of fingertip locations, we design a fingertip refinement network which takes K nearest neighboring points of the estimated fingertip location as input and outputs the refined 3D location of the fingertip. Note that we only refine fingertips for straightened fingers. We first check each finger is bent or straightened by calculating joint angles using the joint locations. For the straightened finger, we find the K nearest neighboring points of the fingertip location in the original point cloud with upper limit of point number to ensure real-time performance. The K nearest neighboring points are then normalized in OBB, which is similar to the method in Sect. 16.3.3. A basic PointNet takes these normalized points as input and outputs the refined fingertip 3D location. During the training stage, we use the ground truth joint locations to calculate joint angles; for the fingertip location used in the nearest neighbor search, we add a 3D random offset within a radius of $r = 15$ mm to the ground truth fingertip location in order to make the fingertip refinement network more robust to inaccurate fingertip estimations. During the testing stage, we use joint locations estimated by the hand pose regression network for calculating joint angles and searching nearest neighboring points.

16.4   Point-Set-Based Point-Wise Regression for 3D Hand Pose Estimation

16.4.1   Overview

In Sect. 16.3, we propose to holistically regress 3D coordinates of hand joints from point sets with the help of PointNet [32, 33]. However, the direct mapping from input representation to 3D hand pose is highly nonlinear and difficult to learn, which makes the holistical regression method difficult to achieve high accuracy [57]. An alternative way is to generate a set of heat-maps representing the probability distributions of joint locations on 2D image plane [58], which has been successfully applied in 2D human pose estimation [23, 65]. However, it is nontrivial to lift 2D heat-maps to 3D joint locations [30, 37, 56]. One straightforward solution is to generate volumetric heat-maps using 3D CNNs, but this solution is computationally inefficient. Wan et al. [62] recently propose a dense pixel-wise estimation method. Apart from generating 2D heat-maps, this method estimates 3D offsets of hand joints for each pixel of the 2D image. However, this method suffers from two limitations. First, as it regresses pixel-wise 3D estimations from 2D images, the proposed method may not fully exploit the 3D spatial information in depth images. Second, generating 3D estimations for background pixels of the 2D image may distract the deep neural network from learning effective features in the hand region.

To tackle these problems, we aim at regressing point-wise estimations directly from 3D point cloud. We define *point-wise estimations* as the offsets from the 3D points in the point cloud to the hand joint locations (Fig. 16.3).

Compared with the holistic regression method proposed in Sect. 16.3 that holistically regresses 3D hand pose parameters from point cloud using a holistic regression PointNet, this point-wise regression method estimates the *point-wise* closeness and offset directions to hand joints from the input point cloud using a stacked point-to-point regression PointNet, which is able to capture local evidence for estimating accurate 3D hand pose.

16.4.2   Point-Wise Estimation Targets

The point-wise estimations can be defined as the offsets from points to hand joint locations. However, estimating offsets for all points in the point set is unnecessary and may make the per-point vote noisy. Thus, we only estimate offsets for the neighboring

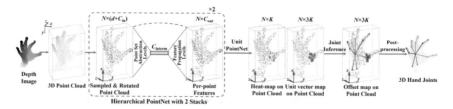

Fig. 16.3 Overview of our proposed point-wise regression method for 3D hand pose estimation from single depth images. We propose to directly take N sampled and normalized 3D hand points as network input and output a set of heat-maps as well as unit vector fields on the input point cloud, reflecting the closeness and directions from input points to J hand joints, respectively. From the network outputs, we can infer point-wise offsets to hand joints and estimate the 3D hand pose with post-processing. We apply the hierarchical PointNet [33] with two-stacked network architecture which feeds the output of one module as input to the next. For illustration purpose, we only visualize the heat-map, unit vector field and offset field of one hand joint

points of the hand joint. We define the element in the target offset fields V for point p_i ($i = 1, \ldots, N$) and ground truth hand joint location ϕ_j^* ($j = 1, \ldots, J$) as

$$V\left(p_i, \phi_j^*\right) = \begin{cases} \phi_j^* - p_i & p_i \in \mathscr{P}_K\left(\phi_j^*\right) \text{ and } \left\|\phi_j^* - p_i\right\| \le r, \\ \mathbf{0} & \text{otherwise}; \end{cases} \qquad (16.6)$$

where $\mathscr{P}_K\left(\phi_j^*\right)$ is a set of K nearest neighboring points (KNN) of the ground truth hand joint location ϕ_j^* in the point set $\mathscr{P}^{obb}$; r is the maximum radius of ball for nearest neighbor search; in our implementation, we set K as 64 and r as 80 mm$/L_{obb}$. We combine KNN with ball query for nearest neighbor search in order to guarantee that both the number of neighboring points and the scale of neighboring region are controllable.

However, it is difficult to train a neural network that directly generates the offset field due to the large variance of offsets. Similar to [62], we decompose the target offset fields V into heat-maps H reflecting per-point closeness to hand joint locations:

$$H\left(p_i, \phi_j^*\right) = \begin{cases} 1 - \left\|\phi_j^* - p_i\right\|/r & p_i \in \mathscr{P}_K\left(\phi_j^*\right) \text{ and } \left\|\phi_j^* - p_i\right\| \le r, \\ 0 & \text{otherwise}; \end{cases}$$
$$(16.7)$$

and unit vector fields U reflecting per-point directions to hand joint locations:

$$U\left(p_i, \phi_j^*\right) = \begin{cases} \left(\phi_j^* - p_i\right)/\left\|\phi_j^* - p_i\right\| & p_i \in \mathscr{P}_K\left(\phi_j^*\right) \text{ and } \left\|\phi_j^* - p_i\right\| \le r, \\ \mathbf{0} & \text{otherwise}. \end{cases}$$
$$(16.8)$$

Different from [62] that generates heat-maps and unit vector fields on 2D images, our proposed method generates heat-maps and unit vector fields on the 3D point cloud, which can better utilize the 3D spatial information in the depth image. In addition, generating heat-maps and unit vector fields on 2D images with large blank background regions may distract the neural network from learning effective features in the hand region. Although this problem can be alleviated by multiplying a binary hand mask in the loss function, our method is able to concentrate on learning effective features of the hand point cloud in a natural way without using any mask, since the output heat-maps and unit vector fields are represented on the hand point cloud.

16.4.3   Point-Wise Regression Network

We exploit the hierarchical PointNet [33] for learning heat-maps and unit vector fields on 3D point cloud. Different from the hierarchical PointNet for point set segmentation adopted in [33], our proposed point-to-point regression network has a two-stacked network architecture in order to better capture the 3D spatial information in the 3D point cloud.

As illustrated in Fig. 16.4, the input of the network is a set of d-dimensional coordinates with C_{in}-dimensional input features, i.e., 3D surface normals that are approximated by fitting a local plane for the nearest neighbors of the query point in the point cloud. Similar to the network architecture for set segmentation proposed in [33], a single module of our network extracts a global feature vector from point cloud using three set abstraction levels and propagates the global feature to point features for original points using three feature propagation levels. In the feature propagation level, we use nearest neighbors of the interpolation point in N_l points to interpolate features for N_{l-1} points [33]. The interpolated C_l-dimensional features of N_{l-1} points are concatenated with the corresponding point features in the set abstraction level and are mapped to C_{l-1}-dimensional features using per-point MLP, of which the weights are shared across all the points. The heat-map and the unit vector field are generated from the point features for the original point set using per-point MLP.

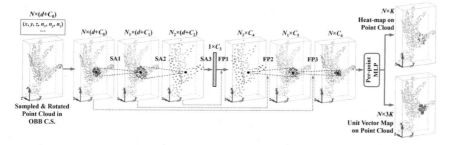

Fig. 16.4 An illustration of a single network module, which is based on the hierarchical Point-Net [33]. Here, "SA" stands for point set abstraction layers; "FP" stands for feature propagation layers; "MLP" stands for multi-layer perceptron network. The dotted shortcuts denote skip links for feature concatenation

Inspired by the stacked hourglass networks for human pose estimation [23], we stack two hierarchical PointNet modules end-to-end to boost the performance of the network. The two hierarchical PointNet modules have the same network architecture and the same hyper-parameters, except for the hyper-parameter in the input layer. The output heat-map and unit vector field of the first module are concatenated with the input and output point features of the first module as the input into the second hierarchical PointNet module. For real-time consideration, we only stack two hierarchical PointNet modules.

We apply intermediate supervision when training the two-stacked hierarchical PointNet. The loss function for each training sample is defined as

$$\mathcal{L} = \sum_{t=1}^{T} \sum_{j=1}^{J} \sum_{i=1}^{N} \left[\left(\hat{H}_{ij}^{(t)} - H\left(p_i, \phi_j^*\right) \right)^2 + \left\| \hat{U}_{ij}^{(t)} - U\left(p_i, \phi_j^*\right) \right\|^2 \right], \quad (16.9)$$

where T is the number of stacked network modules, in this work $T = 2$; $\hat{H}_{ij}^{(t)}$ and $\hat{U}_{ij}^{(t)}$ are elements in the heat-maps and unit vector fields estimated by the tth network module, respectively; $H\left(p_i, \phi_j^*\right)$ and $U\left(p_i, \phi_j^*\right)$ are elements in the ground truth heat-maps and ground truth unit vector fields defined in Eqs. 16.7 and 16.8, respectively.

16.4.4   Hand Pose Inference

During testing, we infer the 3D hand pose from the heat-maps $\hat{H}$ and the unit vector fields $\hat{U}$ estimated by the last hierarchical PointNet module. According to the definition of offset fields, heat-maps and unit vector fields in Eqs. 16.6–16.8, we can infer the offset vector $\hat{V}_{ij}$ from point p_i to joint $\hat{\phi}_j$ as:

$$\hat{V}_{ij} = r \cdot \left(1 - \hat{H}_{ij}\right) \cdot \hat{U}_{ij}. \quad (16.10)$$

According to Eq. 16.6, only the offset vectors for the neighboring points of the hand joint are used for hand pose inference, which can be found from the estimated heat-map reflecting the closeness of points to the hand joint. We denote the estimated heat-map for the jth hand joint as $\hat{H}_j$ that is the jth column of $\hat{H}$. We determine the neighboring points of the jth hand joint as the points corresponding to the largest M values of the heat-map $\hat{H}_j$. The indices of these points in the point set are denoted as $\{i_m\}_{m=1}^{M}$. The hand joint location $\hat{\phi}_j$ can be simply inferred from the corresponding offset vectors $\hat{V}_{i_m j}$ and 3D points p_{i_m} $(m = 1, \ldots, M)$ using weighted average:

$$\hat{\phi}_j = \sum_{m=1}^{M} w_m \left(\hat{V}_{i_m j} + p_{i_m} \right) / \sum_{m=1}^{M} w_m, \quad (16.11)$$

where w_m is the weight of the candidate estimation. In our implementation, we set the weight w_m as the corresponding heat-map value $\hat{H}_{i_m j}$, and set M as 25.

16.4.5   Post-processing

There are two issues in our point-to-point regression method. The first issue is that the estimation is unreliable when the divergence of the M candidate estimations are large in 3D space. This is usually caused by missing depth data near the hand joint. The second issue is that there is no explicit constraint on the estimated 3D hand pose, although the neural network may learn joint constraints in the output heat-maps and unit vector fields.

To tackle the first issue, when the divergence of the M candidate estimations is larger than a threshold, we replace the estimation result with the result of the holistic regression method that directly regresses 3D coordinates of hand joints, since the holistic regression method does not have this issue. In order to save the inference time, instead of training a separate PointNet for direct hand pose regression, we add three fully connected layers for direct hand pose regression to the pretrained two-stacked hierarchical PointNet. The three fully connected layers are trained to directly regress the 3D coordinates of hand joints from the features extracted by the second hierarchical PointNet module. The divergence of the M candidate estimations is defined as the sum of standard deviations of x, y, and z coordinates of candidate estimations. In our implementation, we set the divergence threshold as $7.5 \, \text{mm} / L_{obb}$. Experimental results in Sect. 16.5 will show that although only a small portion of the hand joint estimations requires to be replaced by the direct regression results, this replacement strategy can improve the estimation accuracy to some extent.

To tackle the second issue, we explicitly constrain the estimated 3D hand pose $\hat{\boldsymbol{\Phi}}$ on a lower dimensional space learned by principal component analysis (PCA). By performing PCA on the ground truth 3D joint locations in the training dataset, we can obtain the principal components $\boldsymbol{E} = [\boldsymbol{e}_1, \boldsymbol{e}_2, \ldots, \boldsymbol{e}_H]$ ($H < 3J$) and the empirical mean $\boldsymbol{u}$. The constrained 3D hand pose can be calculated using the following formula:

$$\hat{\boldsymbol{\Phi}}_{cons} = \boldsymbol{E} \cdot \boldsymbol{E}^T \cdot \left(\hat{\boldsymbol{\Phi}} - \boldsymbol{u} \right) + \boldsymbol{u}. \qquad (16.12)$$

In our implementation, we set the number of principle components H as 30. Finally, the estimated 3D hand joint locations in the normalized OBB C.S. are transformed back to joint locations in the camera C.S. $\hat{\boldsymbol{\Phi}}^{cam}$.

16.5   Experiments

We evaluate our proposed methods on three public hand pose datasets: NYU [58], MSRA [47], and ICVL [50].

The NYU dataset [58] contains more than 72 K training frames and 8 K testing frames. Each frame contains 36 annotated joints. Following previous works [10, 27, 58], we estimate a subset of $M = 14$ joints. We segment the hand from the depth image using random decision forest (RDF) similar to [50]. Since the segmented hands may contain arms with various lengths, we augment the training data with random arm lengths.

The MSRA dataset [47] contains more than 76K frames from 9 subjects. Each subject contains 17 gestures. In each frame, the hand has been segmented from the depth image and the ground truth contains $M = 21$ joints. The neural networks are trained on 8 subjects and tested on the remaining subject. We repeat this experiment 9 times for all subjects and report the average metrics. We do not perform any data augmentation on this dataset.

The ICVL dataset [50] contains 22 K training frames and 1.6 K testing frames. The ground truth of each frame contains $M = 16$ joints. We apply RDF for hand segmentation and augment the training data with random arm lengths as well as random stretch factors.

We evaluate the hand pose estimation performance with two metrics: the first metric is the per-joint mean error distance over all test frames; the second metric is the proportion of good frames in which the worst joint error is below a threshold, which is proposed in [54] and is more strict.

All experiments are conducted on a workstation with two Intel Core i7 5930K, 64 GB of RAM and an NVIDIA GTX1080 GPU. The deep neural networks are implemented within the PyTorch framework.

16.5.1   Holistic Regression Versus Point-Wise Regression

To evaluate our proposed point-wise regression method, we compare our holistic regression method proposed in Sect. 16.3 with our point-wise regression method proposed in Sect. 16.4. As shown in Fig. 16.5 (left), the point-wise regression method outperforms the holistic regression method when the error threshold is smaller than 45 mm. But when the error threshold is larger than 45 mm, the point-wise regression method performs worse than the holistic regression method. This may be caused by the large divergence of the candidate estimations in some results, as described in Sect. 16.4.5. By combining the point-wise method with the holistic regression method as described in Sect. 16.4.5, the estimation accuracy can be further improved, as shown in Fig. 16.5 (left). Furthermore, the performance of the combination method is superior to or on par with the holistic regression method over all the error thresholds. In this experiment, only 7.9% of joint locations estimated by point-wise regression

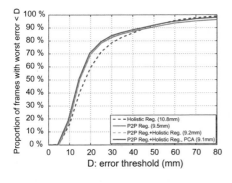
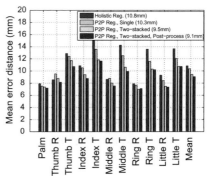

Fig. 16.5 Self-comparison of different methods on NYU dataset [58]. **Left**: the comparison of our point-wise regression method and holistic regression method on the proportion of good frames. We use two-stacked network for point-wise regression in this figure. **Right**: the impact of point-to-point regression method, stacked network architecture, and post-processing methods on the per-joint mean error distance (R: root, T: tip). "P2P Reg." stands for point-to-point regression. The overall mean error distances are shown in parentheses

method are replaced by the results of holistic regression method, which indicates that the estimation results are dominated by the point-wise regression method, and the holistic regression method is complementary with the point-wise regression method. In addition, adding the PCA constraint can further improve the estimation accuracy slightly.

We also evaluate the impact of the stacked network architecture for hierarchical PointNet. As shown in Fig. 16.5 (right), the two-stacked network evidently performs better than the single network module, which indicates the importance of the stacked network architecture on our point-wise regression method. We also observe that the mean error distance on finger tips are larger than those on the other joints. One explanation is that the fingertips are relatively small compared to other hand parts, thus the accurate 3D locations of fingertips are difficult to predict.

16.5.2 Comparisons with Existing Methods

We compare our proposed holistic regression method and point-wise regression method with 16 existing methods: latent random forest (LRF) [50], hierarchical regression with random forest (RDF, Hierarchical) [47], local surface normal based random forest (LSN) [63], collaborative filtering [5], 2D heat-map regression using 2D CNNs (Heat-map) [58], feedback loop based 2D CNNs (Feedback Loop) [27], hand model parameter regression using 2D CNNs (DeepModel) [74], Lie group based 2D CNNs (Lie-X) [69], improved holistic regression with a pose prior using 2D CNNs (DeepPrior++) [24], hallucinating heat distribution using 2D CNNs (Hallucination Heat) [4], multi-view CNNs [9], 3D CNNs [10], crossing nets using deep generative models (Crossing Nets) [61], region ensemble network (REN) [12], pose-guided structured REN (Pose-REN) [3], and dense 3D regression using 2D CNNs (DenseReg) [62]. We evaluate the proportion of good frames over different error thresholds, the per-joint mean error distances as well as the overall mean error distance on NYU [58], ICVL [50] and MSRA [47] datasets, as presented in Figs. 16.6, 16.7, and 16.8, respectively.

As can be seen in Figs. 16.6, 16.7, and 16.8, our method can achieve superior performance on these three datasets. On NYU [58] and ICVL [50] datasets, our method outperforms other methods over almost all the error thresholds and achieves the smallest overall mean error distances on these two datasets. Specifically, on NYU dataset [58], when the error threshold is between 15 and 20 mm, the proportions of good frames of our point-wise regression method is about 15% better than DenseReg [62] and 20% batter than Pose-REN [3]; on ICVL dataset [50], when the error threshold is between 10 and 15 mm, the proportion of good frames of our point-

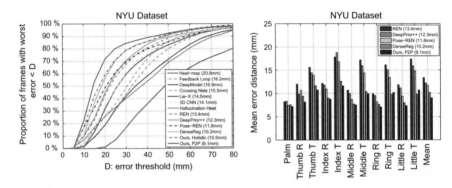

Fig. 16.6 Comparison with existing methods on NYU [58] dataset. **Left**: the proportions of good frames and the overall mean error distances (in parentheses). **Right**: the per-joint mean error distances and the overall mean error distances (R: root, T: tip)

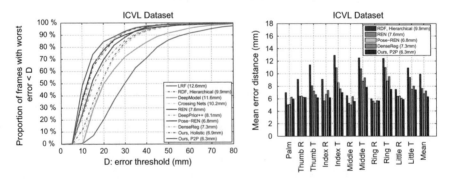

Fig. 16.7 Comparison with existing methods on ICVL [50] dataset. **Left**: the proportions of good frames and the overall mean error distances (in parentheses). **Right**: the per-joint mean error distances and the overall mean error distances (R: root, T: tip)

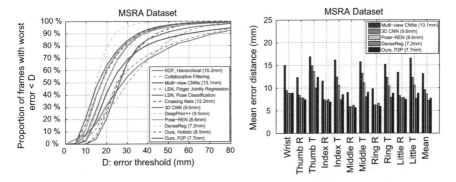

Fig. 16.8 Comparison with existing methods on MSRA [47] dataset. **Left**: the proportions of good frames and the overall mean error distances (in parentheses). **Right**: the per-joint mean error distances and the overall mean error distances (R: root, T: tip)

wise regression method is more than 10% better than those of DenseReg [62] and Pose-REN [3] methods. On MSRA dataset [47], our methods outperform most of other methods over almost all the error thresholds. These experimental results show that our PointNet-based methods perform better than the methods using 2D image or 3D volume as the input. Our PointNet-based methods can extract geometric features of the hand directly from the 3D point cloud, which are more efficient than 2D or 3D CNNs.

16.5.3   Runtime and Model Size

The runtime of our holistic regression method is 20.5 ms per frame on average, including 1.7 ms for farthest point sampling (FPS), 6.5 ms for surface normal approximation, 9.2 ms for the hand pose regression network forward propagation, 3.1 ms for fingertip refinement. Thus, our holistic regression method runs in real time at about 48 fps. In addition, the number of parameters in the hand pose regression network is about 2.3×10^6 (2.3 M). The number of parameters in the fingertip refinement network is about 1.4×10^5 (142 K). In total, there are about 2.5×10^6 (2.5 M) parameters in these two networks. These parameters are stored in 32-bit float and the total size of parameters is 9.8 MB.

The runtime of our point-wise regression method is 23.9 ms per frame on average, including 8.2 ms for point sampling and surface normal calculation, 15.1 ms for the two-stacked hierarchical PointNet forward propagation, 0.6 ms for hand pose inference and post-processing. Thus, our point-wise regression method runs in real time at about 41.8 fps. In addition, the model size of the network is 17.2 MB, including 11.1 MB for the point-wise regression network which is a two-stacked hierarchical PointNet and 6.1 MB for the additional holistic regression module which consists of three fully connected layers.

16.6 Conclusions

In this chapter, we propose a novel approach that directly takes the 3D point cloud of hand as the network input for 3D hand pose estimation. For the network output, we propose two approaches: holistic regression method and point-wise regression method. In the holistic regression method, we holistically regress 3D hand joint locations. In the point-wise regression method, we propose to output heat-maps as well as unit vector fields on the point cloud, reflecting the per-point closeness and directions to hand joints. We infer 3D hand joint locations from the estimated heat-maps and unit vector fields using weighted fusion. Our proposed point-wise regression method can also be easily combined with the holistic regression method to achieve more robust performance. Experimental results on three challenging hand pose datasets show that our method achieves superior accuracy performance in real time.

References

1. Alcover EA, Jaume-i Capó A, Moyà-Alcover B (2018) PROGame: a process framework for serious game development for motor rehabilitation therapy. PloS one 13(5)
2. Ayed I, Ghazel A, Jaume-i Capó A, Moya-Alcover G, Varona J, Martínez-Bueso P (2018) Feasibility of Kinect-based games for balance rehabilitation: A case study. J Healthc Eng
3. Chen X, Wang G, Guo H, Zhang C (2017) Pose guided structured region ensemble network for cascaded hand pose estimation. CoRR. https://arxiv.org/abs/1708.03416
4. Choi C, Kim S, Ramani K (2017) Learning hand articulations by hallucinating heat distribution. In: Proceedings of international conference on computer vision, pp 3104–3113
5. Choi C, Sinha A, Hee Choi J, Jang S, Ramani K (2015) A collaborative filtering approach to real-time hand pose estimation. In: Proceedings of international conference on computer vision, pp 2336–2344
6. Dollár P, Welinder P, Perona P (2010) Cascaded pose regression. In: Proceedings of the IEEE conference on computer vision and pattern recognition, pp 1078–1085
7. Erol A, Bebis G, Nicolescu M, Boyle RD, Twombly X (2005) A review on vision-based full DOF hand motion estimation. In: Proceedings of the IEEE conference on computer vision and pattern recognition. Workshops, pp 75–82
8. Erol A, Bebis G, Nicolescu M, Boyle RD, Twombly X (2007) Vision-based hand pose estimation: a review. Comput Vis Image Underst 108(1):52–73
9. Ge L, Liang H, Yuan J, Thalmann D (2016) Robust 3D hand pose estimation in single depth images: from single-view CNN to multi-view CNNs. In: Proceedings of the IEEE conference on computer vision and pattern recognition, pp 3593–3601
10. Ge L, Liang H, Yuan J, Thalmann D (2017) 3D convolutional neural networks for efficient and robust hand pose estimation from single depth images. In: Proceedings of the IEEE conference on computer vision and pattern recognition, pp 1991–2000
11. Ge L, Liang H, Yuan J, Thalmann D (2018) Real-time 3D hand pose estimation with 3D convolutional neural networks. IEEE Trans. Pattern Anal. Mach. Intell. 1–15. https://doi.org/10.1109/TPAMI.2018.2827052
12. Guo H, Wang G, Chen X, Zhang C, Qiao F, Yang H (2017) Region ensemble network: improving convolutional network for hand pose estimation. In: Proceedings international conference on image processing

13. Hoppe H, DeRose T, Duchamp T, Mcdonald J, Stuetzle W (1992) Surface reconstruction from unorganized points. Comput Graph 26(2):71–78
14. Joo H, Simon T, Sheikh Y (2018) Total capture: A 3D deformation model for tracking faces, hands, and bodies. In: Proceedings of the IEEE conference on computer vision and pattern recognition, pp 8320–8329
15. Keskin C, Kıraç F, Kara YE, Akarun L (2012) Hand pose estimation and hand shape classification using multi-layered randomized decision forests. In: Proceedings european conference on computer vision, pp 852–863
16. Khamis S, Taylor J, Shotton J, Keskin C, Izadi S, Fitzgibbon A (2015) Learning an efficient model of hand shape variation from depth images. In: Proceedings of the IEEE conference on computer vision and pattern recognition, pp 2540–2548
17. Kirac F, Kara YE, Akarun L (2014) Hierarchically constrained 3D hand pose estimation using regression forests from single frame depth data. Pattern Recognit Lett 50:91–100
18. Li P, Ling H, Li X, Liao C (2015) 3D hand pose estimation using randomized decision forest with segmentation index points. In: Proceedings of international conference on computer vision, pp 819–827
19. Liang H, Yuan J, Thalmann D (2014) Parsing the hand in depth images. IEEE Trans Multimed 16(5):1241–1253
20. Liang H, Yuan J, Thalmann D (2015) Resolving ambiguous hand pose predictions by exploiting part correlations. IEEE Trans Circuits Syst Video Technol 25(7):1125–1139
21. Melax S, Keselman L, Orsten S (2013) Dynamics based 3D skeletal hand tracking. In: Proceedings of graphics interface, pp 63–70
22. Moon G, Chang JY, Lee KM (2018) V2V-PoseNet: Voxel-to-voxel prediction network for accurate 3D hand and human pose estimation from a single depth map. In: Proceedings of the IEEE conference on computer vision and pattern Recognition, pp 5079–5088
23. Newell A, Yang K, Deng J (2016) Stacked hourglass networks for human pose estimation. In: proceedings of the European conference on computer vision, pp 483–499
24. Oberweger M, Lepetit V (2017) DeepPrior++: improving fast and accurate 3D hand pose estimation. In: Proceedings of international conference on computer vision. Workshop, pp 585–594
25. Oberweger M, Riegler G, Wohlhart P, Lepetit V (2016) Efficiently creating 3D training data for fine hand pose estimation. In: Proceedings of the IEEE conference on computer vision and pattern recognition, pp 3593–3601
26. Oberweger M, Wohlhart P, Lepetit V (2015) Hands deep in deep learning for hand pose estimation. In: Proceedings of the computer vision. Winter Workshop, pp 21–30
27. Oberweger M, Wohlhart P, Lepetit V (2015) Training a feedback loop for hand pose estimation. In: Proceedings of the international conference computer vision, pp 3316–3324
28. Oikonomidis I, Kyriazis N, Argyros A (2011) Efficient model-based 3D tracking of hand articulations using Kinect. In: Proceedings of the British machine computer vision, pp 101.1–101.11
29. Oikonomidis I, Kyriazis N, Argyros AA (2010) Markerless and efficient 26-DOF hand pose recovery. In: Proceedings of the Asian conference on compute vision, pp 744–757. Springer
30. Pavlakos G, Zhou X, Derpanis KG, Daniilidis K (2017) Coarse-to-fine volumetric prediction for single-image 3D human pose. In: Proceedings of the IEEE conference computer vision pattern recognition, pp 7025–7034
31. Pavlovic VI, Sharma R, Huang TS (1997) Visual interpretation of hand gestures for human-computer interaction: a review. IEEE Trans. Pattern Anal. Mach. Intell. 19(7):677–695
32. Qi CR, Su H, Mo K, Guibas, LJ (2017) PointNet: deep learning on point sets for 3D classification and segmentation. In: Proceedings of the IEEE conference on computer vision and pattern recognition, pp 652–660
33. Qi CR, Yi L, Su H, Guibas LJ (2017) PointNet++: deep hierarchical feature learning on point sets in a metric space. In: Proceedings of the conference neural information processing systems
34. Qian C, Sun X, Wei Y, Tang X, Sun J (2014) Realtime and robust hand tracking from depth. In: Proceedings of the IEEE Conference Computer Vision Pattern Recognition, pp 1106–1113

35. Quam DL (1990) Gesture recognition with a dataglove. Proc. IEEE Conf. Aerosp. Electron. 2:755–760
36. Rad M, Oberweger M, Lepetit V (2018) Feature mapping for learning fast and accurate 3D pose inference from synthetic images. In: Proceedings of the ieee conference computer vision pattern recognition, pp 4663–4672
37. Rogez G, Weinzaepfel P, Schmid C (2017) LCR-net: localization-classification-regression for human pose. In: Proceedings of the IEEE conference computer vision pattern recognition, pp 3433–3441
38. Romero J, Kjellström H, Kragic D (2009) Monocular real-time 3D articulated hand pose estimation. In: Proceedings of the IEEE-RAS conference humanoid robots, pp 87–92
39. Romero J, Kjellström H, Kragic D (2010) Hands in action: real-time 3D reconstruction of hands in interaction with objects. In: Proceedings IEEE Conference Robotics and Automation, pp 458–463
40. Romero J, Tzionas D, Black MJ (2017) Embodied hands: modeling and capturing hands and bodies together. ACM Trans Graph 36(6):245:1–245:17
41. Shakhnarovich G, Viola P, Darrell T (2003) Fast pose estimation with parameter-sensitive hashing. In: Proceedings of the International Conference Computer Vision, pp 750–758
42. Sharp T, Keskin C, Robertson D, Taylor J, Shotton J, Kim D, Rhemann C, Leichter I, Vinnikov A, Wei Y, Freedman D, Kohli P, Krupka E, Fitzgibbon A, Izadi S (2015) Accurate, robust, and flexible real-time hand tracking. In: Proceedings of the 33rd annual ACM conference human factors in computing systems, pp 3633–3642
43. Shotton J, Fitzgibbon A, Cook M, Sharp T, Finocchio M, Moore R, Kipman A, Blake A (2011) Real-time human pose recognition in parts from a single depth image. In: Proceedings IEEE conference computer vision pattern recognition, pp 1297–1304
44. Sinha A, Choi C, Ramani K (2016) Deephand: Robust hand pose estimation by completing a matrix with deep features. In: Proceedings of the IEEE Conference Computer Vision Pattern Recognition, pp 4150–4158
45. Sridhar S, Mueller F, Oulasvirta A, Theobalt C (2015) Fast and robust hand tracking using detection-guided optimization. In: Proceedings of the IEEE conference computer vision pattern recognition, pp 3213–3221
46. Sridhar S, Mueller F, Zollhoefer M, Casas D, Oulasvirta A, Theobalt C (2016) Real-time joint tracking of a hand manipulating an object from RGB-D input. In: Proceedings of the European conference computer vision, pp 294–310
47. Sun X, Wei Y, Liang S, Tang X, Sun J (2015) Cascaded hand pose regression. In: Proceedings of the IEEE conference computer vision pattern recognition, pp 824–832
48. Supancic III JS, Rogez G, Yang Y, Shotton J, Ramanan D (2015) Depth-based hand pose estimation: methods, data, and challenges. In: Proceedings international conference computer vision, pp 1868–1876
49. Tagliasacchi A, Schroeder M, Tkach A, Bouaziz S, Botsch M, Pauly M (2015) Robust articulated-ICP for real-time hand tracking. Comput Graph Forum 34(5):101–114
50. Tang D, Chang HJ, Tejani A, Kim TK (2014) Latent regression forest: structured estimation of 3D articulated hand posture. In: Proceedings of the IEEE conference computer vision pattern recognition, pp 3786–3793
51. Tang D, Taylor J, Kohli P, Keskin C, Kim TK, Shotton J (2015) Opening the black box: hierarchical sampling optimization for estimating human hand pose. In: Proceedings of the international conference computer vision, pp 3325–3333
52. Tang D, Yu TH, Kim TK (2013) Real-time articulated hand pose estimation using semi-supervised transductive regression forests. In: Proceedings of the international conference computer vision, pp 3224–3231
53. Taylor J, Bordeaux L, Cashman T, Corish B, Keskin C, Sharp T, Soto E, Sweeney D, Valentin J, Luff B, Topalian A, Wood E, Khamis S, Kohli P, Izadi S, Banks R, Fitzgibbon A, Shotton J (2016) Efficient and precise interactive hand tracking through joint, continuous optimization of pose and correspondences. ACM Trans Graph 35(4):143:1–143:12

54. Taylor J, Shotton J, Sharp T, Fitzgibbon A (2012) The Vitruvian manifold: Inferring dense correspondences for one-shot human pose estimation. In: Proceedings of the IEEE conference computer vision pattern recognition, pp 103–110
55. Tkach A, Pauly M, Tagliasacchi A (2016) Sphere-meshes for real-time hand modeling and tracking. ACM Trans Graph 35(6):222:1–222:11
56. Tome D, Russell C, Agapito L (2017) Lifting from the deep: Convolutional 3D pose estimation from a single image. In: Proceedings of the IEEE conference computer vision pattern recognition, pp 2500–2509
57. Tompson J, Jain A, LeCun Y, Bregler C (2014) Joint training of a convolutional network and a graphical model for human pose estimation. In: Proceedings neural information processing systems, pp 1799–1807
58. Tompson J, Stein M, Lecun Y, Perlin K (2014) Real-time continuous pose recovery of human hands using convolutional networks. ACM Trans Graph 33(5):169:1–169:10
59. Tzionas D, Ballan L, Srikantha A, Aponte P, Pollefeys M, Gall J (2016) Capturing hands in action using discriminative salient points and physics simulation. Int J Comput Vis 118(2):172–193
60. Verth JMV, Bishop LM (2008) Essential mathematics for games and interactive applications, Second Edition: A Programmer's Guide, 2nd edn. Morgan Kaufmann Publishers Inc., San Francisco, CA
61. Wan C, Probst T, Van Gool L, Yao A (2017) Crossing nets: dual generative models with a shared latent space for hand pose estimation. In: Proceedings of the IEEE conference computer vision pattern recognition, pp 680–689
62. Wan C, Probst T, Van Gool L, Yao A (2018) Dense 3D regression for hand pose estimation. In: Proceedings of the IEEE conference computer vision pattern recognition, pp 5147–5156
63. Wan C, Yao A, Van Gool L (2016) Direction matters: hand pose estimation from local surface normals. In: Proceedings of the European conference computer vision, pp 554–569
64. Wang C, Cannon DJ (1993) A virtual end-effector pointing system in point-and-direct robotics for inspection of surface flaws using a neural network based skeleton transform. Proc Int Conf Robot Autom 3:784–789
65. Wei SE, Ramakrishna V, Kanade T, Sheikh Y (2016) Convolutional pose machines. In: Proceedings IEEE conference computer vision pattern recognition, pp 4724–4732
66. Wu Y, Huang TS (1999) Vision-based gesture recognition: a review. In: International Gesture Workshop, pp 103–115
67. Wu Y, Huang TS (2001) Hand modeling, analysis and recognition. IEEE Signal Process Mag 18(3):51–60
68. Xu C, Cheng L (2013) Efficient hand pose estimation from a single depth image. In: Proceedings of the international conference computer vision, pp 3456 – 3462
69. Xu C, Govindarajan LN, Zhang Y, Cheng L (2016) Lie-X: depth image based articulated object pose estimation, tracking, and action recognition on lie groups. Int J Comput Vis 454–478
70. Ye M, Shen Y, Du C, Pan Z, Yang R (2016) Real-time simultaneous pose and shape estimation for articulated objects using a single depth camera. IEEE Trans Pattern Anal Mach Intell 38(8):1517–1532
71. Ye Q, Yuan S, Kim TK (2016) Spatial attention deep net with partial PSO for hierarchical hybrid hand pose estimation. In: Proceedings European conference computer vision, pp 346–361
72. Yuan S, Garcia-Hernando G, Stenger B, Moon G, Chang JY, Lee KM, Molchanov P, Kautz J, Honari S, Ge L, Yuan J, Chen X, Wang G, Yang F, Akiyama K, Wu Y, Wan Q, Madadi M, Escalera S, Li S, Lee D, Oikonomidis I, Argyros A, Kim TK (2018) Depth-based 3D hand pose estimation: from current achievements to future goals. In: Proceedings of the IEEE conference computer vision pattern recognition, pp 2636–2645
73. Yuan S, Ye Q, Stenger B, Jain S, Kim TK (2017) Bighand2. 2m benchmark: Hand pose dataset and state of the art analysis. In: Proceedings IEEE conference computer vision pattern recognition, pp 2605–2613

74. Zhou X, Wan Q, Zhang W, Xue X, Wei Y (2016) Model-based deep hand pose estimation. In: Proceedings of the international joint conference artificial intelligence, pp 2421–2427
75. Zollhöfer M, Nießner M, Izadi S, Rehmann C, Zach C, Fisher M, Wu C, Fitzgibbon A, Loop C, Theobalt C et al (2014) Real-time non-rigid reconstruction using an RGB-D camera. ACM Trans Graph (TOG) 33(4):156

Chapter 17
RGB-D Object Classification for Autonomous Driving Perception

Cristiano Premebida, Gledson Melotti and Alireza Asvadi

Abstract Autonomous driving systems (ADS) comprise, essentially, sensory perception (including AI-ML-based techniques), localization, decision-making, and control. The cornerstone of an ADS is the sensory perception part, which is involved in most of the essential and necessary tasks for safe driving such as sensor-fusion, environment representation, scene understanding, semantic segmentation, object detection/recognition, and tracking. Multimodal sensor-fusion is an established strategy to enhance safety and robustness of perception systems in autonomous driving. In this work, a fusion of data from color-camera (RGB) and 3D-LIDAR (D-distance), henceforth designated RGB-D, will be particularly addressed, highlighting use-cases on road-users classification using deep learning. 3D-LIDAR data, in the form of point-cloud, can be processed directly by using the PointNet network or, alternatively, by using depth-maps, known as range-view representation, which is a suitable representation to train state-of-the-art Convolutional Neural Network (CNN) models and to make the combination with RGB-images more practical. Experiments are carried out using the KITTI dataset on object classification, i.e., vehicles, pedestrians, cyclists. We report extensive results in terms of classification performance of deep-learning models using RGB, 3D, and RGB-D representations. The results show that RGB-D models have better performance in comparison with 3D and range-view models but, in some circumstances RGB-only achieved superior performance.

C. Premebida (✉)
Department of Aeronautical and Automotive Engineering (AAE),
Loughborough University, Loughborough, UK
e-mail: C.Premebida@lboro.ac.uk

G. Melotti
Department of Electrical and Computer Engineering (DEEC),
University of Coimbra, Coimbra, Portugal
e-mail: gledson.melotti@isr.uc.pt

A. Asvadi
Laboratory of Medical Information Processing (LaTIM),
University of Western Brittany, Brest, France
e-mail: alireza.asvadi@univ-brest.fr

© Springer Nature Switzerland AG 2019
P. L. Rosin et al. (eds.), *RGB-D Image Analysis and Processing*,
Advances in Computer Vision and Pattern Recognition,
https://doi.org/10.1007/978-3-030-28603-3_17

377

17.1   Introduction

RGB-D data analysis and processing in mobile robotics and some autonomous systems applications have been, traditionally, related to the off-the-shelf RGB-D sensors, e.g. MS Kinect and Asus Xtion camera-sensors. The substantial majority of
the RGB-D machine/computer vision applications and datasets are based on these
standalone sensor technologies. In terms of use-cases and applications, as described
in [4, 6], RGB-D vision systems can be involved in one or more of the following:
object detection and tracking, human activity analysis, object and scene recognition, SLAM (Simultaneous Localization And Mapping), localization, hand gesture
analysis. These applications are related to robotics domain and, most of them, to
autonomous driving as well.

In autonomous and automated driving, to date, there is no suitable standalone
RGB-D technology similar to the ones used in mobile robots. Although stereo systems can estimate distance, actually they do not measure distance like radars or
LIDARs sensors. Therefore, in order to develop a suitable RGB-D- based perception
system for autonomous driving, ADAS (Advanced Driver-Assistance Systems) or
related applications in outdoors, a color monocular camera and a LIDAR sensor—
both mounted onboard the vehicle—can be considered. In such a multi-sensor system, the camera contributes to RGB components and D (distance/depth) data comes
from the LIDAR sensor. The use of LIDAR in combination with a camera to provide
an RGB-D representation of the environment brings extra challenges, because the
extrinsic and intrinsic (for the camera) calibration parameters are necessary and, on
the other hand, D-channel's data is sparse—as shown in Fig. 17.1 (second row) and
described in Sect. 17.2.

Sensor technology, together with sensor-fusion and inference algorithms (e.g.,
Bayesian networks, machine learning), play an important role in autonomous driving perception. Although cameras are the most commonly used sensors, deployed
as monocular or stereo systems, they have some disadvantages such as strong sensitivity to external illumination variations, limited field of view, inability to directly
measure distance, or dimension of detected objects [3]. To compensate and complement cameras, LIDARs and radar sensors are the most adopted solution in automated
and self-driving vehicles [5, 10, 13, 16, 22]. But there are some drawbacks as well.
Besides the cost, current LIDAR technologies depend on moving parts (a scanning
mechanism), and their performance degrades in harsh weather conditions (e.g., strong
fog, rain, and snow). Radar, on the other hand, is unable to provide high-resolution
of detected obstacles which hinders recognition.

The implications of sensor-fusion in autonomous driving, for example, camera
and LIDAR perception systems, are positive in the sense that safety and reliability
increase but, such systems need to cope with data alignment, synchronization, and
calibration [12]. A number of camera-LIDAR fusion approaches have been reported
in the literature. For example, Caltagirone et al. [5] proposed a multimodal system for
road detection using fully convolutional neural networks (FCN), camera data, and
LIDAR-based range-view representation. They proposed cross fusion FCN archi-

Fig. 17.1 Sparseness of LIDAR point-cloud, as projected to the image-plane, can be verified in the second row. A dense (non-sparse) LIDAR depth-map, in the third row, can be generated from the original point-cloud. This is an example of range view (RV) map representation. Note, however, that some unsampled pixels are still present

tecture to learn integration levels using the cross connections between the camera and LIDAR processing pipelines. Although existing works on camera (or vision)-based perception have a significant parcel in the current perception systems and ADAS developments, multimodal solutions using camera together with LIDAR are becoming more and more frequent as shown in the recent survey [10].

Perception systems for autonomous driving rely, basically, on sensor data and AI/ML techniques to interpret vehicles' surrounding environments in tasks related to object detection (e.g., pedestrians, cyclists, vehicles detection), road marks and lane detection, traffic sign recognition, obstacle/object detection and tracking, among others [9, 11, 26]. Recently, the work-horse technique for supervised object detection and recognition is deep learning [10, 13]. Convolutional Neural Networks (CNNs) is a deep-learning method which gained remarkable popularity due to impressive image classification performance and its capability of "automatic" feature-map extraction [15]. Under appropriate conditions, i.e., if a LIDAR-mapping representation is provided, a CNN can be directly used on LIDAR data as well [1, 2, 17, 19, 27]. The scientific community normally distinguishes the LIDAR-based representations into two types, range view (RV) and bird's eye view (BV) [8, 21]. The LIDAR-based representation used in this work belongs to the RV category hence, the raw LIDAR data is processed to create a so-called distance/depth-map (DM)—as shown in Fig. 17.1—which can then be fed into a CNN architecture. On the other hand, deep NNs which cope with 3D point-clouds directly are available such as PointNet [7] and LaserNet [21]. However, by transforming the LIDAR data into a 2D image (i.e., RV representation) the LIDAR-camera data integration/fusion can be performed in a straightforward manner, allowing the development of different fusion strategies.

This chapter addresses RGB-D object classification using CNN networks implemented as supervised classifiers, where RGB-D is obtained by combining data from a monocular camera and a LIDAR sensor. The test-case described in this work is a three-class object classification problem, where the categories are cars, cyclists, and pedestrians. Many experiments were conducted on a classification dataset, built up from the KITTI object detection database [12], to assess CNN-models trained under different conditions in terms of input data individually, i.e., RGB, 3D, and DM, and a RGB+D early fusion strategy. Results on object classification, using single-sensor and RGB-D (camera-Lidar) deep-NN models, are reported in terms of ROC (Receiver Operating Characteristic) curves, confusion matrices, and F-score; comparative results using two 8-bit decoding techniques for DM generation are discussed as well.

The remaining of this chapter is organized as follows. 3D LIDAR-based depth-map encoding (in the form of a RV map) using Bilateral filtering is described in Sect. 17.2. The learning models and the experimental results are reported and discussed in Sect. 17.3. Finally, Sect. 17.4 concludes this chapter.

17.2 Depth-Map Encoding for 3D-LIDAR Range-View Representation

A 3D-LIDAR is, in simple terms, a sensing technology composed of a set of laser emitters and receptors, a rotating mechanism, and a detection firmware, which outputs a set of measurement distance/range values, as well as intensity (also known as reflection returns). Most of the current state-of-the-art LIDAR sensors allow high-resolution and full-covered 360° field of view. A 360° LIDAR, for example, the Velodyne with 64 channels, when mounted on the roof of a vehicle allows the observation of the scenery in the form of a 3D point-cloud, as shown in Fig. 17.2 (middle row).

In this chapter, the point-cloud (PC) generated by the LIDAR is defined as the set of points $PC = \{\mathbf{pc}_1, \mathbf{pc}_2, \ldots, \mathbf{pc}_n\}$, in rectangular coordinates, where each element $\mathbf{pc}_i = (x, y, z)_i$, $i = 1, \ldots, n$, represents the position of a point belonging to PC. In order to facilitate and allow direct processing of PC into a CNN classi-

Fig. 17.2 Example of an image obtained through a passive sensor (color camera) in the first row, while the second row shows, for the same scene, the point-cloud obtained by a 3D-LIDAR (Velodyne HDL-64E sensor). The last row shows the projection of the point-cloud in the $2D$ image-plane. The camera and LIDAR data pictured here are based on the KITTI database [12]

fier an "image-like", also called range view (RV), representation of the PC is very convenient. Therefore, assuming the calibration matrices between a LIDAR and an RGB camera, and the camera intrinsic parameters, are known then a set of points P can be obtained by projecting the $3D$ point-cloud to the image-plane. Let us denote $P = \{\mathbf{p}_1, \mathbf{p}_2, \ldots, \mathbf{p}_n\}$ with $\mathbf{p}_i = (u, v, r)_i$, where $(u, v)_i$ represents the position in pixel coordinates and r_i is the range value (range-distance variable) as measured by the LIDAR. The position of $\mathbf{p}_i$, in pixel coordinates, is calculated according to

$$
\begin{bmatrix} u \\ v \\ 1 \end{bmatrix}_i = P_{rect}^{(i)} R_{rect}^{(0)} T_{lidar}^{cam} \mathbf{pc}_i \tag{17.1}
$$

where

- u and v represent the position pixel coordinates;
- P^i_{rect} is projection matrix;
- $R^{(0)}_{rect}$ is rectifying rotation matrix;
- T^{cam}_{lidar} is the matrix containing the matrix of rotation and translation (LIDAR to camera).

Equation 17.1 can be expanded as follows:

$$
\underbrace{\begin{bmatrix} u \\ v \\ 1 \end{bmatrix}}_{\substack{\text{Image} \\ \text{coordinates}}} = \underbrace{\begin{bmatrix} f_u^{(i)} & 0 & c_u^{(i)} & -f_u^{(i)}b_x^{(i)} \\ 0 & f_v^{(i)} & c_v^{(i)} & 0 \\ 0 & 0 & 1 & 0 \end{bmatrix} \times \begin{bmatrix} 1 & R_{12} & R_{13} & 0 \\ R_{21} & 1 & R_{23} & 0 \\ R_{31} & R_{32} & 1 & 0 \\ 0 & 0 & 0 & 1 \end{bmatrix}}_{\substack{\text{Projection} \\ \text{matrix}}} \times \underbrace{\begin{bmatrix} r_{11} & r_{12} & r_{13} & t_x \\ r_{21} & r_{22} & r_{23} & t_y \\ r_{31} & r_{32} & r_{33} & t_z \\ 0 & 0 & 0 & 1 \end{bmatrix}}_{\substack{\text{LIDAR to} \\ \text{camera}}} \times \underbrace{\begin{bmatrix} x_v \\ y_v \\ z_v \\ 1 \end{bmatrix}}_{\substack{\text{LIDAR} \\ \text{coordinates}}}
$$

(17.2)

where f_u and f_v are focal lengths, c_u and c_v are principal point, and $b_x^{(i)}$ denotes a baseline (in meters) with respect to reference camera zero. Figure 17.2 shows an example of the $3D$ point-cloud projected in the $2D$ image-plane. In the first row, there is a $2D$ image obtained by a monocular camera, the second row shows LIDAR data and the last row shows the projection of the $3D$ point-clouds.

The set of points P is then used to build a distance/depth-map (DM), which is equivalent to a range-view representation. Although n's order of magnitude is of thousands of points, still the number of unsampled points in the image-plane is significant.[1] Therefore, to obtain a dense, or high-resolution, depth-map (DM) it is necessary to estimate, as much as possible, the values of r_i in unsampled locations of the map. To estimate the unsampled pixels' values in P, a spatial filtering technique can be used. Thus, given a mask $\mathbf{M}$ with size $m \times m$ pixels, the points in P that belong to $\mathbf{M}$ are weighted to estimate the range pixel's value located in the center of $\mathbf{M}$.

One possible approach to obtain a depth-map is the Bilateral Filter [25]. By applying the sliding window technique principle, which is based on a local mask $\mathbf{M}$, Bilateral filtering is used to estimate unsampled locations in P to achieve a dense depth-map (DM) which will serve, in combination with RGB data, as input to a RGB-D-CNN model on object classification. The DM generation comprises two steps: (1) Upsampling using Bilateral interpolation, and (2) DM 8-bit encoding ("Range Inverse" or "Range Linear").

Figure 17.3 shows the 8-bit depth-map profile using range-inverse and range-linear methods. The main difference between these methods is that range-inverse assigns more bits (i.e., more information) at near ranges while range-linear quantization is homogeneous regardless of the range values. This can be useful because some precision may be lost due to the 8-bit conversion.[2]

---

[1] Considering images of 1392×512 pixels resolution.

[2] More details at https://developers.google.com/depthmap-metadata/encoding.

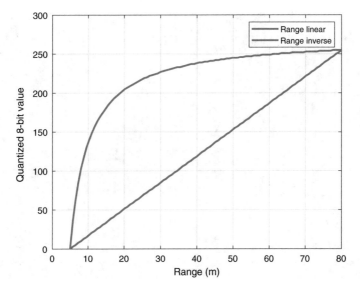

Fig. 17.3 Resulting profile curves, on 8-bit depth-map encoding, using range-inverse (red) and range-linear (blue) techniques

17.2.1   Bilateral Filter for LIDAR-Based Depth-Map

Bilateral filter (BF) [25], a well-known spatial filtering method in image processing, aims to eliminate noise and preserve edges in images. BF name derives from the reason that the filter combines two components: intensity filtering (pixels having similar values) and domain filtering (pixels at nearby spatial locations) [25]. Each output pixel of the filtered image is a function of the pixel values of the original image, taking into account a certain local mask $\mathbf{M}$.

Let $\mathbf{k}_0 = (u, v)_0$ denote the location of interest, which is the center of $\mathbf{M}$, and r_0^* be the variable to be estimated, i.e., the depth/distance (r_i) at $\mathbf{k}_0$. Thus, following the notations in [23], the BF can be expressed by

$$r_0^* = \frac{1}{W} \sum_{k_i \in M} \underbrace{G_{\sigma_s}(||\mathbf{k}_0 - \mathbf{k}_i||)}_{\text{domain weight}} \underbrace{G_{\sigma_r}(|r_0 - r_i|)}_{\text{depth weight}} \times r_i \qquad (17.3)$$

$$W = \sum_{k_i \in M} G_{\sigma_s}(||\mathbf{k}_0 - \mathbf{k}_i||) G_{\sigma_r}(|r_0 - r_i|) \qquad (17.4)$$

where W is a normalization factor that ensures the weights sum to one, G_{σ_s} weights the point $\mathbf{k}_i$ inversely proportional to a distance (here we use the Euclidean distance) between the center of the $\mathbf{M}$ and the sampled locations $\mathbf{k}_i$ to the position of interest $\mathbf{k}_0$, and G_{σ_r} controls the influence of the sampled points based on their values r_i (range

Fig. 17.4 Depth-map using the Bilateral filter with mask size 13 × 13. In the first row, the DM was generated using range-linear quantization while, in the second row, range-inverse was used instead

data in the DM-map). In other words, G_{σ_r} smooths differences in intensities and G_{σ_s} influences smoothing in position. Because BF considers distances in the spatial and intensity (depth) domains, different functions can be applied to each component i.e., spatial location and the pixel depth's value. The gain-components G_{σ_s} and G_{σ_r} can be calculated according to

$$G_{\sigma_s} = \frac{1}{1 + (\|x_0 - x_i\|)} \qquad (17.5)$$

$$G_{\sigma_r} = \frac{1}{1 + (|r_0 - r_i|)}. \qquad (17.6)$$

Figure 17.4 shows an example of a dense depth-map (DM), using BF with a mask size 13 × 13, taking as input the LIDAR-points as given in Fig. 17.2. In the first row, the DM was obtained using range-linear 8-bit encoding while the resulting DM in the second row used range-inverse.

17.3 Experiments and Results

To evaluate single-sensor models, RGB (camera-only) and RV (range-view, or depth-map—DM), and the combined model, i.e., RGB-D, a three-category object classification dataset, containing color images and LIDAR data, was generated from the

KITTI's *2D object detection* database. The experiments are performed using different deep-NN architectures, as classifiers, for the different data representations: RGB, "D" (i.e., DM), and RGB-D. In summary, deep-NN models were trained using camera and LIDAR data separately and in combination, the latter is designated by RGB-D model.

Results are reported in terms of confusion matrix, classification performance measures (F-score and AUC—area under ROC-curve), and plots are shown for the receiver operating characteristic (ROC) curves, allowing a more detailed and accurate analysis of the results on "pedestrians", "car", and "cyclists" classification. F-score and true-positives were calculated considering a threshold of 0.5.

17.3.1 Dataset

A reliable and significant dataset containing labeled camera-images and high-resolution 3D-LIDAR data collected in real-world conditions is a very challenging and demanding work [12, 18, 28]. The KITTI database is a state-of-the-art public available dataset that allows benchmarking object detection using camera (mono and/or stereo) and 3D-LIDAR data gathered in traffic roads and urban scenarios. Based on the *2D object detection* from KITTI, we created a "classification" dataset where the classes are given in the form of 2D bounding box tracklets: car, van, truck, pedestrian and cyclist, tram and misc. We composed the dataset in three classes/categories of interest: pedestrian, car (van, truck, and small car), and cyclist. A 70% split was used for training (10% of that for validation) and the remaining 30% was used as the testing set. Table 17.1 gives a summary of the classification dataset employed in this work.

Depth maps (DMs), using a Bilateral filter approach with a mask size of 13×13, were generated from 3D-LIDAR data to compose the classification dataset corresponding to the D-channel. Figure 17.5 shows some examples of "car", "cyclist", and "pedestrians" in RGB color space and DM's representation. The differences in DMs are due to the 8-bit encoding techniques. Additionally, a point-cloud based dataset was created to allow the training of a PointNet network.

Table 17.1 Summary of the classification dataset

Sub-datasets	Car	Cyclist	Pedestrian	#Total
Training	20,632	1025	2827	24,484
Validation	2293	114	314	2721
Testing	9825	488	1346	11,659
Total	32,750	1627	4487	38,864
% of total	84.3	4.2	11.5	100

Fig. 17.5 In the first row, we have examples of cars, cyclists, and pedestrians as seen by a monocular camera. The second and third lines show the corresponding DMs generated from LIDAR data using Bilateral filter, with mask size of 13×13, and 8-bit linear and inverse range encoding, respectively

17.3.2 Deep Neural Network Models

Experiments were performed using three deep networks, AlexNet [14], Inception $V3$ [24], and PointNet [7]. The first two networks were used on RGB-images, DMs, and RGB-D representations, while the PointNet was trained directly on 3D-points[3] extracted from the LIDAR data. The networks were trained from scratch for the pedestrian, car, and cyclist classes, using the training dataset given in Table 17.1.

The AlexNet CNN architecture used in the experiments on object classification consists of 11×11, 5×5 and three 3×3 convolution layers, with *max* pooling; further details are described in [20]. We used batch normalization in the first two layers, instead of the local normalization scheme, and in the last layer we use the *softmax* activation function with three classes (i.e., $nc = 3$), instead of 1000 classes, and dropout of 50%. The image size should be the same to feed the network, therefore, all RGB-images and DMs were resized to the size of 227×227. The AlexNet network was trained on 30 epochs, with a batch size equal to 64, stochastic gradient descent optimizer with $lr = 0.001$ (learning rate), $decay = 10^{-6}$ (learning rate decay over each update), $momentum = 0.9$, and categorical cross-entropy as loss function.

Inception $V3$, which contains 42 layers, is one of the state-of-the-art CNNs which has been achieved very satisfactory results on image classification. The main contri-

---

[3]Although not being the focus of this chapter, results using PointNet are presented for sake of completeness and comparison.

bution of Inception $V3$ was the idea of introducing convolutional factorization layers (by reducing the number of parameters/connections, for example, two 3×3 convolution layers replaces a 5×5 convolution layer) and a classifier-auxiliary acting as a regularizer, as well as a new structure to image reduction after the convolution layers (grid size reduction), instead of using only *max* pooling [24].

LIDAR-based object recognition uses, on most of the cases, a 2D-like representation of the 3D point-clouds, e.g., RV, BV, or multi-view, to feed and train a CNN model. Conversely, the PointNet can be used to process *unordered* 3D point-clouds directly [7]. PointNet considers permutation invariance (order), transformation invariance and point interaction. Basically, the 3D-LIDAR point set is processed by two multi-layer perceptron (MLP) stages, by performing feature transformations and aggregations, which increase the feature-space dimension to 64 and then to 1024 dimensions; in the second MLP a *max* pooling is applied to create a global feature vector and, to complete the architecture, a $(512, 256, nc)$ MLP-layer is used to process the global feature vector for the subsequent classification/output layer. However, because the input layer has to have the same dimension for all classes the number of LIDAR-points (np) per object, which is the network input, has to be the same as well; therefore, in the classification problem considered here, upsampling and downsampling strategies were necessary to guarantee np is the same regardless the size, distance to the sensor, and the class of the object.

17.3.3   Single-Sensor Models Performance: RGB Versus Depth

Experiments on RGB-images and DMs were performed using Inception V3 and AlexNet architectures, where the CNN's inputs receive color images (a 3-channel model) or DMs (single channel) depending on the model under evaluation. The implemented CNN's architecture and parameters for both LIDAR DM-maps, using range linear (RL) and inverse (RI) quantization techniques, are the same. Additionally, a PointNet-based model was learned using the 3D-points that belong to the labeled-objects. Consequently, and considering single-sensor technology, we have four deep-NN models regarding input data: RGB, DM using range-linear quantization (DM_{RL}), DM using range-inverse (DM_{RI}), and 3D-point based architecture (PointNet). To train the PointNet the labeled examples are in the form of a set of 3D point-sets which were extracted from the input (raw) point-cloud.

The resulting confusion matrices, calculated on the testing set, are given in Table 17.2 for RGB and DMs. Experiments using PointNet were performed by increasing number of points per input-example $np = \{64, 128, 256, 512\}$ points. The results on the testing set, having 1000 epochs during the training, are shown in Table 17.3 where the PointNet-model with $np = 256$ achieved the best classification performance. In terms of average F-score, the performance for $np =$

Table 17.2 Confusion matrices on the testing set: single-sensor modalities

Ground truth class	Inception V3 architecture								
	RGB images			LIDAR DM_{RL}			LIDAR DM_{RI}		
	Ped.	Car	Cyc.	Ped.	Car	Cyc.	Ped.	Car	Cyc.
Pedestrian	**1300**	31	15	**1127**	213	6	**1206**	108	32
Car	45	**9773**	7	265	9511	49	53	**9742**	30
Cyclist	22	19	**447**	210	115	163	55	72	**361**
	AlexNet architecture								
Pedestrian	1295	42	9	1062	254	30	1114	201	31
Car	52	9768	5	38	**9781**	6	87	9729	9
Cyclist	99	30	359	47	123	**318**	84	127	266

Table 17.3 Confusion matrix for a LIDAR-based PointNet model

GT	PointNet—predicted class on the testing set											
	$np = 64$			$np = 128$			$np = 256$			$np = 512$		
	Ped.	Car	Cyc.	Ped.	Car	Cyc.	Ped.	Car	Cyc.	Ped.	Car	Cyc.
Ped.	1173	134	39	1160	146	40	**1174**	140	32	1163	128	55
Car	128	9655	42	111	9676	38	68	**9724**	33	89	9680	56
Cyc.	109	103	276	93	100	295	55	74	**359**	95	102	291

64, 128, **256**, 512 are 82.80%, 84.04%, **88.66%** and 83.54%, respectively. The values in the confusion matrices were calculated using a threshold equal to 0.5.

The ROC curves for AlexNet and Inception models are shown in Fig. 17.6, together with their corresponding value of AUC (Area Under Curve). It can be seen, in terms of DMs representations, that the Inception is more suitable to be used in DM_{RI} while AlexNet works better with DM_{RL}. From the results in Table 17.2, the RGB-CNN achieved the best overall results for all classes. On the other hand, the results yielded by the LIDAR-based representations were not homogeneous. By using DM_{RL}, the AlexNet achieved good results for "car" and 'cyclist" while Inception was superior when using DM_{RI} representation. In terms of LIDAR data quantization, it can be seen that Inception V3 using DM_{RI} produced the best results. In summary, RGB-models perform better than LIDAR-models overall however, concerning LIDAR representation, Inception-DM_{RI} performed better than 3D point-sets (PointNet). Finally, in terms of AUC as per given in Fig. 17.6, the RGB-models attained the overall best performance compared to LIDAR-models.

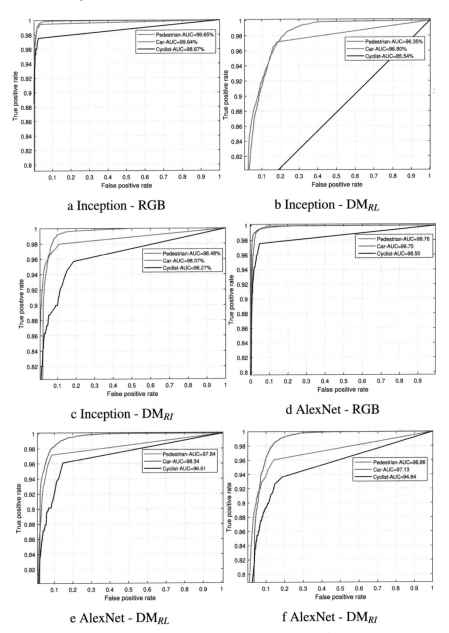

Fig. 17.6 ROCs, on the testing set, calculated for the Inception and AlexNet CNN-architectures having as inputs: RGB (3 channels), DM_{RL}, and DM_{RI} (1 channel). AUC are shown in the legends

Table 17.4 RGB-D object classification performance

Ground truth class	Inception V3						AlexNet					
	RGB-D $_{RL}$			RGB-D $_{RI}$			RGB-D $_{RL}$			RGB-D $_{RI}$		
	Ped.	Car	Cyc.	Ped.	Car	Cyc.	Ped.	Car	Cyc.	Ped.	Car	Cyc.
Pedestrian	**1262**	49	35	1246	57	43	1291	45	10	**1292**	46	8
Car	103	9689	33	74	**9725**	26	60	9748	17	49	**9764**	12
Cyclist	57	49	382	56	42	**390**	80	31	377	40	25	**423**

17.3.4 RGB-D: Camera and LIDAR Data

The confusion matrices calculated on the testing set for CNN-models trained using RGB-D representation i.e., four channel models, are provided in Table 17.4. In terms of true-positives, per class, the model where the DMs were interpolated using range-inverse encoding achieved the best results. Considering the values of AUC and the ROC curves, shown in Fig. 17.7, the performance for both models are very close, however the RGB-D-AlexNet is relatively favored. In summary, when combining camera and LIDAR data to obtain RGB-D models the range-inverse quantization, applied to DMs, achieved better results than range-linear maps.

To allow a more comprehensive analysis of all the deep-networks discussed in this section, Table 17.5 provides the results for the implemented CNN-models in terms of the average F-score (in %). Because of the unbalanced nature of the dataset, F-score is an appropriate measure to summarize classification performance. Based on the values highlighted in bold, RGB-Inception V3 has the overall best performance out of the DMs and RGB-D representations. The AlexNet achieved its best results by incorporating RGB and DM$_{RI}$, i.e., using RGB-D representation, which is close to the RGB-Inception V3. Although the PointNet yielded good performance, DMs representation provided more significant results in terms of LIDAR-based deep-networks. Finally, the RGB-D models demonstrated to be useful and a promising representation specifically when compared to LIDAR-based models and also achieved the best results for the AlexNet architecture.

17.3.4.1 Discussion on Performance with Respect to Objects' Distance

To evaluate classification performance relative to the objects' distance, the RGB-D dataset was organized according to the average distance of the objects as measured by the LIDAR (which is mounted on the vehicle's roof [12]). Figure 17.8 shows the distribution of the number of labeled examples versus the distance—ranging from 5 up to 65 m (in 15 m steps). The distributions show that the majority of the examples are at a distance up to 35 m.

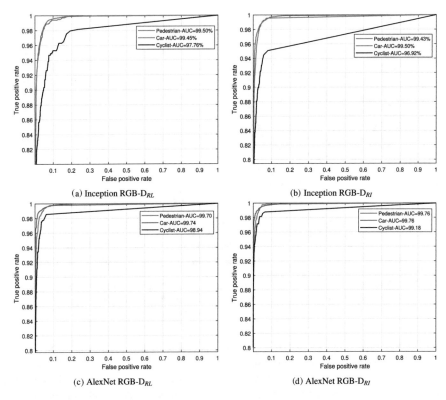

Fig. 17.7 ROC curves for the RGB-D CNN-architectures (4 channels)

Table 17.5 F-score performance (in %), averaged over the three classes, for all the deep-networks discussed in this chapter

	Inception V3					AlexNet					PointNet
	RGB	DM_{RL}	DM_{RI}	$RGBD_{RL}$	$RGBD_{RI}$	RGB	DM_{RL}	DM_{RI}	$RGBD_{RL}$	$RGBD_{RI}$	3D
F_1	**96.24**	73.13	89.55	90.48	90.97	91.83	86.21	83.79	92.24	**94.99**	88.66

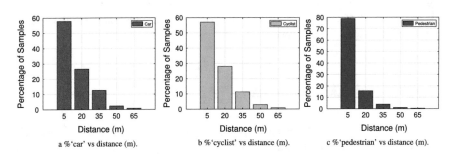

Fig. 17.8 Percentage of classes versus distance, as per measured by the 3D-LIDAR

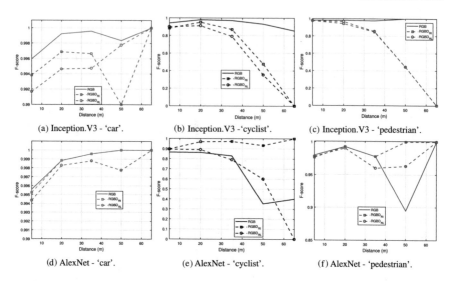

Fig. 17.9 F-score performance versus distance, ranging from 5 up to 70 m. First row gives RGB-D-Inception V3 results, per object class, followed by RGB-D-AlexNet results

The main idea in this section is to show the deep-networks performance on object classification using RGB-D in comparison with RGB inputs. Because LIDAR provides distance/range measurements, an analysis in terms of the objects' distance is relevant to investigate how consistent the CNN results are for increasing distances. The average F-score was the performance metric selected, whilst the RGB-based results serve as the baseline for comparisons. Figure 17.9 shows, for both RGB-D-CNN-models using Inception and AlexNet (dashed-plots), the values of F-score relative to the objects' distance. The plots also show that the RGB-D models are more sensitive to the distance, which is an expected behavior because the LIDAR resolution is strongly affected by the distance; for example, "distant" objects are perceived as a small set of points by the LIDAR. Another conclusion drawn from Fig. 17.9 is that the RGB-D Inception-based networks are more sensitive than the AlexNet models. Finally, the results for the "car" category demonstrated to be more consistent regardless the distance.

17.4 Conclusions and Remarks

RGB-D object classification using deep-networks, based on camera (RGB) and 3D-LIDAR (Depth) data representations, has been addressed in this chapter. Three object classes were considered: pedestrian, cyclist, car. Object labels were extracted from the *KITTI Object database*. For the 3D-LIDAR data, and by using Bilateral filtering, depth-maps (DM) were calculated to allow a direct implementation of *range-view*

2D-CNN-models—AlexNet [14] and Inception V3 [24]. As part of the process to obtain the DMs two 8-bit quantization techniques, range-inverse and range-linear encoding, were implemented and compared in terms of classification performance. Additionally, a PointNet [7] network which operates on *unordered* 3D point-sets directly was used in the experiments as well.

Experiments were conducted to investigate and compare the classification performance of the deep-network models in terms of sensor modalities and data representations. In the single-modality case, i.e., by training the deep-networks using camera-images (RGB) or LIDAR data individually, the AlexNet and the Inception V3 networks were trained and tested on RGB, DM_{RL}, and DM_{RI} representations; RL and RI stand for range-linear and range-inverse quantization respectively. The PointNet, on the other hand, was used on 3D-LIDAR-points directly. Multi-modality sensor data representation i.e., RGB-D, was addressed by aggregating RGB and DM-map into 4-channels input-layers of the CNNs; these models are designated by RGB-D $_{RL}$ and RGB-D $_{RI}$ according to the quantization technique employed. Therefore, RGB-D-based AlexNet and Inception networks were trained, evaluated and compared with the single-modalities networks.

Results of the deep-network models were analyzed in terms of F-score, confusion matrices, and ROC curves. The results on the single-modality case indicate that the RGB-based Inception V3 network achieved the best classification performance in terms of camera versus LIDAR-based models, also for the AlexNet using images which was better than the LIDAR-DMs. LIDAR-wise performance, the Inception model using DM_{RI} was slightly better than the PointNet (LIDAR only) which means the PointNet results are very competitive. The RGB-D network outperformed the LIDAR-based networks, as well as the RGB-AlexNet. This indicates the combination of RGB and LIDAR, in the form of RGB-D input-representation, works well compared to most of the single-modality cases. However, the RGB-Inception V3 demonstrated to be marginally better than the RGB-D models.

Based on the results related to the objects' distance with respect to the sensors onboard the vehicle, the classification performance specifically for the "cyclist" category is negatively affected by the distance increases. In summary, the main message that can be drawn from the results is that the RGB-D outperformed the LIDAR-based models, both range-view CNN and 3D-point PointNet, demonstrating that RGB complements LIDAR.

References

1. Asvadi A, Garrote L, Premebida C, Peixoto P, Nunes UJ (2017) DepthCN: vehicle detection using 3D-LIDAR and ConvNet. In: 2017 IEEE 20th international conference on intelligent transportation systems (ITSC), Yokohama, Japan, pp 1–6
2. Asvadi A, Garrote L, Premebida C, Peixoto P, Nunes UJ (2017) Multimodal vehicle detection: fusing 3D-LIDAR and color camera data. Pattern Recognit Lett
3. Broggi A, Grisleri P, Zani P (2013) Sensors technologies for intelligent vehicles perception systems: a comparison between vision and 3D-LIDAR. In: 2013 16th international IEEE con-

ference on intelligent transportation systems-(ITSC), pp 887–892. IEEE

4. Cai Z, Han J, Liu L, Shao L (2017) RGB-D datasets using Microsoft Kinect or similar sensors: a survey. Multimed Tools Appl 76(3):4313–4355

5. Caltagirone L, Bellone M, Svensson L, Wahde M (2019) LIDAR-camera fusion for road detection using fully convolutional neural networks. Robot Auton Syst 111:125–131

6. Cavallari T, Golodetz S, Lord N, Valentin J, Prisacariu V, Di Stefano L, Torr PHS (2019) Real-time RGB-D camera pose estimation in novel scenes using a relocalisation cascade. IEEE Trans Pattern Anal Mach Intell 1–1

7. Charles RQ, Su H, Kaichun M, Guibas LJ (2017) PointNet: deep learning on point sets for 3D classification and segmentation. In: 2017 IEEE conference on computer vision and pattern recognition (CVPR), pp 77–85

8. Chen X, Ma H, Wan J, Li B, Xia T (2017) Multi-view 3D object detection network for autonomous driving. In: 2017 IEEE conference on computer vision and pattern recognition (CVPR), pp 6526–6534

9. Feng D, Rosenbaum L, Dietmayer K (2018) Towards safe autonomous driving: capture uncertainty in the deep neural network for LIDAR 3D vehicle detection. In: 21st IEEE international conference on intelligent transportation systems (ITSC), USA

10. Feng D, Haase-Schuetz C, Rosenbaum L, Hertlein H, Duffhauss F, Glaeser C, Wiesbeck W, Dietmayer K (2019) Deep multi-modal object detection and semantic segmentation for autonomous driving: datasets, methods, and challenges. arXiv:1902.07830

11. Gao H, Cheng B, Wang J, Li K, Zhao J, Li D (2018) Object classification using CNN-based fusion of vision and LIDAR in autonomous vehicle environment. IEEE Trans Ind Inform 1–1

12. Geiger A, Lenz P, Stiller C, Urtasun R (2013) Vision meets robotics: the KITTI dataset. Int J Robot Res 32(11):1231–1237

13. Janai J, Güney F, Behl A, Geiger A (2017) Computer vision for autonomous vehicles: problems, datasets and state-of-the-art. CoRR. arXiv:1704.05519

14. Krizhevsky A, Sutskever I, Hinton GE (2012) ImageNet classification with deep convolutional neural networks. In: Proceedings of the 25th international conference on neural information processing systems - volume 1, NIPS'12, USA, pp 1097–1105

15. Lecun Y, Bengio Y, Hinton G (2015) Deep learning. Nature 521(7553):436–444

16. Lee SW, Nakatani T (eds) (2016) Sensing technologies required for ADAS/AD applications, 671. In: Third Asia-Pacific symposium, APRES. Springer

17. Li Y, Bu R, Sun M, Wu W, Di X, Chen B (2018) PointCNN: convolution on X-transformed points. In: Bengio S, Wallach H, Larochelle H, Grauman K, Cesa-Bianchi N, Garnett R (eds) Advances in neural information processing systems, vol 31, pp 820–830

18. Maddern W, Pascoe G, Linegar C, Newman P (2017) 1 year, 1000 km: the Oxford RobotCar dataset. Int J Robot Res (IJRR) 36(1):3–15

19. Maturana D, Scherer S (2015) VoxNet: a 3D convolutional neural network for real-time object recognition. In: 2015 IEEE/RSJ international conference on intelligent robots and systems (IROS), pp 922–928

20. Melotti G, Premebida C, Gonçalves NMMDS, Nunes UJC, Faria DR (2018) Multimodal CNN pedestrian classification: a study on combining LIDAR and camera data. In: 21st IEEE international conference on intelligent transportation systems (ITSC), USA

21. Meyer GP, Laddha A, Kee E, Vallespi-Gonzalez C, Wellington CK (2019) LaserNet: an efficient probabilistic 3D object detector for autonomous driving. CoRR. arXiv:1903.08701

22. Miron A, Rogozan A, Ainouz S, Bensrhair A, Broggi A (2015) An evaluation of the pedestrian classification in a multi-domain multi-modality setup. Sensors 15(6):13851–13873

23. Premebida C, Garrote L, Asvadi A, Ribeiro AP, Nunes U (2016) High-resolution LIDAR-based depth mapping using bilateral filter. In: 2016 IEEE 19th international conference on intelligent transportation systems (ITSC), pp 2469–2474

24. Szegedy C, Vanhoucke V, Ioffe S, Shlens J, Wojna Z (2016) Rethinking the inception architecture for computer vision. In: 2016 IEEE conference on computer vision and pattern recognition (CVPR), pp 2818–2826

25. Tomasi C, Manduchi R (1998) Bilateral filtering for gray and color images. In: Proceedings of the IEEE international conference on computer vision, Bombay, India
26. Wang Z, Zhan W, Tomizuka M (2017) Fusing bird view LIDAR point cloud and front view camera image for deep object detection. CoRR. arXiv:1711.06703
27. Yang B, Luo W, Urtasun R (2018) PIXOR: real-time 3D object detection from point clouds. In: Conference on computer vision and pattern recognition (CVPR), pp 7652–7660
28. Yin H, Berger C (2017) When to use what data set for your self-driving car algorithm: an overview of publicly available driving datasets. In: 2017 IEEE 20th international conference on intelligent transportation systems (ITSC), Japan, pp 1–8

Chapter 18
People Counting in Crowded Environment and Re-identification

Emanuele Frontoni, Marina Paolanti and Rocco Pietrini

Abstract Nowadays, detecting people and understanding their behaviour automatically is one of the key aspects of modern intelligent video systems. This interest arises from societal needs. Security and Video Analytics, Intelligent Retail Environment and Activities of Daily Living are just a few of the possible applications. The problem remains largely open due to several serious challenges such as occlusion, change of appearance, complex and dynamic background. Nevertheless, in recent years, privacy concerns are arising making these system designs more challenging, also to cope with different worldwide country regulations. Popular sensors for this task are RGB-D cameras because of their availability, reliability and affordability. Studies have demonstrated the great value (both in accuracy and efficiency) of depth camera in coping with severe occlusions among humans and complex background. In particular, RGB-D cameras show their great potential if used in a top-view configuration achieving high performances even in a crowded environment (considering at least 3 people per square meter in the area of the camera) minimizing occlusions and also being the most privacy-compliant approach. The first step in people detection and tracking is the segmentation to retrieve people silhouette, for this reason different methods will be covered in this chapter, ranging from classical handcraft feature based approaches to deep learning techniques. These techniques also solve the nontrivial problem of blob collision, occurring when two or more people are close enough to form a unique blob from the camera point of view. Multilevel segmentation and water filling algorithms will be presented to the reader in this chapter as handcraft feature based, in addition a deep learning approach is also introduced from the literature. In the methods presented in this chapter, the elaboration occurs live (there is no image recording) and occurs on the edge, following an IoT paradigm. Live analysis

---

E. Frontoni (✉) · M. Paolanti · R. Pietrini
Department of Information Engineering, Universitá Politecnica delle Marche,
Ancona 60121, Italy
e-mail: e.frontoni@univpm.it

M. Paolanti
e-mail: m.paolanti@univpm.it

R. Pietrini
e-mail: r.pietrini@pm.univpm.it

© Springer Nature Switzerland AG 2019
P. L. Rosin et al. (eds.), *RGB-D Image Analysis and Processing*,
Advances in Computer Vision and Pattern Recognition,
https://doi.org/10.1007/978-3-030-28603-3_18

also strengthens the aforementioned concept of privacy compliance. The last part of this chapter is dedicated to person re-identification (re-id), which is the process to determine if different instances or images of the same person, recorded in different moments, belong to the same subject. Person re-id has many important applications in video surveillance, because it saves human efforts on exhaustively searching for a person from large amounts of video sequences. Identification cameras are widely employed in most of the public places like malls, office buildings, airports, stations and museums. These cameras generally provide enhanced coverage and overlay large geospatial areas because they have non-overlapping fields-of-views. Huge amounts of video data, monitored in real time by law enforcement officers are used after the event for forensic purposes, are provided by these networks. An automated analysis of these data improves significantly the quality of monitoring, in addition to processing the data faster. Handcrafted anthropomorphic features coupled with a machine learning approach will be exploited in this chapter, then a deep leaning approach in comparison is presented. Different metrics are then adopted to evaluate the above algorithms and to compare them.

18.1 Introduction

Nowadays, detecting and tracking people is an utmost important and challenging task for various applications. It can be viably used in many interactive and intelligent systems such as visual surveillance and human–computer interaction. Recently, a considerable research has been made towards this topic and robust methods have been developed to track isolated or a small number of humans in case of the existence of transient occlusion [15, 72]. Nonetheless, tracking in crowded situations with a high number of people present in the image is experiencing many issues such as the exhibition of persistent occlusion, change of appearance, dynamic and complex background [41]. Indeed, these issues are the cause of the severe problems in the case of crowded environment since the conventional surveillance technologies cease to understand the image [68].

The methods dealing with people counting problems can be divided into twofold: detection-based methods and mapping-based methods. The first ones refer to running a detector, counting or clustering the output. The different features can include body, head, skin, hair, etc. For effective detection algorithms, they can have a high output accuracy for not highly crowded environments, but are not scalable for large crowds [68]. The mapping-based methods are referring to feature extraction and mapping them to a value. They use edge points, background, texture, optical flow, etc., as the features. Compared to detection-based methods, these methods can be scalable to large crowds. To address people detecting and tracking problems, sensors viably adopted are RGB-D cameras. Compared to conventional cameras, their performance results in increased reliability, availability and affordability. The efficiency and accuracy of depth cameras have been proven to be elevated in cases with severe occlusions among humans and complex background [53]. The combination of high-resolution depth and visual information opens up new opportunities in many applications in the field of activity recognition and people tracking. Tracking and detection results can be significantly improved by the use of reliable depth maps [32].

In existing works, depth cameras are often placed either vertically overhead (top-view configuration) [8], or horizontally at the same level as humans (front-view configuration) [21]. The preferred choice is the RGB-D camera in a top-view configuration since it offers greater suitability compared with a front-view configuration. It moreover reduces the problem of occlusions and has the ability of being privacy preserving since a person's face is not recorded by the camera [32]. In [33], it has been shown that top-view people counting applications are the most accurate (with accuracy up to 99%) even in highly crowded scenarios, defined as situations with more than three people per square meter. However, this configuration is showing also an important limitation: inability to retrieve features connected to the front view, since the front-view configuration has been highly employed by many state-of-the-art approaches [60, 61].

In the literature exist several datasets using RGB-D technology for the study of person re-id mainly in the front-view configuration such as VIPeR [19], the iLIDS multi-camera tracking scenario [58], ETHZ [11], CAVIAR4REID [4, 6]. They cover many aspects of the existing problems such as shape deformation, occlusions, illumination changes, very-low-resolution images and image blurring. The top-view dataset is introduced in [31], called TVPR (Top- View Person Re-identification) dataset.

There have been many vision techniques and algorithms proposed in the literature in the past years for person detection and tracking. In general, we can distinguish the following: segmentation using background subtraction, water filling, statistical algorithms, machine learning, and finally deep learning techniques.

This chapter is organized as follows: Sect. 18.2 is giving the state of the art on the algorithms and approaches for person detection and tracking, Sect. 18.3 is giving results and use cases and in final Sect. 18.4 the conclusions are given.

18.2 Algorithms and Approaches

Many vision techniques and algorithms for person detection and tracking have been proposed during the past years. In this section, we give the state of the art on algorithms and techniques applied for tracking and detecting humans from top-view RGB-D data, covering both early and recent literature. In particular, the approaches related to segmentation using background subtraction, water filling, statistical algorithms, and finally machine learning and deep learning techniques are considered.

18.2.1 Approaches Using Background Subtraction

In most of the approaches, it is necessary to remove the background to obtain better accuracy in the next stages. In re-id, the methods that use the same reference background frame are not useful since data are grabbed from different cameras and with different backgrounds [49]. The most Naïve approach for background elimination method is the manual silhouette segmentation as proposed in [1]. Many works in the literature [48, 64, 65] use Gaussian mixture models (GMMs) for the background classification, introduced by [52]. The limitation is the sensitivity to fast illumination variations. Another approach is proposing the notion of a structure element [23], referring to a probabilistic element of an entire image class and widely employed for background elimination [12, 50]. The main advantage is that it can be used in the case of still images of a dataset with different backgrounds. However, the limitation is that it is time consuming. In [25], the authors use depth information from the Kinect camera, by exploiting the distance between the head and the floor.

In [67], a system is proposed for passenger counting in buses based on stereovision. The counting system involves different steps dedicated to the detection, segmentation, tracking and counting. The height maps have been segmented for highlighting the passengers' heads at different levels, resulting in kernels-binary images containing information related to the heads [34]. It makes use of the idea of computed tomography (CT) and the depth images are segmented to different layers along the transverse plane. The depth images are segmented into K layers as the CT slides with a fixed value of depth spacing between two adjacent layers. Then, based on the classic contour finding algorithm, the region of each slide can be found. Afterwards, an SVM classifier is trained to classify the activities. Another work is proposing a method of low-level segmentation and tracking, namely, the system detects the interactions with products on the shelves but also the movement of the people inside the store [43].

The authors [17] employ Microsoft Kinect depth sensor in an on-ceiling configuration and propose an automatic indoor fall detection method based on the analysis of depth frames. A segmentation algorithm is used to recognize the elements acquired. It extracts the elements and implements a solution to classify all the blobs in the scene. The human subjects are recognized by anthropometric relationships and features. In [10], an approach is presented for low-level body part segmentation based on RGB-D data gathered from the RGB-D sensor. The object classes are certain human body parts. In order to generate data for training the classifier, the authors make use of synthetic representation of the human body in a virtual environment in combination with Kinect skeleton tracking data.

The approach with multiple depth cameras is presented in [55], with the goal to develop real-time indoor surveillance system for tracking. The system tries to overcome the well-known problems such as severe occlusion, similar appearance, illumination changes, etc. It is based on the background subtraction of the stitched top-view images. Different phases have been employed in the detection scheme such as the graph-based segmentation, the head hemiellipsoid model, and the geodesic distance map, resulting in improved robustness and efficiency when compared to other state-of-the-art techniques.

The algorithm proposed in [24] shows an improvement of the classical segmentation techniques. It begins with nearest neighbour interpolation in order to fill the holes in the depth map. After that, the median filter with a 5×5 window on the depth array is executed to smoothen the data. In order to extract the person, the algorithm extracts the floor and removes its corresponding pixels from the depth map. After that, to confirm the presence of the tracked subject as well as to provide head's location, a Support Vector Machine (SVM) based person finder is used. The algorithm shows promising results in achieving high sensitivity and specificity of fall detection in poor lighting conditions. Method for people counting in public transportation has also been presented in [36] using a segmentation approach. Data from Kinect sensor contains an image database of 1–5 persons, with and without body poses of holding a handrail. However, in this case, the image is processed in blocks with the goal to find potential local maxima, in order to find head candidates in the next step. Finally, non-head objects are filtered out.

The approach in [5] employs a novel active sensor based on a Time of Flight (TOF) technology applied in real time people tracking system, successful also in severe low-lighting conditions. A simple background subtraction procedure based on a pixel-wise parametric statistical model is performed. The system has proven to be reliable by the experiments conducted under changing lighting conditions and involving multiple people in close interaction.

A method using top-view camera system is presented in [45], used for human detection. The authors introduce a new feature descriptor to train a head-shoulder detector by the usage of discriminative class scheme, with excellent runtime performance. A final tracking step reliably propagates detection providing stable tracking results.

The papers [38, 39] have addressed the problem of the tracking of 3D human gestures by particle filtering and by using the Xtion PRO-LIVE camera. A hybrid 2D–3D method is proposed, consisting in separating human body in two parts; head and shoulders tracked in the 2D space, and arms tracked in the 3D space.

18.2.2 Water Filling

Water Filling is a computer vision algorithm adopted by many researchers while considering RGB-D cameras in top-view configuration.

In [71], the authors have built a system which uses vertical Kinect sensor for people counting, and the depth information is used to remove the effect of the appearance variation. They propose a novel unsupervised water filling method that can find suitable local minimum regions (people heads) with the property of robustness, locality and scale-invariance, even in crowded scenarios. The limitation is seen in the fact that water filling cannot handle the situation, where some moving object is closer to the sensor than head.

People counting system using water filling technique is also presented in [7]. In this case, the sensor is placed perpendicular to the ceiling. Water filling algorithm is used for the determination of the people's heads. Robot Operating System (ROS) is used to capture depth information from the Kinect sensor, and the images are

processed by using open-source library OpenCV. Some minor contributions have
been obtained such as elimination of chattering, tracking the person lost in the image
for a short time.

Water filling algorithm finds local minimum regions in depth images simulating
the rain and the flooding of ground, with some raindrop, with a uniform distribution.
Moving the raindrops towards the local minimum points puddles are formed since
the water flows to some local minimum regions. Contour lines can be computed
considering the distance from the local minimum as a function of the total raindrops.
A depth image can be seen as a function $f(x, y)$ that can be non-derivable or even
discontinuous, due to the noise of depth sensor. Finding people means to find local
minimum regions in f. The problem can be defined as finding the region A and N
satisfying the following equation [71]:

$$E_A(f(x, y)) + \eta \leqslant E_{N \setminus A}(f(x, y)) \tag{18.1}$$

where $A \in N$, A is the local region and N is its neighbourhood, both of arbitrary
shape, $E(\cdot)$ is an operation to relate the depth information in the region to a real value
reflecting the total depth information in the region. η is a threshold to ensure that
depth in A should be lower than $N \setminus A$ within a tolerance. Zhang et al. [71] define an
additional measure function $g(x, y)$ as

Definition 18.1 $g(x, y)$ is a measure function of $f(x, y) \iff \exists \epsilon > 0, \forall (x_1, y_1),$
(x_2, y_2), s.t. $\|(x_1 - x_2)^2 + (y_1 - y_2)^2\| < \epsilon$, if $f(x_1, y_1) \leqslant f(x_2, y_2)$

$$f(x_1, y_1) + g(x_1, y_1) \leqslant f(x_2, y_2) + g(x_2, y_2) \tag{18.2}$$

$$g(x_1, y_1) \geqslant g(x_2, y_2)$$
$$g(x_1, y_1) \geqslant 0, g(x_2, y_2) \geqslant 0$$

The form of $g(x, y)$ can be trivial, for example, a zero function. The use of $g(x, y)$
helps to infer the $f(x, y)$. Definition of $g(x, y)$ allows us to solve efficiently the
equation and be robust to noise.

A general solution of $g(x, y)$ is not necessary for these contexts, but a proper
nontrivial form is acceptable. The form of the function $f(x, y)$ can be seen as a
land with humps and hollows. In the hump, raindrops flow to the neighbourhood
hollow due to the force of gravity. Step by step the hollow region will be filled
with raindrops. Function $g(x, y)$ represents the quantity of raindrop in the point
(x, y). When the rain stops, regions that collected rain drops can be classified as
hollow. Algorithm 18.1 proposed by Liciotti et at. [30] is an improved version of
the original method proposed in [71]. In particular, the drops are chosen according
to the segmentation of the foreground image (line 4). This procedure improves the
execution time of the algorithm. The main characteristics are depicted in Fig. 18.1.

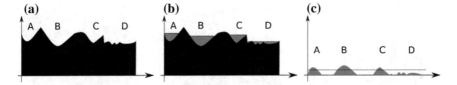

Fig. 18.1 The main characteristics of water filling algorithm. A, B, C correspond to three people, respectively, and D is a noise region (figure a). Region A has smaller scale compared with B and C, and the absolute height of A is larger than noise region D. After the water filling process (figure b), the measure function $g(x, y)$ which reflects the property of $f(x, y)$ is obtained (figure c). Finally, the people are detected by a threshold operation on measure function $g(x, y)$

Algorithm 18.1 Water Filling

1: **function** WATERFILLING($f(x, y), T, K$)
2:    $g(x, y) = 0$
3:    $M, N = size(f(x, y))$
4:    $fg(x, y) = (bg(x, y)â¨f(x, y)) > T$ where $fg(x, y)$ is the foreground and $bg(x, y)$ the background
5:    **for** $k = 1 : K$ **do**
6:       $x = rand(1, M), y = rand(1, N)$ with $(x, y) \in fg(x, y)$
7:       **while** *True* **do**
8:          $d(x_n, y_n) = f(x_n, y_n) + g(x_n, y_n)â¨(f(x, y) + g(x, y))$ where (x_n, y_n) is the neighbourhood of (x, y)
9:          $(x^*, y^*) = arg \min d(x_n, y_n)$
10:         **if** $d(x^*, y^*) < 0$ **then**
11:            $x = x^*, y = y^*$
12:         **else**
13:            $g(x, y) = g(x, y) + 1$
14:            *break*
15:         **end if**
16:      **end while**
17:   **end for**
18:   **return** $g(x, y) > T$
19: **end function**

The total number of raindrops is $K = tMN$, where t is usually set to be 100. Every iteration (line 5), (x, y) is randomly generated through a discrete uniform distribution (line 6). If there is a point (x^*, y^*) in the neighbourhood of (x, y) that satisfies Eq. 18.2 then the raindrop in (x, y) flows towards (x^*, y^*) and the loop is restarted until a local minimum is reached. When a local minimum is reached, the measure function $g(\cdot)$ is increased (line 13). After all the K raindrops find their stable places, measure function $g(x, y)$ is calculated and by applying a threshold T, it is possible to extract the heads of people that are under the camera (line 18).

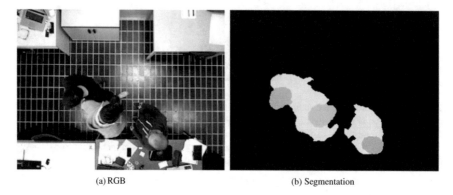

(a) RGB   (b) Segmentation

Fig. 18.2 Multilevel segmentation algorithm. Head recognition (**b**): different colours of the blob highlight the head of the people detected in the scene (**a**). Images from [29]

18.2.3 Multilevel Segmentation

The Multilevel Segmentation algorithm overcomes the limitations of common binary segmentation methods in case of collisions among people. In a normal segmentation, when two people collide they become a single blob (person). Multilevel segmentation ensures that, when a collision occurs, even if two people are in a single blob, their heads are detected and taken into account as discriminant elements [13]. In Fig. 18.2, it is possible to see the head of each person obtained by the multilevel segmentation algorithm. In case of collisions both people's heads are detected in the yellow blob (Figs. 18.2a and b). Multilevel segmentation is explained in detail in the pseudocode Algorithm 18.2. The MULTILEVELSEGM function takes the foreground image $(f(x, y))$ as input. FINDPOINTMAX function calculates the highest point in the image (max) and its location coordinates ($point_{max}$). In line 3, the level counter assumes the *threshold* value, a fixed value corresponding to average height of the human head ([13] adopted the value 10 cm, which is quite reasonable). When the segmentation level becomes negative (above the floor) the iteration stops. In line 5, there is a segmentation function that yields in output a binary image with blobs representative of moving objects that are above the segmentation level ($max - level$). This binary image is the input of FINDCONTOURS, a function that returns a vector of points for each blob. Then, the FILTERCONTOURS function deletes noise (condition on size and shape can be applied). The highest point/depth value (FINDPOINTMAX function) of each blob identified by means of the FILTERMASK function is then inserted in the vector *points*. Finally, MULTILEVELSEGM function returns a vector with all maximum local points. The length of this vector is exactly the number of people in the current frame.

Algorithm 18.2 Multi level segmentation algorithm

1: **function** MULTILEVELSEGM($f(x, y)$)
2:     $(max, point_{max}) = $ FINDPOINTMAX($f(x, y)$)
3:     $level = threshold$
4:     **while** $(max - level) > 0$ **do**
5:         $f_{level}(x, y) = f(x, y) > (max - level)$
6:         $contours = $ FINDCONTOURS($f_{level}(x, y)$)
7:         FILTERCONTOURS($contours$)
8:         **for** each contour $i \in contours$ **do**
9:             $f_{mask}(x, y) = $ FILTERMASK($f_{level}(x, y), i$)
10:            $v_{max}, p_{max} = $ FINDPOINTMAX($f_{mask}(x, y)$)
11:            **if** $p_{max} \notin points$ **then**
12:                $points$.PUSHBACK(p_{max})
13:            **end if**
14:        **end for**
15:        $level = level + threshold$
16:    **end while**
17:    **return** $points$
18: **end function**

18.2.4   Semantic Segmentation with Deep Learning

One of the main problems in computer vision is the semantic segmentation of images, video and 3D data. Semantic segmentation is one of the high-level tasks that leads to complete scene understanding. Scene understanding started with the goal of building machines that can see like humans to infer general principles and current situations from imagery, but it has become much broader than that. Applications such as image search engines, autonomous driving, computational photography, vision for graphics, human–machine interaction, were unanticipated and other applications keep arising as scene understanding technology develops [16]. As a core problem of high-level CV, while it has enjoyed some great success in the past 50 years, a lot more is required to reach a complete understanding of visual scenes. In the past, such a problem has been addressed using different traditional CV and machine learning techniques. Despite the popularity of those kinds of methods, the deep learning marked a significant change so that many CV problems are being tackled using deep architectures, usually Convolutional Neural Networks (CNNs), which are surpassing other approaches by a large margin in terms of accuracy and sometimes even efficiency. This section presents a particular case study describing five approaches from the literature based on CNN architectures and implementation methods for semantic segmentation. In this case, the goal is to segment people heads from a top-view configuration, so different CNN architectures have been tested for this. People heads are always visible from a top-view configuration and thus after successful detection, counting became trivial, because we already have a binary mask to apply common computer vision algorithm to extract contours. In Sect. 18.3, a comparison between the different architectures is reported from [33].

18.2.4.1   U-NET

U-Net architecture proposed in [47] is shown in Fig. 18.3. It is composed of two main parts:

- *contracting* path (left side);
- *expansive* path (right side).

The first path follows the typical architecture of a CNN. It consists of the repeated application of two 3×3 convolutions (unpadded convolutions), each followed by a Rectified Linear Unit (ReLU) and a 2×2 max pooling operation with stride 2 for downsampling. At each downsampling step, the number of feature channels is doubled. Every step in the expansive path consists of an upsampling of the feature map followed by a 2×2 convolution ("up-convolution") that halves the number of feature channels, a concatenation with the corresponding cropped feature map from the contracting path, and two 3×3 convolutions, each followed by a ReLU. At the final layer, a 1×1 convolution is used to map each 32-component feature vector to the desired number of classes. Similarly, the authors of [46] revisited the classic U-Net by removing two levels of max pooling and changing the ReLU activation function with a LeakyReLU (Fig. 18.4). Another U-Net architecture is proposed in [33]. In particular, a batch normalization is added after the first ReLU activation function and after each max pooling and upsampling functions (Fig. 18.5).

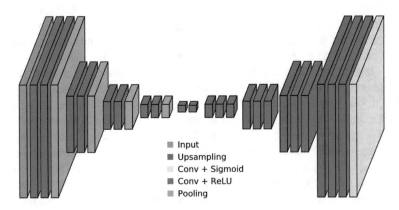

Input
Upsampling
Conv + Sigmoid
Conv + ReLU
Pooling

Fig. 18.3   U-Net architecture

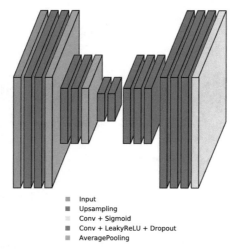

■ Input
■ Upsampling
▫ Conv + Sigmoid
■ Conv + LeakyReLU + Dropout
▪ AveragePooling

Fig. 18.4 U-Net2 architecture

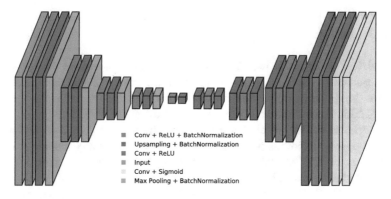

■ Conv + ReLU + BatchNormalization
■ Upsampling + BatchNormalization
■ Conv + ReLU
■ Input
▫ Conv + Sigmoid
▪ Max Pooling + BatchNormalization

Fig. 18.5 U-Net3 architecture [33]

18.2.4.2 SegNet

SegNet, presented by Vijay et al. in [2], is depicted in Fig. 18.6. The architecture consists of a sequence of non-linear processing layers (encoders) and a corresponding set of decoders followed by a pixel-wise classifier. Typically, each encoder consists of one or more convolutional layers with batch normalization and a ReLU non-linearity, followed by non-overlapping max pooling and subsampling. The sparse encoding, due to the pooling process, is upsampled in the decoder using the max pooling indices in the encoding sequence. The max pooling indices are used in the decoders to perform upsampling of low-resolution feature maps. This has the important advantage of retaining high-frequency details in the segmented images and also reducing the total number of trainable parameters in the decoders. The entire architecture can be trained end-to-end using stochastic gradient descent. The

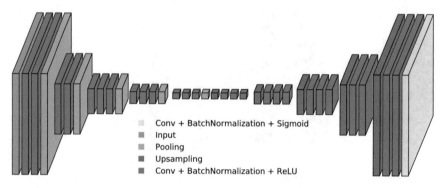

Fig. 18.6 SegNet architecture

raw SegNet predictions tend to be smooth even without a Conditional Random Field (CRF) based post processing.

18.2.4.3 ResNet

He et al. in [22] observed that deepening traditional feed-forward networks often results in an increased training loss. In theory, however, the training loss of a shallow network should be an upper bound on the training loss of a corresponding deep network. This is due to the fact that increasing the depth by adding layers strictly increases the expressive power of the model. A deep network can express all functions that the original shallow network can express by using identity mappings for the added layers. He et al. proposed residual networks that exhibit significantly improved training characteristics. A ResNet is composed of a sequence of residual units (RUs) shown in Fig. 18.7. The output x_n of the *nth* RU in a ResNet is computed as

$$x_n = x_{n-1} + F(x_{n-1}; W_n) \tag{18.3}$$

where $F(x_{n-1}; W_n)$ is the residual, which is parametrized by W_n. In this way, instead of computing the output x_n directly, F only computes a residual that is added to the input x_{n-1}. This design can be referred to skip connection, since there is a connection from the input x_{n-1} to the output x_n that skips the actual computation F. It has been empirically observed that ResNets have superior training properties over traditional feed-forward networks. This can be explained by an improved gradient flow within the network.

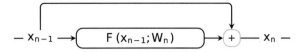

Fig. 18.7 Residual unit

18.2.4.4   FractalNet

Fractal network is introduced by Larsson et al. in [26]. Let C denote the index of a truncated fractal $f_C(\cdot)$ (i.e., a few stacked layers) and the base case of a truncated fractal is a single convolution:

$$f_1(z) = conv(z)$$

According to the expansion rule,

$$z' = conv(z)$$

$$f_{C+1}(z) = conv(conv(z') \oplus f_C(z'))$$

can be defined recursively for the successive fractals, where $\oplus$ is a join operation and $conv(\cdot)$ is a convolution operator. Two blobs are merged by the join operation $\oplus$. As these two blobs contain features from different visual levels, joining them can enhance the discrimination capability of our network. Generally, this operation can be summation, maximization and concatenation. In order to enlarge the receptive field and enclose more contextual information, downsampling and upsampling operations are added in the above expansion rule. In particular, a max pooling with a stride of 2 and a deconvolution also with a stride of 2 are added. After the downsampling operation, the receptive field of a fractal becomes broader. When combining different

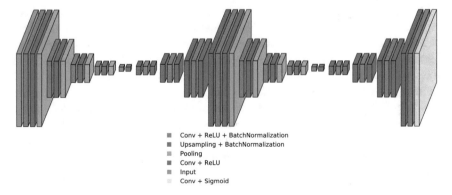

Fig. 18.8 FractalNet architecture

receptive fields through the join operation, the network can harness multi-scale visual cues and promote itself in discriminating. The Fractal Net architecture is depicted in Fig. 18.8.

18.2.5 Re-identification

Person re-id has many important applications in video surveillance, because it saves human efforts on exhaustively searching for a person from large amounts of video sequences. Identification cameras are widely employed in most of public places like malls, office buildings, airports, stations and museums. These cameras generally provide enhanced coverage and overlay large geospatial areas because they have non-overlapping fields-of-views. Huge amounts of video data, monitored in real time by law enforcement officers are used after the event for forensic purposes, are provided by these networks.

In this context, robust modelling of the entire body appearance of the individual is essential, because other classical biometric cues (face, gait) may not be available, due to sensors' scarce resolution or low frame rate. Usually, it is assumed that individuals wear the same clothes between the different sightings. The model has to be invariant to pose, viewpoint, illumination changes and occlusions: these challenges call for specific human-based solutions.

An automated analysis of these data improves significantly the quality of monitoring, in addition to processing the data faster [56]. The behaviour characterization of people in a scene and their long-term activity can be possible using video analysis, which is required for high-level surveillance tasks in order to alert the security personnel. Over the past years, in the field of object recognition a significant amount of research has been performed by comparing video sequences. Colour-based features of video sequences are usually described with the use of a set of keyframes that characterizes well a video sequence. The HSV colour histogram and the RGB colour histogram are robust against the perspective and the variability of resolution [20]. The clothing colour histograms taken over the head, trousers and shirt regions, together with the approximated height of the person, have been used as discriminative features. Research works on person re-id can be divided into two categories: feature-based and learning-based [37]. The use of anthropometric measures for re-id was proposed for the first time in [35]. In this case, height was estimated from RGB cameras as a cue for associating tracks of individuals coming from non-overlapping views. In [18], the authors proposed the use of local motion features to re-identify people across camera views. They obtained correspondence between body parts of different persons through space–time segmentation. On these body parts, colour and edge histograms are extracted. In this approach, person re-id is performed by matching the body parts based on the features and correspondence. Shape and appearance context, which computes the co-occurrence of shape words and visual words for person re-id is proposed in [59]. Human body is partitioned into L parts with the shape context and a learned shape dictionary. Then, these parts are further segmented into

M subregions by a spatial kernel. The histogram of visual words is extracted on each subregion. Consequently, for the person re-id the $L \times M$ histograms are used as visual features. In [12], the appearance of a pedestrian is represented by combining three kinds of features (sampled according to the symmetry and asymmetry axes obtained from silhouette segmentation): the weighted colour histograms, the maximally stable colour regions and recurrent highly structured patches. Another method to face the problem of person re-id is learning discriminant models on low-level visual features. Adaboost is used to select an optimal ensemble of localized features for pedestrian recognition in [20]. The partial least squares method is used to perform person re-id in [51]. Instead, Prosser et al. [44] have used a ranking SVM to learn the ranking model. In the past years, it is well-known to use metric learning for person re-id. A probabilistic relative distance comparison model has been proposed in [73]. It maximizes the probability that the distance between a pair of true match is smaller than the distance between an incorrect match pair. In [40], the authors investigate whether the re-id accuracy of clothing appearance descriptors can be improved by fusing them with anthropometric measures extracted from depth data, using RGB-D sensors, in unconstrained settings. They also propose a dissimilarity-based framework for building and fusing the multimodal descriptors of pedestrian images for re-id tasks, as an alternative to the widely used score-level fusion.

Recently, CNNs are being widely employed to solve the problem of person re-id. Deep Learning models in the person re-id problem are still suffering from the lack of training data samples. The reason for this is that most of the datasets provide only two images per individual [27]. Several CNN models have been proposed in the literature to improve the performance of person re-id. Specifically, two models have been employed in re-id area: a classification model and a Siamese model based on either pair or triplet comparisons.

The model based on classification requires determining the individual identity. In [63], a novel feature extraction model called Feature Fusion Net (FFN) is proposed for pedestrian image representation. The presented model makes use of both CNN feature and handcrafted features. The authors utilize both colour histogram features and texture features. The extracted features are followed by a buffer layer and a fully connected layer which are acting as the fusion layer. The effectiveness was demonstrated on the three challenging datasets. In [62], a hybrid deep architecture for person re-id is presented, composed of Fisher vectors and multiple supervised layers. The network has been trained employing the linear discriminative analysis (LDA) as an objective function, with the goal of maximizing margin between classes. The authors in [66] propose a method based on learning deep feature representations from multiple domains by using CNNs with the aim to discover effective neurons for each training dataset. The authors propose Domain Guided Dropout algorithm in order to improve the feature learning process by discarding useless neurons. They evaluate on various datasets, with the limitation that some neurons are effective only for a specific data set and useless for another one. The authors in [28] designed a multi-scale context-aware network. The network is learning powerful features over the body and body parts. It can capture knowledge of the local context by stacking convolutions of multiple scales in each layer. They also propose to learn and locate deformable pedestrian parts through networks of spatial transformers with new spatial restrictions, instead of using predefined rigid parts.

Since the person re-id research area lacks training instances, Siamese network models have been widely and viably employed. Siamese neural network is a type of neural network architectures which contains two or more identical sub-networks. A Siamese network is employed as pairwise (in the case of two sub-networks), or triplet (the case of three sub-networks). Some examples of pairwise research can be found in [14, 57, 69]. The authors in [57] combined four CNNs, each of them embedding images from different scale or different body part. Each of sub-CNN is trained with adaptive list-wise loss function. In addition, they adopted sharpness parameter and an adaptive margin parameter to automatically focus more on the hard negative samples in the training process. In [69], a Siamese neural network has been proposed to learn pairwise similarity. The method can learn at the same time the colour feature, texture feature and metric in a unified framework. The network is a symmetrical structure containing two sub-networks, which are connected by Cosine function. Binomial deviance is also used to deal with the big variations of person images [14]. The authors propose a novel type of features based on covariance descriptors—the convolutional covariance features. There are three steps, first a hybrid network is trained for person recognition, next another hybrid network is employed to discriminate the gender, and finally the output of the two networks are passed through the coarse-to-fine transfer learning method to a pairwise Siamese network in order to accomplish the final person re-id. In [9], the authors presented a scalable distance driven feature learning framework based on the deep neural network in order to produce feature representation from a raw person images. A CNN network is trained by a set of triplets to produce features that can satisfy the relative distance constraints. In [70], a supervised learning framework is proposed to generate compact and bit-scalable hashing codes from raw images. Training images were organized into a batch of triplet samples, two images with the same label and one with a different label. The deep convolutional neural network is utilized to train the model in an end-to-end fashion, with the simultaneous optimization of the discriminative image features and hash functions. In [54], a three-stage training is proposed: a deep convolutional neural network is first trained on an independent dataset labelled with attributes, then it is fine-tuned on another dataset that is only labelled with person IDs using a particular triplet loss they define, and finally, the updated network predicts attribute labels for the target dataset.

18.2.5.1 Person Re-identification in Top-View Configuration

The re-id in top-view configuration has been studied in [31, 42]. In order to face this task, the authors have built a dataset namely TVPR[1] (Top-View Person Re-identification). An Asus Xtion PRO LIVE RGB-D camera has been used because it allows to acquire colour and depth information in an affordable and fast way. The

---

[1]http://vrai.dii.univpm.it/re-id-dataset.

camera is installed on the ceiling above the area to be analysed. Data of 100 people are collected, acquired across intervals of days and at different times. Each person walked with an average gait within the recording area in one direction, stopping for a few seconds just below the camera, then it turned around and repeated the same route in the opposite direction, always stopping under the camera for a while. This choice is due to its greater suitability compared with a front-view configuration, usually adopted for gesture recognition or even for video gaming. The top-view configuration reduces the problem of occlusions [30] and has the advantage of being privacy preserving, because the face is not recorded by the camera. The process of extraction of a high number of significant features derived from both depth and colour information is presented. The first step is the processing of the data acquired from the RGB-D camera. The camera captures depth and colour images, both with dimensions of 640×480 pixels, at a rate up to approximately 30 fps and illuminates the scene/objects with structured light based on infrared patterns. Seven out of the nine features selected are the anthropometric features extracted from the depth image:

- distance between floor and head, d_1;
- distance between floor and shoulders, d_2;
- area of head surface, d_3;
- head circumference, d_4;
- shoulders circumference, d_5;
- shoulders breadth, d_6;
- thoracic anteroposterior depth, d_7.

The remaining two *colour-based features* are acquired by the colour image, such as in [3], with $n = 10$ bin quantization, for both H channel and S channel.

- colour histogram for the head/hair, H_h;
- colour histogram for the outwear, H_o.

It has also been defined in three descriptors: *TVH*, *TVD* and *TVDH*.

- *TVH* is the colour descriptor:

$$TVH = \{H_h^p, H_o^p\} \qquad (18.4)$$

- *TVD* is the depth descriptor:

$$TVH = \{d_1^p, d_2^p, d_3^p, d_4^p, d_5^p, d_6^p, d_7^p\} \qquad (18.5)$$

- Finally, *TVDH* is the signature of a person defined as:

$$TVDH = \{d_1^p, d_2^p, d_3^p, d_4^p, d_5^p, d_6^p, d_7^p, H_h^p, H_o^p\} \qquad (18.6)$$

Figure 18.9 depicts the set of features considered: anthropometric and the colour-based ones.

The 100 people dataset was acquired in 23 registration sessions. Each of the 23 folders contains the video of one registration session. The recording time [s] for

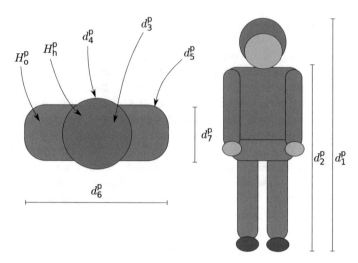

Fig. 18.9 Anthropometric and colour-based features

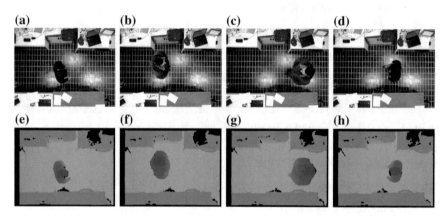

Fig. 18.10 Snapshots of a registration session of the recorded data, in an indoor scenario, with artificial light. People had to pass under the camera installed on the ceiling. The sequences **a–e**, **b–f** correspond to the sequences **d–h**, **c–g** respectively for the training and testing sets of the classes 8–9 for the registration session g003 [31]

the session and the number of persons of that session are reported in Table 18.1. Acquisitions have been performed in 8 days and the total recording time is about 2000 s. Registrations are made in an indoor scenario, where people pass under the camera installed on the ceiling. Another big issue is environmental illumination. In each recording session, the illumination condition is not constant, because it varies in function of the different hours of the day and it also depends on natural illumination due to weather conditions. The video acquisitions, in this scenario, are depicted in Fig. 18.10, which are examples of person registration respectively with sunlight and artificial light. Each person during a registration session walked with an average gait

Table 18.1 Time [s] of registration for each session and the number of people of that session [31]

Session	Time [s]	# People	Session	Time [s]	# People
g001	68.765	4	g013	102.283	6
g002	53.253	3	g014	92.028	5
g003	50.968	2	g015	126.446	6
g004	59.551	3	g016	86.197	4
g005	75.571	4	g017	95.817	5
g006	128.827	7	g018	57.903	3
g007	125.044	6	g019	82.908	5
g008	75.972	3	g020	87.228	4
g009	94.336	4	g021	42.624	2
g010	116.861	6	g022	68.394	3
g011	101.614	5	g023	56.966	3
g012	155.338	7			
			Total	**2004.894**	**100**

within the recording area in one direction, then it turned back and repeated the same route in the opposite direction. This methodology is used for a better split of TVPR in training set (the first passage of the person under the camera) and testing set (when the person passed again under the camera). The recruited people are aged between 19–36 years: 43 females and 57 male; 86 with dark hair, 12 with light hair and 2 are hairless. Furthermore, of these people 55 have short hair, 43 have long hair. The subjects were recorded in their everyday clothing like T-shirts/sweatshirts/shirts, loose-fitting trousers, coats, scarves and hats. In particular, 18 subjects wore coats and 7 subjects wore scarves. All videos have fixed dimensions and a frame rate of about 30 fps. Videos are saved in native *.oni* files, but can be converted to any other format. Colour stream is available in a non-compressed format. Figure 18.11 reports the histogram of each extracted anthropometric feature. Due to the dissimilarity of the analysed subjects a Gaussian curve is obtained from the data. The Cumulative Matching Characteristic (CMC) curve represents the expectation of finding the correct match in the top n matches. It is equivalent to the Receiver Operating Characteristic (ROC) curve in detection problems. This performance metric evaluates recognition problems, by some assumptions about the distribution of appearances in a camera network. It is considered the primary measure of identification performance among biometric researchers. As well-established in recognition and in re-id tasks, for each testing item we ranked the training gallery elements using standard distance metrics. Three distance measures have been examined as the matching distance metrics: the L1 City block, the Euclidean Distance and the Cosine Distance. To evaluate the TVPR, performance results are reported in terms of recognition rate, using the CMC curves, illustrated in Fig. 18.12. In particular, the horizontal axis is the rank of the matching score, and the vertical axis is the probability of correct identification. Considering the dataset, a comparison among TVH and TVD in terms of CMC curves are depicted, to

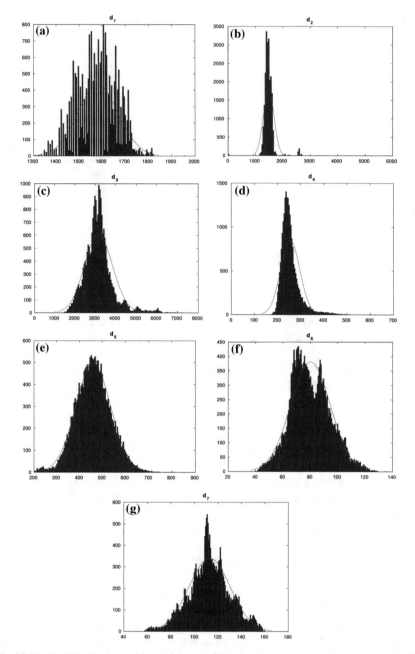

Fig. 18.11 Statistics histogram for each feature (18.11a d_1 distance between floor and head; 18.11b d_2 distance between floor and shoulders; 18.11c d_3 area of head surface; 18.11d d_4 Head circumference, 18.11e d_5 shoulders circumference, 18.11f d_6 shoulders breadth; 18.11g d_7 thoracic antero-posterior depth). The resultant Gaussian curve (in red) is due to the dissimilarity of the analysed subjects [31]

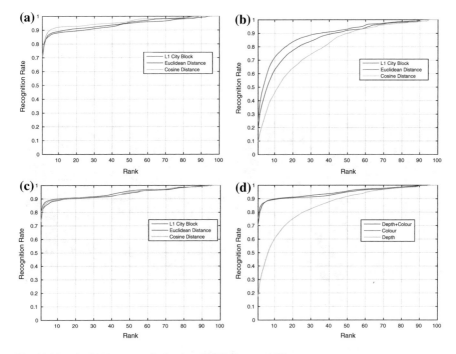

Fig. 18.12   The CMC curves obtained on TVPR Dataset [42]

compare the ranks returned by using these different descriptors. Figure 18.12a provides the CMC obtained for TVH. Figure 18.12b represents the CMC obtained for TVD. These results are compared with the average obtained by TVH and TVD. The average CMC is displayed in Fig. 18.12c. It is observed that the best performance is achieved by the combination of descriptors. In Fig. 18.12d, it can be seen that the combination of descriptors improves the results obtained by each of the descriptor separately. This result is due to the depth contribution that can be more informative. In fact, the depth outperforms the colour, giving the best performance for rank values higher than 15 (Fig. 18.12b). Its better performance suggests the importance and potential of this descriptor.

18.3   Results and Use Cases

In this section, the results of experiments performed for testing the performance of multilevel segmentation and water filling, DCNNs for people counting and re-id feature based approach are reported.

Table 18.2 Image processing algorithms performances

Algorithm	Precision	Recall	F1-score
Multilevel segmentation	0.9390	0.9872	0.9625
Water filling	0.9365	0.7564	0.8369

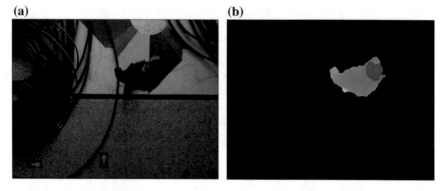

Fig. 18.13 CBSR dataset

In particular, the multilevel segmentation and water filling algorithms are assessed evaluating a restricted part of CBSR Dataset.[2] This dataset includes a total of 3884 images with 6094 heads. It contains depth images after background subtraction and in the ground truth the heads are manually painted as red colour.

Table 18.2 shows the results of algorithms in term of Precision, Recall and F1-score. The algorithms reach high values of performances. However, when the heads are along the edge of image their accuracies are decreased. Instead, the multilevel segmentation algorithm looks more accurate than water filling algorithm (Fig. 18.13).

Regarding the evaluation of deep learning approaches *TVHeads*[3] dataset has been used. It contains depth images of people from top-view configuration. In particular, the purpose of this dataset is to localise the heads of people who are present below the camera. It contains a total of 1815 depth images (16 bit) with a dimension of 320×240 pixels. Furthermore, after an image preprocessing phase, the depth images are also converted, with an appropriate scaling, in order to obtain images (8 bit), where the heads silhouette is highlighted by improving image contrast and brightness (Fig. 18.14).

Each CNN implementation is trained with two types of depth images:

- *16-bit*: original images acquired by depth sensor;
- *8-bit*: scaled images in order to highlight the heads' silhouette, improving the images contrast and brightness.

---

[2]https://goo.gl/MwtWKR.

[3]http://vrai.dii.univpm.it/tvheads-dataset.

(a) 8 bit Depth image.   (b) 16 bit Depth image.   (c) Ground truth.

Fig. 18.14 TVHeads dataset. It consists of 8-bit scaled depth images (**a**), 16-bit original images (**b**) and the corresponding ground truth (**c**) [33]

Table 18.3 Jaccard and Dice indices of different *CNN* architectures. From [33]

Net	Bit	Jaccard Train	Jaccard Validation	Dice Train	Dice Validation
Fractal [26]	8	0.960464	0.948000	0.979833	0.973306
	16	0.961636	0.947762	0.980443	0.973180
U-Net [47]	8	0.896804	0.869399	0.945595	0.930138
	16	0.894410	0.869487	0.944262	0.930188
U-Net2 [46]	8	0.923823	0.939086	0.960403	0.968586
	16	0.923537	0.938208	0.960249	0.968119
U-Net3[33]	8	0.962520	0.931355	**0.980902**	0.964458
	16	0.961540	0.929924	0.980393	0.963690
SegNet [2]	8	0.884182	0.823731	0.938531	0.903347
	16	0.884162	0.827745	0.938520	0.905756
ResNet [22]	8	0.932160	0.856337	0.964889	0.922609
	16	0.933436	0.848240	0.965572	0.917889

Table 18.4 Semantic segmentation results of different ConvNet architectures. From [33]

Net	Bit	Accuracy	Precision	Recall	F1-score
Fractal [26]	8	0.994414	0.991400	0.993120	0.992235
	16	0.994437	0.992667	0.993297	0.992970
U-Net [47]	8	0.992662	0.946475	0.950483	0.948408
	16	0.992569	0.945083	0.948957	0.946938
U-Net2 [46]	8	0.993156	0.970013	0.969206	0.969568
	16	0.993165	0.967884	0.970557	0.969123
U-Net3[33]	8	**0.994572**	0.990451	0.990387	0.990419
	16	0.994559	0.989382	0.989411	0.989396
SegNet [2]	8	0.992683	0.946304	0.953136	0.949625
	16	0.992699	0.946237	0.953342	0.949658
ResNet [22]	8	0.993789	0.968399	0.968374	0.968359
	16	0.993819	0.968765	0.969256	0.968992

Table 18.5 Qualitative result of prediction. From [33]

	8-bit	16-bit	Label
FractalNet [26]			
U-Net [47]			
U-Net2 [46]			
U-Net3 [33]			
SegNet [2]			
ResNet [22]			

In this case, training, test and validation are chosen, respectively, to learn model parameters. Once this phase is completed, the best model is also evaluated over the never before seen test set. In the following experiments, 70%, 10% and 20% of the datasets are chosen, respectively, for training, test and validation. Furthermore, different combinations of hyperparameters are tested, a learning rate equal to 0.001 and an Adam optimization algorithm have been used. Semantic segmentation performances are divided into two different tables. Table 18.3 shows Jaccard and Dice indices for training and for validation, respectively, while Table 18.4 reported the results in terms of accuracy, precision, recall and F1-score. Both tables refer to a learning process conducted during 200 epochs. In Table 18.3, the best CNN architecture is the U-Net3 8-bit version. Indeed, Jaccard index reaches a value equal to 0.962520. The second best is Fractal Net 16-bit version also obtaining higher values as regards validation performances. Table 18.4 reports the best CNN architecture, in terms of accuracy, is U-Net3 8-bit version, while Fractal Net 16-bit version exceeds slightly in precision, recall and F1-score metrics. Qualitative results in Table 18.5.

18.4 Conclusions

The RGB-D cameras installed in top-view configuration have several advantages for tracking and detecting people especially in a heavy crowded environment with values of accuracy that reaches 99%. The aim of this chapter is to demonstrate the potential of these sensors installed in top-view configuration for two tasks: people counting and re-id. These kind of solutions are successfully applied in several applications because of their great suitability compared with a front-view configuration, usually adopted for gesture recognition or even for video gaming. The combination of depth information coupled with visual images provides their success in retail domain.

Future works would include the integration of these systems with an audio framework and the use of other types of RGB-D sensors, such as time of flight (TOF) ones. The system can additionally be integrated as a source of high semantic-level information in a networked ambient intelligence scenario, to provide cues for different problems, such as detecting abnormal speed and dimension outliers, that can alert of a possible uncontrolled circumstance. Further investigation will be devoted to improve the top-view configuration approach for people counting and re-id by extracting other comprehensive features and setting up it for the real-time processing of video images, in particular, in the retail scenario.

References

1. Annesley J, Orwell J, Renno J (2005) Evaluation of MPEG7 color descriptors for visual surveillance retrieval. In: 2005 IEEE international workshop on visual surveillance and performance

evaluation of tracking and surveillance, pp 105–112. https://doi.org/10.1109/VSPETS.2005.
1570904

2. Badrinarayanan V, Kendall A, Cipolla R (2015) Segnet: a deep convolutional encoder-decoder architecture for image segmentation. arXiv preprint arXiv:1511.00561

3. Baltieri D, Vezzani R, Cucchiara R (2013) Learning articulated body models for people re-identification. In: Proceedings of the 21st ACM international conference on multimedia, pp 557–560. ACM

4. Barbosa BI, Cristani M, Del Bue A, Bazzani L, Murino V (2012) Re-identification with RGB-D sensors. In: First international workshop on re-identification

5. Bevilacqua A, Stefano LD, Azzari P (2006) People tracking using a time-of-flight depth sensor. In: 2006 IEEE international conference on video and signal based surveillance, pp 89–89. https://doi.org/10.1109/AVSS.2006.92

6. Cheng DS, Cristani M, Stoppa M, Bazzani L, Murino V (2011) Custom pictorial structures for re-identification. In: Proceedings of the british machine vision conference, pp 68.1–68.11. BMVA Press. http://dx.doi.org/10.5244/C.25.68

7. Coşkun A, Kara A, Parlaktuna M, Ozkan M, Parlaktuna O (2015) People counting system by using Kinect sensor. In: 2015 International symposium on innovations in intelligent systems and applications (INISTA), pp 1–7. https://doi.org/10.1109/INISTA.2015.7276740

8. Dan B, Kim YS, Jung J, Ko S (2012) Robust people counting system based on sensor fusion. IEEE Trans Consum Electron 58(3):1013–1021. https://doi.org/10.1109/TCE.2012.6311350

9. Ding S, Lin L, Wang G, Chao H (2015) Deep feature learning with relative distance comparison for person re-identification. Pattern Recognit 48(10):2993–3003. https://doi.org/10.1016/j.patcog.2015.04.005. http://www.sciencedirect.com/science/article/pii/S0031320315001296

10. Dittrich F, Woern H, Sharma V, Yayilgan S (2014) Pixelwise object class segmentation based on synthetic data using an optimized training strategy. In: 2014 First international conference on networks & soft computing (ICNSC2014), pp 388–394. IEEE

11. Ess A, Leibe B, Gool LV (2007) Depth and appearance for mobile scene analysis. In: 2007 IEEE 11th international conference on computer vision, pp 1–8. https://doi.org/10.1109/ICCV.2007.4409092

12. Farenzena M, Bazzani L, Perina A, Murino V, Cristani M (2010) Person re-identification by symmetry-driven accumulation of local features. In: 2010 IEEE computer society conference on computer vision and pattern recognition, pp 2360–2367. https://doi.org/10.1109/CVPR.2010.5539926

13. Ferracuti N, Norscini C, Frontoni E, Gabellini P, Paolanti M, Placidi V (2019) A business application of RTLS technology in intelligent retail environment: Defining the shopper's preferred path and its segmentation. J Retail Consum Serv 47:184–194

14. Franco A, Oliveira L (2017) Convolutional covariance features: conception, integration and performance in person re-identification. Pattern Recognit 61:593–609. https://doi.org/10.1016/j.patcog.2016.07.013. http://www.sciencedirect.com/science/article/pii/S0031320316301625

15. Frontoni E, Zingaretti P (2005) A vision based algorithm for active robot localization. In: 2005 International symposium on computational intelligence in robotics and automation, pp 347–352. IEEE

16. Garcia-Garcia A, Orts-Escolano S, Oprea S, Villena-Martinez V, Garcia-Rodriguez J (2017) A review on deep learning techniques applied to semantic segmentation. arXiv:1704.06857

17. Gasparrini S, Cippitelli E, Spinsante S, Gambi E (2014) A depth-based fall detection system using a Kinect® sensor. Sensors 14(2):2756–2775. https://doi.org/10.3390/s140202756. http://www.mdpi.com/1424-8220/14/2/2756

18. Gheissari N, Sebastian TB, Hartley R (2006) Person reidentification using spatiotemporal appearance. In: IEEE conference on computer vision and pattern recognition, pp 1528–1535. IEEE

19. Gray D, Brennan S, Tao H (2007) Evaluating appearance models for recognition, reacquisition, and tracking. In: IEEE international workshop on performance evaluation for tracking and surveillance, Rio de Janeiro

20. Gray D, Tao H (2008) Viewpoint invariant pedestrian recognition with an ensemble of localized features. In: European conference on computer vision, pp 262–275. Springer
21. Han J, Pauwels EJ, de Zeeuw PM, de With PHN (2012) Employing a RGB-D sensor for real-time tracking of humans across multiple re-entries in a smart environment. IEEE Trans Consum Electron 58(2):255–263. https://doi.org/10.1109/TCE.2012.6227420
22. He K, Zhang X, Ren S, Sun J (2016) Deep residual learning for image recognition. In: Proceedings of the IEEE conference on computer vision and pattern recognition, pp 770–778
23. Jojic N, Perina A, Cristani M, Murino V, Frey B (2009) Stel component analysis: modeling spatial correlations in image class structure. In: 2009 IEEE conference on computer vision and pattern recognition, pp 2044–2051. https://doi.org/10.1109/CVPR.2009.5206581
24. Kepski M, Kwolek B (2014) Detecting human falls with 3-axis accelerometer and depth sensor. In: 2014 36th Annual International Conference of the IEEE Engineering in Medicine and Biology Society, pp 770–773. https://doi.org/10.1109/EMBC.2014.6943704
25. Kouno D, Shimada K, Endo T (2012) Person identification using top-view image with depth information. In: 2012 13th ACIS international conference on software engineering, artificial intelligence, networking and parallel/distributed computing, pp 140–145. https://doi.org/10.1109/SNPD.2012.47
26. Larsson G, Maire M, Shakhnarovich G (2016) Fractalnet: ultra-deep neural networks without residuals. arXiv:1605.07648
27. Lavi B, Serj MF, Ullah I (2018) Survey on deep learning techniques for person re-identification task. CoRR. arXiv:1807.05284
28. Li D, Chen X, Zhang Z, Huang K (2017) Learning deep context-aware features over body and latent parts for person re-identification
29. Liciotti D, Frontoni E, Mancini A, Zingaretti P (2016) Pervasive system for consumer behaviour analysis in retail environments. Video analytics. Face and facial expression recognition and audience measurement. Springer, Berlin, pp 12–23
30. Liciotti D, Massi G, Frontoni E, Mancini A, Zingaretti P (2015) Human activity analysis for in-home fall risk assessment. In: 2015 IEEE international conference on communication workshop (ICCW), pp 284–289. IEEE
31. Liciotti D, Paolanti M, Frontoni E, Mancini A, Zingaretti P (2017) Person re-identification dataset with RGB-D camera in a top-view configuration. In: Nasrollahi K, Distante C, Hua G, Cavallaro A, Moeslund TB, Battiato S, Ji Q (eds) Video analytics. Face and facial expression recognition and audience measurement. Springer International Publishing, Cham, pp 1–11
32. Liciotti D, Paolanti M, Frontoni E, Zingaretti P (2017) People detection and tracking from an RGB-D camera in top-view configuration: review of challenges and applications. In: Battiato S, Farinella GM, Leo M, Gallo G (eds) New trends in image analysis and processing - ICIAP 2017, pp 207–218. Springer International Publishing, Cham
33. Liciotti D, Paolanti M, Pietrini R, Frontoni E, Zingaretti P (2018) Convolutional networks for semantic heads segmentation using top-view depth data in crowded environment. In: 2018 24th international conference on pattern recognition (ICPR), pp 1384–1389. IEEE
34. Lin S, Liu A, Hsu T, Fu L (2015) Representative body points on top-view depth sequences for daily activity recognition. In: 2015 IEEE international conference on systems, man, and cybernetics, pp 2968–2973. https://doi.org/10.1109/SMC.2015.516
35. Madden C, Piccardi M (2005) Height measurement as a session-based biometric for people matching across disjoint camera views. In: Image and vision computing conference. Wickliffe Ltd
36. Malawski F (2014) Top-view people counting in public transportation using Kinect. Chall Mod Technol 5(4):17–20
37. Messelodi S, Modena CM (2015) Boosting Fisher vector based scoring functions for person re-identification. Image Vis Comput 44:44–58
38. Migniot C, Ababsa F (2013) 3D human tracking in a top view using depth information recorded by the xtion pro-live camera. In: Bebis G, Boyle R, Parvin B, Koracin D, Li B, Porikli F, Zordan V, Klosowski J, Coquillart S, Luo X, Chen M, Gotz D (eds) Advances in visual computing. Springer, Berlin, pp 603–612

39. Migniot C, Ababsa F (2016) Hybrid 3D–2D human tracking in a top view. J R-Time Image Process 11(4):769–784. https://doi.org/10.1007/s11554-014-0429-7
40. Pala F, Satta R, Fumera G, Roli F (2016) Multimodal person reidentification using RGB-D cameras. IEEE Trans Circuits Syst Video Technol 26(4):788–799
41. Paolanti M, Liciotti D, Pietrini R, Mancini A, Frontoni E (2018) Modelling and forecasting customer navigation in intelligent retail environments. J Intell Robot Syst 91(2):165–180
42. Paolanti M, Romeo L, Liciotti D, Pietrini R, Cenci A, Frontoni E, Zingaretti P (2018) Person re-identification with RGB-D camera in top-view configuration through multiple nearest neighbor classifiers and neighborhood component features selection. Sensors 18(10):3471
43. Paolanti M, Romeo L, Martini M, Mancini A, Frontoni E, Zingaretti P (2019) Robotic retail surveying by deep learning visual and textual data. Robot Auton Syst 118:179–188
44. Prosser BJ, Zheng WS, Gong S, Xiang T, Mary, Q (2010) Person re-identification by support vector ranking. In: BMVC, vol 2, p 6
45. Rauter M (2013) Reliable human detection and tracking in top-view depth images. In: 2013 IEEE conference on computer vision and pattern recognition workshops, pp 529–534. https://doi.org/10.1109/CVPRW.2013.84
46. Ravishankar H, Venkataramani R, Thiruvenkadam S, Sudhakar P, Vaidya V (2017) Learning and incorporating shape models for semantic segmentation. In: International conference on medical image computing and computer-assisted intervention, pp 203–211. Springer
47. Ronneberger O, Fischer P, Brox T (2015) U-net: convolutional networks for biomedical image segmentation
48. Roy A, Sural S, Mukherjee J (2012) A hierarchical method combining gait and phase of motion with spatiotemporal model for person re-identification. Pattern Recognit Lett 33(14):1891–1901. https://doi.org/10.1016/j.patrec.2012.02.003. http://www.sciencedirect.com/science/article/pii/S0167865512000359. Novel pattern recognition-based methods for re-identification in biometric context
49. Saghafi MA, Hussain A, Zaman HB, Saad MHM (2014) Review of person re-identification techniques. IET Comput Vis 8(6):455–474. https://doi.org/10.1049/iet-cvi.2013.0180
50. Satta R, Fumera G, Roli F (2011) Exploiting dissimilarity representations for person re-identification. In: Pelillo M, Hancock ER (eds) Similarity-based pattern recognition. Springer, Berlin, pp 275–289
51. Schwartz WR, Davis LS (2009) Learning discriminative appearance-based models using partial least squares. In: 2009 XXII Brazilian symposium on computer graphics and image processing (SIBGRAPI), pp 322–329. IEEE
52. Stauffer C, Grimson WEL (1999) Adaptive background mixture models for real-time tracking. In: Proceedings. 1999 IEEE computer society conference on computer vision and pattern recognition (Cat. No PR00149), vol 2, pp 246–252. https://doi.org/10.1109/CVPR.1999.784637
53. Sturari M, Liciotti D, Pierdicca R, Frontoni E, Mancini A, Contigiani M, Zingaretti P (2016) Robust and affordable retail customer profiling by vision and radio beacon sensor fusion. Pattern Recognit Lett 81:30–40. https://doi.org/10.1016/j.patrec.2016.02.010. http://www.sciencedirect.com/science/article/pii/S016786551600057X
54. Su C, Zhang S, Xing J, Gao W, Tian Q (2016) Deep attributes driven multi-camera person re-identification. In: Leibe B, Matas J, Sebe N, Welling M (eds) Computer vision - ECCV 2016. Springer International Publishing, Cham, pp 475–491
55. Tseng T, Liu A, Hsiao P, Huang C, Fu L (2014) Real-time people detection and tracking for indoor surveillance using multiple top-view depth cameras. In: 2014 IEEE/RSJ international conference on intelligent robots and systems, pp 4077–4082. https://doi.org/10.1109/IROS.2014.6943136
56. Tu PH, Doretto G, Krahnstoever NO, Perera AA, Wheeler FW, Liu X, Rittscher J, Sebastian TB, Yu T, Harding, KG (2007) An intelligent video framework for homeland protection. In: Unattended ground, sea, and air sensor technologies and applications IX, vol 6562, p 65620C. International Society for Optics and Photonics
57. Wang J, Wang Z, Gao C, Sang N, Huang R (2017) DeepList: learning deep features with adaptive listwise constraint for person reidentification. IEEE Trans Circuits Syst Video Technol 27(3):513–524. https://doi.org/10.1109/TCSVT.2016.2586851

58. Wang T, Gong S, Zhu X, Wang S (2014) Person re-identification by video ranking. In: Fleet D, Pajdla T, Schiele B, Tuytelaars T (eds) Computer vision - ECCV 2014. Springer International Publishing, Cham, pp 688–703
59. Wang X, Doretto G, Sebastian T, Rittscher J, Tu P (2007) Shape and appearance context modeling
60. Wang Z, Hu R, Liang C, Yu Y, Jiang J, Ye M, Chen J, Leng Q (2016) Zero-shot person re-identification via cross-view consistency. IEEE Trans Multimed 18(2):260–272. https://doi.org/10.1109/TMM.2015.2505083
61. Wu A, Zheng W, Lai J (2017) Robust depth-based person re-identification. IEEE Trans Image Process 26(6):2588–2603. https://doi.org/10.1109/TIP.2017.2675201
62. Wu L, Shen C, van den Hengel A (2017) Deep linear discriminant analysis on Fisher networks: a hybrid architecture for person re-identification. Pattern Recognit 65:238–250. https://doi.org/10.1016/j.patcog.2016.12.022. http://www.sciencedirect.com/science/article/pii/S0031320316304447
63. Wu S, Chen YC, Li X, Wu AC, You JJ, Zheng WS (2016) An enhanced deep feature representation for person re-identification
64. Xiang JP (2012) Active learning for person re-identification. In: 2012 International conference on machine learning and cybernetics, vol 1, pp 336–340. https://doi.org/10.1109/ICMLC.2012.6358936
65. Xiang ZJ, Chen Q, Liu Y (2014) Person re-identification by fuzzy space color histogram. Multimed Tools Appl 73(1):91–107. https://doi.org/10.1007/s11042-012-1286-7.
66. Xiao T, Li H, Ouyang W, Wang X (2016) Learning deep feature representations with domain guided dropout for person re-identification
67. Yahiaoui T, Meurie C, Khoudour L, Cabestaing F (2008) A people counting system based on dense and close stereovision. In: Elmoataz A, Lezoray O, Nouboud F, Mammass D (eds) Image and signal processing. Springer, Berlin, pp 59–66
68. Ye W, Xu Y, Zhong Z (2007) Robust people counting in crowded environment. In: 2007 IEEE international conference on robotics and biomimetics (ROBIO), pp 1133–1137. https://doi.org/10.1109/ROBIO.2007.4522323
69. Yi D, Lei Z, Li SZ (2014) Deep metric learning for practical person re-identification
70. Zhang R, Lin L, Zhang R, Zuo W, Zhang L (2015) Bit-scalable deep hashing with regularized similarity learning for image retrieval and person re-identification. IEEE Trans Image Process 24:4766–4779. https://doi.org/10.1109/TIP.2015.2467315
71. Zhang X, Yan J, Feng S, Lei Z, Yi D, Li SZ (2012) Water filling: unsupervised people counting via vertical Kinect sensor. In: 2012 IEEE 9th international conference on advanced video and signal-based surveillance, pp 215–220. https://doi.org/10.1109/AVSS.2012.82
72. Zhao T, Nevatia R, Wu B (2008) Segmentation and tracking of multiple humans in crowded environments. IEEE Trans Pattern Anal Mach Intell 30(7):1198–1211. https://doi.org/10.1109/TPAMI.2007.70770
73. Zheng WS, Gong S, Xiang T (2011) Person re-identification by probabilistic relative distance comparison

Appendix
References

1. Cornell grasping dataset. http://pr.cs.cornell.edu/grasping/rect_data/data.php. Accessed 13 Dec 2018
2. MRPT (mobile robot programming toolkit). http://www.mrpt.org
3. OpenSLAM. http://openslam.org/
4. Abobakr A, Hossny M, Abdelkader H, Nahavandi S (2018) RGB-D fall detection via deep residual convolutional LSTM networks. In: Digital image computing: techniques and applications (DICTA), pp 1–7
5. Abrams A, Hawley C, Pless R (2012) Heliometric stereo: shape from sun position. In: European conference on computer vision (ECCV), pp 357–370
6. Achanta R, Hemami S, Estrada F, Susstrunk S (2009) Frequency-tuned salient region detection. In: IEEE conference on computer vision and pattern recognition, pp 1597–1604
7. Achanta R, Shaji A, Smith K, Lucchi A, Fua P, Süsstrunk S (2012) SLIC superpixels compared to state-of-the-art superpixel methods. IEEE Trans Pattern Anal Mach Intell 34(11):2274–2282
8. de Aguiar E, Stoll C, Theobalt C, Ahmed N, Seidel HP, Thrun S (2008) Performance capture from sparse multi-view video. ACM Trans Graph (TOG) 27(3):1
9. Ahmed N (2012) A system for 360 degree acquisition and 3D animation reconstruction using multiple RGB-D cameras. In: International conference on computer animation and social agents
10. Ahmed N (2013) Spatio-temporally coherent 3D animation reconstruction from multi-view RGB-D images using landmark sampling. In: Proceedings of the international multiconference of engineers and computer scientists 2, vol 1, pp 441–445
11. Ahmed N, Junejo I (2014) Using multiple RGB-D cameras for 3D video acquisition and spatio-temporally coherent 3D animation reconstruction. Int J Comput Theory Eng 6

© Springer Nature Switzerland AG 2019   427
P. L. Rosin et al. (eds.), *RGB-D Image Analysis and Processing*,
Advances in Computer Vision and Pattern Recognition,
https://doi.org/10.1007/978-3-030-28603-3

12. Alcover EA, Jaume-i Capó A, Moyà-Alcover B (2018) PROGame: a process framework for serious game development for motor rehabilitation therapy. PloS one 13(5):e0197383

13. Alexa M (2003) Differential coordinates for local mesh morphing and deformation. Vis Comput 19(2):105–114

14. Alexandre LA (2014) 3D object recognition using convolutional neural networks with transfer learning between input channels. In: IAS

15. Alexandrov SV, Prankl J, Zillich M, Vincze M (2016) Calibration and correction of vignetting effects with an application to 3D mapping. In: IEEE/RSJ international conference on intelligent robots and systems (IROS), vol 2016-Novem, pp 4217–4223

16. Alexe B, Deselaers T, Ferrari V (2010) What is an object? In: Conference on computer vision and pattern recognition, pp 73–80

17. Alexiadis DS, Zarpalas D, Daras P (2013) Real-time, full 3-d reconstruction of moving foreground objects from multiple consumer depth cameras. IEEE Trans Multimed 15(2):339–358

18. Alexiadis S, Kordelas G, Apostolakis KC, Agapito JD, Vegas J, Izquierdo E, Daras P (2012) Reconstruction for 3D immersive virtual environments. In: International workshop on image analysis for multimedia interactive services (WIAMIS), pp 1–4

19. Almomani R, Dong M (2013) SegTrack: a novel tracking system with improved object segmentation. In: ICIP, pp 3939–3943

20. Alnowami M, Alnwaimi B, Tahavori F, Copland M, Wells K (2012) A quantitative assessment of using the Kinect for Xbox360 for respiratory surface motion tracking. In: Holmes DR III, Wong KH (eds) Proceedings of SPIE, vol 8316, p 83161T

21. Amer K, Samy M, ElHakim R, Shaker M, ElHelw M (2017) Convolutional neural network-based deep urban signatures with application to drone localization. In: IEEE international conference on computer vision workshop (ICCVW), pp 2138–2145

22. Anand A, Koppula HS, Joachims T, Saxena A (2011) Contextually guided semantic labeling and search for 3D point clouds. CoRR abs/1111.5358

23. Anderson F, Annett M, Bischof WF (2010) Lean on Wii: physical rehabilitation with virtual reality wii peripherals. Stud Health Technol Inform 154(154):229–34

24. Andreasson H, Triebel R, Burgard W (2005) Improving plane extraction from 3D data by fusing laser data and vision. In: International conference on intelligent robots and systems, pp 2656–2661

25. Anguelov D, Srinivasan P, Koller D, Thrun S, Rodgers J, Davis J (2005) SCAPE: shape completion and animation of people. ACM SIGGRAPH 24:408–416

26. Annesley J, Orwell J, Renno, J (2005) Evaluation of MPEG7 color descriptors for visual surveillance retrieval. In: IEEE international workshop on visual surveillance and performance evaluation of tracking and surveillance, pp 105–112

27. Arbelaez P, Maire M, Fowlkes C, Malik J (2009) From contours to regions: an empirical evaluation. In: IEEE conference on computer vision and pattern recognition (CVPR), pp 2294–2301

28. Arbeláez P, Pont-Tuset J, Barron J, Marques F, Malik J (2014) Multiscale combinatorial grouping. In: Computer vision and pattern recognition

29. Arias P, Facciolo G, Caselles V, Sapiro G (2011) A variational framework for exemplar-based image inpainting. Comput Vis 93(3):319–347

30. Armeni I, Sax A, Zamir AR, Savarese S (2017) Joint 2D-3D-semantic data for indoor scene understanding. arXiv:1702.01105

31. Asfour T, Regenstein K, Azad P, Schroder J, Bierbaum A, Vahrenkamp N, Dillmann R (2006) Armar-III: an integrated humanoid platform for sensory-motor control. In: IEEE-RAS international conference on humanoid robots (humanoids)

32. Asif U, Bennamoun M, Sohel FA (2017) RGB-D object recognition and grasp detection using hierarchical cascaded forests. IEEE Trans Robot 33(3):547–564

33. Aşkın A, Atar E, Koçyiğit H, Tosun A (2018) Effects of Kinect-based virtual reality game training on upper extremity motor recovery in chronic stroke. Somatosens Motor Res 35(1):25–32

34. Asteriadis S, Chatzitofis A, Zarpalas D, Alexiadis DS, Daras P (2013) Estimating human motion from multiple Kinect sensors. In: International conference on computer vision/computer graphics collaboration techniques and applications, MIRAGE '13, pp 3:1–3:6

35. Asvadi A, Garrote L, Premebida C, Peixoto P, Nunes UJ (2017) DepthCN: vehicle detection using 3D-LIDAR and ConvNet. In: IEEE international conference on intelligent transportation systems (ITSC), pp 1–6

36. Asvadi A, Garrote L, Premebida C, Peixoto P, Nunes UJ (2017) Multimodal vehicle detection: fusing 3D-LIDAR and color camera data. Pattern Recognit Lett

37. Ataer-Cansizoglu E, Taguchi Y, Ramalingam S (2016) Pinpoint SLAM: a hybrid of 2D and 3D simultaneous localization and mapping for RGB-D sensors. In: IEEE international conference on robotics and automation (ICRA), pp 1300–1307

38. Ataer-Cansizoglu E, Taguchi Y, Ramalingam S, Garaas T (2013) Tracking an RGB-D camera using points and planes. In: IEEE international conference on computer vision workshop (ICCVW), pp 51–58

39. Atapour-Abarghouei A, Breckon T (2017) DepthComp: real-time depth image completion based on prior semantic scene segmentation. In: British machine vision conference (BMVC), pp 1–12

40. Atapour-Abarghouei A, Breckon T (2018) A comparative review of plausible hole filling strategies in the context of scene depth image completion. Comput Graph 72:39–58

41. Atapour-Abarghouei A, Breckon T (2018) Extended patch prioritization for depth filling within constrained exemplar-based RGB-D image completion. In: International conference on image analysis and recognition, pp 306–314

42. Atapour-Abarghouei A, Breckon T (2018) Real-time monocular depth estimation using synthetic data with domain adaptation via image style transfer. In: IEEE conference on computer vision and pattern recognition (CVPR), pp 2800–2810

43. Atapour-Abarghouei A, Payen de La Garanderie G, Breckon TP (2016) Back to Butterworth – a Fourier basis for 3D surface relief hole filling within RGB-D imagery. In: International conference on pattern recognition, pp 2813–2818

44. Auvinet E, Meunier J, Multon F (2012) Multiple depth cameras calibration and body volume reconstruction for gait analysis. In: International conference on information science, signal processing and their applications (ISSPA), pp 478–483

45. Auvinet E, Multon F, Saint-Arnaud A, Rousseau J, Meunier J (2011) Fall detection with multiple cameras: an occlusion-resistant method based on 3-D Silhouette vertical distribution. IEEE Trans Inf Technol Biomed 15(2):290–300

46. Ayed I, Ghazel A, Jaume-i Capó A, Moya-Alcover G, Varona J, Martínez-Bueso P (2018) Feasibility of Kinect-based games for balance rehabilitation: a case study. J Healthc Eng

47. Ayed I, Moyà-Alcover B, Martínez-Bueso P, Varona J, Ghazel A, Jaume-i Capó A (2017) Validación de dispositivos RGBD para medir terapéuticamente el equilibrio: el test de alcance funcional con Microsoft Kinect. Revista Iberoamericana de Automática e Informática Industrial RIAI 14(1):115–120

48. Azizpour H, Laptev I (2012) Object detection using strongly-supervised deformable part models. In: European conference on computer vision (ECCV), pp 836–849

49. Babu BW, Kim S, Yan Z, Ren L (2016) σ-DVO: sensor noise model meets dense visual odometry. In: IEEE international symposium on mixed and augmented reality (ISMAR), pp 18–26

50. Badami I, Stückler J, Behnke S (2013) Depth-enhanced Hough forests for object-class detection and continuous pose estimation. In: ICRA workshop on semantic perception, mapping and exploration (SPME)

51. Badrinarayanan V, Kendall A, Cipolla R (2015) SegNet: a deep convolutional encoder-decoder architecture for image segmentation. arXiv:1511.00561

52. Baek S, Kim KI, Kim TK (2018) Augmented skeleton space transfer for depth-based hand pose estimation. In: IEEE conference on computer vision and pattern recognition (CVPR), pp 8330–8339

53. Baek S, Kim M (2015) Dance experience system using multiple kinects. Int J Future Comput Commun 4(1):45–49

54. Baek S, Kim M (2017) User pose estimation based on multiple depth sensors. In: SIGGRAPH Asia posters, SA '17, pp 1:1–1:2

55. Baek SH, Choi I, Kim MH (2016) Multiview image completion with space structure propagation. In: IEEE conference on computer vision and pattern recognition (CVPR), pp 488–496

56. Bagalà F, Becker C, Cappello A, Chiari L, Aminian K, Hausdorff J, Zijlstra W, Klenk J (2012) Evaluation of accelerometer-based fall detection algorithms on real-world falls. PLoS ONE 7(5)
57. Bailey T, Durrant-Whyte H (2006) Simultaneous localization and mapping (SLAM): Part II. IEEE Robot Autom Mag 13(3):108–117
58. Ballan L, Taneja A, Gall J, Gool LV, Pollefeys M (2012) Motion capture of hands in action using discriminative salient points. In: European conference on computer vision (ECCV), pp 640–653
59. Ballester C, Caselles V, Verdera J, Bertalmio M, Sapiro G (2001) A variational model for filling-in gray level and color images. In: International conference on computer vision, vol 1, pp 10–16
60. Balntas V, Doumanoglou A, Sahin C, Sock J, Kouskouridas R, Kim TK (2017) Pose guided RGBD feature learning for 3D object pose estimation. In: Proceedings of the IEEE international conference on computer vision, pp 3856–3864
61. Baltieri D, Vezzani R, Cucchiara R (2013) Learning articulated body models for people re-identification. In: Proceedings of the ACM international conference on multimedia, pp 557–560
62. Banerjee T, Keller JM, Skubic M, Stone E (2014) Day or night activity recognition from video using fuzzy clustering techniques. IEEE Trans Fuzzy Syst 22(3):483–493
63. Bansal A, Russell B, Gupta A (2016) Marr revisited: 2D–3D alignment via surface normal prediction. arXiv:1604.01347
64. Barbero A, Sra S (2011) Fast Newton-type methods for total variation regularization. In: International conference on machine learning, pp 313–320
65. Barbosa BI, Cristani M, Del Bue A, Bazzani L, Murino V (2012) Re-identification with RGB-D sensors. In: First international workshop on re-identification
66. Barfoot TD (2017) State estimation for robotics. Cambridge University Press
67. Barnes C, Shechtman E, Finkelstein A, Goldman D (2009) Patchmatch: a randomized correspondence algorithm for structural image editing. ACM Trans Graph 28(3):24
68. Barron JT, Malik J (2013) Intrinsic scene properties from a single RGB-D image. IEEE conference on computer vision and pattern recognition (CVPR) pp 17–24
69. Barron JT, Poole B (2016) The fast bilateral solver. In: European conference on computer vision (ECCV), pp 617–632
70. Barrow HG, Tenenbaum JM, Bolles RC, Wolf HC (1977) Parametric correspondence and chamfer matching: two new techniques for image matching. In: Proceedings of the international joint conference on artificial intelligence, vol 2, IJCAI'77, pp 659–663
71. Bäuml B, Schmidt F, Wimböck T, Birbach O, Dietrich A, Fuchs M, Friedl W, Frese U, Borst C, Grebenstein M, Eiberger O, Hirzinger G (2011) Catching flying balls and preparing coffee: humanoid Rollin' Justin performs dynamic and sensitive tasks. In: IEEE international conference on robotics and automation (ICRA)

72. Bay H, Ess A, Tuytelaars T, Van Gool L (2008) Speeded-up robust features (SURF). Comput Vis Image Underst 110(3):346–359

73. Beck S, Kunert A, Kulik A, Froehlich B (2013) Immersive group-to-group telepresence. IEEE Trans Vis Comput Graph 19(4):616–625

74. Beetz M, Klank U, Kresse I, Maldonado A, Mösenlechner L, Pangercic D, Rühr T, Tenorth M (2011) Robotic roommates making pancakes. In: IEEE-RAS international conference on humanoid robots (humanoids), pp 529–536

75. Behnke S (1999) Hebbian learning and competition in the neural abstraction pyramid. In: International joint conference on neural networks (IJCNN), vol 2, pp 1356–1361

76. Behnke S (2001) Learning iterative image reconstruction in the neural abstraction pyramid. Int J Comput Intell Appl 1(4):427–438

77. Behnke S (2003) Discovering hierarchical speech features using convolutional non-negative matrix factorization. In: International joint conference on neural networks (IJCNN), vol 4, pp 2758–2763

78. Behnke S (2003) Hierarchical neural networks for image interpretation. Lecture notes in computer science. Springer

79. Behnke S (2003) A two-stage system for meter value recognition. In: IEEE international conference on image processing (ICIP), pp 549–552

80. Behnke S (2005) Face localization and tracking in the neural abstraction pyramid. Neural Comput Appl 14(2):97–103

81. Belhedi A, Bartoli A, Bourgeois S, Gay-Bellile V, Hamrouni K, Sayd P (2015) Noise modelling in time-of-flight sensors with application to depth noise removal and uncertainty estimation in three-dimensional measurement. IET Comput Vis 9(6):967–977

82. Bell T, Li B, Zhang S (2016) Structured light techniques and applications. American Cancer Society, pp 1–24

83. Bengio Y, Courville A, Vincent P (2013) Representation learning: a review and new perspectives. IEEE Trans Pattern Anal Mach Intell 35(8):1798–1828

84. Beraldin JA, Blais F, Cournoyer L, Godin G, Rioux M (2000) Active 3D sensing. Quaderni della Scuola Normale Superiore di Pisa 10:1–21

85. Berdnikov Y, Vatolin D (2011) Real-time depth map occlusion filling and scene background restoration for projected-pattern based depth cameras. In: Graphic conference IETP

86. Berger K (2013) The role of RGB-D benchmark datasets: an overview. CoRR abs/1310.2053. arXiv:1310.2053

87. Berger K (2014) A state of the art report on multiple RGB-D sensor research and on publicly available RGB-D datasets. In: Computer vision and machine learning with RGB-D sensors. Springer, pp 27–44

88. Berger K, Meister S, Nair R, Kondermann D (2013) A state of the art report on Kinect sensor setups in computer vision. Springer, Berlin/Heidelberg, pp 257–272

89. Berger K, Ruhl K, Schroeder Y, Bruemmer C, Scholz A, Magnor M (2011) Markerless motion capture using multiple color-depth sensors. In: Eisert P, Hornegger J, Polthier K (eds) Vision, modeling, and visualization. The Eurographics Association

90. Bernardini F, Mittleman J (1999) The ball-pivoting algorithm for surface reconstruction. IEEE Trans Vis Comput Graph

91. Berner A, Li J, Holz D, Stückler J, Behnke S, Klein R (2013) Combining contour and shape primitives for object detection and pose estimation of prefabricated parts. In: Proceedings of the international conference on image processing (ICIP)

92. Bertalmio M, Sapiro G, Caselles V, Ballester C (2000) Image inpainting. In: International conference on computer graphics and interactive techniques, pp 417–424

93. Bertalmio M, Vese L, Sapiro G, Osher S (2003) Simultaneous structure and texture image inpainting. IEEE Trans Image Process 12(8):882–889

94. Bescós B, Fácil JM, Civera J, Neira J (2018) DynaSLAM: tracking, mapping, and inpainting in dynamic scenes. IEEE Robot Autom Lett 3(4):4076–4083

95. Besl P, McKay N (1992) A method for registration of 3-D shapes. IEEE Trans Pattern Anal Mach Intell 14(2):239–256

96. Bevilacqua A, Stefano LD, Azzari P (2006) People tracking using a time-of-flight depth sensor. In: IEEE international conference on video and signal based surveillance, pp 89–89

97. Bianchi F, Redmond SJ, Narayanan MR, Cerutti S, Lovell NH (2010) Barometric pressure and triaxial accelerometry-based falls event detection. IEEE Trans Neural Syst Rehabil Eng 18(6):619–627

98. Bier A, Luchowski L (2009) Error analysis of stereo calibration and reconstruction. In: Gagalowicz A, Philips W (eds) Computer vision/computer graphics collaboration techniques. Springer, Berlin/Heidelberg, pp 230–241

99. Blais G, Levine M (1995) Registering multiview range data to create 3D computer objects. IEEE Trans Pattern Anal Mach Intell 17(8):820–824

100. Bleyer M, Rhemann C, Rother C (2012) Extracting 3D scene-consistent object proposals and depth from stereo images. In: European conference on computer vision (ECCV), pp 467–481

101. Bloesch M, Czarnowski J, Clark R, Leutenegger S, Davison AJ (2018) CodeSLAM – learning a compact, optimisable representation for dense visual SLAM. In: IEEE conference on computer vision and pattern recognition (CVPR), pp 2560–2568

102. Blösch M, Weiss S, Scaramuzza D, Siegwart R (2010) Vision based MAV navigation in unknown and unstructured environments. In: IEEE international conference on robotics and automation (ICRA), pp 21–28

103. Bo L, Ren X, Fox D (2011) Depth kernel descriptors for object recognition. In: IROS, pp 821–826

104. Bo L, Ren X, Fox D (2014) Learning hierarchical sparse features for RGB-(D) object recognition. Int J Robot Res 33(4):581–599

105. Boehler W, Bordas Vicent M, Marbs A (2003) Investigating laser scanner accuracy. Int Arch Photogramm Remote Sens Spatial Inf Sci 34(Part 5):696–701
106. Bohren J, Rusu R, Jones E, Marder-Eppstein E, Pantofaru C, Wise M, Mösenlechner L, Meeussen W, Holzer S (2011) Towards autonomous robotic butlers: lessons learned with the PR2. In: IEEE international conference on robotics and automation (ICRA)
107. Bolt RA (1980) "Put-that-there". ACM SIGGRAPH 14(3):262–270
108. Bonde U, Badrinarayanan V, Cipolla R (2014) Robust instance recognition in presence of occlusion and clutter. In: European conference on computer vision (ECCV), pp 520–535
109. Borenstein J, Feng L (1996) Measurement and correction of systematic odometry errors in mobile robots. IEEE Trans Robot Autom 12(6):869–880
110. Borji A (2012) Exploiting local and global patch rarities for saliency detection. In: IEEE conference on computer vision and pattern recognition (CVPR), pp 478–485
111. Borji A (2014) What is a salient object? A dataset and a baseline model for salient object detection. IEEE Trans Image Process 24(2):742–756
112. Borji A, Cheng MM, Jiang H, Li J (2015) Salient object detection: a benchmark. IEEE Trans Image Process 24(12):5706–5722
113. Born F, Masuch M (2017) Increasing presence in a mixed reality application by integrating a real time tracked full body representation. In: International conference on advances in computer entertainment, pp 46–60
114. Borst C, Wimböck T, Schmidt F, Fuchs M, Brunner B, Zacharias F, Giordano PR, Konietschke R, Sepp W, Fuchs S, et al (2009) Rollin' Justin—mobile platform with variable base. In: IEEE international conference on robotics and automation (ICRA)
115. Bose L, Richards A (2016) Fast depth edge detection and edge based RGB-D SLAM. In: IEEE international conference on robotics and automation (ICRA), pp 1323–1330
116. Bose NK, Ahuja NA (2006) Superresolution and noise filtering using moving least squares. IEEE Trans Image Process 15(8):2239–2248
117. Bourke A, O'Brien J, Lyons G (2007) Evaluation of a threshold-based tri-axial accelerometer fall detection algorithm. Gait Posture 26(2):194–199
118. Boutellaa E, Hadid A, Bengherabi M, Ait-Aoudia S (2015) On the use of Kinect depth data for identity, gender and ethnicity classification from facial images. Pattern Recognit Lett 68:270–277
119. Bowman SL, Atanasov N, Daniilidis K, Pappas GJ (2017) Probabilistic data association for semantic slam. In: IEEE international conference on robotics and automation (ICRA), pp 1722–1729
120. Brachmann E, Krull A, Michel F, Gumhold S, Shotton J, Rother C (2014) Learning 6D object pose estimation using 3D object coordinates. In: European conference on computer vision (ECCV), pp 536–551

121. Brachmann E, Michel F, Krull A, Ying Yang M, Gumhold S, et al (2016) Uncertainty-driven 6D pose estimation of objects and scenes from a single RGB image. In: IEEE conference on computer vision and pattern recognition (CVPR), pp 3364–3372

122. Bradski G (2000) Dr. Dobb's journal of software tools

123. Bradski G, Kaehler A (2013) Learning OpenCV: computer vision in C++ with the OpenCV library, 2nd edn. O'Reilly Media, Inc.

124. Breckon T, Fisher R (2005) Plausible 3D colour surface completion using non-parametric techniques. In: Mathematics of surfaces XI, vol 3604, pp 102–120

125. Breckon TP, Fisher R (2005) Non-parametric 3D surface completion. In: International conference on 3D digital imaging and modeling, pp 573–580

126. Breckon TP, Fisher R (2008) 3D surface relief completion via non-parametric techniques. IEEE Trans Pattern Anal Mach Intell 30(12):2249–2255

127. Breckon TP, Fisher R (2012) A hierarchical extension to 3D non-parametric surface relief completion. Pattern Recognit 45:172–185

128. Bregler C, Hertzmann A, Biermann H (2000) Recovering non-rigid 3D shape from image streams. In: IEEE conference on computer vision and pattern recognition (CVPR), pp 3–9

129. Bregler C, Malik J, Pullen K (2004) Twist based acquisition and tracking of animal and human kinematics. Int J Comput Vis (IJCV) 56(3):179–194

130. Broadley R, Klenk J, Thies S, Kenney L, Granat M (2018) Methods for the real-world evaluation of fall detection technology: a scoping review. Sensors 18(7)

131. Broggi A, Grisleri P, Zani P (2013) Sensors technologies for intelligent vehicles perception systems: a comparison between vision and 3D-LIDAR. In: International IEEE conference on intelligent transportation systems (ITSC), pp 887–892

132. Buades A, Coll B, Morel JM (2005) A non-local algorithm for image denoising. In: International conference on computer vision and pattern recognition, vol 2, pp 60–65

133. Buch NE, Orwell J, Velastin SA (2009) 3D extended histogram of oriented gradients (3DHOG) for classification of road users in urban scenes. In: British machine vision conference (BMVC)

134. Budd C, Huang P, Hilton A (2011) Hierarchical shape matching for temporally consistent 3D video. In: 3D imaging, modeling, processing, visualization and transmission (3DIMPVT), pp 172–179

135. Budd C, Huang P, Klaudiny M, Hilton A (2013) Global non-rigid alignment of surface sequences. Int J Comput Vis (IJCV) 102(1–3):256–270

136. Bugeau A, Bertalmío M, Caselles V, Sapiro G (2010) A comprehensive framework for image inpainting. IEEE Trans Image Process 19(10):2634–2645

137. van der Burgh M, Lunenburg J, Appeldoorn R, Wijnands R, Clephas T, Baeten M, van Beek L, Ottervanger R, van Rooy H, van de Molengraft M (2017) Tech united Eindhoven @Home 2017 team description paper. University of Technology Eindhoven

138. Burke JW, McNeill M, Charles DK, Morrow PJ, Crosbie JH, McDonough SM (2009) Optimising engagement for stroke rehabilitation using serious games. Vis Comput 25(12):1085

139. Burrus N (2012) RGBDemo: demo software to visualize, calibrate and process Kinect cameras output. https://github.com/rgbdemo. Accessed Feb 2015

140. Butler DA, Izadi S, Hilliges O, Molyneaux D, Hodges S, Kim D (2012) Shake'n'sense: reducing interference for overlapping structured light depth cameras. In: Proceedings of the SIGCHI conference on human factors in computing systems, CHI '12, pp 1933–1936

141. Cabrera E, Ortiz L, da Silva B, Clua E, Gonçalves L (2018) A versatile method for depth data error estimation in RGB-D sensors. Sensors 18(9)

142. Cadena C, Carlone L, Carrillo H, Latif Y, Scaramuzza D, Neira J, Reid I, Leonard JJ (2016) Past, present, and future of simultaneous localization and mapping: towards the robust-perception age. IEEE Trans Robot 32(6):1309–1332

143. Cagniart C, Boyer E, Ilic S (2009) Iterative mesh deformation for dense surface tracking. In: International conference on computer vision (ICCV) workshops, pp 1465–1472

144. Cagniart C, Boyer E, Ilic S (2010) Free-form mesh tracking: a patch-based approach. In: IEEE conference on computer vision and pattern recognition (CVPR), pp 1339–1346

145. Cagniart C, Boyer E, Ilic S (2010) Probabilistic deformable surface tracking from multiple videos. In: European conference on computer vision (ECCV), pp 326–339

146. Cai JF, Candès EJ, Shen Z (2010) A singular value thresholding algorithm for matrix completion. SIAM J Optim 20(4):1956–1982

147. Cai Y, Ge L, Cai J, Yuan J (2018) Weakly-supervised 3D hand pose estimation from monocular RGB images. In: European conference on computer vision (ECCV)

148. Cai Z, Han J, Liu L, Shao L (2017) RGB-D datasets using Microsoft Kinect or similar sensors: a survey. Multimed Tools Appl 76(3):4313–4355

149. Caltagirone L, Bellone M, Svensson L, Wahde M (2019) LIDAR-camera fusion for road detection using fully convolutional neural networks. Robot Auton Syst 111:125–131

150. Camplani M, Salgado L (2012) Adaptive spatio-temporal filter for low-cost camera depth maps. In: Proceedings of the IEEE international conference on emerging signal processing applications (ESPA), pp 33–36

151. Camplani M, Salgado L, de Imágenes G, et al (2012) Efficient spatio-temporal hole filling strategy for Kinect depth maps. In: Proceedings of SPIE, vol 8290, p 82900E

152. Cao X, Wang F, Zhang B, Fu H, Li C (2016) Unsupervised pixel-level video foreground object segmentation via shortest path algorithm. Neurocomputing 172:235–243

153. Cao X, Zhang C, Fu H, Guo X, Tian Q (2016) Saliency-aware nonparametric foreground annotation based on weakly labeled data. IEEE Trans Neural Netw Learn Syst 27(6):1253–1265

154. Cao Y, Wu Z, Shen C (2017) Estimating depth from monocular images as classification using deep fully convolutional residual networks. IEEE Trans Circuits Syst Video Technol 28(11):3174–3182

155. Cao YP, Liu ZN, Kuang ZF, Kobbelt L, Hu SM (2018) Learning to reconstruct high-quality 3D shapes with cascaded fully convolutional networks. In: European conference on computer vision (ECCV)

156. Jaume-i Capó A, Martínez-Bueso P, Moya-Alcover B, Varona J (2014) Interactive rehabilitation system for improvement of balance therapies in people with cerebral palsy. IEEE Trans Neural Syst Rehabil Eng 22(2):419–427

157. Jaume-i Capó A, Moyà-Alcover B, Varona J (2014) Design issues for vision-based motor-rehabilitation serious games. In: Technologies of inclusive well-being. Springer, pp 13–24

158. Carfagni M, Furferi R, Governi L, Servi M, Uccheddu F, Volpe Y (2017) On the performance of the Intel SR300 depth camera: metrological and critical characterization. IEEE Sens J 17(14):4508–4519

159. Cashman TJ, Fitzgibbon AW (2013) What shape are dolphins? Building 3D morphable models from 2D images. IEEE Trans Pattern Anal Mach Intell 35(1):232–44

160. Castellanos JA, Montiel J, Neira J, Tardós JD (1999) The SPmap: a probabilistic framework for simultaneous localization and map building. IEEE Trans Robot Autom 15(5):948–952

161. Cavallari T, Golodetz S, Lord N, Valentin J, Prisacariu V, Di Stefano L, Torr PHS (2019) Real-time RGB-D camera pose estimation in novel scenes using a relocalisation cascade. IEEE Trans Pattern Anal Mach Intell:1

162. Cavallari T, Golodetz S, Lord NA, Valentin J, Di Stefano L, Torr PH (2017) On-the-fly adaptation of regression forests for online camera relocalisation. In: IEEE conference on computer vision and pattern recognition (CVPR), pp 4457–4466

163. Cavestany P, Rodriguez A, Martinez-Barbera H, Breckon T (2015) Improved 3D sparse maps for high-performance structure from motion with low-cost omnidirectional robots. In: International conference on image processing, pp 4927–4931

164. Chan D, Buisman H, Theobalt C, et al (2008) A noise-aware filter for real-time depth upsampling. In: Proceedings of ECCV workshop on M2SFA2

165. Chan T, Shen J (2000) Mathematical models for local deterministic inpaintings. Technical Report CAM TR 00-11, UCLA

166. Chang A, Dai A, Funkhouser T, Halber M, Niessner M, Savva M, Song S, Zeng A, Zhang Y (2017) Matterport3D: learning from RGB-D data in indoor environments. In: International conference on 3D vision (3DV)

167. Chang AX, Funkhouser TA, Guibas LJ, Hanrahan P, Huang Q, Li Z, Savarese S, Savva M, Song S, Su H, Xiao J, Yi L, Yu F (2015) ShapeNet: an information-rich 3D model repository. CoRR arXiv:1512.03012.

168. Chang K, Liu T, Lai S (2011) From co-saliency to co-segmentation: an efficient and fully unsupervised energy minimization model. In: IEEE conference on computer vision and pattern recognition (CVPR), pp 2129–2136

169. Chang S (2007) Extracting skeletons from distance maps. Int J Comput Sci Netw Secur 7(7)

170. Chang W, Zwicker M (2011) Global registration of dynamic range scans for articulated model reconstruction. ACM Trans Graph (TOG) 30

171. Chatzitofis A, Zarpalas D, Kollias S, Daras P (2019) DeepMoCap: deep optical motion capture using multiple depth sensors and retro-reflectors. Sensors 19:282

172. Chen C, Cai J, Zheng J, Cham TJ, Shi G (2013) A color-guided, region-adaptive and depth-selective unified framework for Kintect depth recovery. In: International workshop on multimedia signal processing, pp 007–012

173. Chen C, Cai J, Zheng J, Cham TJ, Shi G (2015) Kinect depth recovery using a color-guided, region-adaptive, and depth-selective framework. ACM Trans Intell Syst Technol 6(2):12

174. Chen H, Li Y (2018) Progressively complementarity-aware fusion network for RGB-D salient object detection. In: IEEE conference on computer vision and pattern recognition (CVPR), pp 3051–3060

175. Chen H, Li Y (2019) Three-stream attention-aware network for RGB-D salient object detection. IEEE Trans Image Process PP(99):1–12

176. Chen H, Li Y, Su D (2019) Multi-modal fusion network with multi-scale multi-path and cross-modal interactions for RGB-D salient object detection. Pattern Recognit 86:376–385

177. Chen J, Bautembach D, Izadi S (2013) Scalable real-time volumetric surface reconstruction. ACM Trans Graph (TOG) 32(4):113

178. Chen J, Nie S, Ji Q (2013) Data-free prior model for upper body pose estimation and tracking. IEEE Trans Image Process 22(12):4627–4639

179. Chen K, Lai Y, Hu S (2015) 3D indoor scene modeling from RGB-D data: a survey. Comput Vis Media 1(4):267–278

180. Chen K, Lai YK, Wu YX, Martin R, Hu SM (2014) Automatic semantic modeling of indoor scenes from low-quality RGB-D data using contextual information. ACM Trans Graph 33(6):208:1–208:12

181. Chen W, Fu Z, Yang D, Deng J (2016) Single-image depth perception in the wild. In: Advances in neural information processing systems, pp 730–738

182. Chen X, Davis J, Slusallek P (2000) Wide area camera calibration using virtual calibration objects. In: IEEE conference on computer vision and pattern recognition (CVPR), vol 2, pp 520–527

183. Chen X, Kundu K, Zhu Y, Berneshawi A, Ma H, Fidler S, Urtasun R (2015) 3D object proposals for accurate object class detection. In: Proceedings of the international conference on neural information processing systems, NIPS'15, vol 1, pp 424–432

184. Chen X, Ma H, Wan J, Li B, Xia T (2017) Multi-view 3D object detection network for autonomous driving. In: IEEE conference on computer vision and pattern recognition (CVPR), vol 1, p 3

185. Chen X, Wang G, Guo H, Zhang C (2017) Pose guided structured region ensemble network for cascaded hand pose estimation. CoRR abs/1708.03416. arXiv:1708.03416

186. Chen X, Zhou B, Lu F, Wang L, Bi L, Tan P (2015) Garment modeling with a depth camera. ACM Trans Graph (TOG) 34(6):1–12

187. Chen Y, Medioni G (1991) Object modeling by registration of multiple range images. In: Proceedings. IEEE international conference on robotics and automation, vol 3, pp 2724–2729

188. Chen Y, Medioni G (1992) Object modelling by registration of multiple range images. Image Vis Comput 10(3):145–155

189. Chen YQ (2011) Joint reconstruction of 3D shape and non-rigid motion in a region-growing framework. In: International conference on computer vision (ICCV) workshops, pp 1578–1585

190. Cheng DS, Cristani M, Stoppa M, Bazzani L, Murino V (2011) Custom pictorial structures for re-identification. In: British machine vision conference (BMVC), pp 68.1–68.11

191. Cheng MM, Mitra NJ, Huang X, Hu SM (2014) Salientshape: group saliency in image collections. Vis Comput 30(4):443–453

192. Cheng MM, Mitra NJ, Huang X, Torr PH, Hu SM (2014) Global contrast based salient region detection. IEEE Trans Pattern Anal Mach Intell 37(3):569–582

193. Cheng Y, Cai R, Li Z, Zhao X, Huang K (2017) Locality-sensitive deconvolution networks with gated fusion for RGBD indoor semantic segmentation. In: IEEE conference on computer vision and pattern recognition (CVPR), pp 1475–1483

194. Choi C, Christensen HI (2012) 3D pose estimation of daily objects using an RGB-D camera. In: IEEE/RSJ international conference on intelligent robots and systems (IROS), pp 3342–3349

195. Choi C, Christensen HI (2016) RGB-D object pose estimation in unstructured environments. Robot Auton Syst 75:595–613

196. Choi C, Kim S, Ramani K (2017) Learning hand articulations by hallucinating heat distribution. In: IEEE international conference on computer vision (ICCV), pp 3104–3113

197. Choi C, Sinha A, Hee Choi J, Jang S, Ramani K (2015) A collaborative filtering approach to real-time hand pose estimation. In: IEEE international conference on computer vision (ICCV), pp 2336–2344

198. Choi C, Taguchi Y, Tuzel O, Liu MY, Ramalingam S (2012) Voting-based pose estimation for robotic assembly using a 3D sensor. In: IEEE international conference on robotics and automation (ICRA), pp 1724–1731

199. Choi C, Trevor AJB, Christensen HI (2013) RGB-D edge detection and edge-based registration. In: IEEE/RSJ international conference on intelligent robots and systems, pp 1568–1575

200. Choi S, Lee J, Kim J (1997) Volumetric object reconstruction using the 3D-MRF model-based segmentation. IEEE Med Imaging 16(6):887–892

201. Chow CK, Yuen SY (2010) Illumination direction estimation for augmented reality using a surface input real valued output regression network. Pattern Recognit 43(4):1700–1716
202. Chow JCK, Ang KD, Lichti DD, Teskey WF (2012) Performance analysis of a low-cost triangulation-based 3D camera: Microsoft Kinect system. In: International archives of the photogrammetry, remote sensing and spatial information sciences—ISPRS archives, vol 39, pp 175–180
203. Choy CB, Xu D, Gwak J, Chen K, Savarese S (2016) 3D-R2N2: a unified approach for single and multi-view 3D object reconstruction. In: Leibe B, Matas J, Sebe N, Welling M (eds) European conference on computer vision (ECCV), pp 628–644
204. Chua CS, Guan H, Ho YK (2002) Model-based 3D hand posture estimation from a single 2d image. Image Vis Comput 20(3):191–202
205. Chuan CH, Regina E, Guardino C (2014) American sign language recognition using leap motion sensor. In: International conference on machine learning and applications, pp 541–544
206. Çiçek Ö, Abdulkadir A, Lienkamp SS, Brox T, Ronneberger O (2016) 3D U-Net: learning dense volumetric segmentation from sparse annotation. In: Ourselin S, Joskowicz L, Sabuncu MR, Unal G, Wells W (eds) Medical image computing and computer-assisted intervention – MICCAI 2016, pp 424–432
207. Cinbis RG, Verbeek J, Schmid C (2013) Segmentation driven object detection with Fisher vectors. In: IEEE international conference on computer vision (ICCV), pp 2968–2975
208. Cippitelli E, Fioranelli F, Gambi E, Spinsante S (2017) Radar and RGB-depth sensors for fall detection: a review. IEEE Sens J 17(12):3585–3604
209. Cippitelli E, Gambi E, Gasparrini S, Spinsante S (2016) TST fall detection dataset v1. In: IEEE Dataport
210. Cippitelli E, Gambi E, Gasparrini S, Spinsante S (2016) TST fall detection dataset v2. In: IEEE Dataport
211. Cippitelli E, Gasparrini S, Gambi E, Spinsante S (2014) A depth-based joints estimation algorithm for get up and go test using Kinect. In: IEEE international conference on consumer electronics (ICCE), pp 226–227
212. Cippitelli E, Gasparrini S, Gambi E, Spinsante S, Wåhslény J, Orhany I, Lindhy T (2015) Time synchronization and data fusion for RGB-depth cameras and inertial sensors in AAL applications. In: IEEE international conference on communication workshop (ICCW), pp 265–270
213. Cippitelli E, Gasparrini S, Santis AD, Montanini L, Raffaeli L, Gambi E, Spinsante S (2015) Comparison of RGB-D mapping solutions for application to food intake monitoring. Springer International Publishing, pp 295–305
214. Cippitelli E, Gasparrini S, Spinsante S, Gambi E (2015) Kinect as a tool for gait analysis: validation of a real-time joint extraction algorithm working in side view. Sensors 15(1):1417–1434
215. Clark RA, Pua YH, Bryant AL, Hunt MA (2013) Validity of the Microsoft Kinect for providing lateral trunk lean feedback during gait retraining. Gait Posture 38(4):1064–1066

216. Coşkun A, Kara A, Parlaktuna M, Ozkan M, Parlaktuna O (2015) People counting system by using Kinect sensor. In: International symposium on innovations in intelligent systems and applications (INISTA), pp 1–7

217. Cogollor JM, Hughes C, Ferre M, Rojo J, Hermsdörfer J, Wing A, Campo S (2012) Handmade task tracking applied to cognitive rehabilitation. Sensors 12(10):14214–14231

218. Collado-Mateo D, Dominguez-Muñoz FJ, Adsuar JC, Merellano-Navarro E, Gusi N (2017) Exergames for women with fibromyalgia: a randomised controlled trial to evaluate the effects on mobility skills, balance and fear of falling. PeerJ 5:e3211

219. Comport AI, Meilland M, Rives P (2011) An asymmetric real-time dense visual localisation and mapping system. In: International conference on computer vision (ICCV) workshops, pp 700–703

220. Concha A, Civera J (2015) An evaluation of robust cost functions for RGB direct mapping. In: European conference on mobile robots (ECMR)

221. Concha A, Civera J (2017) RGBDTAM: a cost-effective and accurate RGB-D tracking and mapping system. In: IEEE/RSJ international conference on intelligent robots and systems (IROS), pp 6756–6763

222. Concha A, Hussain MW, Montano L, Civera J (2014) Manhattan and piecewise-planar constraints for dense monocular mapping. In: Robotics: science and systems

223. Concha A, Loianno G, Kumar V, Civera J (2016) Visual-inertial direct SLAM. In: IEEE international conference on robotics and automation (ICRA), pp 1331–1338

224. Cong P, Xiong Z, Zhang Y, Zhao S, Wu F (2015) Accurate dynamic 3D sensing with Fourier-assisted phase shifting. Sel Top Signal Process 9(3):396–408

225. Cong R, Lei J, Fu H, Cheng MM, Lin W, Huang Q (2018) Review of visual saliency detection with comprehensive information. IEEE Trans Circuits Syst Video Technol PP(99):1–19

226. Cong R, Lei J, Fu H, Huang Q, Cao X, Hou C (2017) Co-saliency detection for RGBD images based on multi-constraint feature matching and cross label propagation. IEEE Trans Image Process 27(2):568–579

227. Cong R, Lei J, Fu H, Huang Q, Cao X, Ling N (2018) HSCS: hierarchical sparsity based co-saliency detection for RGBD images. IEEE Trans Multimed PP(99):1–12

228. Cong R, Lei J, Fu H, Lin W, Huang Q, Cao X, Hou C (2017) An iterative co-saliency framework for RGBD images. IEEE Trans Cybern (99):1–14

229. Cong R, Lei J, Zhang C, Huang Q, Cao X, Hou C (2016) Saliency detection for stereoscopic images based on depth confidence analysis and multiple cues fusion. IEEE Signal Process Lett 23(6):819–823

230. Cordts M, Omran M, Ramos S, Rehfeld T, Enzweiler M, Benenson R, Franke U, Roth S, Schiele B (2016) The cityscapes dataset for semantic urban scene understanding. In: IEEE conference on computer vision and pattern recognition (CVPR), pp 3213–3223

231. Corke P (2017) Robotics, vision and control: fundamental algorithms in MAT-LAB® second, completely revised, chap 1. Springer, pp 15–41

232. Coroiu ADCA, Coroiu A (2018) Interchangeability of Kinect and Orbbec sensors for gesture recognition. In: IEEE international conference on intelligent computer communication and processing (ICCP), pp 309–315

233. Crabb R, Tracey C, Puranik A, Davis J (2008) Real-time foreground segmentation via range and color imaging. In: IEEE conference on computer vision and pattern recognition workshops, pp 1–5

234. Creative Commons (2019) Creative commons attribution license (CC BY 4.0). https://creativecommons.org/licenses/by/4.0/. Accessed 25 Jun 2019

235. Criminisi A, Pérez P, Toyama K (2004) Region filling and object removal by exemplar-based image inpainting. IEEE Trans Image Process 13(9):1200–1212

236. Cruz L, Lucio D, Velho L (2012) Kinect and RGBD images: challenges and applications. In: SIBGRAPI conference on graphics, patterns and images tutorials, pp 36–49

237. Curless B, Levoy M (1996) A volumetric method for building complex models from range images. In: ACM SIGGRAPH, pp 303–312

238. Da Gama A, Chaves T, Figueiredo L, Teichrieb V (2012) Guidance and movement correction based on therapeutics movements for motor rehabilitation support systems. In: Symposium on virtual and augmented reality, pp 191–200

239. Dabov K, Foi A, Katkovnik V, Egiazarian K (2007) Image denoising by sparse 3D transform-domain collaborative filtering. IEEE Trans Image Process 16(8):2080–2095

240. Dai A, Chang AX, Savva M, Halber M, Funkhouser T, Nießner M (2017) ScanNet: richly-annotated 3D reconstructions of indoor scenes. In: IEEE conference on computer vision and pattern recognition (CVPR)

241. Dai A, Nießner M, Zollhöfer M, Izadi S, Theobalt C (2017) BundleFusion: real-time globally consistent 3D reconstruction using on-the-fly surface reintegration. ACM Trans Graph 36(3):24:1–24:18

242. Dai A, Qi CR, Nießner M (2017) Shape completion using 3D-encoder-predictor CNNs and shape synthesis. In: IEEE conference on computer vision and pattern recognition (CVPR), pp 5868–5877

243. Dai J, He K, Sun J (2014) Convolutional feature masking for joint object and stuff segmentation. CoRR abs/1412.1283. arXiv:1412.1283

244. Dal Mutto C, Zanuttigh P, Cortelazzo GM (2012) Time-of-flight cameras and Microsoft Kinect™. Springer briefs in electrical and computer engineering. Springer, USA

245. Dalal N, Triggs B (2005) Histograms of oriented gradients for human detection. In: IEEE conference on computer vision and pattern recognition (CVPR)

246. Damen D, Gee A, Mayol-Cuevas W, Calway A (2012) Egocentric real-time workspace monitoring using an RGB-D camera. In: IEEE/RSJ international conference on intelligent robots and systems, pp 1029–1036

247. Dan B, Kim Y, Suryanto, Jung J, Ko S (2012) Robust people counting system based on sensor fusion. IEEE Trans Consum Electron 58(3):1013–1021

248. Daponte P, DeMarco J, DeVito L, Pavic B, Zolli S (2011) Electronic measurements in rehabilitation. In: IEEE international symposium on medical measurements and applications, pp 274–279

249. Darabi S, Shechtman E, Barnes C, Goldman DB, Sen P (2012) Image melding: combining inconsistent images using patch-based synthesis. ACM Trans Graph 31(4):82–1

250. Daribo I, Saito H (2011) A novel inpainting-based layered depth video for 3DTV. IEEE Trans Broadcast 57(2):533–541

251. Davison AJ (2003) Real-time simultaneous localisation and mapping with a single camera. In: IEEE international conference on computer vision (ICCV), vol 2, pp 1403–1410

252. Davison AJ, Reid ID, Molton ND, Stasse O (2007) MonoSLAM: real-time single camera SLAM. IEEE Trans Pattern Anal Mach Intell 29(6):1052–1067

253. Debard G, Mertens M, Goedemé T, Tuytelaars T, Vanrumste B (2017) Three ways to improve the performance of real-life camera-based fall detection systems. J Sens 2017

254. Delage E, Lee H, Ng AY (2006) A dynamic Bayesian network model for autonomous 3D reconstruction from a single indoor image. In: IEEE conference on computer vision and pattern recognition (CVPR), vol 2, pp 2418–2428

255. Demiröz BE, Salah AA, Akarun L (2014) Coupling fall detection and tracking in omnidirectional cameras. In: Park HS, Salah AA, Lee YJ, Morency LP, Sheikh Y, Cucchiara R (eds) Human behavior understanding. Springer, pp 73–85

256. Deng J, Dong W, Socher R, Li LJ, Li K, Fei-Fei L (2009) Imagenet: a large-scale hierarchical image database. In: IEEE conference on computer vision and pattern recognition (CVPR), pp 248–255

257. Deng T, Bazin JC, Martin T, Kuster C, Cai J, Popa T, Gross M (2014) Registration of multiple RGBD cameras via local rigid transformations. http://www.cs.utah.edu/~martin/calibration.pdf

258. Deng Z, Latecki LJ (2017) Amodal detection of 3D objects: inferring 3D bounding boxes from 2D ones in RGB-depth images. In: IEEE conference on computer vision and pattern recognition (CVPR), vol 2, p 2

259. Desingh K, Krishna KM, Rajan D, Jawahar C (2013) Depth really matters: improving visual salient region detection with depth. In: British machine vision conference (BMVC)

260. Diebel J, Thrun S (2015) An application of Markov random fields to range sensing. In: NIPS

261. Ding L, Sharma G (2017) Fusing structure from motion and lidar for dense accurate depth map estimation. In: International conference on acoustics, speech and signal processing, pp 1283–1287

262. Ding M, Fan G (2016) Articulated and generalized gaussian kernel correlation for human pose estimation. IEEE Trans Image Process 25(2):776–789

263. Ding S, Lin L, Wang G, Chao H (2015) Deep feature learning with relative distance comparison for person re-identification. Pattern Recognit 48(10):2993–3003

264. Dittrich F, Woern H, Sharma V, Yayilgan S (2014) Pixelwise object class segmentation based on synthetic data using an optimized training strategy. In: First international conference on networks & soft computing (ICNSC2014), pp 388–394

265. Dollár P, Welinder P, Perona P (2010) Cascaded pose regression. In: IEEE conference on computer vision and pattern recognition (CVPR), pp 1078–1085

266. Dong C, Loy CC, He K, Tang X (2016) Image super-resolution using deep convolutional networks. IEEE Trans Pattern Anal Mach Intell 38(2):295–307

267. Dong H, Figueroa N, El Saddik A (2014) Towards consistent reconstructions of indoor spaces based on 6D RGB-D odometry and KinectFusion. In: IEEE/RSJ international conference on intelligent robots and systems, pp 1796–1803

268. Dong W, Shi G, Li X, Peng K, Wu J, Guo Z (2016) Color-guided depth recovery via joint local structural and nonlocal low-rank regularization. IEEE Trans Multimed 19(2):293–301

269. Dong Y, Carin L (2003) Quantization of multiaspect scattering data: target classification and pose estimation. IEEE Trans Signal Process 51(12):3105–3114

270. Dou M, Davidson P, Fanello SR, Khamis S, Kowdle A, Rhemann C, Tankovich V, Izadi S (2017) Motion2Fusion: real-time volumetric performance capture. ACM Trans Graph 36(6):246:1–246:16

271. Dou M, Fuchs H (2014) Temporally enhanced 3D capture of room-sized dynamic scenes with commodity depth cameras. In: IEEE virtual reality (VR), pp 39–44

272. Dou M, Fuchs H, Frahm J (2013) Scanning and tracking dynamic objects with commodity depth cameras. In: IEEE international symposium on mixed and augmented reality (ISMAR), pp 99–106

273. Dou M, Khamis S, Degtyarev Y, Davidson P, Fanello SR, Kowdle A, Escolano SO, Rhemann C, Kim D, Taylor J, Kohli P, Tankovich V, Izadi S (2016) Fusion4d: real-time performance capture of challenging scenes. ACM Trans Graph (TOG)

274. Doumanoglou A, Kouskouridas R, Malassiotis S, Kim TK (2016) Recovering 6D object pose and predicting next-best-view in the crowd. In: IEEE conference on computer vision and pattern recognition (CVPR), pp 3583–3592

275. Downs SH, Black N (1998) The feasibility of creating a checklist for the assessment of the methodological quality both of randomised and non-randomised studies of health care interventions. J Epidemiol Commun Health 52(6):377–384

276. Droeschel D, Behnke S (2011) 3D body pose estimation using an adaptive person model for articulated ICP. In: International conference on intelligent robotics and applications (ICIRA), pp 157–167

277. Droeschel D, Nieuwenhuisen M, Beul M, Holz D, Stückler J, Behnke S (2016) Multilayered mapping and navigation for autonomous micro aerial vehicles. J Field Robot 33(4):451–475

278. Droeschel D, Stückler J, Behnke S (2011) Learning to interpret pointing gestures with a time-of-flight camera. In: Human robot interaction (HRI)

279. Droeschel D, Stückler J, Behnke S (2014) Local multi-resolution representation for 6D motion estimation and mapping with a continuously rotating 3D laser scanner. In: IEEE international conference on robotics and automation (ICRA), pp 5221–5226

280. Droeschel D, Stückler J, Holz D, Behnke S (2011) Towards joint attention for a domestic service robot – person awareness and gesture recognition using time-of-flight cameras. In: IEEE international conference on robotics and automation (ICRA)

281. Drost B, Ilic S (2012) 3D object detection and localization using multimodal point pair features. In: International conference on 3D imaging, modeling, processing, visualization & transmission, pp 9–16

282. Drost B, Ulrich M, Navab N, Ilic S (2010) Model globally, match locally: efficient and robust 3D object recognition. In: IEEE conference on computer vision and pattern recognition (CVPR), pp 998–1005

283. Dryanovski I, Morris W, Xiao J (2011) An open-source pose estimation system for micro-air vehicles. In: IEEE international conference on robotics and automation (ICRA), pp 4449–4454

284. Duda RO, Hart PE (1972) Use of the Hough transformation to detect lines and curves in pictures. Commun ACM 15(1):11–15

285. Duncan PW, Weiner DK, Chandler J, Studenski S (1990) Functional reach: a new clinical measure of balance. J Gerontol 45(6), M192–M197

286. Durand F, Dorsey J (2002) Fast bilateral filtering for the display of high-dynamic-range images. ACM Trans Graph (TOG) 21(3):257–266

287. Durfee WK, Savard L, Weinstein S (2007) Technical feasibility of teleassessments for rehabilitation. IEEE Trans n Neural Syst Rehabil Eng 15(1):23–29

288. Durrant-Whyte H, Bailey T (2006) Simultaneous localization and mapping: Part I. IEEE Robot Autom Mag 13(2):99–110

289. Schapire RE (2013) Explaining AdaBoost, pp 37–52

290. Efros AA, Freeman WT (2001) Image quilting for texture synthesis and transfer. In: Conference on computer graphics and interactive techniques, pp 341–346

291. Efros AA, Leung TK (1999) Texture synthesis by non-parametric sampling. In: International conference on computer vision, vol 2, pp 1033–1038

292. Eigen D, Fergus R (2015) Predicting depth, surface normals and semantic labels with a common multi-scale convolutional architecture. In: IEEE international conference on computer vision (ICCV)

293. Eigen D, Puhrsch C, Fergus R (2014) Depth map prediction from a single image using a multi-scale deep network. In: Advances in neural information processing systems, pp 2366–2374

294. Eisemann E, Durand F (2004) Flash photography enhancement via intrinsic relighting. ACM Trans Graph (TOG) 23(3):673–678

295. Eitel A, Springenberg JT, Spinello L, Riedmiller MA, Burgard W (2015) Multimodal deep learning for robust RGB-D object recognition. CoRR abs/1507.06821

296. El-laithy RA, Huang J, Yeh M (2012) Study on the use of microsoft Kinect for robotics applications. In: Position location and navigation symposium, pp 1280–1288

297. Elgammal A, Harwood D, Davis L (2000) Non-parametric model for background subtraction. In: European conference on computer vision (ECCV), pp 751–767

298. Endres F, Hess J, Engelhard N, Sturm J, Burgard W (2012) An evaluation of the RGB-D SLAM system. In: IEEE international conference on robotics and automation (ICRA)

299. Endres F, Hess J, Sturm J, Cremers D, Burgard W (2014) 3-D mapping with an RGB-D camera. IEEE Trans Robot 30(1):177–187

300. Engel J, Koltun V, Cremers D (2018) Direct sparse odometry. IEEE Trans Pattern Anal Mach Intell 40(3):611–625

301. Engelcke M, Rao D, Wang DZ, Tong CH, Posner I (2017) Vote3deep: fast object detection in 3D point clouds using efficient convolutional neural networks. In: IEEE international conference on robotics and automation (ICRA), pp 1355–1361

302. Enzweiler M, Gavrila DM (2011) A multilevel mixture-of-experts framework for pedestrian classification. IEEE Trans Image Process 20(10):2967–2979

303. Eppner C, Höfer S, Jonschkowski R, Martín-Martín R, Sieverling A, Wall V, Brock O (2016) Lessons from the Amazon Picking Challenge: four aspects of building robotic systems. In: Robotics: science and systems

304. Erhan D, Szegedy C, Toshev A, Anguelov D (2014) Scalable object detection using deep neural networks. In: IEEE conference on computer vision and pattern recognition (CVPR)

305. Eric N, Jang JW (2017) Kinect depth sensor for computer vision applications in autonomous vehicles. In: International conference on ubiquitous and future networks, ICUFN, pp 531–535

306. Erol A, Bebis G, Nicolescu M, Boyle RD, Twombly X (2005) A review on vision-based full DOF hand motion estimation. In: IEEE conference on computer vision and pattern recognition workshops (CVPRW), pp 75–82

307. Erol A, Bebis G, Nicolescu M, Boyle RD, Twombly X (2007) Vision-based hand pose estimation: a review. Comput Vis Image Underst 108(1):52–73

308. Ess A, Leibe B, Gool LV (2007) Depth and appearance for mobile scene analysis. In: IEEE international conference on computer vision, pp 1–8

309. Esser SK, Merolla PA, Arthur JV, Cassidy AS, Appuswamy R, Andreopoulos A, Berg DJ, McKinstry JL, Melano T, Barch DR, di Nolfo C, Datta P, Amir A, Taba B, Flickner MD, Modha DS (2016) Convolutional networks for fast, energy-efficient neuromorphic computing. Proc Natl Acad Sci

310. Everingham M, Van Gool L, Williams C, Winn J, Zisserman A (2010) The PASCAL visual object classes (VOC) challenge. In: IEEE conference on computer vision and pattern recognition (CVPR)

311. Fácil JM, Ummenhofer B, Zhou H, Montesano L, Brox T, Civera J (2019) CAM-Convs: camera-aware multi-scale convolutions for single-view depth. In: IEEE conference on computer vision and pattern recognition (CVPR)

312. Factory 42 (2019) "Hold the world" with David Attenborough. https://www.factory42.uk/. Accessed 28 Jun 2019

313. Faion F, Friedberger S, Zea A, Hanebeck UD (2012) Intelligent sensor-scheduling for multi-kinect-tracking. In: IEEE/RSJ international conference on intelligent robots and systems, pp 3993–3999

314. Fan X, Liu Z, Sun G (2014) Salient region detection for stereoscopic images. In: ICDSP, pp 454–458

315. Fang H, Xie S, Tai YW, Lu C (2017) RMPE: regional multi-person pose estimation. In: IEEE international conference on computer vision (ICCV), pp 2334–2343

316. Fang Y, Wang J, Narwaria M, Le Callet P, Lin W (2014) Saliency detection for stereoscopic images. IEEE Trans Image Process 23(6):2625–2636

317. Farenzena M, Bazzani L, Perina A, Murino V, Cristani M (2010) Person re-identification by symmetry-driven accumulation of local features. In: IEEE on computer vision and pattern recognition, pp 2360–2367

318. Fechteler P, Eisert P (2011) Recovering articulated pose of 3D point clouds. In: European conference on visual media production (CVMP), p 2011

319. Fehrman B, McGough J (2014) Depth mapping using a low-cost camera array. In: Southwest symposium on image analysis and interpretation, pp 101–104

320. Fei-Fei L, Fergus R, Perona P (2004) Learning generative visual models from few training examples: an incremental bayesian approach tested on 101 object categories. In: 2004 conference on computer vision and pattern recognition workshop, pp 178–178

321. Felzenszwalb PF, Girshick RB, McAllester D, Ramanan D (2010) Object detection with discriminatively trained part-based models. IEEE Trans Pattern Anal Mach Intell 32(9):1627–1645

322. Felzenszwalb PF, Huttenlocher DP (2004) Efficient graph-based image segmentation. Comput Vis 59(2):167–181

323. Felzenszwalb PF, Zabih R (2011) Dynamic programming and graph algorithms in computer vision. IEEE Trans Pattern Anal Mach Intell 33(4):721–40

324. Feng D, Barnes N, You S, McCarthy C (2016) Local background enclosure for RGB-D salient object detection. In: IEEE conference on computer vision and pattern recognition (CVPR), pp 2343–2350

325. Feng D, Haase-Schuetz C, Rosenbaum L, Hertlein H, Duffhauss F, Glaeser C, Wiesbeck W, Dietmayer K (2019) Deep multi-modal object detection and semantic segmentation for autonomous driving: datasets, methods, and challenges. arXiv:1902.07830

326. Feng D, Rosenbaum L, Dietmayer K (2018) Towards safe autonomous driving: capture uncertainty in the deep neural network for LIDAR 3D vehicle detection. In: IEEE international conference on intelligent transportation systems (ITSC)

327. Ferracuti N, Norscini C, Frontoni E, Gabellini P, Paolanti M, Placidi V (2019) A business application of RTLS technology in intelligent retail environment: defining the shopper's preferred path and its segmentation. J Retail Consum Serv 47:184–194

328. Ferstl D, Reinbacher C, Ranftl R, Rüther M, Bischof H (2013) Image guided depth upsampling using anisotropic total generalized variation. In: IEEE international conference on computer vision (ICCV), pp 993–1000

329. Ferstl D, Riegler G, Rüether M, Bischof H (2014) CP-Census: a novel model for dense variational scene flow from RGB-D data. In: British machine vision conference (BMVC), pp 18.1–18.11

330. Figueiredo M, Bioucas J, Nowak R (2007) Majorization-minimization algorithms for wavelet-based image restoration. IEEE Trans Image Process 16(12):2980–2991

331. Firman M, Mac Aodha O, Julier S, Brostow GJ (2016) Structured prediction of unobserved voxels from a single depth image. In: IEEE conference on computer vision and pattern recognition (CVPR)

332. Fischler MA, Bolles RC (1981) Random sample consensus: a paradigm for model fitting with applications to image analysis and automated cartography. Commun ACM 24(6):381–395

333. Fisher SS (1987) Telepresence master glove controller for dexterous robotic end-effectors. In: Casasent DP (ed) Proceedings of SPIE, vol 726, p 396

334. Fitzgibbon A (2003) Robust registration of 2D and 3D point sets. Image Vis Comput 21(13–14):1145–1153

335. Flores E, Tobon G, Cavallaro E, Cavallaro FI, Perry JC, Keller T (2008) Improving patient motivation in game development for motor deficit rehabilitation. In: Proceedings of the international conference on advances in computer entertainment technology, pp 381–384

336. Foix S, Alenya G, Torras C (2011) Lock-in time-of-flight (ToF) cameras: a survey. IEEE Sensors J 11(9):1917–1926

337. Forsyth DA, Ponce J (2002) Computer vision: a modern approach. Prentice Hall Professional Technical Reference

338. Fox D (2016) The 100-100 tracking challenge. Keynote at ICRA conference

339. Franco A, Oliveira L (2017) Convolutional covariance features: conception, integration and performance in person re-identification. Pattern Recognit 61:593–609

340. Franco JS, Boyer E (2011) Learning temporally consistent rigidities. In: IEEE conference on computer vision and pattern recognition (CVPR), pp 1241–1248

341. Freedman B, Shpunt A, Machlin M, Arieli Y (2012) depth mapping using projected patterns. US8150142B2 Patent

342. Friedman JH, Bentley JL, Finkel RA (1977) An algorithm for finding best matches in logarithmic expected time. ACM Trans Math Softw 3(3):209–226

343. Friedman LM, Furberg C, DeMets DL, Reboussin D, Granger CB (1998) Fundamentals of clinical trials, vol 3. Springer

344. Friedman N, Geiger D, Goldszmidt M (1997) Bayesian network classifiers. Mach Learn 29(2–3):131–163

345. Frontoni E, Zingaretti P (2005) A vision based algorithm for active robot localization. In: International symposium on computational intelligence in robotics and automation, pp 347–352

346. Fu D, Zhao Y, Yu L (2010) Temporal consistency enhancement on depth sequences. In: Picture coding symposium, pp 342–345

347. Fu H, Xu D, Lin S (2017) Object-based multiple foreground segmentation in RGBD video. IEEE Trans Image Process 26(3):1418–1427

348. Fu H, Xu D, Lin S, Liu J (2015) Object-based RGBD image co-segmentation with mutex constraint. In: IEEE conference on computer vision and pattern recognition (CVPR), pp 4428–4436

349. Fu H, Xu D, Zhang B, Lin S, Ward R (2015) Object-based multiple foreground video co-segmentation via multi-state selection graph. IEEE Trans Image Process 24(11):3415–3424

350. Fuhrmann A, Kretz J, Burwik P (2013) Multi sensor tracking for live sound transformation. In: Proceedings of the international conference on new interfaces for musical expression. Graduate School of Culture Technology, KAIST, pp 358–362

351. Fuhrmann S, Goesele M (2014) Floating scale surface reconstruction. In: ACM SIGGRAPH, July

352. Furukawa Y, Curless B, Seitz SM, Szeliski R (2009) Reconstructing building interiors from images. In: Proceedings of ICCV, pp 80–87

353. Furukawa Y, Ponce J (2008) Dense 3D motion capture from synchronized video streams. In: IEEE conference on computer vision and pattern recognition (CVPR)

354. Furukawa Y, Ponce J (2009) Dense 3D motion capture for human faces. In: IEEE conference on computer vision and pattern recognition (CVPR), pp 1674–1681

355. Gabel M, Gilad-Bachrach R, Renshaw E, Schuster A (2012) Full body gait analysis with Kinect. In: Engineering in Medicine and Biology Society (EMBC), annual international conference of the IEEE, pp 1964–1967

356. Gal Y, Ghahramani Z (2016) Dropout as a Bayesian approximation: representing model uncertainty in deep learning. In: International conference on machine learning (ICML), pp 1050–1059

357. Galen SS, Pardo V, Wyatt D, Diamond A, Brodith V, Pavlov A (2015) Validity of an interactive functional reach test. Games Health J 4(4):278–284

358. Gall J, Lempitsky VS (2009) Class-specific Hough forests for object detection. In: IEEE conference on computer vision and pattern recognition (CVPR)

359. Gall J, Stoll C, de Aguiar E, Theobalt C, Rosenhahn B, Seidel HP (2009) Motion capture using joint skeleton tracking and surface estimation. In: IEEE conference on computer vision and pattern recognition (CVPR), pp 1746–1753

360. Gálvez-López D, Tardos JD (2012) Bags of binary words for fast place recognition in image sequences. IEEE Trans Robot 28(5):1188–1197

361. Gangwal OP, Djapic B (2010) Real-time implementation of depth map post-processing for 3D-TV in dedicated hardware. In: International conference on consumer electronics, pp 173–174

362. Gao H, Cheng B, Wang J, Li K, Zhao J, Li D (2018) Object classification using CNN-based fusion of vision and LIDAR in autonomous vehicle environment. IEEE Trans Ind Inform:1

363. Gao X, Zhang T (2015) Robust RGB-D simultaneous localization and mapping using planar point features. Robot Auton Syst 72:1–14

364. Garcia F, Aouada D, Mirbach B, Ottersten B (2012) Real-time distance-dependent mapping for a hybrid tof multi-camera rig. IEEE J Sel Top Signal Process 6(5):425–436

365. Garcia F, Aouada D, Mirbach B, Solignac T, Ottersten B (2015) Unified multi-lateral filter for real-time depth map enhancement. Image Vis Comput 41:26–41

366. Garcia F, Aouada D, Solignac T, Mirbach B, Ottersten B (2013) Real-time depth enhancement by fusion for RGB-D cameras. IET Comput Vis 7(5):335–345

367. Garcia GM, Husain F, Schulz H, Frintrop S, Torras C, Behnke S (2016) Semantic segmentation priors for object discovery. In: International conference on pattern recognition (ICPR)

368. Garcia NM, Garcia NC, Sousa P, Oliveira D, Alexandre C, Felizardo V (2014) TICE.Healthy: a perspective on medical information integration. In: IEEE-EMBS international conference on biomedical and health informatics (BHI), pp 464–467

369. Garcia-Garcia A, Orts-Escolano S, Oprea S, Villena-Martinez V, Garcia-Rodriguez J (2017) A review on deep learning techniques applied to semantic segmentation. arXiv:1704.06857

370. Garcia-Hernando G, Yuan S, Baek S, Kim TK (2018) First-person hand action benchmark with RGB-D videos and 3D hand pose annotations. In: IEEE conference on computer vision and pattern recognition (CVPR), pp 409–419

371. Garg R, Carneiro G, Reid I (2016) Unsupervised CNN for single view depth estimation: geometry to the rescue. In: European conference on computer vision, pp 740–756

372. Garg R, Roussos A, Agapito L (2013) A variational approach to video registration with subspace constraints. Int J Comput Vis (IJCV) 104(3):286–314

373. Garg R, Roussos A, Agapito L (2013) Dense variational reconstruction of non-rigid surfaces from monocular video. In: IEEE conference on computer vision and pattern recognition (CVPR), pp 1272–1279

374. Garland M, Heckbert P (1998) Simplifying surfaces with color and texture using quadric error metrics. In: Conference on visualization

375. Garro V, Mutto CD, Zanuttigh P, Cortelazzo GM (2009) A novel interpolation scheme for range data with side information. In: Conference on visual media production, pp 52–60

376. Garro V, Zanuttigh P, Cortelazzo G (2009) A new super resolution technique for range data. Associazione Gruppo Telecomunicazioni e Tecnologie dellInformazione

377. Gasparrini S, Cippitelli E, Gambi E, Spinsante S, Wåhslén J, Orhan I, Lindh T (2016) Proposal and experimental evaluation of fall detection solution based on wearable and depth data fusion. In: Loshkovska S, Koceski S (eds) ICT innovations. Springer, pp 99–108

378. Gasparrini S, Cippitelli E, Spinsante S, Gambi E (2014) A depth-based fall detection system using a Kinect® sensor. Sensors 14(2):2756–2775

379. Gasparrini S, Cippitelli E, Spinsante S, Gambi E (2015) Depth cameras in AAL environments: technology and real-world applications. IGI Global, vols 2–4

380. Gatys LA, Ecker AS, Bethge M (2016) Image style transfer using convolutional neural networks. In: IEEE conference on computer vision and pattern recognition (CVPR), pp 2414–2423

381. Gavrila D, Davis LS (1996) 3-d model-based tracking of humans in action: a multi-view approach. In: IEEE conference on computer vision and pattern recognition (CVPR)

382. Ge L, Cai Y, Weng J, Yuan J (2018) Hand pointnet: 3D hand pose estimation using point sets. In: IEEE conference on computer vision and pattern recognition (CVPR), pp 8417–8426

383. Ge L, Liang H, Yuan J, Thalmann D (2017) 3D convolutional neural networks for efficient and robust hand pose estimation from single depth images. In: IEEE conference on computer vision and pattern recognition (CVPR), pp 1991–2000

384. Ge L, Liang H, Yuan J, Thalmann D (2018) Real-time 3D hand pose estimation with 3D convolutional neural networks. IEEE Trans Pattern Anal Mach Intell:1–15

385. Ge L, Liang H, Yuan J, Thalmann D (2018) Robust 3D hand pose estimation from single depth images using multi-view CNNs. IEEE Trans Image Process 27(9):4422–4436

386. Ge L, Ren Z, Yuan J (2018) Point-to-point regression pointnet for 3D hand pose estimation. In: European conference on computer vision (ECCV)

387. Ge S, Fan G (2015) Articulated non-rigid point set registration for human pose estimation from 3D sensors. MDPI AG, pp 15218–15245

388. Gee AP, Mayol-Cuevas WW (2012) 6D relocalisation for RGBD cameras using synthetic view regression. In: British machine vision conference (BMVC)

389. Geerse DJ, Coolen B, Roerdink M (2015) Kinematic validation of a multi-Kinect v2 instrumented 10-meter walkway for quantitative gait assessments. PLoS One 10:e0139913. Accessed 01 Feb 2019
390. Geiger A, Lenz P, Stiller C, Urtasun R (2013) Vision meets robotics: the KITTI dataset. Int J Robot Res 32(11):1231–1237
391. Geiger A, Lenz P, Urtasun R (2012) Are we ready for autonomous driving? The KITTI vision benchmark suite. In: Conference on computer vision and pattern recognition (CVPR)
392. Geiselhart F, Otto M, Rukzio E (2016) On the use of multi-depth-camera based motion tracking systems in production planning environments. Procedia CIRP 41:759–764. Research and innovation in manufacturing: key enabling technologies for the factories of the future – proceedings of the 48th CIRP conference on manufacturing systems
393. Geng J (2011) Structured-light 3D surface imaging: a tutorial. Adv Opt Photon 3(2):128–160
394. Getto R, Fellner DW (2015) 3D object retrieval with parametric templates. In: Proceedings of the eurographics workshop on 3D object retrieval, 3DOR '15, pp 47–54
395. Gheissari N, Sebastian TB, Hartley R (2006) Person reidentification using spatiotemporal appearance. In: IEEE conference on computer vision and pattern recognition, pp 1528–1535
396. Ghiasi G, Lee H, Kudlur M, Dumoulin V, Shlens J (2017) Exploring the structure of a real-time, arbitrary neural artistic stylization network. In: British machine vision conference (BMVC), pp 1–12
397. Ghose A, Chakravarty K, Agrawal AK, Ahmed N (2013) Unobtrusive indoor surveillance of patients at home using multiple Kinect sensors. In: Proceedings of the ACM conference on embedded networked sensor systems, SenSys '13, pp 40:1–40:2
398. Ghose A, Sinha P, Bhaumik C, Sinha A, Agrawal A, Dutta Choudhury A (2013) Ubiheld: ubiquitous healthcare monitoring system for elderly and chronic patients. In: Proceedings of the ACM conference on pervasive and ubiquitous computing adjunct publication, UbiComp '13 Adjunct, pp 1255–1264
399. Gidaris S, Komodakis N (2016) Attend refine repeat: active box proposal generation via in-out localization. CoRR abs/1606.04446
400. Girshick R (2015) Fast R-CNN. In: IEEE international conference on computer vision (ICCV), pp 1440–1448
401. Girshick R, Donahue J, Darrell T, Malik J (2014) Rich feature hierarchies for accurate object detection and semantic segmentation. In: IEEE conference on computer vision and pattern recognition (CVPR), pp 580–587
402. Girshick R, Iandola F, Darrell T, Malik J (2015) Deformable part models are convolutional neural networks. In: IEEE conference on computer vision and pattern recognition (CVPR)

403. Girshick RB, Donahue J, Darrell T, Malik J (2016) Region-based convolutional networks for accurate object detection and segmentation. IEEE Trans Pattern Anal Mach Intell 38(1):142–158
404. Glocker B, Shotton J, Criminisi A, Izadi S (2015) Real-time RGB-D camera relocalization via randomized ferns for keyframe encoding. IEEE Trans Vis Comput Graph 21(5):571–583
405. Godard C, Mac Aodha O, Brostow GJ (2017) Unsupervised monocular depth estimation with left-right consistency. In: IEEE conference on computer vision and pattern recognition (CVPR), pp 6602–6611
406. Gokturk SB, Yalcin H, Bamji C (2004) A time-of-flight depth sensor – system description, issues and solutions. In: Conference on computer vision and pattern recognition workshop, pp 35–35
407. Gong S, Cristani M, Yan S, Loy CC (2014) Person re-identification. Springer
408. Goodfellow IJ, Pouget-Abadie J, Mirza M, Xu B, Warde-Farley D, Ozair S, Courville AC, Bengio Y (2014) Generative adversarial nets. In: Advances in neural information processing systems (NIPS), pp 2672–2680
409. Google: Google Project Tango. http://www.google.com/atap/project-tango. Accessed Aug 2012
410. Gortler SJ, Grzeszczuk R, Szeliski R, Cohen MF (1996) The lumigraph. In: Conference on computer graphics and interactive techniques, pp 43–54
411. Grau O (2011) Fast volumetric visual hull computation. In: International conference on computer vision (ICCV) workshops, pp 1658–1664
412. Gräve K, Behnke S (2014) Bayesian exploration and interactive demonstration in continuous state MAXQ-learning. In: IEEE international conference on robotics and automation (ICRA)
413. Gray D, Brennan S, Tao H (2007) Evaluating appearance models for recognition, reacquisition, and tracking. In: IEEE international workshop on performance evaluation for tracking and surveillance, Rio de Janeiro
414. Gray D, Tao H (2008) Viewpoint invariant pedestrian recognition with an ensemble of localized features. In: European conference on computer vision (ECCV), pp 262–275
415. Griffin G, Holub A, Perona P (2007) Caltech-256 object category dataset. Tech. Rep. 7694, California Institute of Technology. http://authors.library. caltech.edu/7694
416. Grunnet-Jepsen A, Winer P, Takagi A, Sweetser J, Zhao K, Khuong T, Nie D, Woodfill J (2019) Using the realsense D4xx depth sensors in multi-camera configurations. White paper. https://www.intel.ca/content/www/ca/en/support/articles/000028140/emerging-technologies/intel-realsense-techn ology.html/. Accessed 01 July 2019
417. Gu K, Wang S, Yang H, Lin W, Zhai G, Yang X, Zhang W (2016) Saliency-guided quality assessment of screen content images. IEEE Trans Multimed 18(6):1098–1110
418. Gu S, Zuo W, Guo S, Chen Y, Chen C, Zhang L (2017) Learning dynamic guidance for depth image enhancement. In: IEEE conference on computer vision and pattern recognition (CVPR), pp 3769–3778

419. Guillemaut JY, Hilton A (2010) Joint multi-layer segmentation and reconstruction for free-viewpoint video applications. Int J Comput Vis (IJCV) 93(1):73–100

420. Guillemot C, Le Meur O (2014) Image inpainting: overview and recent advances. Signal Process Mag 31(1):127–144

421. Guo C, Li C, Guo J, Cong R, Fu H, Han P (2019) Hierarchical features driven residual learning for depth map super-resolution. IEEE Trans Image Process 28(5):2545–2557

422. Guo H, Wang G, Chen X, Zhang C (2017) Towards good practices for deep 3D hand pose estimation. CoRR abs/1707.07248. arXiv:1707.07248

423. Guo H, Wang G, Chen X, Zhang C, Qiao F, Yang H (2017) Region ensemble network: improving convolutional network for hand pose estimation. In: Proceedings of the international conference on image processing

424. Guo J, Ren T, Bei J (2016) Salient object detection for RGB-D image via saliency evolution. In: IEEE international conference on multimedia and expo (ICME), pp 1–6

425. Guo K, Xu F, Wang Y, Liu Y, Dai Q (2015) Robust non-rigid motion tracking and surface reconstruction using L0 regularization. In: IEEE international conference on computer vision (ICCV), vol 1, pp 3083–3091

426. Guo K, Xu F, Yu T, Liu X, Dai Q, Liu Y (2017) Real-time geometry, albedo and motion reconstruction using a single RGBD camera. ACM Trans Graph (TOG)

427. Guo R, Hoiem D (2013) Support surface prediction in indoor scenes, pp 2144–2151

428. Guo X, Liu D, Jou B, Zhu M, Cai A, Chang SF (2013) Robust object co-detection. In: IEEE conference on computer vision and pattern recognition (CVPR), pp 3206–3213

429. Gupta S, Arbeláez P, Girshick R, Malik J (2015) Aligning 3D models to RGB-D images of cluttered scenes. In: IEEE conference on computer vision and pattern recognition (CVPR), pp 4731–4740

430. Gupta S, Arbeláez P, Malik J (2013) Perceptual organization and recognition of indoor scenes from RGB-D images. In: IEEE conference on computer vision and pattern recognition, pp 564–571

431. Gupta S, Girshick R, Arbeláez P, Malik J (2014) Learning rich features from RGB-D images for object detection and segmentation. In: European conference on computer vision (ECCV), pp 345–360

432. Gupta S, Hoffman J, Malik J (2016) Cross modal distillation for supervision transfer. In: IEEE conference on computer vision and pattern recognition (CVPR), pp 2827–2836

433. Gutierrez-Gomez D, Guerrero JJ (2018) RGBiD-SLAM for accurate real-time localisation and 3D mapping. arXiv:1807.08271

434. Gutiérrez-Gómez D, Mayol-Cuevas W, Guerrero JJ (2015) Inverse depth for accurate photometric and geometric error minimisation in RGB-D dense visual odometry. In: IEEE international conference on robotics and automation (ICRA), pp 83–89

435. Gutierrez-Gomez D, Mayol-Cuevas W, Guerrero JJ (2016) Dense RGB-D visual odometry using inverse depth. Robot Auton Syst 75:571–583
436. Guzman-Rivera A, Kohli P, Glocker B, Shotton J, Sharp T, Fitzgibbon A, Izadi S (2014) Multi-output learning for camera relocalization. In: IEEE conference on computer vision and pattern recognition (CVPR), pp 1114–1121
437. Hailey D, Roine R, Ohinmaa A, Dennett L (2011) Evidence of benefit from telerehabilitation in routine care: a systematic review. J Telemed Telecare 17(6):281–287
438. Halme RJ, Lanz M, Kämäräinen J, Pieters R, Latokartano J, Hietanen A (2018) Review of vision-based safety systems for human–robot collaboration. In: Procedia CIRP, vol 72, pp 111–116
439. Han J, Chen H, Liu N, Yan C, Li X (2018) CNNs-based RGB-D saliency detection via cross-view transfer and multiview fusion. IEEE Trans Cybern 48(11):3171–3183
440. Han J, Pauwels EJ, de Zeeuw PM, de With PHN (2012) Employing a RGB-D sensor for real-time tracking of humans across multiple re-entries in a smart environment. IEEE Trans Consum Electron 58(2):255–263
441. Han J, Zhang D, Cheng G, Liu N, Xu D (2018) Advanced deep-learning techniques for salient and category-specific object detection: a survey. IEEE Signal Process Mag 35(1):84–100
442. Han S, Liu B, Wang R, Ye Y, Twigg CD, Kin K (2018) Online optical marker-based hand tracking with deep labels. ACM Trans Graph 37(4):1–10
443. Han S, Vasconcelos N (2006) Image compression using object-based regions of interest. In: ICIP, pp 3097–3100
444. Han X, Li Z, Huang H, Kalogerakis E, Yu Y (2017) High-resolution shape completion using deep neural networks for global structure and local geometry inference. In: IEEE international conference on computer vision (ICCV)
445. Handa A, Whelan T, McDonald J, Davison AJ (2014) A benchmark for RGB-D visual odometry, 3D reconstruction and SLAM. In: IEEE international conference on robotics and automation (ICRA), pp 1524–1531
446. Hane C, Zach C, Cohen A, Angst R, Pollefeys M (2013) Joint 3D scene reconstruction and class segmentation. IEEE conference on computer vision and pattern recognition (CVPR), pp 97–104
447. Hansard M, Lee S, Choi O, et al (2013) Time-of-flight cameras. Springer
448. Harris C, Stephens M (1988) A combined corner and edge detector. In: Proceedings of Alvey vision conference, pp 147–151
449. Hartley RI, Zisserman A (2000) Multiple view geometry in computer vision. Cambridge University Press
450. Hays J, Efros AA (2007) Scene completion using millions of photographs. ACM Trans Graph 26(3):4
451. He D, Wang L (1990) Texture unit, texture spectrum, and texture analysis. IEEE Trans Geosci Remote Sens 28(4):509–512
452. He K, Gkioxari G, Dollár P, Girshick R (2017) Mask R-CNN. In: IEEE conference on computer vision and pattern recognition (CVPR), pp 2961–2969

453. He K, Sun J, Tang X (2012) Guided image filtering. IEEE Trans Pattern Anal Mach Intell 35(6):1397–1409

454. He K, Zhang X, Ren S, Sun J (2015) Delving deep into rectifiers: surpassing human-level performance on imagenet classification. In: IEEE international conference on computer vision (ICCV), pp 1026–1034

455. He K, Zhang X, Ren S, Sun J (2016) Deep residual learning for image recognition. In: IEEE conference on computer vision and pattern recognition (CVPR), pp 770–778

456. He Y, Chiu W, Keuper M, Fritz M (2017) STD2P: RGBD semantic segmentation using spatio-temporal data-driven pooling. In: IEEE conference on computer vision and pattern recognition (CVPR), pp 7158–7167

457. He Y, Liang B, Zou Y, He J, Yang J (2017) Depth errors analysis and correction for time-of-flight (ToF) cameras. Sensors 17(1)

458. Heikkilä J (2000) Geometric camera calibration using circular control points. IEEE Trans Pattern Anal Mach Intell 22(10):1066–1077

459. Heitz G, Gould S, Saxena A, Koller D (2009) Cascaded classification models: combining models for holistic scene understanding. In: Advances in neural information processing systems, pp 641–648

460. Henry P, Krainin M, Herbst E, Ren X, Fox D (2012) RGB-D mapping: using Kinect-style depth cameras for dense 3D modeling of indoor environments. Int J Robot Res 31(5):647–663

461. Herbst E, Ren X, Fox D.: RGB-D flow: dense 3-D motion estimation using color and depth. cs.washington.edu

462. Hermann A, Sun J, Xue Z, Rühl SW, Oberländer J, Roennau A, Zöllner JM, Dillmann R (2013) Hardware and software architecture of the bimanual mobile manipulation robot HoLLiE and its actuated upper body. In: IEEE/ASME international conference on advanced intelligent mechatronics (AIM)

463. Hermans A, Floros G, Leibe B (2014) Dense 3D semantic mapping of indoor scenes from RGB-D images. In: IEEE international conference on robotics and automation (ICRA)

464. Hernandez C, Perbet F, Pham M, Vogiatzis G, Woodford OJ, Maki A, Stenger B, Cipolla R (2011) Live 3D shape reconstruction, recognition and registration. In: International conference on computer vision (ICCV) workshops, p 729

465. Hernandez M, Choi J, Medioni G (2015) Near laser-scan quality 3-D face reconstruction from a low-quality depth stream. Image Vis Comput 36:61–69

466. Herrera D, Kannala J, Heikkilä J (2011) Accurate and practical calibration of a depth and color camera pair. In: Computer analysis of images and patterns, pp 437–445

467. Herrera D, Kannala J, Heikkilä J (2012) Joint depth and color camera calibration with distortion correction. IEEE Trans Pattern Anal Mach Intell 34(10):2058–2064

468. Herrera D, Kannala J, Heikkilä J, et al (2013) Depth map inpainting under a second-order smoothness prior. In: Scandinavian conference on image analysis, pp 555–566

469. Hervieu A, Papadakis N, Bugeau A, Gargallo P, Caselles V (2010) Stereoscopic image inpainting: distinct depth maps and images inpainting. In: International conference on pattern recognition, pp 4101–4104

470. Hettiarachchi A, Wigdor D (2016) Annexing reality: enabling opportunistic use of everyday objects as tangible proxies in augmented reality. In: Proceedings of the CHI conference on human factors in computing systems, pp 1957–1967

471. Hickson S, Birchfield S, Essa I, Christensen H (2014) Efficient hierarchical graph-based segmentation of RGBD videos. In: IEEE conference on computer vision and pattern recognition (CVPR), pp 344–351

472. Hilton A, Stoddart A, Illingworth J, Windeatt T (1998) Implicit surface-based geometric fusion. Comput Vis Image Underst 69(3):273–291

473. Hilton A, Stoddart AJ, Illingworth J, Windeatt T (1996) Marching triangles: range image fusion for complex object modelling. In: International conference on image processing, vol 2, pp 381–384

474. Hilton A, Stoddart AJ, Illingworth J, Windeatt T (1996) Reliable surface reconstruction from multiple range images. In: European conference on computer vision (ECCV), pp 117–126

475. Hinterstoisser S, Holzer S, Cagniart C, Ilic S, Konolige K, Navab N, Lepetit V (2011) Multimodal templates for real-time detection of texture-less objects in heavily cluttered scenes. In: IEEE international conference on computer vision (ICCV), pp 858–865

476. Hinterstoisser S, Lepetit V, Ilic S, Holzer S, Bradski G, Konolige K, Navab N (2012) Model based training, detection and pose estimation of texture-less 3D objects in heavily cluttered scenes. In: Proceedings of ACCV, pp 548–562

477. Hinterstoisser S, Lepetit V, Rajkumar N, Konolige K (2016) Going further with point pair features. In: European conference on computer vision (ECCV), pp 834–848

478. Hinton GE, Osindero S, Teh YW (2006) A fast learning algorithm for deep belief nets. Neural Comput 18(7):1527–1554

479. Hinton GE, Salakhutdinov RR (2006) Reducing the dimensionality of data with neural networks. Science 313(5786):504–507

480. Hirschmuller H (2008) Stereo processing by semi-global matching and mutual information. IEEE Trans Pattern Anal Mach Intell 30:328–341

481. Hirschmuller H, Scharstein D (2007) Evaluation of cost functions for stereo matching. In: IEEE conference on computer vision and pattern recognition (CVPR), pp 1–8

482. Hodan T, Haluza P, Obdržálek Š, Matas J, Lourakis M, Zabulis X (2017) T-LESS: an RGB-D dataset for 6D pose estimation of texture-less objects. In: IEEE winter conference on applications of computer vision (WACV), pp 880–888

483. Hodaň T, Zabulis X, Lourakis M, Obdržálek Š, Matas J (2015) Detection and fine 3D pose estimation of texture-less objects in RGB-D images. In: IEEE/RSJ international conference on intelligent robots and systems (IROS), pp 4421–4428

484. Hoffman G (2010) Anticipation in human–robot interaction. In: AAAI spring symposium: it's all in the timing

485. Hoffman J, Gupta S, Leong J, Guadarrama S, Darrell T (2016) Cross-modal adaptation for RGB-D detection. In: IEEE international conference on robotics and automation (ICRA), pp 5032–5039

486. Höft N, Schulz H, Behnke S (2014) Fast semantic segmentation of RGB-D scenes with GPU-accelerated deep neural networks. In: German conference on AI

487. Hoiem D, Efros AA, Hebert M (2005) Automatic photo pop-up. ACM Trans Graph (TOG) 24:577–584

488. Hoiem D, Efros AA, Hebert M (2005) Geometric context from a single image. In: IEEE international conference on computer vision (ICCV), vol 1, pp 654–661

489. Holz D, Topalidou-Kyniazopoulou A, Stückler J, Behnke S (2015) Real-time object detection, localization and verification for fast robotic depalletizing. In: International conference on intelligent robots and systems (IROS), pp 1459–1466

490. Hong S, Kim Y (2018) Dynamic pose estimation using multiple RGB-D cameras. Sensors 18(11)

491. Hoppe H, DeRose T, Duchamp T, McDonald JA, Stuetzle W (1992) Surface reconstruction from unorganized points. In: ACM SIGGRAPH, pp 71–78

492. Horaud R, Hansard M, Evangelidis G, Ménier C (2016) An overview of depth cameras and range scanners based on time-of-flight technologies. Mach Vis Appl 27(7):1005–1020

493. Horn BK, Hilden HM, Negahdaripour S (1988) Closed-form solution of absolute orientation using orthonormal matrices. JOSA A 5(7):1127–1135

494. Hornáček M, Fitzgibbon A, Rother C (2014) SphereFlow: 6 DoF scene flow from RGB-D pairs. In: IEEE conference on computer vision and pattern recognition (CVPR), pp 3526–3533

495. Hossny M, Filippidis D, Abdelrahman W, Zhou H, Fielding M, Mullins J, Wei L, Creighton D, Puri V, Nahavandi S (2012) Low cost multimodal facial recognition via Kinect sensors. In: Proceedings of the land warfare conference (LWC): potent land force for a joint maritime strategy. Commonwealth of Australia, pp 77–86

496. Hou Q, Cheng MM, Hu X, Borji A, Tu Z, Torr P (2017) Deeply supervised salient object detection with short connections. In: IEEE conference on computer vision and pattern recognition (CVPR), pp 5300–5309

497. Houseago C, Bloesch M, Leutenegger S (2019) KO-Fusion: dense visual SLAM with tightly-coupled kinematic and odometric tracking. In: IEEE international conference on robotics and automation (ICRA)

498. Hsiao M, Westman E, Kaess M (2018) Dense planar-inertial SLAM with structural constraints. In: IEEE international conference on robotics and automation (ICRA), pp 6521–6528

499. Hsiao M, Westman E, Zhang G, Kaess M (2017) Keyframe-based dense planar SLAM. In: IEEE international conference on robotics and automation (ICRA)

500. HTC Corp. (2019) HTC vive wireless adapter. https://www.vive.com/us/wireless-adapter//. Accessed 14 Jun 2019

501. Hu J, Ozay M, Zhang Y, Okatani T (2018) Revisiting single image depth estimation: toward higher resolution maps with accurate object boundaries. arXiv:1803.08673

502. Hu RZL, Hartfiel A, Tung J, Fakih A, Hoey J, Poupart P (2011) 3D pose tracking of walker users' lower limb with a structured-light camera on a moving platform. In: IEEE conference on computer vision and pattern recognition workshops (CVPRW), pp 29–36

503. Hu SM, Cai JX, Lai YK (2019) Semantic labeling and instance segmentation of 3D point clouds using patch context analysis and multiscale processing. IEEE Trans Vis Comput Graph

504. Hua BS, Pham QH, Nguyen DT, Tran MK, Yu LF, Yeung SK (2016) SceneNN: a scene meshes dataset with aNNotations. In: International conference on 3D vision (3DV)

505. Huang AS, Bachrach A, Henry P, Krainin M, Maturana D, Fox D, Roy N (2017) Visual odometry and mapping for autonomous flight using an RGB-D camera. Springer Tracts Adv Robot 100:235–252

506. Huang CM, Mutlu B (2016) Anticipatory robot control for efficient human-robot collaboration. In: ACM/IEEE international conference on human–robot interaction (HRI), pp 83–90

507. Huang G, Liu Z, v. d. Maaten L, Weinberger KQ (2017) Densely connected convolutional networks. In: IEEE conference on computer vision and pattern recognition (CVPR), pp 2261–2269

508. Huang J, Cakmak M (2017) Code3: a system for end-to-end programming of mobile manipulator robots for novices and experts. In: Proceedings of the ACM/IEEE international conference on human–robot interaction, pp 453–462

509. Huang L, Yang Y, Deng Y, Yu Y (2015) Densebox: unifying landmark localization with end to end object detection. CoRR abs/1509.04874

510. Huang P, Budd C, Hilton A (2011) Global temporal registration of multiple non-rigid surface sequences. In: IEEE conference on computer vision and pattern recognition (CVPR), pp 3473–3480

511. Huang Q, Wang W, Neumann U (2018) Recurrent slice networks for 3D segmentation on point clouds. In: IEEE conference on computer vision and pattern recognition (CVPR), pp 2626–2635

512. Huang X, Wang L, Huang J, Li D, Zhang M (2009) A depth extraction method based on motion and geometry for 2D to 3D conversion. In: Intelligent information technology application, vol 3, pp 294–298

513. Huber PJ (2011) Robust statistics. Springer
514. Huhle B, Fleck S, Schilling A (2007) Integrating 3D time-of-flight camera data and high resolution images for 3DTV applications. In: Proceedings of IEEE 3DTV conference, pp 1–4
515. Huhle B, Jenke P, Straßer W (2008) On-the-fly scene acquisition with a handy multi-sensor system. IJISTA 5(3/4):255–263
516. Huhle B, Schairer T, Jenke P, Straser W (2010) Fusion of range and color images for denoising and resolution enhancement with a non-local filter. Comput Vis Image Underst 114(12):1336–1345
517. Huhle B, Schairer T, Jenke P, et al (2008) Robust non-local denoising of colored depth data. In: IEEE conference on computer vision and pattern recognition workshops (CVPRW), pp 1–7
518. Hui T, Loy CC, Tang X (2016) Depth map super-resolution by deep multi-scale guidance. In: European conference on computer vision (ECCV), pp 353–369
519. Husain F, Schulz H, Dellen B, Torras C, Behnke S (2016) Combining semantic and geometric features for object class segmentation of indoor scenes. IEEE Robot Autom Lett 2(1):49–55
520. Ihler A, McAllester D (2009) Particle belief propagation. In: Artificial intelligence and statistics, pp 256–263
521. Ihrke I, Kutulakos KN, Lensch H, Magnor M, Heidrich W (2010) Transparent and specular object reconstruction. In: Computer graphics forum, vol 29, pp 2400–2426
522. Iizuka S, Simo-Serra E, Ishikawa H (2017) Globally and locally consistent image completion. ACM Trans Graph 36(4):107
523. Inc. S (2015) ZED stereo camera. https://www.stereolabs.com/. Accessed Sept 2015
524. Innmann M, Zollhöfer M, Nießner M, Theobalt C, Stamminger M (2016) VolumeDeform: real-time volumetric non-rigid reconstruction. In: European conference on computer vision (ECCV), pp 362–379
525. Intel (2018) Intel RealSense SDK. https://software.intel.com/en-us/intel-realsense-sdk
526. Intel Corp. (2017) Intel RealSense. https://realsense.intel.com/. Accessed 21 Jan 2019
527. Intel Corp. (2019) Intel volumetric content studio large. https://newsroom.intel.com/wp-content/uploads/sites/11/2018/01/intel-studios-fact-sheet.pdf. Accessed 21 Jan 2019
528. Intel Corp. (2019) Intel volumetric content studio small. https://realsense.intel.com/intel-realsense-volumetric-capture/. Accessed 21 Jan 2019
529. Iocchi L, Holz D, Ruiz-del Solar J, Sugiura K, van der Zant T (2015) RoboCup@Home: analysis and results of evolving competitions for domestic and service robots. Artif Intell 229:258–281
530. Islam AT, Scheel C, Pajarola R, Staadt O (2017) Robust enhancement of depth images from depth sensors. Comput Graph 68:53–65

531. Itti L, Koch C, Niebur E (1998) A model of saliency-based visual attention for rapid scene analysis. IEEE Trans Pattern Anal Mach Intell 20(11):1254–1259

532. Izadi S, Kim D, Hilliges O, Molyneaux D, Newcombe R, Kohli P, Shotton J, Hodges S, Freeman D, Davison A, Fitzgibbon A (2011) KinectFusion: real-time 3D reconstruction and interaction using a moving depth camera. In: Proceedings of ACM symposium on user interface software and technology, pp 559–568

533. Engel J, Sturm J, Cremers D (2014) Scale-aware navigation of a low-cost quadrocopter with a monocular camera. Robot Auton Syst (RAS) 62(11):1646–1656

534. Jackson PT, Atapour-Abarghouei A, Bonner S, Breckon T, Obara B (2018) Style augmentation: data augmentation via style randomization, pp 1–13. arXiv:1809.05375

535. Jacob H, Padua F, Lacerda A, Pereira A (2017) Video summarization approach based on the emulation of bottom-up mechanisms of visual attention. J Intell Inf Syst 49(2):193–211

536. Jaderberg M, Simonyan K, Zisserman A, Kavukcuoglu K (2015) Spatial transformer networks. In: Proceedings of the conference on neural information processing systems

537. Jaimez M, Gonzalez-Jimenez J (2015) Fast visual odometry for 3-d range sensors. IEEE Trans Robot 31(4):809–822

538. Jaimez M, Kerl C, Gonzalez-Jimenez J, Cremers D (2017) Fast odometry and scene flow from RGB-D cameras based on geometric clustering. In: IEEE international conference on robotics and automation (ICRA), pp 3992–3999

539. Jaimez M, Souiai M, Gonzalez-Jimenez J, Cremers D (2015) A primal-dual framework for real-time dense RGB-D scene flow. In: IEEE international conference on robotics and automation (ICRA), vol 2015-June, pp 98–104

540. Jain A, Singh A, Koppula HS, Soh S, Saxena A (2016) Recurrent neural networks for driver activity anticipation via sensory-fusion architecture. In: IEEE international conference on robotics and automation (ICRA)

541. Jain A, Tompson J, Andriluka M, Taylor GW, Bregler C (2014) Learning human pose estimation features with convolutional networks. CoRR. arXiv:1312.7302

542. Jain A, Zamir AR, Savarese S, Saxena A (2016) Structural-RNN: deep learning on spatio-temporal graphs. In: IEEE conference on computer vision and pattern recognition (CVPR)

543. Janai J, Güney F, Behl A, Geiger A (2017) Computer vision for autonomous vehicles: problems, datasets and state-of-the-art. CoRR abs/1704.05519

544. Janarthanan V, Jananii G (2012) A detailed survey on various image inpainting techniques. Adv Image Process 2(2):1

545. Jang JH, Hong KS (2001) Linear band detection based on the Euclidean distance transform and a new line segment extraction method. Pattern Recognit 34(9):1751–1764

546. JCGM (2012) The international vocabulary of metrology—basic and general concepts and associated terms (VIM), 3rd edn. JCGM (Joint Committee for Guides in Metrology), pp 1–92

547. Jenke P, Wand M, Bokeloh M, Schilling A, Straß er W (2006) Bayesian point cloud reconstruction. Comput Graph Forum 25(3):379–388

548. Jeong S, Ban SW, Lee M (2008) Stereo saliency map considering affective factors and selective motion analysis in a dynamic environment. Neural Netw 21(10):1420–1430

549. Jermyn IH, Kurtek S, Laga H, Srivastava A (2017) Elastic shape analysis of three-dimensional objects. Synth Lect Comput Vis 12(1):1–185

550. Ji M, Gall J, Zheng H, Liu Y, Fang L (2017) SurfaceNet: an end-to-end 3D neural network for multiview stereopsis. In: IEEE international conference on computer vision (ICCV)

551. Ji P, Li H, Dai Y, Reid I (2017) 'Maximizing rigidity' revisited: a convex programming approach for generic 3D shape reconstruction from multiple perspective views. In: IEEE international conference on computer vision (ICCV), pp 929–937

552. Ji S, Xu W, Yang M, Yu K (2013) 3D convolutional neural networks for human action recognition. IEEE Trans Pattern Anal Mach Intell 35(1):221–231

553. Jia J, Tang CK (2003) Image repairing: robust image synthesis by adaptive n-d tensor voting. In: IEEE conference on computer vision and pattern recognition (CVPR), vol 1, pp I–643

554. Jiang H (2014) Finding approximate convex shapes in RGBD images. In: European conference on computer vision (ECCV), pp 582–596

555. Jiang H, Xiao J (2013) A linear approach to matching cuboids in RGBD images. In: IEEE conference on computer vision and pattern recognition (CVPR), pp 2171–2178

556. Jiang R, Gu X (2011) Multiscale, curvature-based shape representation for surfaces. In: IEEE international conference on computer vision (ICCV), pp 1887–1894

557. Jiang Y, Lim M, Zheng C, Saxena A (2012) Learning to place new objects in a scene. Int J Robot Res 31(9):1021–1043

558. Jiang Z, Hou Y, Yue H, Yang J, Hou C (2018) Depth super-resolution from RGB-D pairs with transform and spatial domain regularization. IEEE Trans Image Process 27(5):2587–2602

559. Johnson A, Hebert M (1999) Using spin images for efficient object recognition in cluttered 3D scenes. IEEE Trans Pattern Anal Mach Intell 21(5):433–449

560. Johnson A, Kang SB (1999) Registration and integration of textured 3D data. Image Vis Comput 17:135–147

561. Johnson J, Alahi A, Fei-Fei L (2016) Perceptual losses for real-time style transfer and super-resolution. In: European conference on computer vision, pp 694–711

562. Jojic N, Frey BJ (2001) Learning flexible sprites in video layers. In: IEEE conference on computer vision and pattern recognition (CVPR), pp 199–206

563. Jojic N, Perina A, Cristani M, Murino V, Frey B (2009) Stel component analysis: modeling spatial correlations in image class structure. In: IEEE conference on computer vision and pattern recognition, pp 2044–2051

564. Jones B, Sodhi R, Murdock M, Mehra R, Benko H, Wilson A, Ofek E, MacIntyre B, Raghuvanshi N, Shapira L (2014) Roomalive: magical experiences enabled by scalable, adaptive projector-camera units. In: Proceedings of the annual ACM symposium on user interface software and technology, UIST '14, pp 637–644

565. Joo H, Simon T, Li X, Liu H, Tan L, Gui L, Banerjee S, Godisart T, Nabbe B, Matthews I, Kanade T, Nobuhara S, Sheikh Y (2017) Panoptic studio: a massively multiview system for social interaction capture. IEEE Trans Pattern Anal Mach Intell 41(1):190–204

566. Joo H, Simon T, Sheikh Y (2018) Total capture: a 3D deformation model for tracking faces, hands, and bodies. In: IEEE conference on computer vision and pattern recognition (CVPR), pp 8320–8329

567. Joulin A, Bach F, Ponce J (2010) Discriminative clustering for image co-segmentation. In: IEEE conference on computer vision and pattern recognition (CVPR), pp 1943–1950

568. Ju R, Ge L, Geng W, Ren T, Wu G (2014) Depth saliency based on anisotropic center-surround difference. In: IEEE international conference on image processing (ICIP), pp 1115–1119

569. Ju R, Liu Y, Ren T, Ge L, Wu G (2015) Depth-aware salient object detection using anisotropic center-surround difference. Signal Process: Image Commun 38:115–126

570. Jung HY, Suh Y, Moon G, Lee KM (2016) A sequential approach to 3D human pose estimation: separation of localization and identification of body joints. In: Proceedings of the European conference on computer vision, pp 747–761

571. Jung Y, Yeh SC, Stewart J (2006) Tailoring virtual reality technology for stroke rehabilitation: a human factors design. In: CHI'06 extended abstracts on human factors in computing systems, pp 929–934

572. Kaenchan S, Mongkolnam P, Watanapa B, Sathienpong S (2013) Automatic multiple Kinect cameras setting for simple walking posture analysis. In: International computer science and engineering conference (ICSEC), pp 245–249

573. Kaess M (2015) Simultaneous localization and mapping with infinite planes. In: IEEE international conference on robotics and automation, pp 4605–4611

574. Kaess M, Johannsson H, Roberts R, Ila V, Leonard JJ, Dellaert F (2012) iSAM2: incremental smoothing and mapping using the Bayes tree. Int J Robot Res 31(2):216–235

575. Kainz B, Hauswiesner S, Reitmayr G, Steinberger M, Grasset R, Gruber L, Veas E, Kalkofen D, Seichter H, Schmalstieg D (2012) OmniKinect: real-time dense volumetric data acquisition and applications. In: Proceedings of the ACM symposium on virtual reality software and technology, VRST '12, pp 25–32

576. Kangas M, Vikman I, Wiklander J, Lindgren P, Nyberg L, Jämsä T (2009) Sensitivity and specificity of fall detection in people aged 40 years and over. Gait Posture 29(4):571–574

577. Kappel G, Pröll B, Reich S, Retschitzegger W (2006) Web engineering. Wiley, New York

578. Karahan AY, Tok F, Taskin H, Küçüksaraç S, Basaran A, Yildirim P (2015) Effects of exergames on balance, functional mobility, and quality of life of geriatrics versus home exercise programme: randomized controlled study. Centr Eur J Public Health 23:S14

579. Karpathy A, Toderici G, Shetty S, Leung T, Sukthankar R, Fei-Fei L (2014) Large-scale video classification with convolutional neural networks. In: IEEE conference on computer vision and pattern recognition (CVPR)

580. Karsch K, Liu C, Kang SB (2014) Depth transfer: depth extraction from video using non-parametric sampling. IEEE Trans Pattern Anal Mach Intell 36(11):2144–2158

581. Kasturi S, Jo K (2017) Human fall classification system for ceiling-mounted Kinect depth images. In: International conference on control, automation and systems (ICCAS), pp 1346–1349

582. Kazhdan M, Bolitho M, Hoppe H (2006) Poisson surface reconstruction. In: Proceedings of the fourth eurographics symposium on geometry processing, pp 61–70

583. Keays S, Bullock-Saxton J, Newcombe P, Bullock M (2006) The effectiveness of a pre-operative home-based physiotherapy programme for chronic anterior cruciate ligament deficiency. Physiother Res Int 11(4):204–218

584. Kehl W, Manhardt F, Tombari F, Ilic S, Navab N (2017) SSD-6D: making RGB-based 3D detection and 6D pose estimation great again. In: Proceedings of the international conference on computer vision (ICCV), pp 22–29

585. Kehl W, Milletari F, Tombari F, Ilic S, Navab N (2016) Deep learning of local RGB-D patches for 3D object detection and 6D pose estimation. In: European conference on computer vision (ECCV), pp 205–220

586. Keller M, Lefloch D, Lambers M, Izadi S, Weyrich T, Kolb A (2013) Real-time 3D Reconstruction in dynamic scenes using point-based fusion. In: International conference on 3D vision (3DV), pp 1–8

587. Kendall A, Badrinarayanan V, Cipolla R (2015) Bayesian SegNet: model uncertainty in deep convolutional encoder-decoder architectures for scene understanding. CoRR abs/1511.02680

588. Kendall A, Cipolla R (2017) Geometric loss functions for camera pose regression with deep learning. CoRR abs/1704.00390

589. Kepski M, Kwolek B (2014) Detecting human falls with 3-axis accelerometer and depth sensor. In: Annual international conference of the IEEE Engineering in Medicine and Biology Society, pp 770–773

590. Kepski M, Kwolek B (2014) Fall detection using ceiling-mounted 3D depth camera. In: International conference on computer vision theory and applications (VISAPP), vol 2, pp 640–647

591. Kerl C, Stuckler J, Cremers D (2015) Dense continuous-time tracking and mapping with rolling shutter RGB-D cameras. In: IEEE conference on computer vision and pattern recognition (CVPR), pp 2264–2272

592. Kerl C, Sturm J, Cremers D (2013) Dense visual SLAM for RGB-D cameras. In: IEEE/RSJ international conference on intelligent robots and systems (IROS), pp 2100–2106

593. Kerl C, Sturm J, Cremers D (2013) Robust odometry estimation for RGB-D cameras. In: IEEE international conference on robotics and automation (ICRA)

594. Keselman L, Woodfill JI, Grunnet-Jepsen A, Bhowmik A (2017) Intel® RealSense™ stereoscopic depth cameras. In: IEEE conference on computer vision and pattern recognition workshops (CVPRW), pp 1267–1276

595. Keskin C, Kıraç F, Kara YE, Akarun L (2012) Hand pose estimation and hand shape classification using multi-layered randomized decision forests. In: Proceedings of the European conference on computer vision, pp 852–863

596. Khamis S, Taylor J, Shotton J, Keskin C, Izadi S, Fitzgibbon A (2015) Learning an efficient model of hand shape variation from depth images. In: IEEE conference on computer vision and pattern recognition (CVPR), pp 2540–2548

597. Khan S, Bennamoun M, Sohel F, Togneri R (2014) Geometry driven semantic labeling of indoor scenes. In: European conference on computer vision (ECCV), pp 679–694

598. Khan S, Rahmani H, Shah SAA, Bennamoun M (2018) A guide to convolutional neural networks for computer vision. Morgan and Claypool Publishers

599. Khan SH, He X, Bennamoun M, Sohel F, Togneri R (2015) Separating objects and clutter in indoor scenes. In: IEEE conference on computer vision and pattern recognition (CVPR), pp 4603–4611

600. Khoshelham K (2012) Accuracy analysis of Kinect depth data. In: ISPRS – international archives of the photogrammetry, remote sensing and spatial information sciences, vol XXXVIII-5, pp 133–138

601. Khoshelham K, Elberink SO (2012) Accuracy and resolution of Kinect depth data for indoor mapping applications. Sensors 12(2):1437–1454

602. Kilner J, Neophytou A, Hilton A (2012) 3D scanning with multiple depth sensors. In: International conference on 3D body scanning technologies, pp 295–301

603. Kim B, Xu S, Savarese S (2013) Accurate localization of 3D objects from RGB-D data using segmentation hypotheses. In: IEEE conference on computer vision and pattern recognition (CVPR), pp 3182–3189

604. Kim C, Kim P, Lee S, Kim HJ (2018) Edge-based robust RGB-D visual odometry using 2-D edge divergence minimization. In: IEEE/RSJ international conference on intelligent robots and systems (IROS), pp 6887–6894

605. Kim C, Zimmer H, Pritch Y, Sorkine-Hornung A, Gross M (2013) Scene reconstruction from high spatio-angular resolution light fields. ACM Trans Graph (TOG) 32(4):1

606. Kim E, Medioni G (2011) 3D object recognition in range images using visibility context. In:IEEE/RSJ international conference on intelligent robots and systems (IROS), pp 3800–3807

607. Kim G, Xing E, Fei-Fei L, Kanade T (2011) Distributed cosegmentation via submodular optimization on anisotropic diffusion. In: IEEE international conference on computer vision (ICCV), pp 169–176

608. Kim J (2014) Object detection using RGB-D data for interactive robotic manipulation. In: International conference on ubiquitous robots and ambient intelligence (URAI), pp 339–343

609. Kim JK, Fessler JA, Zhang Z (2012) Forward-projection architecture for fast iterative image reconstruction in X-ray ct. IEEE Trans Signal Process 60(10):5508–5518

610. Kim K, Bolton J, Girouard A, Cooperstock J, Vertegaal R (2012) TeleHuman: effects of 3D perspective on gaze and pose estimation with a life-size cylindrical telepresence pod. In: Proceedings of the SIGCHI conference on human factors in computing systems, CHI '12, pp 2531–2540

611. Kim P, Coltin B, Kim HJ (2018) Linear RGB-D SLAM for planar environments. In: European conference on computer vision (ECCV), pp 350–366

612. Kim P, Coltin B, Kim HJ (2018) Low-drift visual odometry in structured environments by decoupling rotational and translational motion. In: IEEE international conference on robotics and automation (ICRA), pp 7247–7253

613. Kim Y, Baek S, Bae BC (2017) Motion capture of the human body using multiple depth sensors. ETRI J 39(2):181–190

614. Kim Y, Ham B, Oh C, Sohn K (2016) Structure selective depth superresolution for RGB-D cameras. IEEE Trans Image Process 25(11):5227–5238

615. Kim YM, Mitra NJ, Yan DM, Guibas L (2012) Acquiring 3D indoor environments with variability and repetition. ACM Trans Graph 31(6):138:1–138:11

616. Kim YM, Theobalt C, Diebel J, Kosecka J, Miscusik B, Thrun S (2009) Multi-view image and tof sensor fusion for dense 3D reconstruction. In: IEEE international conference on computer vision workshop (ICCVW), pp 1542–1549

617. Kirac F, Kara YE, Akarun L (2014) Hierarchically constrained 3D hand pose estimation using regression forests from single frame depth data. Pattern Recognit Lett 50:91–100

618. Kitchenham B (2004) Procedures for performing systematic reviews. Keele, UK, Keele University 33(2004):1–26

619. Kitsikidis A, Dimitropoulos K, Douka S, Grammalidis N (2014) Dance analysis using multiple Kinect sensors. In: International conference on computer vision theory and applications (VISAPP), vol 2, pp 789–795

620. Kittmann R, Fröhlich T, Schäfer J, Reiser U, Weißhardt F, Haug A (2015) Let me introduce myself: I am Care-O-bot 4. In: Mensch und Computer

621. Klaudiny M, Budd C, Hilton A (2012) Towards optimal non-rigid surface tracking. In: Fitzgibbon A, Lazebnik S, Perona P, Sato Y, Schmid C (eds) European conference on computer vision (ECCV). Lecture notes in computer science, vol 7575, pp 743–756

622. Klaudiny M, Hilton A (2012) High-detail 3D capture and non-sequential alignment of facial performance. In: International conference on 3D imaging, modeling, processing, visualization & transmission, pp 17–24

623. Klein G, Murray D (2007) Parallel tracking and mapping for small AR workspaces. In: International symposium on mixed and augmented reality (ISMAR), pp 225–234

624. Klein G, Murray D (2008) Improving the agility of keyframe-based SLAM. In: Forsyth D, Torr P, Zisserman A (eds) European conference on computer vision (ECCV). Lecture notes in computer science, vol 5303. Springer, Berlin/Heidelberg, pp 802–815

625. Klingensmith M, Dryanovski I, Srinivasa S, Xiao J (2015) Chisel: real time large scale 3D reconstruction onboard a mobile device using spatially hashed signed distance fields. In: Robotics: science and systems, vol 4

626. Klingensmith M, Sirinivasa SS, Kaess M (2016) Articulated robot motion for simultaneous localization and mapping (ARM-SLAM). IEEE Robot Autom Lett 1(2):1156–1163

627. Klose S, Heise P, Knoll A (2013) Efficient compositional approaches for real-time robust direct visual odometry from RGB-D data. In: IEEE/RSJ international conference on intelligent robots and systems (IROS), pp 1100–1106

628. Koch C, Ullman S (1987) Shifts in selective visual attention: towards the underlying neural circuitry. In: Matters of intelligence, pp 115–141. Springer

629. Koenig S, Ardanza A, Cortes C, De Mauro A, Lange B (2014) Introduction to low-cost motion-tracking for virtual rehabilitation. In: Emerging therapies in neurorehabilitation. Springer, pp 287–303

630. Kolb A, Barth E, Koch R, et al (2010) Time-of-flight cameras in computer graphics. In: Wiley online library, computer graphics forum, vol 29, pp 141–159

631. Kolkmeier J, Harmsen E, Giesselink S, Reidsma D, Theune M, Heylen D (2018) With a little help from a holographic friend: the OpenIMPRESS mixed reality telepresence toolkit for remote collaboration systems. In: Proceedings of the ACM symposium on virtual reality software and technology, VRST '18, pp 26:1–26:11

632. Koller O, Ney H, Bowden R (2016) Deep hand: how to train a CNN on 1 million hand images when your data is continuous and weakly labelled. In: IEEE conference on computer vision and pattern recognition (CVPR), pp 3793–3802

633. Komodakis N, Tziritas G (2007) Image completion using efficient belief propagation via priority scheduling and dynamic pruning. IEEE Trans Image Process 16(11):2649–2661

634. Kong S, Fowlkes C (2018) Recurrent scene parsing with perspective understanding in the loop. In: IEEE conference on computer vision and pattern recognition (CVPR), pp 956–965

635. Konolige K (2010) Projected texture stereo

636. Kopf J, Cohen MF, Lischinski D, Uyttendaele M (2007) Joint bilateral upsampling. ACM Trans Graph (TOG) 26(3)

637. Koppula HS, Anand A, Joachims T, Saxena A (2011) Semantic labeling of 3D point clouds for indoor scenes. In: Shawe-Taylor J, Zemel RS, Bartlett PL, Pereira FCN, Weinberger KQ (eds) NIPS, pp 244–252
638. Koppula HS, Gupta R, Saxena A (2013) Learning human activities and object affordances from RGB-D videos. Int J Robot Res 32(8):951–970
639. Koppula HS, Jain A, Saxena A (2016) Anticipatory planning for human-robot teams. In: Experimental robotics
640. Kouno D, Shimada K, Endo T (2012) Person identification using top-view image with depth information. In: ACIS international conference on software engineering, artificial intelligence, networking and parallel/distributed computing, pp 140–145
641. Kowalski M, Naruniec J, Daniluk M (2015) Livescan3D: a fast and inexpensive 3D data acquisition system for multiple Kinect v2 sensors. In: International conference on 3D vision, pp 318–325
642. Kramer J, Burrus N, Echtler F, Daniel HC, Parker M (2012) Object modeling and detection. Apress, pp 173–206
643. Kreylos O (2010) Movies – 2 Kinects 1 box. http://idav.ucdavis.edu/~okreylos/ResDev/Kinect/Movies.html. Accessed 22 Jun 2019
644. Krizhevsky A, Sutskever I, Hinton GE (2012) ImageNet classification with deep convolutional neural networks. In: NIPS, pp 1097–1105
645. Krueger V, Rovida F, Grossmann B, Petrick R, Crosby M, Charzoule A, Garcia GM, Behnke S, Toscano C, Veiga G (2018) Testing the vertical and cyber-physical integration of cognitive robots in manufacturing. Robot Comput-Integr Manuf 57:213–229
646. Krull A, Brachmann E, Michel F, Ying Yang M, Gumhold S, Rother C (2015) Learning analysis-by-synthesis for 6D pose estimation in RGB-D images. In: Proceedings of the IEEE international conference on computer vision, pp 954–962
647. Kumar DP, Yun Y, Gu YH (2016) Fall detection in RGB-D videos by combining shape and motion features. In: IEEE international conference on acoustics, speech and signal processing (ICASSP), pp 1337–1341
648. Kumar S, Dai Y, Li H (2017) Monocular dense 3D reconstruction of a complex dynamic scene from two perspective frames. In: IEEE international conference on computer vision (ICCV), pp 4659–4667
649. Kumar V, Mukherjee J, Mandal SKD (2016) Image inpainting through metric labeling via guided patch mixing. IEEE Trans Image Process 25(11):5212–5226
650. Kümmerle R, Grisetti G, Strasdat H, Konolige K, Burgard W (2011) g2o: a general framework for graph optimization. In: IEEE international conference on robotics and automation (ICRA), pp 3607–3613
651. Kurillo G, Bajcsy R (2008) Wide-area external multi-camera calibration using vision graphs and virtual calibration object. In: Second ACM/IEEE international conference on distributed smart cameras, pp 1–9

652. Kuse M, Shaojie Shen (2016) Robust camera motion estimation using direct edge alignment and sub-gradient method. In: IEEE international conference on robotics and automation (ICRA), pp 573–579

653. Kuznietsov Y, Stückler J, Leibe B (2017) Semi-supervised deep learning for monocular depth map prediction. In: IEEE conference on computer vision and pattern recognition (CVPR), pp 6647–6655

654. Kwolek B, Kepski M (2014) Human fall detection on embedded platform using depth maps and wireless accelerometer. Comput Methods Progr Biomed 117(3):489–501

655. de La Gorce M, Fleet DJ, Paragios N (2011) Model-based 3D hand pose estimation from monocular video. IEEE Trans Pattern Anal Mach Intell 33(9):1793–1805

656. Lachat E, Macher H, Landes T, Grussenmeyer P (2015) Assessment and calibration of a RGB-D camera (Kinect v2 Sensor) towards a potential use for close-range 3D modeling. Remote Sens 7(10):13070–13097

657. Ladicky L, Shi J, Pollefeys M (2014) Pulling things out of perspective. In: IEEE conference on computer vision and pattern recognition (CVPR), pp 89–96

658. Laga H, Guo Y, Tabia H, Fisher RB, Bennamoun M (2019) 3D shape analysis: fundamentals, theory, and applications. Wiley

659. Laga H, Mortara M, Spagnuolo M (2013) Geometry and context for semantic correspondences and functionality recognition in man-made 3D shapes. ACM Trans Graph (TOG) 32(5):150

660. Laga H, Xie Q, Jermyn IH, Srivastava A (2017) Numerical inversion of SRNF maps for elastic shape analysis of genus-zero surfaces. IEEE Trans Pattern Anal Mach Intell 39(12):2451–2464

661. Lahoud J, Ghanem B (2017) 2D-driven 3D object detection in RGB-D images. In: IEEE international conference on computer vision (ICCV)

662. Lai K, Bo L, Fox D (2014) Unsupervised feature learning for 3D scene labeling. In: IEEE international conference on robotics and automation (ICRA)

663. Lai K, Bo L, Ren X, Fox D (2011) A large-scale hierarchical multi-view RGB-D object dataset. In: IEEE international conference on robotics and automation (ICRA), pp 1817–1824

664. Lai K, Bo L, Ren X, Fox D (2012) Detection-based object labeling in 3D scenes. In: IEEE international conference on robotics and automation (ICRA)

665. Lai K, Bo L, Ren X, Fox D (2013) RGB-D object recognition: features, algorithms, and a large scale benchmark. In: Consumer depth cameras for computer vision. Springer, pp 167–192

666. Lai P, Tian D, Lopez P (2010) Depth map processing with iterative joint multilateral filtering. In: Picture coding symposium, pp 9–12

667. Laidlow T, Bloesch M, Li W, Leutenegger S (2017) Dense RGB-D-inertial SLAM with map deformations. In: IEEE/RSJ international conference on intelligent robots and systems (IROS), pp 6741–6748

668. Laina I, Rupprecht C, Belagiannis V, Tombari F, Navab N (2016) Deeper depth prediction with fully convolutional residual networks. In: International conference on 3D vision, pp 239–248

669. Lang C, Nguyen TV, Katti H, Yadati K, Kankanhalli M, Yan S (2012) Depth matters: influence of depth cues on visual saliency. In: European conference on computer vision (ECCV), pp 101–115

670. Lange B, Koenig S, McConnell E, Chang CY, Juang R, Suma E, Bolas M, Rizzo A (2012) Interactive game-based rehabilitation using the Microsoft Kinect. In: Virtual reality short papers and posters (VRW). IEEE, pp 171–172

671. Langmann B, Hartmann K, Loffeld O (2012) Depth camera technology comparison and performance evaluation. In: International conference on pattern recognition applications and methods (ICPRAM), vol 2, pp 438–444

672. Larsson G, Maire M, Shakhnarovich G (2016) Fractalnet: ultra-deep neural networks without residuals. arXiv:1605.07648

673. Lavi B, Serj MF, Ullah I (2018) Survey on deep learning techniques for person re-identification task. CoRR abs/1807.05284

674. Le P, Košecka J (2017) Dense piecewise planar RGB-D SLAM for indoor environments. In: IEEE/RSJ international conference on intelligent robots and systems (IROS), pp 4944–4949

675. Le QV, Ranzato M, Monga R, Devin M, Corrado G, Chen K, Dean J, Ng AY (2012) Building high-level features using large scale unsupervised learning. In: International conference on machine learning (ICML)

676. LeapMotion: LeapMotion sensor. http://www.leapmotion.com. Accessed Aug 2012

677. LeCun Y, Bengio Y, Hinton G (2015) Deep learning. Nature 521(7553):436–444

678. LeCun Y, Bottou L, Bengio Y, Haffner P (1998) Gradient-based learning applied to document recognition. Proc IEEE 86(11):2278–2324

679. LeCun Y, Kavukcuoglu K, Farabet C (2010) Convolutional networks and applications in vision. In: Proceedings of IEEE international symposium on circuits and systems, pp 253–256

680. Lee HC, Huang CL, Ho SH, Sung WH (2017) The effect of a virtual reality game intervention on balance for patients with stroke: a randomized controlled trial. Games Health J 6(5):303–311

681. Lee J, Shin SY (1999) A hierarchical approach to interactive motion editing for human-like figures. In: ACM SIGGRAPH, vol 99, pp 39–48

682. Lee JH, Choi I, Kim MH (2016) Laplacian patch-based image synthesis. In: IEEE conference on computer vision and pattern recognition (CVPR), pp 2727–2735

683. Lee S, Ho Y (2013) Joint multilateral filtering for stereo image generation using depth camera. The era of interactive media, pp 373–383

684. Lee SB, Ho YS (2009) Discontinuity-adaptive depth map filtering for 3D view generation. In: International conference on immersive telecommunications, p 8

685. Lee SH, de Croon G (2018) Stability-based scale estimation for monocular SLAM. IEEE Robot Autom Lett 3(2):780–787

686. Lee SH, Yoon C, Chung SG, Kim HC, Kwak Y, Park Hw, Kim K (2015) Measurement of shoulder range of motion in patients with adhesive capsulitis using a Kinect. PloS one 10(6):e0129398

687. Lee SW, Nakatani T (eds) (2016) Sensing technologies required for ADAS/AD applications, 671, vol 1. Springer

688. Lei J, Duan J, Wu F, Ling N, Hou C (2018) Fast mode decision based on grayscale similarity and inter-view correlation for depth map coding in 3D-HEVC. IEEE Trans Circuits Syst Video Technol 28(3):706–718

689. Lei J, Wu M, Zhang C, Wu F, Ling N, Hou C (2017) Depth-preserving stereo image retargeting based on pixel fusion. IEEE Trans Multimed 19(7):1442–1453

690. Lei Z, Chai W, Zhao S, Song H, Li F (2017) Saliency detection for RGB-D images using optimization. In: International conference on computer science and education (ICCSE), pp 440–443

691. Leibe B, Leonardis A, Schiele B (2008) Robust object detection with interleaved categorization and segmentation. Int J Comput Vis 77(1–3):259–289

692. Leidner D, Dietrich A, Schmidt F, Borst C, Albu-Schäffer A (2014) Object-centered hybrid reasoning for whole-body mobile manipulation. In: IEEE international conference on robotics and automation (ICRA)

693. Lepetit V (2015) Hashmod: a hashing method for scalable 3D object detection. In: British machine vision conference (BMVC)

694. Lerma C, Kosecká J (2015) Semantic parsing for priming object detection in indoors RGB-D scenes. Int J Robot Res 34:582–597

695. Leung T, Malik J (2001) Representing and recognizing the visual appearance of materials using three-dimensional textons. Int J Comput Vis 43(1):29–44

696. Levi Z, Gotsman C (2014) Smooth rotation enhanced as-rigid-as-possible mesh animation. IEEE Trans Vis Comput Graph 21(2):264–277

697. Levin A, Lischinski D, Weiss Y (2008) A closed-form solution to natural image matting. IEEE Trans Pattern Anal Mach Intell 30(2):228–42

698. Li B (2016) 3D fully convolutional network for vehicle detection in point cloud. CoRR abs/1611.08069. arXiv:1611.08069

699. Li B, Dai Y, He M (2018) Monocular depth estimation with hierarchical fusion of dilated CNNs and soft-weighted-sum inference. Pattern Recognit

700. Li B, Zhang T, Xia T (2016) Vehicle detection from 3D lidar using fully convolutional network. arXiv:1608.07916

701. Li C, Guo J, Cong R, Pang Y, Wang B (2016) Underwater image enhancement by dehazing with minimum information loss and histogram distribution prior. IEEE Trans Image Process 25(12):5664–5677

702. Li C, Wand M (2016) Combining markov random fields and convolutional neural networks for image synthesis. In: IEEE conference on computer vision and pattern recognition (CVPR), pp 2479–2486

703. Li D, Chen X, Zhang Z, Huang K (2017) Learning deep context-aware features over body and latent parts for person re-identification. arXiv:1710.06555

704. Li F, Yu J, Chai J (2008) A hybrid camera for motion deblurring and depth map super-resolution. In: IEEE conference on computer vision and pattern recognition (CVPR), pp 1–8

705. Li H, Adams B, Guibas LJ, Pauly M (2009) Robust single-view geometry and motion reconstruction. ACM Trans Graph (TOG) 28(5):1

706. Li H, Liu H, Cao N, Peng Y, Xie S, Luo J, Sun Y (2017) Real-time RGB-D image stitching using multiple Kinects for improved field of view. Int J Adv Robot Syst 14(2). https://doi.org/1729881417695560

707. Li H, Luo L, Vlasic D, Peers P, Popović J, Pauly M, Rusinkiewicz S (2012) Temporally coherent completion of dynamic shapes. ACM Trans Graph (TOG) 31(1)

708. Li K, Dai Q, Xu W, Yang J, Jiang J (2011) Three-dimensional motion estimation via matrix completion. IEEE Trans Syst Man Cybern:1–13

709. Li N, Ye J, Ji Y, Ling H, Yu J (2017) Saliency detection on light field. IEEE Trans Pattern Anal Mach Intell 39(8):1605–1616

710. Li P, Ling H, Li X, Liao C (2015) 3D hand pose estimation using randomized decision forest with segmentation index points. In: IEEE international conference on computer vision (ICCV), pp 819–827

711. Li S, Pathirana PN, Caelli T (2014) Multi-kinect skeleton fusion for physical rehabilitation monitoring. In: Annual international conference of the IEEE Engineering in Medicine and Biology Society, pp 5060–5063

712. Li W, Saeedi S, McCormac J, Clark R, Tzoumanikas D, Ye Q, Huang Y, Tang R, Leutenegger S (2018) InteriorNet: mega-scale multi-sensor photo-realistic indoor scenes dataset. In: British machine vision conference (BMVC)

713. Li W, Zhang Z, Liu Z (2010) Action recognition based on a bag of 3D points. In: IEEE conference on computer vision and pattern recognition (CVPR) workshop human communicative behavior analysis, pp 9–14

714. Li Y, Bu R, Sun M, Wu W, Di X, Chen B (2018) PointCNN: convolution on X-transformed points. In: Bengio S, Wallach H, Larochelle H, Grauman K, Cesa-Bianchi N, Garnett R (eds) Advances in neural information processing systems, vol 31, pp 820–830

715. Li Y, Huang JB, Ahuja N, Yang MH (2016) Deep joint image filtering. In: European conference on computer vision (ECCV), pp 154–169

716. Li Y, Min D, Do M, Lu J (2016) Fast guided global interpolation for depth and motion. In: European conference on computer vision (ECCV), pp 717–733

717. Li Y, Pirk S, Su H, Qi CR, Guibas LJ (2016) FPNN: field probing neural networks for 3D data. CoRR abs/1605.06240

718. Li Y, Wu X, Chrysathou Y, Sharf A, Cohen-Or D, Mitra NJ (2011) Globfit: consistently fitting primitives by discovering global relations. ACM Trans Graph 30(4):52:1–52:12

719. Li Y, Xue T, Sun L, Liu J (2012) Joint example-based depth map super-resolution. In: IEEE international conference on multimedia and expo, pp 152–157

720. Li Z, Gan Y, Liang X, Yu Y, Cheng H, Lin L (2016) LSTM-CF: unifying context modeling and fusion with LSTMs for RGB-D scene labeling. In: European conference on computer vision (ECCV), pp 541–557

721. Li Z, Guo J, Cheong L, Zhou S (2013) Perspective motion segmentation via collaborative clustering. In: IEEE international conference on computer vision (ICCV), vol 2

722. Liang H, Wang J, Sun Q, Liu Y, Yuan J, Luo J, He Y (2016) Barehanded music: real-time hand interaction for virtual piano. In: ACM SIGGRAPH, pp 87–94

723. Liang H, Yuan J, Thalmann D (2014) Parsing the hand in depth images. IEEE Trans Multimed 16(5):1241–1253

724. Liang H, Yuan J, Thalmann D (2015) Resolving ambiguous hand pose predictions by exploiting part correlations. IEEE Trans Circuits Syst Video Technol 25(7):1125–1139

725. Liang H, Yuan J, Thalmann D, Thalmann NM (2015) AR in hand: egocentric palm pose tracking and gesture recognition for augmented reality applications. In: Proceedings of the ACM international conference on multimedia, pp 743–744

726. Liao B, Xiao C, Pang Z (2013) Efficient feature tracking of time-varying surfaces using multi-scale motion flow propagation. Comput-Aided Des 45(11):1394–1407

727. Liao M, Wang H, Gong M (2009) Modeling deformable objects from a single depth camera. In: IEEE international conference on computer vision (ICCV), pp 167–174

728. Liciotti D, Contigiani M, Frontoni E, Mancini A, Zingaretti P, Placidi V (2014) Shopper analytics: a customer activity recognition system using a distributed RGB-D camera network. In: International workshop on video analytics for audience measurement in retail and digital signage, pp 146–157

729. Liciotti D, Frontoni E, Mancini A, Zingaretti P (2016) Pervasive system for consumer behaviour analysis in retail environments. In: Video analytics. Face and facial expression recognition and audience measurement. Springer, pp 12–23

730. Liciotti D, Massi G, Frontoni E, Mancini A, Zingaretti P (2015) Human activity analysis for in-home fall risk assessment. In: IEEE international conference on communication workshop (ICCW), pp 284–289

731. Liciotti D, Paolanti M, Frontoni E, Mancini A, Zingaretti P (2017) Person re-identification dataset with RGB-D camera in a top-view configuration. In: Nasrollahi K, Distante C, Hua G, Cavallaro A, Moeslund TB, Battiato S, Ji Q (eds) Video analytics. Face and facial expression recognition and audience measurement. Springer, pp 1–11

732. Liciotti D, Paolanti M, Frontoni E, Zingaretti P (2017) People detection and tracking from an RGB-D camera in top-view configuration: review of challenges and applications. Lecture notes in computer science (including subseries Lecture notes in artificial intelligence and Lecture notes in bioinformatics), LNCS, vol 10590, pp 207–218

733. Liciotti D, Paolanti M, Pietrini R, Frontoni E, Zingaretti P (2018) Convolutional networks for semantic heads segmentation using top-view depth data in crowded environment. In: Proceedings – international conference on pattern recognition, pp 1384–1389
734. Lien J, Gillian N, Karagozler ME, Amihood P, Schwesig C, Olson E, Raja H, Poupyrev I (2016) Soli: ubiquitous gesture sensing with millimeter wave radar. ACM Trans Graph 35(4):142:1–142:19
735. Lightman K (2016) Silicon gets sporty. IEEE Spectr 53(3):48–53
736. Lim B, Son S, Kim H, Nah S, Lee KM (2017) Enhanced deep residual networks for single image super-resolution. In: IEEE conference on computer vision and pattern recognition workshops (CVPRW), pp 1132–1140
737. Lin D, Chen G, Cohen-Or D, Heng P, Huang H (2017) Cascaded feature network for semantic segmentation of RGB-D images. In: IEEE international conference on computer vision (ICCV), pp 1320–1328
738. Lin D, Fidler S, Urtasun R (2013) Holistic scene understanding for 3D object detection with RGBD cameras. In: Proceedings of the IEEE international conference on computer vision, pp 1417–1424
739. Lin M, Chen Q, Yan S (2013) Network in network. CoRR abs/1312.4400. arXiv:1312.4400
740. Lin S, Chen Y, Lai YK, Martin RR, Cheng ZQ (2016) Fast capture of textured full-body avatar with RGB-D cameras. Vis Comput 32(6):681–691
741. Lin S, Liu A, Hsu T, Fu L (2015) Representative body points on top-view depth sequences for daily activity recognition. In: IEEE international conference on systems, man, and cybernetics, pp 2968–2973
742. Lin TY, Dollár P, Girshick RB, He K, Hariharan B, Belongie SJ (2017) Feature pyramid networks for object detection. In: IEEE conference on computer vision and pattern recognition (CVPR), vol 1, p 4
743. Lin Z, Chen M, Ma Y (2010) The augmented lagrange multiplier method for exact recovery of corrupted low-rank matrices. arXiv:1009.5055
744. Lin Z, Liu R, Su Z (2011) Linearized alternating direction method with adaptive penalty for low-rank representation. In: Proceedings of advances in neural information processing systems, pp 612–620
745. Lindlbauer D, Mueller J, Alexa M (2017) Changing the appearance of real-world objects by modifying their surroundings. In: Proceedings of the CHI conference on human factors in computing systems, pp 3954–3965
746. Lindner M, Kolb A, Hartmann K (2007) Data-fusion of PMD-based distance-information and high-resolution RGB-images. In: International symposium on signals, circuits and systems (ISSCS), vol 1, pp 1–4
747. Lindner M, Schiller I, Kolb A, Koch R (2010) Time-of-flight sensor calibration for accurate range sensing. Comput Vis Image Underst 114(12):1318–1328
748. Liu B, Gould S, Koller D (2010) Single image depth estimation from predicted semantic labels. In: IEEE conference on computer vision and pattern recognition (CVPR), pp 1253–1260

749. Liu D, Sara E, Sun W (2001) Nested auto-regressive processes for MPEG-encoded video traffic modeling. IEEE Trans Circuits Syst Video Technol 11(2):169–183

750. Liu F, Shen C, Lin G (2015) Deep convolutional neural fields for depth estimation from a single image. In: IEEE conference on computer vision and pattern recognition (CVPR), pp 5162–5170

751. Liu F, Yang J, Yue H (2016) Moiré pattern removal from texture images via low-rank and sparse matrix decomposition. In: Proceedings of IEEE visual communications and image processing (VCIP), pp 1–4

752. Liu J, Gong X, Liu J (2012) Guided inpainting and filtering for Kinect depth maps. In: International conference on pattern recognition, pp 2055–2058

753. Liu J, Liu Y, Zhang G, Zhu P, Chen YQ (2015) Detecting and tracking people in real time with RGB-D camera. Pattern Recognit Lett 53:16–23

754. Liu L, Chan S, Nguyen T (2015) Depth reconstruction from sparse samples: representation, algorithm, and sampling. IEEE Trans Image Process 24(6):1983–1996

755. Liu M, Salzmann M, He X (2014) Discrete-continuous depth estimation from a single image. In: IEEE conference on computer vision and pattern recognition (CVPR), pp 716–723

756. Liu MY, Tuzel O, Taguchi Y (2013) Joint geodesic upsampling of depth images. In: IEEE conference on computer vision and pattern recognition (CVPR), pp 169–176

757. Liu MY, Tuzel O, Veeraraghavan A, Taguchi Y, Marks TK, Chellappa R (2012) Fast object localization and pose estimation in heavy clutter for robotic bin picking. Int J Robot Res 31(8):951–973

758. Liu S, Lai P, Tian D, Gomila C, Chen CW (2010) Joint trilateral filtering for depth map compression. In: Visual communications and image processing, p 77440F

759. Liu S, Wang Y, Wang J, Wang H, Zhang J, Pan C (2013) Kinect depth restoration via energy minimization with TV 21 regularization. In: International conference on image processing, pp 724–724

760. Liu W, Chen X, Yang J, Wu Q (2016) Robust color guided depth map restoration. IEEE Trans Image Process 26(1):315–327

761. Liu W, Chen X, Yang J, Wu Q (2016) Variable bandwidth weighting for texture copy artifact suppression in guided depth upsampling. IEEE Trans Circuits Syst Video Technol 27(10):2072–2085

762. Liu X, Zhai D, Chen R, Ji X, Zhao D, Gao W (2018) Depth restoration from RGB-D data via joint adaptive regularization and thresholding on manifolds. IEEE Trans Image Process 28(3):1068–1079

763. Liu X, Zhai D, Chen R, Ji X, Zhao D, Gao W (2018) Depth super-resolution via joint color-guided internal and external regularizations. IEEE Trans Image Process 28(4):1636–1645

764. Liu Y, Lasang P, Siegel M, Sun Q (2015) Geodesic invariant feature: a local descriptor in depth. IEEE Trans Image Process 24(1):236–248

765. Liu Y, Ye G, Wang Y, Dai Q, Theobalt C (2014) Human performance capture using multiple handheld Kinects. Springer, pp 91–108

766. Liu Z, Zhang C, Tian Y (2016) 3D-based deep convolutional neural network for action recognition with depth sequences. Image Vis Comput 55:93–100

767. Lo KH, Wang YCF, Hua KL (2017) Edge-preserving depth map upsampling by joint trilateral filter. IEEE Trans Cybern 48(1):371–384

768. Lorensen W, Cline H (1987) Marching cubes: a high resolution 3D surface construction algorithm. In: ACM SIGGRAPH, vol 21, pp 163–169

769. Lourido BP, Gelabert SV (2008) La perspectiva comunitaria en la fisioterapia domiciliaria: una revisión. Fisioterapia 30(5):231–237

770. Low KL (2004) Linear least-squares optimization for point-to-plane ICP surface registration. Tech. Rep., Department of Computer Science University of North Carolina at Chapel Hill (February)

771. Lowe DG (1999) Object recognition from local scale-invariant features. In: Proceedings of the ICCV, vol 2, pp 1150–1157

772. Lowe DG (2004) Distinctive image features from scale-invariant keypoints. Int J Comput Vis 60(2):91–110

773. Lozano-Quilis JA, Gil-Gómez H, Gil-Gómez JA, Albiol-Pérez S, Palacios-Navarro G, Fardoun HM, Mashat AS (2014) Virtual rehabilitation for multiple sclerosis using a Kinect-based system: randomized controlled trial. JMIR Serious Games 2(2)

774. Lu J, Min D, Pahwa RS, Do MN (2011) A revisit to MRF-based depth map super-resolution and enhancement. In: Proceedings of the ICASSP, pp 985–988

775. Lu J, Shi K, Min D, Lin L, Do MN (2012) Cross-based local multipoint filtering. In: IEEE conference on computer vision and pattern recognition (CVPR), pp 430–437

776. Lu S, Ren X, Liu F (2014) Depth enhancement via low-rank matrix completion. In: IEEE conference on computer vision and pattern recognition (CVPR), pp 3390–3397

777. Lu Y, Song D (2015) Robust RGB-D odometry using point and line features. In: IEEE international conference on computer vision (ICCV), pp 3934–3942

778. Lu Y, Song D (2015) Robustness to lighting variations: an RGB-D indoor visual odometry using line segments. In: IEEE/RSJ international conference on intelligent robots and systems (IROS), pp 688–694

779. Lucas BD, Kanade T (1981) An iterative image registration technique with an application to stereo vision. In: Proceedings of the international joint conference on artificial intelligence, vol 2, pp 674–679

780. Lun R, Zhao W (2015) A survey of applications and human motion recognition with Microsoft Kinect. Int J Pattern Recognit Artif Intell

781. Ma L, Kerl C, Stückler J, Cremers D (2016) CPA-SLAM: consistent plane-model alignment for direct RGB-D SLAM. In: IEEE international conference on robotics and automation (ICRA), pp 1285–1291

782. Ma L, Stückler J, Kerl C, Cremers D (2017) Multi-view deep learning for consistent semantic mapping with RGB-D cameras. In: IEEE/RSJ international conference on intelligent robots and systems (IROS), pp 598–605

783. Ma S, Goldfarb D, Chen L (2011) Fixed point and Bregman iterative methods for matrix rank minimization. Math Progr 128(1–2):321–353

784. Ma Y, Guo Y, Lei Y, Lu M, Zhang J (2017) Efficient rotation estimation for 3D registration and global localization in structured point clouds. Image Vis Comput 67:52–66

785. Ma Y, Worrall S, Kondoz AM (2008) Automatic video object segmentation using depth information and an active contour model. In: Workshop on multimedia signal processing, pp 910–914

786. Mac Aodha O, Campbell ND, Nair A, Brostow GJ (2012) Patch based synthesis for single depth image super-resolution. In: European conference on computer vision (ECCV), pp 71–84

787. Maclean N, Pound P, Wolfe C, Rudd A (2002) The concept of patient motivation: a qualitative analysis of stroke professionals' attitudes. Stroke 33(2):444–448

788. Madden C, Piccardi M (2005) Height measurement as a session-based biometric for people matching across disjoint camera views. In: Image and vision computing conference

789. Maddern W, Pascoe G, Linegar C, Newman P (2017) 1 year, 1000km: the Oxford robotcar dataset. Int J Robot Res (IJRR) 36(1):3–15

790. Madsen K, Nielsen HB, Tingleff O (2004) Methods for non-linear least squares problems, 2nd edn, p 60

791. Magic Leap Inc. (2019) Introducing spatiate to magic leap one. https://www.magicleap.com/news/product-updates/spatiate-on-magic-leap-one/. Accessed 14 Jun 2019

792. Magnor M, Grau O, Sorkine-Hornung O, Theobalt C (2015) Digital representations of the real world: how to capture, model, and render visual reality. A. K. Peters, Ltd.

793. Maimone A, Fuchs H (2011) Encumbrance-free telepresence system with real-time 3D capture and display using commodity depth cameras. In: Proceedings of the IEEE international symposium on mixed and augmented reality (ISMAR), pp 137–146

794. Maimone A, Fuchs H (2011) A first look at a telepresence system with room-sized real-time 3D capture and life-sized tracked display wall. In: Proceedings of ICAT 2011, pp 4–9 (in press)

795. Maimone A, Fuchs H (2012) Real-time volumetric 3D capture of room-sized scenes for telepresence. In: 3DTV conference: the true vision – capture, transmission and display of 3D video (3DTV-CON), pp 1–4

796. Maimone A, Fuchs H (2012) Reducing interference between multiple structured light depth sensors using motion. IEEE Virtual Real (VR):51–54

797. Maki BE, Sibley KM, Jaglal SB, Bayley M, Brooks D, Fernie GR, Flint AJ, Gage W, Liu BA, McIlroy WE, et al (2011) Reducing fall risk by improving

balance control: development, evaluation and knowledge-translation of new approaches. J Saf Res 42(6):473–485

798. Malawski F (2014) Top-view people counting in public transportation using Kinect. Chall Mod Technol 5(4):17–20

799. Malleson C (2015) Dynamic scene modelling and representation from video and depth. Ph.D. thesis, CVSSP, University of Surrey

800. Malleson C, Bazin JC, Wang O, Beeler T, Bradley D, Hilton A, Sorkine-Hornung A (2015) FaceDirector: continuous control of facial performance in video. In: IEEE international conference on computer vision (ICCV)

801. Malleson C, Collomosse J (2011) Volumetric 3D graphics on commodity displays using active gaze tracking John Collomosse. In: IEEE international conference on computer vision workshop (ICCVW), pp 399–405

802. Malleson C, Collomosse J (2013) Virtual volumetric graphics on commodity displays using 3D viewer tracking. Int J Comput Vis (IJCV) 101(2):519–532

803. Malleson C, Guillemaut J, Hilton A (2018) Hybrid modelling of non-rigid scenes from RGBD cameras. IEEE Trans Circuits Syst Video Technol:1

804. Malleson C, Hilton A, Guillemaut, Jy (2012) Evaluation of KinectFusion for set modelling. In: European conference on visual media production (CVMP)

805. Malleson C, Klaudiny M, Guillemaut JY, Hilton A (2014) Structured representation of non-rigid surfaces from single view 3D point tracks. In: International conference on 3D vision (3DV), pp 625–632

806. Malleson C, Klaudiny M, Hilton A, Guillemaut JY (2013) Single-view RGBD-based reconstruction of dynamic human geometry. In: International conference on computer vision (ICCV) workshops, pp 307–314

807. Mallick T, Das PP, Majumdar AK (2014) Characterizations of noise in Kinect depth images: a review. IEEE Sens J 14(6):1731–1740

808. Mankoff KD, Russo TA (2013) The Kinect: a low-cost, high-resolution, short-range 3D camera. Earth Surface Processes Landforms 38(9):926–936

809. Margolin R, Zelnik-Manor L, Tal A (2014) How to evaluate foreground maps? In: IEEE conference on computer vision and pattern recognition (CVPR), pp 248–255

810. Marks R (2011) 3D spatial interaction for entertainment. In: IEEE symposium on 3D user interfaces (3DUI)

811. Martín RM, Lorbach M, Brock O (2014) Deterioration of depth measurements due to interference of multiple RGB-D sensors. In: IEEE/RSJ international conference on intelligent robots and systems, pp 4205–4212

812. Martínez-Aranda S, Fernández-Pato J, Caviedes-Voullième D, García-Palacín I, García-Navarro P (2018) Towards transient experimental water surfaces: a new benchmark dataset for 2D shallow water solvers. Adv Water Resour 121:130–149

813. Marzahl C, Penndorf P, Bruder I, Staemmler M (2012) Unobtrusive fall detection using 3D images of a gaming console: concept and first results. In: Ambient assisted living. Springer, pp 135–146

814. Mastorakis G, Makris D (2014) Fall detection system using Kinect's infrared sensor. J Real-Time Image Process 9(4):635–646

815. Mathieu M, Couprie C, LeCun Y (2015) Deep multi-scale video prediction beyond mean square error. arXiv:1511.05440

816. Mattausch O, Panozzo D, Mura C, Sorkine-Hornung O, Pajarola R (2014) Object detection and classification from large-scale cluttered indoor scans. Comput Graph Forum 33(2):11–21

817. Maturana D, Scherer S (2015) 3D convolutional neural networks for landing zone detection from LiDAR. In: IEEE international conference on robotics and automation (ICRA), pp 3471–3478

818. Maturana D, Scherer S (2015) VoxNet: a 3D convolutional neural network for real-time object recognition. In: IEEE/RSJ international conference on intelligent robots and systems (IROS), pp 922–928

819. Matyunin S, Vatolin D, Berdnikov Y, Smirnov M (2011) Temporal filtering for depth maps generated by Kintect depth camera. In: 3DTV conference, pp 1–4

820. Mazuran M, Burgard W, Tipaldi GD (2016) Nonlinear factor recovery for long-term SLAM. Int J Robot Res 35(1–3):50–72

821. McCormac J, Handa A, Davison A, Leutenegger S (2017) SemanticFusion: dense 3D semantic mapping with convolutional neural networks. In: IEEE international conference on robotics and automation (ICRA), pp 4628–4635

822. McCormac J, Handa A, Leutenegger S, Davison A (2017) SceneNet RGB-D: can 5M synthetic images beat generic imageNet pre-training on indoor segmentation? In: IEEE international conference on computer vision (ICCV)

823. McElhone M, Stückler J, Behnke S (2013) Joint detection and pose tracking of multi-resolution surfel models in RGB-D. In: European conference on mobile robots

824. Meeussen W, Wise M, Glaser S, Chitta S, McGann C, Mihelich P, Marder-Eppstein E, Muja M, Eruhimov V, Foote T, Hsu J, Rusu RB, Marthi B, Bradski G, Konolige K, Gerkey BP, Berger E (2010) Autonomous door opening and plugging in with a personal robot. In: IEEE international conference on robotics and automation (ICRA), pp 729–736

825. Mehta SP, Roy JS (2011) Systematic review of home physiotherapy after hip fracture surgery. J Rehabil Med 43(6):477–480

826. Meilland M, Comport AI (2013) On unifying key-frame and voxel-based dense visual SLAM at large scales. In: IEEE/RSJ international conference on intelligent robots and systems, pp 3677–3683

827. Meilland M, Comport AI (2013) Super-resolution 3D tracking and mapping. In: IEEE international conference on robotics and automation, pp 5717–5723

828. Melax S, Keselman L, Orsten S (2013) Dynamics based 3D skeletal hand tracking. In: Proceedings of the graphics interface, pp 63–70

829. Melotti G, Premebida C, da S. Gonçalves NMM, Nunes UJC, Faria DR (2018) Multimodal CNN pedestrian classification: a study on combining LIDAR and camera data. In: IEEE international conference on intelligent transportation systems (ITSC)

830. Memmesheimer R, Seib V, Paulus D (2017) homer@UniKoblenz: Winning team of the RoboCup@Home open platform league 2017. In: Robot world cup, pp 509–520

831. Meng X, Gao W, Hu Z (2018) Dense RGB-D SLAM with multiple cameras. Sensors 18(7)

832. Mentiplay BF, Perraton LG, Bower KJ, Pua YH, McGaw R, Heywood S, Clark RA (2015) Gait assessment using the Microsoft Xbox One Kinect: concurrent validity and inter-day reliability of spatiotemporal and kinematic variables. J Biomech 48(10):2166–2170

833. Menze M, Geiger A (2015) Object scene flow for autonomous vehicles. In: Conference on computer vision and pattern recognition (CVPR)

834. Merrell P, Schkufza E, Li Z, Agrawala M, Koltun V (2011) Interactive furniture layout using interior design guidelines. ACM Trans Graph 30(4):87:1–87:10

835. MeshLab: MeshLab. http://meshlab.sourceforge.net. Accessed Apr 2015

836. Messelodi S, Modena CM (2015) Boosting Fisher vector based scoring functions for person re-identification. Image Vis Comput 44:44–58

837. Meyer GP, Laddha A, Kee E, Vallespi-Gonzalez C, Wellington CK (2019) LaserNet: an efficient probabilistic 3D object detector for autonomous driving. CoRR abs/1903.08701. arXiv:1903.08701

838. Miao D, Fu J, Lu Y, Li S, Chen CW (2012) Texture-assisted Kinect depth inpainting. In: International symposium on circuits and systems, pp 604–607

839. Michel F, Kirillov A, Brachmann E, Krull A, Gumhold S, Savchynskyy B, Rother C (2017) Global hypothesis generation for 6D object pose estimation. In: IEEE conference on computer vision and pattern recognition (CVPR)

840. Microsoft Corp. (2019) Microsoft HoloLens – mixed reality technology for business. https://www.microsoft.com/en-us/hololens. Accessed 14 Jun 2019

841. Microsoft Corp. (2019) Mixed reality capture studios. https://www.microsoft.com/en-us/mixed-reality/capture-studios. Accessed 27 Jun 2019

842. Middlebury datasets (2005) http://vision.middlebury.edu/stereo/data/

843. Migniot C, Ababsa F (2013) 3D human tracking in a top view using depth information recorded by the xtion pro-live camera. In: Bebis G, Boyle R, Parvin B, Koracin D, Li B, Porikli F, Zordan V, Klosowski J, Coquillart S, Luo X, Chen M, Gotz D (eds) Advances in visual computing. Springer, Berlin/Heidelberg, pp 603–612

844. Migniot C, Ababsa F (2016) Hybrid 3D–2D human tracking in a top view. J Real-Time Image Process 11(4):769–784

845. Miller S, Teichman A, Thrun S (2013) Unsupervised extrinsic calibration of depth sensors in dynamic scenes. In: IEEE/RSJ international conference on intelligent robots and systems (IROS), pp 2695–2702

846. Min D, Choi S, Lu J, Ham B, Sohn K, Do MN (2014) Fast global image smoothing based on weighted least squares. IEEE Trans Image Process 23(12):5638–5653

847. Min D, Lu J, Do M (2011) Depth video enhancement based on joint global mode filtering. IEEE Trans Image Process 21(3):1176–1190

848. Min D, Lu J, Do MN (2012) Depth video enhancement based on weighted mode filtering. IEEE Trans Image Process 21(3):1176–1190

849. Miron A, Rogozan A, Ainouz S, Bensrhair A, Broggi A (2015) An evaluation of the pedestrian classification in a multi-domain multi-modality setup. Sensors 15(6):13,851–13,873

850. Mishra A, Shrivastava A, Aloimonos Y (2012) Segmenting "simple" objects using RGB-D. In: IEEE international conference on robotics and automation (ICRA), pp 4406–4413

851. Mitra N, Flöry S, Ovsjanikov M (2007) Dynamic geometry registration. In: Eurographics symposium on geometry processing

852. Molnár B, Toth CK, Detrekői A (2012) Accuracy test of Microsoft Kinect for human morphologic measurements. ISPRS – Int Arch Photogramm Remote Sens Spatial Inf Sci XXXIX-B3:543–547

853. Mondragón IF, Campoy P, Martinez C, Olivares-Méndez MA (2010) 3D pose estimation based on planar object tracking for UAVs control. In: IEEE international conference on robotics and automation (ICRA), pp 35–41

854. Montani C, Scateni R, Scopigno R (1994) A modified look-up table for implicit disambiguation of marching cubes. Vis Comput 10(6):353–355

855. Moon G, Chang JY, Lee KM (2018) V2V-PoseNet: voxel-to-voxel prediction network for accurate 3D hand and human pose estimation from a single depth map. In: IEEE conference on computer vision and pattern recognition (CVPR), pp 5079–5088

856. Morell-Gimenez V, Saval-Calvo M, Villena Martinez V, Azorin-Lopez J, Rodriguez J, Cazorla M, Orts S, Guilló A (2018) A survey of 3D rigid registration methods for RGB-D cameras, pp 74–98

857. Motion L (2018) Leap motion. https://www.leapmotion.com

858. Moya-Alcover G, Elgammal A, Jaume-i-Capó A, Varona J (2017) Modeling depth for nonparametric foreground segmentation using RGBD devices. Pattern Recognit Lett 96:76–85

859. Mueller F, Bernard F, Sotnychenko O, Mehta D, Sridhar S, Casas D, Theobalt C (2018) GANerated hands for real-time 3D hand tracking from monocular RGB. In: IEEE conference on computer vision and pattern recognition (CVPR), pp 49–59

860. Mueller M, Zilly F, Kauff P (2010) Adaptive cross-trilateral depth map filtering. In: 3DTV conference, pp 1–4

861. Müller AC, Behnke S (2014) Learning depth-sensitive conditional random fields for semantic segmentation of RGB-D images. In: IEEE international conference on robotics and automation (ICRA), pp 6232–6237

862. Mur-Artal R, Montiel JMM, Tardós JD (2015) ORB-SLAM: a versatile and accurate monocular SLAM system. IEEE Trans Robot 31(5):1147–1163

863. Mur-Artal R, Tardós JD (2017) ORB-SLAM2: an open-source SLAM system for monocular, stereo, and RGB-D cameras. IEEE Trans Robot 33(5):1255–1262

864. Muybridge E, Wikipedia (1878) Sallie gardner at a gallop. https://en.wikipedia. org/wiki/Sallie_Gardner_at_a_Gallop. Accessed 21 Jan 2019

865. Myronenko A, Song X (2010) Point set registration: coherent point drift. IEEE Trans Pattern Anal Mach Intell 32(12):2262–2275

866. Nakahara H, Yonekawa H, Sato S (2017) An object detector based on multiscale sliding window search using a fully pipelined binarized CNN on an FPGA. In: International conference on field programmable technology (ICFPT), pp 168–175

867. Nan L, Xie K, Sharf A (2012) A search-classify approach for cluttered indoor scene understanding. ACM Trans Graph 31(6):137:1–137:10

868. Neumann D, Lugauer F, Bauer S, Wasza J, Hornegger J (2011) Real-time RGB-D mapping and 3-D modeling on the GPU using the random ball cover data structure. In: International conference on computer vision (ICCV) workshops, pp 1161–1167

869. Neumann DA (2013) Kinesiology of the musculoskeletal system-e-book: foundations for rehabilitation. Elsevier Health Sciences

870. Newcombe R, Davison A (2010) Live dense reconstruction with a single moving camera. In: IEEE conference on computer vision and pattern recognition (CVPR), pp 1498–1505

871. Newcombe R, Lovegrove S, Davison A (2011) DTAM: dense tracking and mapping in real-time. In: IEEE international conference on computer vision (ICCV), pp 2320–2327

872. Newcombe RA, Fox D, Seitz SM (2015) DynamicFusion: reconstruction and tracking of non-rigid scenes in real-time. In: IEEE conference on computer vision and pattern recognition (CVPR), pp 343–352

873. Newcombe RA, Izadi S, Hilliges O, Molyneaux D, Kim D, Davison AJ, Kohi P, Shotton J, Hodges S, Fitzgibbon A (2011) Kinectfusion: real-time dense surface mapping and tracking. In: IEEE international symposium on mixed and augmented reality, pp 127–136

874. Newell A, Yang K, Deng J (2016) Stacked hourglass networks for human pose estimation. In: European conference on computer vision (ECCV), pp 483–499

875. Nguyen CV, Izadi S, Lovell D (2012) Modeling Kinect sensor noise for improved 3D reconstruction and tracking. In: International conference on 3D imaging, modeling, processing, visualization & transmission, pp 524–530

876. Nguyen H, Ciocarlie M, Hsiao K, Kemp C (2013) ROS commander: flexible behavior creation for home robots. In: IEEE international conference on robotics and automation (ICRA), pp 467–474

877. Nguyen HT, Do MN (2005) Image-based rendering with depth information using the propagation algorithm. In: International conference on acoustics, speech and signal processing, pp 589–592

878. Nguyen K, Fookes C, Sridharan S, Tistarelli M, Nixon M (2018) Super-resolution for biometrics: a comprehensive survey. Pattern Recognit 78:23–42

879. Nguyen QH, Do MN, Patel SJ (2009) Depth image-based rendering from multiple cameras with 3D propagation algorithm. In: International conference on immersive telecommunications, p 6

880. Ni M, Lei J, Cong R, Zheng K, Peng B, Fan X (2017) Color-guided depth map super resolution using convolutional neural network. IEEE Access 2:26666–26672

881. Nießner M, Zollhöfer M, Izadi S, Stamminger M (2013) Real-time 3D reconstruction at scale using voxel hashing. ACM Trans Graph (TOG) 32(6):169

882. Nießner M, Zollhöfer M, Izadi S, Stamminger M (2013) Real-time 3D reconstruction at scale using voxel hashing. ACM Trans Graph 32(6):169:1–169:11

883. Nieuwenhuisen M, Behnke S (2013) Human-like interaction skills for the mobile communication robot Robotinho. Int J Soc Robot 5(4):549–561

884. Nieuwenhuisen M, Droeschel D, Holz D, Stückler J, Berner A, Li J, Klein R, Behnke S (2013) Mobile bin picking with an anthropomorphic service robot. In: IEEE international conference on robotics and automation (ICRA)

885. Nieuwenhuisen M, Steffens R, Behnke S (2011) Local multiresolution path planning in soccer games based on projected intentions. In: RoboCup 2011: robot soccer world cup XV. LNCS, vol 7416. Springer, pp 495–506

886. Nintendo (2008) Consolidated financial highlights. www.nintendo.co.jp/ir/pdf/2008/080124e.pdf

887. Niu Y, Geng Y, Li X, Liu F (2012) Leveraging stereopsis for saliency analysis. In: IEEE conference on computer vision and pattern recognition (CVPR), pp 454–461

888. del Nogal ML, González-Ramírez A, Palomo-Iloro A (2005) Evaluación del riesgo de caídas. Protocolos de valoración clínica. Revista Española de Geriatría y Gerontología 40:54–63

889. NVidia: CUDA. http://www.nvidia.com/cuda. Accessed Feb 2012

890. Oberweger M, Lepetit V (2017) DeepPrior++: improving fast and accurate 3D hand pose estimation. In: Proceedings of the international conference on computer vision workshop, pp 585–594

891. Oberweger M, Riegler G, Wohlhart P, Lepetit V (2016) Efficiently creating 3D training data for fine hand pose estimation. In: IEEE conference on computer vision and pattern recognition (CVPR), pp 3593–3601

892. Oberweger M, Wohlhart P, Lepetit V (2015) Hands deep in deep learning for hand pose estimation. In: Proceedings of the computer vision winter workshop, pp 21–30

893. Oberweger M, Wohlhart P, Lepetit V (2015) Training a feedback loop for hand pose estimation. In: IEEE international conference on computer vision (ICCV), pp 3316–3324

894. Oculus (2018) Oculus. https://www.oculus.com/

895. Oesau S, Lafarge F, Alliez P (2014) Indoor scene reconstruction using feature sensitive primitive extraction and graph-cut. ISPRS J Photogram Remote Sens 90:68–82

896. Oh J, Guo X, Lee H, Lewis RL, Singh S (2015) Action-conditional video prediction using deep networks in atari games. In: Cortes C, Lawrence ND, Lee DD, Sugiyama M, Garnett R (eds) NIPS, pp 2863–2871

897. Ohtake Y, Belyaev A, Seidel HP (2003) A multi-scale approach to 3D scattered data interpolation with compactly supported basis functions. In: Shape modeling international, SMI '03, pp 153

898. Oikonomidis I, Kyriazis N, Argyros A (2011) Efficient model-based 3D tracking of hand articulations using Kinect. In: British machine vision conference (BMVC), pp 101.1–101.11

899. Oikonomidis I, Kyriazis N, Argyros AA (2010) Markerless and efficient 26-DOF hand pose recovery. In: Proceedings of the Asian conference on computer vision, pp 744–757

900. van den Oord A, Kalchbrenner N, Vinyals O, Espeholt L, Graves A, Kavukcuoglu K (2016) Conditional image generation with PixelCNN decoders. CoRR abs/1606.05328

901. Open source computer vision (OpenCV). http://opencv.org

902. OpenNI: OpenNI. www.openni.org. Accessed Feb 2012

903. Ortiz L, Cabrera E, Gonçalves L (2018) Depth data error modeling of the ZED 3D vision sensor from stereolabs. Electron Lett Comput Vis Image Anal 17

904. Orts-Escolano S, Rhemann C, Fanello S, Chang W, Kowdle A, Degtyarev Y, Kim D, Davidson PL, Khamis S, Dou M, Tankovich V, Loop C, Cai Q, Chou PA, Mennicken S, Valentin J, Pradeep V, Wang S, Kang SB, Kohli P, Lutchyn Y, Keskin C, Izadi S (2016) Holoportation: virtual 3D teleportation in real-time. In: Proceedings of the annual symposium on user interface software and technology, UIST '16, pp 741–754

905. Ouerhani N, Hugli H (2000) Computing visual attention from scene depth. In: Proceedings of the international conference on pattern recognition, ICPR-2000, vol 1, pp 375–378

906. Overmyer SP (1991) Revolutionary vs. evolutionary rapid prototyping: balancing software productivity and HCI design concerns, vol 4400. Center of Excellence in Command, Control, Communications and Intelligence (C3I), George Mason University

907. Owen J, Eccles B, Choo B, et al (2001) The application of auto-regressive time series modelling for the time-frequency analysis of civil engineering structures. Eng Struct 23(5):521–536

908. Oxford Active Vision Group: InfiniTAM. http://www.robots.ox.ac.uk/~victor/infinitam/download.html. Accessed June 2015

909. Pala F, Satta R, Fumera G, Roli F (2016) Multimodal person reidentification using RGB-D cameras. IEEE Trans Circuits Syst Video Technol 26(4):788–799

910. Palasek P, Yang H, Xu Z, Hajimirza N, Izquierdo E, Patras I (2015) A flexible calibration method of multiple Kinects for 3D human reconstruction. In: IEEE international conference on multimedia expo workshops (ICMEW), pp 1–4

911. Panahi L, Ghods V (2018) Human fall detection using machine vision techniques on RGB-D images. Biomedical Signal Processing and Control 44:146–153

912. Paolanti M, Liciotti D, Pietrini R, Mancini A, Frontoni E (2018) Modelling and forecasting customer navigation in intelligent retail environments. J Intell Robot Syst 91(2):165–180

913. Paolanti M, Romeo L, Liciotti D, Pietrini R, Cenci A, Frontoni E, Zingaretti P (2018) Person re-identification with RGB-D camera in top-view configuration through multiple nearest neighbor classifiers and neighborhood component features selection. Sensors 18(10):3471

914. Paolanti M, Romeo L, Martini M, Mancini A, Frontoni E, Zingaretti P (2019) Robotic retail surveying by deep learning visual and textual data. Robot Auton Syst 118:179–188

915. Papachristou A, Zioulis N, Zarpalas D, Daras P (2018) Markerless structure-based multi-sensor calibration for free viewpoint video capture

916. Papazov C, Haddadin S, Parusel S, Krieger K, Burschka D (2012) Rigid 3D geometry matching for grasping of known objects in cluttered scenes. Int J Robot Res 31(4):538–553

917. Park J, Kim H, Tai Y, Brown M, Kweon I (2011) High quality depth map upsampling for 3D-TOF cameras. In: IEEE international conference on computer vision (ICCV), pp 1623–1630

918. Parker S, Shirley P, Livnat Y, Hansen C, Sloan PP (1998) Interactive ray tracing for isosurface rendering. In: Conference on visualization, pp 233–238

919. Pastor L, Rodríguez A, Espadero JM, Rincón L (2001) 3D wavelet-based multiresolution object representation. Pattern Recognit 34(12):2497–2513

920. Patel R, Curtis R, Romero B, Correll N (2016) Improving grasp performance using in-hand proximity and contact sensing. In: Robotic grasping and manipulation challenge, pp 146–160

921. Pathak D, Krahenbuhl P, Donahue J, Darrell T, Efros AA (2016) Context encoders: feature learning by inpainting. In: IEEE conference on computer vision and pattern recognition (CVPR), pp 2536–2544

922. Pavel MS, Schulz H, Behnke S (2015) Recurrent convolutional neural networks for object-class segmentation of RGB-D video. In: International joint conference on neural networks (IJCNN)

923. Pavlakos G, Zhou X, Derpanis KG, Daniilidis K (2017) Coarse-to-fine volumetric prediction for single-image 3D human pose. In: IEEE conference on computer vision and pattern recognition (CVPR), pp 7025–7034

924. Pavlovic VI, Sharma R, Huang TS (1997) Visual interpretation of hand gestures for human–computer interaction: a review. IEEE Trans Pattern Anal Mach Intell 19(7):677–695

925. Pei D, Liu H, Liu Y, Sun F (2013) Unsupervised multimodal feature learning for semantic image segmentation. In: IJCNN, pp 1–6

926. Pellegrini S, Schindler K, Nardi D (2008) A generalisation of the ICP algorithm for articulated bodies. In: British machine vision conference (BMVC), Lm

927. Pellegrini S, Schindler K, Nardi D (2008) A generalization of the ICP algorithm for articulated bodies. In: British machine vision conference (BMVC)

928. Peng H, Li B, Xiong W, Hu W, Ji R (2014) RGBD salient object detection: a benchmark and algorithms. In: European conference on computer vision (ECCV), pp 92–109

929. Peng J, Hazan T, McAllester D, Urtasun R (2011) Convex max-product algorithms for continuous MRFs with applications to protein folding. In: International conference on machine learning, pp 729–736

930. Pepik B, Stark M, Gehler P, Schiele B (2012) Teaching 3D geometry to deformable part models. In: IEEE conference on computer vision and pattern recognition (CVPR), pp 3362–3369

931. Perona P, Malik J (1990) Scale-space and edge detection using anisotropic diffusion. IEEE Trans Pattern Anal Mach Intell 12(7):629–639

932. Petit A, Lippiello V, Siciliano B (2015) Tracking fractures of deformable objects in real-time with an RGB-D sensor. In: International conference on 3D vision, pp 632–639

933. Petschnigg G, Szeliski R, Agrawala M, Cohen M, Hoppe H, Toyama K (2004) Digital photography with flash and no-flash image pairs. ACM Trans Graph (TOG) 23:664–672

934. Pham TH, Kyriazis N, Argyros AA, Kheddar A (2017) Hand-object contact force estimation from markerless visual tracking. IEEE Trans Pattern Anal Mach Intell

935. Pham TT, Reid I, Latif Y, Gould S (2015) Hierarchical higher-order regression forest fields: an application to 3D indoor scene labelling. In: Proceedings of the IEEE international conference on computer vision, pp 2246–2254

936. Pire T, Fischer T, Castro G, De Cristóforis P, Civera J, Berlles JJ (2017) S-PTAM: stereo parallel tracking and mapping. Robot Auton Syst 93:27–42

937. Planinc R, Kampel M (2013) Introducing the use of depth data for fall detection. Pers Ubiquitous Comput 17(6):1063–1072

938. Platinsky L, Davison AJ, Leutenegger S (2017) Monocular visual odometry: sparse joint optimisation or dense alternation? In: IEEE international conference on robotics and automation (ICRA), pp 5126–5133

939. Po LM, Zhang S, Xu X, Zhu Y (2011) A new multi-directional extrapolation hole-filling method for depth-image-based rendering. In: International conference on image processing, pp 2589–2592

940. Pons-Moll G, Pujades S, Hu S, Black MJ (2017) Clothcap: seamless 4d clothing capture and retargeting. ACM Trans Graph (TOG) 36(4):73:1–73:15

941. Pont-Tuset J, Arbeláez P, Barron J, Marques F, Malik J (2015) Multiscale combinatorial grouping for image segmentation and object proposal generation. arXiv:1503.00848

942. Popat K, Picard RW (1993) Novel cluster-based probability model for texture synthesis, classification, and compression. In: Visual communications, pp 756–768

943. Premebida C, Garrote L, Asvadi A, Ribeiro AP, Nunes U (2016) High-resolution LIDAR-based depth mapping using Bilateral Filter. In: IEEE inter-

national conference on intelligent transportation systems (ITSC), pp 2469–2474

944. Pritch Y, Kav-Venaki E, Peleg S (2009) Shift-map image editing. In: International conference on computer vision, vol 9, pp 151–158

945. Proença PF, Gao Y (2018) Probabilistic RGB-D odometry based on points, lines and planes under depth uncertainty. Robot Auton Syst 104:25–39

946. Prosser BJ, Zheng WS, Gong S, Xiang T, Mary Q (2010) Person re-identification by support vector ranking. In: British machine vision conference (BMVC), vol 2, p 6

947. Pulli K (1999) Multiview registration for large data sets. In: 3-D digital imaging and modeling, pp 160–168

948. Qi CR, Liu W, Wu C, Su H, Guibas LJ (2018) Frustum pointnets for 3D object detection from RGB-D data. In: IEEE conference on computer vision and pattern recognition (CVPR), pp 918–927

949. Qi CR, Su H, Mo K, Guibas LJ (2017) PointNet: deep learning on point sets for 3D classification and segmentation. In: IEEE conference on computer vision and pattern recognition (CVPR), pp 652–660

950. Qi CR, Su H, Nießner M, Dai A, Yan M, Guibas LJ (2016) Volumetric and multi-view CNNs for object classification on 3D data. CoRR. arXiv:1604.03265

951. Qi CR, Yi L, Su H, Guibas LJ (2017) PointNet++: deep hierarchical feature learning on point sets in a metric space. In: Proceedings of the conference on neural information processing systems

952. Qi F, Han J, Wang P, Shi G, Li F (2013) Structure guided fusion for depth map inpainting. Pattern Recognit Lett 34(1):70–76

953. Qi X, Liao R, Jia J, Fidler S, Urtasun R (2018) 3D graph neural networks for RGBD semantic segmentation. In: IEEE international conference on computer vision (ICCV), pp 5209–5218

954. Qian C, Sun X, Wei Y, Tang X, Sun J (2014) Realtime and robust hand tracking from depth. In: IEEE conference on computer vision and pattern recognition (CVPR), pp 1106–1113

955. Qu L, He S, Zhang J, Tian J, Tang Y, Yang Q (2017) RGBD salient object detection via deep fusion. IEEE Trans Image Process 26(5):2274–2285

956. Quam DL (1990) Gesture recognition with a dataglove. In: Proceedings of the IEEE conference on aerospace and electronics, vol 2, pp 755–760

957. Quigley M, Gerkey B, Conley K, Faust J, Foote T, Leibs J, Berger E, Wheeler R, Ng A (2009) ROS: an open-source robot operating system. In: IEEE international conference on robotics and automation (ICRA)

958. Rad M, Lepetit V (2017) BB8: a scalable, accurate, robust to partial occlusion method for predicting the 3D poses of challenging objects without using depth. In: IEEE international conference on computer vision (ICCV), pp 3848–3856

959. Rad M, Oberweger M, Lepetit V (2018) Feature mapping for learning fast and accurate 3D pose inference from synthetic images. In: IEEE conference on computer vision and pattern recognition (CVPR), pp 4663–4672

960. Rafighi A, Seifi S, Meruvia-Pastor O (2015) Automatic and adaptable registration of live RGBD video streams. In: International conference on motion in games

961. Rander P, Narayanan PJ, Kanade T (1997) Virtualized reality: constructing time-varying virtual worlds from real world events. In: Proceedings. Visualization, pp 277–283

962. Ranftl R, Vineet V, Chen Q, Koltun V (2016) Dense monocular depth estimation in complex dynamic scenes. In: Conference on computer vision and pattern recognition (CVPR), pp 4058–4066

963. Raposo C, Lourenço M, Antunes M, Barreto JP (2013) Plane-based odometry using an RGB-D camera. In: British machine vision conference (BMVC)

964. Rauter M (2013) Reliable human detection and tracking in top-view depth images. In: IEEE conference on computer vision and pattern recognition workshops, pp 529–534

965. Ravishankar H, Venkataramani R, Thiruvenkadam S, Sudhakar P, Vaidya V (2017) Learning and incorporating shape models for semantic segmentation. In: International conference on medical image computing and computer-assisted intervention, pp 203–211

966. Redmon J, Divvala S, Girshick R, Farhadi A (2016) You only look once: unified, real-time object detection. In: IEEE conference on computer vision and pattern recognition (CVPR), pp 779–788

967. Ren J, Gong X, Yu L, Zhou W, Yang MY (2015) Exploiting global priors for RGB-D saliency detection. In: IEEE conference on computer vision and pattern recognition workshops (CVPRW), pp 25–32

968. Ren S, He K, Girshick RB, Sun J (2015) Faster R-CNN: towards real-time object detection with region proposal networks. CoRR abs/1506.01497

969. Ren X, Bo L, Fox D (2012) RGB-(D) scene labeling: features and algorithms. In: IEEE conference on computer vision and pattern recognition (CVPR), pp 2759–2766

970. Ren Z, Sudderth EB (2016) Three-dimensional object detection and layout prediction using clouds of oriented gradients. In: IEEE conference on computer vision and pattern recognition (CVPR), pp 1525–1533

971. Ren Z, Sudderth EB (2018) 3D object detection with latent support surfaces. In: IEEE conference on computer vision and pattern recognition (CVPR)

972. Ren Z, Yuan J, Meng J, Zhang Z (2013) Robust part-based hand gesture recognition using Kinect sensor. IEEE Trans Multimed 15(5):1110–1120

973. Ricciuti M, Spinsante S, Gambi E (2018) Accurate fall detection in a top view privacy preserving configuration. Sensors (Switzerland) 18(6)

974. Richard MMOBB, Chang MYS (2001) Fast digital image inpainting. In: International conference on visualization, imaging and image processing, pp 106–107

975. Richardt C, Stoll C, Dodgson NA, Seidel HP, Theobalt C (2012) Coherent spatiotemporal filtering, upsampling and rendering of RGBZ videos. In: Computer graphics forum, vol 31, pp 247–256

976. Rico J, Crossan A, Brewster S (2011) Gesture based interfaces: practical applications of gestures in real world mobile settings. In: England D (ed) Whole body interaction, chap 14. Springer, London, pp 173–186

977. Riegler G, Ulusoy AO, Geiger A (2017) Octnet: learning deep 3D representations at high resolutions. In: IEEE conference on computer vision and pattern recognition (CVPR), pp 3577–3586

978. Ringbeck T, Möller T, Hagebeuker B (2007) Multidimensional measurement by using 3D PMD sensors. Adv Radio Sci 5:135

979. Rios-Cabrera R, Tuytelaars T (2013) Discriminatively trained templates for 3D object detection: a real time scalable approach. In: Proceedings of the IEEE international conference on computer vision, pp 2048–2055

980. Rodríguez-Gonzálvez P, Rodríguez-Martín M, Ramos LF, González-Aguilera D (2017) 3D reconstruction methods and quality assessment for visual inspection of welds. Autom Constr 79:49–58

981. Rogez G, Supancic JS, Ramanan D (2015) Understanding everyday hands in action from RGB-D images. In: IEEE international conference on computer vision (ICCV), pp 3889–3897

982. Rogez G, Weinzaepfel P, Schmid C (2017) LCR-net: localization-classification-regression for human pose. In: IEEE conference on computer vision and pattern recognition (CVPR), pp 3433–3441

983. Romero J, Kjellström H, Kragic D (2009) Monocular real-time 3D articulated hand pose estimation. In: Proceedings of the IEEE-RAS conference on humanoid robots, pp 87–92

984. Romero J, Kjellström H, Kragic D (2010) Hands in action: real-time 3D reconstruction of hands in interaction with objects. In: Proceedings of the IEEE conference on robotics and automation, pp 458–463

985. Romero J, Tzionas D, Black MJ (2017) Embodied hands: modeling and capturing hands and bodies together. ACM Trans Graph 36(6):245:1–245:17

986. Ronneberger O, Fischer P, Brox T (2015) U-net: convolutional networks for biomedical image segmentation. In: Proceedings of the international conference on medical image computing and computer-assisted intervention, pp 234–241

987. Rosen DM, Carlone L, Bandeira AS, Leonard JJ (2019) SE-Sync: a certifiably correct algorithm for synchronization over the special euclidean group. Int J Robot Res 38(2–3)

988. Rosten E, Drummond T (2006) Machine learning for high-speed corner detection. In: European conference on computer vision (ECCV), pp 430–443

989. Roth H, Marsette V (2012) Moving volume KinectFusion. British machine vision conference (BMVC), pp 112.1–112.11

990. Rother C, Minka T, Blake A, Kolmogorov V (2006) Cosegmentation of image pairs by histogram matching-incorporating a global constraint into MRFs. In: IEEE conference on computer vision and pattern recognition (CVPR), pp 993–1000

991. Rougier C, Meunier J, St-Arnaud A, Rousseau J (2011) Robust video surveillance for fall detection based on human shape deformation. IEEE Trans Circuits Syst Video Technol 21(5):611–622

992. Rouhani M, Sappa AD (2011) Correspondence free registration through a point-to-model distance minimization. In: IEEE international conference on computer vision (ICCV), pp 2150–2157

993. Rousseeuw PJ (1984) Least median of squares regression. Am Stat Assoc 79(388):871–880

994. Roy A, Sural S, Mukherjee J (2012) A hierarchical method combining gait and phase of motion with spatiotemporal model for person re-identification. Pattern Recognit Lett 33(14):1891–1901. Novel pattern recognition-based methods for re-identification in biometric context

995. Rublee E, Rabaud V, Konolige K, Bradski G (2011) ORB: an efficient alternative to SIFT or SURF. In: IEEE international conference on computer vision (ICCV)

996. Rumelhart DE, Hinton GE, Williams RJ (1988) Learning representations by back-propagating errors. Cognit Model 5(3):1

997. Rünz M, Buffier M, Agapito L (2018) MaskFusion: real-time recognition, tracking and reconstruction of multiple moving objects. In: IEEE international symposium on mixed and augmented reality (ISMAR), pp 10–20

998. Rusinkiewicz S, Hall-Holt O, Levoy M (2002) Real-time 3D model acquisition. ACM Trans Graph (TOG) 21(3)

999. Rusinkiewicz S, Levoy M (2001) Efficient variants of the ICP algorithm. In: International conference on 3-D digital imaging and modeling, pp 145–152

1000. Russakovsky O, Deng J, Su H, Krause J, Satheesh S, Ma S, Huang Z, Karpathy A, Khosla A, Bernstein M, Berg AC, Fei-Fei L (2015) ImageNet large scale visual recognition challenge. Int J Comput Vis (IJCV) 115(3):211–252

1001. Russell C, Fayad J, Agapito L (2011) Energy based multiple model fitting for non-rigid structure from motion. In: IEEE conference on computer vision and pattern recognition (CVPR), pp 3009–3016

1002. Russell C, Yu R, Agapito L (2014) Video Pop-up: monocular 3D reconstruction of dynamic scenes. In: European conference on computer vision (ECCV), pp 583–598

1003. Rusu RB, Cousins S (2011) 3D is here: Point Cloud Library (PCL). In: IEEE international conference on robotics and automation (ICRA)

1004. Rutishauser M, Stricker M, Trobina M (1994) Merging range images of arbitrarily shaped objects. In: IEEE conference on computer vision and pattern recognition (CVPR), pp 573–580

1005. Sabov A, Krüger J (2008) Identification and correction of flying pixels in range camera data. In: Conference on computer graphics, pp 135–142

1006. Saghafi MA, Hussain A, Zaman HB, Saad MHM (2014) Review of person re-identification techniques. IET Comput Vis 8(6):455–474

1007. Sahin C, Kim TK (2018) Category-level 6D object pose recovery in depth images. In: IEEE European conference on computer vision workshop (ECCVW)

1008. Sahin C, Kim TK (2019) Recovering 6D object pose: a review and multi-modal analysis. In: ECCV workshops, pp 15–31

1009. Sahin C, Kouskouridas R, Kim TK (2016) Iterative Hough forest with histogram of control points for 6 DoF object registration from depth images. In: IEEE/RSJ international conference on intelligent robots and systems (IROS), pp 4113–4118

1010. Sahin C, Kouskouridas R, Kim TK (2017) A learning-based variable size part extraction architecture for 6D object pose recovery in depth images. Image Vis Comput 63:38–50

1011. Salas-Moreno R, Glocker B, Kelly P, Davison A (2014) Dense planar SLAM. In: International symposium on mixed and augmented reality (ISMAR)

1012. Salas-Moreno RF, Newcombe RA, Strasdat H, Kelly PH, Davison AJ (2013) SLAM++: simultaneous localisation and mapping at the level of objects. IEEE conference on computer vision and pattern recognition (CVPR), pp 1352–1359

1013. Salvi J, Matabosch C, Fofi D, Forest J (2007) A review of recent range image registration methods with accuracy evaluation. Image Vis Comput 25(5):578–596

1014. Salzmann M, Pilet J, Ilic S, Fua P (2007) Surface deformation models for non-rigid 3D shape recovery. IEEE Trans Pattern Anal Mach Intell 29(8):1481–7

1015. Sanchez V, Zakhor A (2012) Planar 3D modeling of building interiors from point cloud data. In: Proceedings of the international conference on image processing (ICIP), pp 1777–1780

1016. Sandlund M, McDonough S, Häger-Ross C (2009) Interactive computer play in rehabilitation of children with sensorimotor disorders: a systematic review. Dev Med Child Neurol 51(3):173–179

1017. Sarbolandi H, Lefloch D, Kolb A (2015) Kinect range sensing: structured-light versus time-of-flight Kinect. Comput Vis Image Underst 139:1–20

1018. Sarbolandi H, Lefloch D, Kolb A (2015) Kinect range sensing: structured-light versus time-of-flight kinect. Comput Vis Image Underst

1019. Satnik A, Izquierdo E (2018) Real-time multi-view volumetric reconstruction of dynamic scenes using Kinect v2. In: 3DTV conference: the true vision – capture, transmission and display of 3D video (3DTV-CON), pp 1–4

1020. Satta R, Fumera G, Roli F (2011) Exploiting dissimilarity representations for person re-identification. In: Pelillo M, Hancock ER (eds) Similarity-based pattern recognition. Springer, Berlin/Heidelberg, pp 275–289

1021. Sattler T, Leibe B, Kobbelt L (2011) Fast image-based localization using direct 2D-to-3D matching. In: IEEE international conference on computer vision (ICCV), pp 667–674

1022. Savva M, Chang AX, Hanrahan P, Fisher M, Nießner M (2014) SceneGrok: inferring action maps in 3D environments. ACM Trans Graph (TOG) 33(6)

1023. Savva M, Chang AX, Hanrahan P, Fisher M, Nießner M (2016) PiGraphs: learning interaction snapshots from observations. ACM Trans Graph (TOG) 35(4)

1024. Saxena A, Chung SH, Ng AY (2006) Learning depth from single monocular images. In: Advances in neural information processing systems, pp 1161–1168

1025. Saxena A, Sun M, Ng AY (2009) Make3D: learning 3D scene structure from a single still image. IEEE Trans Pattern Anal Mach Intell 31(5):824–840

1026. Scharstein D, Szeliski R, Zabih R (2002) A taxonomy and evaluation of dense two-frame stereo correspondence algorithms. Int J Comput Vis (IJCV) 47(1):7–42

1027. Schenk F, Fraundorfer F (2017) Combining edge images and depth maps for robust visual odometry. In: British machine vision conference (BMVC)

1028. Scherer D, Müller AC, Behnke S (2010) Evaluation of pooling operations in convolutional architectures for object recognition. In: International conference on artificial neural networks (ICANN), pp 92–101

1029. Scherer SA, Zell A (2013) Efficient onbard RGBD-SLAM for autonomous MAVs. In: IEEE/RSJ international conference on intelligent robots and systems, pp 1062–1068

1030. Schops T, Sattler T, Pollefeys M (2019) BAD SLAM: bundle adjusted direct RGB-D SLAM. In: IEEE conference on computer vision and pattern recognition (CVPR), pp 134–144

1031. Schröder M, Maycock J, Botsch M (2015) Reduced marker layouts for optical motion capture of hands. In: Proceedings of the ACM SIGGRAPH conference on motion in games, pp 7–16

1032. Schröder M, Maycock J, Ritter H, Botsch M (2014) Real-time hand tracking using synergistic inverse kinematics. In: Proceedings of the international conference on robotics and automation, pp 5447–5454

1033. Schröder M, Waltemate T, Maycock J, Röhlig T, Ritter H, Botsch M (2017) Design and evaluation of reduced marker layouts for hand motion capture. Comput Anim Virtual Worlds

1034. Schröder Y, Scholz A, Berger K, Ruhl K, Guthe S, Magnor M (2011) Multiple Kinect studies. Technical Report, Computer Graphics Lab, TU Braunschweig. http://www.digibib.tu-bs.de/?docid=00041359. Accessed 15 Sept 2011

1035. Schulz H, Behnke S (2012) Deep learning – layer-wise learning of feature hierarchies. German J Artif Intell 26(4):357–363

1036. Schulz H, Behnke S (2012) Learning object-class segmentation with convolutional neural networks. In: European symposium on artificial neural networks

1037. Schulz H, Behnke S (2014) Structured prediction for object detection in deep neural networks. In: International conference on artificial neural networks, pp 395–402

1038. Schulz H, Cho K, Raiko T, Behnke S (2015) Two-layer contractive encodings for learning stable nonlinear features. Neural Netw 64:4–11

1039. Schulz H, Höft N, Behnke S (2015) Depth and height aware semantic RGB-D perception with convolutional neural networks. In: ESANN

1040. Schulz H, Waldvogel B, Sheikh R, Behnke S (2015) CURFIL: random forests for image labeling on GPU. In: International conference on computer vision theory and applications (VISAPP), pp 156–164

1041. Schwartz WR, Davis LS (2009) Learning discriminative appearance-based models using partial least squares. In: XXII Brazilian symposium on computer graphics and image processing (SIBGRAPI), pp 322–329

1042. Schwarz LA, Mkhitaryan A, Mateus D, Navab N (2012) Human skeleton tracking from depth data using geodesic distances and optical flow. Image Vis Comput 30(3):217–226

1043. Schwarz M, Milan A, Periyasamy AS, Behnke S (2018) RGB-D object detection and semantic segmentation for autonomous manipulation in clutter. Int J Robot Res 37(4–5):437–451

1044. Schwarz M, Schulz H, Behnke S (2015) RGB-D object recognition and pose estimation based on pre-trained convolutional neural network features. In: IEEE international conference on robotics and automation (ICRA), pp 1329–1335

1045. Schwarz M, Stückler J, Behnke S (2014) Mobile teleoperation interfaces with adjustable autonomy for personal service robots. In: ACM/IEEE international conference on human–robot interaction (HRI), pp 288–289

1046. Scona R, Jaimez M, Petillot YR, Fallon M, Cremers D (2018) StaticFusion: background reconstruction for dense RGB-D SLAM in dynamic environments. In: IEEE international conference on robotics and automation (ICRA), pp 1–9

1047. Scona R, Nobili S, Petillot YR, Fallon M (2017) Direct visual SLAM fusing proprioception for a humanoid robot. In: IEEE/RSJ international conference on intelligent robots and systems (IROS), pp 1419–1426

1048. Seer S, Brändle N, Ratti C (2012) Kinects and human Kinetics: a new approach for studying crowd behavior. CoRR abs/1210.2838. arXiv:1210.2838

1049. Segal A, Haehnel D, Thrun S (2009) Generalized-ICP. In: Robotics: science and systems

1050. Seifi S (2014) DeReEs: real-time registration of RGBD images using image-based feature detection and robust 3D correspondence estimation and refinement. http://research.library.mun.ca/8462/

1051. Seitz SM, Curless B, Diebel J, Scharstein D, Szeliski R (2006) A comparison and evaluation of multi-view stereo reconstruction algorithms. In: Proceedings of the conference on computer vision and pattern recognition, vol 1, pp 519–528

1052. Sermanet P, Eigen D, Zhang X, Mathieu M, Fergus R, LeCun Y (2013) OverFeat: integrated recognition, localization and detection using convolutional networks. CoRR abs/1312.6229

1053. Shakhnarovich G, Viola P, Darrell T (2003) Fast pose estimation with parameter-sensitive hashing. In: IEEE international conference on computer vision (ICCV), pp 750–758

1054. Shao L, Han J, Xu D, Shotton J (2013) Computer vision for RGB-D sensors: Kinect and its applications (special issue intro.). IEEE Trans Cybern 43(5):1314–1317

1055. Shao T, Xu W, Zhou K, Wang J, Li D, Guo B (2012) An interactive approach to semantic modeling of indoor scenes with an RGBD camera. ACM Trans Graph 31(6):136:1–136:11

1056. Sharma A, Grau O, Fritz M (2016) VConv-DAE: deep volumetric shape learning without object labels. In: Hua G, Jégou H (eds) Computer vision – ECCV workshops, pp 236–250

1057. Sharp T, Keskin C, Robertson D, Taylor J, Shotton J, Kim D, Rhemann C, Leichter I, Vinnikov A, Wei Y, et al (2015) Accurate, robust, and flexible real-time hand tracking. In: ACM conference on human factors in computing systems, pp 3633–3642

1058. Shelhamer E, Long J, Darrell T (2017) Fully convolutional networks for semantic segmentation. IEEE Trans Pattern Anal Mach Intell 39(4):640–651

1059. Shen CH, Fu H, Chen K, Hu SM (2012) Structure recovery by part assembly. ACM Trans Graph 31(6):180:1–180:11

1060. Shen J, Xu W, Luo Y, Su PC, Cheung SCS (2014) Extrinsic calibration for wide-baseline RGB-D camera network. In: IEEE International workshop on multimedia signal processing (MMSP), pp 1–6

1061. Shen X, Zhou C, Xu L, Jia J (2015) Mutual-structure for joint filtering. In: IEEE conference on computer vision and pattern recognition (CVPR), pp 3406–3414

1062. Sheng H, Liu X, Zhang S (2016) Saliency analysis based on depth contrast increased. In: IEEE international conference on acoustics, speech and signal processing (ICASSP), pp 1347–1351

1063. Sheng L, Ngan KN, Li S (2014) Temporal depth video enhancement based on intrinsic static structure. In: International conference on image processing, pp 2893–2897

1064. Shi B, Bai S, Zhou Z, Bai X (2015) Deeppano: deep panoramic representation for 3-d shape recognition. IEEE Signal Process Lett 22(12):2339–2343

1065. Shi J, Tomasi C (1994) Good features to track. In: IEEE conference on computer vision and pattern recognition, pp 593–600

1066. Shi W, Caballero J, Huszar F, Totz J, Aitken AP, Bishop R, Rueckert D, Wang Z (2016) Real-time single image and video super-resolution using an efficient sub-pixel convolutional neural network. In: IEEE conference on computer vision and pattern recognition (CVPR), pp 1874–1883

1067. Shi Y, Xu K, Niessner M, Rusinkiewicz S, Funkhouser T (2018) PlaneMatch: patch coplanarity prediction for robust RGB-D reconstruction. arXiv:1803.08407

1068. Shi Z, Sun Y, Xiong L, Hu Y, Yin B (2015) A multisource heterogeneous data fusion method for pedestrian tracking. Math Probl Eng 2015(150541):1–10

1069. Shih MC, Wang RY, Cheng SJ, Yang YR (2016) Effects of a balance-based exergaming intervention using the Kinect sensor on posture stability in individuals with Parkinson's disease: a single-blinded randomized controlled trial. J Neuroeng Rehabil 13(1):78

1070. Shin JH, Park SB, Jang SH (2015) Effects of game-based virtual reality on health-related quality of life in chronic stroke patients: a randomized, controlled study. Comput Biol Med 63:92–98

1071. Shotton J, Girshick R, Fitzgibbon A, Sharp T, Cook M, Finocchio M, Moore R, Kohli P, Criminisi A, Kipman A, Blake A (2013) Efficient human pose estimation from single depth images. IEEE Trans Pattern Anal Mach Intell 35(12):2821–2840

1072. Shotton J, Girshick R, Fitzgibbon A, Sharp T, Cook M, Finocchio M, Moore R, Kohli P, Criminisi A, Kipman A, et al (2013) Efficient human pose estimation from single depth images. IEEE Trans Pattern Anal Mach Intell 35(12):2821–2840

1073. Shotton J, Glocker B, Zach C, Izadi S, Criminisi A, Fitzgibbon A (2013) Scene coordinate regression forests for camera relocalization in RGB-D images. In: IEEE conference on computer vision and pattern recognition (CVPR), pp 2930–2937

1074. Shotton J, Sharp T, Kipman A, Fitzgibbon AW, Finocchio M, Blake A, Cook M, Moore R (2013) Real-time human pose recognition in parts from single depth images. Commun ACM 56(1):116–124

1075. Si L, Wang Q, Xiao Z (2014) Matching cost fusion in dense depth recovery for camera-array via global optimization. In: International conference on virtual reality and visualization, pp 180–185

1076. Silberman N, Fergus R (2011) Indoor scene segmentation using a structured light sensor. In: ICCV workshops, pp 601–608

1077. Silberman N, Hoiem D, Kohli P, Fergus R (2012) Indoor segmentation and support inference from RGBD images. In: European conference on computer vision (ECCV), pp 746–760

1078. Silberman N, Hoiem D, Kohli P, Fergus R (2012) Indoor segmentation and support inference from RGBD images. In: European conference on computer vision (ECCV), pp 746–760

1079. Silberman S (2003) Matrix2. https://www.wired.com/2003/05/matrix2/. Accessed 25 Jun 2019

1080. Simonyan K, Zisserman A (2014) Two-stream convolutional networks for action recognition in videos. CoRR abs/1406.2199

1081. Simonyan K, Zisserman A (2014) Very deep convolutional networks for large-scale image recognition. arXiv:1409.1556

1082. Sin H, Lee G (2013) Additional virtual reality training using Xbox Kinect in stroke survivors with hemiplegia. Am J Phys Med Rehabil 92(10):871–880

1083. Singh A, Sha J, Narayan KS, Achim T, Abbeel P (2014) BigBIRD: a large-scale 3D database of object instances. In: IEEE international conference on robotics and automation (ICRA), pp 509–516

1084. Sinha A, Choi C, Ramani K (2016) DeepHand: robust hand pose estimation by completing a matrix with deep features. In: IEEE conference on computer vision and pattern recognition (CVPR), pp 4150–4158

1085. Sinha A, Unmesh A, Huang Q, Ramani K (2017) SurfNet: generating 3D shape surfaces using deep residual networks. In: IEEE conference on computer vision and pattern recognition (CVPR)

1086. Sivic J, Zisserman A (2003) Video Google: a text retrieval approach to object matching in videos. In: IEEE international conference on computer vision (ICCV), p 1470

1087. Slavcheva M, Baust M, Cremers D, Ilic S (2017) KillingFusion: non-rigid 3D reconstruction without correspondences. In: Conference on computer vision and pattern recognition (CVPR), pp 5474–5483

1088. Snavely N, Seitz SM, Szeliski R (2006) Photo tourism: exploring photo collections in 3D. ACM Trans Graph (TOG) 25(3):835–846

1089. Socher R, Huval B, Bath B, Manning C, Ng AY (2012) Convolutional-recursive deep learning for 3D object classification. In: NIPS, pp 665–673

1090. Sock J, Kasaei SH, Lopes LS, Kim TK (2017) Multi-view 6D object pose estimation and camera motion planning using RGBD images. In: IEEE international conference on computer vision workshop (ICCVW), pp 2228–2235

1091. Solà J, Deray J, Atchuthan D (2018) A micro Lie theory for state estimation in robotics. arXiv:1812.01537

1092. Song H, Liu Z, Du H, Sun G (2016) Depth-aware saliency detection using discriminative saliency fusion. In: IEEE international conference on acoustics, speech and signal processing (ICASSP), pp 1626–1630

1093. Song H, Liu Z, Du H, Sun G, Le Meur O, Ren T (2017) Depth-aware salient object detection and segmentation via multiscale discriminative saliency fusion and bootstrap learning. IEEE Trans Image Process 26(9):4204–4216

1094. Song H, Liu Z, Xie Y, Wu L, Huang M (2016) RGBD co-saliency detection via bagging-based clustering. IEEE Signal Process Lett 23(12):1722–1726

1095. Song S, Lichtenberg SP, Xiao J (2015) Sun RGB-D: a RGB-D scene understanding benchmark suite. In: IEEE conference on computer vision and pattern recognition (CVPR), pp 567–576

1096. Song S, Xiao J (2014) Sliding shapes for 3D object detection in depth images. In: European conference on computer vision (ECCV), pp 634–651

1097. Song S, Xiao J (2016) Deep sliding shapes for amodal 3D object detection in RGB-D images. In: IEEE conference on computer vision and pattern recognition (CVPR)

1098. Song S, Yu F, Zeng A, Chang A, Savva M, Funkhouser T (2017) Semantic scene completion from a single depth image. In: IEEE conference on computer vision and pattern recognition (CVPR), pp 190–198

1099. Song W, Yun S, Jung SW, Won CS (2016) Rotated top-bottom dual-Kinect for improved field of view. Multimed Tools Appl 75(14):8569–8593

1100. Sorkine O (2005) Laplacian mesh processing. Eurographics state-of-the-art report (Section 4)

1101. Sorkine O, Cohen-Or D, Lipman Y, Alexa M, Rossl C, Seidel H (2004) Laplacian surface editing. In: Eurographics symposium on geometry processing, pp 175–184

1102. Soucy M, Laurendeau D (1995) A general surface approach to the integration of a set of range views. IEEE Trans Pattern Anal Mach Intell 17(4):344–358

1103. Spinello L, Arras KO (2011) People detection in RGB-D data. In: IROS

1104. Springenberg JT, Dosovitskiy A, Brox T, Riedmiller M (2014) Striving for simplicity: the all convolutional net. CoRR abs/1412.6806. arXiv:1412.6806

1105. Sridhar S, Mueller F, Oulasvirta A, Theobalt C (2015) Fast and robust hand tracking using detection-guided optimization. In: IEEE conference on computer vision and pattern recognition (CVPR), pp 3213–3221

1106. Sridhar S, Mueller F, Zollhoefer M, Casas D, Oulasvirta A, Theobalt C (2016) Real-time joint tracking of a hand manipulating an object from RGB-D input. In: Proceedings of the European conference on computer vision, pp 294–310

1107. Sridhar S, Oulasvirta A, Theobalt C (2013) Interactive markerless articulated hand motion tracking using rgb and depth data. In: IEEE international conference on computer vision (ICCV), pp 2456–2463

1108. Srivastava N, Hinton G, Krizhevsky A, Sutskever I, Salakhutdinov R (2014) Dropout: a simple way to prevent neural networks from overfitting. J Mach Learn Res 15:1929–1958

1109. Srivastava N, Mansimov E, Salakhutdinov R (2015) Unsupervised learning of video representations using LSTMs. In: International conference on machine learning (ICML), pp 843–852

1110. Starck J, Hilton A (2007) Surface capture for performance-based animation. Comput Graph Appl 27(3):21–31

1111. Starck JL, Elad M, Donoho DL (2005) Image decomposition via the combination of sparse representations and a variational approach. IEEE Trans Image Process 14(10):1570–1582

1112. Stauffer C, Grimson WEL (1999) Adaptive background mixture models for real-time tracking. In: IEEE conference on computer vision and pattern recognition, vol 2, pp 246–252

1113. Steffens R, Nieuwenhuisen M, Behnke S (2014) Continuous motion planning for service robots with multiresolution in time. In: International conference on intelligent autonomous systems (IAS), pp 203–215

1114. Steinbrucker F, Kerl C, Cremers D, Sturm J (2013) Large-scale multi-resolution surface reconstruction from RGB-D sequences. In: IEEE international conference on computer vision (ICCV), pp 3264–3271

1115. Steinbruecker F, Sturm J, Cremers D (2011) Real-time visual odometry from dense RGB-D images. In: Workshop on live dense reconstruction with moving cameras at the international conference on computer vision (ICCV)

1116. Stenger B, Mendonça PR, Cipolla R (2001) Model-based 3D tracking of an articulated hand. In: IEEE conference on computer vision and pattern recognition (CVPR), vol 2, pp II–310

1117. Stenger B, Thayananthan A, Torr PHS, Cipolla R (2006) Model-based hand tracking using a hierarchical bayesian filter. IEEE Trans Pattern Anal Mach Intell 28(9):1372–1384

1118. Stereolabs, Inc. (2019) ZED camera and SDK overview. https://www.stereolabs.com/zed/docs/ZED_Datasheet_2016.pdf. Accessed 21 Jan 2019

1119. Sterzentsenko V, Karakottas A, Papachristou A, Zioulis N, Doumanoglou A, Zarpalas D, Daras P (2018) A low-cost, flexible and portable volumetric capturing system. In: International conference on signal-image technology internet-based systems (SITIS), pp 200–207

1120. Stoyanov T, Magnusson M, Andreasson H, Lilienthal AJ (2012) Fast and accurate scan registration through minimization of the distance between compact 3D NDT representations. Int J Robot Res 31(12):1377–1393

1121. Stoyanov T, Mojtahedzadeh R, Andreasson H, Lilienthal AJ (2013) Comparative evaluation of range sensor accuracy for indoor mobile robotics and automated logistics applications. Robot Auton Syst 61(10):1094–1105

1122. Strasdat H (2012) Local accuracy and global consistency for efficient visual SLAM. Ph.D. thesis, Department of Computing, Imperial College London

1123. Strasdat H, Montiel J, Davison AJ (2010) Scale drift-aware large scale monocular SLAM. Robot: Sci Syst VI 2(3):7

1124. Stroucken S (2013) Graph-basierte 3D-Kartierung von Innenräumen mit einem RGBD-Multikamera-System. Diplomarbeit, Universität Bonn, Computer Science VI

1125. Stückler J, Behnke S (2011) Following human guidance to cooperatively carry a large object. In: IEEE-RAS international conference on humanoid robots (humanoids)

1126. Stückler J, Behnke S (2012) Integrating depth and color cues for dense multi-resolution scene mapping using RGB-D cameras. In: IEEE conference on multisensor fusion and integration for intelligent systems (MFI), pp 162–167

1127. Stückler J, Behnke S (2013) Hierarchical object discovery and dense modelling from motion cues in RGB-D video. In: International conference on artificial intelligence (IJCAI)

1128. Stückler J, Behnke S (2014) Adaptive tool-use strategies for anthropomorphic service robots. In: IEEE-RAS international conference on humanoid robots (humanoids)

1129. Stückler J, Behnke S (2014) Efficient deformable registration of multi-resolution surfel maps for object manipulation skill transfer. In: IEEE international conference on robotics and automation (ICRA)

1130. Stückler J, Behnke S (2014) Multi-resolution surfel maps for efficient dense 3D modeling and tracking. J Vis Commun Image Represent 25(1):137–147

1131. Stückler J, Behnke S (2015) Efficient dense rigid-body motion segmentation and estimation in RGB-D video. Int J Comput Vis 113(3):233–245

1132. Stückler J, Droeschel D, Gräve K, Holz D, Schreiber M, Topalidou-Kyniazopoulou A, Schwarz M, Behnke S (2014) Increasing flexibility of mobile manipulation and intuitive human–robot interaction in RoboCup@ Home. In: RoboCup 2013: robot world cup XVII, pp 135–146. Springer

1133. Stückler J, Schwarz M, Behnke S (2016) Mobile manipulation, tool use, and intuitive interaction for cognitive service robot Cosero. Front Robot AI 3:58

1134. Stückler J, Schwarz M, Schadler M, Topalidou-Kyniazopoulou A, Behnke S (2016) NimbRo Explorer: semi-autonomous exploration and mobile manipulation in rough terrain. J Field Robot 33(4):411–430

1135. Stückler J, Steffens R, Holz D, Behnke S (2013) Efficient 3D object perception and grasp planning for mobile manipulation in domestic environments. Robot Auton Syst 61(10):1106–1115

1136. Stückler J, Waldvogel B, Schulz H, Behnke S (2015) Dense real-time mapping of object-class semantics from RGB-D video. J Real-Time Image Process 10(4):599–609

1137. Sturari M, Liciotti D, Pierdicca R, Frontoni E, Mancini A, Contigiani M, Zingaretti P (2016) Robust and affordable retail customer profiling by vision and radio beacon sensor fusion. Pattern Recognit Lett 81:30–40

1138. Sturm J, Engelhard N, Endres F, Burgard W, Cremers D (2012) A benchmark for the evaluation of RGB-D SLAM systems. In: Proceedings of the international conference on intelligent robot systems (IROS)

1139. Sturm P, Ramalingam S, Tardif JP, Gasparini S, Barreto, J.a (2011) Camera models and fundamental concepts used in geometric computer vision. Found Trends Comput Graph Vis 6(1–2):1–183

1140. Su C, Zhang S, Xing J, Gao W, Tian Q (2016) Deep attributes driven multi-camera person re-identification. In: Leibe B, Matas J, Sebe N, Welling M (eds) European conference on computer vision (ECCV). Springer, pp 475–491

1141. Su H, Maji S, Kalogerakis E, Learned-Miller E (2015) Multi-view convolutional neural networks for 3D shape recognition. In: IEEE international conference on computer vision (ICCV), pp 945–953

1142. Su H, Qi CR, Li Y, Guibas LJ (2015) Render for CNN: viewpoint estimation in images using CNNs trained with rendered 3D model views. In: IEEE international conference on computer vision (ICCV)

1143. Sun D, Roth S, Black MJ (2010) Secrets of optical flow estimation and their principles. In: IEEE conference on computer vision and pattern recognition (CVPR)

1144. Sun D, Sudderth EB, Pfister H (2015) Layered RGBD scene flow estimation. In: Conference on computer vision and pattern recognition (CVPR), 07–12 June, pp 548–556

1145. Sun H, Meng Z, Tao PY, Ang MH (2018) Scene recognition and object detection in a unified convolutional neural network on a mobile manipulator. In: IEEE international conference on robotics and automation (ICRA), pp 1–5

1146. Sun J, Liu X, Wan W, Li J, Zhao D, Zhang H (2015) Database saliency for fast image retrieval. IEEE Trans Multimed 17(3):359–369

1147. Sun J, Zheng N, Shum H (2003) Stereo matching using belief propagation. IEEE Trans Pattern Anal Mach Intell 25(7):787–800

1148. Sun L, Zhao C, Stolkin R (2017) Weakly-supervised DCNN for RGB-D object recognition in real-world applications which lack large-scale annotated training data. arXiv:1703.06370

1149. Sun X, Wei Y, Liang S, Tang X, Sun J (2015) Cascaded hand pose regression. In: IEEE conference on computer vision and pattern recognition (CVPR), pp 824–832

1150. Sundaram N, Brox T, Keutzer K (2010) Dense point trajectories by GPU-accelerated large displacement optical flow. In: European conference on computer vision (ECCV)

1151. Sünderhauf N, Pham TT, Latif Y, Milford M, Reid I (2017) Meaningful maps with object-oriented semantic mapping. In: IEEE/RSJ international conference on intelligent robots and systems (IROS), pp 5079–5085

1152. Supancic III JS, Rogez G, Yang Y, Shotton J, Ramanan D (2015) Depth-based hand pose estimation: methods, data, and challenges. In: IEEE international conference on computer vision (ICCV), pp 1868–1876

1153. Suthar R, Patel MKR (2014) A survey on various image inpainting techniques to restore image. Int J Eng Res Appl 4(2):85–88

1154. Svoboda T, Hug H, Van Gool L (2002) ViRoom – low cost synchronized multicamera system and its self-calibration. In: Pattern recognition. Springer, pp 515–522

1155. Svoboda T, Martinec D, Pajdla T (2005) A convenient multicamera self-calibration for virtual environments. Presence 14(4):407–422

1156. Szegedy C, Vanhoucke V, Ioffe S, Shlens J, Wojna Z (2016) Rethinking the inception architecture for computer vision. In: IEEE conference on computer vision and pattern recognition (CVPR), pp 2818–2826

1157. Szeliski R, Zabih R, Scharstein D, Veksler O, Kolmogorov V, Agarwala A, Tappen M, Rother C (2006) A comparative study of energy minimization methods for Markov random fields. In: European conference on computer vision (ECCV), pp 1–17

1158. Tagliasacchi A, Schroeder M, Tkach A, Bouaziz S, Botsch M, Pauly M (2015) Robust articulated-ICP for real-time hand tracking. Comput Graph Forum 34(5):101–114

1159. Taguchi Y, Jian Y, Ramalingam S, Feng C (2013) Point-plane SLAM for hand-held 3D sensors. In: IEEE international conference on robotics and automation, pp 5182–5189

1160. Tam GKL, Cheng ZQ, Lai YK, Langbein FC, Liu Y, Marshall AD, Martin RR, Sun X, Rosin PL (2013) Registration of 3D point clouds and meshes: a survey from rigid to nonrigid. IEEE Trans Vis Comput Graph 19:1199–1217

1161. Tang D, Chang HJ, Tejani A, Kim TK (2014) Latent regression forest: structured estimation of 3D articulated hand posture. In: IEEE conference on computer vision and pattern recognition (CVPR), pp 3786–3793

1162. Tang D, Taylor J, Kohli P, Keskin C, Kim TK, Shotton J (2015) Opening the black box: hierarchical sampling optimization for estimating human hand pose. In: IEEE international conference on computer vision (ICCV), pp 3325–3333

1163. Tang D, Yu TH, Kim TK (2013) Real-time articulated hand pose estimation using semi-supervised transductive regression forests. In: IEEE international conference on computer vision (ICCV), pp 3224–3231

1164. Tao MW, Srinivasan PP, Malik J, Rusinkiewicz S, Ramamoorthi R (2015) Depth from shading, defocus, and correspondence using light-field angular coherence. In: IEEE conference on computer vision and pattern recognition (CVPR), pp 1940–1948

1165. Tatarchenko M, Dosovitskiy A, Brox T (2016) Multi-view 3D models from single images with a convolutional network. In: Leibe B, Matas J, Sebe N, Welling M (eds) European conference on computer vision (ECCV), pp 322–337

1166. Tateno K, Tombari F, Laina I, Navab N (2017) CNN-SLAM: real-time dense monocular SLAM with learned depth prediction. In: IEEE conference on computer vision and pattern recognition (CVPR)

1167. Tateno K, Tombari F, Navab N (2015) Real-time and scalable incremental segmentation on dense SLAM. In: IEEE/RSJ international conference on intelligent robots and systems (IROS), pp 4465–4472

1168. Taylor D (1996) Virtual camera movement: the way of the future? Am Cinematogr 77(9):93–100

1169. Taylor J, Bordeaux L, Cashman T, Corish B, Keskin C, Sharp T, Soto E, Sweeney D, Valentin J, Luff B, Topalian A, Wood E, Khamis S, Kohli P, Izadi S, Banks R, Fitzgibbon A, Shotton J (2016) Efficient and precise interactive hand tracking through joint, continuous optimization of pose and correspondences. ACM Trans Graph (TOG) 35(4):143:1–143:12

1170. Taylor J, Shotton J, Sharp T, Fitzgibbon A (2012) The Vitruvian manifold: inferring dense correspondences for one-shot human pose estimation. In: IEEE conference on computer vision and pattern recognition (CVPR), pp 103–110

1171. Tejani A, Tang D, Kouskouridas R, Kim TK (2014) Latent-class Hough forests for 3D object detection and pose estimation. In: European conference on computer vision (ECCV), pp 462–477

1172. Tekin B, Sinha SN, Fua P (2018) Real-time seamless single shot 6D object pose prediction. In: IEEE conference on computer vision and pattern recognition (CVPR), pp 292–301

1173. Telea A (2004) An image inpainting technique based on the fast marching method. Graphics Tools 9(1):23–34

1174. Tevs A, Berner A, Wand M, Ihrke I, Bokeloh M, Kerber J, Seidel, H.p (2011) Animation cartography – intrinsic reconstruction of shape and motion. ACM Trans Graph (TOG)

1175. The SCENE consortium: EU FP7 project SCENE. www.3d-scene.eu. Accessed Nov 2014

1176. Theobalt C, Albrecht I, Haber J, Magnor M, Seidel HP (2004) Pitching a baseball: tracking high-speed motion with multi-exposure images. ACM Trans Graph 23(3):540–547

1177. Thrun S, Montemerlo M (2006) The graph SLAM algorithm with applications to large-scale mapping of urban structures. Int J Robot Res 25(5–6):403–429

1178. Tippetts B, Lee DJ, Lillywhite K, Archibald J (2016) Review of stereo vision algorithms and their suitability for resource-limited systems. Real-Time Image Process 11(1):5–25

1179. Tkach A, Pauly M, Tagliasacchi A (2016) Sphere-meshes for real-time hand modeling and tracking. ACM Trans Graph 35(6):222:1–222:11

1180. Tomasi C, Manduchi R (1998) Bilateral filtering for gray and color images. In: IEEE international conference on computer vision (ICCV), pp 839–846

1181. Tome D, Russell C, Agapito L (2017) Lifting from the deep: convolutional 3D pose estimation from a single image. In: IEEE conference on computer vision and pattern recognition (CVPR), pp 2500–2509

1182. Tompson J, Goroshin R, Jain A, LeCun Y, Bregler C (2015) Efficient object localization using convolutional networks. In: IEEE conference on computer vision and pattern recognition (CVPR), pp 648–656

1183. Tompson J, Jain A, LeCun Y, Bregler C (2014) Joint training of a convolutional network and a graphical model for human pose estimation. In: Proceedings of the neural information processing systems, pp 1799–1807

1184. Tompson J, Stein M, Lecun Y, Perlin K (2014) Real-time continuous pose recovery of human hands using convolutional networks. ACM Trans Graph (TOG) 33(5):169:1–169:10

1185. Tong J, Zhou J, Liu L, Pan Z, Yan H (2012) Scanning 3D full human bodies using Kinects. IEEE Trans Vis Comput Graph 18(4):643–650

1186. Torralba A, Freeman W (2002) Properties and applications of shape recipes

1187. Toshev A, Shi J, Daniilidis K (2007) Image matching via saliency region correspondences. In: IEEE conference on computer vision and pattern recognition (CVPR), pp 1–8

1188. Toshev A, Szegedy C (2014) Deeppose: human pose estimation via deep neural networks. In: IEEE conference on computer vision and pattern recognition (CVPR), pp 1653–1660

1189. Treisman AM, Gelade G (1980) A feature-integration theory of attention. Cognit Psychol 12(1):97–136

1190. Triggs B, Mclauchlan PF, Hartley RI, Fitzgibbon AW (2000) Bundle adjustment – a modern synthesis. Synthesis 34099:298–372

1191. Tsai C, Wang C, Wang W (2013) Design and implementation of a RANSAC RGB-D mapping algorithm for multi-view point cloud registration. In: CACS international automatic control conference, pp 367–370

1192. Tseng T, Liu A, Hsiao P, Huang C, Fu L (2014) Real-time people detection and tracking for indoor surveillance using multiple top-view depth cameras. In: IEEE/RSJ international conference on intelligent robots and systems, pp 4077–4082

1193. Tu PH, Doretto G, Krahnstoever NO, Perera AA, Wheeler FW, Liu X, Rittscher J, Sebastian TB, Yu T, Harding KG (2007) An intelligent video framework for homeland protection. In: Unattended ground, sea, and air sensor technologies and applications IX, vol 6562, p 65620C

1194. Tu Z, Guo Z, Xie W, Yan M, Veltkamp RC, Li B, Yuan J (2017) Fusing disparate object signatures for salient object detection in video. Pattern Recognit 72:285–299

1195. Turk G, Levoy M (1994) Zippered polygon meshes from range images. In: Proceedings of the annual conference on computer graphics and interactive techniques, pp 311–318

1196. Türkbey TA, Kutlay Ş, Gök H (2017) Clinical feasibility of Xbox KinectTM training for stroke rehabilitation: a single-blind randomized controlled pilot study. J Rehabil Med 49(1):22–29

1197. Tzionas D, Ballan L, Srikantha A, Aponte P, Pollefeys M, Gall J (2016) Capturing hands in action using discriminative salient points and physics simulation. Int J Comput Vis 118(2):172–193

1198. Uenohara M, Kanade T (1995) Vision-based object registration for real-time image overlay. In: Computer vision, virtual reality and robotics in medicine, pp 13–22

1199. Uijlings JR, Sande KE, Gevers T, Smeulders AW (2013) Selective search for object recognition. Int J Comput Vis 104(2):154–171

1200. Vahrenkamp N, Asfour T, Dillmann R (2012) Simultaneous grasp and motion planning: humanoid robot ARMAR-III. Robot Autom Mag

1201. Valentin J, Nießner M, Shotton J, Fitzgibbon A, Izadi S, Torr PH (2015) Exploiting uncertainty in regression forests for accurate camera relocalization. In: IEEE conference on computer vision and pattern recognition (CVPR), pp 4400–4408

1202. Varona J, Jaume-i Capó A, Gonzèlez J, Perales FJ (2008) Toward natural interaction through visual recognition of body gestures in real-time. Interact Comput 21(1–2):3–10

1203. Verth JMV, Bishop LM (2008) Essential mathematics for games and interactive applications, second edition: a programmer's guide, 2nd edn. Morgan Kaufmann Publishers Inc.

1204. Vese L, Osher S (2003) Modeling textures with total variation minimization and oscillating patterns in image processing. J Sci Comput 19(3):553–572

1205. Vicente S, Rother C, Kolmogorov V (2011) Object cosegmentation. In: IEEE conference on computer vision and pattern recognition (CVPR), pp 2217–2224

1206. Vijayanagar KR, Loghman M, Kim J (2014) Real-time refinement of Kinect depth maps using multi-resolution anisotropic diffusion. Mobile Netw Appl 19(3):414–425

1207. Villena-Martínez V, Fuster-Guilló A, Azorín-López J, Saval-Calvo M, Mora-Pascual J, Garcia-Rodriguez J, Garcia-Garcia A (2017) A quantitative comparison of calibration methods for RGB-D sensors using different technologies. Sensors 17(2)

1208. Vineet V, Miksik O, Lidegaard M, Nießner M, Golodetz S, Prisacariu VA, Kähler O, Murray DW, Izadi S, Pérez P, et al (2015) Incremental dense semantic stereo fusion for large-scale semantic scene reconstruction. In: IEEE international conference on robotics and automation (ICRA), pp 75–82

1209. Viola P, Jones MJ (2004) Robust real-time face detection. Int J Comput Vis 57(2):137–154

1210. Volino M, Hilton A (2013) Layered view-dependent texture maps. In: European conference on visual media production (CVMP)

1211. Wachsmuth S, Lier F, Meyer zu Borgsen S, Kummert J, Lach L, Sixt D (2017) ToBI-Team of Bielefeld a human–robot interaction system for RoboCup@ home 2017

1212. Wan C, Probst T, Van Gool L, Yao A (2017) Crossing nets: dual generative models with a shared latent space for hand pose estimation. In: IEEE conference on computer vision and pattern recognition (CVPR), pp 680–689

1213. Wan C, Probst T, Van Gool L, Yao A (2018) Dense 3D regression for hand pose estimation. In: IEEE conference on computer vision and pattern recognition (CVPR), pp 5147–5156

1214. Wan C, Yao A, Van Gool L (2016) Direction matters: hand pose estimation from local surface normals. In: European conference on computer vision (ECCV), pp 554–569

1215. Wan J, Athitsos V, Jangyodsuk P, Escalante HJ, Ruan Q, Guyon I (2014) CSMMI: class-specific maximization of mutual information for action and gesture recognition. IEEE Trans Image Process 23(7):3152–3165

1216. Wand M, Adams B, Ovsjanikov M, Berner A, Bokeloh M, Jenke P, Guibas L, Seidel HP, Schilling A (2009) Efficient reconstruction of nonrigid shape and motion from real-time 3D scanner data. ACM Trans Graph (TOG) 28(2):1–15

1217. Wand M, Jenke P, Huang Q, Bokeloh M (2007) Reconstruction of deforming geometry from time-varying point clouds. In: Symposium on geometry processing

1218. Wand MP, Jones MC (1993) Comparison of smoothing parameterizations in bivariate kernel density estimation. J Am Stat Assoc 88(422):520–528

1219. Wang A, Cai J, Lu J, Cham TJ (2015) MMSS: multi-modal sharable and specific feature learning for RGB-D object recognition. In: IEEE conference on computer vision and pattern recognition (CVPR), pp 1125–1133

1220. Wang A, Lu J, Wang G, Cai J, Cham T (2014) Multi-modal unsupervised feature learning for RGB-D scene labeling. In: European conference on computer vision (ECCV), pp 453–467

1221. Wang A, Wang M (2017) RGB-D salient object detection via minimum barrier distance transform and saliency fusion. IEEE Signal Process Lett 24(5):663–667

1222. Wang C, Cannon DJ (1993) A virtual end-effector pointing system in point-and-direct robotics for inspection of surface flaws using a neural network based skeleton transform. In: Proceedings of the international conference on robotics and automation, vol 3, pp 784–789

1223. Wang D, Pan Q, Zhao C, Hu J, Xu Z, Yang F, Zhou Y (2017) A study on camera array and its applications. IFAC-PapersOnLine 50(1):10323–10328

1224. Wang DZ, Posner I (2015) Voting for voting in online point cloud object detection. In: Robotics: science and systems

1225. Wang J, An P, Zuo Y, You Z, Zhang Z (2014) High accuracy hole filling for Kinect depth maps. In: SPIE/COS photonics Asia, p 92732L

1226. Wang J, Wang Z, Gao C, Sang N, Huang R (2017) DeepList: learning deep features with adaptive listwise constraint for person reidentification. IEEE Trans Circuits Syst Video Technol 27(3):513–524

1227. Wang J, Wang Z, Tao D, See S, Wang G (2016) Learning common and specific features for RGB-D semantic segmentation with deconvolutional networks. In: European conference on computer vision (ECCV), pp 664–679

1228. Wang J, Yang J (2015) Reflection removal for stele images via sparse signal decomposition. In: Proceedings of the IEEE visual communications and image processing (VCIP)

1229. Wang JYA, Adelson EH (1994) Representing moving images with layers. IEEE Trans Image Process 3(5):625–638

1230. Wang L, Huang Z, Gong Y, Pan C (2017) Ensemble based deep networks for image super-resolution. Pattern Recognit 68:191–198

1231. Wang L, Qiao Y, Tang X (2015) Action recognition with trajectory-pooled deep-convolutional descriptors. In: IEEE conference on computer vision and pattern recognition (CVPR)

1232. Wang O, Finger J, Qingxiong Y, Davis J, Ruigang Y (2007) Automatic natural video matting with depth. Pacific conference on computer graphics and applications, pp 469–472

1233. Wang O, Schroers C, Zimmer H, Gross M, Sorkine-Hornung A (2014) VideoSnapping: interactive synchronization of multiple videos. In: ACM SIGGRAPH

1234. Wang P, Li W, Gao Z, Zhang J, Tang C, Ogunbona PO (2016) Action recognition from depth maps using deep convolutional neural networks. IEEE Trans Hum-Mach Syst 46(4):498–509

1235. Wang P, Li W, Gao Z, Zhang Y, Tang C, Ogunbona P (2017) Scene flow to action map: a new representation for RGB-D based action recognition with convolutional neural networks. arXiv:1702.08652

1236. Wang RY, Popović J (2009) Real-time hand-tracking with a color glove. ACM Trans Graph 28(3):63:1–63:8

1237. Wang S, Song J, Lien J, Poupyrev I, Hilliges O (2016) Interacting with soli: exploring fine-grained dynamic gesture recognition in the radio-frequency spectrum. In: Proceedings of the annual symposium on user interface software and technology, pp 851–860

1238. Wang T, Gong S, Zhu X, Wang S (2014) Person re-identification by video ranking. In: Fleet D, Pajdla T, Schiele B, Tuytelaars T (eds) European conference on computer vision (ECCV), pp 688–703

1239. Wang W, Huang Q, You S, Yang C, Neumann U (2017) Shape inpainting using 3D generative adversarial network and recurrent convolutional networks. In: IEEE international conference on computer vision (ICCV)

1240. Wang W, Lai Q, Fu H, Shen J, Ling H (2019) Salient object detection in the deep learning era: an in-depth survey. arXiv:1904.09146

1241. Wang W, Neumann U (2018) Depth-aware CNN for RGB-D segmentation. In: European conference on computer vision (ECCV), pp 144–161

1242. Wang W, Shen J, Porikli F (2015) Saliency-aware geodesic video object segmentation. In: IEEE conference on computer vision and pattern recognition (CVPR), pp 3395–3402

1243. Wang W, Shen J, Yang R, Porikli F (2017) Saliency-aware video object segmentation. IEEE Trans Pattern Anal Mach Intell 40(1):20–33

1244. Wang W, Shen J, Yu Y, Ma KL (2017) Stereoscopic thumbnail creation via efficient stereo saliency detection. IEEE Trans Vis Comput Graph 23(8):2014–2027

1245. Wang W, Yu R, Huang Q, Neumann U (2018) SGPN: similarity group proposal network for 3D point cloud instance segmentation. In: IEEE conference on computer vision and pattern recognition (CVPR), pp 2569–2578

1246. Wang X, Dong W, Zhou M, Li R, Zha H (2016) Edge enhanced direct visual odometry. In: British machine vision conference (BMVC), pp 35.1–35.11

1247. Wang X, Doretto G, Sebastian T, Rittscher J, Tu P (2007) Shape and appearance context modeling. In: IEEE international conference on computer vision (ICCV), pp 1–8

1248. Wang X, Fan B, Chang S, Wang Z, Liu X, Tao D, Huang TS (2017) Greedy batch-based minimum-cost flows for tracking multiple objects. IEEE Trans Image Process 26(10):4765–4776

1249. Wang X, Gao L, Song J, Shen H (2017) Beyond frame-level CNN: saliency-aware 3-D CNN with LSTM for video action recognition. IEEE Signal Process Lett 24(4):510–514

1250. Wang X, Han TX, Yan S (2009) An HOG-LBP human detector with partial occlusion handling. In: IEEE international conference on computer vision, pp 32–39

1251. Wang X, Liu L, Li G, Dong X, Zhao P, Feng X (2018) Background subtraction on depth videos with convolutional neural networks. In: International joint conference on neural networks (IJCNN), pp 1–7

1252. Wang X, Türetken E, Fleuret F, Fua P (2016) Tracking interacting objects using intertwined flows. IEEE Trans Pattern Anal Mach Intell 38(11):2312–2326

1253. Wang X, Yu K, Wu S, Gu J, Liu Y, Dong C, Qiao Y, Loy CC (2018) ESRGAN: enhanced super-resolution generative adversarial networks. In: Computer vision – ECCV workshops, pp 63–79

1254. Wang Y, Li K, Yang J, Ye X (2017) Intrinsic decomposition from a single RGB-D image with sparse and non-local priors. In: IEEE international conference on multimedia and expo, pp 1201–1206

1255. Wang Y, Ren T, hua Zhong S, Liu Y, Wu G (2018) Adaptive saliency cuts. Multimed Tools Appl 77:22213–22230

1256. Wang Y, Zhang J, Liu Z, Wu Q, Chou P, Zhang Z, Jia Y (2015) Completed dense scene flow in RGB-D space. In: Asian conference on computer vision (ACCV) workshops, vol 9009, pp 191–205

1257. Wang Y, Zhang Q, Zhou Y (2014) RGB-D mapping for indoor environment. In: IEEE conference on industrial electronics and applications, pp 1888–1892

1258. Wang Z, Zhan W, Tomizuka M (2017) Fusing bird view LIDAR point cloud and front view camera image for deep object detection. CoRR abs/1711.06703. arXiv:1711.06703

1259. Ward IR, Jalwana MAAK, Bennamoun M (2019) Improving image-based localization with deep learning: the impact of the loss function. CoRR abs/1905.03692. arXiv:1905.03692

1260. Wei LY, Lefebvre S, Kwatra V, Turk G (2009) State of the art in example-based texture synthesis. In: Eurographics state of the art report, pp 93–117

1261. Wei SE, Ramakrishna V, Kanade T, Sheikh Y (2016) Convolutional pose machines. In: IEEE conference on computer vision and pattern recognition (CVPR), pp 4724–4732

1262. Weik S (1997) Registration of 3-D partial surface models using luminance and depth information. In: International conference on recent advances in 3-D digital imaging and modeling

1263. Weiss A, Hirshberg D, Black MJ (2011) Home 3D body scans from noisy image and range data. In: IEEE international conference on computer vision (ICCV), pp 1951–1958

1264. Wen C, Qin L, Zhu Q, Wang C, Li J (2014) Three-dimensional indoor mobile mapping with fusion of two-dimensional laser scanner and rgb-d camera data. IEEE Geosci Remote Sens Lett 11(4):843–847

1265. Wen Y, Sheng B, Li P, Lin W, Feng DD (2019) Deep color guided coarse-to-fine convolutional network cascade for depth image super-resolution. IEEE Trans Image Process 28(2):994–1006

1266. Wexler Y, Shechtman E, Irani M (2007) Space-time completion of video. IEEE Trans Pattern Anal Mach Intell 29(3):463–476

1267. Wheeler MD, Ikeuchi K (1995) Iterative estimation of rotation and translation using the quaternion. Carnegie-Mellon University, Department of Computer Science

1268. Whelan T, Johannsson H, Kaess M, Leonard JJ, McDonald J (2013) Robust real-time visual odometry for dense RGB-D mapping. In: IEEE international conference on robotics and automation (ICRA), pp 5724–5731

1269. Whelan T, Kaess M, Fallon M (2012) Kintinuous: spatially extended Kinect-Fusion. In: RSS workshop on RGB-D: advanced reasoning with depth cameras

1270. Whelan T, Kaess M, Johannsson H, Fallon M, Leonard JJ, McDonald J (2015) Real-time large-scale dense RGB-D SLAM with volumetric fusion. Int J Robot Res 34(4–5):598–626

1271. Whelan T, Kaess M, Johannsson H, Fallon MF, Leonard JJ, McDonald J (2015) Real-time large-scale dense RGB-D SLAM with volumetric fusion. Int J Robot Res 34(4–5):598–626

1272. Whelan T, Kaess M, Leonard JJ, McDonald J (2013) Deformation-based loop closure for large scale dense RGB-D SLAM. In: IEEE/RSJ international conference on intelligent robots and systems (IROS), pp 548–555

1273. Whelan T, Leutenegger S, Salas-Moreno RF, Glocker B, Davison AJ (2015) ElasticFusion: dense SLAM without a pose graph. In: Robotics: science and systems (RSS)

1274. Whelan T, Salas-Moreno RF, Glocker B, Davison AJ, Leutenegger S (2016) ElasticFusion: real-time dense SLAM and light source estimation. Int J Robot Res 35(14):1697–1716

1275. Whyte O, Sivic J, Zisserman A (2009) Get out of my picture! internet-based inpainting. In: British machine vision conference (BMVC), pp 1–11

1276. Wikipedia (2019) Multiple-camera setup. https://en.wikipedia.org/wiki/Multiple-camera_setup. Accessed 25 Jun 2019

1277. Wisspeintner T, van der Zant T, Iocchi L, Schiffer S (2009) RoboCup@Home: scientific competition and benchmarking for domestic service robots. Interact Stud 10(3):392–426

1278. Wohlhart P, Lepetit V (2015) Learning descriptors for object recognition and 3D pose estimation. In: IEEE conference on computer vision and pattern recognition (CVPR), pp 3109–3118

1279. Wu A, Zheng W, Lai J (2017) Robust depth-based person re-identification. IEEE Trans Image Process 26(6):2588–2603

1280. Wu C, Stoll C, Valgaerts L, Theobalt C (2013) On-set performance capture of multiple actors with a stereo camera. ACM Trans Graph (TOG) 32(6):1–11

1281. Wu CJ, Quigley A, Harris-Birtill D (2017) Out of sight: a toolkit for tracking occluded human joint positions. Pers Ubiquitous Comput 21(1):125–135

1282. Wu H (2011) Robust consistent correspondence between 3D non-rigid shapes based on "dual shape-DNA". IEEE international conference on computer vision (ICCV), pp 587–594

1283. Wu L, Shen C, van den Hengel A (2017) Deep linear discriminant analysis on Fisher networks: a hybrid architecture for person re-identification. Pattern Recognit 65:238–250

1284. Wu P, Liu Y, Ye M, Li J, Du S (2017) Fast and adaptive 3D reconstruction with extensively high completeness. IEEE Trans Multimed 19(2):266–278

1285. Wu S, Chen YC, Li X, Wu AC, You JJ, Zheng WS (2016) An enhanced deep feature representation for person re-identification. arXiv:1604.07807

1286. Wu X, Yu C, Shi Y (2018) Multi-depth-camera sensing and interaction in smart space. In: IEEE SmartWorld, ubiquitous intelligence computing, advanced trusted computing, scalable computing communications, cloud big data computing, internet of people and smart city innovation (SmartWorld/SCALCOM/UIC/ATC/CBDCom/IOP/SCI), pp 718–725

1287. Wu Y, Huang TS (1999) Vision-based gesture recognition: a review. In: International gesture workshop, pp 103–115

1288. Wu Y, Huang TS (2000) View-independent recognition of hand postures. In: IEEE conference on computer vision and pattern recognition (CVPR), pp 88–94

1289. Wu Y, Huang TS (2001) Hand modeling, analysis and recognition. IEEE Signal Process Mag 18(3):51–60

1290. Wu Y, Lin J, Huang TS (2005) Analyzing and capturing articulated hand motion in image sequences. IEEE Trans Pattern Anal Mach Intell 27(12):1910–1922

1291. Wu Y, Wu Y, Gkioxari G, Tian Y (2018) Building generalizable agents with a realistic and rich 3D environment. arXiv:1801.02209

1292. Wu Y, Ying S, Zheng L (2018) Size-to-depth: a new perspective for single image depth estimation. arXiv:1801.04461

1293. Wu Z, Song S, Khosla A, Tang X, Xiao J (2014) 3D ShapeNets for 2.5d object recognition and next-best-view prediction. CoRR

1294. Wu Z, Song S, Khosla A, Yu F, Zhang L, Tang X, Xiao J (2015) 3D ShapeNets: a deep representation for volumetric shapes. In: IEEE conference on computer vision and pattern recognition (CVPR), pp 1912–1920

1295. Xia C, Li J, Chen X, Zheng A, Zhang Y (2017) What is and what is not a salient object? Learning salient object detector by ensembling linear exemplar regressors. In: IEEE conference on computer vision and pattern recognition (CVPR), pp 4142–4150

1296. Xiang JP (2012) Active learning for person re-identification. In: International conference on machine learning and cybernetics, vol 1, pp 336–340

1297. Xiang S, Yu L, Yang Y, Liu Q, Zhou J (2015) Interfered depth map recovery with texture guidance for multiple structured light depth cameras. Image Commun 31(C):34–46

1298. Xiang Y, Kim W, Chen W, Ji J, Choy C, Su H, Mottaghi R, Guibas L, Savarese S (2016) ObjectNet3D: a large scale database for 3D object recognition. In: European conference on computer vision (ECCV), pp 160–176

1299. Xiang Y, Mottaghi R, Savarese S (2014) Beyond Pascal: a benchmark for 3D object detection in the wild. In: IEEE winter conference on applications of computer vision (WACV), pp 75–82

1300. Xiang Y, Schmidt T, Narayanan V, Fox D (2017) PoseCNN: a convolutional neural network for 6D object pose estimation in cluttered scenes. arXiv:1711.00199

1301. Xiang ZJ, Chen Q, Liu Y (2014) Person re-identification by fuzzy space color histogram. Multimed Tools Appl 73(1):91–107

1302. Xiao J, Furukawa Y (2012) Reconstructing the world's museums. In: European conference on computer vision (ECCV)

1303. Xiao J, Hays J, Ehinger KA, Oliva A, Torralba A (2010) SUN database: large-scale scene recognition from abbey to zoo. In: Conference on computer vision and pattern recognition, pp 3485–3492

1304. Xiao J, Owens A, Torralba A (2013) SUN3D: a database of big spaces reconstructed using SfM and object labels. In: IEEE international conference on computer vision (ICCV)

1305. Xiao T, Li H, Ouyang W, Wang X (2016) Learning deep feature representations with domain guided dropout for person re-identification.

1306. Xie J, Feris RS, Yu SS, Sun MT (2015) Joint super resolution and denoising from a single depth image. IEEE Trans Multimed 17(9):1525–1537

1307. Xie J, Girshick R, Farhadi A (2016) Deep3D: fully automatic 2D-to-3D video conversion with deep convolutional neural networks. In: European conference on computer vision, pp 842–857

1308. Xie L, Lee F, Liu L, Yin Z, Yan Y, Wang W, Zhao J, Chen Q (2018) Improved spatial pyramid matching for scene recognition. Pattern Recognit 82:118–129

1309. Xie Q, Remil O, Guo Y, Wang M, Wei M, Wang J (2018) Object detection and tracking under occlusion for object-level RGB-D video segmentation. IEEE Trans Multimed 20(3):580–592

1310. Xu C, Cheng L (2013) Efficient hand pose estimation from a single depth image. In: IEEE international conference on computer vision (ICCV), pp 3456–3462

1311. Xu C, Govindarajan LN, Zhang Y, Cheng L (2016) Lie-X: depth image based articulated object pose estimation, tracking, and action recognition on lie groups. Int J Comput Vis:454–478

1312. Xu F, Yan Z, Xiao G, Zhang K, Zuo W (2018) JPEG image super-resolution via deep residual network. In: Intelligent computing methodologies – international conference, ICIC 2018, Wuhan, China, 15–18 August 2018. Proceedings, Part III, pp 472–483

1313. Xu J, Yuan J, Wu Y (2009) Multimodal partial estimates fusion. In: IEEE international conference on computer vision (ICCV), pp 2177–2184

1314. Xu T, Zhou Y, Zhu J (2018) New advances and challenges of fall detection systems: a survey. Appl Sci 8(3)

1315. Xu X, Po LM, Cheung CH, Feng L, Ng KH, Cheung KW (2013) Depth-aided exemplar-based hole filling for DIBR view synthesis. In: International symposium on circuits and systems, pp 2840–2843

1316. Xue H, Zhang S, Cai D (2017) Depth image inpainting: improving low rank matrix completion with low gradient regularization. IEEE Trans Image Process 26(9):4311–4320

1317. Yahiaoui T, Meurie C, Khoudour L, Cabestaing F (2008) A people counting system based on dense and close stereovision. In: Elmoataz A, Lezoray O, Nouboud F, Mammass D (eds) Image and signal processing. Springer, Berlin/Heidelberg, pp 59–66

1318. Yan J, Pollefeys M (2008) A factorization-based approach for articulated nonrigid shape, motion and kinematic chain recovery from video. IEEE Trans Pattern Anal Mach Intell 30(5):865–77

1319. Yan Q, Xu L, Shi J, Jia J (2013) Hierarchical saliency detection. In: IEEE conference on computer vision and pattern recognition (CVPR), pp 1155–1162

1320. Yan X, Yang J, Yumer E, Guo Y, Lee H (2016) Perspective transformer nets: learning single-view 3D object reconstruction without 3D supervision. In: Lee DD, Sugiyama M, Luxburg UV, Guyon I, Garnett R (eds) Advances in neural information processing systems, pp 1696–1704

1321. Yang B, Luo W, Urtasun R (2018) PIXOR: real-time 3D object detection from point clouds. In: IEEE conference on computer vision and pattern recognition (CVPR), pp 7652–7660

1322. Yang B, Wen H, Wang S, Clark R, Markham A, Trigoni N (2017) 3D object reconstruction from a single depth view with adversarial learning. In: IEEE international conference on computer vision workshop (ICCVW)

1323. Yang C, Lu X, Lin Z, Shechtman E, Wang O, Li H (2017) High-resolution image inpainting using multi-scale neural patch synthesis. In: IEEE conference on computer vision and pattern recognition (CVPR), pp 4076–4084

1324. Yang J, Liu F, Yue H, Fu X, Hou C, Wu F (2017) Textured image demoiréing via signal decomposition and guided filtering. IEEE Trans Image Process 26(7):3528–3541

1325. Yang J, Ye X, Frossard P (2018) Global auto-regressive depth recovery via iterative non-local filtering. IEEE Trans Broadcast

1326. Yang J, Ye X, Li K, Hou C, Wang Y (2014) Color-guided depth recovery from RGB-D data using an adaptive autoregressive model. IEEE Trans Image Process 23(8):3443–3458

1327. Yang J, Ye X, Li K, et al (2012) Depth recovery using an adaptive color-guided auto-regressive model. In: European conference on computer vision (ECCV), pp 158–171

1328. Yang L, Zhang L, Dong H, Alelaiwi A, Saddik AE (2015) Evaluating and improving the depth accuracy of Kinect for Windows v2. IEEE Sensors J 15(8):4275–4285

1329. Yang NE, Kim YG, Park RH (2012) Depth hole filling using the depth distribution of neighboring regions of depth holes in the Kinect sensor. In: International conference on signal processing, communication and computing, pp 658–661

1330. Yang Q (2012) A non-local cost aggregation method for stereo matching. In: IEEE conference on computer vision and pattern recognition (CVPR), pp 1402–1409

1331. Yang Q, Tan KH, Ahuja N (2009) Real-time O(1) bilateral filtering. In: Proceedings of CVPR (1), pp 557–564

1332. Yang Q, Tan KH, Culbertson B, Apostolopoulos J (2010) Fusion of active and passive sensors for fast 3D capture. In: International workshop on multimedia signal processing, pp 69–74

1333. Yang Q, Wang L, Ahuja N (2010) A constant-space belief propagation algorithm for stereo matching. In: IEEE conference on computer vision and pattern recognition (CVPR), pp 1458–1465

1334. Yang Q, Yang R, Davis J, Nister D (2007) Spatial-depth super resolution for range images. In: IEEE conference on computer vision and pattern recognition (CVPR), pp 1–8

1335. Yang Q, Yang R, Davis J, et al (2007) Spatial depth super resolution for range images. In: IEEE conference on computer vision and pattern recognition (CVPR), pp 1–8

1336. Yang S, Kuang ZF, Cao YP, Lai YK, Hu SM (2019) Probabilistic projective association and semantic guided relocalization for dense reconstruction. In: IEEE international conference on robotics and automation (ICRA)

1337. Yang S, Yi X, Wang Z, Wang Y, Yang X (2015) Visual SLAM using multiple RGB-D cameras. In: IEEE international conference on robotics and biomimetics (ROBIO), pp 1389–1395

1338. Ye G, Liu Y, Deng Y, Hasler N, Ji X, Dai Q, Theobalt C (2013) Free-viewpoint video of human actors using multiple handheld Kinects. IEEE Trans Cybern 43(5):1370–1382

1339. Ye G, Liu Y, Wu D, Li K, Deng Y, Deng W, Wu C.: Performance capture of interacting characters with handheld Kinects. In: European conference on computer vision (ECCV), pp 1–14

1340. Ye M, Shen Y, Du C, Pan Z, Yang R (2016) Real-time simultaneous pose and shape estimation for articulated objects using a single depth camera. IEEE Trans Pattern Anal Mach Intell 38(8):1517–1532

1341. Ye Q, Yuan S, Kim TK (2016) Spatial attention deep net with partial PSO for hierarchical hybrid hand pose estimation. In: Proceedings of the European conference on computer vision, pp 346–361

1342. Ye W, Xu Y, Zhong Z (2007) Robust people counting in crowded environment. In: IEEE international conference on robotics and biomimetics (ROBIO), pp 1133–1137

1343. Ye X, Duan X, Li H (2018) Depth super-resolution with deep edge-inference network and edge-guided depth filling. In: IEEE international conference on acoustics, speech and signal processing, ICASSP, pp 1398–1402

1344. Ye X, Song X, Yang J, Hou C, Wang Y (2016) Depth recovery via decomposition of polynomial and piece-wise constant signals. In: Proceedings of the IEEE visual communications and image processing (VCIP)

1345. Yeh RA, Chen C, Lim TY, G. SA, Hasegawa-Johnson M, Do MN (2017) Semantic image inpainting with deep generative models. In: IEEE conference on computer vision and pattern recognition (CVPR), pp 6882–6890

1346. Yi D, Lei Z, Li SZ (2014) Deep metric learning for practical person re-identification. arXiv:1407.4979

1347. Yi L, Kim VG, Ceylan D, Shen IC, Yan M, Su H, Lu C, Huang Q, Sheffer A, Guibas L (2016) A scalable active framework for region annotation in 3D shape collections. In: SIGGRAPH Asia

1348. Yin H, Berger C (2017) When to use what data set for your self-driving car algorithm: an overview of publicly available driving datasets. In: IEEE international conference on intelligent transportation systems (ITSC), pp 1–8

1349. Yokozuka M, Oishi S, Thompson S, Banno A (2019) VITAMIN-E: visual tracking and mapping with extremely dense feature points. In: IEEE conference on computer vision and pattern recognition (CVPR), pp 9641–9650

1350. Yu J, Lin Z, Yang J, Shen X, Lu X, Huang TS (2018) Generative image inpainting with contextual attention. In: IEEE conference on computer vision and pattern recognition (CVPR), pp 1–15

1351. Yu LF, Yeung SK, Tang CK, Terzopoulos D, Chan TF, Osher SJ (2011) Make it home: automatic optimization of furniture arrangement. ACM Trans Graph 30(4):86:1–86:12

1352. Yu M, Yu Y, Rhuma A, Naqvi S, Wang L, Chambers J (2013) An online one class support vector machine-based person-specific fall detection system for monitoring an elderly individual in a room environment. IEEE J Biomed Health Inform 17(6):1002–1014

1353. Yuan S, Garcia-Hernando G, Stenger B, Moon G, Chang JY, Lee KM, Molchanov P, Kautz J, Honari S, Ge L, Yuan J, Chen X, Wang G, Yang F, Akiyama K, Wu Y, Wan Q, Madadi M, Escalera S, Li S, Lee D, Oikono-midis I, Argyros A, Kim TK (2018) Depth-based 3D hand pose estimation: from current achievements to future goals. In: IEEE conference on computer vision and pattern recognition (CVPR), pp 2636–2645

1354. Yuan S, Ye Q, Stenger B, Jain S, Kim TK (2017) BigHand2.2M benchmark: hand pose dataset and state of the art analysis. In: IEEE conference on computer vision and pattern recognition (CVPR), pp 2605–2613

1355. Yun Y, Innocenti C, Nero G, Lindén H, Gu IYH (2015) Fall detection in RGB-D videos for elderly care. In: International conference on E-health networking, application services (HealthCom), pp 422–427

1356. Zach C, Gallup D, Frahm J (2008) Fast gain-adaptive KLT tracking on the GPU. IEEE conference on computer vision and pattern recognition (CVPR) (1)

1357. Zach C, Pock T, Bischof H (2007) A globally optimal algorithm for robust TV-L 1 range image integration. In: IEEE international conference on computer vision (ICCV), pp 1–8

1358. Zhan H, Garg R, Weerasekera CS, Li K, Agarwal H, Reid I (2018) Unsuper-vised learning of monocular depth estimation and visual odometry with deep feature reconstruction. In: IEEE conference on computer vision and pattern recognition (CVPR), pp 340–349

1359. Zhang C, Cai Q, Chou PA, Zhang Z, Martin-Brualla R (2013) Viewport: a distributed, immersive teleconferencing system with infrared dot pattern. IEEE MultiMedia 20(1):17–27

1360. Zhang C, Zhang Z (2014) Calibration between depth and color sensors for commodity depth cameras. In: Computer vision and machine learning with RGB-D sensors. Springer, pp 47–64

1361. Zhang D, Fu H, Han J, Borji A, Li X (2018) A review of co-saliency detection algorithms: fundamentals, applications, and challenges. ACM Trans Intell Syst Technol 9(4):1–31

1362. Zhang D, Yao Y, Liu D, Chen Y, Zang D (2013) Kinect-based 3D video conference system. In: Global high tech congress on electronics (GHTCE). IEEE, pp 165–169

1363. Zhang G, Jia J, Bao H (2011) Simultaneous multi-body stereo and segmen-tation. In: IEEE international conference on computer vision (ICCV), pp 826–833

1364. Zhang G, Jia J, Hua W, Bao H (2011) Robust bilayer segmentation and motion/depth estimation with a handheld camera. IEEE Trans Pattern Anal Mach Intell 33(3):603–617

1365. Zhang J, Kaess M, Singh S (2014) Real-time depth enhanced monocular odometry. In: IEEE/RSJ international conference on intelligent robots and systems (IROS), pp 4973–4980

1366. Zhang J, Singh S (2014) Loam: lidar odometry and mapping in real-time. In: Robotics: science and systems conference (RSS), pp 109–111

1367. Zhang L, Shen P, Zhang S, Song J, Zhu G (2016) Depth enhancement with improved exemplar-based inpainting and joint trilateral guided filtering. In: International conference on image processing, pp 4102–4106

1368. Zhang L, Sturm J, Cremers D, Lee D (2012) Real-time human motion tracking using multiple depth cameras. IEEE/RSJ international conference on intelligent robots and systems pp 2389–2395

1369. Zhang L, Tam WJ, Wang D (2004) Stereoscopic image generation based on depth images. In: International conference on image processing, vol 5, pp 2993–2996

1370. Zhang M, Fan Y (2014) Computational biomechanics of the musculoskeletal system. CRC Press

1371. Zhang R, Isola P, Efros AA (2016) Colorful image colorization. In: European conference on computer vision, pp 649–666

1372. Zhang R, Lin L, Zhang R, Zuo W, Zhang L (2015) Bit-scalable deep hashing with regularized similarity learning for image retrieval and person re-identification. IEEE Trans Image Process 24:4766–4779

1373. Zhang SH, Zhang SK, Liang Y, Hall P (2019) A survey of 3D indoor scene synthesis. J Comput Sci Technol 34(3):594–608

1374. Zhang X, Lin W, Xiong R, Liu X, Ma S, Gao W (2016) Low-rank decomposition-based restoration of compressed images via adaptive noise estimation. IEEE Trans Image Process 25(9):4158–4171

1375. Zhang X, Wu X (2008) Image interpolation by adaptive 2-D autoregressive modeling and soft-decision estimation. IEEE Trans Image Process 17(6):887–896

1376. Zhang X, Yan J, Feng S, Lei Z, Yi D, Li SZ (2012) Water filling: unsupervised people counting via vertical Kinect sensor. In: IEEE international conference on advanced video and signal-based surveillance, pp 215–220

1377. Zhang Y, Bai M, Kohli P, Izadi S, Xiao J (2017) Deepcontext: context-encoding neural pathways for 3D holistic scene understanding. In: Proceedings of the IEEE international conference on computer vision, pp 1192–1201

1378. Zhang Y, Funkhouser T (2018) Deep depth completion of a single RGB-D image. In: IEEE conference on computer vision and pattern recognition (CVPR), pp 175–185

1379. Zhang Y, Li L, Cong R, Guo X, Xu H, Zhang J (2018) Co-saliency detection via hierarchical consistency measure. In: ICME, pp 1–6

1380. Zhang Y, Zhao D, Ji X, et al (2009) A spatio-temporal auto regressive model for frame rate upconversion. IEEE Trans Circuits Syst Video Technol 19(9):1289–1301

1381. Zhang Z (1997) Parameter estimation techniques: a tutorial with application to conic fitting. Image Vis Comput 15:59–76

1382. Zhang Z (1999) Flexible camera calibration by viewing a plane from unknown orientations. In: IEEE international conference on computer vision (ICCV), pp 0–7

1383. Zhang Z (2000) A flexible new technique for camera calibration. IEEE Trans Pattern Anal Mach Intell 22(11):1330–1334

1384. Zhang Z (2012) Microsoft Kinect sensor and its effect. IEEE Multimed 19(2):4–10

1385. Zhao B, An P, Liu C, Yan J, Li C, Zhang Z (2014) Inpainting algorithm for Kinect depth map based on foreground segmentation. J Electron (China) 31(1):41–49

1386. Zhao L, Liang J, Bai H, Wang A, Zhao Y (2017) Simultaneously color-depth super-resolution with conditional generative adversarial network. CoRR abs/1708.09105

1387. Zhao T, Nevatia R, Wu B (2008) Segmentation and tracking of multiple humans in crowded environments. IEEE Trans Pattern Anal Mach Intell 30(7):1198–1211

1388. Zhao W, Chai J, Xu YQ (2012) Combining marker-based mocap and RGB-D camera for acquiring high-fidelity hand motion data. In: Proceedings of the ACM SIGGRAPH/eurographics symposium on computer animation, pp 33–42

1389. Zhao Yang, Liu Zicheng, Cheng Hong (2013) RGB-depth feature for 3D human activity recognition. China Commun 10(7):93–103

1390. Zheng B, Zhao Y, Yu JC, Ikeuchi K, Zhu SC (2013) Beyond point clouds: scene understanding by reasoning geometry and physics. In: IEEE conference on computer vision and pattern recognition (CVPR), pp 3127–3134

1391. Zheng C, Cham TJ, Cai J (2018) T2net: synthetic-to-realistic translation for solving single-image depth estimation tasks. In: European conference on computer vision, pp 767–783

1392. Zheng H, Bouzerdoum A, Phung SL (2013) Depth image super-resolution using multi-dictionary sparse representation. In: IEEE international conference on image processing (ICIP), pp 957–961

1393. Zheng WS, Gong S, Xiang T (2011) Person re-identification by probabilistic relative distance comparison. In: IEEE conference on computer vision and pattern recognition (CVPR), pp 649–656

1394. Zhou H, Ummenhofer B, Brox T (2018) DeepTAM: deep tracking and mapping. In: European conference on computer vision (ECCV), pp 822–838

1395. Zhou Q, Miller S, Koltun V (2013) Elastic fragments for dense scene reconstruction. In: IEEE international conference on computer vision (ICCV), Figure 2

1396. Zhou QY, Koltun V (2013) Dense scene reconstruction with points of interest. ACM Trans Graph 32(4):112:1–112:8

1397. Zhou QY, Koltun V (2014) Color map optimization for 3D reconstruction with consumer depth cameras. ACM Trans Graph 33(4):155:1–155:10

1398. Zhou T, Brown M, Snavely N, Lowe DG (2017) Unsupervised learning of depth and ego-motion from video. In: IEEE conference on computer vision and pattern recognition (CVPR), pp 6612–6619

1399. Zhou W, Yu L (2016) Binocular responses for no-reference 3D image quality assessment. IEEE Trans Multimed 18(6):1077–1084

1400. Zhou X, Wan Q, Zhang W, Xue X, Wei Y (2016) Model-based deep hand pose estimation. In: Proceedings of the international joint conference on artificial Intelligence, pp 2421–2427

1401. Zhou Y, Li H, Kneip L (2019) Canny-VO: visual odometry with RGB-D cameras based on geometric 3-D–2-D edge alignment. IEEE Trans Robot 35(1):184–199

1402. Zhou Y, Tuzel O (2018) VoxelNet: end-to-end learning for point cloud based 3D object detection. In: IEEE conference on computer vision and pattern recognition (CVPR), pp 4490–4499

1403. Zhu C, Li G (2018) A multilayer backpropagation saliency detection algorithm and its applications. Multimed Tools Appl, pp 1–17

1404. Zhu J, Wang L, Davis J (2011) Reliability fusion of time-of-flight depth and stereo geometry for high quality depth maps. IEEE Trans Pattern Anal Mach Intell 33(7):1400–1414

1405. Zhu J, Wang L, Gao J, et al (2010) Spatial-temporal fusion for high accuracy depth maps using dynamic MRFs. IEEE Trans Pattern Anal Mach Intell 32(5):899–909

1406. Zhu JY, Park T, Isola P, Efros AA (2017) Unpaired image-to-image translation using cycle-consistent adversarial networks. In: International conference on computer vision, pp 2242–2251

1407. Zhu M, Derpanis KG, Yang Y, Brahmbhatt S, Zhang M, Phillips C, Lecce M, Daniilidis K (2014) Single image 3D object detection and pose estimation for grasping. In: IEEE international conference on robotics and automation (ICRA), pp 3936–3943

1408. Zhuo W, Salzmann M, He X, Liu M (2015) Indoor scene structure analysis for single image depth estimation. In: IEEE conference on computer vision and pattern recognition (CVPR), pp 614–622

1409. Zoccolillo L, Morelli D, Cincotti F, Muzzioli L, Gobbetti T, Paolucci S, Iosa M (2015) Video-game based therapy performed by children with cerebral palsy: a cross-over randomized controlled trial and a cross-sectional quantitative measure of physical activity. Eur J Phys Rehabil Med 51(6):669–676

1410. Zollhöfer M, Dai A, Innmann M, Wu C, Stamminger M, Theobalt C, Nießner M (2015) Shading-based refinement on volumetric signed distance functions. ACM Trans Graph (TOG)

1411. Zollhöfer M, Nießner M, Izadi S, Rhemann C (2014) Real-time non-rigid reconstruction using an RGB-D camera. In: ACM SIGGRAPH

1412. Zollhöfer M, Stotko P, Görlitz A, Theobalt C, Nießner M, Klein R, Kolb A (2018) State of the art on 3D reconstruction with RGB-D cameras. Comput Graph Forum (Eurographics State of the Art Reports 2018) 37(2)

1413. Zou Y, Chen W, Wu X, Liu Z (2012) Indoor localization and 3D scene recon-struction for mobile robots using the Microsoft Kinect sensor. In: IEEE inter-national conference on industrial informatics (INDIN), pp 1182–1187

1414. Zubizarreta J, Aguinaga I, Montiel J (2019) Direct sparse mapping. arXiv:1904.06577

1415. Zuo Y, Wu Q, Zhang J, An P (2016) Explicit modeling on depth-color incon-sistency for color-guided depth up-sampling. In: IEEE international confer-ence on multimedia and expo (ICME), pp 1–6

1416. Zuo Y, Wu Q, Zhang J, An P (2017) Explicit edge inconsistency evaluation model for color-guided depth map enhancement. IEEE Trans Circuits Syst Video Technol PP(99):1–1

1417. Zuo Y, Wu Q, Zhang J, An P (2017) Minimum spanning forest with embedded edge inconsistency measurement for color-guided depth map upsampling. In: IEEE international conference on multimedia and expo (ICME), pp 211–216

1418. Zwicker M, Pfister H, van Baar J, Gross M (2001) Surface splatting. In: Conference on computer graphics and interactive techniques, pp 371–378

Index

© Springer Nature Switzerland AG 2019
P. L. Rosin et al. (eds.), *RGB-D Image Analysis and Processing*,
Advances in Computer Vision and Pattern Recognition,
https://doi.org/10.1007/978-3-030-28603-3

Printed in the United States
By Bookmasters